NCERT BIOLOGY

REVISION WORK BOOK

Most Effective Revision & Concept Zipper for >>>>

NEET & CUET

Vol. 1 CLASS XI

Authors
Juhi Bhatia
Kanika Narag

Super 6

ADVANTAGES OF REVISION WORK BOOKS

1. Learn with fun while practicing with Self Assessment.
2. Different question types are helpful in increasing the learning and understanding about **Core Concepts** and **Conceptual Applications**.
3. Figure based small methodical questions also help in increasing **figure visualisation**.
4. Innovative style of practice in Workbook manner helps in breaking the **monotonicity** of subject.
5. Complete sync with NCERT along with **Competition Connect** and **Competition Edge Up** helps in building the foundation for the preparation of competitions like NEET and CUET.
6. Questions with one word or maximum one sentence long answers are very helpful in **Faster Revision** and **Confidence Boost Up**.

ARIHANT PRAKASHAN (SERIES), MEERUT

卐 **Administrative & Production Offices**

Regd. Office
'Ramchhaya' 4577/15, Agarwal Road, Darya Ganj, New Delhi -110002
Tele: 011- 47630600, 43518550

卐 **Head Office**
Kalindi, TP Nagar, Meerut (UP) - 250002
Tel: 0121-7156203, 7156204

卐 **Sales & Support Offices**
Agra, Ahmedabad, Bengaluru, Bareilly, Chennai, Delhi, Guwahati, Hyderabad, Jaipur, Jhansi, Kolkata, Lucknow, Nagpur & Pune.

卐 **PRICE** ₹410.00

卐 PO No. : TXT-59-T064900-05-25

Published by Arihant Publications (India) Ltd.

For further information about the books published by Arihant, log on to www.arihantbooks.com or e-mail at info@arihantbooks.com

Follow us on    

FAB 4 Features

TOPIC 1

Diversity in The Living World

NCERT Tracker
Every topic is tagged with NCERT page numbers for better syncing with NCERT.

1. Each different kind of plant, animal or organism that you see, represents a ________ (genus/species).
2. In a given habitat, we have 20 plant species and 20 animal species. Should we call it as variety or biodiversity? ________
3. There is a need to standardise the naming of living organisms such that a particular organism is known by the same name all over the world. This process is called ________

***13.** Which of the following is the correct representation of scientific name of mangoes?

(a) *mangifera indica* Linn. ☐
(b) *Mangifera Indica* linn. ☐
(c) *Mangifera Indica* Linn. ☐
(d) *Mangifera indica* Linn. ☐

Important Concept Tagging
Every question which is based on the important concept from NEET & CUET point of view is marked with *.

COMPETITION CONNECT

Topic 1. Modifications of Root [NCERT (old) Pg. 67]

1. ________ (Tap/Adventitious) roots of carrot, turnip and ________ (tap/adventitious) roots of sweet potato get swollen and store food. ________ ________
2. The hanging structure of banyan tree is called ________.
3. Identify the type of root arising from the plant shown in the following figure. ________

Competition Connect
Supplement containing related portions of old NCERT which are present in NEET/CUET syllabus but removed from latest NCERT.

COMPETITION EDGE UP

1. *In the taxonomic categories, which hierarchical arrangement in ascending order is correct in case of animals?* **[NCERT Pg. 8, NEET 2022]**
   (a) *Kingdom, class, phylum, family, order, genus, species* ☐
   (b) *Kingdom, order, class, phylum, family, genus, species* ☐
   (c) *Kingdom, order, phylum, class, family, genus, species* ☐
   (d) *Kingdom, phylum, class, order, family, genus, species* ☐
2. *Which one of the following belongs to the family-Muscidae?* **[NCERT Pg. 8, NEET 2021]**
   (a) *Housefly* ☐
   (b) *Firefly* ☐
4. *Select the correctly written scientific name of mango which was first described by Carolus Linnaeus.* **[NCERT Pg. 5, NEET (National) 2019)]**
   (a) *Mangifera indica Linn.* ☐
   (b) *Mangifera indica* ☐
   (c) *Mangifera Indica* ☐
   (d) *Mangifera indica Car. Linn.* ☐
5. *The common characteristics between tomato and potato will be maximum at the level of their* **[NEET 2016]**
   (a) *family* ☐ (b) *order* ☐
   (c) *division* ☐ (d) *genus* ☐
6. *Study the four statements (I-IV) given below and select the two correct ones out of them*

Competition Edge Up
Selected PYQs in Sync with NCERT Chapter.

CONTENTS

Chapter 01

The Living World

Scan and take Chapter Test

TOPIC 1

Diversity in The Living World

1. Each different kind of plant, animal or organism that you see, represents a ____________ (genus/species).

2. In a given habitat, we have 20 plant species and 20 animal species. Should we call it as variety or biodiversity? ____________

3. There is a need to standardise the naming of living organisms such that a particular organism is known by the same name all over the world. This process is called ____________

4. Consider the following statements.

Statement I An unknown organism right after its discovery is first identified.

Statement II Only after identification and characterisation, an unknown organism is named.

Choose the correct option from the following.

(a) Statement I is true, but statement II is false ☐

(b) Both statements I and II are true ☐

5. Nomenclature is possible only when the organism is ____________ correctly.

***6.** Give full forms of the following abbreviations.

(i) ICBN ____________

(ii) ICZN ____________

***7.** What are the two components in a scientific name?

____

***8.** Binomial nomenclature was given by ____________

***9.** In *Mangifera indica*, the word *Mangifera* is a ____________

***10.** Scientific names are printed in ____________ and are derived from ____________.

***11.** The first word in a scientific name denoting genus starts with a ____________ letter, while the second word denoting species starts with a ____________ letter.

*Concepts of all questions bearing * are important for NEET & CUET*

***12.** Given below are few statements. Identify the correct statement.

I. For hand written scientific names the genus and species should be separately underlined.
II. Scientific names are Italicised and written in Latin.
III. The first word in a biological name represents the genus, while the second component denotes the specific epithet.
IV. Name of the author appears before the specific epithet.

Choose the correct answer from the options given below.

(a) I and III ☐ (b) II and III ☐
(c) III and IV ☐ (d) I and IV ☐

***13.** Which of the following is the correct representation of scientific name of mangoes?

(a) *mangifera indica* Linn. ☐ (b) *Mangifera Indica* linn. ☐
(c) *Mangifera Indica* Linn. ☐ (d) *Mangifera indica* Linn. ☐

***14.** What does Linn., represent in the biological name *Mangifera indica* Linn ?

____

15. Choose the odd one out from the following scientific names.

Panthera tigris. Mangifera indica, Panthera leo, Columba LIVEA

____

16. The process by which anything grouped into convenient categories based on some easily observable character is called _______________

***17.** The scientific term for different categories like plants and mammals is _______________

18. _______________ (Systematics/Taxonomy) takes into account evolutionary relationships between organisms.

19. Choose the odd one out from the following.

Characterisation, Identification, Classification, Nomenclature, Systematics

____

20. Consider the following statements.

Statement I Classification allows us to link organisms with their ancestors.

Statement II Systematics gives us an idea about the origin of a species.

Choose the correct option from the following.

(a) Statement I is true, but statement II is false ☐
(b) Both statements I and II are true ☐

21. In the given image which of the organism represents the common ancestor of the remaining?

W Z Y X

S

(a) *X* ☐
(b) *W* ☐
(c) *S* ☐
(d) *Y* and *Z* ☐

TOPIC 2

Taxonomic Categories

***22.** Ascending and descending arrangement of taxonomic categories is known as classification.
(*Rewrite the statement after correcting the underlined word.*)

____

***23.** A taxonomic group of any ranking is ______________ (category/taxon).

24. The taxonomic categories are distinct biological ______________ and not merely ______________ aggregates.

***25.** Species is considered as the ______________ (smallest/largest) taxon of taxonomy.

26. Individual of which taxa interbreed freely? ______________

***27.** In *Solanum tuberosum,* first and second words stand for ______________, respectively.

***28.** Consider the following statements.

Statement I *melongena* and *nigrum* bear similarity at the genus level.

Statement II Leopard and tigers are unrelated organisms in the evolution tree.

Choose the correct option from the following.

(a) Statement I is true, but statement II is false ☐

(b) Both statements I and II are true ☐

29. How many of the given plants belong to genus–*Solanum*?

Potato, Brinjal, Datura, Tulip

____

30. Give the scientific name of lion, leopard and tiger.

____

***31.** Family comprises of related species which has more characters in common in comparison to species of other genera.

True ☐ False ☐

***32.** Which of the plants do not belong to Solanaceae?

(a) Brinjal ☐ (b) *Datura* ☐

(c) *Petunia* ☐ (d) Wheat ☐

33. Write one similarity and one difference between cats and tigers on the basis of classification. ______________

34. The suffix used for plant family is ______________ and for animal family is ______________.

35. Study the chart alongside and choose the correct combination from the following.

(a) *A* – Polymoniales, *B* – Poaceae ☐
(b) *A* – Polymoniales, *B* – Solanaceae ☐
(c) *A* – Poales, *B* – Solanaceae ☐
(d) *A* – Poales, *B* – Poaceae ☐

A
Convolvulaceae | B
Datura | *Petunia*

36. 'Order' related to 'Brinjal' is ____________

37. Give the name of the category given in bracket on the basis of the adjoining information.

(i) *Felis* and *Panthera* (Family) ____________
(ii) Solanaceae and Convolvulaceae (Order) ____________

38. Suffix used for plant order is ____________

39. Consider the following statements.

Statement I Gorillas, gibbons, monkeys and humans belong to two different orders.

Statement II Animals of the same order show fewer similarities than those of the same class.

Choose the correct option from the following.

(a) Statement I is true, but statement II is false ☐
(b) Both statements I and II are false ☐

40. In case of plants, classes with a few similar characters are assigned to a higher category called ____________ (phylum/division).

41. If two plants belong to the same division, but different orders, they may belong to the same ____________ (family/class)

***42.** Write the missing taxonomic categories in ascending order.

Kingdom ← Phylum ← ____________ ← Order ← ____________ ← Genus ← Species

***43.** As we go higher from species to kingdom then what will happen to the number of common characteristics? ____________

44. The given figure represents taxonomic hierarchy. Maximum similarity of characteristics is observed in which of the following?

(a) Z and S ☐
(b) X and Y ☐
(c) A and S ☐
(d) A and Z ☐

A
Z | S
X | Y

***45.** All of the following belong to the same taxonomic hierarchy except

(a) Sapindales ☐ (b) Carnivora ☐
(c) Muscidae ☐ (d) Primata ☐

46. Match Column I with Column II.

	Column I		Column II
A.	Order	1.	Plantae
B.	Class	2.	Poaceae
C.	Kingdom	3.	Diptera
D.	Family	4.	Mammalia

Choose the correct option.

	A	B	C	D			A	B	C	D
(a)	3	4	1	2		(b)	3	2	1	4
(c)	3	4	2	1		(d)	3	2	4	1

47. Which of the following represents the correct descending order of taxonomic hierarchy?

(a) Anacardiaceae, Diptera, *Musca domestica*, Angiospermae

(b) Angiospermae, Diptera, Anacardiaceae, *Musca domestica*

(c) *Musca domestica*, Anacardiaceae, Diptera, Angiospermae

(d) Angiospermae, *Musca domestica*, Diptera, Anacardiaceae

48. Given below are few statements. Identify the incorrect ones.

I. A class contains fewer organisms compared to a family.

II. Chordata and Arthropoda bear fewer similarities between them.

III. Family includes related orders.

IV. Order is the assemblage of families which exhibit many similar characters.

Choose the correct answer from the options given below.

(a) I, II and IV (b) II, III and IV

(c) I, III and IV (d) II and IV

49. Write the next higher taxonomic hierarchy for the following taxonomic groups.

(i) Pisces, Amphibia, Aves, Mammalia ____________

(ii) Liliales, Poales, Commelinales ____________

***50.** Recognise the following flowchart and write the missing taxonomic hierarchy.

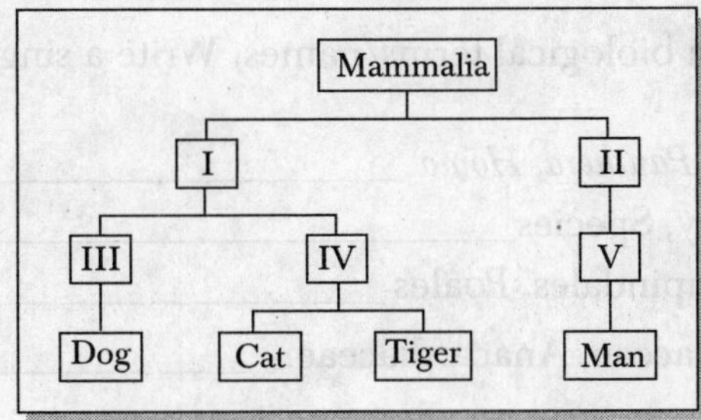

I. ____________ II. ____________

III. ____________ IV. ____________

V. ____________

51. Find the odd one out for housefly classification.

Musca, Chordata, Muscidae, Diptera, Insecta

____

52. Arrange the following taxonomic categories in ascending order.

I. Poaceae II. Poales III. Monocotyledonae
IV. *Triticum aestivum* V. Angiospermae

____

53. Consider the following statements.

Statement I *Petunia* and *Datura* have fewer similarities than Convolvulaceae and Solanaceae.

Statement II Wheat and mango relates only at the level of kingdom.

Choose the correct option from the following.

(a) Statement I is true, but statement II is false ☐
(b) Both statements I and II are false ☐

***54.** Match the following columns.

	Column I (Taxonomic categories)		Column II (Examples)
A.	Family	1.	*tuberosum*
B.	Kingdom	2.	Polymoniales
C.	Order	3.	Plantae
D.	Species	4.	Solanaceae

A. ______________ B. ______________
C. ______________ D. ______________

55. Consider the categories given in the box and group together those which belong to the similar hierarchy.

Cicer, Petunia, Asteraceae, Primata, Rodentia, Solanaceae

____

56. Given below are certain biological terms/names. Write a single collecting term for each group.

(i) *Mangifera, Solanum, Panthera, Homo* ______________
(ii) Class, Order, Family, Species ______________
(iii) Primata, Diptera, Sapindales, Poales ______________
(iv) Poaceae, Convolvulaceae, Anacardiaceae. ______________

COMPETITION CONNECT

What is Living ? [NCERT (Old) Pg. 3-5]

1. What are the twin characteristics of growth?

____

2. Multicellular and unicellular organisms grow by _______________ (cell division/cellular organisation).

3. In plants, the growth by cell division occurs *A* whereas in animals, the growth is seen *B*

	A	B
(a)	only upto a certain age	continuously throughout their lifespan
(b)	continuously throughout their lifespan	only upto a certain age
(c)	continuously	continuously
(d)	only upto a certain age	only upto a certain age

(a) ☐ (b) ☐ (a) ☐ (b) ☐

4. Growth is a common feature exhibited by both living and non-living.

True ☐ False ☐

5. Consider the following statements.

Statement I In majority of higher animals and plants, growth and reproduction are mutually exclusive events.

Statement II Non-living objects also grow by increase in body mass.

Choose the correct option from the following.

(a) Statement I is true, but statement II is false ☐

(b) Both statements I and II are true ☐

6. Non-living organisms perform growth by _______________

7. Match the following columns.

Column I (Organisms)	Column II (Modes of reproduction)
A. Fungi	1. Asexual spores
B. *Amoeba*	2. Binary fission
C. *Hydra* and yeast	3. True regeneration
D. *Planaria*	4. Budding

A. _______________ B. _______________ C. _______________ D. _______________

8. Write a common mode of reproduction in the following.

Fungi, Filamentous algae, Protonema of mosses

____

9. For unicellular organisms like bacteria, unicellular algae or *Amoeba*, _______________ is synonymous with _______________.

10. Out of the given organisms, how many of them do not reproduce?

Mules, Worker bees, Infertile human couple, Horse

____

11. The sum total of all chemical reactions occurring in our body is called ____________

12. Metabolic reactions can be demonstrated outside the body in cell-free system.

True ☐ False ☐

13. Consider the following statements.

Statement I An isolated metabolic reaction performed in test tube outside the body an organism is neither living nor non-living.

Statement II Metabolism cannot be a defining feature of all living organisms without exception.

Choose the correct option from the following.

(a) Statement I is true, but statement II is false ☐

(b) Both statements I and II are false ☐

14. Isolated metabolic reactions *in vitro* are not living things, but surely living reactions.

True ☐ False ☐

15. ____________ affects reproduction in seasonal breeders in both plant and animals.

16. Human being is the only organism who is aware of himself, i.e. has metabolism.

(*Rewrite the statement after correcting the underlined word.*)

____

17. How many (in number) of the following are the defining characteristics of living organisms?

Growth, Reproduction, Metabolism, Consciousness, Cellular organisation

____

18. Choose the correct sequence for organisational complexity of living beings from simple to complex form.

(a) Atomic level → Cellular level → Molecular level → Tissues → Organ → Individual → Organ system ☐

(b) Atomic level → Molecular level → Cellular level → Tissue → Organ → Organ system → Individual ☐

(c) Atomic level → Cellular level → Molecular level → Tissue → Organ → Organ system → Individual ☐

(d) Molecular level → Atomic level → Cellular level → Tissue → Organ → Organ system → Individual ☐

19. Read the following statements and select the correct ones.

I. Fungi, filamentous algae and protonema of mosses have a common mode of reproduction.
II. For unicellular organisms like *Amoeba* reproduction in antonymous with growth.
III. Isolated metabolic reactions *in vitro* are not living things, but surely living reactions.
IV. Human beings are not the only organisms who are aware of themselves.
V. Living organisms are self-replicating, evolving and self- regulating interactive system capable of responding to external stimuli.

Choose the correct answer from the options given below.

(a) II and IV ☐ (b) I, III and V ☐

(c) I, II and III ☐ (d) I and V ☐

Assertion-Reason Questions

The following questions consist of two statements- Assertion (A) and Reason (R). Answer these questions by selecting the appropriate options given below.
(a) Both A and R are true and R is the correct explanation of A
(b) Both A and R are true, but R is not the correct explanation of A
(c) A is true, but R is false
(d) A is false, but R is true

1. Assertion (A) The term biodiversity refers to the number and types of organisms present on earth.

Reason (R) The number of species that are known and described range between 17. 8-18.8 million.

(a) ☐ (b) ☐ (c) ☐ (d) ☐

***2. Assertion** (A) One person in Delhi and other in Texas would call a tiger *Panthera tigris*.

Reason (R) The system of binomial nomenclature was introduced to avoid confusion.

(a) ☐ (b) ☐ (c) ☐ (d) ☐

***3. Assertion** (A) Nomenclature of an organism is preceded by identification.

Reason (R) The ICBN has laid down the principles for nomenclature of plants.

(a) ☐ (b) ☐ (c) ☐ (d) ☐

***4. Assertion** (A) Scientific names are derived from Latin and are written in Italics.

Reason (R) On hand written papers, the genus and species are separately underlined.

(a) ☐ (b) ☐ (c) ☐ (d) ☐

5. Assertion (A) A species that is newly discovered needs to be classified first before it is named.

Reason (R) Classification allows organisms to be sorted based on similarities and dissimilarities.

(a) ☐ (b) ☐ (c) ☐ (d) ☐

***6. Assertion** (A) Every organism on this planet has a definite taxon.

Reason (R) Structural information of the cell is enough to assign a taxa.

(a) ☐ (b) ☐ (c) ☐ (d) ☐

7. Assertion (A) Two dissimilar organisms found in nature might be linked through evolution.

Reason (R) Systematics allows us to study the evolutionary relationship between organisms.

(a) ☐ (b) ☐ (c) ☐ (d) ☐

8. Assertion (A) Species represent the smallest unit of classification.

Reason (R) Species show reproductive isolation.

(a) ☐ (b) ☐ (c) ☐ (d) ☐

9. Assertion (A) Members of a genus can interbreed freely.

Reason (R) A genus is formed by aggregation of closely related species.

(a) ☐ (b) ☐ (c) ☐ (d) ☐

***10. Assertion** (A) *Panthera* and *Felis* are placed under the same family–Canidae.

Reason (R) The two related genera are placed under the same family.

(a) ☐ (b) ☐ (c) ☐ (d) ☐

Case Based Questions

***1.** The given schematic represents a taxonomic hierarchy. Study the image carefully and answer the questions that follows:

Leopard Cats Dogs
A B C
D E
X

(i) Which of the following group would have the highest number of organisms?

(a) D and E ☐ (b) A, B and C ☐
(c) X ☐ (d) A and B ☐

(ii) Which of the following would have more similarities in properties ?

(a) A and B ☐ (b) B and C ☐
(c) A and C ☐ (d) D and E ☐

(iii) Choose the correct combination from the following.

(a) D – Canidae, E – Felidae ☐
(b) D – Felidae, E – Canidae ☐
(c) B – *Canis,* C – *Felis* ☐
(d) A – *Felis,* B – *Panthera* ☐

(iv) Identify 'X'.

(a) Omnivora ☐ (b) Carnivora ☐
(c) Primata ☐ (d) Mammalia ☐

***2.** Given below is the figure of an organism. Identify the organism and answer the questions that follows.

(i) Choose the correct statement regarding the organism.

(a) It belong to order– Muscidae and class- Insecta ☐

(b) Its scientific name is *Musca melongena*, in which the former denotes genus ☐

(c) It belongs to class– Diptera and order– Insecta ☐

(d) It belongs to family–Muscidae and class– Insecta ☐

(ii) The given organisms belong to order ...A... and phylum ...B...

	A	B
(a)	Insecta	Arthropoda
(b)	Muscidae	Diptera
(c)	Insecta	Muscidae
(d)	Diptera	Arthropoda

(a) ☐ (b) ☐ (c) ☐ (d) ☐

(iii) Given below are few statements regarding the figure given above. Identify the correct ones, and choose the correct option.

I. This organism comes under the order–Animalia.

II. It belongs to phylum - Arthropoda.

III. It has four pairs of jointed legs.

IV. It belong to order- Poales.

(a) Only II ☐ (b) I and II ☐

(c) III and IV ☐ (d) Only III ☐

COMPETITION EDGE UP

1. In the taxonomic categories, which hierarchical arrangement in ascending order is correct in case of animals? **[NCERT Pg. 8, NEET 2022]**

(a) Kingdom, class, phylum, family, order, genus, species ☐

(b) Kingdom, order, class, phylum, family, genus, species ☐

(c) Kingdom, order, phylum, class, family, genus, species ☐

(d) Kingdom, phylum, class, order, family, genus, species ☐

2. Which one of the following belongs to the family-Muscidae? **[NCERT Pg. 8, NEET 2021]**

(a) Housefly ☐

(b) Firefly ☐

(c) Grasshopper ☐

(d) Cockroach ☐

3. Which of the following is against the rules of ICBN? **[NCERT Pg. 4, NEET (Odisha) 2019]**

(a) Handwritten scientific names should be underlined ☐

(b) Every species should have a generic name and a specific epithet ☐

(c) Scientific names are in Latin and should be Italicised ☐

(d) Generic and specific names should be written by starting with small letters ☐

4. Select the correctly written scientific name of mango which was first described by Carolus Linnaeus. **[NCERT Pg. 5, NEET (National) 2019)]**

(a) Mangifera indica Linn. ☐

(b) Mangifera indica ☐

(c) Mangifera Indica ☐

(d) Mangifera indica Car. Linn. ☐

5. The common characteristics between tomato and potato will be maximum at the level of their **[NEET 2016]**

(a) family ☐ (b) order ☐

(c) division ☐ (d) genus ☐

6. Study the four statements (I-IV) given below and select the two correct ones out of them. **[NCERT (Old) Pg 4, 5, 6, NEET 2016, Phase II]**

I. Definition of biological species was given by Ernst Mayr.

II. Photoperiod does not affect reproduction in plants.

III. Binomial nomenclature system was given by RH Whittaker.

IV. In unicellular organisms, reproduction is synonymous with growth.

The two correct statements are

(a) II and III ☐ (b) III and IV ☐

(c) I and IV ☐ (d) I and II ☐

Chapter 02

Biological Classification

Scan and take Chapter Test

TOPIC 1

Introduction and Kingdom-Monera

1. Biological classification was first proposed by ____________________ who used simple morphological characters to classify plants and animals.

2. Aristotle divided animals into two groups on the basis of the presence and absence of _______________ (WBCs/RBCs/Lymphocytes).

3. Two kingdom classification system was given by ____________________

4. The demerit of two kingdom system is that it does not distinguish between the eukaryotes and prokaryotes, unicellular and multicellular organisms and photosynthetic and non-photosynthetic organisms.

True ☐ False ☐

5. Out of the following how many criteria were used for five kingdom classification?

Cell structure, Body organisation, Mode of nutrition, Reproduction, Phylogenetic relationship, Nuclear membrane composition.

____

6. Consider the following statements.

Statement I Five kingdom classification by RH Whittaker did not take into account the phylogeny of organisms.

Statement II The two kingdom classification by Linnaeus failed to consider the prokaryotic and eukaryotic nature.

Choose the correct option from the following.

(a) Statement I is true, but statement II is false ☐

(b) Statement I is false, but statement II is true ☐

7. The three domain classification divides the kingdom __________ into two domains.

8. Earlier classification systems included bacteria, Blue-Green Algae (BGA), fungi, mosses, ferns, gymnosperms under plants. Name the character which unified all these organisms in one kingdom. ____________________

*Concepts of all questions bearing * are important for NEET & CUET*

9. Study the following table carefully and write the correct words for *A*, *B*, *C* and *D*.

Characters	Monera	Protista	Fungi	Plantae	Animalia
Cell type	(*A*)	Eukaryotic	Eukaryotic	Eukaryotic	Eukaryotic
Cell wall	(*B*)	Present in some	Present	Present	Absent
Nuclear membrane	Absent	Present	Present	Present	(*C*)
Body organisation	Cellular	Cellular	(*D*)	Tissue/Organ	Tissue/Organ/ Organ system

A. ____________ B. ____________ C. ____________ D ____________

10. In the given diagram, *A*, *B* and *C* are autotrophs, heterotrophs and both (autotrophs and heterotrophs), respectively.

Write down how many of the kingdoms out of the five kingdoms belong to *A*, *B* and *C*?

A *C* *B*

A. ____________

B. ____________

C. ____________

11. The sole members of kingdom–Monera are ____________.

12. Write true and false for the given statements with respect to bacteria.

(i) They are the most abundant microorganisms found almost everywhere.

True ☐ False ☐

(ii) They cannot survive in extreme habitats like hotsprings, desert, snow and deep sea.

True ☐ False ☐

(iii) Many of them live in or on other organisms as parasites.

True ☐ False ☐

13. Write the names of different bacteria according to shapes given below.

A *B* *C* *D*

A. ____________

B. ____________

C. ____________

D. ____________

14. Bacterial structure is very ____________, but they are very ____________ in behaviour.

15. According to the mode of nutrition,

(i) The bacteria which depend on other organisms or on dead organic matter for food are ____________.

(ii) The bacteria which synthesise their own food from inorganic substrate are____________.

***16.** Name the two types of autotrophic nutrition performed by bacteria.

____

***17.** Match the following columns.

Column I (Types of Archaebacteria)	Column II (Habitats)
A. Halophiles	1. Hotsprings and extreme acidity
B. Thermoacidophiles	2. Extreme salty areas
C. Methanogens	3. Marshy areas

A. ____________ B. ____________ C. ____________.

***18.** Which of the following bacteria can be a source of an enzyme that can be used at very high temperatures?

(a) Acidophiles ☐ (b) Thermoacidophiles ☐
(c) Methanogens ☐ (d) Cyanobacteria ☐

***19.** Read the following characters.

(i) Found in the gut of ruminants.
(ii) Commercially used for methane (biogas) production.

Above characters are related to group of organisms collectively called as ____________.

***20.** Consider the following statements.

Statement I Biogas production requires aerobic digestion by methane forming methanogens.

Statement II Methanogens are archaea that tolerate high temperature and salt concentration.

Choose the correct option from the following.

(a) Statement I is true, but statement II is false ☐
(b) Statement I is false, but statement II is true ☐

21. Name the bacterial group which is also known as 'True bacteria'. ____________.

***22.** The cyanobacteria are also referred to as ____________.

***23.** Cyanobacteria have chlorophyll ____________ (*a*/*b*/*c*) similar to green plants.

***24.** Blue-green algae are unicellular, colonial or filamentous, freshwater/marine or terrestrial algae.

True ☐ False ☐

***25.** Specialised cells present in cyanobacteria for fixing atmospheric nitrogen is known as ____________.

***26.** Which of the following structures are the site of the below reaction?

$$\underset{\text{Atmospheric nitrogen}}{N_2} + 12\,ATP \xrightarrow{\text{Nitrogenase}} \underset{\text{Ammonia}}{2NH_3} + 12\,ADP + \underset{\text{Inorganic phosphate}}{12P_i}$$

(a) Fruiting bodies ☐ (b) Pellicle ☐
(c) Heterocyst ☐ (d) Dikaryon ☐

***27.** Identify the following organism 'X' and its structures A and B.

A. ____________________

B. ____________________

X. ____________________

***28.** Choose the odd one out with respect to eubacteria.

Spirulina, Methanococcus, Nostoc, Anabaena

____

***29.** Given below are characteristics of eubacteria, write whether these are photosynthetic autotrophic bacteria or chemosynthetic autotrophic bacteria.

(i) Oxidise various nitrates, nitrites, ammonia and use the released energy for their ATP production. ____________________

(ii) Form blooms in polluted water bodies. ____________________

(iii) Play a great role in recycling of nutrients like nitrogen, phosphorus, iron and sulphur.

____

30. Identify the incorrect statement about heterotrophic bacteria.

(a) They are helpful in making curd from milk. ☐

(b) They play a great role in recycling nutrients. ☐

(c) The help in nitrogen fixation in leguminous roots. ☐

(d) These aid in decomposition. ☐

***31.** Given below are some economic importance of heterotrophic bacteria. How many of them are correct?

Antibiotic production, Curd making, Coagulation of blood, Decomposition, Biogas production, Nitrogen-fixation.

____

32. Choose the odd one out with respect to disease caused by bacteria.

Cholera, Typhoid, Citrus canker, Influenza

____

33. Identify the below 'X' process in bacteria and write its parts A, B and C.

A. ____________________

B. ____________________

C. ____________________

X. ____________________

34. Sometimes under unfavourable conditions, bacteria produce <u>fragments</u>.
(*Rewrite the statement after correcting the underlined word.*)

____

35. "Organism A reproduce by adopting a primitive type of DNA transfer from one species to another while B is the smallest living pathogen that affects animals and plants". With respect to the above statement.

Choose the correct option.

(a) Organism A is mycoplasma and organism B is bacteria ☐

(b) Both organism A and organsism B represent mycoplasma ☐

(c) Organism A is bacteria and organism B is mycoplasma ☐

(d) Both organism A and organism B denote bacteria ☐

***36.** Name the organism based on the following characters.

(i) Lack cell wall

(ii) Anaerobic

(iii) Smallest cell (0.1-0.15 μm in length)

____

37. Consider the following statements.

Statement I Mycoplasma are smallest living cells that possess cell wall.

Statement II Most of the mycoplasma are pathogenic to man.

Choose the concet option from the following.

(a) Statement I is true, but statement II is false ☐

(b) Statement I is false, but statement II is true ☐

***38.** Consider the following statements.

I. Heterotrophic bacteria are most abundant in nature.

II. The majority of heterotrophic bacteria are important nitrogen fixers.

III. Bacteria reproduce mainly by fission. Sometimes under favourable conditions they produce spores.

IV. Mycoplasma can survive in anoxic conditions and can be pathogenic to animals.

Choose the option with incorrect statements.

(a) II and IV ☐ (b) II and III ☐

(c) I and IV ☐ (d) I and III ☐

TOPIC 2

Kingdom-Protista

NCERT Pg. 14-16

39. In which kingdom, chrysophytes, dinoflagellates, euglenoids, slime moulds and protozoans are included?

____

40. How many of the given features are correct with respect to members of kingdom- Protista?

Single-celled, Eukaryotic, Membrane bound organelles, Lacks nucleus, Terrestrial, Connecting link between plants, animals and fungi

____

41. Complete the following analogy given below with respect to Protista.
Asexual reproduction : ____________ Sexual reproduction: ____________ .

42. Write the common biological term.

Diatoms, Desmids, Golden algae

____

43. The cell wall is composed of two thin overlapping shells which fit together like a soap case in ________________ .

44. Siliceous frustules of diatoms being indestructible piles up at the bottom of ocean and forms a thick bed over billions of years. Such a thick bed is known as ________________ .

45. Which of the following is not the economic importance of 'Diatomaceous earth' or 'Diatomite'.

Polishing, Filtering oil and syrups, Biogas production, Making sound and fireproof rooms, Insulation material in refrigerators, Source of sodium silicate.

____

46. ____________ are the chief producers in the oceans.

47. Dinoflagellates are mostly marine and (saprophytic/photosynthetic) organisms.

48. Dinoflagellates appear yellow, green, brown, blue or red depending on the main pigments present in their cells.

True ☐ False ☐

49. Which protist group possesses two flagella, one lies longitudinally and other transversely?

____

50. Identify the dinoflagellate based on the given features.
(i) Form 'red tides' in warm coastal water.
(ii) Release toxin to kill prey.
(iii) Cell wall has stiff cellulosic plates on the outer surface.

____

51. Euglenoids have flexible body due to the presence of ________ and bear ________ flagella.

52. In contrary to the rigidity observed in plant cells, euglenoids have a more flexible structure due to the presence of________________ rich layer.

(a) hemicellulose ☐ (b) chitin ☐
(c) pectin ☐ (d) protein ☐

53. Write the number of flagella in euglenoids.________________

54. *Euglena* is called a plant due to the presence of ________________ and an animal due to ________________ nutrition.

55. Which group of organisms is represented by the given figure?

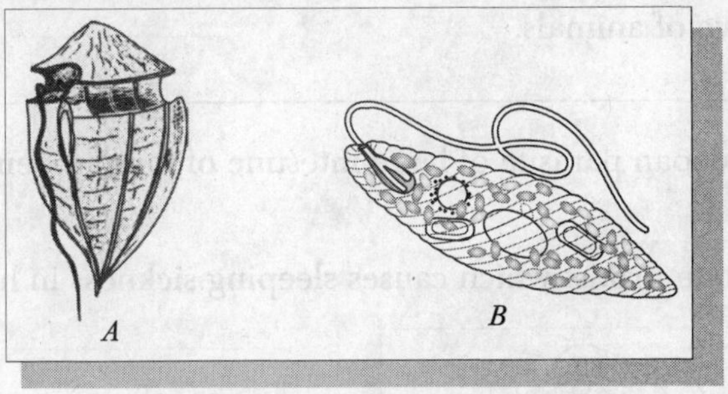

A ________________

B ________________

56. Consider the following statements.

Statement I *Euglena* are conditional heterotrophs when exposed to conditions like absence of sunlight.

Statement II The fine texture of diatomaceous earth is used in filtration of oils and syrups.

Choose the correct option from the following.

(a) Statement I is true, but statement II is false ☐
(b) Statement I is false, but statement II is true ☐
(c) Both statements I and II are true ☐
(d) Both statements I and II are false ☐

***57.** The slime moulds are ________________ (photosynthetic protists/saprophytic protists).

58. The body of slime moulds moves along the decaying twigs and leaves engulfing organic material.

True ☐ False ☐

59. The multinucleate slimy mass of protoplasm forming the body of slime moulds is known as <u>myxamoeba</u>.
(*Rewrite the statement after correcting the underlined word.*)

____

***60.** Plasmodial slime mould under unfavourable conditions differentiates and forms fruiting bodies, i.e. ________________ bearing spores. A spore possesses a cell wall made up of ________________. These spores are dispersed *via* ________________.

61. Consider the following statements.

Statement I Many protozoans belonging to the Protista group can be pathogenic to humans.

Statement II Dehydration can stimulate the formation of fruiting bodies in many slime moulds.

Choose the correct option from the following.

(a) Statement I is true, but statement II is false ☐

(b) Both statements I and II are true ☐

62. Name the protist group based on the given below characters.

(i) Heterotrophs (ii) Predators or Parasites

(iii) Believed to be primitive relative of animals.

____

63. ______________ is a protozoan parasite of large intestine of human beings and causes the disease dysentery.

64. Identify the given figure of protozoan protist which causes sleeping sickness in human.

____

65. Identify the given figure *'X'* and write the name of structures *A*, *B*, *C* and *D*.

A. ______________

B. ______________

C. ______________

D. ______________

X. ______________

66. All of the following bear flagella for locomotion, except

(a) *Gonyaulax* ☐ (b) *Paramecium* ☐

(c) *Euglena* ☐ (d) *Trypanosoma* ☐

67. Write the names of the group of protozoan based on their characters.

(i) They move to capture their prey by forming pseudopodia and some marine forms have silica shells on their surface. ______________

(ii) Actively moving organisms having a cavity (gullet) that opens to the outside of the cell surface. ______________

68. The sporozoans are all internal ________________ that typically have an infective cyst stage in their life cycle. An example of sporozoan is the genus ____________, which causes malaria.

69. Match the following columns.

	Column I (Groups of protozoan)		Column II (Examples)
A.	Amoeboid	1.	*Paramecium*
B.	Flagellated	2.	*Plasmodium*
C.	Ciliated	3.	*Entamoeba*
D.	Sporozoans	4.	*Trypanosoma*

A.__________ B.__________ C.__________ D.__________

TOPIC 3

Kingdom-Fungi

NCERT Pg. 16-18

70. The fungi constitute a unique kingdom of __________ organisms.

71. Give one an example of each

(i) Edible fungi __________ (ii) Poisonous fungi __________

72. A unicellular fungi, __________ is used to make bread and beer.

73. The causal organism of wheat rust is __________ (*Ustilago/Puccinia*).

74. Fungi prefer to grow in __________ environment.

75. With the exception of <u>mushrooms</u>, all other fungi are filamentous.
(*Rewrite the statement after correcting the underlined word*).

____

***76.** Except yeast, the bodies of fungi consist of long, slender, thread-like structure called __________, which form a network called __________.

77. Coenocytic hyphae have septal walls in its filaments.

True ☐ False ☐

78. Describe the correct condition as represented in the provided image:

A *B*

(a) *A* – Coenocytic, *B* – Septate ☐
(b) *A* – Septate, *B* – Coenocytic ☐
(c) *A* – Aseptate, *B* – Septate ☐
(d) *A* – Coenocytic, *B* – Aseptate ☐

79. Fungal cell walls composed of ________ and ________.

***80.** The lichens live as symbionts having ________ and ________ as symbiotic partners.

***81.** Consider the following statements.

Statement I In the absence of cross walls, a mycelium forms a continuous multinucleate cytoplasmic structure.

Statement II Mycorrhizal association between plants and fungi provides benefit only to the fungal species.

Choose the correct option from the following.

(a) Statement I is true, but statement II is false ☐

(b) Statement I is false, but statement II is true ☐

(c) Both statements I and II are true ☐

(d) Both statements I and II are false ☐

82. Write the biological term for the following sentences.

(i) Fungi that absorb soluble organic matter from dead substrates. ________

(ii) Fungi that absorb nutrients directly from the cytoplasm of living host. ________

(iii) Association of fungi with roots of higher plants. ________

***83.** Given below is the flowchart of the types of reproduction in fungi.

Reproduction

Vegetative means	Asexual spores	Sexual spores
(i) ________	(i) ________	(i) ________
(ii) ________	(ii) ________	(ii) ________
(iii) ________	(iii) ________	(iii) ________

Write the correct words in the blanks given.

***84.** Name the three steps of sexual cycle in fungi.

***85.** In fungi, the fusion of protoplasms between two motile or non-motile gametes is called cytokinesis. (*Rewrite the statement after correcting the underlined word.*)

____

***86.** Given below are few statements choose the correct ones.

I. Fusion of protoplasms only between two motile gametes is called plasmogamy.

II. Fusion of two nuclei is called karyogamy.

III. Karyogamy results in the formation of zygospores that bear two copies of the genome.

IV. Meiosis in zygote results in the formation of haploid spores.

Choose the correct answer from the options given below.

(a) I and II ☐ (b) II and III ☐

(c) II, III and IV ☐ (d) II and IV ☐

***87.** In fungi, karyogamy is the fusion of two ________.

88. Which of the following represents an incorrect match ?

(a) Basidiocarp – $2n$ ☐ (b) Ascocarp - $2n$ ☐

(c) Zygospore - $2n$ ☐ (d) Conidia - $2n$ ☐

***89.** Dikaryophase is a specific property of __________ and __________ classes of fungi.

***90.** The morphology of mycelium, mode of spore formation and type of fruiting bodies forms the basis of classification of fungi.

True ☐ False ☐

91. Members of __________ are found in aquatic habitats and on decaying wood in moist and damp places or as obligate parasites.

92. Name the class of fungi which shows all the three types of sexual reproduction.

Isogamous, Anisogamous, Oogamous

____

93. In Phycomycetes, zygospore is formed by the fusion of two gametes. These gametes are similar in morphology, i.e. __________ or dissimilar, i.e. __________.

94. Consider the following statements.

Statement I Zoospores are exogenously produced in the sporangium of Phycomycetes.

Statement II The gametes produced by *Rhizopus* and *Mucor* are always isogamous in nature.

Choose the correct option from the following.

(a) Statement I is true, but statement II is false ☐

(b) Both statements I and II are false ☐

95. Identify the fungi shown below in figures *A*, *B* and *C*.

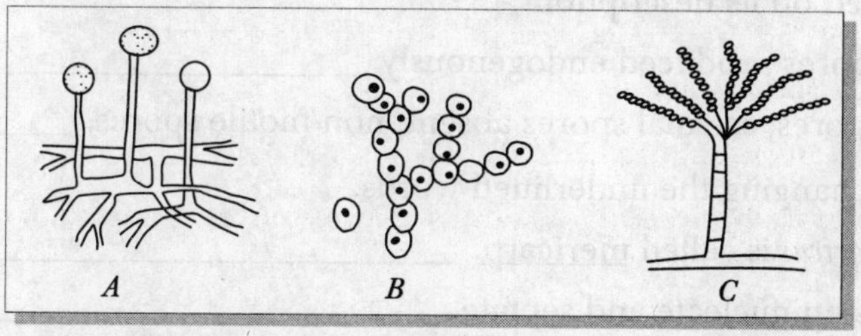

A. __________

B. __________

C. __________

96. Consider the following statements.

Statement I The mycelium of Ascomycetes has a discontinuous cytoplasm separated by cross walls.

Statement II In *Penicillium* the haploid conidia germinates to produce the haploid mycelium.

Choose the correct option from the following.

(a) Statement I is true, but statement II is false ☐

(b) Both statements I and II are true ☐

***97.** In *Penicillium*, the asexual reproduction takes place by __________.

***98.** The wonder drug penicillin, is extracted from which of the species of *Penicillium*? ____________

***99.** Categorise the types of spores into their production types in fungi.

Zoospores, Aplanospores, Conidia, Ascospores, Basidiospores

(i) Exogenous ____________.

(ii) Endogenous ____________

***100.** In Ascomycetes, ascospores are produced in a sac called ____________

101. Which fungus is used extensively in biochemical and genetic works? ____________

***102.** Name the class of fungi on the basis of their characters.

(i) They are saprophytic, decomposers, parasitic or coprophilous (growing on dung). ____________

(ii) They grow in soil, on logs and tree stumps and live in plant bodies as parasites. ____________

103. Name the common class of these fungi.

Mushroom, Bracket fungi, Smut fungi

____

104. In which class of fungi, asexual spores are generally not found, but vegetative reproduction by fragmentation is common?

____

***105.** The basidiospores are ____________ produced on the ____________.

106. How many basidiospores are produced from the basidium? ____________

***107.** Name the type of fungi, based on its description.

Description 1. True fungi, spores produced endogenously ____________.

Description 2. Exogenous spores, asexual spores absent, non-motile spores. ____________.

108. Rewrite the statements by changing the underlined words.

(i) The fruiting body of *Agaricus* is called mericarp. ____________

(ii) Coenocytic mycelium is uninucleate and septate. ____________

(iii) The parasitic fungi on mustard is *Mucor*. ____________

109. Write the scientific names of the following fungi.

(i) Bread mould ____________

(ii) Mushroom ____________

(iii) Smut ____________

(iv) Rust fungus ____________

110. Consider the following statements.

Statement I Imperfect fungi are so named because the mycelium structure is not properly known.

Statement II Deuteromycetes can follow parasitic or saprophytic modes of nutrition.

Choose the correct option from the following.

(a) Statement I is true, but statement II is false ☐

(b) Statement I is false, but statement II is true ☐

111. Choose the odd one out.

Phycomycetes, Ascomycetes, Zygomycetes, Basidiomycetes, Deuteromycetes

____

***112.** Most of the members of the class-Ascomycetes are decomposers of litter and help in mineral cycling. (*Rewrite the statement after correcting the underlined word.*)

____

***113.** Which of the following is not a correct combination of fungi and its respective asexual spore?

(a) *Albugo*– aplanospores ☐ (b) *Penicillium*– conidia ☐

(c) *Agaricus* – basidiospores ☐ (d) *Trichoderma* – conidia ☐

***114.** Rewrite the statements after correcting the underlined word.

(i) In Phycomycetes, asexual reproduction takes place by zoospores (motile) and conidiophores (non-motile).

____

(ii) In Ascomycetes, asexual spores are conidia and sexual spores are basidiospores.

____

(iii) In Deuteromycetes, sex organs are absent, but plasmogamy is brought about by the fusion of two vegetative cells. ______________________________

***115.** Match the following columns.

Column I (Fungi classes)		Column II (Common names)	
A.	Ascomycetes	1.	Club fungi
B.	Basidiomycetes	2.	Sac fungi
C.	Deuteromycetes	3.	Algae fungi
D.	Phycomycetes	4.	Fungi imperfecti

A.__________ B.__________ C.__________ D.__________

116. Fill in the table for classification of fungi.

Fungi classes	Features	Members
(A)	Mycelium septate and branched	*Neurospora*
Phycomycetes	(B)	*Rhizopus*
Deuteromycetes	Mycelium septate and branched	(C)
(D)	Mycelium branched and septate	(E)

A.__________ B.__________ C.__________

D.__________ E.__________

TOPIC 4

Kingdom-Plantae and Animalia

NCERT Pg. 19

117. In kingdom–Plantae, few members are partially heterotrophic like insectivorous plants or parasites. With reference to the above statement give examples of insectivorous plant and the parasitic plant. ______________________

118. Give a common term.

Bryophytes, Pteridophytes, Gymnosperms, Angiosperms

____

119. Life cycle of plants have two distinct phases, the diploid ______________ and the haploid ______________ (sporophytic/gametophytic).

120. State true or false.

(i) Animals show definite growth pattern and grow into adults that have a definite shape and size.

True ☐ False ☐

(ii) All animals have elaborated sensory and neuromotor mechanisms.

True ☐ False ☐

(iii) Sexual reproduction is followed by embryological development in animals.

True ☐ False ☐

121. Out of the words/features given in the box, choose the correct ones for describing plants and animals.

Chlorophyll, Cellulose present, Glycogen present, Holozoic nutrition, Mobility, Alternation of generation

Kingdom–Plantae	Kingdom–Animalia
______________	______________
______________	______________
______________	

TOPIC 5

Viruses, Viroids, Prions and Lichens

NCERT Pg. 19-21

122. Name the acellular organisms not included in five kingdom classification of Whittaker.

____

123. Viruses are ______________ (non-cellular/cellular) organisms that are characterised by having an inner crystalline structure outside the living cell.

***124.** Viruses infect, by taking over the machinery of the host cell to replicate themselves and then kill the host cell.

True ☐ False ☐

125. The name 'virus' means ____________

126. Given below is the diagram of a virus. Identify the virus '*X*' and write its parts *A* and *B*.

A. ____________

B. ____________

X. ____________

127. Name the scientists who said that 'viruses are smaller than bacteria'.

____

128. Match the following columns.

Column I (Scientists)	Column II (Contributions)
A. Pasteur	1. *Contagium vivum fluidum*
B. Beijerinek	2. Crystallisation of viruses
C. Stanley	3. Virus means venom

A. ____________ B. ____________ C. ____________

129. The genetic material of viruses consists of ____________

***130.** No virus contains both RNA and DNA.

True ☐ False ☐

***131.** Consider the following statements.

Statement I Viruses can capture the host cell machinery and direct them to produce progeny viruses.

Statement II RNA viruses owing to the nature of the genome, can mutate faster than DNA viruses.

Choose the correct option from the following.

(a) Statement I is true, but statement II is false ☐

(b) Both statements I and II are true ☐

***132.** Rewrite the statements by changing the underlined word.

(i) Virus is an infectious <u>lipoprotein particle</u>. ____________

(ii) Bacteriophage is a <u>*ds* RNA virus</u>. ____________

(iii) Virus that attacks bacteria is called <u>prions</u>. ____________

***133.** The genetic material of virus is *ss*RNA, *ds*RNA, *ss*DNA and *ds*DNA. Out of these the genetic material of viral that infect.

(i) Plants ______________________

(ii) Animals ______________________

134. Identify the virus *'X'* and name its structures marked as *A, B, C, D* and *E*.

A. ______________________

B. ______________________

C. ______________________

D. ______________________

E. ______________________

X. ______________________

135. Where is the genetic material of the given structure placed?

(a) R ☐

(b) P ☐

(c) S ☐

(d) Q ☐

***136.** Name the scientific term for the statements given below.

(i) The protein coat of a virus. ______________________

(ii) The subunit of capsid. ______________________

137. Write a common term for the diseases mentioned in the box given below.

Common cold (flu), Mumps, Herpes, Influenza

138. Complete the following analogy given below.

Tobacco mosaic disease : Plant viral disease : : ________ : Animal viral disease

139. Out of the following symptoms, how many are shown by plants infected with virus?

Mosaic formation, Leaf rolling and curling, Leaf spots Yellowing and vein clearing, Dwarfing, Stunted growth

____

***140.** Name the microorganism discovered by TO Diener in 1971, which is smaller than viruses.

____

***141.** Viroids are infectious agents made up of free ________ (DNA/RNA) that lacks ________ (protein/carbohydrate) coat found in virus.

***142.** TO Diener discovered a popular disease in plants called ________ caused by ________.

***143.** Certain infectious neurological diseases are transmitted by abnormally folded proteins called ________ (virions/prions).

144. Dementia related to CJD in humans occur due to

(a) misfolded protein ☐ (b) unfolded protein ☐
(c) deletion of a protein ☐ (d) clumping of a protein ☐

***145.** The other name of Bovine Spongiform Encephalopathy (BSE) is ________.

***146.** The full form of CJD in humans is ________

***147.** The algal and fungal components of a lichen are respectively called ________ and ________.

***148.** Write one function of each

(i) Algal component of lichen. ________

(ii) Fungal component of lichen. ________

***149.** Lichens grow very well in ________ (less/more) polluted areas.

***150.** Consider the following statements.

Statement I The phycobiont absorbs mineral nutrient for its partner mycobiont in the mutualistic association.

Statement II Lichens accumulate in areas with high Air Quality Index (AQI) and are indicators of pollution.

Choose the correct option from the following.

(a) Statement I is true, but statement II is false ☐
(b) Both statements I and II are false ☐

151. Write the correct term against each statement from the box given below.

Viroid, Prions, Virus, Lichen

(i) Proteinaceous infectious particles with small amount of nucleic acid. ________
(ii) Small infectious agent with low molecular weight . ________

Assertion-Reason Questions

The following questions consist of two statements- Assertion (A) and Reason (R). Answer these questions by selecting the appropriate option given below.
(a) Both A and R are true and R is the correct explanation of A
(b) Both A and R are true, but R is not the correct explanation of A
(c) A is true, but R is false
(d) A is false, but R is true

***1.** **Assertion** (A) Hot springs and volcanic sites also showcase a diversity in the microbial population.

Reason (R) Archaebacteria like thermoacidophiles and acidophiles are adapted to survive extreme conditions including those found in volcanoes.

(a) ☐ (b) ☐ (c) ☐ (d) ☐

***2.** **Assertion** (A) Chemosynthetic bacteria recycle nutrients like iron and sulphur.

Reason (R) Chemosynthetic bacteria depends on other organisms for food and are hence heterotrophic.

(a) ☐ (b) ☐ (c) ☐ (d) ☐

***3.** **Assertion** (A) Diatoms and golden algae can resist destruction by a large extent due to the nature of their cell wall.

Reason (R) The cell wall is overlapped and embedded with silica.

(a) ☐ (b) ☐ (c) ☐ (d) ☐

4. **Assertion** (A) Oceans which show red tides can be of scenic beauty, but could probably be dead.

Reason (R) The flexibility of *Euglena* is due to the protein rich layer called pellicle instead of cell wall.

(a) ☐ (b) ☐ (c) ☐ (d) ☐

***5.** **Assertion** (A) Ascomycetes and Basidiomycetes in their life cycle do not always have a single nucleus.

Reason (R) The fungal fruiting bodies undergo equational division and as a result, form haploid spores in them.

(a) ☐ (b) ☐ (c) ☐ (d) ☐

***6.** **Assertion** (A) *Claviceps* are sac fungi with a mycelium which is aseptate and coenocytic.

Reason (R) Ascospores are produced endogenously in the asci which are arranged in the ascocarps.

(a) ☐ (b) ☐ (c) ☐ (d) ☐

***7.** **Assertion** (A) The Basidiomycetes often pass through a dikaryotic phase after plasmogamy.

Reason (R) The fusion of the nucleus causes an intermediate stage with two nuclei condition.

(a) ☐ (b) ☐ (c) ☐ (d) ☐

***8.** **Assertion** (A) Viruses contain a protein coat made up of monomeric units around their genetic material.

Reason (R) The protein coat called capsid is responsible for the virulence and is integrated in the host genome.

(a) ☐ (b) ☐ (c) ☐ (d) ☐

Case Based Questions

1. The image illustrates the life cycle of mushrooms. Study the image carefully and answer the following questions:

(i) What is the ploidy of structure labelled as X?

(a) $2n$ ☐ (b) n ☐ (c) $4n$ ☐ (d) $3n$ ☐

(ii) Which of the following process converts A to X?

(a) Mitosis ☐ (b) Meiosis ☐
(c) Germination ☐ (d) Pollination ☐

(iii) Choose the correct combination.

(a) P – Karyogamy Q – Plasmogamy ☐ (b) P – Plasmogamy Q – Karyogamy ☐
(c) P – Fertilisation Q – Plasmogamy ☐ (d) P – Karyogamy Q – Fertilisation ☐

***2.** A rabbit that has developed tumours on its body was selected for an experiment. The blood from this rabbit was collected and was injected into another healthy rabbit. Tumours were seen to develop on the latter as well. On close investigation of the blood sample, it showed crystalline structures with a proteinaceous coat. With reference to the provided information, answer the following.

(i) To which kingdom can the isolated microorganisms be placed?

(a) Protista ☐ (b) Monera ☐
(c) Protozoa ☐ (d) No specific kingdom ☐

(ii) What is the purpose of the protein coat?

(a) Virulence ☐ (b) Pathogenicity ☐
(c) Protection of genome ☐ (d) Replication ☐

(iii) What cannot be the possible infectious agent in the isolated particle?

(a) *ss* RNA ☐ (b) *ds*RNA ☐
(c) *ds* DNA ☐ (d) *t*DNA ☐

COMPETITION EDGE UP

1. Which one of the following is not a criterion for classification of fungi? [NEET 2024]

(a) Morphology of mycelium
(b) Mode of nutrition
(c) Mode of spore formation
(d) Fruiting body

2. Match List I and List II. [NEET 2024]

	List I		List II
A.	Rhizopus	i.	Mushroom
B.	Ustilago	ii.	Smut fungus
C.	Puccinia	iii.	Bread mould
D.	Agaricus	iv.	Rust fungus

Choose the correct answer from the options given below.

(a) A-iii, B-ii, C-iv, D-i
(b) A-i, B-iii, C-ii, D-iv
(c) A-iii, B-ii, C-i, D-iv
(d) A-iv, B-iii, C-ii, D-i

3. Which of the following is a correct statement? [NCERT Pg. 13, NEET 2022]

(a) Bacteria are exclusively heterotrophic organisms
(b) Slime moulds are saprophytic organisms classified under kingdom–Monera
(c) Mycoplasma have DNA, Ribosome and cell wall
(d) Cyanobacteria are a group of autotrophic organisms classified under kingdom–Monera

4. Which of the following statements is correct? [NCERT Pg. 17, NEET 2021]

(a) Some of the organisms can fix atmospheric nitrogen in specialised cells called sheath cells
(b) Fusion of two cells is called Karyogamy
(c) Fusion of protoplasms between two motile or non-motile gametes is called plasmogamy
(d) Organisms that depend on living plants are called saprophytes

5. Which of the following is incorrect about cyanobacteria? [NCERT Pg. 13, NEET 2020]

(a) They are photoautotrophs
(b) They lack heterocysts
(c) They often form blooms in polluted water bodies
(d) They have chlorophyll-a similar to green plants

6. Which of the following is correct about viroids? [NCERT Pg. 21, NEET 2020]

(a) They have free RNA without protein coat
(b) They have DNA with protein coat
(c) They have free DNA without protein coat
(d) They have RNA with protein coat

7. Which of the following statements is incorrect? [NEET 2019]

(a) Morels and truffles are edible delicacies
(b) Claviceps is a source of many alkaloids and LSD
(c) Conidia are produced exogenously and ascospores endogenously
(d) Yeasts have filamentous bodies with long thread-like hyphae

8. Match Column I with Column II. [NEET 2019]

	Column I		Column II
A.	Saprophyte	1.	Symbiotic association of fungi with plant roots
B.	Parasite	2.	Decomposition of dead organic materials
C.	Lichens	3.	Living on living plants or animals
D.	Mycorrhiza	4.	Symbiotic association of algae and fungi

Choose the correct answer from the options given below

	A	B	C	D
(a)	1	2	3	4
(b)	3	2	1	4
(c)	2	1	3	4
(d)	2	3	4	1

Chapter 03

Plant Kingdom

Scan and take Chapter Test

TOPIC 1

Introduction to Plants

NCERT Pg. 23-24

1. Blue-green algae are the members of the plant kingdom.

True ☐ False ☐

2. Which of the following is included in plant kingdom?

Algae, Fungi, Angiosperm, Gymnosperm, Bryophytes, Pteridophytes, Lichen

____

3. Find the odd one out with respect to criteria of earliest system of classification.

Habit, Colour, Shape of leaves, Embryology

4. Name the scientist who gave artificial system of classification.

____

5. Artificial systems gave equal weightage to _______________ and _______________ characters.

6. Natural system of classification is based on natural affinities among the organisms and consider both _______________ and _______________ features.

7. Name the scientists who gave natural system of classification.

____

8. Phylogenetic classification system is based on _______________ relationships between various organisms.

9. Organisms belonging to same taxa have a common ancestor.

True ☐ False ☐

Concept: all questions bearing * are important for NEET & CUET

10. Match the following columns.

Column I (Classification systems)	Column II (Features)
A Chemotaxonomy	1. Numbers and codes
B. Cytotaxonomy	2. Evolutionary relationship
C. Numerical taxonomy	3. Cytological information
D. Phylogenetic system	4. Chemical constituents of plants

A. ________ B. ________ C. ________ D ________

11. Consider the following statements.

Statement I Numerical taxonomy has made handling large amount of data at the same time possible.

Statement II Chromosome structure, number and behaviour is considered in chemotaxonomy.

Choose the correct option from the following.

(a) Statement I is true, but statement II is false ☐

(b) Statement I is false, but statement II is true ☐

TOPIC 2

Algae

NCERT Pg. 24-28

12. Chlorophyll- bearing, simple, thalloid, autotrophic and largely aquatic organisms are called as ________.

13. Write a common term for the symbiotic association of algae and fungi.

____

14. Name all the reproductive methods used by algae.

____

***15.** Write an example for the following.

(i) Unicellular algae ________

(ii) Colonial forms of algae ________

(iii) Filamentous forms of algae ________

16. Asexual reproduction in algae occurs by fragmentation.
(*Rewrite the statement after correcting the underlined word.*)

____

17. Each fragment after the fragmentation develops into a thallus, ranging in size from unicellular forms to complex giants.

True ☐ False ☐

18. Name the most common spore formed in algae during asexual reproduction.

____

19. Complete the following analogy.

Flagellated forms : ____________ : : Non-flagellated forms : ____________

20. Write the technical term for the fusion of gametes, which are similar in size.

____

21. Which of the following is the incorrect combination from the following?

(a) Isogamous : *Ulothrix* ☐ (b) Anisogamous : *Eudorina* ☐

(c) Oogamous : *Volvox* ☐ (d) Isogamous : *Fucus* ☐

22. Consider the alongside given Venn diagram. '*P*' denotes the area of similarity between the two algal species.

Volvox 'P' Fucus

This may be due to

(a) Presence of zoospores ☐

(b) Flagellated forms ☐

(c) Fusion between large non-motile female and smaller motile male gamete/oogamy ☐

(d) Anisogamy ☐

23. Non-motile and similar gametes are found in ____________ (*Spirogyra/ Chlamydomonas*).

24. Fusion between one large, non-motile female gamete and smaller, motile male gamete is termed anisogamous, e.g. *Volvox*.

(*Rewrite the statement after correcting the underlined word.*)

____

25. Large amount of CO_2 fixation on the earth is carried out by ____________ through photosynthesis.

26. ____________ are the primary producers of energy-rich compounds which form the basis of the food cycles of all aquatic animals.

***27.** The examples of marine algae used as food are ____________ and ____________.

***28.** Write the scientific term for the water holding substances produced by marine brown and red algae. ____________

***29.** Name the commercial product obtained from algae used to grow microbes.

____

***30.** Name the two species of algae from which agar is obtained.

____

***31.** ____________ is a unicellular alga, rich in proteins and is used as food supplement by space travellers.

***32.** Name the three main classes of algae.

____

***33.** Match column I with column II.

Column I (Algae)	Column II (Commercial importance)
A. Phaeophyceae	1. Ice-creams
B. Rhodophyceae	2. Algin
C. *Gelidium*	3. Carrageen
D. *Chlorella*	4. Space food

A B C D
(a) 2 3 1 4 ☐
(b) 2 3 4 1 ☐
(c) 2 4 3 1 ☐
(d) 2 1 3 4 ☐

***34.** Complete the flowchart given below.

Algae → *A* → Green algae; *B* → Brown algae; Rhodophyceae → *C*

A. ____________ B. ____________ C. ____________

35. Name the chlorophyll pigments in the class–Chlorophyceae.

____

36. Find the odd one out with respect to shape of chloroplast in Chlorophyceae.

Cup-shaped, Plate-like, Discoid, Reticulate, Hexagonal, Spiral

____

37. Name the storage body located in the chloroplast containing starch and protein.

____

***38.** Algae store food in the form of oil droplets.

True ☐ False ☐

39. Green algae usually have a rigid cell wall made of an inner layer of ____________ and an outer layer of ____________.

40. Vegetative reproduction in Chlorophyceae takes place by budding.

True ☐ False ☐

41. Flagellated zoospores are produced in megasporangia.

True ☐ False ☐

42. Consider the following statements.

Statement I *Ulothrix* and *Chara* can store starch and proteins in special storage bodies called pyrenoids.

Statement II *Volvox* forms daughter colonies when showing asexual reproduction.

Choose the correct option from the following.

(a) Statement I is true, but statement II is false ☐

(b) Both statements I and II are true ☐

***43.** Write any two examples of algae belonging to class–Chlorophyceae.

____

***44.** Name the class of algae that is found primarily in marine habitats.

____

***45.** Write an example for simple branched, filamentous forms of brown algae.

____

***46.** Name the two pigments other than chlorophyll, present in members of Phaeophyceae.

____

***47.** Colour of the members of phaeophyceae depend upon the amount of pigment named

____

***48.** Consider the following statements.

Statement I The shades of brown observed in *Fucus* is due to the different amounts of phycoerythrin present.

Statement II Stored food in *Ectocarpus* and *Dictyota* can be in the form mannitol or laminarin.

Choose the correct option from the following.

(a) Statement I is true, but statement II is false ☐

(b) Statement I is false, but statement II is true ☐

***49.** Food is stored as proteins in Phaeophyceae.

True ☐ False ☐

***50.** The carbohydrates can be stored in the form of ____________ and ____________ in brown algae.

***51.** Name the gelatinous coating covering the cellulosic wall in vegetative cells of brown algae.

____

52. Write the structure attaching the brown algae to the substratum.

____

53. ____________ (Stipe/Holdfast) is the part attaching the plant body to substratum.

54. Choose the correct combination with respect to the provided image:

(a) *A* – Stipe, *B* – Holdfast ☐

(b) *A* – Holdfast, *B* – Stipe ☐

(c) *A* – Stipe, *B* – Frond ☐

(d) *A* – Frond, *B* – Stipe ☐

55. In brown algae, a leaf-like photosynthetic organ called stalk is present.
(*Rewrite the statement after correcting the underlined word.*)

____

56. Asexual reproduction in brown algae occurs by monoflagellated zoospores.

True ☐ False ☐

57. The pear-shaped forms of gametes in brown algae are called ______________

***58.** Write any two examples of brown algae. ______________

***59.** Study the figure given below and answer the following questions.

(i) Name the plant. ______________

(ii) Identify *A*, *B* and *C*.

A. ______________

B. ______________

C. ______________

***60.** Study the figure given below and answer the following questions.

(i) Name the plant. ______________

(ii) Identify *A*, *B* and *C*.

A. ______________

B. ______________

C. ______________

***61.** Study the figure given below and answer the following questions.

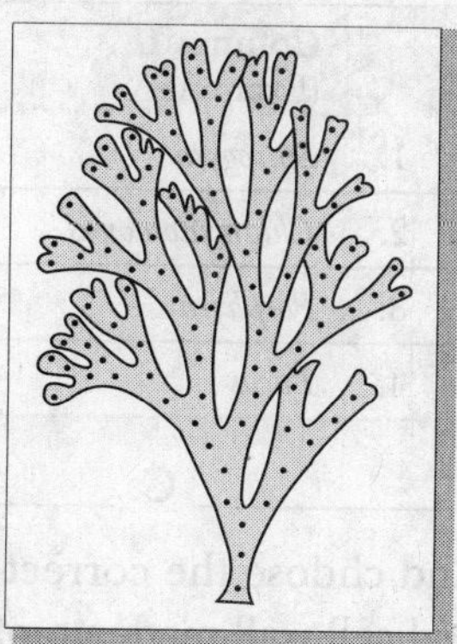

(i) Identify the algal species. ____________________

(ii) Name the pigment found in the cells of this species. ____________________

***62.** Name the predominant pigment in red algae. ____________________

***63.** Red algae do not occur at deep ocean depths.

True ☐ False ☐

64. The thalli of most red algae are unicellular.

True ☐ False ☐

65. The food is stored as ____________________ in red algae which is similar to ____________________ and ____________________ in structure.

66. Red algae reproduce asexually by non-motile spores.

True ☐ False ☐

67. Red algae reproduce sexually by motile gametes.

True ☐ False ☐

68. Sexual reproduction is ____________________ (isogamous, oogamous, anisogamous) in Rhodophyceae.

***69.** Write any two examples of Rhodophyceae. ____________________

***70.** Study the figure given below and identify the algal species.

71. Match the following columns.

	Column I (Features)		Column II (Examples)
A	Unicellular (motile)	1.	*Spirogyra*
B.	Pyriform gametes	2.	*Chlamydomonas*
C.	Filamentous	3.	*Porphyra*
D.	Chlorophyll-*a*, *d*	4.	*Fucus*

A. ____________ B. ____________ C. ____________ D. ____________

72. Read the following statements and choose the correct ones.

I. Green algae usually have a rigid cell wall made up of an inner layer of pectose and an outer layer of cellulose.

II. The sexual reproduction in Chlorophyceae may be isogamous, anisogamous or oogamous.

III. Phaeophyceae possess chlorophyll *a*, *c*, carotenoid and xanthophyll.

IV. In Phaeophyceae the food is stored as floridean starch.

V. The red algae usually reproduce vegetatively by fragmentation.

Choose the correct answer from the options given below.

(a) II, III and IV ☐ (b) II, III and V ☐

(c) I, II and III ☐ (d) II and IV ☐

73. Read the table carefully and fill up the blanks.

Classes	Major pigments	Stored food	Cell wall	Flagellar number and position of insertions
Chlorophyceae	(A)	Starch	Cellulose	2-8, equal, apical
Phaeophyceae	Chlorophyll-*a* and *c*, fucoxanthin	Mannitol, laminarin	(C)	2, unequal, lateral
Rhodophyceae	Chlorophyll-*a* and *d*, phycoerythrin	(B)	Cellulose	(D)

A. ____________ B. ____________ C. ____________ D. ____________

TOPIC 3

Bryophytes

NCERT Pg. 28-30

74. Bryophytes are also called ____________ of the plant kingdom.

75. Bryophytes live in soil, but depend on water for sexual reproduction.

True ☐ False ☐

***76.** The plant body of bryophytes are less differentiated than that of algae.

True ☐ False ☐

77. Name the structure in bryophytes that attach the plant body to substratum.

____

78. Bryophytes lack true root, stem or leaves.

True ☐ False ☐

***79.** The main plant body of bryophytes is the gametophyte.

True ☐ False ☐

80. The pre-dominant phase in the plant body of bryophyte is__________which is________.

81. Complete the following analogy.
Female : Male : : ________________________ : Antheridium

82. Name the biflagellated unicellular structure in antheridium which comes in contact with archegonium. ________________________________

83. In bryophytes, the multicellular body produced by zygote is called ______________.

***84.** The ________________________ is not free-living, but attached to the photosynthetic ________________________ and derives nourishment from it. (sporophyte/gametophyte).

***85.** Which of the following is correct about mosses?

(a) The gametophyte is haploid while the sporophyte is diploid ☐

(b) Both the gametophyte and sporophyte are diploid ☐

(c) Both the gametophyte and sporophyte are haploid ☐

(d) The gametophyte is diploid while the sporophyte is haploid. ☐

***86.** Sporophyte undergoes ________________________ to produce haploid spores which germinate to produce ________________________.

87. Name the moss which had long been used as fuel. ________________________________

88. Consider the following statements.

Statement I Peat obtained from *Funaria*, a moss, can be used as packing material due to their water holding capacity.

Statement II A flask shaped structure present in bryophytes that forms antherozoids is antheridium.

Choose the correct option from the following.

(a) Statement I is true, but statement II is false ☐

(b) Both statements I and II are false ☐

89. Mosses and ________________________ are the first organisms to colonise rocks.

90. Write the two divisions of bryophytes.

____

91. The plant body of a liverwort is haploid, e.g. *Marchantia*.
(*Rewrite the statement after correcting the underlined word.*)

____

92. Name the specialised structures formed in liverworts for asexual reproduction.

____

93. Consider the given image. Which of the following options shows presence of structure '*P*'?

(a) *Funaria* ☐

(b) *Polytrichum* ☐

(c) *Sphagnum* ☐

(d) *Marchantia* ☐

P

***94.** Gemmae are multicellular, green, asexual buds developed in small receptacles called ___________________ located on the thalli.

***95.** Gemma gets detached from the parent body and germinate to form new individuals.

True ☐ False ☐

96. During sexual reproduction in liverwort, male and female sex organs are produced on same thalli only.

True ☐ False ☐

***97.** Find the odd one out with respect to sporophyte of liverwort.

Capsule, Seta, Holdfast, Foot

____

98. After meiosis, the spore formation takes place within the ____________

99. Consider the following figure for the structural details of bryophyte. Answer the following questions.

(i) Identify *A*, *B* and *C*.

A
B
C

A. ________________________

B. ________________________

C. ________________________

(ii) Identify the ploidy of thallus structure shown.________________________

***100.** Name the first stage of life cycle of mosses.________________________

***101.** ______________ stage in mosses develops from secondary protonema on a lateral bud.

102. Leafy stage of mosses is attached to soil through multicellular and branched buds.
(*Rewrite the statement after correcting the underlined word.*)

____

***103.** Leafy stage does not bear sex organs.

True ☐ False ☐

104. Vegetative reproduction in mosses occurs by ________________________ and ________________________ in the ________________________.

***105.** Consider the following statements.

Statement I The protonema stage is obtained directly from the spores and is haploid.

Statement II Gametophyte is the pre-dominant stage in the life cycle of a moss.

Choose the correct option from the following.

(a) Statement I is true, but statement II is false ☐

(b) Both statements I and II are true ☐

***106.** The gametophyte in mosses is more elaborate than that in liverworts.

(*Rewrite the statement after correcting the underlined word.*)

____

107. *Funaria* and *Sphagnum* are called liverworts.

True ☐ False ☐

108. *Sphagnum* is also called as ____________________ (club moss/ peat moss).

109. Consider the following figure for structural details of moss. Answer the following questions.

(i) Identify *A*, *B*, *C*, *D* and *E*.

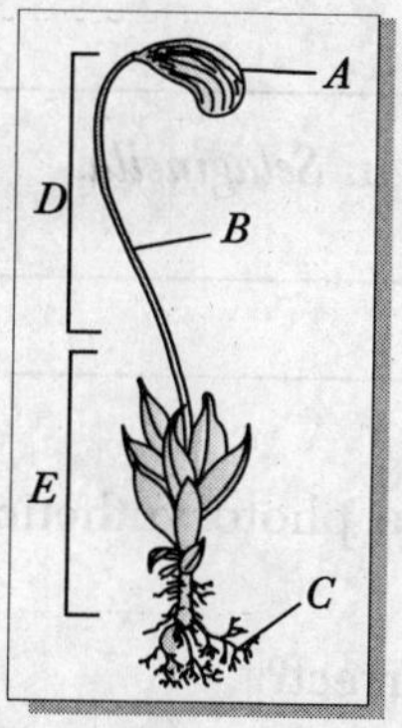

A *A*
D *D*
B *B*
E *E*
C *C*

A. ____________________

B. ____________________

C. ____________________

D. ____________________

E. ____________________

(ii) The given plant is ____________________

110. Consider the structural details shown in the following figure. Answer the following questions.

(i) Identify *A* and *B*.

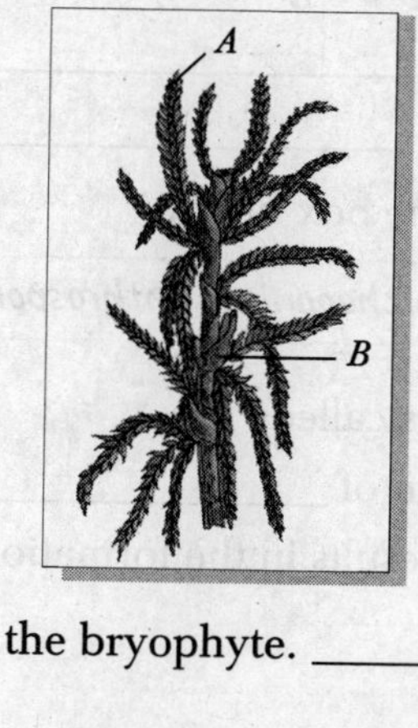

A
B

A. ____________________

B. ____________________

(ii) Name the bryophyte. ____________________

TOPIC 4

Pteridophytes

NCERT Pg. 30-32

111. ____________ are mainly used for medicinal purposes and as soil binders.

112. Pteridophytes are the first <u>aquatic</u> plants to possess vascular tissues.
(*Rewrite the statement after correcting the underlined word.*)
____

113. Which of the following tissues allow pteridophytes to adapt to terrestrial habitats?

(a) Apical meristem ☐ (b) Xylem and phloem ☐
(c) Parenchyma ☐ (d) Collenchyma ☐

***114.** In pteridophytes, dominant phase in the life cycle is ____________.

***115.** The main plant body is a ____________ which is differentiated into true root, stem and leaves.

116. The leaves in ferns are ____________ (macrophylls/ microphylls)

117. Write the technical name for the leaf-like appendages found in sporangia.
____

***118.** Write the compact arrangements of sporophyll found in *Selaginella.*
____

119. Spores are produced in spore mother cells by ____________ (equational/ reductional) division.

***120.** Germination of spores gives rise to small, multicellular photosynthetic thalloid gametophytes called ____________.

121. Which of the following statements about ferns is incorrect?

(a) The sporophyll in *Equisetum* is arranged into a compact structure called strobili. ☐
(b) The spore mother cells of the sporangia divide mitotically to produce spores. ☐
(c) Spores germinate to form photosynthetic gametophyte called prothallus. ☐
(d) Unlike mosses, the main plant body in ferns is the diploid sporophyte. ☐

122. Write any two reasons which restrict pteridophytic plant growth in limited area.

(i) ____________
(ii) ____________

***123.** Complete the following, using the words given in the box below.

Archegonium, Archesporium, Antherozoids, Anthers, Archegonia, Anthrospore, Antheridia.

The gametophytes bear male and female sex organs called ____________ and ____________, respectively. Fusion of ____________ with the egg present in the ____________ results in the formation of zygote.

***124.** Arrange the correct sequence of reproductive structures in pteridophytes.

Strobili → Sporophyll → Sporangia → Spores → Spore mother cell

____

***125.** Pteridophytes with spores of similar kinds are called ___________

***126.** Heterospory is the production of ___________

127. Consider the following statements.

Statement I The antherozoids of ferns released from antheridia travel to the archegonium by water.

Statement II *Selaginella* and *Salvinia* produce two types of spores, macrospores and microspores.

Choose the correct option from the following.

(a) Statement I is true, but statement II is false ☐

(b) Both statements I and II are true ☐

***128.** Identify *A*, *B* and *C* in the following figure.

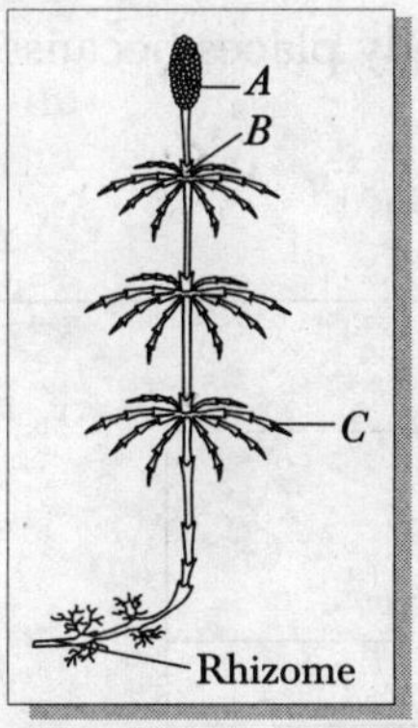

A. ___________

B. ___________

C. ___________

***129.** Go through the following figures and identify these plants (*A*, *B* and *C*).

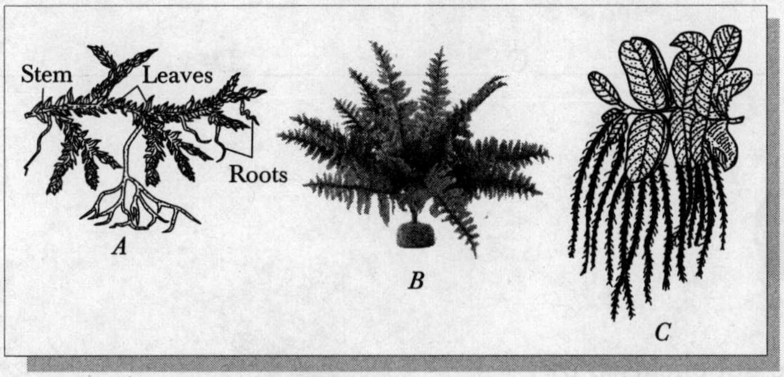

A. ___________

B. ___________

C. ___________

130. Megaspore germinates to give rise to female gametophyte.

True ☐ False ☐

131. The female gametophytes are retained in parent ___________ in heterosporous pteridophytes.

132. The development of zygote into young embryo take place within the ______________.

133. Development of zygote into embryo within the female gametophyte is a precursor to the ______________, which is important for evolution.

134. Consider the following statements.

Statement I Evolutionary history claims pteridophytes to have succeeded plants having the property of seed habit.

Statement II Presence of macrophylls is observed in *Selaginella* while ferns show the presence of microphylls.

Choose the correct option from the following.

(a) Statement I is true, but statement II is false ☐

(b) Both statements I and II are false ☐

135. Seed habit is linked to ______________.

136. Write the four classes of pteridophytes.

____

***137.** In *Dryopteris,* transport of male gametes requires ______________.

138. *Selaginella* and *Adiantum* are found in moist and shady places because both require sunlight for fertilisation.

(*Rewrite the statement after correcting the underlined phrase.*)

____

139. Match the following columns.

Column I (Pteridophyte class)		Column II (Examples)
A. Psilopsida	1.	*Dryopteris, Pteris, Adiantum*
B. Lycopsida	2.	*Equisetum*
C. Sphenopsida	3.	*Selaginella*
D. Pteropsida	4.	*Psilotum*

A. ______ B. ______ C. ______ D. ______

TOPIC 5 Gymnosperms

NCERT Pg. 32-33

***140.** In gymnosperms, ovules are not enclosed by ______________.

141. Name the gymnosperm species which is one of the tallest tree species. ______________

142. The roots of gymnosperm are generally ______________ (tap/fibrous) roots.

***143.** Name the association of roots of gymnosperm and fungi. ______________

144. Small specialised roots called ______________ roots are associated with N_2-fixing cyanobacteria in *Cycas.*

145. Consider the following statements.

Statement I *Pinus* shows the presence of mycorrhiza while *Cycas* bear coralloid roots.

Statement II In gymnosperms, the seeds that develop post-fertilisation are not covered.

Choose the correct option from the following.

(a) Statement I is true, but statement II is false ☐

(b) Both statements I and II are true ☐

146. In conifers, the needle-like leaves increase the surface area which ultimately reduces water loss.

True ☐ False ☐

147. Write any two adaptations of leaves in gymnosperms that help them in reducing water loss.

(i) ________________ (ii) ________________

148. The gymnosperms are homosporous.

True ☐ False ☐

149. The ________________ microspore and megaspore that are borne on within sporangia are arranged spirally along an axis to form ________________.

150. Write other names of cones in gymnosperms. ________________

151. Name the strobili bearing microsporophylls and microsporangia.

____

152. The reduced male gametophyte present in gymnosperm is called________________

153. The male or female cones may be borne on the same trees.

True ☐ False ☐

154. The male cones and megasporophylls are borne on same trees in *Cycas*.

True ☐ False ☐

155. The male strobili of *Pinus* and *Cycas* bear

(a) megasporophyll and megasporangia ☐

(b) megasporophyll and microsporangia ☐

(c) microsporophyll and microsporangia ☐

(d) microsporophyll and megasporangia ☐

156. Complete the paragraph using the words given below in the box.

Megaspore mother cell, Integument, Nucellus, Ovary, Ovule, Microspore mother cell

The ________________ is differentiated from one of the cells of the ________________. The nucellus is protected by envelopes and the composite structure is called an ________________.

157. The megaspore mother cell divides ________________ (meiotically/ mitotically) to form ________________ (two, four, eight) megaspores.

158. The megasporangium develops into a multicellular female gametophyte that bears two or more ________________

159. Consider the following statements.

Statement I The development of pollen grains occurs within the megasporangia of the megasporophyll in gymnosperms.

Statement II Out of the four megaspores produced, only one develops into a female gametophyte in gymnosperms.

Choose the correct option from the following.

(a) Statement I is true, but statement II is false ☐

(b) Statement I is false, but statement II is true ☐

160. The female gametophyte is retained within megasporangium.

True ☐ False ☐

161. The gametophytes have an independent free-living existence in gymnosperms.

True ☐ False ☐

162. Complete the following sequence.

Pollen grain released from (A) → (B) carrying male gametes grow towards (C) → Following fertilisation, zygote develops into (D) and ovule develops into (E)

A. ________________ B. ________________ C. ________________

D. ________________ E. ________________

163. Consider the following figure and answer the following questions.

(i) Name the plant. ________________

(ii) Identify *A*, *B* and *C*.

A. ________________

B. ________________

C. ________________

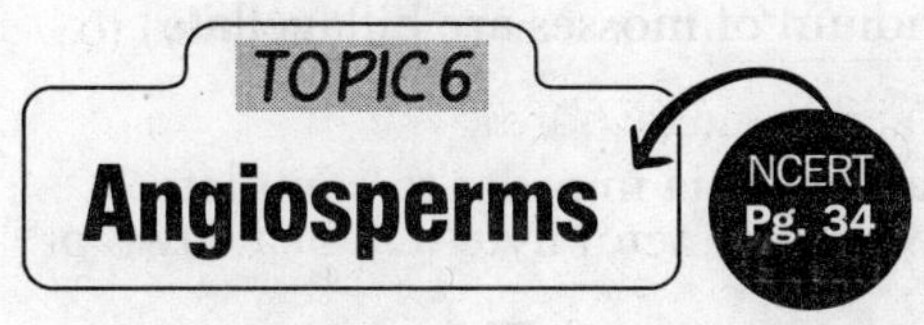

164. In angiosperms, pollen grains and ovules are developed in specialised structures called ________

165. Seeds are enclosed by flowers in angiosperms.

True ☐ False ☐

166. Consider the following statements.

Statement I Angiosperms produce seeds that are well protected by a seed coat.

Statement II Angiosperms are exceptionally large group of plants covering a variety of habitat.

Choose the correct option from the following.

(a) Statement I is true, but statement II is false ☐

(b) Both statements I and II are true ☐

167. Complete the following analogy.

Tallest angiosperm : Smallest angiosperm : : *Eucalyptus* : ________

168. Name the class of angiosperm that possess two cotyledons, ________

169. Write the two divisions of angiosperms.

(i) ________ (ii) ________

170. Germination would result in rupturing of the seed coat in

(a) *Sequoia* ☐ (b) *Cycas* ☐ (c) *Eucalyptus* ☐ (d) *Cedrus* ☐

Assertion-Reason Questions

The following questions consist of two statements- Assertion (A) and Reason (R). Answer these questions by selecting the appropriate option given below.

(a) Both A and R are true and R is correct explanation of A

(b) Both A and R are true, but R is not the correct explanation of A

(c) A is true, but R is false

(d) A is false, but R is true

***1.** **Assertion** (A) Oceans found in the warmer areas of the earth particularly in the tropics often turn red.

Reason (R) The stored food in *Polysiphonia* and *Gelidium* is red coloured floridean starch.

(a) ☐ (b) ☐ (c) ☐ (d) ☐

***2.** **Assertion** (A) Antherozoids produced by the antheridium of mosses are biflagellate structures.

Reason (R) The antherozoids get transferred to the archegonia in order to complete fertilisation.

(a) ☐ (b) ☐ (c) ☐ (d) ☐

***3.** **Assertion** (A) The sporophyte of *Marchantia* is differentiated into foot, seta and capsule.

Reason (R) The sporophyte of liverworts contains a single copy of the genome and are haploid.

(a) ☐ (b) ☐ (c) ☐ (d) ☐

***4.** **Assertion** (A) The main plant body in *Selaginella* and ferns is diploid and produces spores by meiosis.

Reason (R) It develops from zygote formed after fusion of haploid male and female gametes.

(a) ☐ (b) ☐ (c) ☐ (d) ☐

5. **Assertion** (A) Pteridophytes are widely distributed and colonise different habitats on earth.

Reason (R) : Ferns can thrive in cool, damp environment and require water for fertilisation.

(a) ☐ (b) ☐ (c) ☐ (d) ☐

***6.** **Assertion** (A) Gymnosperms are said to have a mutualistic relationship with many bacteria and fungi.

Reason (R) The megaspore mother cell in *Cycas* undergoes reduction division to form four megaspores.

(a) ☐ (b) ☐ (c) ☐ (d) ☐

***7.** **Assertion** (A) The female gametophyte in *Pinus* and *Cedrus* do not have an independent existence.

Reason (R) The female gametophyte in gymnosperms remains within the megasporangia of the sporophyte.

(a) ☐ (b) ☐ (c) ☐ (d) ☐

8. **Assertion** (A) The primary reproductive organ of an angiosperm is the flower.

Reason (R) Unlike gymnosperms, angiosperms bear seeds which are covered by a seed coat.

(a) ☐ (b) ☐ (c) ☐ (d) ☐

Case Based Questions

1. A land area 'A' underwent drastic soil erosion due to heavy rainfall. Knowing the importance of plant diversity, scientists added a species of plant 'P' to note the changes occurring in the area thereafter. Given below are graphical representations of two conditions before and after addition of the new species. Study the graphs and answer the questions that follow

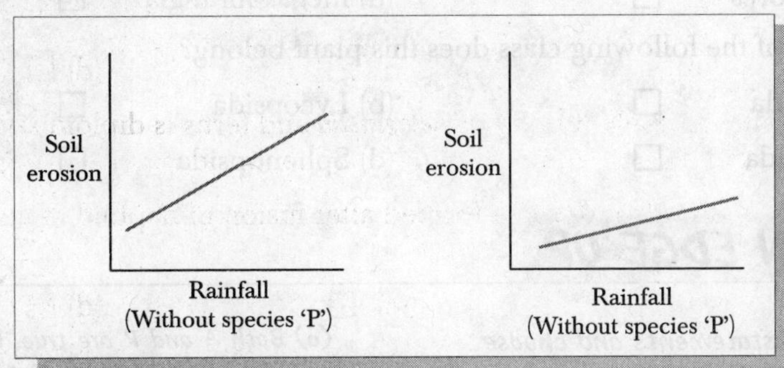

(i) Identify the species of plant 'P' added by the scientist to combat the condition

(a) *Sphagnum* ☐ (b) *Marchantia* ☐
(c) *Volvox* ☐ (d) *Ulothrix* ☐

(ii) Which characteristic of the species 'P' makes it useful for preventing soil erosion?

(a) It provides peat ☐ (b) Its capacity to hold water ☐
(c) It colonises rock ☐ (d) It is used as fuel ☐

(iii) What conclusion can be drawn from the given graphs?

(a) Soil erosion remains the same ☐
(b) Soil erosion has increased after adding species '*P*' ☐
(c) Soil erosion has reduced after adding species '*P*' ☐
(d) Soil erosion was less before adding species '*P*' ☐

2. Consider the given image and answer the following questions.

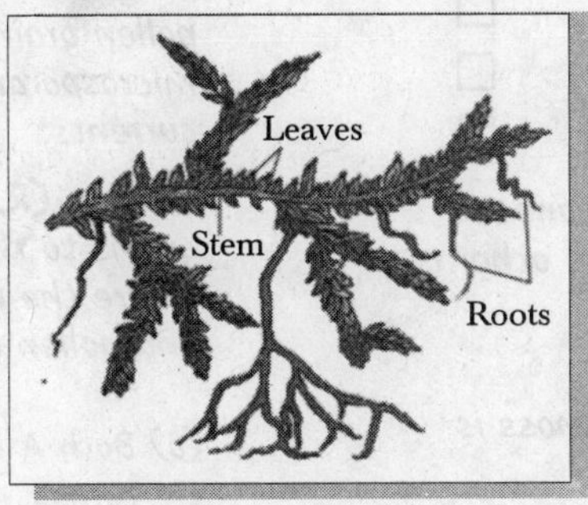

(i) Which of the following structures is not associated with the given plant?

(a) Microspores ☐ (b) Macrospores ☐
(c) Gemma cups ☐ (d) Strobili ☐

(ii) Which of the following is not a characteristic associated with the gametophyte of this plant?

(a) Multicellular ☐ (b) Thalloid ☐

(c) Photosynthetic ☐ (d) Symbiotic ☐

(iii) The male gametophytes of this plant germinate from

(a) microspores ☐ (b) microsporangia ☐

(c) megaspores ☐ (d) megasporangia ☐

(iv) To which of the following class does this plant belong?

(a) Psilopsida ☐ (b) Lycopsida ☐

(c) Pteropsida ☐ (d) Sphenopsida ☐

COMPETITION EDGE UP

1 Read the following statements and choose the set of correct statements: **[NCERT Pg. 26,27 NEET 2024]**

A. Asexual reproduction occurs usually by biflagellate zoospores.

B. Sexual reproduction is by oogamous method only.

C. Stored food is in the form of carbohydrates which is either mannitol or laminarin.

D. The major pigments found are chlorophyll a, c and carotenoids and xanthophyll.

E. Vegetative cells have a celluloic wall, usually covered on the outside by gelatinous coating of algin.

Choose the correct answer from the options given below.

(a) A, B, C and D only ☐

(b) B, C, D and E only ☐

(c) A, C, D and E only ☐

(d) A, B, C and E only ☐

2 Given below are two statements, one is labelled as **Assertion** (A) and the other is labelled as **Reason** (R).

Assertion (A) The first stage of gametophyte in the life cycle of moss is protonema stage.

Reason (R) Protonema develops directly from spores produced in capsule.

In the light of the above statements, choose the most appropriate answer from the options given below **[NEET 2023]**

(a) Both A and R are true, but R is not the correct explanation of A ☐

(b) A is true, but R is false ☐

(c) A is false, but R is true ☐

(d) Both A and R are true and R is the correct explanation of A ☐

3 Identify the pair of heterosporous pteridophytes among the following. **[NEET 2023]**

(a) Selaginella and Salvinia ☐

(b) Psilotum and Salvinia ☐

(c) Equisetum and Salvinia ☐

(d) Lycopodium and Selaginella ☐

4 Given below are two statements, one is labelled as **Assertion (A)** and the other is labelled as **Reason (R).**

Assertion (A) In gymnosperms, the pollen grains are released from the microsporangium and carried by air currents.

Reason (R) Air currents carry the pollen grains to the mouth of the archegonia where the male gametes are discharged and pollen tube is not formed. **[NCERT Pg.33, NEET 2023]**

(a) Both A and R are true, R is not the correct explanation of A ☐

(b) A is true, but R is false ☐

(c) A is false, but R is true ☐

(d) Both A and R are true and R is the correct explanation of A ☐

5 Hydrocolloid carrageen is obtained from [NCERT Pg. 26, NEET 2016, 22]

(a) Phaeophyceae and Rhodophyceae ☐
(b) Rhodophyceae only ☐
(c) Phaeophyceae only ☐
(d) Chlorophyceae and Phaeophyceae ☐

6 Which of the following is incorrectly matched? [NCERT Pg. 27, NEET 2022]

(a) Ulothrix—Mannitol ☐
(b) Porphyra—Floridean starch ☐
(c) Volvox—Starch ☐
(d) Ectocarpus—Fucoxanthin ☐

7 Which of the following plants is monoecious? [NEET 2021]

(a) Cycas circinalis ☐
(b) Carica papaya ☐
(c) Chara ☐
(d) Marchantia polymorpha ☐

8 Which of the following algae contains mannitol as reserve food material ? [NCERT Pg. 27, NEET 2021]

(a) Ectocarpus ☐
(b) Gracilaria ☐
(c) Volvox ☐
(d) Ulothrix ☐

9 Which of the following algae produces carrageen? [NCERT Pg. 26, NEET 2021]

(a) Green algae ☐
(b) Brown algae ☐
(c) Red algae ☐
(d) Blue-green algae ☐

10 Genera like Selaginella and Salvinia produce two kinds of spores. Such plants are known as [NCERT Pg. 32, NEET 2021]

(a) heterosporous ☐
(b) homosorus ☐
(c) heterosorus ☐
(d) homosporous ☐

11 Which of the following pairs is of unicellular algae? [NCERT Pg. 26, NEET (Sep.) 2020]

(a) Gelidium and Gracilaria ☐
(b) Anabaena and Volvox ☐
(c) Chlorella and Spirulina ☐
(d) Laminaria and Sargassum ☐

12 Phycoerythrin is the major pigment in [NCERT Pg. 27, NEET (Oct.) 2020]

(a) red algae ☐
(b) blue-green algae ☐
(c) green algae ☐
(d) brown algae ☐

Chapter 04

Animal Kingdom

Scan and take Chapter Test

TOPIC 1

Basis of Classification

NCERT Pg. 37-39

1. All members of kingdom–Animalia are multicellular and exhibit the same pattern of organisation of cells.

True ☐ False ☐

***2.** Consider the following.

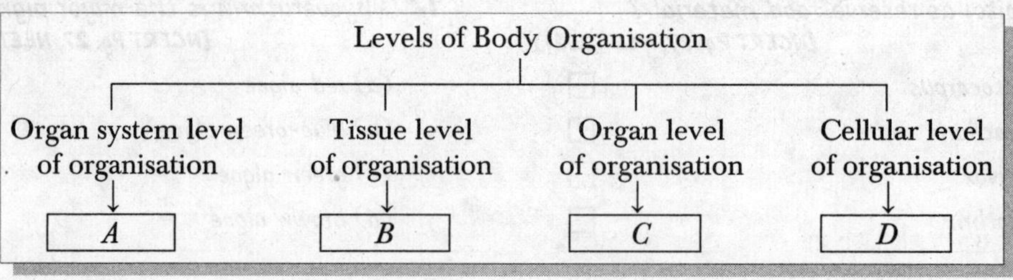

Name the animal phylums showing the above level of body organisation.

A.________ B.________ C.________ D.________

3. Division of labour is completely absent among the cells in phylum ________.

***4.** Names the type of symmetry found in animal's world.

____

***5.** In the given diagram, *A* shows the bilateral symmetry and *B* represents radial symmetry. Based on it, identify the phylums at *A*, *B* and *C*.

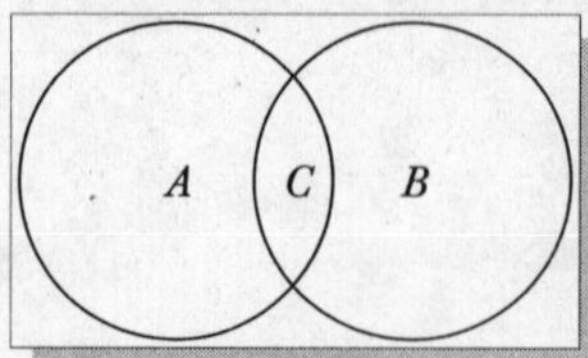

A. ________

B. ________

C. ________

*Concepts of all questions bearing * are important for NEET & CUET*

***6.** Choose the correct combination from the following.

(a) Coelenterates – bilateral symmetry ; Platyhelminthes – radial symmetry ☐

(b) Coelenterates – bilateral symmetry; Platyhelminthes – bilateral symmetry ☐

(c) Coelenterates – radial symmetry ; Platyhelminthes – radial symmetry ☐

(d) Coelenterates – radial symmetry ; Platyhelminthes – bilateral symmetry ☐

***7.** Identify the type of symmetry in animals, *A* and *B*.

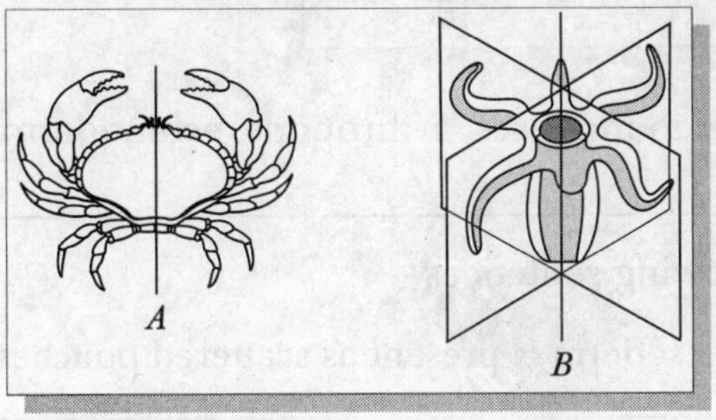

A *B*

A. ____________

B. ____________

***8.** Identify the germ layers, *A*, *B*, *C* and *D* in the diagram given below.

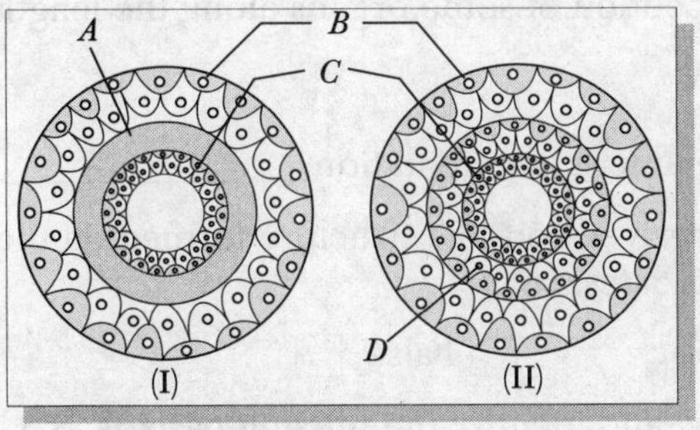

A *B* *C* *D* (I) (II)

A. ____________

B. ____________

C. ____________

D. ____________

***9.** Consider the given image and mention which of the following organisms shows this type of arrangement of cells.

(a) Coelenterates ☐

(b) Platyhelminthes ☐

(c) Aschelminthes ☐

(d) Annelids ☐

***10.** Rewrite the following statements after correcting the underlined word.

(i) Animals in which the cells are arranged into two embryonic layers, i.e. an external ectoderm and an internal endoderm, are called <u>bilaterally symmetrical</u>.

____

(ii) Animals in which the developing embryo has a third germinal layer <u>mesoglea</u>, in between ectoderm and endoderm are called triploblastic.

____

***11.** ____________ is the space between the wall of alimentary canal and body wall enclosed by the layer of mesoderm on both sides.

***12.** The figures given below show the types of coelom. Identify them and write the correct group of organisms which possess them.

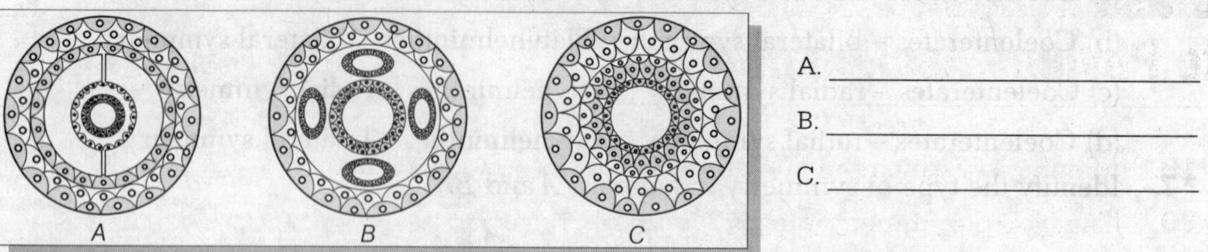

***13.** Name the type of coelom present in molluscs, arthropods, echinoderms and chordates.

____

***14.** Give biological term for the following sentences.

(i) Type of coelom in which the mesoderm is present as scattered pouches in between the ectoderm and endoderm. ____________

(ii) The animals in which the body cavity is absent. ____________

15. Division of body with serial repetition of some organs along the length of an animal is known as ____________.

16. Name an animal exhibiting metameric segmentation. ____________

17. Notochord is a mesodermally derived rod-like structure formed on the ventral side during embryonic development in chordates.

True ☐ False ☐

***18.** Study the flowchart given below and identify the missing parts *A, B, C, D* and *E*.

Kingdom | **Levels of Organisation** | **Symmetry** | **Body cavity or Coelom** | **Phylum**

Animalia (multicellular)
- (A) — Mostly asymmetrical — Acoelomata — Porifera
- Tissue/Organ/Organ system
  - Radial — (B) — Coelenterata (Cnidaria); Ctenophora
  - (C)
    - Without body cavity (acoelomates) — Platyhelminthes
    - With false coelom (pseudocoelomates) — (D)
    - (E) — Annelida; Arthropoda; Mollusca; *Echinodermata; Hemichordata; Chordata

A. ____________
B. ____________
C. ____________
D. ____________
E. ____________

TOPIC 2

Classification of Animals : Phylum–Porifera to Phylum–Aschelminthes

19. Members of which phylum are commonly known as sponges? ______________

20. The type of symmetry mostly found in sponges is ______________

21. Presence of water transport or canal system is a characteristic of phylum __________.

22. In sponges, the water enters through minute pores called __________ into the central cavity, __________ from where it goes out through the __________.

23. Out of the given characters, how many are present in sponges?

Internal fertilisation, Indirect development, Sessile, Extracellular digestion, Hermaphrodite, Generally marine, Cellular organisation

____

24. Consider the following statements.

Statement I *Sycon* has a water canal system that helps in gathering food and removal of wastes.

Statement II The spongocoel of the phylum-Porifera are lined by collar cells or choanocytes.

Choose the correct option from the following.

(a) Statement I is true, but statement II is false ☐

(b) Both statements I and II are true ☐

25. Give the scientific name for the collar cells lining the spongocoel and canals in poriferans.

____

26. Which of the following statements about *Sycon* is correct?

(a) Water enters in their body through osculum ☐

(b) Water exits from their body through ostia ☐

(c) Skeleton is made up of spongin fibres ☐

(d) Fertilisation takes place outside the body. ☐

27. Name the structures which support the body of sponges as a skeleton.

____

28. Animals which do not have separate sexes are called as ______________, i.e. eggs and sperms are produced by the same individual.

29. Complete the following analogy related to sponges.

Sexual reproduction: Gametes :: Asexual reproduction : ______________

30. Sponges have a larval stage which is morphologically distinct from the adult.

True ☐ False ☐

31. Identify the figures and write their names.

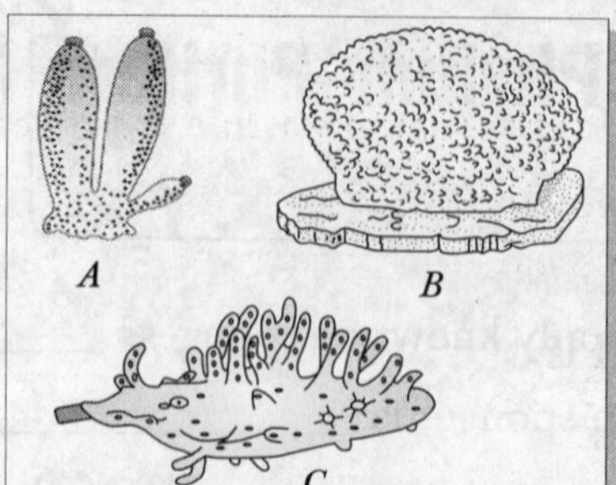

A. ____________

B. ____________

C. ____________

32. When development of an organism occurs through larval stage it is called as________.

33. Identify the phylum based on given features.

(i) Sessile or free–swimming.

(ii) Tissue level organisation and diploblastic.

(iii) Have central gastro-vascular cavity.

(iv) Digestion is extracellular and intracellular.

____

34. (i) Identify the diagram given below and also write its function.

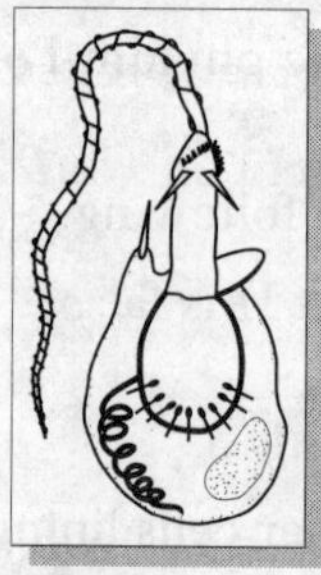

____

(ii) The stinging cell found in the above shown structure is called ________.

35. Name the structure marked as '*X*' in the given diagram of *Adamsia.*

X. ____________

36. Answer the following questions.

(i) Name the cnidarian possessing a skeleton made up of calcium carbonate. ________

(ii) Mention the type of digestion found in coelenterates. ________

37. Consider the following statements.

Statement I Nematocysts present in the cnidoblasts are important for catching prey.

Statement II The polyps can form medusae sexually while the reverse occurs asexually.

Choose the correct option from the following.

(a) Statement I is true, but statement II is false ☐

(b) Statement I is false, but statement II is true ☐

38. *Aurelia* has__________type of body form.

39. Sessile polyps produce medusae ____________ and free-swimming medusae form the polyps ______________.

40. Cnidarians exhibit alternation of generation between their polyp and medusa forms. This process is known as ______________.

41. Identify the structures *A* and *B* .

A. ______________________

B. ______________________

42. Consider the provided image and mention which of the following is correct about the given body form.

(a) They are sessile like *Adamsia* ☐

(b) They are free swimming like *Aurelia* ☐

(c) They are sessile like *Aurelia* ☐

(d) They are free swimming like *Adamsia* ☐

43. Give the scientific name of the following.

(i) Portuguese man of war ______________

(ii) Sea anemone ______________

(iii) Sea pen ______________

(iv) Sea fan ______________

(v) Brain coral ______________

***44.** Ctenophores are commonly known as ______________________ and are exclusively marine forms.

***45.** State True or False.

(i) Ctenophores are exclusively marine, radially symmetrical and diploblastic animals.

True ☐ False ☐

(ii) Ctenophores bear eight external rows of ciliated comb-plates which help in locomotion.

True ☐ False ☐

(iii) Ctenophores exhibit intracellular digestion only.

True ☐ False ☐

***46.** Give the scientific term for the property of emission of light by the body of an organism.

____

***47.** Consider the following statements.

Statement I In *Pleurobrachia* and *Ctenoplana* reproduction takes place only by asexual method.

Statement II Chemiluminescence is the property whereby living organisms can emit light.

Choose the correct option from the following.

(a) Statement I is true, but statement II is false ☐

(b) Both statements I and II are false ☐

***48.** Choose the correct option for the given animal.

(i) Scientific name is ______________ (*Pleurobrachia/Ctenoplana*).

(ii) Bioluminescence is ______________ (present/absent).

(iii) Reproduction occurs only by ______________ means (sexual/asexual).

(iv) Fertilisation is ______________ (internal/external).

(v) Development is ______________ (direct/indirect).

49. Choose the odd one out with respect to phylum–Platyhelminthes.

Bilateral symmetry, Coelomate, Triploblastic, Flatworms, Organ level of organisation

____

50. Flatworms are mostly endoparasites, found in animals, having structures like ______________ and ______________ for adhesion .

51. Nephridium is present in liver fluke for excretion and osmoregulation.
(*Rewrite the statement after correcting the underlined word.*)

____

52. State True or False.

(i) *Planaria* possesses high regeneration capacity.

True ☐ False ☐

(ii) Common name of *Fasciola* is tapeworm.

True ☐ False ☐

53. Identify the diagram given below and choose the correct option regarding it.

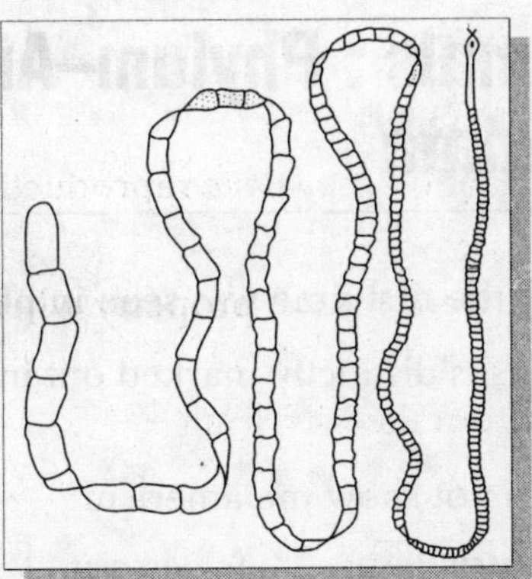

(a) It ingest food particles through suckers present on their body ☐

(b) It absorb nutrients from the host directly through their body surface ☐

(c) It consist of nematocytes which help in gathering the food particles ☐

(d) It is diploblastic and have organ level of organisation ☐

54. Identify the phylum based on the given features.

(i) Bilateral symmetry (ii) Triploblastic

(iii) Internal fertilisation (iv) Development direct or indirect

(v) Muscular pharynx

____

55. Write three features present in phylum–Aschelminthes but not present in phylum–Platyhelminthes.

____

56. Consider the following statements.

Statement I Members of phylum-Aschelminthes can be both free-living or parasitic.

Statement II Development in Aschelminthes is always indirect.

Choose the correct option from the following.

(a) Statement I is true, but statement II is false ☐

(b) Statement I is false, but statement II is true ☐

57. Consider the given images and state the reason how one can easily distinguish between the males and females of this species?

Male Female

(a) Males are longer than females ☐

(b) Females are longer than males ☐

(c) Symmetry in females is radial while in males is bilateral ☐

(d) Symmetry in females is bilateral while in males is radial ☐

58. Name the animal phylum in which organ system level of body organisation appeared first time.

____

TOPIC 3

Classification of Animals : Phylum–Annelida to Phylum–Hemichordata

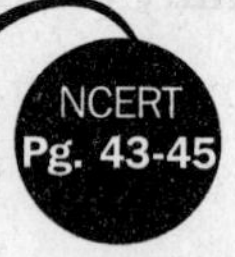

***59.** Presence of true coelom for the first time was seen in phylum ____________.

***60.** The body surface of annelids is distinctly marked out into segments which are called as ____________.

***61.** Which of the following does not show metamerism?

(a) *Hirudinaria* ☐ (b) *Nereis* ☐ (c) *Ascaris* ☐ (d) *Pheretima* ☐

62. Name the lateral appendages present in *Nereis* which help in swimming.

____

63. Read the following statement and choose the incorrect ones.

I. Lateral appendages called parapodia in *Pheretima* help them in swimming.
II. Segmented body in characteristic of *Nereis* and earthworm, but not leeches.
III. Annelids possess longitudinal and circular muscles which help in locomotion.
IV. An open circulatory system is present in annelids.

Choose the correct answer from the options given below.

(a) I, II and III ☐ (b) I and II ☐ (c) III and IV ☐ (d) I, II and IV ☐

64. Name the structure which help in the osmoregulation and excretion in annelids.

____

65. In annelids, neural system consists of paired ganglia connected by lateral nerves to a double ventral nerve cord.

True ☐ False ☐

66. Choose the odd one out with respect to monoecious annelid.

Earthworm, Leeches, Nereis

____

***67.** The largest phylum of animal kingdom is ____________

***68.** All of the following are the exclusive features of members of which phylum?

(i) Chitinous exoskeleton (ii) Jointed appendages
(iii) Presence of respiratory system

____

***69.** Consider the given image and state which of the substance covers the body of the given animal?

(a) Cellulose ☐
(b) Pectin ☐
(c) Chitin ☐
(d) Lignin ☐

70. Body of an arthropod is divided into ________, ________ and ________.

71. Consider the following statements.

Statement I The body of insects can be divided into head, thorax and abdomen.

Statement II Statocysts and compound eyes are unique features of the largest phylum.

Choose the correct option from the following.

(a) Statement I is true, but statement II is false ☐

(b) Both statements I and II are true ☐

***72.** How many features belong to phylum-Arthropoda?

Open circulatory system, Eyes may be simple or compound, Mostly oviparous, Development direct or indirect, Radial symmetry, Triploblastic, Coelomate, Mostly dioecious

____

***73.** Which of the following is true about the insect phylum?

(a) Bilaterally symmetrical, triploblastic, segmented and coelomate ☐

(b) Bilaterally symmetrical, diploblastic, segmented and coelomate ☐

(c) Bilaterally symmetrical, triploblastic, unsegmented and coelomate ☐

(d) Bilaterally symmetrical, triploblastic, segmented and acoelomate ☐

***74.** Choose the odd one out with respect to sensory structures of arthropod.

Malpighian tubules, Compound eyes, Antenna, Statocysts

____

75. Fill in the blank.

Balancing organs of aquatic arthropods are ________.

76. Name the excretory organ in arthropods. ________

***77.** Complete the following analogy given below.

(i) ________ : Organism produces silk :: *Laccifer* : Organism produces lac.

(ii) Gregarious pest : *Locusta* : : Vector : ________

78. Match the following columns.

Column I (Animals)	Column II (Common names)
A. *Pheretima*	1. Silkworm
B. *Bombyx*	2. Honeybee
C. *Apis*	3. Blood sucking leech
D. *Hirudinaria*	4. Earthworm

A.________ B.________ C.________ D.________

***79.** The body of second largest phylum of animal kingdom is covered by________.

80. The soft spongy layer of skin over the visceral hump of molluscs is known as ________.

***81.** Members of phylum–Mollusca can be distinguished from other invertebrate by the presence of mantle and unsegmented body.

True ☐ False ☐

***82.** Body of a mollusc is covered by a __________ shell with a distinct __________, __________ and visceral hump.

83. Exchange of gases in molluscs occurs through feathery gills present in the visceral hump. (*Rewrite the statement after correcting the underlined word.*)

____

84. In molluscs, the mouth contains a file-like rasping organ for feeding called __________

***85.** Radula or rasping organ is present in all except

(a) *Pila* ☐ (b) *Pinctada* ☐ (c) *Sepia* ☐ (d) *Limulus* ☐

86. Consider the following statements.

Statement I Feather-like gills present in the mantle cavity are involved with respiration only.

Statement II The sensory tentacles of a snail are located at the anterior region of the head.

Choose the correct option from the following:

(a) Statement I is true, but statement II is false ☐

(b) Statement I is false, but statement II is true ☐

***87.** Study the following table carefully and identify *A, B, C, D* and *E*.

Phylums	Excretory organs	Circulatory systems	Respiratory organs
Ⓐ	Nephridia	Closed	Skin
Arthropoda	Ⓑ	Ⓒ	Lungs/Gills tracheal system
Ⓓ	Feather-like gills	Open	Ⓔ

A. __________ B. __________ C. __________ D. __________

E. __________

***88.** Match the following columns.

	Column I (Molluscs)		Column II (Scientific names)
A.	Apple snail	1.	*Dentalium*
B.	Pearl oyster	2.	*Pila*
C.	Cuttle fish	3.	*Octopus*
D.	Devil fish	4.	*Sepia*
E.	Tusk shell	5.	*Pinctada*

A. __________ B. __________ C. __________ D. __________

E. __________

89. Identify the organisms, *A*, *B* and *C* along with their respective phyla.

(*A*) (*B*) (*C*)

	Organisms	Phyla
A.	____________	____________
B.	____________	____________
C.	____________	____________

***90.** Complete the following analogy given below.

__________ : Larvae :: Radial : : Adults

***91.** Choose the odd one out feature of echinoderm

Spiny bodies, All marines, Coelomate, Tissue level organisation.

____

***92.** Name the most distinctive system in the animals of phylum–Echinodermata.

____

93. Digestive system in echinoderms is complete with mouth on the lower (ventral) side and anus on the upper (dorsal) side.

True ☐ False ☐

***94.** Water vascular system performs all the following functions, except

(a) locomotion ☐ (b) capture of food ☐ (c) excretion ☐ (d) respiration ☐

***95.** Give the scientific names and their respective phyla.

(i) Sea lily ____________ (ii) Sea urchin ____________

(iii) Sea cucumber ____________

***96.** Choose the correct option for the given animal and fill the blanks given below.

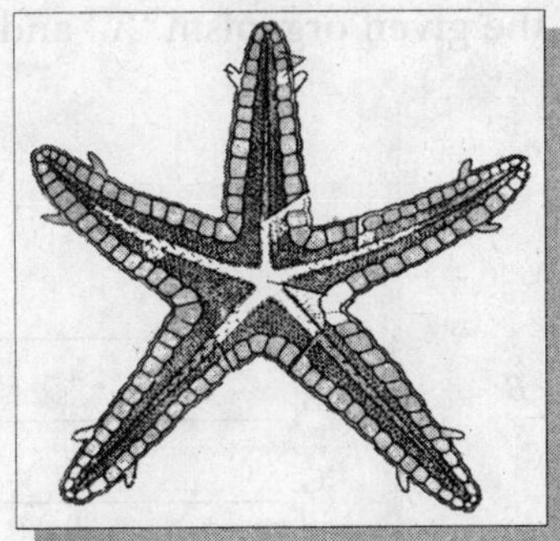

(i) Excretory system is ____________ (present/absent)

(ii) Germ layer is ____________ (triploblastic/diploblastic)

(iii) Reproduction by ____________ (sexual/asexual method)

(iv) Sexes are ____________ (dioecious/monoecious)

(v) Scientific name is ____________ *(Asterias/ Ophiura)*

***97.** Consider the following statements.

Statement I *Ophiura* and *Cucumaria* have a water vascular system that serves various purposes.

Statement II A well developed excretory system is present in most members of the phylum–Echinodermata.

Choose the correct option from the following.

(a) Statement I is true, but statement II is false ☐

(b) Statement I is false, but statement II is true ☐

98. Hemichordates are now placed as separate phylum under non-chordates.

True ☐ False ☐

99. Hemichordates have a rudimentary structure in the collar region called proboscis, that is similar to notochord. (*Rewrite the statement after correcting the underlined word.*)

____

100. Consider the given image and state which of the following is a distinctive feature of this animal?

(a) Notochord ☐

(b) Nerve cord ☐

(c) Vertebral column ☐

(d) Stomocord ☐

101. ________________ is the phylum which consists of a small group of worm–like marine animals with organ system level of organisation.

102. Choose the odd one out with respect to feature in *Saccoglossus.*

Triploblastic, Coelomate, Gills, Closed circulation, Bilaterally symmetrical

____

103. Write the scientific name of the given organism '*X*' and correctly name its parts, *A*, *B* and *C*.

A
B
C

A. ____________________

B. ____________________

C. ____________________

104. Match column I with column II.

Column I Animals	Column II Excretory organ/cells
A. *Pheretima*	1. Proboscis
B. *Laccifer*	2. Feather like gills
C. *Aplysia*	3. Malpighian tubules
D. *Balanoglossus*	4. Nephridia

A B C D
(a) 4 3 2 1 ☐
(b) 4 3 1 2 ☐
(c) 4 1 2 3 ☐
(d) 4 1 3 2 ☐

105. Consider the following statements.

Statement I The body of *Balanoglossus* can be divided into proboscis, collar and trunk.

Statement II In animals belonging to Hemichordata, fusion of gametes takes place outside the body.

Choose the correct option from the following.

(a) Statement I is true, but statement II is false ☐
(b) Both statements I and II are true ☐

106. Sexes are separate, fertilisation is external and development is indirect in which two phyla of non-chordates? ______________

TOPIC 4
Classification of Animals : Phylum–Chordata

NCERT Pg. 45-51

107. Write the three fundamental chracteristics of phylum–Chordata.

____

***108.** The diagram given below represents the characteristics of a Chordata. Identify and write the name of the structures marked as *A*, *B*, *C* and *D*.

A. ______________
B. ______________
C. ______________
D. ______________

***109.** __________ possess notochord throughout their life, but __________ have it only in larval stage.

110. In which of the following organism notochord extends from head to tail region?

(a) *Ascidia* ☐ (b) *Lancelet* ☐ (c) *Salpa* ☐ (d) *Doliolum* ☐

***111.** Select the correct options for the given animal.

(i) Heart is ____________ (dorsal heart/ventral heart)

(ii) Colelom is ____________ (acoelomate/pseudocoelomate/coelomate)

(iii) Position ____________ (vertebrates/invertebrates)

(iv) Sub-phylum is ____________ (urochordates/cephalochordates)

(v) Scientific name is ____________ (*Ascidia*/ *Doliolum*)

***112.** In vertebrates, embryonic notochord is replaced by a ____________ in the adult.

***113.** State True or False.

(i) All chordates are vertebrates, but all vertebrates are not chordates.

True ☐ False ☐

(ii) Tunicata is an alternative name of urochordata.

True ☐ False ☐

114. Complete the following analogy given below.

Kidneys : Chordates :: ____________ : Hemichordates.

115. A common characteristic of all vertebrates without exception is the presence of ____________ (exoskeleton/skull).

***116.** Study the flow chart given below and identify the missing parts *A, B, C, D* and *E*.

Phylum-Chordata
Sub-phyla
A | *B* → Protochordates
Vertebrata → Agnatha | Gnathostomata
Agnatha → Class → Extinct | *C*
Gnathostomata → Superclass → *D* | *E*
D → Class: 1. Chondrichthyes 2. Osteichthyes
E → Class: 1. Amphibia 2. Reptilia 3. Aves 4. Mammalia

A. ____________

B. ____________

C. ____________

D. ____________

E. ____________

117. Name the class of jawless vertebrates which are marine, but migrate for spawning to freshwater. ____________

118. Consider the following statements.

Statement I *Petromyzon* of class-Cyclostomata uses paired gill slits for respiration.

Statement II Lamprey and hagfish show direct development in the ocean habitats.

Choose the correct option from the following.

(a) Statement I is true, but statement II is false ☐

(b) Statement I is false, but statement II is true ☐

119. ______________ (*Carcharodon/ Clarias*) are cold-blooded animals in which male pelvic fins bear claspers for copulation.

120. Name the Chondrichthyes with the following characters.

(i) Electric organs ______________ (ii) Poison sting ______________

***121.** Write the scientific names of the following.

(i) Flying fish ______________

(ii) Angel fish ______________

(iii) Dog fish ______________

(iv) Saw fish ______________

(v) Fighting fish ______________

(vi) Hag fish ______________

(vii) Star fish ______________

122. The heart of fishes is ________ chambered with ________ auricle and ________ ventricle.

123. Name the structure that prevents the bony fishes from sinking. ______________

124. Cartilaginous fishes have to swim constantly because they lack ______________.

***125.** Write true or false about the given animal (vertebrate).

(i) It belongs to class–Reptilia.

True ☐ False ☐

(ii) It is a cold-blooded animal.

True ☐ False ☐

126. Complete the following analogy given below.

Bony fish : : Osteichthyes : Cartilaginous fish : ______________

***127.** Consider the following statements.

Statement I There are eight pairs of gills in rohu and catla for respiration.

Statement II Gills are covered by operculum on each side in bony fishes.

Choose the correct option from the following.

(a) Statement I is true, but statement II is false ☐

(b) Statement I is false, but statement II is true ☐

128. Identify the given images and mark the correct combination from the following.

(*A*) (*B*)

(a) *A* – Placoid scales, *B* – Cycloid scales ☐

(b) *A* – Cycloid scales, *B* – Placoid scales ☐

(c) *A* – Ctenoid scales, *B* – Placoid scales ☐

(d) *A* – Ctenoid scales, *B* – Cycloid scales ☐

129. Match the following columns.

Fishes		Features	
A.	Cartilaginous fishes	1.	Usually external fertilisation
B.	Bony fishes	2.	Internal fertilisation
		3.	Mostly oviparous
		4.	Mostly viviparous

A.____________ B. ____________

***130.** Fill in the in the table with correct differences.

Cyclostomes	Chondrichthyes	Osteichthyes
(A)	Ventral mouth	(B)
(C)	(D)	Cycloid/Ctenoid scales
(E)	(F)	Marine and freshwater
(G)	5-7 paires of gills without operculum	(H)

A.____________ B. ____________ C. ____________ D. ____________

E.____________ F. ____________ G. ____________ H.____________

***131.** Identify the diagrams and answer the questions as follows.

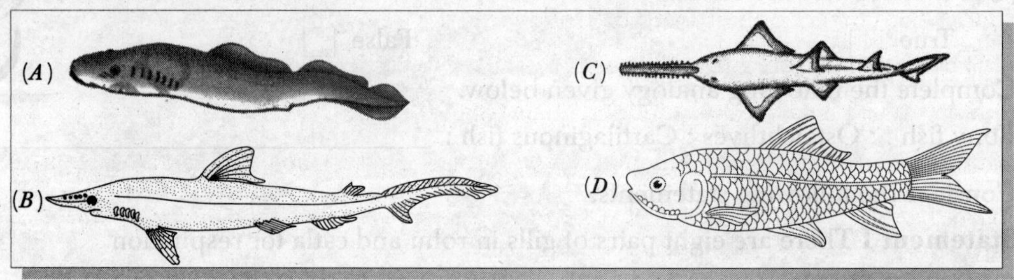

(i) Which fish has air bladder? ____________

(ii) Which fishes are cartilaginous and bony, respectively? ____________

(iii) From the following fishes given above, which one is ectoparasite? ____________

(iv) Which fish has paired fins? ____________

(v) Which fish lives in freshwater and possesses operculum. ____________

(vi) Write names of each *A*, *B*, *C* and *D* above. ____________

132. Fill in the blanks with respect to amphibians.

(i) Body of amphibians is divisible into ____________ and ____________.

(ii) A ____________ represents the ear.

(iii) Alimentary canal, urinary and reproductive tracts open into a common chamber called ____________ which opens to the outside.

(iv) Heart is ____________ chambered with ____________ and ____________.

133. Choose the odd one out with respect to respiration in amphibians.

Gills, Lungs, Skin, Nephridia

____

134. All of the following acts as a respiratory organ in amphibians, except

(a) skin ☐ (b) lungs ☐ (c) gills ☐ (d) operculum ☐

135. Choose the correct option for the given animal.

(i) Scientific name of animal is _______________ (*Rana tigrina/Rana tigris*)

(ii) Fertilisation is _______________ (internal /external)

(iii) Respiration occurs by under water _______________ (lungs/gills)

(iv) Development is _______________ (indirect/direct)

136. The mode of locomotion in reptiles is _______________

137. Name the class of vertebrates possessing dry and cornified skin with epidermal scales or scutes._______________

138. Consider the following statements.

Statement I Reptiles have a dry and cornified skin, epidermal scales or scutes.

Statement II Reptiles are homeotherms while amphibians are poikilotherms.

Choose the correct option from the following:

(a) Statement I is true, but statement II is false ☐

(b) Statement I is false, but statement II is true ☐

139. Out of the below features, which is not present in amphibians, but found in reptiles?

Poikilotherms, 3-chambered heart, Oviparous, Tympanum, Two pairs of limbs, Direct development, Internal fertilisation

____

140. Name two reptiles based on the features listed below.

(i) Four-chambered heart _______________

(ii) Shed their scales as skin cast _______________

(iii) Limbless reptiles _______________

141. Give common names for the following.

(i) *Testudo* _______________

(ii) *Bufo* _______________

(iii) *Hyla* _______________

(iv) *Calotes* _______________

(v) *Hemidactylus* _______________

(vi) *Bangarus* _______________

***142.** The bones of birds are long and hollow with air cavities. These types of bones are called as ________.

***143.** In birds, the hindlimbs are modified into wings and forelimbs are modified for walking, swimming or clasping the tree branches.

True ☐ False ☐

***144.** The skin of class–Aves is dry without glands, except the ________ gland present at the base of tail.

***145.** Name the additional chambers found in the digestive tracts of birds.

____

***146.** Name the structures in birds.

(i) Respiration ________

(ii) Feeding, seed crushing, flesh tearing, etc. ________

***147.** Match the following columns.

Column I (Aves)	Column II (Common names)
A. *Corvus*	1. Pigeon
B. *Columba*	2. Crow
C. *Aptenodytes*	3. Vulture
D. *Neophron*	4. Penguin

A. ________ B. ________ C. ________ D. ________

***148.** Write the scientific names of birds *A-D* and identify which among the following is a flightless bird?

A B C D

A. ________

B. ________

C. ________

D. ________

***149.** Write three common features present in all mammals.

____

***150.** How many features are common to both mammals and Aves?

Development direct, Internal fertilisation, Four-chambered heart, Teeth present, Viviparous, Homoiothermous

____

151. Read the following statement and choose the correct ones.

I. External ears or pinnae are characteristics of most reptiles.

II. All mammals bear mammary glands and are viviparous in nature.

III. All mammals have two pair of limbs, adapted for walking, running, climbing, burrowing, swimming or flying.

IV. The skin of mammals is unique in possessing hair.

Choose the correct answer from the options given below.

(a) I and II ☐ (b) II an d IV ☐

(c) II and III ☐ (d) III and IV ☐

152. Write the names and mention one feature of each given mammals, not present in other the two.

A B C

A. ______

B. ______

C. ______

***153.** Which character is present in bats, but not in birds?

Homoiothermy, Four-chambered heart, Gizzard, Diaphragm

______

154. Which of the following is the only oviparous mammal?

(a) *Balaenoptera* ☐ (b) *Delphinus* ☐

(c) *Ornithorhynchus* ☐ (d) *Pteropus* ☐

***155.** How many organisms in the list given below respire through gills?

Sponges, Coelentrates, Flatworms, Aquatic arthropods, Molluscs, Fishes, Tadpoles, Reptiles, Aves, Mammals

______

156. Complete the missing difference.

	Class–Insecta	Class–Mammalia
Phylum	(A)	(B)
Examples	(C)	(D)

A. ______ B. ______ C. ______ D. ______

157. Respiration in all mammals occurs *via*. ______

158. Write the names of any one mammal adapted for the given features and habitat.

(i) Flying ______

(ii) Swimming ______

(iii) Climbing ______

(iv) Burrowing ______

Assertion-Reason Questions

The following questions consist of two statements- Assertion (A) and Reason (R). Answer these questions by selecting the appropriate option given below.
(a) Both A and R are true and R is correct explanation of A
(b) Both A and R are true, but R is not the correct explanation of A
(c) A is true, but R is false
(d) A is false, but R is true

***1.** **Assertion** (A) Cnidoblasts present on the tentacles of *Adamsia* are used for capturing prey.

Reason (R) Cnidarians have special mechanisms which they use for defense against predators.

(a) ☐ (b) ☐ (c) ☐ (d) ☐

***2.** **Assertion** (A) Platyhelminthes are generally hermaphrodite.

Reason (R) In Platyhelminthes, fertilisation is internal.

(a) ☐ (b) ☐ (c) ☐ (d) ☐

***3.** **Assertion** (A) Animals belonging to the phylum-Aschelminthes are pseudocoelomates.

Reason (R) In Aschelminthes mesoderm is present as scattered pouches between ectoderm and endoderm.

(a) ☐ (b) ☐ (c) ☐ (d) ☐

***4.** **Assertion** (A) Alimentary canal in Aschelminthes is complete with a well-developed muscular pharynx.

Reason (R) An excretory tube removes body wastes from the body cavity through the excretory pore.

(a) ☐ (b) ☐ (c) ☐ (d) ☐

***5.** **Assertion** (A) The visceral hump of animals belonging to Mollusca, is enclosed within a calcareous shell.

Reason (R) Body of a *Pila* is unsegmented with distinct head, visceral hump and a muscular foot.

(a) ☐ (b) ☐ (c) ☐ (d) ☐

***6.** **Assertion** (A) Starfish and sea urchin show both radial and bilateral symmetry in different growth phases .

Reason (R) *Asterias* has a complete digestive system with dorsally located mouth and ventrally located anus.

(a) ☐ (b) ☐ (c) ☐ (d) ☐

***7.** **Assertion** (A) Chordates differ from non-chordates in having a ectodermally derived notochord.

Reason (R) Heart is ventral in chordates while, if present, it is dorsally located in non-chordates.

(a) ☐ (b) ☐ (c) ☐ (d) ☐

***8. Assertion** (A) The great white shark in its habitat is observed to be swimming constantly.

Reason (R) Air bladder which provides buoyancy to bony fishes are absent in Chondrichthyes.

(a) ☐ (b) ☐ (c) ☐ (d) ☐

9. Assertion (A) The cloaca in frogs is a common chamber that connects the alimentary, urinary and reproductive tracts.

Reason (R) Amphibians like frogs are warm blooded animals that show external fertilisation .

(a) ☐ (b) ☐ (c) ☐ (d) ☐

***10. Assertion** (A) Birds have a bony endoskeleton with long pneumatic bones.

Reason (R) Hollow bones contain air cavities that make the body light for flight.

(a) ☐ (b) ☐ (c) ☐ (d) ☐

Case Based Questions

1. Rama in his crop field, introduced an organism '*X*' that belong to kingdom- Animalia. It brought about a gradual change in the nutrient availability for his crops. Due to this his crops showed sufficient increase in yield. Observe the bar graph given below for nutrient availability over a time span of 4 years (2020-2023).

(i) Select the incorrect statement regarding organism '*X*'.

(a) The body surface is distinctly marked out into segments or metameres ☐

(b) It possess lateral appendages called parapodia which help in locomotion ☐

(c) A closed circulatory system is present ☐

(d) It is monoecious ☐

(ii) Which type of excretory organ is present in organism '*X*'?

(a) An excretory tube ☐ (b) Nephridia ☐

(c) Malpighian tubules ☐ (d) Flame cells ☐

(iii) Organism 'X' possess neural system which consists of '*A*' connected by lateral nerves to a '*B*' nerve cord. Identify '*A*' and '*B*' and choose the correct option.

	A	B
(a)	paired ganglia	double ventral
(b)	singular ganglion	double ventral
(c)	paired ganglia	single ventral
(d)	paired ganglia	double dorsal

(a) ☐ (b) ☐ (c) ☐ (d) ☐

***2.** Observe the given image carefully and answer the following questions:

(i) Identify the correct classification of the provided animal.

(a) Cyclostomata of Gnathostomata ☐

(b) Cyclostomata of Agnatha ☐

(c) Chondricthyes of Gnathostomata ☐

(d) Chondricthyes of Agnatha ☐

(ii) How is the given animal different from catla?

(a) They are jawless, devoid of scales and paired fins ☐

(b) They are jawless, but contain placoid scales ☐

(c) They bear jaws, but are devoid of scales and fins ☐

(d) They are jawless, placoid scales and bear paired fins ☐

(iii) Which of the following explains their feeding mechanism?

(a) Predation ☐ (b) Endoparasite ☐

(c) Ectoparasite ☐ (d) Saprotrophic ☐

(iv) Which of the following is true about the given animal?

(a) Embryo – notochord; Adult – nerve cord ☐

(b) Embryo – notochord; Adult – vertebral column ☐

(c) Embryo – nerve cord; Adult – notochord ☐

(d) Embryo – vertebral column; Adult – notochord ☐

COMPETITION EDGE UP

1. The following are the statements about non-chordates.

A. Pharynx is perforated by gill slits.

B. Notochord is absent.

C. Central nervous system is dorsal.

D. Heart is dorsal if present.

E. Post anal tail is absent.

Choose the most appropriate answer from the options given below.

[NCERT Pg. 46, NEET 2024]

(a) A and C only ☐

(b) A, B and D only ☐

(c) B, D and E only ☐

(d) B, C and D only ☐

2. Match List I with List II.

	List I		List II
A.	Pleurobrachia	I.	Mollusca
B.	Radula	II.	Ctenophora
C.	Stomochord	III.	Osteichthyes
D.	Air bladder	IV.	Hemichordata

Choose the correct answer from the options given below.

[NCERT Pg. 42, 44, 45, 47, NEET 2024]

(a) A-IV, B-II, C-III, D-I ☐

(b) A-II, B-I, C-IV, D-III ☐

(c) A-II, B-IV, C-I, D-III ☐

(d) A-IV, B-III, C-II, D-I ☐

3. Match List I with List II.

	List I		List II
A.	Pterophyllum	I.	Hag fish
B.	Myxine	II.	Saw fish
C.	Pristis	III.	Angel fish
D.	Exocoetus	IV.	Flying fish

Choose the correct answer from the options given below.

[NCERT Pg. 47, 48, NEET 2024]

(a) A-II, B-I, C-III, D-IV ☐

(b) A-III, B-I, C-II, D-IV ☐

(c) A-IV, B-I, C-II, D-III ☐

(d) A-III, B-II, C-I, D-IV ☐

4. Select the correct statements with reference to chordates.

[NCERT Pg. 46, NEET 2023]

A. Presence of a mid-dorsal, solid and double nerve cord.

B. Presence of closed circulatory system.

C. Presence of paired pharyngeal gillslits.

D. Presence of dorsal heart.

E. Triploblastic pseudocoelomate animals.

Choose the correct answer from the options given below

(a) B and C only ☐

(b) B, D and E only ☐

(c) C, D and E only ☐

(d) A, C and D only ☐

5. Radial symmetry is not found in adults of phylum **[NCERT Pg. 45, NEET 2023]**

(a) Hemichordata ☐

(b) Coelenterata ☐

(c) Echinodermata ☐

(d) Ctenophora ☐

6. Read the following statements.

[NCERT Pg. 42, 43, 45, NEET 2021]

I. Metagenesis is observed in helminths.

II. Echinoderms are triploblastic and coelomate animals.

III. Round worms have organ-system level of body organisation.

IV. Comb plates present in ctenophores help in digestion.

V. Water vascular system is characteristic of echinoderms.

Choose the correct answer from the options given below.

(a) III, IV and V are correct ☐

(b) I, II and III are correct ☐

(c) I, IV and V are correct ☐

(d) II, III and V are correct ☐

7. Which one of the following organisms bears hollow and pneumatic long bones?

[NCERT Pg. 49, 50, NEET 2021]

(a) Neophron ☐

(b) Hemidactylus ☐

(c) Macropus ☐

(d) Ornithorhynchus ☐

8. Match the following columns and select the correct option. [NCERT Pg. 42, 44, 45, NEET (Sep.) 2020]

	Column I		Column II
A.	Gregarious, polyphagous pest	1.	Asterias
B.	Adult with radiol symmetry and larva with bilateral symmetry	2.	Scorpion
C.	Book lungs	3.	Ctenoplana
D.	Bioluminescence	4.	Locusta

A B C D
(a) 4 1 2 3 ☐
(b) 3 2 1 4 ☐
(c) 2 1 3 4 ☐
(d) 1 3 2 4 ☐

9. Which of the following options does correctly represent the characteristic features of phylum-Annelida? [NCERT Pg. 43, NEET (Oct.) 2020]

(a) Triploblastic, unsegmented body and bilaterally symmetrical ☐
(b) Triploblastic, segmented body and bilaterally symmetrical ☐
(c) Triploblastic, flattened body and acoelomate condition ☐
(d) Diploblastic, mostly marine and radially symmetrical ☐

10. Match the following organisms with their respective characteristics. [NCERT Pg. 42, 44, 45, NEET (National) 2019]

	Column I		Column II
A.	Pila	1	Flame cells
B.	Bombyx	2	Comb plates
C.	Pleurobrachia	3	Radula
D.	Taenia	4	Malpighian tubules

Select the correct option from the following

A B C D
(a) 3 4 2 1 ☐
(b) 2 4 3 1 ☐
(c) 3 2 4 1 ☐
(d) 3 2 1 4 ☐

Chapter 05

Morphology of Flowering Plants

Scan and take Chapter Test

TOPIC 1

Introduction and The Root

1. The angiosperms show a large diversity in ______________. They all are characterised by the presence of ______________, ______________, ______________, ______________ and ______________.

2. The underground part of the flowering plant is the ______________ system, while the portion above the ground is the ______________ system.

3. The direct elongation of the radicle leads to the formation of primary root in majority of the monocotyledonous plants.

True ☐ False ☐

4. The primary root bears lateral roots of several orders that are referred to as ______________, ______________, etc, roots.

5. Refer to the given figure and answer the following questions.

(i) Identify *A*, *B* and *C* parts.

A. ______________

B. ______________

C. ______________

(ii) Root *A* and *B* constitute which type of root system? ______________

(iii) In ______________ (monocot/dicot) plants, *A* is short-lived.

*Concepts of all questions bearing * are important for NEET & CUET*

6. Consider the following Venn diagram where region '*P*' denotes similarity between both the flowers.

Which of the following will be most accurate for '*P*'?

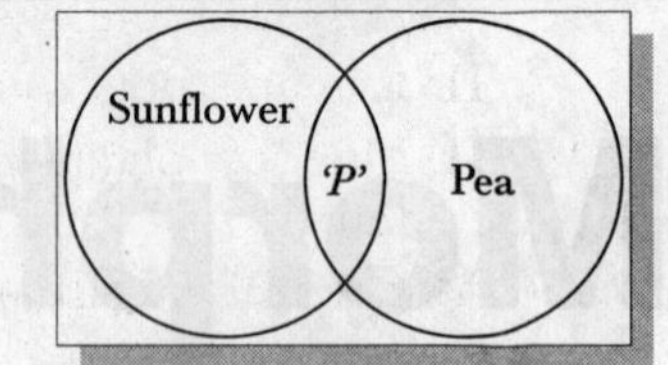

(a) Presence of fibrous roots

(b) Presence of tap roots

(c) Presence of more number of roots

(d) Presence of more root hairs

***7.** Match the following columns.

Column I (Types of root system)		Column II (Features)		Column III (Examples)
(i) Tap root	a.	Root arises from parts of the plant other than the radicle	1	*Monstera*
(ii) Adventitious	b.	Root originate form the base of the stem	2.	Mustard
(iii) Fibrous	c.	Consists of primary and secondary root	3.	Wheat

(i) ________ (ii) ________ (iii) ________

8. How many of the following functions given are related to the root system?

Absorption of water, Food production, Food storage, Plant growth regulator production

____

9. Root is covered at the apex by a thimble-like structure called ________.

10. Match the following columns with the labelled parts of the regions of the root tip.

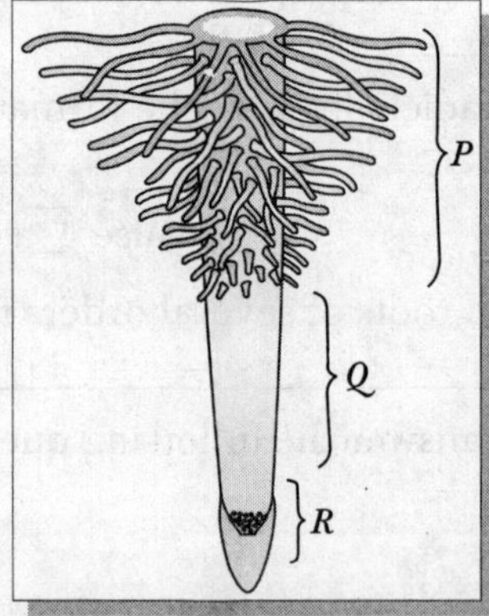

Column I (Regions of the root)		Column II (Regions of the root)		Column III (Features)
(i) Region of meristematic activity	a.	*Q*	1.	Cell form very fine and delicate, thread like structure called root hairs
(ii) Region of elongation	b.	*P*	2.	Cells are small, thin-walled with dense cytoplasm
(iii) Region of maturation	c.	*R*	3.	Cells undergo rapid elongation and enlargement

(i) ________ (ii) ________ (iii) ________

11. Consider the following statements w.r.t. roots.

I. Primary roots is often found growing inside the soil.

II. Primary roots and its branches form the tap root system.

III. Monocot plants have a long lived primary root arising from the plant parts other than radicle.

IV. Epidermal cells arising from the region of elongation, beat root hairs.

Identify the set of incorrect statements.

(a) II and III ☐ (b) II and IV ☐ (c) I and III ☐ (d) III and IV ☐

TOPIC 2

The Stem

NCERT Pg. 59

12. The stem is the ____________ part of the axis bearing branches, leaves, flowers and fruits.

13. Where does the stem develop from? ____________

14. The region of the stem where leaves are borne is called ____________ while ____________ are the portion between two nodes.

15. The stem bears buds, which may be terminal or axillary.

True ☐ False ☐

16. Give any two main functions of stem.

(i) ____________

(ii) ____________

TOPIC 3

The Leaf

NCERT Pg. 59-61

17. Name the lateral and generally flattened structure borne on the stem.

____

18. Leaf develops at the node and bears a bud in its axil. The ____________ later develops into a branch.

19. Leaves originate from ____________ and are arranged in an ____________ order.

20. Consider the diagram of leaf and answer the following questions.

(i) Identity the labelled parts *A, B, C, D* and *E.*

A. ____________

B. ____________

C. ____________

D. ____________

E. ____________

(ii) Name the structure which attaches leaf to the stem.

(iii) In ______________, structure D expands into a sheath covering the stem partially or wholly.

21. In which plants, swollen leaf base pulvinus is found? ______________

22. ______________ (Stipules/Petioles) are the small leaf-like structure.

23. Name the structure of leaf which allows leaf blades to flutter in wind.

____

24. The ______________ or the ______________ is the green expanded part of the leaf with veins and veinlets and the middle prominent vein is called ______________

25. Observe the given image carefully and choose the correct option which best describes the structure that allows the leaf blades to flutter in wind thereby cooling them

(a) D ☐ (b) C ☐ (c) A ☐ (d) B ☐

26. Pulvinus provides rigidity to the leaf blade and acts as channels of transport for water, minerals and food materials.

(Rewrite the statement after correcting the underlined word.)

____

27. The arrangement of veins and the veinlets in the lamina of leaf is termed as

______________.

28. In ______________ venation, the veinlets form a network and in ______________ venation, the vein runs parallel to each other (parallel/reticulate).

29. In which of the following plants, the veinlets in the lamina are observed in a parallel fashion?

(a) Gram ☐ (b) Pea ☐ (c) Wheat ☐ (d) Bean ☐

30. Leaf with the entire lamina or when incised, the incisions do not touch the midrib, is known as ______________ leaf.

31. In ______________ leaf, the incisions of the lamina reach up to the midrib breaking it into a number of leaflets.

32. A bud is present in the axil of petiole in both simple and compound leaves, but not in the axil of leaflets of simple leaf.

True ☐ False ☐

33. A number of leaflets are present on a rachis in ______________ compound leaf.

34. In ______________ compound leaves, the leaflets are attached at the tip of petiole.

35. Identify the type of leaves and species in which these are found from the given figures.

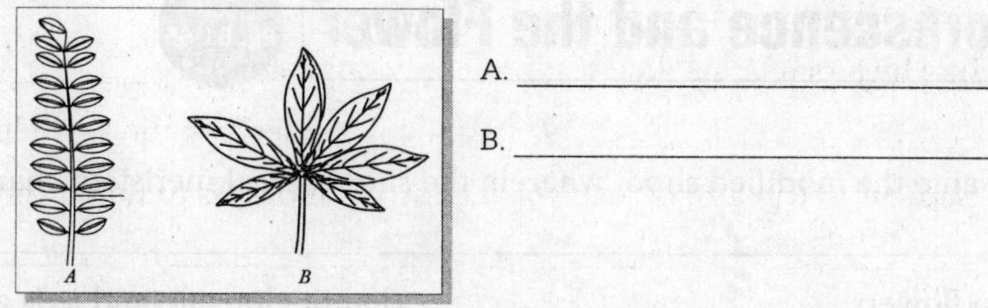

A. ______________________

B. ______________________

***36.** Venation is the pattern of arrangement of leaves on the stem or branch.
(*Rewrite the statement after correcting the underlined word.*)

____

***37.** In alternate type of phyllotaxy, a single leaf arises at each node in __________ manner.

***38.** How many leaves arise from a single node of *Alstonia*?

(a) One ☐ (b) A pair ☐
(c) More than two ☐ (d) Four ☐

***39.** In opposite type of phyllotaxy, a pair of leaves arise at each and lies ______________________ to each other.

***40.** In opposite phyllotaxy, more than two leaves arise at a node and form a whorl.

True ☐ False ☐

***41.** Match the following columns.

Column I (Types of phyllotaxy)	Column II (Figures of phyllotaxy)	Column II (Examples)
(i) Opposite	a.	1. *Alstonia*
(ii) Alternate	b.	2. Guava
(iii) Whorled	c.	3. China rose

(i) ______________ (ii) ______________ (iii) ______________

TOPIC 4

Inflorescence and the Flower

42. Name the modified shoot wherein the shoot apical meristem changes to floral meristem.

____

43. In flowers, ______________ do not elongate and axis gets condensed.

44. The apex of flower produces different kinds of floral appendages vertically at successive nodes instead of leaves.
(*Rewrite the statement after correcting the underlined word.*)

____

45. When a shoot tip transforms into a flower, it is always solitary.

True ☐ False ☐

46. The arrangement of flower on the floral axis is known as ______________.

47. The main axis continues to grow in ______________ (acropetal/basipetal) succession in racemose inflorescence.

48. The main axis terminates into a flower and flowers are borne in a (acropetal/basipetal) succession in cymose inflorescence.

49. Consider the given image and choose the incorrect statement from the following options.

(a) New flowers are produced at the base ☐

(b) The main axis has limited growth ☐

(c) Older flowers are borne at the top ☐

(d) They show acropetal succession ☐

50. Identify the type of inflorescence in the given figures.

A B

A. ______________

B. ______________

51. A typical flower has three different kinds of whorls arranged successively on the swollen end of the pedicel called thalamus.

True ☐ False ☐

52. Name the accessory and reproductive organs of a flower.

____

53. A _______________ flower has both androecium and gynoecium, while _______________ flowers have either only stamens or carpels (unisexual/bisexual).

54. Complete the following analogy with respect to floral symmetry.

Actinomorphic : Zygomorphic :: _______________ : Bilateral symmetry

55. How many of the following flowers can be divided into two equal radial halves in any radial plane passing through the centre?

Mustard, Bean, Datura, Chilli

____

56. Actinomorphic flower can be divided into two similar halves only in one particular vertical plane.

True ☐ False ☐

57. Pea, gulmohur, bean and *Cassia* have _______________ flower.

58. The flower of _______________ is _______________ and cannot be divided into two similar halves by any vertical plane passing through the centre.

59. A flower may be trimerous, tetramerous or pentamerous when the floral appendages are in multiples of _______ (3/4), _______ (4/5), _______ (5/6), respectively.

60. Flowers with reduced leaf found at the base of the pedicel are called ebracteate and without these are called bracteate. (*Rewrite the statement after correcting the underlined words.*)

____

61. Match Column I with Column II.

	Column I		Column II
A.	Actinomorphic	1.	Plum
B.	Ebracteate	2.	Radial symmetry
C.	Epigynous	3.	Inferior ovary
D.	Half inferior	4.	Without bracts

	A	B	C	D			A	B	C	D	
(a)	2	4	3	1	☐	(b)	2	4	1	3	☐
(c)	2	1	3	4	☐	(d)	2	1	4	3	☐

62. In _______________ flower, the gynoecium is situated in the centre and other parts of the flower are located on the rim of the thalamus.

63. In perigynous flowers, the margin of thalamus grows upward enclosing the ovary completely and getting fused with it.

True ☐ False ☐

64. Match the following columns.

Column I (Types of flower)	Column II (Positions of ovary)	Column III (Structural details)
(i) Hypogynous	a. Half inferior	1.
(ii) Epigynous	b. Inferior	2.
(iii) Perigynous	c. Superior	3.

(i) ________ (ii) ________ (iii) ________

65. A group of species is given below. Differentiate the following on the basis of position of floral parts on thalamus.

Guava, China rose, Cucumber, Peach, Plum, Brinjal, Mustard, Ray florets of sunflower

66. The ________ is the outermost whorl of the flower and the members are called ________.

67. When sepals are united, calyx is known as polysepalous and when they are free, it is termed as gamosepalous.

True ☐ False ☐

68. Identify the flower parts *A* to *E* in the given diagram.

A ________ B. ________ C. ________ D. ________

E. ________

69. Match the following columns.

	Column I (Parts of a flower)		Column II (Structures)
A.	Calyx	1.	
B.	Androecium	2.	
C.	Corolla	3.	
D.	Gynoecium	4.	

A. __________

B. __________

C. __________

D. __________

70. Petals are usually brightly coloured to attract ____________ for ____________.

71. Placentation is the mode of arrangement of sepals or petals in a floral bud.

(*Rewrite the statement after correcting the underlined word.*)

____

72. In ____________ (imbricate/valvate) aestivation, sepals or petals in a whorl just touch one another at the margin without overlapping.

73. Name the aestivation in which one margin of the appendage overlaps that of the next one.

____

74. How many of the following species possess aestivation in which the margins of sepals/petals overlaps one another but not in any particular direction.

Pea, Cassia, China rose, Gulmohar

75. Which of the following arrangements show the presence of wings and keel?

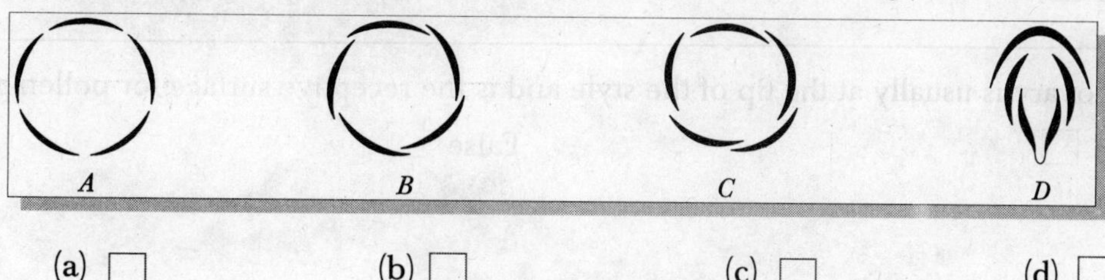

(a) ☐ (b) ☐ (c) ☐ (d) ☐

76. Identify the types of aestivation *A-E* in the given diagram.

A B C D

A. ______________

B. ______________

C. ______________

D. ______________

77. In angiosperms each anther is usually trilobed and each lobe has two chambers.

True ☐ False ☐

78. Where are pollen grains produced? ______________

79. The sterile stamen is called ______________ in which pollen grains are absent.

80. Consider the following statements.

Statement I A staminode of a flower is unable to produce pollen grains and hence cannot take part in reproduction.

Statement II If stamens are attached to the perianth as in the flowers of lily, it is called epipetalous.

Choose the correct option from the following.

(a) Statement I is true, but statement II is false ☐

(b) Statement I is false, but statement II is true ☐

81. Complete the following analogy with respect to stamen position.

Epipetalous : Epiphyllous :: Brinjal : ______________

82. In which situation, do stamens remain free? ______________

83. The stamens may be united into one bunch, i.e. ______________ or two bundles, i.e ______________ or into more than two bundles, i.e. ______________.

84. What is the arrangement of stamens in Citrus called?

(a) Epiphyllous ☐ (b) Syncarpous ☐

(c) Polyadelphous ☐ (d) Epipetalous ☐

85. Complete the following analogy.

Monoadelphous : Diadelphous : Polyadelphous :: ______________ : ______________ : *Citrus*

86. The three parts of a carpel are ______________, ______________ and ______________.

87. Stigma is the enlarged basal part, ovary is the elongated tube which connects the ovary to the style. (*Rewrite the statement after correcing the underlined words.*)

____

88. The ovary is usually at the tip of the style and is the receptive surface for pollen grains.

True ☐ False ☐

89. The ovary bears one or more ovules attached to a flattened cushion-like structure called ________________ (ovary wall/placenta).

90. In ________________ (syncarpous/apocarpous) situation, more than one carpel is present and they are free.

91. In ________________ situation, more than one carpel is present and they are fused to each other.

***92.** The arrangement of ovules within the ovary is known as ________________.

***93.** In parietal placentation, the placenta forms a ridge along the ventral suture of the ovary and the ovules are borne on this ridge forming two rows.

True ☐ False ☐

***94.** When the placenta is axial and the ovules are attached to it in a multilocular ovary, then the placentation is said to be ________________ (marginal/axile).

***95.** Name the placentation in which the ovules develop on the inner wall of the ovary or on peripheral part.

____

***96.** Ovary is one chambered, but it becomes two chambered due to the formation of ________________ in ________________ placentation.

***97.** In basal placentation, the ovules are borne on central axis and septa are absent.
(*Rewrite the statement after correcting the underlined word.*)

____

***98.** Name the placentation in which the placenta develops at the base of ovary and contains single large ovule.

____

***99.** Consider the following image and state which of the following is correct about the given arrangement of ovules.

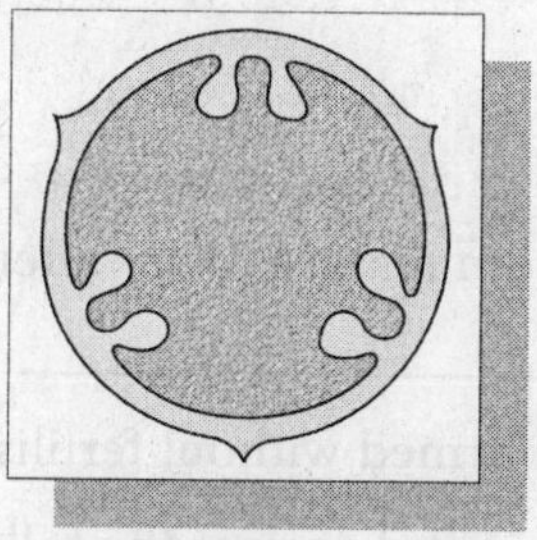

(a) Ovules are borne on a ridge forming two rows ☐
(b) Ovules are attached to the placenta in a multilocular ovary ☐
(c) Ovary becomes two chambered due to false septum ☐
(d) The placenta develops at the base of ovary ☐

***100.** Match the following columns.

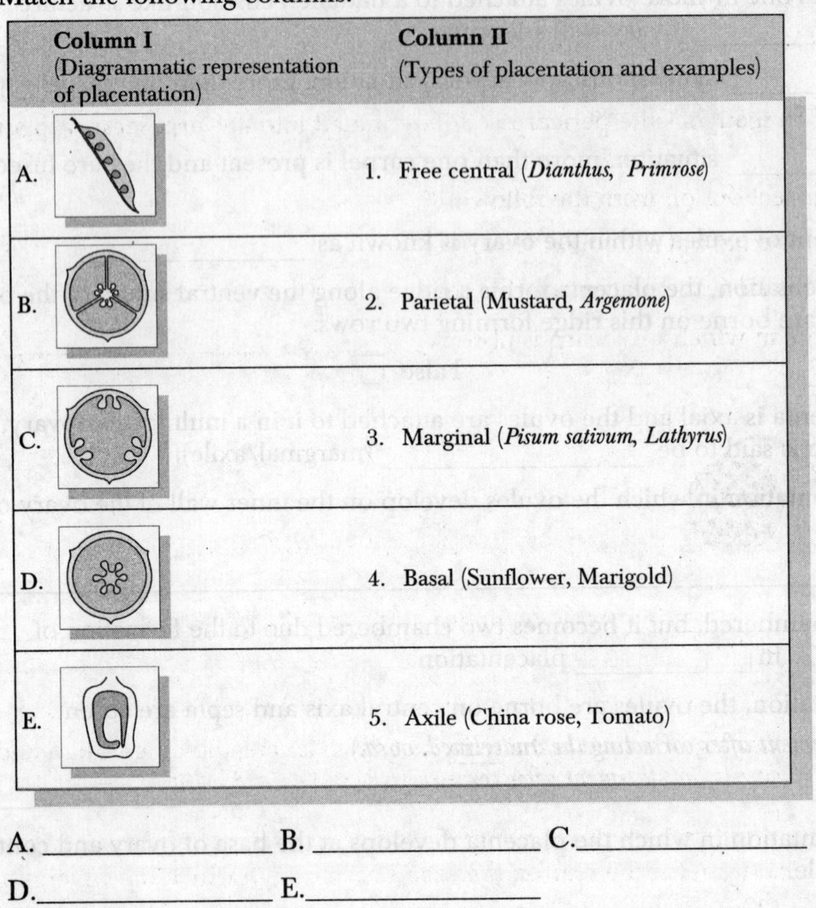

Column I (Diagrammatic representation of placentation)	Column II (Types of placentation and examples)
A.	1. Free central (*Dianthus*, *Primrose*)
B.	2. Parietal (Mustard, *Argemone*)
C.	3. Marginal (*Pisum sativum*, *Lathyrus*)
D.	4. Basal (Sunflower, Marigold)
E.	5. Axile (China rose, Tomato)

A. ______ B. ______ C. ______

D. ______ E. ______

TOPIC 5 The Fruit

NCERT Pg. 65-67

101. Name the structure developed from mature ovary after fertilisation.

______

102. The ______ fruits are formed without fertilisation of the ovary.

103. Consider the diagram given below and answer the following questions.

(i) Identify the labelled parts *A*, *B*, *C* and *D*.

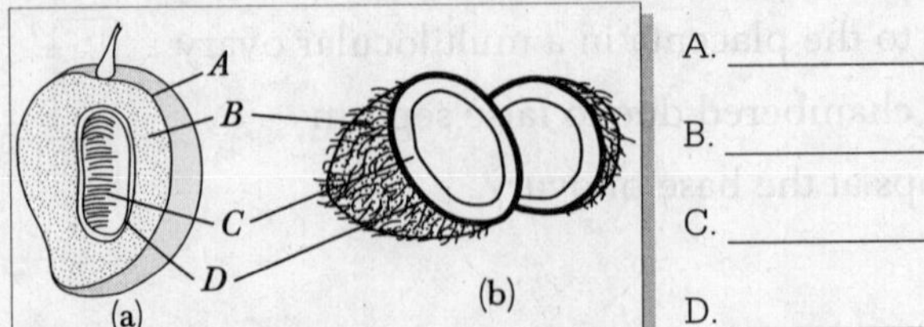

A. ______

B. ______

C. ______

D. ______

(ii) In which of the given fruit mesocarp is fleshy? ______

(iii) Identify the type of fruit represented by (a) and (b).

***104.** Consider the following statements.

Statement I Coconut develops from monocarpellary inferior ovaries and bear single seed.

Statement II In mangoes the pericarp is differentiated into epicarp, mesocarp and an endocarp.

Choose the correct option from the following.

(a) Statement I is true, but statement II is false ☐

(b) Statement I is false, but statement II is true ☐

***105.** Name the drupe in which mesocarp is fibrous.________________

TOPIC 6 The Seed

NCERT Pg. 66-67

106. A seed is the ____________ ovule made up of a ____________ and an ____________.

107. The embryo is made up of a ____________, an ____________ and one or two ____________.

108. The outermost covering of a seed is the testa it has two layers, the outer hilum and the inner tegmen. (*Rewrite the statement after correcting the underlined words.*)

____

***109.** Give the biological term for the scar on the seed coat through which the developing seeds were attached to the fruit ____________.

***110.** Consider the given image and mark the structure which represents the point of attachment of the seeds to the fruit.

(a) Only *C* ☐

(b) B and *C* ☐

(c) Only B ☐

(d) *A* ☐

D
B
C

***111.** A small pore above the hilum is called ____________.

112. Answer the following questions, considering the given figures.

(i) Identify the labelled parts of dicot seed (*A-F*).

A B C D E F

A. ____________

B. ____________

C. ____________

D. ____________

E. ____________

F. ____________

(ii) Which of the above labelled parts is fleshy and full of reserve food?____________

113. Complete the following analogy with respect to seed structure.

Endospermic : Non-endospermic : : Castor : ______________

114. Give a common collective term for the following species.

Pisum sativum, Gram, Bean

____

115. In ______________ (dicotyledonous/ monocotyledonous) seed, seed coat is membranous and generally fused with the fruit wall.

116. The outer covering of endosperm separates the embryo by a proteinaceous layer called ______________ .

117. Consider the following statements and choose the set of correct statements.

I. Castor's embryo derives nourishment from the endosperm formed by double fertilisation.

II. The embryo is situated at one end of the endosperm.

III. The fruit is a characteristic feature of both gymnosperms and angiosperms.

IV. The cotyledons are stony and full of reserve food materials.

Codes

(a) I and III ☐ (b) I and II ☐
(c) III and IV ☐ (d) II and IV ☐

118. Dicotyledonous seeds consist of one large and shield-shaped cotyledon known as scutellum.

True ☐ False ☐

119. The plumule and radicle are enclosed in sheaths known as ______________ and ______________, respectively.

120. In the figure given below, some parts are wrongly labelled. Correct the wrongly labelled parts and write them in front of their correct labels.

Scutellum (A)
Endosperm (B)
Plumule (C)
Coleoptile (D)
Coleorhiza (E)
Radicle (F)

A. ______________
B. ______________
C. ______________
D. ______________
E. ______________
F. ______________

121. Consider the following statements.

Statement I Maize grains have a single large cotyledon called the scutellum.

Statement II The aleurone layer that separates the embryo is rich in starch.

Choose the correct option from the following.

(a) Statement I is true, but statement II is false ☐

(b) Statement I is false, but statement II is true ☐

122. Name any two species in which part 'A' of the given figure, is present in mature seed.

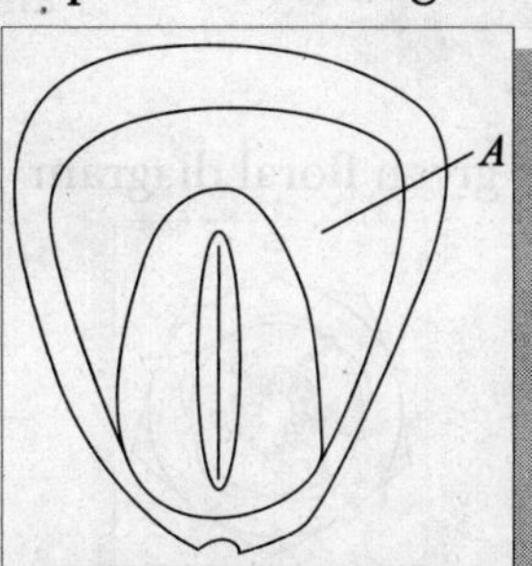

123. Consider the given image and choose the option that represents the part of the seed which encloses the structure which emerges as the root.

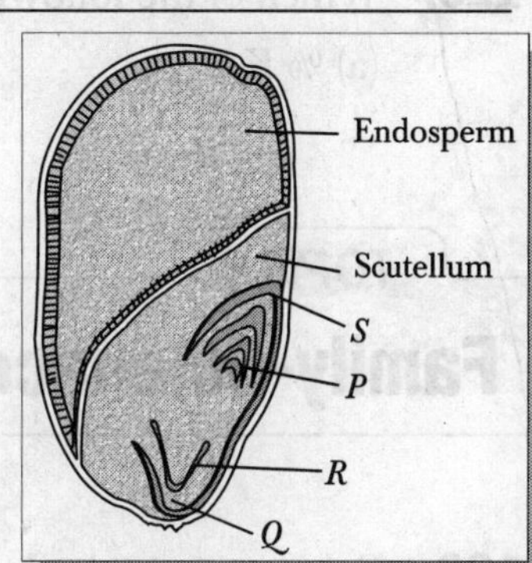

(a) P 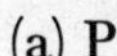

(b) Q 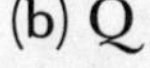

(c) S 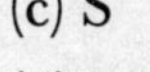

(d) R 

TOPIC 7

Semi-Technical Description of a Typical Flowering Plant

NCERT Pg. 67-68

***124.** Write the symbol of the following character of a flower.

(i) Bracteate ____________________

(ii) Calyx ____________________

(iii) Corolla ____________________

(iv) Perianth ____________________

(v) Androecium ____________________

(vi) Gynoecium ____________________

(vii) Superior ovary ____________________

(viii) Inferior ovary ____________________

(ix) Actinomorphic ____________________

(x) Zygomorphic ____________________

***125.** A ____________ provides information about the ____________ of parts of a flower, their ____________ and the relation they have with each another.

126. The position of the mother axis with respect to the flower is represented by a dot on the bottom of the floral diagram.

True ☐ False ☐

127. The floral formula shows ______________ and ______________ within parts of whorls and between whorls.

***128.** Write the floral formula of the given floral diagram.

$\oplus$

____

129. Which of the following represents an actinomorphic flower with free 5 sepals?

(a) % K_5 ☐ (b) % $K_{(5)}$ ☐ (c) $\oplus$ K_5 ☐ (d) + $K_{(5)}$ ☐

TOPIC 8

Family-Solanaceae

NCERT Pg. 68-69

130. Solanaceae is also known as______________.

***131.** Select the odd one out from the following features with respect to Solanaceae family

Herbaceous, Aerial, Erect, Non-endospermic, Cylindrical branched, Solid or Hollow

____

***132.** What are the features of the leaves of given flowering twig of *Solanum nigrum*?

____

***133.** The inflorescence of *Solanum nigrum* is solitary or ______________ (racemose/cymose).

***134.** The calyx and corolla of *Solanum nigrum* are five in number, united and with imbricate aestivation.

True ☐ False ☐

***135.** Consider the following statements.

Statement I Plants belonging to Solanaceae have pinnately compound leaves that show opposite phyllotaxy.

Statement II Potato plants are gamosepalous, gamopetalous, epipetalous with imbricate aestivation.

Choose the correct option from the following.

(a) Statement I is true, but statement II is false ☐

(b) Both statements I and II are false ☐

***136.** Answer the following questions after considering the floral parts and floral diagram given below.

(i) The floral diagram belongs to ____________ plant.

(ii) The gynoecium is ____________ (monocarpellary/ bicarpellary), ____________ (apocaropus/ syncarpous), ovary superior with axile placentation.

(iii) There are ____________ stamens with ____________ condition.

(iv) Write their floral formula.____________

137. How many of the following species belong to Solanaceae family?

Belladonna, Ashwagandha, Tomato, Brinjal, Lily, Chilli, Tobacco

____

138. Complete the following analogy with respect to economic importance of Solanaceae family.

(i) Medicine : Fumigatory :: ____________ : Tobacco

(ii) Ornamental : Spice :: ____________ : Chilli

COMPETITION CONNECT

Topic 1. Modifications of Root [NCERT (Old) Pg. 67]

1. ________________ (Tap/Adventitious) roots of carrot, turnip and ________________ (tap/adventitious) roots of sweet potato get swollen and store food. ________________

   ____

2. The hanging structure of banyan tree is called ________________.

3. Identify the type of root arising from the plant shown in the following figure.

   ____

4. The stems of maize and sugarcane have supporting roots coming out of the lower nodes of the stem and are called clinging roots.
   (*Rewrite the statement after correcting the underlined word.*)

   ____

5. Consider the following image and mention the function of the structure shown:

   (a) Respiration ☐
   (b) Support ☐
   (c) Photosynthesis ☐
   (d) Absorption ☐

6. Prop roots come out of the ground and grow vertically upwards.

   True ☐ False ☐

7. Consider the following diagram of modification of root and answer the following questions.

(i) These roots are found in mangroove species, e.g. ____________________ growing in swampy areas.

(ii) These roots prove to be advantageous for the plants.

True ☐ False ☐

8. Identify the mismatched pair.

(a) Prop roots – Provide support ☐

(b) Stilt roots – Originate from stem's nodal part ☐

(c) Pneumatophores – Help in storing food ☐

(d) Edible roots – Sweet potato ☐

9. A type of modified ____________________ root that arises from the internode of stem, grows and becomes fleshy and tuberous, serving as storage for reserve food material is observed in ____________________ .

Topic 2. Modifications of Stem [NCERT (Old) Pg. 68-69]

10. Give a common property possessed by the following plant species.

Potato, Ginger, Turmeric, Jimikand, Colocasia

____

11. Choose the correct combination of plants and their modified stems from the following.

(a) Cucumber – tendrils, *Citrus* – thorns ☐

(b) *Citrus* – tendrils, Cucumber – thorns ☐

(c) Cucumber – tendrils, *Citrus* – tendrils ☐

(d) *Citrus* – thorns, Cucumber – thorns ☐

____

12. Stem suckers develop from axillary buds are slender, spirally coiled and help plants to climb. (*Rewrite the statement after correcting the underlined word.*)

____

13. Give a common collective term for the structure possessed by the following plant species.

Cucumber, Pumpkin, Watermelon, Grapevine

____

14. Consider the following statements.

Statement I The underground stem of *Colocasia* is modified to store food.

Statement II Potato is a modified stem while sweet potato is a modified root.

Choose the correct option from the following.

(a) Statement I is true, but statement II is false ☐

(b) Both statements I and II are true ☐

15. Axillary buds of stems are modified into woody, straight and pointed ____________ (bulbils/thorns) which protect plants from browsing animals.

16. The tendrils of cucumber and grapevines help them to climb.

True ☐ False ☐

17. Which type of stem modification is found in *Citrus* and *Bougainvillea*?

____

18. Some plants of arid regions modify their stems into ______________ or ______________ structures, containing chlorophyll.

19. Name the stem modification in which underground stems of some plants spread to new niches and when older parts die new plants are formed.

____

20. Which type of stem modification is shown in the following figure of *Oxalis* sp.?

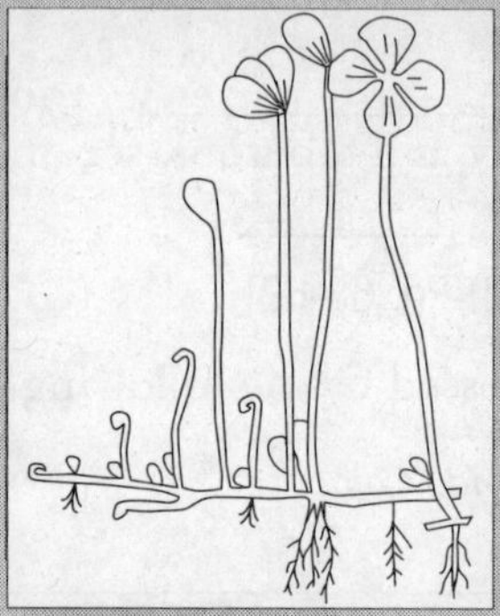

____

21. In <u>suckers</u>, a slender lateral branch arises from the base of the main axis and after growing aerially it arches downwards to touch the ground.

(*Rewrite the statement after correcting the underlined word.*)

____

22. ______________ (Runners/Offsets) are lateral branches with short internodes and each node bearing a rosette of leaves and a tuft of roots.

23. Stolons are the lateral branches originating from the basal and underground portion of the stem, grow horizontally and give rise to leafy shoots.

True ☐ False ☐

24. Match the following columns.

	Column I (Types of stem modification)		Column II (Examples)
A.	Runners	1.	Mint, jasmine
B.	Sucker	2.	*Pistia*, *Eichhornia*
C.	Stolon	3.	Banana, pineapple, *Chrysanthemum*
D.	Offset	4.	Grass, strawberry

A. ______________ B. ______________ C.______________ D ______________

Topic 3. Modifications of Leaves [NCERT (Old) Pg. 71]

25. The ______________ of Australian *Acacia* expand, become green and synthesise food, because their ______________ are small and short-lived.

26. ______________ and ______________ have modified their leaves for trapping insects.

27. Identify the type of leaf modifications in the given diagrams (*A* to *C*).

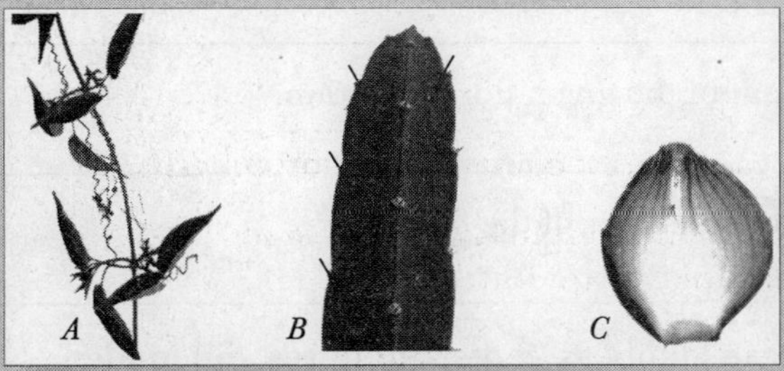

A. ______________________

B. ______________________

C. ______________________

28. Consider the following statements.

Statement I In peas, stem is modified into tendrils that support them in climbing.

Statement II Cacti has a lot of spines which serve as a defensive structure against animals.

Choose the correct option from the following.

(a) Statement I is true, but statement II is false ☐

(b) Statement I is false, but statement II is true ☐

Topic 4. Description of Some Important Families [NCERT (Old) Pg. 78-81]

29. Answer the following questions considering the given figure.

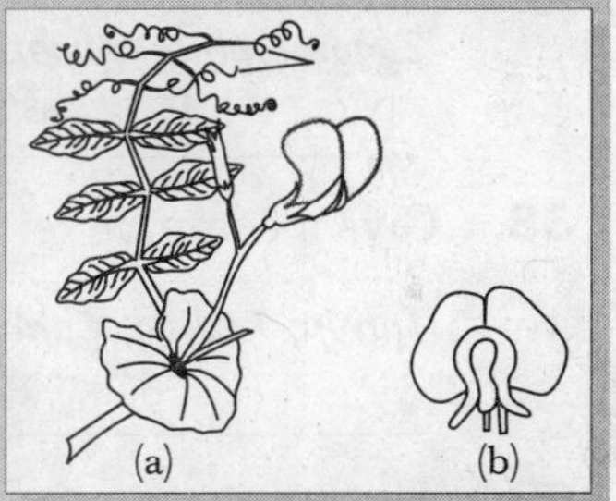

(i) Write the feature of their leaves.

____

(ii) Plant (a) shows ______________________ inflorescence.

(iii) Flowers are unisexual and actinomorphic.

True ☐ False ☐

(iv) Identify plant twig (a). ______________________

30. How many of the following features of corolla are not related to corolla of pea?

5 petals, Gamopetalous, Papilionaceous, Twisted aestivation, Vexillary aestivation

____

31. The calyx of pea flower are five in number with polysepalous or valvate/imbricate condition.

True ☐ False ☐

32. Consider the given floral diagram and answer the following questions.

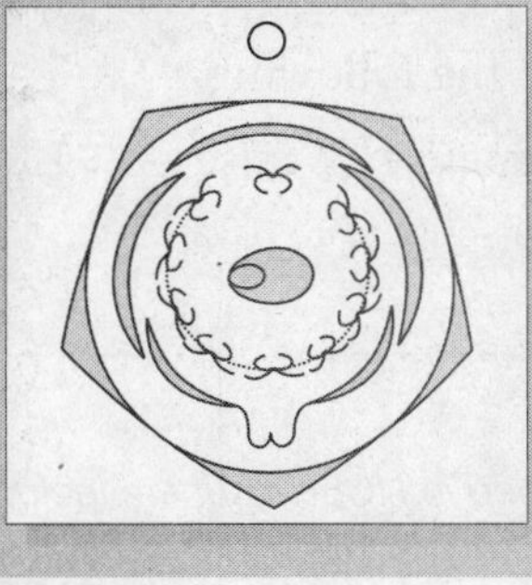

(i) Write all the features of androecium of the given floral diagram.

____

(ii) Write all the features of gynoecium of the given floral diagram.

____

(iii) Write the floral formula of any one member of the family.

____

33. Give example of each from Fabaceae family as (i) dye, (ii) fibres, (iii) fodder, (iv) medicine, (v) ornamentals.

____

34. Give a common collective feature for the following species.

Gram, Arhar, Sem, Moong, Soybean, Groundnut

____

***35.** The flowers of the Malvaceae family are unisexual

True ☐ False ☐

***36.** *Hibiscus* flowers are______________(actinomorphic/zygomorphic)

***37.** How many of the following features belong to members of Malvaceae family?

Zygomorphic, Epipetalous, Syncarpous, Monocarpellary, Diadelphous

____

38. Give a common term for the following.

Turnip, Radish, Cabbage, Mustard

____

***39.** The other name for Crucifereae family is____________(Brassicaceae/Leguminoseae)

***40.** The position of ovary in radish is superior

True ☐ False ☐

***41.** How does the seed of a cabbage plant gets nourishment?

____

***42.** Name the placentation in family-Compositae____________.

***43.** Consider the following statements.

Statement I Sunflower plants have sessile small flowers called florets.

Statement II Sunflower has a superior ovary and is referred to as hypogynous.

Choose the correct option from the following.

(a) Statement I is true, but statement II is false ☐

(b) Statement I is false, but statement II is true ☐

***44.** Ray florets of sunflower are___________ while ___________ disc florets are________.

(Zygomorphic/actinomorphic)

***Note** *Some families are not described in NCERT but are included in NEET syllabus.*

***45.** How many of the following features belong to compositae family?

Ebracteate, Epipetalous, Syncarpous, Bicarpellary, Epigynous

____

***46.** The other name for Gramineae is____________.

***47.** Give four examples of plants belonging to Graminae family. __________.

***48.** The wheat family shows____________venation and have _____cotyledon (s).

***49.** The Gramineae family has____________(superior/inferior) ovary and are________ (hypogynous/epigynous).

***50.** Mention two economic importance of Poaceae.

____

***51.** Which of the following about Graminaea is not true?

(a) Flowers have 3-6 androecium and are polyandrous ☐

(b) Ovary is superior and hypogynous ☐

(c) Flowers contain a stalk or pedicel ☐

(d) Ovaries show basal placentation ☐

52. Choose the correct combination from the following:

(a) Malvaceae – actinomorphic, Gramineae – actinomorphic ☐

(b) Malvaceae – actinomorphic, Graminae – zygomorphic ☐

(c) Malvaceae – zygomorphic, Gramineae – zygomorphic ☐

(d) Malvaceae – zygomorphic, gramineae – actinomorphic ☐

***Note** *Some families are not described in NCERT but are included in NEET syllabus.*

Assertion-Reason Questions

The following questions consist of two statements- Assertion (A) and Reason (R). Answer these questions by selecting the appropriate option given below.

(a) Both A and R are true and R is the correct explanation of A

(b) Both A and R are true, but R is not the correct explanation of A

(c) A is true, but R is false

(d) A is false, but R is true

1. **Assertion** (A) The fine thread like structures present in the region of elongation are the root hairs.

Reason (R) Root hairs increase the surface area of absorption of water and minerals from the soil.

(a) ☐ (b) ☐ (c) ☐ (d) ☐

2. **Assertion** (A) In potato, ginger and turmeric, the underground stem stores food inside them.

Reason (R) These underground stems are adaptations for efficient food storage.

(a) ☐ (b) ☐ (c) ☐ (d) ☐

3. **Assertion** (A) The veins and veinlets in the lamina allow food to be distributed to other parts of the plant.

Reason (R) Veins and veinlets act as channels of transport for water, minerals and food materials.

(a) ☐ (b) ☐ (c) ☐ (d) ☐

***4.** **Assertion** (A) Phyllotaxy is the arrangement of leaves on a branch or stem of a plant.

Reason (R) In guava plants, more than two leaves arise from a single node and form a whorl.

(a) ☐ (b) ☐ (c) ☐ (d) ☐

***5.** **Assertion** (A) In flowers of guava and cucumber the ovary occupies an inferior position.

Reason (R) The calyx, corolla and androecium in epigynous flowers arise above the ovary.

(a) ☐ (b) ☐ (c) ☐ (d) ☐

***6.** **Assertion** (A) The arrangement of ovules within the ovary in *Dianthus* and *Primrose* is free central.

Reason (R) Ovules attach to the ovary wall by means of a cushion-like tissue called placenta.

(a) ☐ (b) ☐ (c) ☐ (d) ☐

7. **Assertion** (A) Castor seeds do not undergo double fertilisation and hence there is no endosperm formation.

Reason (R) Endosperm is a food storing tissue and provides nourishment to the developing embryo.

(a) ☐ (b) ☐ (c) ☐ (d) ☐

8. **Assertion** (A) Monocot seeds like maize do not contain endosperm and derive nourishment from the scutellum.

Reason (R) Maize seeds have their seed coat fused with the fruit wall and contain a protein rich layer.

(a) ☐ (b) ☐ (c) ☐ (d) ☐

9. **Assertion** (A) Floral formula proves to be of much importance to us.

Reason (R) Floral formula is a symbolic and numeric representation sending information on the type of symmetry, level of ovary, type and number of organs, etc.

(a) ☐ (b) ☐ (c) ☐ (d) ☐

10. **Assertion** (A) Members of the Malvaceae family include okra and cotton.

Reason (R) Flowers of Malvaceae family have many carpels and all the carpels remain free from one another.

(a) ☐ (b) ☐ (c) ☐ (d) ☐

Case Based Questions

***1.** Consider the following image and answer the following questions.

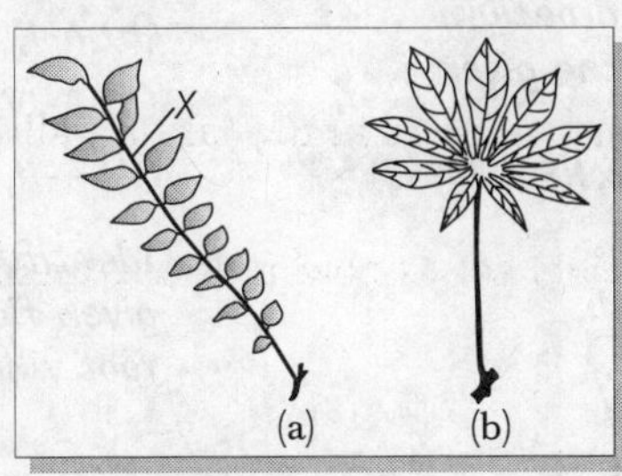

(i) Identify the structure labelled as X.

(a) Pedicel ☐ (b) Petiole ☐
(c) Thalamus ☐ (d) Rachis ☐

(ii) What type leaves are represented in the image(a)?

(a) Simple leaf ☐ (b) Pinnately compound ☐
(c) Palmately compound ☐ (d) Simple compound ☐

(iii) What is the term given for arrangement of leaves on a stem?

(a) Aestivation ☐ (b) Inflorescence ☐
(c) Phyllotaxy ☐ (d) Placentation ☐

(iv) Which plant represents type of leaf shown in image (b)?

(a) Neem ☐ (b) Walnut ☐
(c) Silk cotton ☐ (d) *Cassia* sp. ☐

***2.** A particular species of plant is collected from the wild and has the following characteristics.

1. Bisexual and zygomorphic
2. Five sepals which are united
3. Five petals which are free
4. Diadelphous androecium
5. Monocarpellary, ovary
6. Superior ovary

With respect to the given information, answer the following questions.

(i) Based on the condition of the ovary, the given plant is

(a) hypogynous ☐ (b) perigynous ☐
(c) epigynous ☐ (d) hypergynous ☐

(ii) Choose the correct combination of sepals and petals of the flower.

(a) Polypetalous and gamosepalous ☐ (b) Gamopetalous and Polysepalous ☐
(c) Gamosepalous and gamopetalous ☐ (d) Polysepalous and polypetalous ☐

(iii) Which of the following best represents the floral formula of the plant?

(a) $\oplus$ ⚥ $K_{(5)}\ \widehat{C_{(5)}\ A_5}\ \underline{G}_{(2)}$ ☐ (b) $\oplus$ ♂ $K_{(5)}\ C_{(5)}\ A_5\ \underline{G}_{(2)}$ ☐
(c) % ⚥ $K_5\ \widehat{C_{(5)}A_5}\ \underline{G}_{(2)}$ ☐ (d) % ⚥ $K_{(5)}\ C_{(1+2+(2))}\ A_{(9)+1}\ \underline{G}_1$ ☐

COMPETITION EDGE UP

1. Identify the type of flowers based on the position of calyx, corolla and androecium with respect to the ovary from the given figures (A) and (B).
[NCERT Pg. 62, NEET 2024]

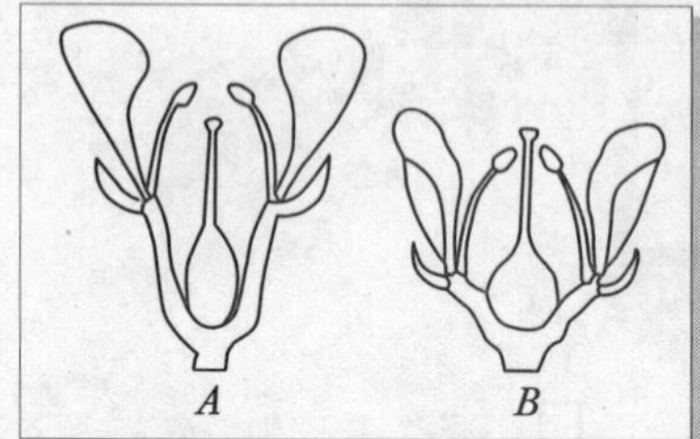

(a) (A) Epigynous; (B) Hypogynous ☐
(b) (A) Hypogynous; (B) Epigynous ☐
(c) (A) Perigynous; (B) Epigynous ☐
(d) (A) Perigynous; (B) Perigynous ☐

2. Match List I with List II.

	List I (Types of Stamens)		List II (Example)
A.	Monoadelphous	I.	Citrus
B.	Diadelphous	II.	Pea
C.	Polyadelphous	III.	Lily
D.	Epiphyllous	IV.	China rose

Choose the correct answer from the options given below.
[NCERT Pg. 64, NEET 2024]

(a) A-IV, B-II, C-I, D-III ☐
(b) A-IV, B-I, C-II, D-III ☐
(c) A-I, B-II, C-IV, D-III ☐
(d) A-III, B-I, C-IV, D-II ☐

3. Match List I with List II.

	List I		List II
A.	Rose	I.	Twisted aestivation
B.	Pea	II.	Perigynous flower
C.	Cotton	III.	Drupe
D.	Mango	IV.	Marginal placentation

Choose the correct answer from the options given below.
[NCERT Pg. 74, 75, 76, NEET 2024]

(a) A-II, B-IV, C-I, D-III ☐
(b) A-I, B-II, C-III, D-IV ☐
(c) A-IV, B-III, C-II, D-I ☐
(d) A-II, B-III, C-IV, D-I ☐

4. Identify the part of the seed from the given figure which is destined to form root when the seed germinates.
[NCERT Pg. 67, NEET 2024]

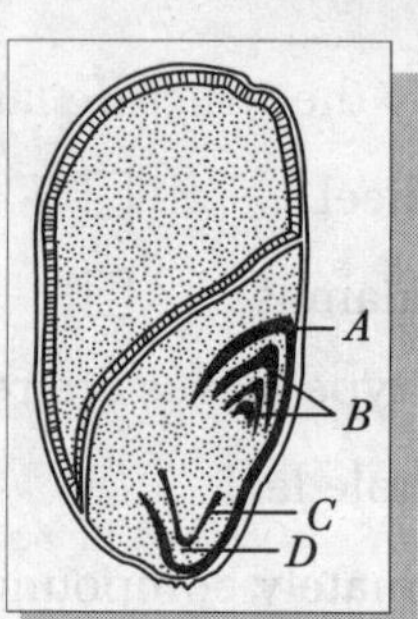

(a) A ☐ (b) B ☐
(c) C ☐ (d) D ☐

5. Axile placentation is observed in
[NCERT Pg. 65, NEET 2023]

(a) China rose, beans and lupin ☐
(b) Tomato, Dianthus and pea ☐
(c) China rose, Petunia and lemon ☐
(d) Mustard, cucumber and primrose ☐

6. Given below are two statements; One is labelled as **Assertion (A)** and the other is labelled as **Reason (R)**.

Assertion (A) A flower is defined as modified shoot wherein the shoot apical meristem changes to floral meristem.

Reason (R) Internode of the shoot gets condensed to produce different floral appendages laterally at successive nodes instead of leaves.

In the light of the above statements, choose the correct answer from the options given below.
[NEET 2023]

(a) Both A and R are true, but R is not the correct explanation of A ☐
(b) A is true, but R is false ☐
(c) A is false, but R is true ☐
(d) Both A and R are true and R is the correct explanation of A ☐

7. *Family-Fabaceae differs from Solanaceae and Liliaceae. With respect to the stamens pick out the characteristics specific to family-Fabaceae, but not found in Solanaceae or Liliaceae.*
[NCERT (Old) Pg. 79, NEET 2023]

(a) Polyadelphous and epipetalous stamens ☐
(b) Monoadelphous and monothecous anthers ☐
(c) Epiphyllous and dithecous anthers ☐
(d) Diadelphous and dithecous anthers ☐

8. *Identify the correct set of statements.*
[NCERT (Old) Pg. 67, NEET 2022]

I. The leaflets are modified into pointed hard thorns in Citrus and Bougainvillea.
II. Axillary buds form slender and spirally coiled tendrils in cucumber and pumpkin.
III. Stem is flattened and fleshy in Opuntia and modified to perform the function of leaves.
IV. Rhizophora shows vertically upward growing roots that help to get oxygen for respiration.
V. Subaerially growing stems in grasses and strawberry help in vegetative propagation.

Choose the correct answer from the options given below.

(a) I and IV ☐
(b) II, III, IV and V ☐
(c) I, II, IV and V ☐
(d) II and III ☐

9. *The flowers are zygomorphic in*
[NCERT Pg. 62, NEET 2022]

I. Mustard II. Gulmohar
III. Cassia IV. Datura V. Chilly

Choose the correct answer from the options given below.

(a) (II) and (III) ☐
(b) (IV) and (V) ☐
(c) (III), (IV) and (V) ☐
(d) (I), (II) and (III) ☐

10. *Which one of the following plants shows vexillary aestivation and diadelphous stamens?* **[NCERT (Old) Pg. 79, NEET 2022]**

(a) Pisum sativum ☐
(b) Allium cepa ☐
(c) Solanum nigrum ☐
(d) Colchicum autumnale ☐

11. *Identify the correct features of mango and coconut fruits.*
[NCERT Pg. 65, 66, NEET (Oct.) 2020]

(i) In both fruit is a drupe.
(ii) Endocarp is edible in both.
(iii) Mesocarp in coconut is fibrous and in mango it is fleshy.
(iv) In both, fruit develops from monocarpellary ovary.

Select the correct option.

(a) (i), (iii) and (iv) ☐
(b) (i), (ii) and (iii) ☐
(c) (i) and (iv) ☐
(d) (i) and (ii) ☐

Chapter 06

Anatomy of Flowering Plants

1. Name all the types of tissue system on the basis of their structure and location.

____

2. The epidermal tissue system forms the outermost covering of the whole plant body and comprises of __________, __________ and __________.

3. The outermost layer of the primary plant body is mesophyll.
(*Rewrite the statement after correcting the underlined word.*)

____

4. Epidermis is made up of round, compactly arranged cells, and forms a continuous layer.
True ☐ False ☐

5. Epidermal cells are __________ with a small amount of cytoplasm lining the cell wall and a large __________.

6. The outside of the epidermis is covered with a waxy thick layer that prevents the loss of water and is known as __________

7. Cuticle is absent in roots. (*Give reason*)

____

8. Stomata regulate the process of __________ and __________.

9. Stomata are structures present in________that help in gaseous exchange.

(a) fundamental tissue ☐
(b) guard cells ☐
(c) leaf epidermis ☐
(d) roof epidermis ☐

*Concepts of all questions bearing * are important for NEET & CUET*

10. Bean-shaped guard cells are found in monocot and dumb-bell-shaped guard cells are found in dicot.

True ☐ False ☐

11. In dicot leaves, stomata are scattered whereas in monocot, these are arranged in rows.

True ☐ False ☐

12. The outer walls of guard cells are ____________ and the inner walls are highly ____________.

13. The ____________ (subsidiary cells/guard cells) possess chloroplast and regulate the opening and closing of stomata.

14. A few epidermal cells in the vicinity of the guard cells become specialised in their shape and size and are known as guard cells.
(*Rewrite the statement after correcting the underlined words.*)

____

15. Which of the following is not a part of the stomatal apparatus?

(a) Stomatal aperture ☐ (b) Guard cells ☐

(c) Epidermal cells ☐ (d) Subsidiary cells ☐

16. Which stomata given in the following figure belongs to monocot leaves?

A B

A. ☐

B. ☐

17. The unicellular elongations of the epidermal cells that absorb water and minerals from the soil is known as ____________

18. Name the epidermal hair which is present on stem. ____________

19. The trichomes in the shoot system are usually unicellular.

True ☐ False ☐

20. In some plants, trichomes may be secretory in nature.

True ☐ False ☐

21. The trichomes help in preventing water loss occurring due to ____________.

22. Identify the incorrect feature about trichomes.

(a) Secretory nature ☐ (b) Help in preventing water loss ☐

(c) Unicellular elongations ☐ (d) Branched or unbranched ☐

23. Ground tissue constitutes epidermis and vascular bundle.

True ☐ False ☐

24. Ground tissue consists of simple tissues such as ________, ________ and ________.

25. Name the cells of ground tissue which contain chloroplast. ________

26. Identify the odd one out from the following terms.

Epidermis, Mesophyll, Stomata, Trichomes

____

27. The vascular system consists of complex tissues, like the ________ and the ________.

28. Cambium is absent in dicot plants.

True ☐ False ☐

29. If cambium is present between xylem and phloem it is known as <u>closed</u> vascular bundle. (*Rewrite the statement after correcting the underlined word.*)

____

30. Secondary growth is absent in monocots. (*Give reason*)

____

31. Consider the given image and choose the plant which shows the given arrangement.

(a) Monocot stem ☐

(b) Dicot stem ☐

(c) Monocot root ☐

(d) Dicot root ☐

32. Study the figures *A* and *B* given below and identify the characteristics which correctly describe them.

(i) Open vascular bundle ________

(ii) Closed vascular bundle ________

(iii) Present in monocots ________

(iv) Forms secondary tissues ________

(v) Do not form secondary tissues ________

(vi) Xylem and phloem are situated on the same radius ________

33. In radial arrangement, xylem and phloem are arranged in ________ manner along different ________.

34. Name the vascular bundle in which xylem and phloem are jointly situated along the same radii. ________

35. Consider the following statements.

Statement I The arrangement of xylem and phloem in an alternate manner along the different radii is a characteristic of stems.

Statement II In open type, xylem and phloem tissue is separated by a cambium layer that causes secondary growth.

Choose the correct option from the following.

(a) Statement I is true, but statement II is false ☐

(b) Statement I is false, but statement II is true ☐

36. Identify the types of vascular bundle on the basis of given scenarios.

(i) Vascular bundle common in stems and leaves. ____________

(ii) Vascular bundle common in root. ____________

(iii) Phloem located only on the outer side of xylem. ____________

37. Which of the following statements is incorrect w.r.t vascular tissue system?

(a) The vascular tissue system in constituted by xylem and phloem. ☐

(b) Monocotyledons like grass, presence of open vascular bundles. ☐

(c) Conjoint type of vascular bundles are more common in stems and roots. ☐

(d) The conjoint vascular bundles usually have phloem located on the outer side of xylem. ☐

TOPIC 2

Anatomy of Dicotyledonous and Monocotyledonous Plants : Root

NCERT Pg. 73-74

38. The outermost layer of dicotyledonous root is <u>cortex</u>.
(Rewrite the statement after correcting the underlined word.)

____

39. Unicellular root hairs protrude from ____________.

40. Name the region of dicotyledonous root where several layers of thin-walled parenchyma cell with intercellular spaces are present. ____________

41. Complete the following analogy.

Cortex : ____________ : : Several layers : Single layer

42. Which layer of dicot roots possess barrel-shaped cell without any intercellular spaces?

____

43. The tangential as well as radial wall of the endodermal cells possess deposition of water impermeable material, i.e. suberin in the form of <u>starch sheath</u>.
(Rewrite the statement after correcting the underlined words.)

____

44. Lateral roots and vascular cambium originate from ____________. These are thick-walled ____________ cells.

45. In dicot root, pith is large.

True ☐ False ☐

46. Consider the following figure of TS of dicot root. Which of the following parts represent cortex, endodermis and xylem?

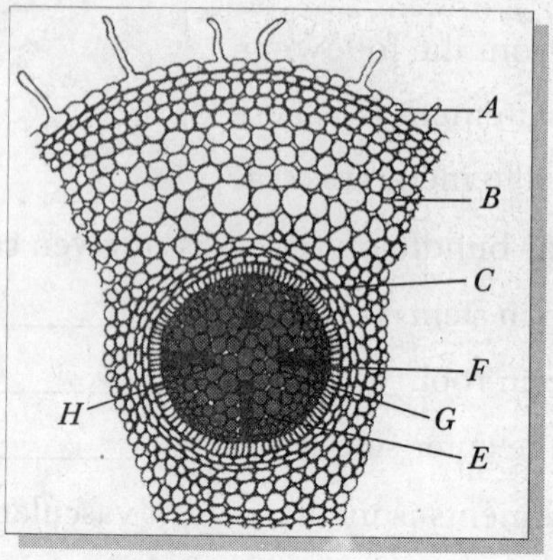

47. Consider the following statements.

Statement I Pericycle is the thin walled parenchymatous layer present inner to the endodermis.

Statement II The sclerenchymatous cells between xylem and phloem in dicot root forms the conjuctive tissue.

Choose the correct option from the following.

(a) Statement I is true, but statement II is false ☐

(b) Both statements I and II are false ☐

48. Rearrange the sequence of internal tissue of dicot root from outer side to inner side.

Epidermis, Root hair, Endodermis, Cortex, Phloem, Pith, Pericycle

____

49. Consider the image given in Q. no. 46 and mention which of the following denotes the collective term for structures *C* to *H*?

(a) Pericycle ☐ (b) Pith ☐ (c) Hypodermis ☐ (d) Stele ☐

50. Identify the odd one out from the given terms.

Cortex, Endoderm, Pericycle, Vascular bundle, Pith

____

51. Your are given a slide of root in which, vascular bundles are radial, xylem is exarch, vascular bundle vary from diarch to hexarch. Identify the root.____________________

52. Vascular bundles in monocot roots are ____________________ and xylem is in ________________ condition.

53. Which of the following is not correct about monocot root?

(a) Six or more xylem bundles are usually present ☐

(b) Pith is larger and more developed than dicot root ☐

(c) Monocot roots do not show secondary growth ☐

(d) Vascular bundles are conjoint open type. ☐

54. Consider the following figure of TS of monocot root. In which of the following part, Casparian strip is present?

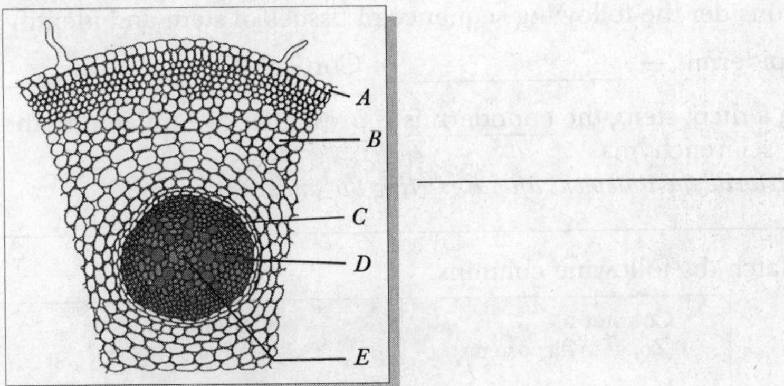

55. Consider the following statements.

Statement I Monocot roots are devoid of epidermal appendages that help in absorption of water and minerals.

Statement II Monocot roots are of closed type and do not show secondary growth of xylem and phloem.

Choose the correct option from the following.

(a) Statement I is true, but statement II is false ☐

(b) Statement I is false, but statement II is true ☐

56. Read the following characteristics and mark them as dicot or monocot root.

(i) There are usually more than six xylem bundles ____________.

(ii) Pith is large and well-developed ____________.

(iii) Secondary growth is present ____________.

TOPIC 3

Anatomy of Dicotyledonous and Monocotyledonous Plants : Stem

57. Epidermis of dicot stem bears trichomes and few stomata.

True ☐ False ☐

58. In dicot stem, cortex is categorised into three zones, i.e. ____________, ____________ and ____________.

59. The hypodermis of a dicot stem is made up of ____________ cells.

60. Which of the following combinations is correct with respect to dicot stems?

(a) Hypodermis – collenchyma ; Cortical layer – parenchyma ☐

(b) Hypodermis – parenchyma ; Cortical layer – collenchyma ☐

(c) Hypodermis – collenchyma ; Cortical layer – collenchyma ☐

(d) Hypodermis –parenchyma ; Cortical layer – parenchyma ☐

61. The endodermis is rich in ______________ and the layer is also known as ______________.

62. Consider the following sequence of tissues of stem and identify *A* and *B*.

Epidermis → ______________ → Cortical layer → ______________ → Pericycle

63. In a dicot stem, the <u>endodermis</u> is present above phloem in the form of semilunar patches of sclerenchyma.

(*Rewrite the statement after correcting the underlined word.*)

____

64. Match the following columns.

Column I (Zones in dicot stems)		Column II (Characteristics)	
A.	Hypodermis	1.	Rounded thin-walled parenchymatous
B.	Cortical layer	2.	Provides mechanical strength
C.	Endodermis	3.	Semilunar patches of sclerenchyma
D.	Pericycle	4.	Innermost layer of cortex

A. ______________ B. ______________ C. ______________ D. ______________

65. Consider the following figure of dicot stem, identify parts *A, B, C* and *D*.

A. ______________
B. ______________
C. ______________
D. ______________

66. Consider the given image in Q. no. 65 and state the cell type that makes up structure *D*.

(a) Parenchyma ☐ (b) Collenchyma ☐
(c) Sclerenchyma ☐ (d) Aerenchyma ☐

67. Some parenchymatous cells are radially placed between the vascular bundles, these are known as <u>xylem rays</u>.

(*Rewrite the statement after correcting the underlined words.*)

____

68. The vascular bundles in dicot stem are scattered.

True ☐ False ☐

69. Consider the following statements.

Statement I Vascular bundles in dicot stems are arranged in a ring system, characteristic to them.

Statement II Each vascular bundle in a dicot stem is conjoint, open and with endarch protoxylem.

Choose the correct option from the following.

(a) Statement I is true, but statement II is false ☐

(b) Both statements I and II are true ☐

70. ________ (Pericycle/Pith) consists of a large number of rounded, parenchymatous cells with large intercellular spaces that occupy central portion of the dicot stem. ________

71. Consider the following figure of TS of stem and identify the parts *A–F*.

A. ________

B. ________

C. ________

D. ________

E. ________

F. ________

72. Consider the following statements.

I. The hypodermis of a monocot and dicot stem contain collenchymatous cells.

II. Monocot stems have scattered vascular bundles, each surrounded by a sclerenchymatous bundle sheath.

III. In dicot stem, each vascular bundle is conjoint, open and with exarch protoxylem.

IV. Sclerenchymatous cells with less intracellular space which occupy the central portion of the stem constitute the pith.

Identify the option with incorrect statements.

(a) I, II and III ☐ (b) I, II and IV ☐

(c) I and IV ☐ (d) I, III and IV ☐

73. Complete the following analogy.

Monocot stem hypodermis : Dicot stem hypodermis : : ________ : Collenchymatous.

74. Vascular bundles in monocot stem are conjoint and ________.

75. Consider the following figure of TS of stem and answer the questions that follows.

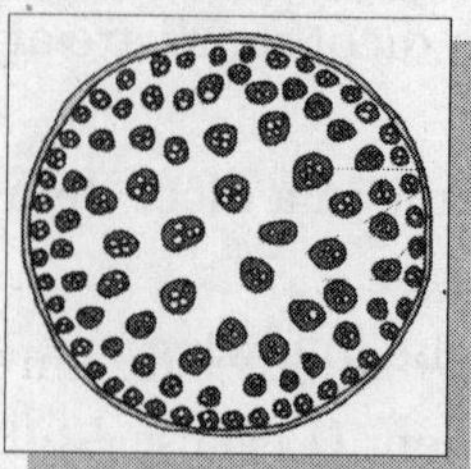

This figure represents ______________ (monocot/dicot) stem.

76. Consider the following images and choose the correct option from the following.

(a) A can show secondary growth ☐ (b) A does not contain cambium ☐

(c) B can show secondary growth ☐ (d) B contains cambium ☐

TOPIC 4

Dorsiventral (Dicotyledonous) **and Isobilateral** (Monocotyledonous) **Leaf**

NCERT Pg. 76-77

77. Dicotyledonous leaf is also known as isobilateral leaf.

True ☐ False ☐

78. Complete the following analogy of leaf surface.

Upper surface : Lower surface : : ______________ : Abaxial.

79. Consider the following diagram of TS of a dicot leaf and identify its parts *A*, *B* and *C*.

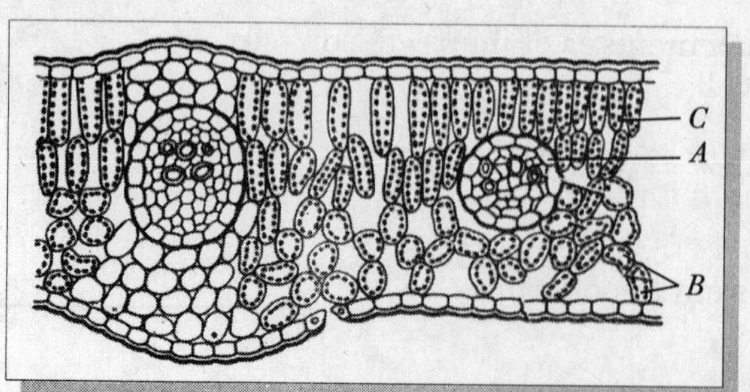

80. The abaxial surface of leaf bears less stomata than the adaxial in dicot.

True ☐ False ☐

81. The tissue between the upper and the lower epidermis in dicot leaves is called as

____

82. Consider the provided image and mark the structure P that surrounds the vascular bundles:

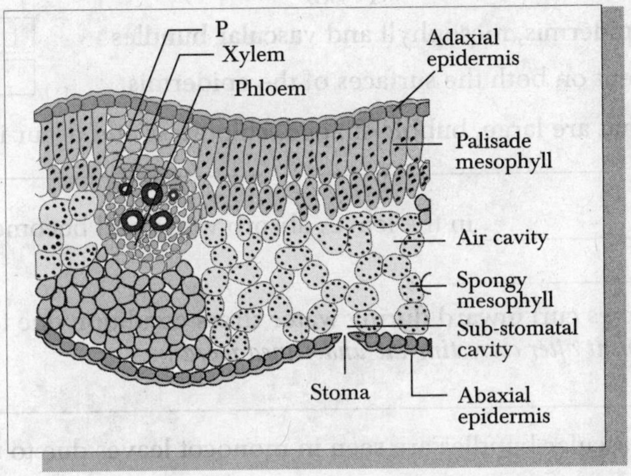

(a) Epidermis ☐ (b) Endodermis ☐

(c) Bundle sheath ☐ (d) Cuticle ☐

83. Identify the type of parenchyma in the following sentences.

(i) Parenchyma placed on adaxial surface.______________________

(ii) Oval or round and loosely arranged parenchyma. ________________

84. Vascular bundles in leaves found at _______________ and _______________.

85. Consider the following statements:

Statements I The epidermis which covers both the upper surface (adaxial epidermis) and lower surface (abaxial epidermis) of the dicot leaf has a conspicuous cuticle.

Statements II The vascular bundles are surrounded by a layer of thick walled bundle sheath cells in a monocot leaf.

Choose the correct option from the following:

(a) Statement I is true, but statement II is false ☐

(b) Statement I is false, but statement II is true ☐

86. The vascular bundles are surrounded by a layer of thick-walled ________________________ cells.

87. Monocot leaf is also known as <u>bulliform leaf</u>.
(*Rewrite the statement after correcting the underlined word.*)

____

88. The epidermis on both side contains ________________ and the mesophyll is usually not differentiated into ________________ and ________________ parenchyma in isobilateral leaf.

89. Which of the following is common to both dicot and monocot leaves?

(a) Presence of large empty and colorless bulliform cells ☐

(b) Air cavities present between the spongy mesophyll cells ☐

(c) Presence of epidermis, mesophyll and vascular bundles ☐

(d) Stomata present on both the surfaces of the epidermis ☐

90. Name the cells that are large, bubble-shaped, colourless and occur in groups on the upper surface in grasses. ________________

91. The ________________ in the leaves absorb water and become turgid and the leaf surface is ________________.

92. The monocot leaves curl inward during water stress condition due to <u>secondary xylem.</u>
(*Rewrite the statement after correcting the underlined words.*)

____

93. Similar sizes of vascular bundles are seen in monocot leaves due to the

________________.

94. Consider the following figure of TS of monocot leaf, identify its parts *A*, *B* and *C*.

A. ________________

B. ________________

C. ________________

95. Given below are few characteristic features related to leaf.

Dorsoventral orientation, dumb-bell shaped guard cells, sufficient intercellular space, equal number of stomata on both surfaces.

How many of these features represent monocot leaves?

(a) 3 ☐ (b) 0 ☐ (c) 4 ☐ (d) 2 ☐

COMPETITION CONNECT

Topic 1. Introduction and Meristematic Tissues [NCERT (Old) Pg. 84-85]

1. Study of internal structure of plant is called ______________________________

2. ______________________ deals with the ontogeny, structure and distribution of various types of tissues in roots, stems, leaves, flowers and fruits.

3. On the basis of anatomy, monocots and dicots are different.

True ☐ False ☐

4. Can you explain plant adaptations to diverse environment by studying the plant anatomy? (Yes/No). ______________________________

5. Name the two major groups of plant tissue. ______________________________

6. In plants, some regions show active cell division, these regions are called __________.

7. Mark the given features as present or absent considering the features of meristematic tissue.

(i) Undifferentiated cells __________ (ii) Intercellular spaces __________

(iii) Thick cell wall __________

8. Name the meristem which is found on the tips of roots and shoots.

____

9. In the figure of shoot apex meristem, name the structures *A*, *B*, *C* and *D*.

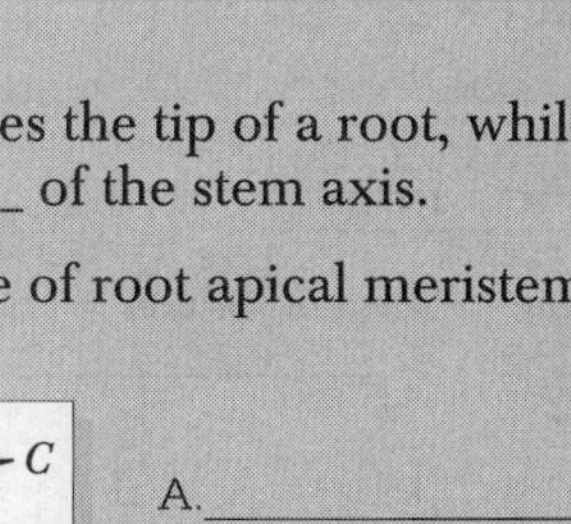

____

10. Root apical meristem occupies the tip of a root, while the shoot apical meristem occupies the ______________________ of the stem axis.

11. Consider the following figure of root apical meristem, identify its parts *A* – *E*.

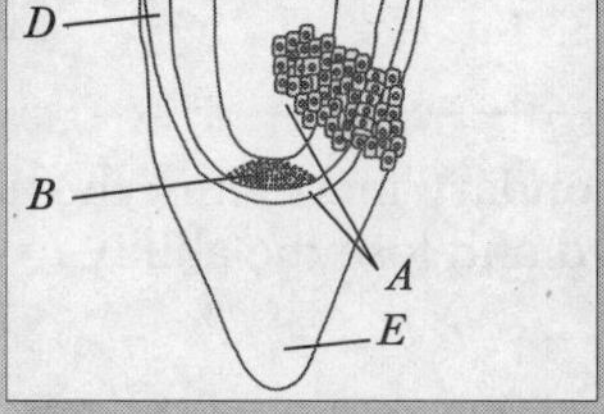

A. ______________________________

B. ______________________________

C. ______________________________

D. ______________________________

E. ______________________________

12. Bud that develops in the axil of a leaf of a plant is known as ____________________.
These buds give rise to ____________________.

13. Name the meristems which are present between mature tissue, that help in longitudinal growth of plants. ____________________

14. Intercalary meristem occurs at the base of the ____________________ and ____________________.

15. Bamboo can grow very fast upto approximately 60 cm/day. (*Give reason*)

____

16. If we pluck the upper part of grasses, which meristem helps the grasses to rejuvenate their parts. ____________________

17. ____________________ and ____________________ furnish the development of primary plant body.

18. Name the meristem which is known as cylindrical meristem, increase thickness of plants and their cells divide periclinally. ____________________

19. Name the meristem which is also known as secondary meristem. ____________________

20. You are given a slide of woody axis, in which parts can you see lateral meristems?

____

21. Consider the following statements.

Statement I Secondary meristem appears in a plant much later than primary meristem.

Statement II Fascicular vascular cambium is a type of lateral meristem found in plants.

Choose the correct option from the following.

(a) Statement I is true, but statement II is false ☐

(b) Both statements I and II are true ☐

22. Length of petiole increases due to the division of intercalary meristem.

True ☐ False ☐

23. Complete the following flowchart with suitable words.

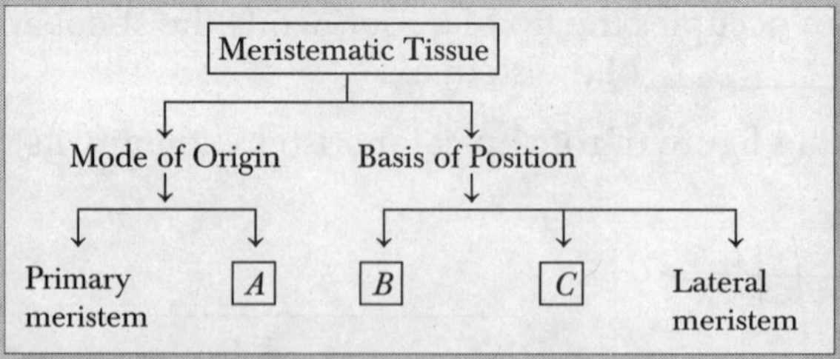

Meristematic Tissue
- Mode of Origin
  - Primary meristem
  - A
- Basis of Position
  - B
  - C
  - Lateral meristem

A. ____________________ B. ____________________ C. ____________________

24. Following divisions of cells in both primary and secondary meristems, the newly formed cells become structurally and functionally specialised and lose the ability to divide. Such cells are termed as ____________________.

25. During the formation of the primary plant body, specified region of the apical meristem produces ____________________, ____________________ and ____________________ tissues.

Topic 2. Permanent Tissues [NCERT (Old) Pg. 86-88]

26. The cells of permanent tissue have definite shape, size and function and are actively dividing.

True ☐ False ☐

27. Name the type of permanent tissue on the basis of sentences given below.

(i) Permanent tissues having all cells similar in structure and function. ______________

(ii) Permanent tissues having many different types of cells. ______________

28. From the given box, identify how many of these are related to simple tissues?

Sclerenchyma, Parenchyma, Xylem, Phloem, Collenchyma

____

29. You are given a simple tissue slide in which cells are isodiametric, have thin cell wall and small intercellular spaces. Name the tissue on the basis of above illustration.

____

30. Parenchymatous cell walls are ____________ and made up of ____________.

31. Parenchyma played various roles in plants, e.g. ______________________, storage, ______________________, etc.

32. Consider the following statements.

Statement I Parenchyma cells are only specialised for storage and secretion.

Statement II Parenchyma cells have lost their division capacity during differentiation.

Choose the correct option from the following.

(a) Statement I is true, but statement II is false ☐

(b) Statement I is false, but statement II is true ☐

33. Parenchymatous cells are ______________________ (living/dead).

34. In the given figure identify '*X*'.

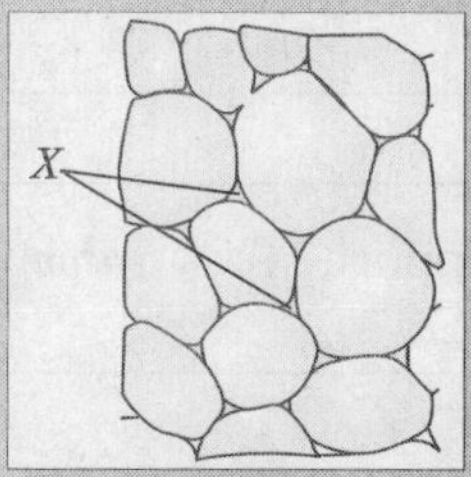

X. ______________________________

35. In dicotyledonous plants, ______________________ (sclerenchyma/collenchyma) is present below the epidermis.

36. Consider the following diagram. Which of the following is not a deposition found in these type of cells?

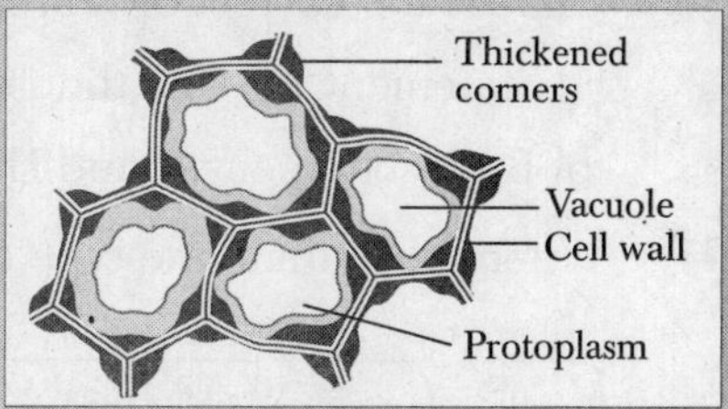

(a) Hemicellulose ☐ (b) Cellulose ☐

(c) Suberin ☐ (d) Pectin ☐

37. Name the tissue which provides mechanical support to the plant and are oval, spherical and polygonal in shape.

____

38. How many of these characters are not related to sclerenchyma?

Lignified cell walls, Oval cells, Dead cells, Having protoplasts, Containing chloroplast

____

39. Name the type of sclerenchyma which are thick walled, elongated and pointed cells, generally occurring in groups in various parts of plants. ______________

40. Sclereids are found in the mesocarp of coconut.
(*Rewrite the statement after correcting the underlined word.*)

____

41. The ______________ (fibres/sclereids) have reduced lumen and thick cell wall and cells are oval, spherical and cylindrical in shape.

42. The pulp of guava has gritty texture. (*Give reason*)

____

43. Consider the given figure of sclereid, answer the questions that follows.

(i) Identify *A* and *B*.

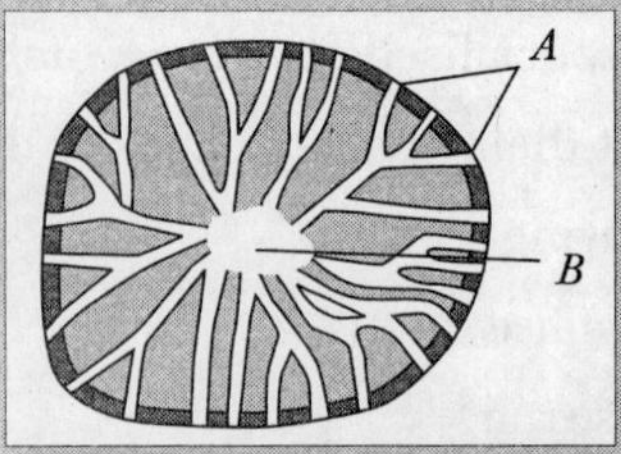

A. ______________

B. ______________

(ii) These are found in leaves of ______________ and seed coats of ______________ .

44. Some biological terms are given below, write a single collective term for each group.

(i) Chlorenchyma, Aerenchyma ______________

(ii) Fibres, Sclereids ______________

45. The sclerenchyma tissue provides mechanical support. (*Give reason*)

____

46. Consider the following statements.

Statement I Sclerenchyma provides mechanical strength to petiole of leaves.

Statement II Sclereids are dead cells with a wide lumen at the centre.

Choose the correct option from the following.

(a) Statement I is true, but statement II is false ☐

(b) Both statements I and II are false ☐

47. When more than one type of cells work together and form a unit it is known as

______________________________ .

48. A leaf is not able to receive water due to injury. Which organ is injured? ______________

49. Xylem is a conducting tissue in plants, it also provides ____________

50. Choose odd one out from the following terms.

Tracheids, Vessels, Xylem fibres, Xylem parenchyma, Sieve tube

____

51. ____________ (Companion cells/Tracheids) are dead with lignified cell wall and are elongated with tapering ends.

52. Tracheids are the most advance type of conductive element in xylem.

True ☐ False ☐

53. Which of the following is a major constituent of tracheid walls?

(a) Cutin ☐ (b) Lignin ☐

(c) Pectin ☐ (d) Suberin ☐

54. Name the xylem element which is not present in gymnosperms.____________

55. Which of the following figures represent tracheid and vessel?

A *B*

A. ____________

B. ____________

56. Vessels are long cylindrical xylem elements, their walls are ____________ and ____________ of protoplasm.

57. The side wall of the vessel is ____________

58. Consider the following statements.

Statement I Vessels form an interconnected system through perforations in their common wall.

Statement II Xylem vessels are cylindrical cells with lignified cell walls and devoid of protoplasm.

Choose the correct option from the following.

(a) Statement I is true, but statement II is false ☐

(b) Both statements I and II are true ☐

59. Name the xylem element in which central lumen is void____________

60. The only living element of xylem is ____________

61. Vessels of xylem are mainly involved in the storage of starch, fat and water conduction. (*Rewrite the statement after correcting the underlined word.*)

____

62. Which of the xylem element is responsible for radial conduction of water?

____

63. Identify the type of xylem on the basis of arrangement of primary xylem.

(i) Primary xylem formed first ______________

(ii) Primary xylem formed later ______________

64. In endarch condition of primary xylem, metaxylem is found at ______________ and protoxylem at ______________.

65. Complete the following analogy.

______________ : Root : : Endarch : Exarch

66. In exarch condition, protoxylem lies towards the centre whereas metaxylem lies towards the periphery.

True ☐ False ☐

67. Write four components of phloem in angiosperm.

____

68. ______________ cells in gymnosperms are analogous to the companion cells of angiosperm.

69. Consider the following figure, identify parts *A*, *B* and *C*.

A ______________

B ______________

C ______________

A. ______________

B. ______________

C. ______________

70. Gymnospermic cells lack <u>phloem fibres</u>.
(*Rewrite the statement after correcting the underlined word.*)

____

71. The mature sieve element is unique in having ______________ cytoplasm, a large vacuole, but lacks a ______________.

72. A mature sieve element is ______________ (living/dead).

73. The nucleus of companion cells controls the functions of ______________

74. Name the phloem element which is conjoint to sieve tube elements ______________

75. Which of the following is not true about companion cells?

(a) They are parenchymatous in nature ☐

(b) They are present in all vascular plants. ☐

(c) They do not lack nucleus at maturity ☐

(d) They maintain pressure gradient in sieve tubes. ☐

76. Consider the following statements.

I. Phloem parenchyma is made up of elongated, tapering cylindrical cells which have dense cytoplasm but lack nucleus.
II. Phloem parenchyma is absent in most of the dicotyledons.
III. Xylem parenchyma stores latex, resin and mucilage.
IV. Bast fibres are made up of sclerenchymatous cells and are absent in primary phloem.
V. End walls of sieve tube are perforated in sieve-like manner to form the sieve plates.

Choose the option with incorrect set of statements:

(a) I, IV and V ☐ (b) II, III and IV ☐
(c) I, II and III ☐ (d) II, IV and V ☐

77. How many of these are parenchymatous in nature?

Companion cells, Phloem parenchyma, Phloem fibres

____

78. Match the following columns.

	Column I (Types of phloem element)		Column II (Functions)
A.	Companion cells	1.	Provide strength
B.	Phloem parenchyma	2.	Maintain pressure gradient
C.	Phloem fibres	3.	Reserve food material

A. ______________ B. ______________ C. ______________

79. Name the element which is present in secondary phloem, but absent in primary phloem ______________

80. The cell wall of phloem fibres is ______________, these fibres lose their ______________ and become ______________.

81. The hemp's phloem fibres are ______________ (lignified/silicate), whereas fibres of flax are made up of ______________ (calcium/cellulose).

82. Protophloem is first formed primary phloem, it has narrow ______________

83. A phloem which has bigger sieve tubes. ______________

Topic 3. Secondary Growth [NCERT (Old) Pg. 94-98]

84. Most dicotyledonous plants increase in girth due to primary growth.
(*Rewrite the statement after correcting the underlined word.*)

____

85. In young stem, vascular cambium is present in ______________, later it forms a ______________.

86. Which of the following tissue is not responsible for the increase in the diameter of stems and roots in woody plants?

(a) Apical meristem ☐ (b) Cork cambium ☐
(c) Vascular cambium ☐ (d) Interfascicular cambium ☐

87. Name the cambium which is present between primary xylem and primary phloem.

____

88. Interfascicular cambium is formed by the cells of xylem and phloem.

True ☐ False ☐

89. Consider the following statements.

Statement I The cambial ring becomes active and begins to cut off new cells only towards the inner side.

Statement II The cells cut off towards pith, mature into secondary phloem.

Choose the correct option from the following.

(a) Statement I is true, but statement II is false ☐

(b) Both statements I and II are false ☐

90. Identify parts *A*, *B*, *C* and *D* from the following figure.

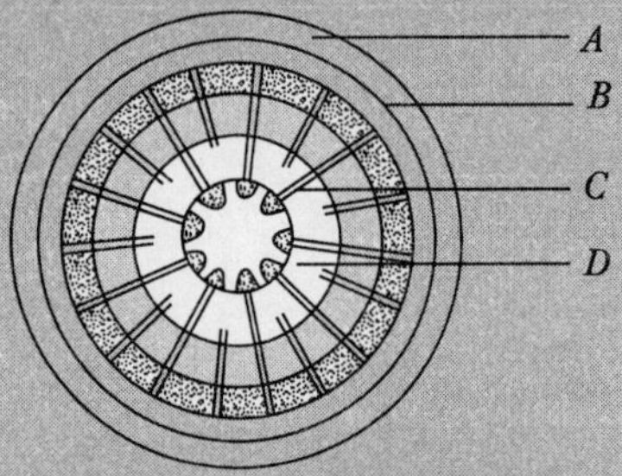

A. ______________________

B. ______________________

C. ______________________

D. ______________________

91. Due to less activity of cambium in winter, it produces fewer xylary elements having broad vessels.

True ☐ False ☐

92. During the spring season, the activity of cambium increases hence it produces large number of xylary elements. The wood formed during this season is called ______________ or ______________.

93. Name the wood in which the greater part of secondary xylem is dark brown due to the deposition of tannins, resins, etc., and it is hard and durable.

____

94. Heart wood is involved in the conduction of water and minerals.
(*Rewrite the statement after correcting the underlined word.*)

____

95. Out of the following options, which one correctly describes the characteristics of spring wood and autumn wood?

(a) Spring wood - dark colour, high density
Autumn wood - light colour, low density ☐

(b) Spring wood - light colour, wide vessels
Autumn wood - dark colour, narrow vessels ☐

(c) Spring wood - light colour, high density
Autumn wood - dark colour, low density ☐

(d) Spring wood - dark colour, narrow vessels
Autumn wood - light colour, wide vessels ☐

96. Match the following columns.

Column I		Column II	
A.	Secondary xylem	1.	Narrow vessels
B.	Secondary phloem	2.	Highly lignified walls
C.	Spring wood	3.	Lighter in colour
D.	Autumn wood	4.	Cells cut off towards pith
E.	Heart wood	5.	Wider vessels
F.	Sap wood	6.	Cells cut off towards periphery

A. ______ B. ______ C.______ D.______ E.______ F.______

97. Find out the correct statement w.r.t. cork cambium?

(a) It is the primary meristem responsible for root growth ☐

(b) It develops from the vascular tissue and produces secondary xylem ☐

(c) It arises in the outer cortex of woody plants and forms cork for protection ☐

(d) It is another term for the apical meristem in stems ☐

98. ______________ is made up of narrow, thin-walled and ______________ cells.

99. Phellogen cuts off cells on both sides, i.e. outer cell is known as phelloderm and inner cell is known as phellem.

True ☐ False ☐

100. Give a collective term for the following words. *Phellogen, Phellem, Phelloderm*

____

101. ______________ is a non-technical term that refers to all tissues exterior to the vascular cambium.

102. Soft bark is formed at the end of the season.

(*Rewrite the statement after correcting the underlined word.*)

____

103. Name the structure in which parenchymatous cells rupture the epidermis to form the lens-shaped opening. ______________

104. Consider the following figure of lenticel, identify parts *A* and *B*.

A

B

A. ______________________________

B. ______________________________

105. Hydathodes permit the exchange of gases between the outer atmosphere and internal tissue system of the stem.

(*Rewrite the statement after correcting the underlined word.*)

____

106. Consider the following figure of a typical dicot root. Identify parts *A*, *B*, *C* and *D*.

A ____________________

B. ____________________

C. ____________________

D. ____________________

Assertion-Reason Questions

The following questions consist of two statements- Assertion (A) and Reason (R). Answer these questions by selecting the appropriate option given below.

(a) Both A and R are true and R is the correct explanation of A

(b) Both A and R are true, but R is not the correct explanation of A

(c) A is true, but R is false

(d) A is false, but R is true

1. Assertion (A) Parts of grasses grazed by herbivorous animals are quickly regenerated.

Reason (R) Intercalary meristem occurs between mature tissues and in the internodal regions.

(a) ☐ (b) ☐ (c) ☐ (d) ☐

2. Assertion (A) Parenchyma cells have a thin wall made up of cellulose.

Reason (R) The thin cells of parenchyma are loosely packed, with intercellular spaces.

(a) ☐ (b) ☐ (c) ☐ (d) ☐

3. Assertion (A) The husk of coconut and seed coats of legumes are generally hard.

Reason (R) Sclerenchyma is a complex tissue that provides mechanical strength.

(a) ☐ (b) ☐ (c) ☐ (d) ☐

4. Assertion (A) In stems protoxylem lies towards the periphery while metaxylem lies towards the centre.

Reason (R) The type of primary xylem present in stems is endarch, while those present in roots is exarch.

(a) ☐ (b) ☐ (c) ☐ (d) ☐

5. Assertion (A) The stomatal pore is lined by guard cells with outer thick walls and inner thin walls.

Reason (R) The stomatal apparatus consists of the stomatal pore, guard cells and subsidiary cells.

(a) ☐ (b) ☐ (c) ☐ (d) ☐

6. **Assertion** (A) Monocot plants lack the ability to form secondary xylem and phloem tissues.

Reason (R) Vascular bundles having presence of cambium between xylem and phloem are of open type.

(a) ☐ (b) ☐ (c) ☐ (d) ☐

7. **Assertion** (A) In dicot roots, the inner layer of cortex forms compactly arranged endodermis.

Reason (R) The endodermal cells have a deposition of water permeable waxy material called suberin.

(a) ☐ (b) ☐ (c) ☐ (d) ☐

8. **Assertion** (A) The innermost layer of the cortex in dicot stems is the endodermis, also called the starch sheath.

Reason (R) The endodermal cells which make up the innermost layer of cortex store starch grains.

(a) ☐ (b) ☐ (c) ☐ (d) ☐

9. **Assertion** (A) The abaxial surface of a dorsiventral leaf has more number of stomata.

Reason (R) Presence of more number in the lower side prevents excess loss of water.

(a) ☐ (b) ☐ (c) ☐ (d) ☐

10. **Assertion** (A) During secondary growth, more secondary xylem is produced compared to secondary phloem.

Reason (R) The vascular cambium is generally more active on its inner side.

(a) ☐ (b) ☐ (c) ☐ (d) ☐

Case Based Questions

1. The figure given below shows a transverse section of a stem. Study the figure and answer the following questions.

(i) Which type of tissues do not make up the structure *A* ?

(a) Collenchyma ☐ (b) Parenchyma ☐

(c) Sclerenchyma ☐ (d) Complex permanent ☐

(ii) Which of the following is correct about structure *B* ?

(a) Conjoint Open ☐ (b) Radial Open ☐
(c) Radial closed ☐ (d) Conjoint closed ☐

(iii) The structure that surrounds structure *B* is made up of

(a) Parenchyma ☐ (b) Collenchyma ☐
(c) Sclerenchyma ☐ (d) Chlorenchyma ☐

2. Scientists while performing research on annual rings, found different growth patterns in trees *A* and *B* growing in different regions.

Based on the given information answer the following questions by choosing the right answer from options below.

(i) Tree *A* showed a concentric pattern of alternate light and dark bands, whereas nothing of such type was visible in tree *B*. What conclusion one can draw from this?

(a) Tree *A* is a temperate dweller ☐
(b) Tree *B* is a temperate dweller ☐
(c) Tree *A* hails from a tropical region ☐
(d) Tree *B* is oak and hails from tropical area ☐

(ii) The most accurate point of difference between trees *A* and *B* consists of all except

(a) active cambium during spring ☐
(b) more xylary elements with narrow vessels ☐
(c) large number of xylary elements ☐
(d) late wood with few xylary elements ☐

(iii) Identify the incorrect statements w.r.t. annual rings.

(a) Number of annual rings gives the age of trees ☐
(b) Dicots growing in dry regions show growth of spring and early wood ☐
(c) Study of the age of tree is dendrochronology ☐
(d) Activity of vascular cambium, responsible for annual rings, it affected by environmental factors ☐

COMPETITION EDGE UP

1. Given below are two statements.

Statement I Parenchyma is living, but collenchyma is dead tissue.

Statement II Gymnosperms lack xylem vessels, but presence of xylem vessels is the characteristic of angiosperms.

In the light of the above statements, choose the correct answer from the options given below.

[NCERT (Old) Pg. 86, 87, NEET 2024]

(a) Both Statement I and Statement II are true ☐

(b) Both Statement I and Statement II are false ☐

(c) Statement I is true, but Statement II is false ☐

(d) Statement I is false, but Statement II is true ☐

2. In the given figure, which component has thin outer walls and highly thickened inner walls? **[NCERT Pg. 72, NEET 2024]**

(a) C ☐ (b) D ☐ (c) A ☐ (d) B ☐

3. Bulliform cells are responsible for **[NCERT Pg. 77, NEET 2024]**

(a) inward curling of leaves in monocots. ☐

(b) protecting the plant from salt stress. ☐

(c) increased photosynthesis in monocots. ☐

(d) providing large spaces for storage of sugars. ☐

4. Given below are two statements.

Statement I Endarch and exarch are the terms often used for describing the position of secondary xylem in the plant body.

Statement II Exarch condition is the most common feature of the root system.

In the light of the above statements, choose the most appropriate answer from the options given below

[NCERT (Old) Pg. 87, NEET 2023]

(a) Both statement I and statement II are incorrect. ☐

(b) Statement I is correct, but statement II is incorrect. ☐

(c) Statement I is incorrect, but statement II is correct. ☐

(d) Both statement I and statement II are correct. ☐

5. Identify the correct statements.

[NCERT (Old) Pg. 96, 97, NEET 2023]

A. Lenticels are the lens-shaped openings permitting the exchange of gases.

B. Bark formed early in the season is called hard bark.

C. Bark is a technical term that refers to all tissues exterior to vascular cambium.

D. Bark refers to periderm and secondary phloem.

E. Phellogen is single-layered in thickness.

Choose the correct answer from the options given below.

(a) A and D only ☐

(b) A, B and D only ☐

(c) B and C only ☐

(d) B, C and E only ☐

6. Read the following statements about the vascular bundles.

I. In roots, xylem and phloem in a vascular bundle are arranged in an alternate manner along the different radii.

II. Conjoint closed vascular bundles do not possess cambium.

III. In open vascular bundles, cambium is present in between xylem and phloem.

IV. The vascular bundles of dicotyledonous stem possess endarch protoxylem.

V. In monocotyledonous root, usually there are more than six xylem bundles present.

Choose the correct answer from the options given below

[NCERT Pg. 73, 74, 76, NEET 2022]

(a) II, III, IV and V ☐

(b) I, II, III and IV ☐

(c) I, III, IV and V ☐

(d) I, II, III IV and V ☐

7. *In old trees, the greater part of secondary xylem is dark brown and resistant to insect attack due to*

   I. secretion of secondary metabolites and their deposition in the lumen of vessels.

   II. deposition of organic compounds like tannins and resins in the central layers of stem.

   III. deposition of suberin and aromatic substances in the outer layer of stem.

   IV. deposition of tannins, gum, resin and aromatic substances in the peripheral layers of stem.

   V. presence of parenchyma cells, functionally active xylem elements and essential oils.

   Choose the correct answer from the options given below.

   [NCERT (Old) Pg. 96, NEET 2022]

   (a) III and IV ☐ (b) IV and V ☐
   (c) II and IV ☐ (d) I and II ☐

8. Match the List I with List II.

   [NCERT (Old) Pg. 84, 86, 87, NEET 2021]

	List I		List II
A.	Cells with active cell division capacity	1.	Vascular tissues
B.	Tissue having all cells similar in structure and function	2.	Meristematic tissue
C.	Tissue having different types of cells	3.	Sclereids
D.	Dead cells with highly thickened walls and narrow lumen	4.	Simple tissue

   Select the correct answer from the options given below.

	A	B	C	D	
(a)	2	4	1	3	☐
(b)	4	3	2	1	☐
(c)	1	2	3	4	☐
(d)	3	2	4	1	☐

9. The transverse section of a plant shows following anatomical features.

   [NCERT Pg. 76, NEET (Sep.) 2020]

   I. Large number of scattered vascular bundles surrounded by bundle sheath.

   II. Large conspicuous parenchymatous ground tissue.

   III. Vascular bundles conjoint and closed.

   IV. Phloem parenchyma absent.

   Identify the category of plant and its part.

   (a) Monocotyledenous root ☐
   (b) Dicotyledenous stem ☐
   (c) Dicotyledenous root ☐
   (d) Monocotyledenous stem ☐

10. Identify the incorrect statement.

   [NCERT (Old) Pg. 96, NEET 2020]

   (a) Sapwood is involved in conduction of water and minerals from root of leaf ☐
   (b) Sapwood is the intermost secondary xylem and is lighter in colour ☐
   (c) due to deposition of tannins, resins, oil, etc. heart wood is dark in colour ☐
   (d) Heart wood does not conduct water, but gives mechanical support ☐

Chapter 07

Structural Organisation in Animals

Scan and take Chapter Test

TOPIC 1

Organ and Organ System, Frog

NCERT Pg. 80-84

1. A human heart consists of __________, __________, _______ and ______________ tissues.

2. Consider the following statements.

   Statement I Cells tissues, organs and organ systems exhibit division of labour are contribute to survival of body.

   Statement II Basic tissues forming an organisation, hamper the coordinated activites of millions of cells in an organism.

   Choose the correct option from the following.

   (a) Statement I is true, but statement II is false ☐

   (b) Statement I is false, but statement II is true ☐

3. The frogs have the ability to change their colour to hide themselves from their enemies. This protective colouration is called ______________________ .

4. What is the probable reason for aestivation observed in animals like frogs?

   (a) To hide from their enemies ☐

   (b) To avoid extreme cold ☐

   (c) To protect against extreme heat ☐

   (d) To blend with the surrounding ☐

5. Choose the odd one out related to *Rana tigrina* habits.

   Camouflage, Aestivation, Hibernation, Endothermy

   ____

6. The skin of frog is slippery and smooth due to the presence of gelatin.

   True ☐ False ☐

*Concepts of all questions bearing * are important for NEET & CUET*

7. Body of a frog is divisible into ________ and ________ .

8. Refer to the given figure and answer the questions that follow.

(i) Name the membrane that is found at site *A* and help to protect eyes under water.

____

(ii) Number of digits at site *B* is ________

(iii) Number of digits at site *C* is ________

(iv) Functions of *B* and *C* is ________

9. Match Column I with Column II based on the morphological features of a frog.

Column I	Column II
A. Nictitating membrane	1. Sexual dimorphism
B. Copulatory pads	2. Receives sound
C. Slippery skin	3. Protects eyes
D. Tympanum	4. Mucus

	A	B	C	D			A	B	C	D
(a)	3	1	4	2	☐	(b)	3	2	4	1	☐
(c)	3	2	1	4	☐	(d)	3	1	2	4	☐

10. Male frog can be distinguished from female frog by the presence of

(i) hindlimb that ends in five digits. ☐

(ii) vocal sacs and copulatory pad on first digit of forelimb. ☐

(Tick ✓ the most appropriate option)

11. The alimentary canal of frog is short because frogs are ________

12. State whether the statements are True or False.

(i) In frog, excess of the bile juice secreted by the liver is stored in intestine.

True ☐ False ☐

(ii) In frog, for the digestion of food, walls of the stomach secrete pepsin and rennin.

True ☐ False ☐

(iii) In frogs, digested food is absorbed by villi and microvilli in intestine.

True ☐ False ☐

13. Which of the following correctly represents the organ and its secretion?

(a) Gall bladder – bile ; Stomach – HCl ☐

(b) Liver – bile ; Stomach – HCl ☐

(c) Pancreas – bile ; Stomach – HCl ☐

(d) Intestine – bile ; Stomach – HCl ☐

14. Given below is the diagram of internal organs of frog. Identify the missing parts labelled as *A* to *F*.

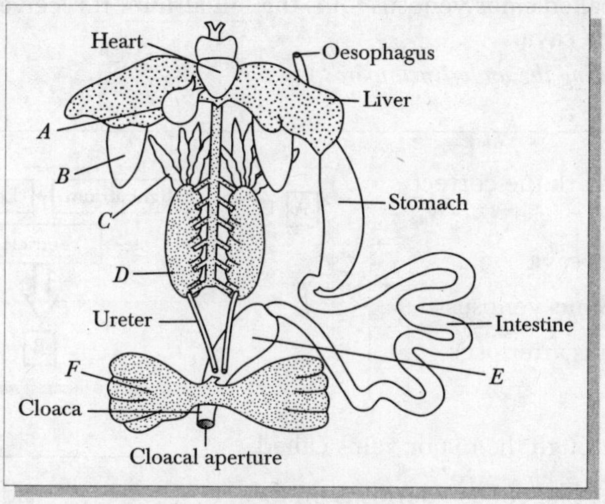

Heart, Oesophagus, Liver, *A*, *B*, *C*, Stomach, *D*, Ureter, Intestine, *F*, *E*, Cloaca, Cloacal aperture

A. ____________________

B. ____________________

C. ____________________

D. ____________________

E. ____________________

F. ____________________

15. Consider the following statements.

Statement I The pancreas in frogs is a rudimentary structure since it is not involved in digestion.

Statement II The villi and microvilli present in the intestinal wall allows absorption of digested food.

Choose the correct option from the following.

(a) Statement I is true, but statement II is false ☐

(b) Statement I is false, but statement II is true ☐

16. State, whether the statements are True or False.

(i) Frogs respire on land and in the water by two different methods. In water, lungs act as aquatic respiratory organ (cutaneous respiration).

True ☐ False ☐

(ii) In frog, dissolved oxygen in the water is exchanged through the skin by diffusion.

True ☐ False ☐

(iii) On land, the buccal cavity, skin and lungs act as the respiratory organs.

True ☐ False ☐

17. During aestivation and hibernation in frogs, gaseous exchange takes place through ____________________.

18. The blood vascular system of the frog is ____________ (open type/closed type).

19. Three-chambered heart of the frog contains ____________________

20. Identify the incorrect set of statements with respect to frog.

I. Ventral side of the frog is generally olive green with dark irregular spots.
II. Alimentary canal in case of frogs, is short since the length of intestine is reduced.
III. Frogs respire on land and in water in the same way.
IV. Apart from a well-developed closed type blood vascular system, the frog has a lymphatic system as well.

Codes

(a) I and IV ☐ (b) I and II ☐ (c) I and III ☐ (d) II and III ☐

21. In frog, a triangular structure called sinus venosus joins the left atrium. It receives blood through major veins called vena cava.
(*Rewrite the statement after correcting the underlined words.*)

____

***22.** Refer to the given image and mark the correct combination.

(a) A – Sinus venosus, B – Vena cava ☐
(b) A – Conus arteriosus, B – Sinus venosus ☐
(c) A – Sinus venosus, B – Conus arteriosus ☐
(d) A – Aorta, B – Vena cava ☐

23. Right atrium receives blood through the major veins called ______________.

24. In frog, ventricle opens into sac-like conus arteriosus on the ______________ side of heart.

25. In frog, blood from the heart is carried to all parts of body by arteries. The ______________ collect blood from different parts of the body to the heart.

26. In frog, a special venous connection is present between liver and ______________

27. Complete the following analogy given below.
Liver and intestine : Hepatic portal system : : Kidney : ______________

28. Give biological term for the following sentences.
(i) The respiration through lungs in frog. ______________
(ii) The membrane that covers the heart of the frog. ______________

29. Consider the following statements.

Statement I The lymphatic system of frogs consists of lymph, lymph channels and lymph nodes.

Statement II The composition of lymph is similar to that of blood except that it does not contain proteins.

Choose the correct option from the following.

(a) Statement I is true, but statement II is false ☐
(b) Statement I is false, but statement II is true ☐

30. How many of the listed components are found in blood vascular system of frog?

Arteries, Veins, Capillaries, Heart, Blood without RBC and WBC

____

31. Excretory system of the frog consists of ______________

***32.** Choose the right word.

(i) In male frog, ureters act as ______________ (urinogenital ducts/cloaca).

(ii) Structural and functional unit of kidney in the frog ______________ (nephrons/bidder's canal).

(iii) In frogs, cloaca is an opening of ______________ (excretory ducts only/excretory and reproductive ducts)

(iv) The frog is ______________ (ureotelic animal/uricotelic animal).

33. The system for control and coordination in frogs comprises______________

34. The number of pairs of cranial nerves arising from the brain of frog is ______________

35. Fill the blanks for different parts of the brain in frog.

(i) The three major components of the forebrain are ______________

(ii) The midbrain of the frog is characterised by a pair of ______________

(iii) Hindbrain of a frog consists of ______________

36. Consider the following statements.

Statement I The brain in frogs is protected by a bony cranium and forms the central nervous system along with spinal cord.

Statement II The medulla oblongata of the hindbrain passes through the foramen magnum and continues into spinal cord.

Choose the correct option from the following.

(a) Statement I is true, but statement II is false ☐

(b) Both statements I and II are true ☐

37. In frogs, sensory papillae, taste buds and nasal epithelium are ______________, while eyes and internal ears are well-organised structures.

38. Which of the following pairs is not correctly matched?

(a) Hearing – Tympanum with external ears ☐

(b) Touch – Sensory papillae ☐

(c) Balancing – Ears ☐

(d) Vision – Simple eyes ☐

39. Match Column I with Column II.

Column I	Column II
A. Tympanum	1. Smell
B. Sensory papillae	2. Touch
C. Nasal epithelium	3. Taste
D. Taste buds	4. Balance

	A	B	C	D			A	B	C	D	
(a)	4	2	3	1	☐	(b)	4	2	1	3	☐
(c)	2	4	3	1	☐	(d)	2	4	1	3	☐

40. Match Column I with Column II.

Column I	Column II
A. Optic lobes	1. Forebrain
B. Unpaired diencephalon	2. Well organised
C. Eyes and ears	3. Midbrain
D. Nasal epithelium	4. Cellular aggregations around nerve endings.

A. __________ B. __________
C. __________ D. __________

41. The number of vasa efferentia that arises from testes in frog's male reproductive system is __________

42. How many of the listed products in male frogs are passed through cloaca?

Sperms, Urine, Faecal matter, Blood

____

***43.** Fill the correct route for the passage of sperms in male frogs.

Testes → *A* → Kidney → *B* → Urinogenital duct → *C*

A. __________ B. __________ C. __________.

44. Consider the following statements.

Statement I A pair of vasa efferentia arises from the testis in frogs and opens into the Bidder's canal.

Statement II In female frogs a pair of oviduct arising from the ovaries opens into the cloaca separately.

Choose the correct option from the following.

(a) Statement I is true, but statement II is false ☐

(b) Statement I is false, but statement II is true ☐

45. Identify the missing parts labelled as *A*, *B*, *C*, *D* and *E* in the given figure of male reproductive system of frog.

A. __________
B. __________
C. __________
D. __________
E. __________

46. Identify the missing parts labelled as *A* to *E* in the following figure of female reproductive system of frog.

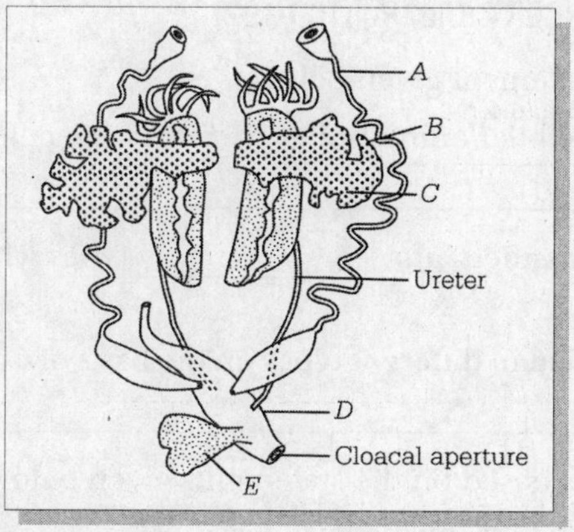

A. ____________

B. ____________

C. ____________

D. ____________

E. ____________

F. ____________

47. In female frogs, ovaries are not connected with kidneys functionally.

True ☐ False ☐

48. A mature female lays how many ova at a time? ____________

49. Which of the following about the female reproductive system of frogs is not correct?

(a) A mature female frog can lay about 2500 to 3000 ova or eggs at a time. ☐

(b) Ovaries are situated near kidneys but do not have any functional connection with it. ☐

(c) A pair of oviduct arising from the ovaries opens into the cloaca separately. ☐

(d) Fertilisation takes place inside the female body in the water. ☐

50. Fill the blanks w.r.t frog.

(i) Fertilisation is ____________ (external/internal).

(ii) Development involves larval stage called ____________

(iii) Tadpole undergoes ____________ to form the adult.

(iv) Edible part of frog body in some countries is ____________

51. Consider the following statements and choose the set of incorrect statements.

I. Lungs in frogs are a pair of elongated, pink coloured sac like structures present in the thorax region.

II. Frog has different types of sense organs like sensory papillae, nasal epithelium, eye and tympanum with internal ears.

III. Cloaca is represented by a moderate sized chamber, used to pass faecal matter, urine and sperms to the exterior.

IV. Hindlimbs end in four digits and are comparatively larger than forelimbs that have five digits.

Codes

(a) I and III ☐ (b) III and IV ☐

(c) II and IV ☐ (d) I and II ☐

COMPETITION CONNECT

Topic 1 : Introduction and Epithelial Tissue [NCERT (Old) Pg. 100-102]

1. Give the scientific term for the statement given below.
A group of similar cells in multicellular animals that perform a specific function.

____

2. In animals, tissues are broadly classified into ____________ types while in plants, tissues are of ____________ types.

3. Animal tissues are broadly classified in different types on the basis of

____

4. Identify the type of animal tissues based on the statements given below.
(i) Cells are compactly packed with little intercellular space.
(ii) It forms covering or lining of external and internal surfaces.
(iii) It helps in protection, secretion, absorption, sensation, etc.

____

5. Fill in the blanks for the types of epithelium.
(i) The ________________ consists of two or more cell layers and has protective function as it does in our skin.
(ii) The ________________ is composed of a single layer of cells and functions as a lining for body cavities, ducts and tubes.

6. On the basis of structural modification of the cells, simple epithelium is further divided into three types *viz* ______________________________

7. Recognise each cell type shown below.

A. ____________
B. ____________
C. ____________
D. ____________

***8.** Match the following columns.

	Column I (Structures)		Column II (Names)		Column III (Locations)
A.	Tall and slender cells	1.	Cuboidal epithelium	K.	Bronchioles
B.	Flattened cells with irregular boundaries	2.	Columnar epithelium	L.	Tubular parts of nephrons
C.	Cilia on their free surface	3.	Squamous epithelium	M.	Lining of intestine
D.	Cube-like cells	4.	Ciliated epithelium	N.	Walls of blood vessels

A. ____________ B. ____________ C. ____________ D. ____________

9. Based on the location given below, write the names of epithelial tissue.

(i) Ducts of glands ________________

(ii) Fallopian tubes ________________

(iii) Air sacs of lungs ________________

(iv) Lining of stomach ________________

10. Based on the function given below, write the names of epithelial tissue.

(i) Helps in forming a diffusion boundary ________________

(ii) Helps in secretion and absorption ________________

(iii) Helps to move particles or mucus in a specific direction over the epithelium

____

11. Fallopian tube and respiratory tract contain which type of epithelium? ________________

12. Some of the columnar or cuboidal cells get specialised for secretion and are called ________________ epithelium. It is of two types, i.e. ________________.

***13.** From the list of characters (i), (ii) and (iii), choose the appropriate characteristics for glands *A* and *B*.

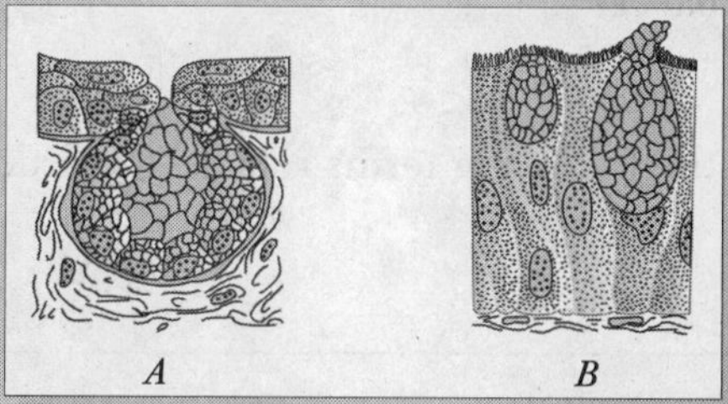

A *B*

(i) **Cellular level** Unicellular/Multicellular

(ii) **Organisation** Isolated cells /Cluster of cells

(iii) **Type and location** Goblet cells of alimentary canal / Cells of salivary gland

A. ________________ *B.* ________________

***14.** Match Column I with Column II

Column I	Column II
A. Cuboidal epithelium	1. Kidney tubules
B. Ciliated epithelium	2. Bronchioles
C. Compound epithelium	3. Salivary gland
D. Glandular epithelium	4. Salivary duct

	A	B	C	D			A	B	C	D
(a)	1	2	4	3		(b)	1	2	3	4
(c)	1	3	2	4		(d)	1	3	4	2

15. On the basis of the mode of pouring of their secretions, glands are divided into two categories, namely ________________

16. Give examples of exocrine glands.

____

17. Ductless glands in human beings secrete ____________________ (mucus/hormones).

18. Complete the following analogy given below.

Exocrine glands : Glands with ducts : : ____________________ : Ductless glands.

19. Read the following properties and find out how many of these are related to the figure given below?

(i) Multilayered epithelium.

(ii) Play major role in secretion and absorption.

(iii) Main function to provide protection against chemical and mechanical stresses.

(iv) They cover the dry surface of skin, moist surface of buccal cavity and pharynx.

____

20. State, whether the following statements are True or False.

(i) All cells in epithelium are held together with little intercellular material.

True ☐ False ☐

(ii) In nearly all animal tissues, specialised junctions provide both structural and functional links between individual cells.

True ☐ False ☐

21. Give common term for the following terms related to tissues.

Tight, Adhering, Gap

____

***22.** Match the following columns.

	Column I (Cell junctions)		Column II (Functions)
A.	Adhering junction	1.	Helps to stop substances from leaking across a tissue
B.	Gap junction	2.	Performs cementing to keep neighbouring cells together
C.	Tight junction	3.	Facilitates the cells to communicate with each other

A. ____________________ B. ____________________ C. ____________________

Topic 2 : Connective Tissues [NCERT (Old) Pg. 102-104]

23. In all connective tissues except ____________________, the cells secrete fibres of structural proteins called collagen or elastin.

24. Identify the tissue '*X*' and write its structures labelled as *A* to *D*.

A, *B*, *C*, *D*, *X*

X. ____________________

A. ____________________

B. ____________________

C. ____________________

D. ____________________

25. For the following statements choose the right option(s) from the bracket.

(i) It provides strength, elasticity and flexibility to the tissue. (Fibres, Blood, Bones)

___

(ii) These cells secrete modified polysaccharides, which accmulate between cells and fibres and act as a matrix or ground substances. (Fibres, Bone, Adipose, Cartilage).

___

26. Which tissue has cells and fibres loosely arranged in a semi-fluid ground substance?

___

***27.** Which connective tissue often serves as a support framework for epithelium, contains fibroblast (cells that produce and secrete fibres), macrophages and mast cells?

___

28. The excess nutrients which are not used immediately are converted into fats and stored in

___

***29.** Identify the tissue '*X*' and write its structures labelled as *A*, *B* and C.

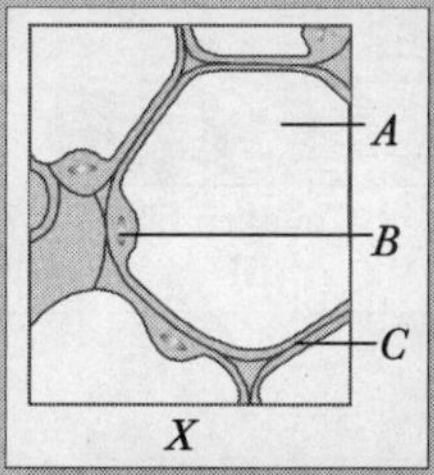

A
B
C
X

X. ___

A. ___

B. ___

C. ___

***30.** Read the statements carefully and name the respective tissue.

(i) Fibres and fibroblasts are compactly packed ___

(ii) The collagen fibres are present in rows between many parallel bundles of fibres

___

(iii) It has fibroblasts and many fibres (mostly collagen) that are oriented differently

___

31. Consider the following statements.

Statement I In tendons collagen fibres are present in rows between many parallel bundles of fibres.

Statement II Skin is a dense regular connective tissue that has fibroblasts and collagen oriented differently.

Choose the correct option from the following.

(a) Statement I is true, but statement II is false ☐

(b) Statement I is false, but statement II is true ☐

***32.** Consider the following image, and mark the option that correctly identifies the cell that secrete fibres.

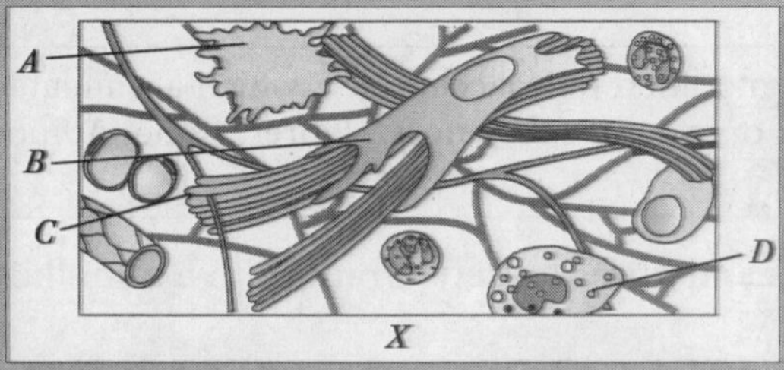

A
B
C
D
X

(a) A ☐ (b) B ☐ (c) C ☐ (d) D ☐

33. Identify the figure *A* and *B*, respectively.

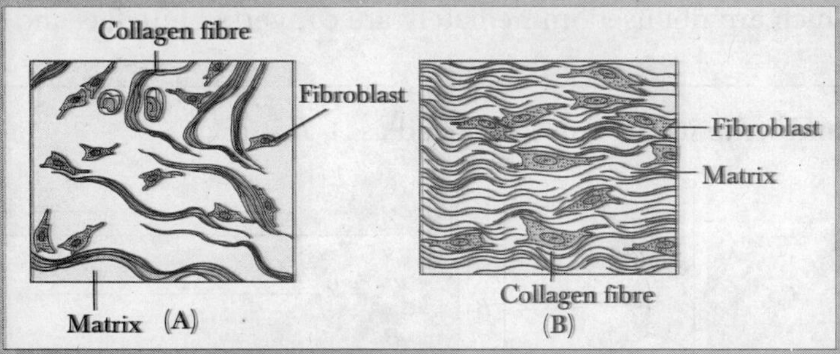

Collagen fibre
Fibroblast
Matrix (A)
Fibroblast
Matrix
Collagen fibre
(B)

A. ______________

B. ______________

***34.** Match the following columns.

Column I		Column II
A. Tendon	1.	Loose connective tissue
B. Cartilage	2.	Dense regular connective tissue
C. Areolar tissue	3.	Dense irregular connective tissue
D. Skin	4.	Specialised connective tissue

A. ______________ B. ______________ C. ______________ D. ______________

35. The intercellular material of <u>bone</u> is solid and pliable and resists compression. Cells of this tissue are enclosed in small cavities within the matrix.
(*Rewrite the statement after correcting the underlined word.*)

____

36. Give three locations where cartilage is present in the body.

____

37. Give the scientific term for the following statement.

A hard and non-pliable ground substance rich in calcium salts and collagen fibres which provides structural framework to the body.______________

38. The bone cells, i.e. ______________ are present in the spaces called ______________ .

39. The site of production of Red Blood Cells (RBCs) in adult humans is

____

40. Name a fluid connective tissue which helps in transport of various substances.

____

41. In the given diagram of TS of cartilage, identify the parts labelled as *A* and *B*.

A. _______________

B. _______________

42. Match the following columns.

	Column I (Connective tissues)		Column II (Functions)
A.	Tendons	1.	Attach one bone to another
B.	Ligaments	2.	Weight bearing function
C.	Bones	3.	Attach skeletal muscle to bones
D.	Blood	4.	Contain formed elements

A. _______ B. _______ C. _______ D. _______

Topic 3. Muscle Tissue [NCERT (Old) Pg. 104-105]

43. Each muscle is made of many long cylindrical fibres arranged in parallel arrays. These fibres are composed of numerous fine fibrils, called _______________.

44. Match the following columns.

	Column I (Figures)		Column II (Names)		Column III (Locations)
A.		1.	Striated muscle	K.	Wall of blood vessels
B.		2.	Smooth muscle	L.	Nodal tissue
C.		3.	Cardiac muscle	M.	Biceps

A. _______ B. _______ C. _______

45. Complete the following table.

Skeletal muscles	Smooth muscles	Cardiac muscles
(A)	Uninucleate	(B)
Striated and cylindrical	(C)	(D)
(E)	(F)	Involuntary
(G)	Slow contraction and do not get fatigued	(H)
(I)	(J)	Present only in the heart

A. ____________ B. ____________

C. ____________ D. ____________

E. ____________ F. ____________

G. ____________ H. ____________

I. ____________ J. ____________

46. Communication junctions or intercalated discs allow the cardiac muscle to contract as a unit.

True ☐ False ☐

Topic 4 : Neural Tissue [NCERT (Old) Pg. 105-106]

47. Which animal tissue exerts the greatest control over the body's responsiveness to changing conditions?

____

48. Name the excitable cells of the body which are known as the unit of neural system.

____

49. Write down the correct labels *A* to *D* for the given neural tissue.

A
B
C
D

A. ____________

B. ____________

C. ____________

D. ____________

50. Which cell of neural system protect and support neurons?

____

51. In human body, neuroglia cells are present in ____________

Topic 5. Cockroach [NCERT (Old) Pg. 111-115]

52. The word anatomy is conventionally used for the study of internal organs in animals.

True ☐ False ☐

53. *Periplaneta* belongs to class ____________ of phylum ____________.

54. The body of cockroach is segmented and divisible into ____________________

55. Exoskeleton of cockroach is formed of ____________________ (keratin/chitin).

56. In each segment of cockroach, the exoskeleton has hardened plates called ____________________.

57. Complete the following analogy related to cockroach.

Dorsal sclerites : Tergites : : Ventral sclerites : ____________________

58. Flexibility of the cockroach body is due to arthrodial membrane or articular membrane.

True ☐ False ☐

59. Write the correct names for the labels *A* to *E* in the figure of cockroach.

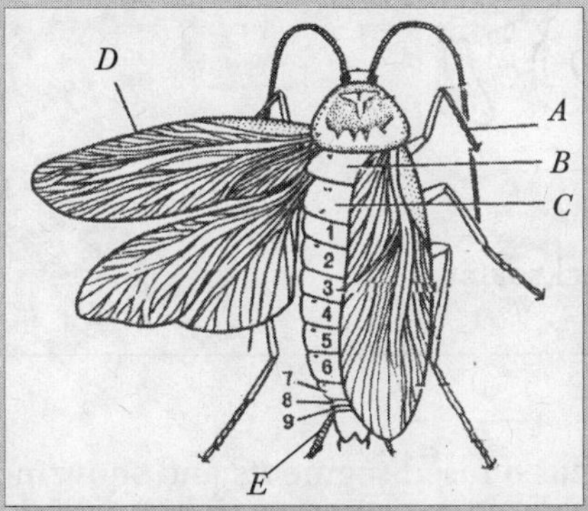

A. ____________________

B. ____________________

C. ____________________

D. ____________________

E. ____________________

60. How many segments of cockroach body are fused to form its head? ____________________

61. Triangular head of cockroach shows great mobility in all directions due to ____________________

62. The mouth parts of cockroach are of ____________________ and ____________________ type.

63. Hypopharynx of cockroach acts as a ____________________.

64. Correctly identify and label the mouth parts of cockroach in the given diagram.

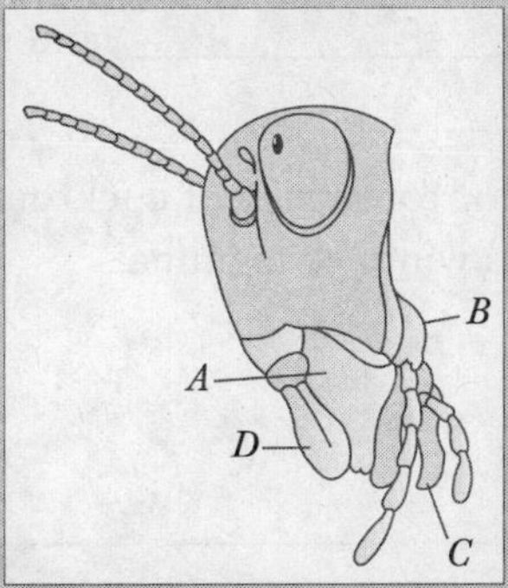

A. ____________________

B. ____________________

C. ____________________

D. ____________________

65. Identify the correct match pair.

(a) Labrum – lower lip ☐ (b) Labium – upper lip ☐

(c) Hypopharynx – tongue ☐ (d) Tegmina – hind wings ☐

66. Identify the parts labelled as *A, B, C, D* and *E* in the given figure related with mouthparts of the cockroach.

A. ______
B. ______
C. ______
D. ______
E. ______

67. The number of thoracic segments in cockroach is ______

68. Consider the following statements.

Statement I The head of a cockroach has 8 fused segments and show mobility in all directions.

Statemnet II A cockroach head is connected with thorax by a short extension of mesothorax.

Choose the correct option from the following.

(a) Statement I is true, but statement II is false ☐

(b) Both statements I and II are false ☐

69. In cockroach,

(i) Pair of walking legs arises from ______ .

(ii) First pair of wings arises from ______ and second pair of wings arises from ______ .

70. How many statements are correct for forewings of cockroach?

(i) They are also called mesothoracic wings or tegmina.
(ii) Opaque, dark and leathery.
(iii) Cover the hindwings when at rest.
(iv) Used in flight.

______

71. The abdomen in male and female consists of ______ segments.

***72.** In female cockroach, shape of the 7th sternum is ______.

73. In female cockroach, the 7th sternum together with the 8th and 9th sterna forms a ______

74. In female cockroach, anterior part of the genital pouch contains ______.

75. In both the sexes of cockroaches, the 10th segment bears a pair of jointed filamentous structure called ______________ .

***76.** Identify the missing parts labelled as *A* to *E* in the given figure of alimentary canal of cockroach.

Pharynx
A
Salivary reservoir
Oesophagus
B
C
Hepatic caeca
Mesenteron or midgut
D
E
Colon
Rectum

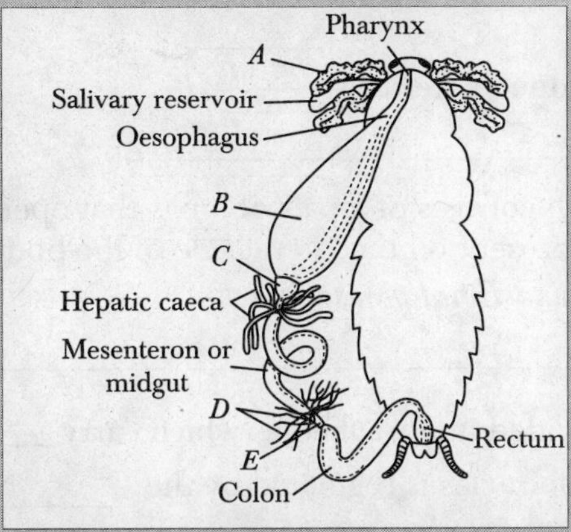

A. ______________
B. ______________
C. ______________
D. ______________
E. ______________

77. Among the following options, which one is used for storing food?

Crop, Gastric caeca, Gizzard, Oesophagus

____

***78.** In the digestive system of cockroach, gastric caecum is present at the junction of <u>midgut and hindgut</u> which secrete digestive juice.
(*Rewrite the statement after correcting the underlined phrase.*)

____

79. How many Malpighian tubules are present in cockroach? ______________

80. Thin Malpighian tubules in cockroach are present at the junction of

____

81. Which part of the cockroach helps in the removal of excretory products from the haemolymph?

____

82. Write the correct sequence of atleast 7 structures in the alimentary canal of cockroach starting from mouth.

____

***83.** Identify the parts labelled as *A*, *B* and *C* in the given figure of open circulatory system of cockroach.

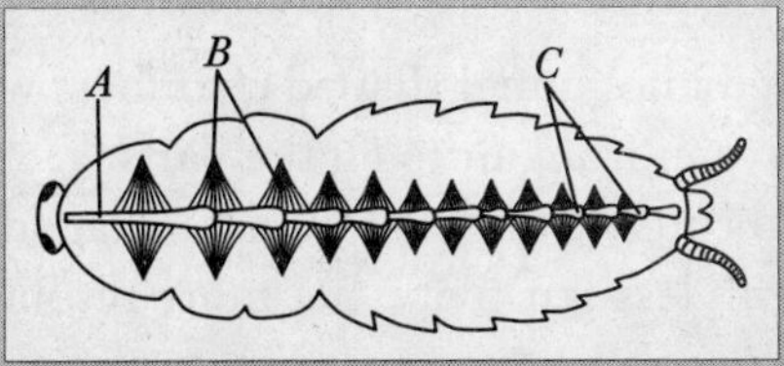

A *B* *C*

A. ______________
B. ______________
C. ______________

84. Blood of a cockroach contains erythrocytes and plasma.

True ☐ False ☐

85. Heart of cockroach consists of elongated muscular tube lying along mid dorsal line and __________________ (caecum/abdomen).

86. Complete the flowchart of blood circulation in cockroach.

Blood from sinus ⟶ *A* ⟶ Pumped anteriorly ⟶ *B*

A. __________________ B. __________________

87. The respiratory system of the cockroach consists of a pair of lungs that open through 10 pairs of small holes called spiracles present on the lateral side of the body. (*Rewrite the statement after correcting the underlined phrase.*)

____

88. Tracheal tubes in cockroach are sub-divided into tracheoles which carry ________ from the air to all the parts. The opening of spiracles is regulated by the ____________.

89. Exchange of gases takes place in cockroaches by the process of ______________.

90. In addition to the Malpighian tubules, excretion of waste products in cockroach occurs by three other structures *viz,* ______________________________

***91.** The nervous system of cockroach consists of a series of fused, segmentally arranged ganglia joined by paired longitudinal connectives on the ventral side.

True ☐ False ☐

***92.** In the head region of the cockroach, brain is represented by ____________________

93. Choose the odd one out related to sense organ pair in cockroach.

Antennae and eyes, Maxillary palp and labial palps, Antennae and anal cerci, Mandible

____

94. The position of compound eyes of cockroaches with respect to head is ____________. Each eye consists of about ____________ ommatidia.

95. In cockroach, with the help of antenna it can receive several images of an object. This kind of vision is known as mosaic vision. (*Rewrite the statement after correcting the underlined words.*)

____

96. Consider the following statements.

I. Heart of cockroach is differentiated into funnel shaped chambers with ostia on either side.
II. In cockroach, tracheoles carry oxygen from air to all the parts.
III. Each compound eye of cockroach consists of about 20000 hexagonal ommatidia.
IV. Cockroach show mosaic vision with less senstivity, but more resolution.

Identify the option with incorrect set of statements.

(a) I and II ☐ (b) I and III ☐ (c) II and III ☐ (d) III and IV ☐

97. The vision of cockroach is

(i) less sensitive with high resolution ☐

(ii) more sensitive with less resolution ☐

98. Refer to the diagram of male cockroach's reproductive system and identify the missing parts labelled as *A* to *D*.

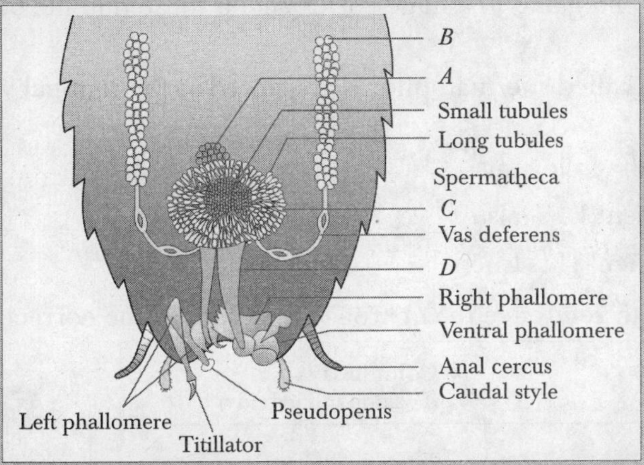

A. ____________________

B. ____________________

C. ____________________

D. ____________________

99. Identify the missing parts labelled as *A* to *E* in the given diagram of female reproductive system of cockroach.

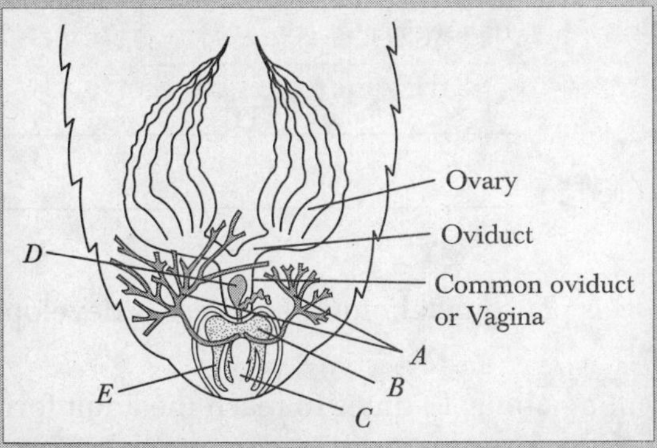

A. ____________________

B. ____________________

C. ____________________

D. ____________________

E. ____________________

100. Name the accessory gland in 6th-7th abdominal segments of male cockroach.

____

101. Answer the following.

(i) The external genitalia of cockroach are represented by ____________________.

(ii) Chitinous asymmetrical structure surrounding the male gonopore is ____________________.

102. Answer the following.

(i) In male cockroaches, sperms are stored in which part of the reproductive system?

____

(ii) Name the structure which are glued together in the form of bundle and are discharged during copulation. ____________________

103. The characteristic of female cockroach is one pair of spermatheca present in the 6th segment and open in genital chamber.

True ☐ False ☐

***104.** Consider the following statements.

Statement I The mushroom shaped gland in a male cockroach, is located in the 6th-7th thoracic segment.

Statement II Bundles of sperms called spermatophores are stored in the seminal vesicles of male cockroaches.

Choose the correct option from the following.

(a) Statement I is true, but statement II is false ☐

(b) Statement I is false, but statement II is true ☐

105. Match the following columns with reference to cockroach and choose the correct option.

	Column I (Body parts of cockroach)		Column II (Position in the body)
A.	Pair of testes	1.	6th segment
B.	Pair of spermatheca	2.	2nd-6th abdominal segment
C.	Two ovaries	3.	4th-6th abdominal segment
D.	Total abdominal segments	4.	10th segment

A. ________ B. ________ C. ________ D. ________

106. In cockroach, 14-16 fertilised eggs are stored in ________

107. Consider the following statements.

Statement I Development of *P. americana* is paurometabolous, i.e. there is development through larval stage.

Statement II The nymph grows by moulting about 13 times to reach the adult form of cockroaches.

Choose the correct option from the following:

(a) Statement I is true, but statement II is false ☐

(b) Statement I is false, but statement II is true ☐

108. ________ are present in nymphal stage of cockroaches.

109. What external changes are visible after the last moult of a cockroach nymph?

____

110. Choose the correct option for cockroach.

(i) Omnivorous/Herbivorous ________

(ii) Monoecious/Dioecious ________

(iii) Coelomate/Pseudocoelomate ________

(iv) Economically important/Serious pest and vector of several diseases ________

Assertion-Reason Questions

The following questions consist of two statements : Assertion (A) and Reason (R). Answer these questions by selecting the appropriate option given below.
(a) Both A and R are true and R is the correct explanation of A
(b) Both A and R are true, but R is not the correct explanation of A
(c) A is true, but R is false
(d) A is false, but R is true

***1. Assertion** (A) Tubular parts of nephrons are made up of glandular epithelium.

Reason (R) Tubular parts of nephrons are mostly involved in secretion and absorption.

(a) ☐ (b) ☐ (c) ☐ (d) ☐

2. Assertion (A) Most of the epithelial cells are packed together with little intercellular material.

Reason (R) Gap junctions allow intercellular communication by connecting the cytoplasm.

(a) ☐ (b) ☐ (c) ☐ (d) ☐

3. Assertion (A) In cockroaches two antennae arise from sockets located behind the eyes.

Reason (R) Antennae have sensory receptors that help in monitoring the environment.

(a) ☐ (b) ☐ (c) ☐ (d) ☐

***4. Assertion** (A) Cockroaches have a ring of 100-150 yellow coloured Malpighian tubules.

Reason (R) Malpighian tubules help in removal of urea from the haemolymph.

(a) ☐ (b) ☐ (c) ☐ (d) ☐

5. Assertion (A) If the head of a cockroach is cut off, it will survive for six to seven days.

Reason (R) Head of cockroach has a bit of the nervous system while the rest situated along the ventral part of its body.

(a) ☐ (b) ☐ (c) ☐ (d) ☐

6. Assertion (A) Frogs undergo aestivation and hibernation, respectively.

Reason (R) During this period, they protect them from extreme heat and cold.

(a) ☐ (b) ☐ (c) ☐ (d) ☐

7. Assertion (A) : Sexual dimorphism is the phenomenon by which males and females of a species can be distinguished.

Reason (R) : Female frogs bear a copulatory pad on the first digit of the forelimbs which are absent in male frogs.

(a) ☐ (b) ☐ (c) ☐ (d) ☐

***8. Assertion** (A) Frogs have a short alimentary canal.

Reason (R) Short-alimentary canal in frogs is a well-suited adaptation to their carnivorous diet.

(a) ☐ (b) ☐ (c) ☐ (d) ☐

9. **Assertion** (A) Despite the absence of external ears in frogs, they are able to hear and is aware of their surroundings.

Reason (R) Tympanum present in frogs plays a dual role in hearing as well as maintaining balance or equilibrium.

(a) ☐ (b) ☐ (c) ☐ (d) ☐

10. **Assertion** (A) Cloaca in female frogs is used to pass faecal matter, urine and eggs out of the body.

Reason (R) Cloaca in frogs is a common opening for urinary, reproductive and alimentary canal.

(a) ☐ (b) ☐ (c) ☐ (d) ☐

Case Based Questions

1. During a study on frog respiration, researchers observe differences in respiratory behaviours between frogs in a terrestrial environment and those in an aquatic habitat. They notice that frogs in the aquatic environment primarily use their skin for gas exchange, while those in the terrestrial environment rely more on their lungs.

Based on the above case. Answer the questions that follows

(i) Which environmental factor is most critical for maintaining effective skin respiration in frogs?

(a) Temperature ☐ (b) Humidity ☐
(c) Light intensity ☐ (d) pH of water ☐

(ii) Which adaptation allows the frog to respire through their skin efficiently?

(a) Presence of gills ☐ (b) Keratinised skin ☐
(c) Mucus secretion ☐ (d) Cutaneous respiration ☐

(iii) Which of the following is not a benefit of cutaneous respiration for frogs?

(a) Allows for gas exchange outside the water ☐
(b) Provides an alternative means of respiration when submerged ☐
(c) Facilitates efficient exchange of gases through the skin ☐
(d) Protect against dessication and dry environments ☐

2. Identify the alongside diagram and answer the following questions.

(i) Which of the following hold structure P to structure Q?

(a) Epithelium ☐ (b) Mesorchium ☐
(c) Pericardium ☐ (d) Mesentery ☐

(ii) Where does the structure X open?

(a) Bidders canal ☐ (b) Haversian canal ☐
(c) Epididymis ☐ (d) Glomerulus ☐

(iii) Which of the following is not released through the structure S?

(a) Fecal matter ☐ (b) Sperm ☐
(c) Digested food ☐ (d) Urine ☐

COMPETITION EDGE UP

1. Match List I with List II.

List I		List II
A. Unicellular glandular epithelium	I.	Salivary glands
B. Compound epithelium	II.	Pancreas
C. Multicellular glandular epithelium	III.	Goblet cells of alimentary canal
D. Endocrine glandular epithelium	IV.	Moist surface of buccal cavity

Choose the correct answer from the options given below.

[NCERT (Old) Pg. 102, NEET 2024]

(a) A-II, B-I, C-III, D-IV ☐
(b) A-IV, B-III, C-I, D-II ☐
(c) A-III, B-IV, C-I, D-II ☐
(d) A-II, B-I, C-IV, D-III ☐

2. In both sexes of cockroach, a pair of jointed filamentous structures called anal cerci are present on

[NCERT Pg. 112, NEET 2024]

(a) 5th segment ☐
(b) 10th segment ☐
(c) 8th and 9th segment ☐
(d) 11th segment ☐

3. Match List I with List II related to digestive system of cockroach.

List I		List II
A. The structures used for storing of food	I.	Gizzard
B. Ring of 6-8 blind tubules at junction of foregut and midgut.	II.	Gastric caeca
C. Ring of 100-150 yellow coloured thin filaments at junction of midgut and hindgut.	III.	Malpighian tubules
D The structures used for grinding the food.	IV.	Crop

Choose the correct answer from the options given below.

[NCERT (Old) Pg. 113, 114, NEET 2024]

(a) A-IV, B-II, C-III, D-I ☐
(b) A-I, B-II, C-III, D-IV ☐
(c) A-IV, B-III, C-II, D-I ☐
(d) A-III, B-II, C-IV, D-I ☐

4. Match List I with List II.

List I		List II
A. Mast cells	I.	Ciliated epithelium
B. Inner surface of bronchiole	II.	Areolar connective tissue
C. Blood	III.	Cuboidal epithelium
D. Tubular part of nephron	IV.	Specialised connective tissue

Choose the correct answer from the options given below. **[NEET 2023]**

(a) A-II, B-III, C-I, D-IV ☐
(b) A-II, B-I, C-IV, D-III ☐
(c) A-III, B-IV, C-II, D-I ☐
(d) A-I, B-II, C-IV, D-III ☐

5. Given below are two statements.

Statement I Ligaments are dense irregular tissue.

Statement II Cartilage is dense regular tissue.

In the light of the above statements, choose the correct answer from the options given below.

[NCERT (Old) Pg. 103, NEET 2023]

(a) Both statement I and statement II are false ☐
(b) Statement I is true, but statement II is false ☐
(c) Statement I is false, but statement II is true ☐
(d) Both statement I and statement II are true ☐

6. *Which of the following is characteristic feature of cockroach regarding sexual dimorphism?* **[NCERT (Old) Pg. 115, NEET 2023]**

(a) Presence of anal styles ☐

(b) Presence of sclerites ☐

(c) Presence of anal cerci ☐

(d) Dark brown body colour and anal cerci ☐

7. *Which of the following is not a connective tissue?* **[NCERT (Old) Pg. 103, NEET 2022]**

(a) Adipose tissue ☐ (b) Cartilage ☐

(c) Neuroglia ☐ (d) Blood ☐

8. *Tegmina in cockroach arises from* **[NCERT (Old) Pg. 112, NEET 2022]**

(a) mesothorax ☐

(b) metathorax ☐

(c) prothorax and mesothorax ☐

(d) prothorax ☐

9. *Which of the following statements wrongly represents the nature of smooth muscle?* **[NCERT (Old) Pg. 105, NEET 2021]**

(a) These muscles have no striations ☐

(b) They are involuntary muscles ☐

(c) Communication among the cells is performed by intercalated discs ☐

(d) These muscles are present in the wall of blood vessels ☐

10. *Which of the following characteristic is incorrect with respect to cockroach?* **[NCERT (Old) Pg. 113, NEET 2021]**

(a) A ring of gastric caeca is present at the junction of midgut and hindgut ☐

(b) Hypopharynx lies within the cavity enclosed by the mouth parts ☐

(c) In females, 7th – 9th sterna together form a genital pouch ☐

(d) 10th abdominal segment in both sexes bears a pair of anal cerci ☐

Chapter 08

Cell : The Unit of Life

Scan and take Chapter Test

TOPIC 1 What is a Cell ?; Cell Theory

NCERT Pg. 87-89

1. Living organisms composed of a single cell are called as ____________ and organisms composed of many cells are called as ____________.

2. Tissue is the fundamental, structural and functional basic unit of all living organisms. (*Rewrite the statement after correcting the underlined word.*)

   ____

3. Name the scientist who first saw and described a living cell.

   ____

*4. Who is known as Father of Cytology? ____________

5. Discovery of ____________ revealed the minute structural details of the cell.

6. ____________ (von Mohl/Matthias Schleiden) examined a large number of plants, observed that all plants are composed of different kinds of cells.

7. Theodor Schwann studied different types of fungal cells. (*Rewrite the statement after correcting the underlined word.*)

   ____

8. What is the unique character of the plant cells according to Schwann?

   ____

9. The bodies of animal and plants are composed of ____________ and ____________.

*Concepts of all questions bearing * are important for NEET & CUET*

10. Match the following columns.

	Column I (Scientists)		Column II (Discoveries made by)
A.	Matthias Schleiden	1.	*Omnis cellula-e-cellula*
B.	Anton van Leeuwenhoek	2.	German botanist
C.	Theodore Schwann	3.	Live cell
D.	Rudolf Virchow	4.	British zoologist

A.__________ B.__________ C. __________. D __________

***11.** Schleiden and Schwann together formulated __________ which did not explain as to how __________.

***12.** What is the meaning of *omnis cellula-e-cellula*?

____

13. Schleiden and Schwann gave final shape of cell theory, according to which all living organisms are composed of cells and arises from pre-existing cells.

True ☐ False ☐

14. Regarding cell theory what is common between the following ?

RBCs, Seive tubes, Viruses

____

15. __________ (Nucleus/Cytoplasm) is a dense membrane bound structure which lies inside the cell.

16. A cell with membrane bound nucleus is known as __________

17. In both prokaryotic and eukaryotic cells, a semifluid matrix called mesosomes occupies the maximum volume of the cell.

(Rewrite the statement after correcting the underlined word.)

____

18. Identify the part of cell on the basis of given characters.

(i) Main arena of cellular activities in all living cells.

(ii) Various reactions take place in it.

____

19. How many of these organelles is/are present in prokaryotic cells?

Endoplasmic reticulum, Golgi complex, Lysosomes, Mitochondria, Ribosomes, Microbodies

____

20. Identify the odd one out from the given series.

Chloroplast, Mitochondria, Lysosomes, Rough ER.

____

21. __________ (Centrosomes/Mesosomes) is a non-membrane bound organelle present in animal cells, which helps in cell division.

22. The largest isolated single cell is the egg of kiwi.

(Rewrite the statement after correcting the underlined word.)

____

23. Match the following columns.

Column I (Types of cell)	Column II (Approximately size of cells)
A. *Mycoplasma*	1. 3 – 5 μm
B. Nerve cell	2. 7.0 μm
C. Bacteria	3. 0.3 μm
D. Red blood cell	4. 30– 90 cm

A. ____________ B. ____________ C. ____________ D. ____________

24. Match column I with column II.

	Column I		Column II
A.	Leukocytes	1.	Oval
B.	Mesophyll	2.	Elongated
C.	Neurons	3.	Amoeboid
D.	Tracheids	4.	Branched

A B C D
(a) 3 1 4 2 ☐
(b) 3 2 4 1 ☐
(c) 3 1 2 4 ☐
(d) 3 2 1 4 ☐

25. Match the following analogy with respect to size.
Smallest cell : *Mycoplasma* : : Longest cell : ____________.

26. ____________ is the smallest human cell.

27. Among multicellular organisms, human red blood cells are about ____________ in diameter.

28. Write the shape of the cells for given diagrams.

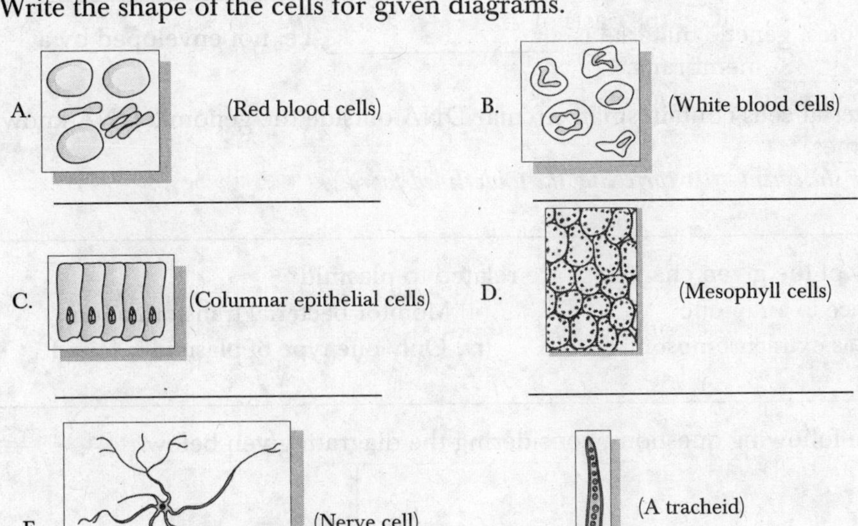

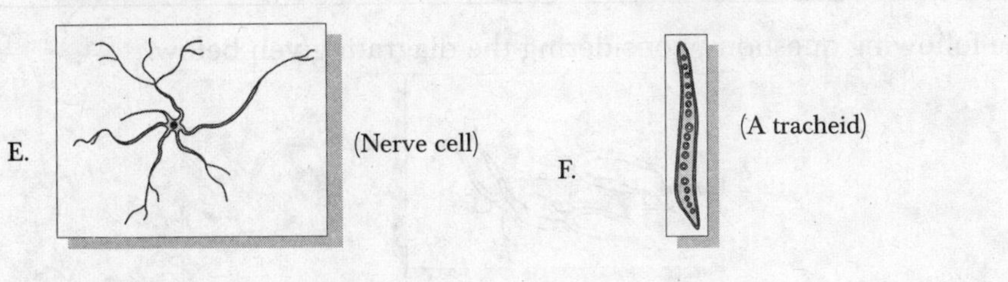

29. Consider the following statements.

Statement I The smallest living cell is Mycoplasma that measures about 0.3 μ.

Statement II The shape of a cell is due to the function it performs.

Choose the correct option from the following.

(a) Statement I is true, but statement II is false ☐

(b) Both statements I and II are true ☐

TOPIC 2

Prokaryotic Cells

NCERT Pg. 89-91

30. How many of the following characters are related to prokaryotic cell?

(i) Smaller
(ii) Multiply more rapidly
(iii) Vary greatly in shape and size
(iv) Have defined nucleus
(v) Contains peroxisomes

____

31. Complete the following diagrammatic analogy with respect to the structure of bacteria.

[figure] : Rod shape : : [figure] : ____________

***32.** Find the odd one out from the following series.

Staphylococcus, Mycoplasma, Bacillus, Spirillum

____

33. In prokaryotes, genetic material is ____________, i.e. not enveloped by a ____________ membrane.

34. Many bacterial cells contain small circular DNA outside the genomic DNA known as carboxysomes.

(*Rewrite the statement after correcting the underlined word.*)

____

35. How many of the given characters are related to plasmid?

(i) Resistance to antibiotic
(ii) Monitor bacterial transformation
(iii) Known as extrachromosomal DNA
(iv) Only one type of plasmid is found

____

36. Answer the following questions, considering the diagram given below.

(i) The cell represents a ________________ (eukaryotic/prokaryotic) cell.

(ii) The size of this cell range between 7μm - 9μm.

True ☐ False ☐

37. The bacterial cell envelope consists of a tightly bound ________________ (two/three) layered structure.

38. Bacteria can be classified into ____________ groups on the basis of the differences in the cell envelope.

39. Name the scientist who developed staining procedure of bacteria.

____

40. Bacteria that take up the Gram stain are known as ________________ others that do not are called ________________.

41. The composition and thickness of glycocalyx is same among different bacteria.

True ☐ False ☐

42. ________________ is the loose sheath of glycocalyx present on bacterial cell.

43. When glycocalyx is tough and thick it is called ____________ (chondrions/capsule).

44. How many of the following characters are not related to the bacterial cell wall?

(i) Determines the shapes of the cell

(ii) Provides structural support

(iii) Helps in bursting of cell

____

45. The ________________ (ribosome/plasma membrane) of prokaryotes is structurally similar to the eukaryotes.

46. Rearrange the following sequence of layer of bacterial cell envelope from outside to inside.

Cell wall → Plasma membrane → Glycocalyx.

____

47. ________________(Basal body/Mesosome) is formed by the extensions of plasma membrane into the cell.

48. How many of these given structures are the extensions of mesosomes?

Hook, Pili, Lamellae, Tubules, Filament, Form of vesicles

____

49. How many of the following processes are carried out by mesosome?

(i) Cell wall formation

(ii) DNA replication

(iii) Respiration

(iv) Secretion processes

(v) Increase surface area of plasma membrane

(vi) Enzymatic activity

(vii) Reproduction

____

50. In PPLO, chromatophores contain pigments which are membranous extensions into the cytoplasm.
(*Rewrite the statement after correcting the underlined word.*)

____

51. Bacterial cell contains one or more ______________ for cellular locomotion.

52. Flagellum is a thin filamentous extension that arise from the cytoplasm and penetrate cell wall.

True ☐ False ☐

53. Consider the following statements.

Statement I Bacterial cells often possess long tubular structures called flagella for locomotion.

Statement II The capsule is laid down just interior to the cell wall of a bacteria for protection.

Choose the correct option from the following.

(a) Statement I is true, but statement II is false ☐

(b) Statement I is false, but statement II is true ☐

54. In bacteria, flagellum is composed of three parts, i.e. ______________, ______________ and ______________.

55. Which is the longest structural component of the flagella? ______________

56. Match the following columns.

Column I (Parts of bacterial cell)	Column II (Characteristics)
A. Mesosome	1. Bristle-like fibres
B. Pili	2. Elongated tubular structure
C. Fimbriae	3. Chondroid

A. ______________ B. ______________ C. ______________

57. In some bacteria, ______________ (fimbriae/pili) attach the bacteria to rocks and also to the host tissues.

58. Which of the following allows the bacteria to adhere to the host cell surface?

Chromosomal DNA
P
Ribosomes
Q
S
Plasma membrane
Cytoplasm
R

(a) P ☐ (b) Q ☐ (c) R ☐ (d) S ☐

59. In prokaryotes, ribosomes are associated with the ________ (plasmid/ plasma membrane) of the cell.

60. Write the size of ribosomes in prokaryotes.________

61. Consider the following statements.

Statement I Prokaryotic ribosomes are made up of two subunits and carryout translation.

Statement II The 50 S and 30 S subunits of a prokaryote join to form the 80 S ribosomes.

Choose the correct option from the following.

(a) Statement I is true, but statement II is false ☐

(b) Statement I is false, but statement II is true ☐

62. The prokaryotic ribosome is made up of 40% *r*RNA and 60% ribosomal protein.

True ☐ False ☐

63. Several ribosomes may attach to a single *m*RNA and form a chain called ________.

64. Name the structure which stores reserve material in the cytoplasm of prokaryotic cell.

____

65. Give a common biological term for the following series.

Phosphate granules, Cyanophycean granules, Glycogen granules

____

66. Name two bacteria in which gas vacuoles are found. ________

TOPIC 3

Eukaryotic Cells

NCERT Pg. 91-102

67. Which type of cell is found in all protists, plants, animals and fungi?

____

68. You have given a cell, which shows following properties.

(i) Compartmentalisation of cytoplasm
(ii) Membrane bound organelle
(iii) Nucleus with nuclear envelope
(iv) Cytoskeletal structure

Identify the cell.

____

69. Eukaryotic genetic material is organised inside the nucleus.

True ☐ False ☐

70. The ________ possesses cell wall, large central vacuole and plastids.

71. Name the organelle which is present in animal cell, but absent in plant cell.

____

72. Consider the following figure of plant cell, identify the organelles *A, B, C* and *D.*

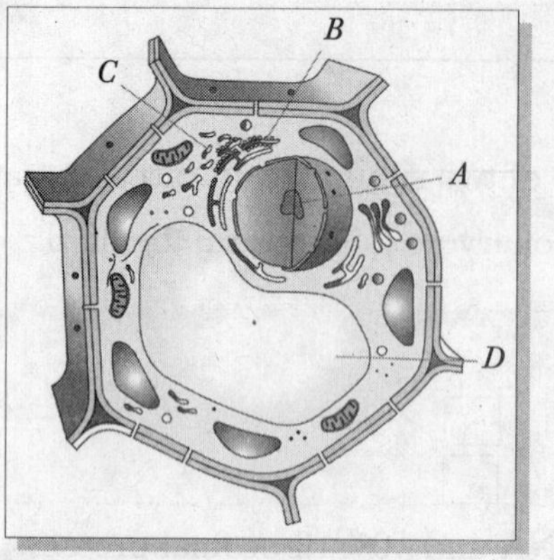

A. ____________________
B. ____________________
C. ____________________
D. ____________________

73. Consider the following figure of animal cell, identify which alphabets represent the organelle centriole, microvilli and ribosomes?

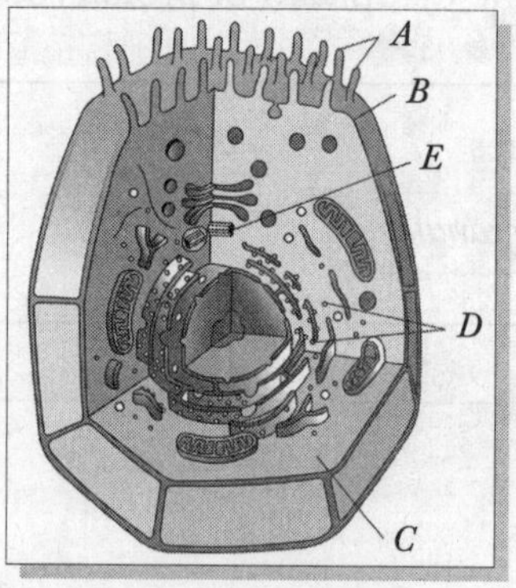

A. ____________________
B. ____________________
C. ____________________
D. ____________________
E. ____________________

74. The detailed structure of the cell membrane was studied only after the discovery of the <u>compound</u> microscope.

(*Rewrite the statement after correcting the underlined words.*)

____

75. ____________ are the major lipids that are arranged in a bilayer membrane of eukaryotic cell.

76. In bilayer membrane, the lipids polar head lies towards the inner side and tails towards the outer side.

True ☐ False ☐

77. Complete the following analogy with respect to membrane structure.

Hydrophobic : Tail of lipid : : Hydrophilic : ____________

78. Lipid layer in plasma membrane protects the non-polar tail of ____________ hydrocarbon from the aqueous environment.

79. Match the following columns.

Column I (Components of cell membrane)	Column II (Compositions of cell membrane)
A. Protein	1. 1 – 2%
B. Lipid	2. 58 – 59%
C. Carbohydrate	3. 40%

A. ________ B. ________ C. ________

80. The membrane proteins are of two types, i.e. ________ and ________ protein.

81. Name the protein which lie on the surface of the membrane.

____

82. The ________ proteins are partially or totally buried in the membrane.

83. Consider the given diagram of the fluid mosaic model of the plasma membrane

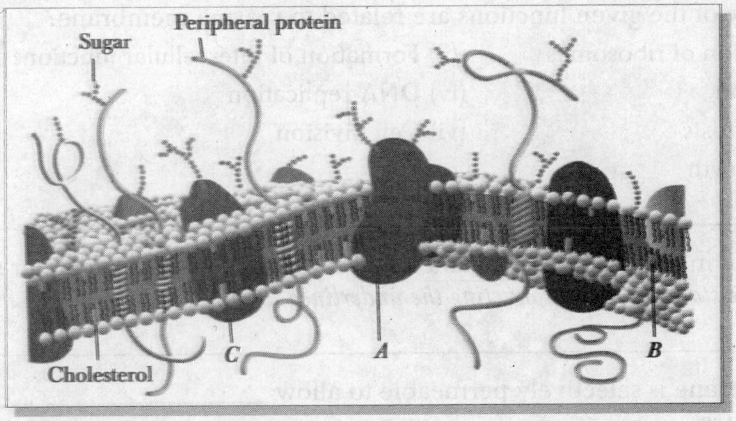

Which of the following would correctly describe the difference of label A and C?

(a) Position on the membrane ☐ (b) Nature of the substance ☐

(c) Distance between the two ☐ (d) Ratio of the substances ☐

84. Integral membrane proteins are easy to extract.

True ☐ False ☐

85. Singer and Nicolson proposed a cell membrane structure model known as unit membrane model.

True ☐ False ☐

86. According to the Fluid Mosaic Model (FMM), the quasi-fluid nature of lipid enables the ________ movement of protein within the overall bilayer.

87. The <u>rigidity</u> of membrane is measured by the ability of protein movement within the bilayer.

(*Rewrite the statement after correcting the underlined word.*)

____

88. Consider the following diagram of structure of plasma membrane and answer the given questions.

(i) Identify parts *A, B, C* and *D.*

A. ____________

B. ____________

C. ____________

D. ____________

(ii) Which model is represented by this figure? ____________

89. Glycolipids and cholesterol are usually present in the membrane of the plant cells.

True ☐ False ☐

90. How many of the given functions are related to plasma membrane?

(i) Formation of ribosomes (ii) Formation of intercellular junctions
(iii) Secretion (iv) DNA replication
(v) Endocytosis (vi) Cell division
(vii) Cell growth

____

91. The plasma membrane is <u>permeable</u> to all molecules present on either side of it. (*Rewrite the statement after correcting the underlined word.*)

____

92. Cell membrane is selectively permeable to allow ____________. This is contrast to skin, which is ____________.

93. Consider the following statements.

Statement I The cell membrane has a hydrophilic core that prevents polar molecules to cross the membrane freely.

Statement II Small hydrophobic molecules can simply diffuse into and out of the cell through the membrane.

Choose the correct option from the following.

(a) Statement I is true, but statement II is false ☐

(b) Statement I is false, but statement II is true ☐

94. In ____________ (active/passive) transport, many molecules can move briefly across the membrane without any requirement of energy.

95. Name the solutes which can move across the membrane *via* simple diffusion.

____

96. In ____________ process, solutes move from higher concentration to the lower.

97. Movement of water from higher concentration to the lower *via* membrane is called ______________ (active transport/osmosis).

98. The polar molecules require a carrier lipid of the membrane to facilitate their transport across the non-polar lipid bilayer.
(*Rewrite the statement after correcting the underlined word.*)

____

99. The process of movement of molecules with the help of carrier protein is called ______________ (active transport/facilitated diffusion).

100. Give one example of facilitated diffusion in human body. ______________.

101. In ______________ transport, molecules and ions move across the membrane against the concentration gradient.

102. A process of transport which require energy in the form of ATP is known as facilitated diffusion.

True ☐ False ☐

103. Give one example in which active transport operates in human body.

____

104. Match the following columns.

	Column I (Functions of plasma membrane)		Column II (Features)
A.	Endocytosis	1.	Materials are transported out of cells
B.	Phagocytosis	2.	Intake of liquid particles
C.	Pinocytosis	3.	Intake of solid particles
D.	Exocytosis	4.	Materials are transported into cells

A. ______ B. ______ C. ______ D. ______

105. The cell wall is a ______________(living/non-living) rigid structure.

106. Name two organisms in which the cell wall functions as an outer covering of plasma membrane. ______________

107. The plasma membrane gives shape to the cell and protects the cell from mechanical damage and infection.

True ☐ False ☐

108. The cell wall helps in cell to cell interaction and to transport macromolecules.

True ☐ False ☐

109. How many of the given components are found involved in algal cell wall?

Pectin, Cellulose, Chitin, Galactans, Mannans, Calcium carbonate, Silicic acid

____

110. **Match the following columns.**

Column I (Cell walls)	Column II (Chemical constituents)
A. Fungal cell wall	1. Cellulose, galactans, mannans
B. Plant cell wall	2. Cellulose, hemicellulose, pectins
C. Algal cell wall	3. Glucosamine, chitin

A. ________ B. ________ C. ________

111. **Consider the following statements.**

Statement I The middle lamella made of calcium phosphate glues the adjacent plant cells.

Statement II Presence of the cell wall prevents bursting of the plant cells in hypotonic solution.

Choose the correct option from the following.

(a) Statement I is true, but statement II is false ☐

(b) Statement I is false, but statement II is true ☐

112. **If plasmodesmata is not formed , which of the following would be affected the most?**

(a) Formation of secondary walls ☐

(b) Rigidity to the cell ☐

(c) Resistance against pathogens ☐

(d) Transport of nutrients ☐

113. **Rearrange the sequence of cell wall layers from inside to outside.**

Primary wall, Middle lamella, Secondary wall

____

114. **The cell wall of a young plant cell contains secondary wall.**
(*Rewrite the statement after correcting the underlined words.*)

115. **The middle lamella ________________ the different neighbouring cells together.**

116. **The plasmodesmata cannot cross the cell wall and middle lamella.**

True ☐ False ☐

117. **Name the structure which connects the cytoplasm of neighbouring cells.**

____

118. **Find the odd one out with respect to organelles related to endomembrane system.**

Endoplasmic reticulum, Peroxisomes, Golgi complex, Lysosomes

____

***119.** **Many of the membranous organelles are considered as a part of endomembrane system because their functions are**

____.

***120.** Name the cell organelle which is present as network or reticulum of tiny tubular structures.

____

***121.** Endoplasmic reticulum divides the intracellular space into two distinct compartments, i.e. __________ and __________.

***122.** Name the organelle which is attached to the outer surface of Endoplasmic Reticulum (ER).

____

***123.** Complete the following analogy with respect to cell organelles.

Rough Endoplasmic Reticulum (RER) : Ribosome present : : Smooth Endoplasmic Reticulum (SER) : __________

***124.** RER is frequently observed in the cells actively involved in <u>lipid</u> synthesis and secretion. (*Rewrite the statement after correcting the underlined word.*)

____

***125.** The __________ (RER/SER) are extensive and continuous with the outer membrane of the nucleus.

***126.** Which molecule is/are synthesised in smooth endoplasmic reticulum?

____

***127.** Identify the labelled parts *A* and *B* in the following diagram of endoplasmic reticulum.

Nucleus

Nuclear pore

A

Ribosome

B

A. __________

B. __________

128. Consider the following statements.

Statement I The smooth endoplasmic reticulum are distant to the nuclear envelope.

Statement II Only RER is involved in membrane biogenesis or formation of plasma membrane.

Choose the correct option from the following.

(a) Statement I is true, but statement II is false ☐

(b) Statement I is false, but statement II is true ☐

129. Who first observed the Golgi apparatus? __________

***130.** The ________________ are densely stained reticular structure near the nucleus.

***131.** The Golgi apparatus consist of many elongated, round or cisternae.

True ☐ False ☐

***132.** The diameter of cisternae range from ____________ to ____________.

***133.** The cisternae of Golgi apparatus remain stacked perpendicular to each other and present in varied number.
(*Rewrite the statement after correcting the underlined word.*)

____

***134.** Identify the given figure and labelled part.

A. ______________________

***135.** Consider the following statements.

Statement I Secretory vesicles emerge from the *trans* face of the Golgi and fuse with the membrane.

Statement II The ER and Golgi are placed at proximity to allow transport of molecules across and out of the cell.

Choose the correct option from the following.

(a) Statement I is true, but statement II is false ☐

(b) Both statements I and II are true ☐

136. The convex cisternae of Golgi apparatus lies towards the ____________________ and concave cisternae lies towards the ____________________.

137. Complete the following analogy related with cisternae of Golgi apparatus.

Cis : ________________ : : *Trans* : Maturing

138. The *cis* and *trans* faces of the organelle are entirely

(i) different, but interconnected ☐

(ii) similar, but separated ☐

139. If the Golgi apparatus is removed from the cell which of the following functions will not be altered?

(a) Secretion of proteins to the extracellular space ☐

(b) Formation of the plasma membrane ☐

(c) Packaging of the lysosomal enzymes ☐

(d) All of the above would be altered ☐

140. The principle function of Golgi apparatus is ____________________ of material.

***141.** The Golgi apparatus remains in close association with the endoplasmic reticulum for
(i) protein and lipid synthesis (ii) packaging of material

____

***142.** Materials are packed in the form of <u>tubules</u> in Golgi apparatus.
(Rewrite the statement after correcting the underlined word.)

____

***143.** The proteins on the endoplasmic reticulum are modified in the cisternae of the Golgi apparatus.

True ☐ False ☐

144. The modified protein of Golgi apparatus is released from __________ *(cis/ trans)* face.

145. A number of proteins synthesised by ribosomes on the endoplasmic reticulum are packed by Golgi apparatus.

True ☐ False ☐

***146.** Golgi apparatus is the important site of formation of __________ and __________.

***147.** Lysosomes are membrane bound __________ structure.

***148.** Lysosomes are formed by the process of packaging in the endoplasmic reticulum.

True ☐ False ☐

***149.** Name the enzyme which is present in isolated lysosomal vesicles.

150. Give a common term for the following enzymes.

Lipases, Proteases, Carbohydrases

____

***151.** A self destruct signal in a cell in response to incoming threat by a virulent pathogen would activate which of the following cell organelle?

(a) Vacuoles ☐ (b) Golgi body ☐ (c) Ribosomes ☐ (d) Lysosomes ☐

***152.** Hydrolytic enzymes of lysosomes are optimally active at __________(basic/acidic) pH.

***153.** Lysosomal enzymes are capable of digesting carbohydrates, proteins, lipids and nucleic acids.

True ☐ False ☐

***154.** Lysosomes are also known as suicidal bags because they cause autoimmune diseases. ☐

Or

They are capable of digesting the substances of their own cell. ☐
(Tick ✓ the most suitable box)

***155.** In electron microscope, you see a membrane bound space in the cytoplasm. What is it?

____

156. How many of the following materials are present in vacuoles?

Glycogen, Water, Sap, Carbon dioxide, Anthocyanin, Permeases, Lipoprotein, Excretory product

____

157. The vacuole is bound by a single membrane called __________ (cytoplast/tonoplast).

158. The vacuoles can occupy up to 20% of the volume of plant cell.
(*Rewrite the statement after correcting the underlined word.*)

____

159. The tonoplast facilitates the transport of a number of ions and other materials from higher concentration to the lower concentration.

True ☐ False ☐

160. Consider the following statements.

Statement I Turgidity of a plant cell occurs due to the excess water stored in the vacuoles.

Statement II Movement of ions across the tonoplast occurs actively from vacuoles to the cytoplasm.

Choose the correct option from the following.

(a) Statement I is true, but statement II is false ☐

(b) Statement I is false, but statement II is true ☐

161. Mark the sign of less than/greater than/equal (>/</=) in given box.

Ions concentration of cytoplasm ☐ Ions concentration of vacuole

***162.** In *Amoeba*, the __________ is important for excretion.

163. The __________ contains digestive enzymes in protists.

***164.** Match the following columns.

	Column I (Types of vacuoles)		Column II (Features)
A.	Food vacuole	1.	Helps in osmoregulation
B.	Contractile vacuole	2.	Contains hydrolases enzyme
C.	Sap vacuole	3.	Found in green bacteria
D.	Gas vacuole	4.	Contains dissolved salts and pigments

A. ______ B. ______ C. ______ D. ______

165. Mitochondria are easily visible under the microscope without staining.

True ☐ False ☐

166. A __________ (senescent cell/meristematic cell) contains high number of mitochondria.

167. The __________ and __________ of mitochondria varies from cell to cell.

168. What is the typical size and shape of a mitochondria?

____

***169.** Each mitochondrion is a __________ (single/double) membrane bound structure.

***170.** The outer membrane and the inner membrane of mitochondria divide its lumen distinctly into __________ aqueous compartments.

***171.** Identify the labelled parts *A*, *B* and *C* in the LS of mitochondria given below.

A. ____________

B. ____________

C. ____________

***172.** The inner compartment of mitochondria is filled with a dense homogeneous substance called cristae.
(*Rewrite the statement after correcting the underlined word.*)

____

***173.** Which of the structures in figure of Q. no. 171, if deleted from the provided organelle would slow down the active processes inside the cell?

(a) A ☐ (b) B ☐ (c) C ☐ (d) None of these ☐

174. The continuous limiting boundary of mitochondria is formed by ____________ (outer membrane/inner membrane).

***175.** Name the mitochondrial membrane which form number of infoldings called cristae towards the matrix. ____________

***176.** The ____________ (cristae/matrix) increase the surface area of mitochondria.

***177.** Name the organelle which is the site of aerobic respiration. ____________

***178.** Mitochondria produce cellular energy in the form of ____________, hence they are called ____________ of the cell.

***179.** Name the part of mitochondria which contain single circular DNA, RNA, ribosomes, and the components required for the protein synthesis. ____________

180. Consider the following statements.

Statement I Mitochondria are autonomously replicating organelles due to the presence of their own DNA and ribosomes.

Statement II An increased number of mitochondria is observed in the sperm cells to facilitate anaerobic respiration.

Choose the correct option from the following.

(a) Statement I is true, but statement II is false ☐

(b) Statement I is false, but statement II is true ☐

***181.** Name the type of ribosome found in mitochondria. ____________

182. The mitochondria divide by budding.
(*Rewrite the statement after correcting the underlined word.*)

____

***183.** ____________ are found in all plant cells and in euglenoids. These are easily observed under microscope.

184. The plants possess different colour due to the ____________ present in plastids.

***185.** Plastids can be of three types, i.e. ______________, ______________ and ______________.

***186.** Match the following columns.

Column I (Types of plastids)	Column II (Features)
A. Chloroplasts	1. Carotenoid
B. Chromoplasts	2. Chlorophyll
C. Leucoplasts	3. Colourless

A. ______________ B. ______________ C. ______________

187. Complete the following analogy.

Elaioplast : Oils : : ______________ : Protein

188. Identify the odd one out from the following series.

Elaioplast, Rhodoplast, Amyloplast, Aleuroplast

____

***189.** Match column I with column II.

Column I	Column II
A. Amyloplast	1. Carotenoids
B. Elaioplast	2. Starch
C. Chromoplast	3. Oils
D. Aleuroplast	4. Proteins

	A	B	C	D			A	B	C	D	
(a)	2	3	1	4	☐	(b)	2	3	4	1	☐
(c)	2	4	1	3	☐	(d)	2	4	3	1	☐

190. Give example of two carotenoid pigments that give the parts of the plant a yellow, orange or red colour.______________

191. Given below are few statements. Choose the correct ones.

I. Based on the number of pigments plastids can be classified into chloroplasts, chromoplasts and leucoplasts.

II. The chloroplasts contain chlorophyll and carotenoid pigments which are responsible for trapping light energy essential for photosynthesis.

III. In the chromoplasts water soluble carotenoid pigments like carotene, xanthophyll and others are present.

IV. The leucoplasts are the colourless plastids of varied shapes and sizes with stored nutrients.

V. Amyloplasts store carbohydrates, elaioplasts store oils and fats, whereas aleuroplasts store proteins.

Choose the correct answer from the options given below

(a) I and III ☐ (b) II, IV and V ☐

(c) II, III and IV ☐ (d) I, II and III ☐

192. Majority of the chloroplasts of the green plants are found in the __________ (epidermis/mesophyll) cells of the leaves.

193. The number of chloroplast in *Chlamydomonas* and mesophyll cells are __________ and __________, respectively.

194. Chloroplasts are double membrane bound organelles.

True ☐ False ☐

195. In chloroplast the __________ (inner membrane/outer membrane) is relatively less permeable.

***196.** The space enclosed by the inner membrane of the chloroplast is called thylakoids. (*Rewrite the statement after correcting the underlined word.*)

____

***197.** The thylakoids are the organised flattened membranous sacs present in the __________ of chloroplast.

***198.** By considering the given figure of chloroplast, answer the following questions.

A

B

C

(i) Part *A* are arranged in stacks like piles of coins to form part *B*. What is part *B* ?

____

(ii) The single unit of part *B* is part *A*. What is part *A*? __________

(iii) Name the labelled part *C*. __________

199. The flat membranous tubules connecting the thylakoids of the different grana is called __________.

***200.** The membrane of the thylakoids encloses a space called a lumen.

True ☐ False ☐

***201.** The __________ (thylakoid/stroma) contains enzymes required for the synthesis of carbohydrates and proteins.

202. The chloroplast contains small, double-stranded circular DNA molecules and peroxisomes. *(Rewrite the statement after correcting the underlined word.)*

____

203. Complete the following analogy with respect to ribosome.

Chloroplast ribosome : 70S : : __________ : 80S

204. __________ are the granular structures that were first observed under the electron microscope as dense particles.

205. Name the scientist who first observed ribosomes. __________

***206.** Name the organelle which is not surrounded by any membrane and composed of RNA and proteins. ____________

***207.** Consider the following diagrams of ribosomes and write the names of cells in which these ribosomes are found?

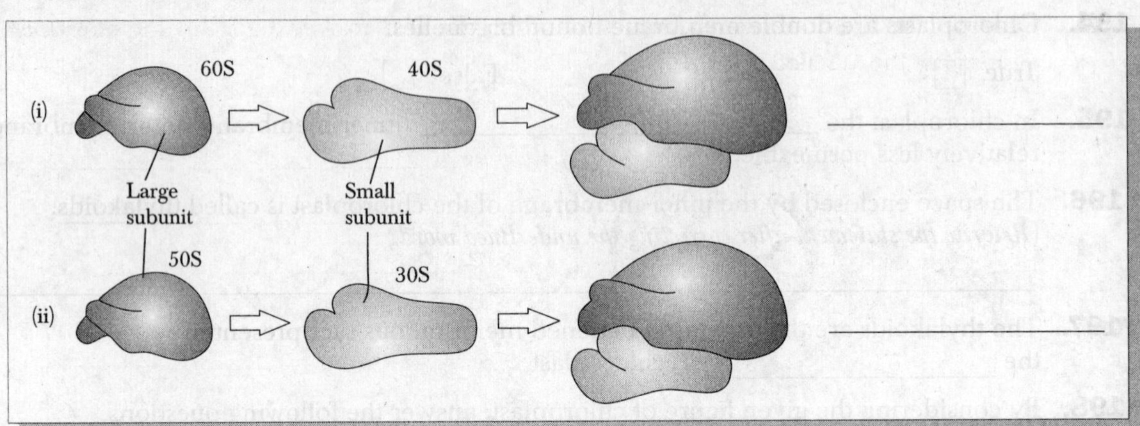

***208.** What is the final coefficient of ribosome shown in figure, in Q. no. 207.

(i) ____________ (ii) ____________

***209.** The S (Svedberg's unit) indirectly measures ________ and ________ of ribosomal units.

210. The ribosomes are organised by the nucleosome and made up of only proteins.

True ☐ False ☐

211. The sedimentation coefficient is a measure of weight of the subunits of ribosomes.

True ☐ False ☐

***212.** ____________ (Centrosome/Cytoskeleton) is an elaborate network of filamentous proteinaceous structures present in the cytoplasm.

***213.** How many given functions are related to cytoskeleton?

Mechanical support, Protein synthesis, Motility, Shape of the cell

____

***214.** Give a collecting term for the following series.

Microtubules, Microfilaments, Intermediate filaments

____

215. Name the hair-like outgrowths of the cell membrane. ____________

216. Cilia are long structures which work like oars, causing the movement of either the cell or the surrounding fluid.

True ☐ False ☐

217. Flagella are comparatively ____________ and help in cell ____________.

218. The prokaryotic and eukaryotic flagella are structurally ____________ (similar/different).

219. Cilium and flagellum are covered with ____________ (plasma membrane/cell wall)

220. The core of flagella/cilia is called the ____________. It possesses a number of ____________ running parallel to the long axis.

221. Write the arrangement of axonemal microtubules. ____________

222. Consider the figure of internal structure of flagella and answer the following questions.

(i) Identify the labelled parts *A, B, C, D* and *E*.

E
B
D
A
C

A. ____________

B. ____________

C. ____________

D. ____________

E. ____________

(ii) How many pairs of microtubules are found in this figure? ____________

223. Which of the following connects the central tubule with the peripheral doublets in a cilia?

(a) Radial hub ☐ (b) Radial spoke ☐ (c) Linkers ☐ (d) Bridge ☐

224. The central microtubules are connected by ____________ (connective/bridges) and is enclosed by a central sheath.

225. The central sheath is connected to one of the tubules of each peripheral doubles by a interdoublet bridge. (*Rewrite the statement after correcting the underlined words.*)

____

226. How many radial spokes are found in cilia/flagella? ____________

227. The cilium and flagellum emerge from lomasome like structure called the hook bodies. (*Rewrite the statement after correcting the underlined words.*)

____

228. Consider the following statements.

Statement I The 9+2 arrangement of the axonemal microtubules are a characteristic of cilia.

Statement II The cilia and the flagella give rise to the basal bodies that form the centrioles.

Choose the correct option from the following.

(a) Statement I is true, but statement II is false ☐

(b) Statement I is false, but statement II is true ☐

229. Which of the following are responsible for basal body formation?

(a) Peripheral doublets of cilia ☐

(b) Peripheral triplets of centrioles ☐

(c) Peripheral triplets of cilia ☐

(d) Peripheral doublets of centrioles ☐

230. The two cylindrical structures of a centrosome are called axoneme.

True ☐ False ☐

***231.** What is the surrounding material of centrioles? ____________

***232.** The centriole in a centrosome lie ____________ (parallel/perpendicular) to each other to form a structure like cartwheel.

233. Centrioles made up of nine evenly spaced peripheral fibrils of ____________ protein. These peripheral fibrils form a ____________.

234. Identify the structures of centriole that are being described in statements (i) and (ii).

(i) This is central part of the centriole, it is proteinaceous in nature.

____

(ii) It connects the hub to the tubules of the peripheral triplets.

____

235. The centrioles form the basal body of ____________ and ____________.

236. The centrioles form the ____________ during cell division in animals.

237. Consider the following statements.

Statement I The cartwheel structure of the centrosomes contains inter-linked triplet fibrils at the periphery.

Statement II Removal of centrioles from an animal cell can interfere with chromosomal segregation during cell division.

Choose the correct option from the following.

(a) Statement I is true, but statement II is false ☐

(b) Both statements I and II are true ☐

238. What is the name proposed by Flemming to the material of the nucleus stained by basic dye?

____

239. The interphase nucleus has highly extended and elaborated ____________ fibres called chromatin, nuclear matrix and one or more spherical bodies called ____________.

***240.** Nucleus is enveloped by nuclear envelope, it consists of two parallel membranes with a space between them called the ____________ (paranuclear/perinuclear) space.

***241.** The nuclear envelope forms a barrier between the materials present inside the nucleus and that of the cytoplasm.

True ☐ False ☐

***242.** The outer membrane of nucleus attaches with endoplasmic reticulum and bears centrosome on it.

(*Rewrite the statement after correcting the underlined word.*)

____

***243.** Consider the following image of nucleus and answer the following questions.

(i) Identify the labelled parts *A, B, C* and *D.*

C
B
A
D

A. ______________

B. ______________

C. ______________

D. ______________

(ii) Which of the labelled parts provide passage for the movement of RNA and protein in both direction from nucleus and cytoplasm? ______________

(iii) Which of the labelled part contains chromatin? ______________

***244.** Nuclear pores are formed by the fusion of ______________ (2/3) membranes of nuclear envelope.

***245.** What would happen if nucleolus is deleted from a cell?

(a) Chromosomes would fail to segregate during mitosis

(b) Spindle formation would not take place

(c) Ribosomes would not be synthesised

(d) All of the above

____

***246.** How many nucleus are present in erythrocytes of mammals and sieve tube cells of vascular plants? ______________

***247.** Name the spherical structure present in the nucleoplasm. ______________

248. The content of nucleolus is not continuous with rest of the nucleoplasm because it is membrane bound structure.

True ☐ False ☐

***249.** When nucleus undergoes protein synthesis, it contains more and large ______________.

***250.** Match the following columns.

	Column I (Structures of a nucleus)		Column II (Characteristics)
A.	Nuclear membrane	1.	It is dark staining granular structure
B.	Nucleoplasm	2.	It is octagonal
C.	Nucleolus	3.	It is also known as karyotheca
D.	Nuclear pore	4.	It is non-staining part

A. ______________ B. ______________ C. ______________ D. ______________

251. Complete the following analogy with respect to nucleus.

Uninucleate : *Amoeba* : : Binucleate : ______________

252. In the interphase, nucleus contains ____________, but during the different stages of cell division, it gets condensed into ____________

253. What does a chromatin contain ? ____________

254. A single human cell has approximately ________ (2/3) metre long thread of DNA distributed among its ________ (46/48) chromosomes.

***255.** The primary constriction of a chromosome is termed as satellite.
(*Rewrite the statement after correcting the underlined word.*)

____

256. Which of the following structures are involved in the attachment of spindle to the chromosomes during cell division?

(a) Centromere ☐ (b) Centriole ☐
(c) Kinetochore ☐ (d) Nucleosome ☐

***257.** Considering the following diagram, answer the following questions.

(i) '*A*' is a disc-shaped structure present on the side of centromere. What is '*A*'? ____________

(ii) Identify the labelled part *B*.

____

***258.** Chromatids of a chromosome are held together by ____________.

***259.** Match the following columns.

Column I	Column II
A.	1. Telocentric
B.	2. Sub-metacentric
C.	3. Metacentric
D.	4. Acrocentric

A. ________ B. ________ C. ________ D. ________

***260.** Identify the types of chromosomes from the following statements.

(i) The chromosome has middle centromere that forms two equal arms of the chromosome.

____

(ii) The chromosome has terminal centromere. ____________

***261.** The ________________ (telocentric/sub-metacentric) chromosome has centromere slightly away from the middle of the chromosome resulting into one shorter arm and one longer arm.

***262.** The telocentric chromosome has centromere situated close to its ends forming one extremely short and one very long arm.
(*Rewrite the statement after correcting the underlined word.*)

____

263. A few chromosomes have non-staining secondary constrictions at a constant location, it gives the appearance of a small fragment called kinetochore.

True ☐ False ☐

264. Consider the following statements and choose the incorrect ones.

I. The metacentric chromosome has centromere slightly away from the middle of the chromosome resulting into one shorter arm and one longer arm.
II. In sub-metacentric chromosome, the centromere is situated close to its end forming one extremely short and one very long arm.
III. The telocentric chromosome has a terminal centromere.
IV. Microscopic image of plant and animal cells will reveal minute vesicles loaded with enzymes.

Choose the correct answer from the options given below.

(a) I and II ☐ (b) II and III ☐
(c) III and IV ☐ (d) I and IV ☐

265. ________________ are membrane bound minute vesicles that contain various enzymes.

Assertion-Reason Questions

The following questions consist of two statements- Assertion (A) and Reason (R). Answer these questions by selecting the appropriate option given below.
(a) Both A and R are true and R is the correct explanation of A
(b) Both A and R are true, but R is not the correct explanation of A
(c) A is true, but R is false
(d) A is false, but R is true

***1.** **Assertion** (A) The cell theory proposed by Schwann and Schleiden in 1839 was incomplete.

Reason (R) The idea about how cells were formed was added by Virchow in the third postulate.

(a) ☐ (b) ☐ (c) ☐ (d) ☐

2. **Assertion** (A) Bacterial cells can prevent bursting when placed in a hypotonic solution.

Reason (R) The outermost glycocalyx provides resistance against the water pressure within the cell.

(a) ☐ (b) ☐ (c) ☐ (d) ☐

3. Assertion (A) Prokaryotic cells lack important organelles like mitochondria and hence cannot perform cellular respiration.

Reason (R) Extensions of the plasma membrane in the form of vesicles and tubules form mesosomes.

(a) ☐ (b) ☐ (c) ☐ (d) ☐

4. Assertion (A) The presence of polysomes in a cell can confirm its prokaryotic nature.

Reason (R) The bacterial system has a 70 S ribosome made up of individual 50 S and 30 subunits.

(a) ☐ (b) ☐ (c) ☐ (d) ☐

5. Assertion (A) Lateral movement of proteins is allowed in the plasma membrane due to the fluidity of phospholipids.

Reason (R) Integral membrane proteins are easier to extract out of the membrane compared to the peripheral ones.

(a) ☐ (b) ☐ (c) ☐ (d) ☐

***6. Assertion** (A) The hydrolases present in the lysosomal compartments are activated at neutral pH.

Reason (R) Hydrolases can degrade biomolecules and even digest the entire cell during starvation.

(a) ☐ (b) ☐ (c) ☐ (d) ☐

***7. Assertion** (A) The number of mitochondria is significantly more in the muscle, heart and sperm cells.

Reason (R) Mitochondria have their own genetic material and ribosomes and are hence semi-autonomous.

(a) ☐ (b) ☐ (c) ☐ (d) ☐

Case Based Questions

1. Carrier proteins are responsible for the facilitated diffusion of sugars and amino acids across the plasma membrane. The uptake of glucose is one of the most important transport functions of the plasma membrane.

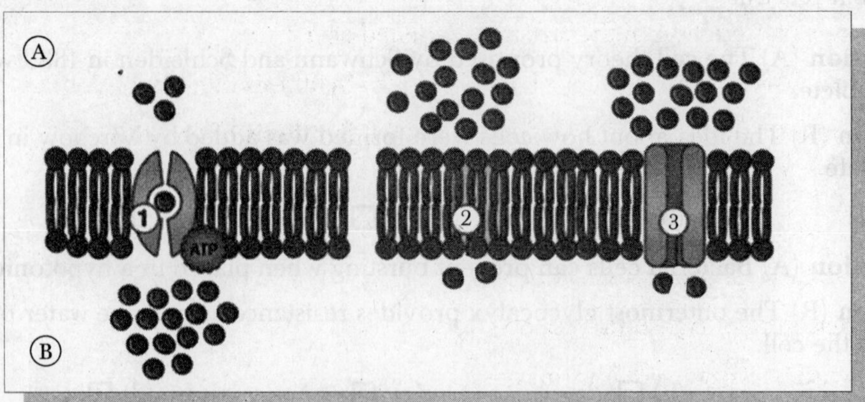

The image represents transport process through the plasma membrane. Observe the image carefully and answer the following questions:

(i) Choose the correct combination:

(a) 1 – channel, 3 – pump ☐ (b) 1 – pump, 3 – channel ☐
(c) 1 – pump, 2 – pump ☐ (d) 1 – channel, 2 – channel ☐

(ii) What would be the correct direction of transport ?

(a) A to B in 1 ☐ (b) B to A in 1 ☐
(c) B to A in 2 ☐ (d) B to A in 3 ☐

(iii) In which of the following is a carrier involved?

(a) 1 and 2 ☐ (b) 2 and 3 ☐ (c) Only 3 ☐ (d) Only 2 ☐

(iv) Which of the following can be transported by 2?

(a) Na^+ ☐ (b) K^+ ☐ (c) Glucose ☐ (d) CO_2 ☐

2. With reference to the provided image, answer the following questions:

(i) Identify the structure labelled as X?

(a) Nucleus ☐ (b) Golgi ☐ (c) Vacuole ☐ (d) Microbodies ☐

(ii) What is the function of the structure labelled as Y?

(a) Synthesis of lipid ☐ (b) Synthesis of carbohydrates ☐
(c) Synthesis of nucleic acids ☐ (d) Synthesis of proteins ☐

(iii) Which of the following is not a function of A?

(a) Divides the intracellular space into distinct compartments. ☐
(b) Synthesis and secretion of proteins ☐
(c) Packaging of lysosomal vesicles ☐
(d) Synthesis of steroidal hormones ☐

COMPETITION EDGE UP

1. Match List I with List II.

	List I		List II
A.	Nucleolus	I.	Site of formation of glycolipid
B.	Centriole	II.	Organisation like the cartwheel
C.	Leucoplasts	III.	Site for active ribosomal RNA synthesis
D.	Golgi apparatus	IV.	For storing nutrients

Choose the correct answer from the options given below:

[NCERT Pg. 95, 97, 99, 100, NEET 2024]

(a) A-III, B-II, C-IV, D-I ☐

(b) A-II, B-III, C-I, D-IV ☐

(c) A-III, B-IV, C-II, D-I ☐

(d) A-I, B-II, C-III, D-IV ☐

2. The DNA present in chloroplast is

[NCERT Pg. 97, 98, NEET 2024]

(a) linear, double-stranded ☐

(b) circular, double-stranded ☐

(c) linear, single-stranded ☐

(d) circular, single-stranded ☐

3. Match List I with List II.

	List I		List II
A.	Axoneme	I.	Centriole
B.	Cartwheel pattern	II.	Cilia and flagella
C.	Crista	III.	Chromosome
D.	Satellite	IV.	Mitochondria

Choose the correct answer from the options given below.

[NCERT Pg. 96, 97, 100, 102, NEET 2024]

(a) A-IV, B-III, C-II, D-I ☐

(b) A-IV, B-II, C-III, D-I ☐

(c) A-II, B-IV, C-I, D-III ☐

(d) A-II, B-I, C-IV, D-III ☐

4. Given below are two statements.

Statement I Mitochondria and chloroplasts both are double membranes bound organelles.

Statement II Inner membrane of mitochondria is relatively less permeable, as compared to chloroplast.

In the light of the above statements, choose the most appropriate answer from the options given below.

[NCERT Pg. 96, 97, 98, NEET 2024]

(a) Both statement I and statement II are true ☐

(b) Both statement I and statement II are false ☐

(c) Statement I is true, but statement II is false ☐

(d) Statement I is false, but statement II is true ☐

5. Which of the following are not considered as the part of endomembrane system?

[NCERT Pg. 95, NEET 2023]

A. Mitochondria

B. Endoplasmic reticulum

C. Chloroplast

D. Golgi complex

E. Peroxisomes

Choose the most appropriate answer from the options given below.

(a) A, C and E only ☐

(b) A and D only ☐

(c) A, D and E only ☐

(d) B and D only ☐

6. Which of the following functions is carried out by cytoskeleton in a cell?

[NCERT Pg. 98, NEET 2023]

(a) Protein synthesis ☐

(b) Motility ☐

(c) Transportation ☐

(d) Nuclear division ☐

7. Given below are two statements.

[NCERT Pg. 88, NEET 2022]

Statement I Mycoplasma can pass through less than 1 micron filter size.

Statement II Mycoplasma are bacteria with cell wall.

In the light of the above statements, choose the most appropriate answer from the options given below

(a) Both statements I and statement II are incorrect ☐
(b) Statement I is correct, but statement II is incorrect ☐
(c) Statement I is incorrect, but statement II is correct ☐
(d) Both statement I and statement II are correct ☐

8. Which of the following statements with respect to endoplasmic reticulum is incorrect? [NCERT Pg. 95, NEET 2022]
(a) SER is devoid of ribosomes ☐
(b) In prokaryotes, only RER are present ☐
(c) SER are the sites for lipid synthesis ☐
(d) RER has ribosomes attached to ER ☐

9. When the centromere is situated in the middle of two equal arms of chromosomes, the chromosome is referred as [NCERT Pg. 101, NEET 2021]
(a) metacentric ☐
(b) telocentric ☐
(c) sub-metacentric ☐
(d) acrocentric ☐

10. Which of the following statements about inclusion bodies is incorrect? [NCERT Pg. 91, NEET 2020]
(a) These are involved in ingestion of food particles ☐
(b) They lie free in the cytoplasm ☐
(c) These represent reserve material in cytoplasm ☐
(d) They are not bound by any membrane ☐

11. Which is the important site of formation of glycoproteins and glycolipids in eukaryotic cells? [NCERT Pg. 96, NEET (Sep.) 2020]
(a) Peroxisomes ☐
(b) Golgi bodies ☐
(c) Polysomes ☐
(d) Endoplasmic reticulum ☐

Chapter 09

Biomolecules

Scan and take Chapter Test

TOPIC 1

How to Analyse Chemical Composition?

1. Name the four major elements obtained by the elemental analysis of plant tissue, animal tissue or a microbial paste ____________________

2. The relative abundance of carbon and hydrogen with respect to other elements is higher in living organisms than in earth's crust.

True ☐ False ☐

3. Complete the following table of comparison of elements present in non-living and living matter.

Elements	% weight of earth's crust	% weight of human body
(i) Hydrogen	(a) 0.14	(1) (A)
(ii) Carbon	(b) 0.03	(2) (B)
(iii) Oxygen	(c) (C)	(3) 65.0
(iv) Nitrogen	(d) Very little	(4) (D)
(v) Sodium	(e) (E)	(5) 0.2

A. ____________________ B. ____________________

C. ____________________ D. ____________________

E. ____________________

4. For chemical analysis of living tissue, it is grinded in ____________________ using a mortar and a pestle.

5. Consider the following flowchart of the process of chemical analysis of living tissue and answer the questions that follows.

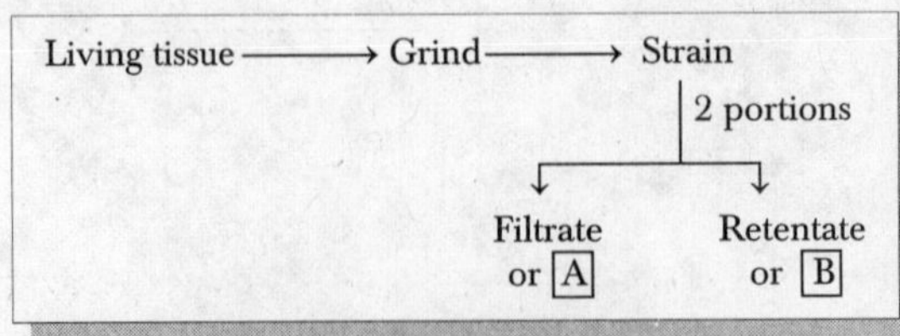

*Concepts of all questions bearing * are important for NEET & CUET*

(i) Name the material used for straining. ______________

(ii) Identify *A* and *B* portion.

A. ______________ B. ______________

(iii) Which of the following portion contains organic compounds?

____

6. After isolating and purifing a compound from tissues, the extracted material undergoes various ______________ techniques.

7. What information (any two) is provided by analytical techniques of organic compounds?

____

8. ______________ (Biomolecules/Micromolecules) are carbon compounds obtained from living tissues.

9. The weight of a living tissue is called ______________.

10. The inorganic materials of living organisms are obtained from ______________.

11. Consider the following process and answer the given questions.

$$\text{Living tissue} \longrightarrow \text{Drying} \longrightarrow \boxed{A} \xrightarrow{CO_2,\ \text{water vapour}} \text{Ash}$$

(i) Identify process '*A*' ______________.

(ii) Name any two inorganic elements present in ash. ______________.

12. Name any two inorganic compounds which are present in the acid soluble fraction of living tissue. ______________

13. Elemental analysis gives elemental composition of living tissues in the form of ______________, ______________, ______________, ______________ etc.

14. The analysis for compounds gives an idea of the kind of ______________ and ______________ constituents.

15. Two students, one from chemistry and other one from biology did an experiment on analysis of compound. Write the results of these experiments on the basis of chemistry and biology.

(i) ______________

(ii) ______________

16. Proteins are organic compounds containing an amino group and an acidic group as substituents on the same carbon, i.e. the α-carbon.
(*Rewrite the statement after correcting the underlined word.*)

____

***17.** Amino acids are also known as ______________ because they contain an amino group and an acidic group on the α-carbon.

***18.** Amino acids are substituted methanes because

(i) Amino acids are derived from methane.

(ii) Four valence position in amino acids are occupied by four substitutent groups similar to hydrogen and carbon atoms in methane.

____

19. The α-carbon of amino acid has four substituted groups *viz*, ________, ________, ________ and a ________ designated as *R*-group.

20. On the basis of nature of carboxyl group, amino acids are of several types.

True ☐ False ☐

21. How many amino acids are found in nature which form various proteins? ________

***22.** Complete the following analogy with respect to amino acid structure.

Hydrogen : Methyl group : : ________ : Alanine

***23.** Match the following columns.

Column I (Types of amino acid)	Column II (Structures of amino acid)
A. Serine	1. COOH / H—C—NH_2 / CH_3
B. Alanine	2. COOH / H—C—NH_2 / CH_2 / COOH
C. Glycine	3. COOH / H—C—NH_2 / CH_2OH
D. Aspartic acid	4. COOH / H—C—NH_2 / H

A. ________ B. ________

C. ________ D. ________

24. In amino acid serine, a methyl group is present at the *R*-group position. (*Rewrite the statement after correcting the underlined word.*)

____

***25.** The physical and chemical properties of amino acids are only dependent on the *R* group i.e. functional group.

True ☐ False ☐

***26.** The number of ________ (amino/*R*-groups) and carboxyl groups differentiate the amino acids into acidic and basic.

***27.** Complete the following analogy with respect to nature of amino acids.

Lysine : Glutamic acid : : ________ : Acidic

28. The amino acids having one amino group and one carboxylic group is ________________ (alcoholic/neutral) in nature.

***29.** Identify the odd one out with respect to nature of amino acids.

Glycine, Valine, Leucine, Arginine, Alanine

____

30. Consider the following statements.

Statement I The *R* group of an amino acid is variable, with the simplest being hydrogen in glycine.

Statement II Valine is a positively charged basic amino acid while lysine is a neutral amino acid.

Choose the correct option from the following.

(a) Statement I is true, but statement II is false ☐

(b) Statement I is false, but statement II is true ☐

***31.** What is the nature of amino acid having an extra carboxylic group? ________________

***32.** Give a common collective term for the following amino acids on the basis of their nature.

Phenylalanine, Tyrosine, Tryptophan

____

33. The specific property of amino acids is the ionisable nature of ________________ and ________________ group.

34. Which of the following correctly describes a zwitter ion?

(a) Molecule with one functional group attached to right ☐

(b) Molecule with additional – ve charge ☐

(c) Molecule with overall charge as 0 ☐

(d) Molecule with an additional + ve charge ☐

35. Answer the following questions considering the given equation.

$$\underset{(A)}{H_3\overset{+}{N}-\underset{}{\overset{R}{\overset{|}{CH}}}-COOH} \rightleftharpoons \underset{(B)}{H_3\overset{+}{N}-\overset{R}{\overset{|}{CH}}-COO^-} \rightleftharpoons \underset{(C)}{H_2N-\overset{R}{\overset{|}{CH}}-COO^-}$$

(i) Which of the following structure is the zwitter ionic form? ________________

(ii) Which of the following structure is found in acidic pH? ________________

(iii) Which of the following structure is an anion? ________________

***36.** Lipids are water ________________ (soluble/insoluble) and could be simple ________________ (fatty acids/glycerols).

***37.** A fatty acid has a ________________ group attached to an *R*-group.

***38.** Complete the following analogy.
Palmitic acid : ________________ : : Arachidonic acid : 20

***39.** Lipids can be fatty acids having a________group attached to R group. The R-group can be________or________or even higher number of $-CH_2$ with C atoms varying from________.

(a) Methyl group; $-CH_4$; $-C_2H_5$, 1 to 16 ☐

(b) Carboxyl group; $-C_3H_8$; $-CH_4$, 1 to 19 ☐

(c) Methyl group; $-C_2H_5$; $-CH_3$; 1 to 16 ☐

(d) Carboxyl group; $-CH_3$; $-C_2H_5$; 1 to 19. ☐

***40.** How many double bonds are present in the fatty acids given below?

(i) Saturated ____________________

(ii) Unsaturated ____________________

***41.** Glycerol is a form of simple lipid called ____________________

***42.** Many lipids have both glycerol and fatty acids, where the faty acids are esterified with glycerol.

True ☐ False ☐

43. Esterified lipids are of three types, *viz*, ____________, ____________ and ____________

44. Consider the following statements.

Statement I Unsaturated fatty acids have one or more double bonds, while saturated fatty acids have a single bond.

Statement II Fats and oils can be distinguished based on the difference in their melting points.

Choose the correct option from the following.

(a) Statement I is true, but statement II is false ☐

(b) Both statements I and II are true ☐

***45.** Oils have <u>higher</u> melting point and hence remain as liquid in winters.
(*Rewrite the statement after correcting the underlined word.*)

____

***46.** Phospholipids have phosphorus and a ____________ (carbonated/ phosphorylated) organic compound. These are found in ____________.

47. Complete the following analogy with respect to organic acid.

Saturated fatty acid : ____________ : : Unsaturated fatty acid : Oleic acid

***48.** Identify the missing boxes of the lipids from following structure.

(i) CH_3 —(A)— COOH
Palmitic acid

(i) A. ____________

(ii)
CH_2 —(A)
|
CH — OH
|
CH_2 —(B)
Glycerol

(ii) A. ____________

B. ____________

____

***49.** Consider the following structure.

$$\begin{array}{l} \qquad\qquad\qquad\quad O \\ \qquad\qquad\qquad\quad \| \\ \quad O \qquad CH_2-O-C-R_1 \\ \quad \| \qquad\quad | \\ R_2-C-O-CH \qquad\ O \\ \qquad\qquad\quad | \qquad\quad \| \\ \qquad\qquad CH_2-O-P-O-CH_2-CH_2 \\ \qquad\qquad\qquad\qquad | \qquad\qquad\quad | \\ \qquad\qquad\qquad\quad OH \qquad CH_3-N^{+}-CH_3 \\ \qquad\qquad\qquad\qquad\qquad\qquad\quad | \\ \qquad\qquad\qquad\qquad\qquad\qquad CH_3 \end{array}$$

Which of the following represents the correct combination of the name and the location of the given structure?

(a) Cholesterol, cell membrane ☐ (b) Lecithin, cell membrane ☐

(c) Cholesterol, cytoplasm ☐ (d) Lecithin, cytoplasm ☐

***50.** In the structure of triglycerides, how many oxygen atoms are bounded by double bond?

____

51. Answer the following question considering the given chemical structure of a lipid.

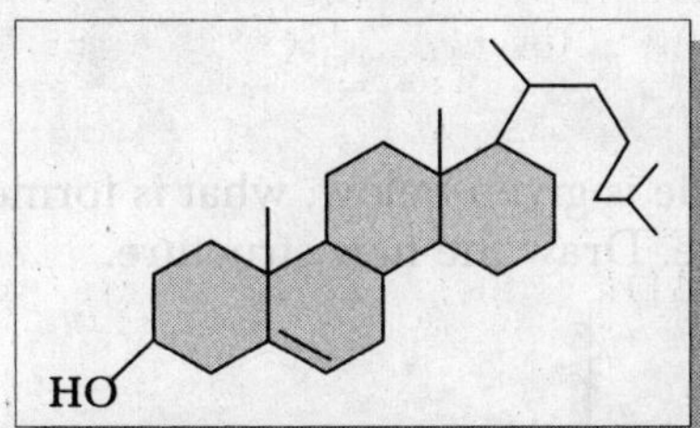

(i) Identify the structure ______________________________.

(ii) The given compound is a______________(steroid/monosaccharide)

52. Give a collective term for the following sequence.

Adenine, Guanine, Cytosine, Uracil, Thymine

____

53. Complete the following analogy.

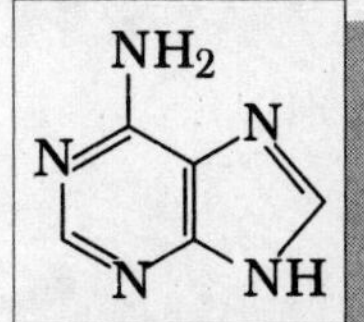

: Adenine : : __________ : Uracil

54. The nitrogen base molecule is joined to the sugar molecule by a glycosidic bond to form ____________________ (nucleosides/nucleotides).

55. Give a common collective term for the following sequence.

Adenosine, Guanosine, Thymidine, Uridine, Cytidine

____

56. The nucleoside combines with a phosphate group at 5' position by an ester bond to form a ________________ (nucleoside/nucleotide).

57. Give a common collective term for the following sequence.

Adenylic acid, Thymidylic acid, Guanylic acid, Uridylic acid, Cytidylic acid

____

58. Consider the following statements.

Statement I Adenylic acid is a nucleoside while adenosine is a nucleotide.

Statement II Nucleosides have a sugar, phosphate and a nitrogenous base.

Choose the correct option from the following.

(a) Statement I is true, but statement II is false ☐

(b) Both statements I and II are false ☐

59. Complete the following analogy with respect to nucleic acid.

HOCH$_2$ O Adenine

OH OH

: ________________ : : Adenosine : Uridine

60. The structure of a nucleotide is given below, what is formed if phosphate group is removed from this structure. Draw the new structure.

O
||
HO–P–OCH$_2$ O Adenine
|
OH

OH OH

____

61. A nucleotide differs from a nucleoside by the presence of

(a) Deoxyribose sugar ☐ (b) Ribose sugar ☐

(c) Phosphate ☐ (d) Thymine ☐

62. Nucleic acid, e.g. DNA and RNA consist of <u>nucleosides</u> only.
(*Rewrite the statement after correcting the underlined word.*)

____

TOPIC 2

Primary and Secondary Metabolites

NCERT Pg. 108

63. ______________ are the intermediate products produced during metabolism, catalysed by various enzymes that occur naturally within cells.

***64.** The metabolites which are required for the growth and maintenance of cellular functions are called secondary metabolites.

True ☐ False ☐

65. How many of the following are primary metabolites?

Alanine, Thiamine, Morphine, Ricin, Uridine

____

66. The primary metabolites consist of vitamins, amino acids, nucleosides and organic acids.

True ☐ False ☐

67. All the compounds other than primary metabolites in plant, fungal and microbial cells are called ______________

***68.** Match the following columns.

Column I (Secondary metabolites)		Column II (Types)	
A.	Pigments	1.	Morphine, Codeine
B.	Alkaloids	2.	Abrin, Ricin
C.	Toxins	3.	Vinblastin, Curcumin
D.	Lectins	4.	Carotenoids, Anthocyanin
E.	Drug	5.	Rubber, gum, Cellulose
F.	Terpenoids	6.	Concanavalin-A
G.	Polymeric substances	7.	Monoterpenes

A. ________ B. ________ C. ________ D. ________

E. ________ F. ________ G. ________

***69.** Name any five secondary metabolites which are useful to humans.

____

70. Match column I with column II.

Column I (Secondary metabolite)		Column II (Example)	
A.	Alkaloids	1.	Guanosine
B.	Terpenoide	2.	Guanylic acid
C.	Nucleoside	3.	Ricin
D.	Nucleotide	4.	Codeine
		5.	Diterpenes

	A	B	C	D			A	B	C	D	
(a)	4	5	1	2	☐	(b)	4	3	1	2	☐
(c)	4	5	2	1	☐	(d)	4	3	2	1	☐

TOPIC 3

Biomacromolecules

NCERT Pg. 108-109

71. The compounds found in acid soluble pool have molecular weight ranging from ______ to ______ Daltons (Da).

72. The molecular weight of compounds found in acid insoluble pool is approximately 10 thousand Daltons and above excluding lipids.

True ☐ False ☐

73. ________________ (Biomolecules/Biomacromolecules) have molecular weights less than one thousand Dalton.

74. Complete the following analogy.

Biomolecules : ______________ : : Biomacromolecule : Acid insoluble

75. (i) The molecular weight of lipids do not exceed ______________ Da.

(ii) Lipids are extracted from the acid ______________ (soluble /insoluble) fraction.

(iii) Lipids are often found in macromolecular fraction during separation because

(a) They themselves are macromolecules.

(b) They are found in cell membranes which get broken into pieces and form water insoluble vesicles.

____

76. The biomacromolecules are formed by ______________ of the micromolecules.

77. The acid soluble pool roughly represents the ______________ (cytoplasmic/mitochondrial) composition and acid insoluble pool represents macromolecules from cytoplasm and organelles.

78. Match the following columns.

	Column I (Compositions of cells)		Column II (% of the total cellular mass)
A.	Water	1.	2
B.	Lipids	2.	1
C.	Nucleic acid	3.	5-7
D.	Ions	4.	70-90

A.______________ B. ______________ C. ______________

D.______________

79. Rearrange the following compounds on the basis of abundance in living organisms in decreasing order.

Protein, Water, Lipid, Carbohydrate

____

TOPIC 4

Proteins

NCERT Pg. 109-110

***80.** Proteins are linear chains of ____________ linked by ____________ bonds.

81. Name the polymer which have only one type of monomer repeating '*n*' number of times.
____

82. What is the source of essential amino acids? ____________

83. ____________ (Essential/Non-essential) amino acids are not synthesised in our body and have to be supplied through diet.

84. Complete the following analogy with respect to category of amino acids.
Essential amino acid : Valine : : Non-essential amino acid : ____________

***85.** Match the following columns.

	Column I (Proteins)		Column II (Functions)
A.	Collagen	1.	Enzyme
B.	Trypsin	2.	Sensory reception
C.	Insulin	3.	Intercellular ground substance
D.	Antibody	4.	Enables glucose transport into cells
E.	Receptor	5.	Hormone
F.	GLUT-4	6.	Fights infectious agents

A.____________ B.____________ C.____________
D.____________ E.____________ F.____________

***86.** Complete the following analogy.
Collagen : Animal : : ____________ : Plant

***87.** Consider the following statements.

Statement I The amino acids that are taken into the body through diet are the non-essential amino acids while essential ones are synthesised by our own body.

Statement II Ribulose bisphosphate carboxylase-oxygenase is the most abundant protein in the whole biosphere.

Choose the correct option from the following.

(a) Statement I is true, but statement II is false ☐

(b) Statement I is false, but statement II is true ☐

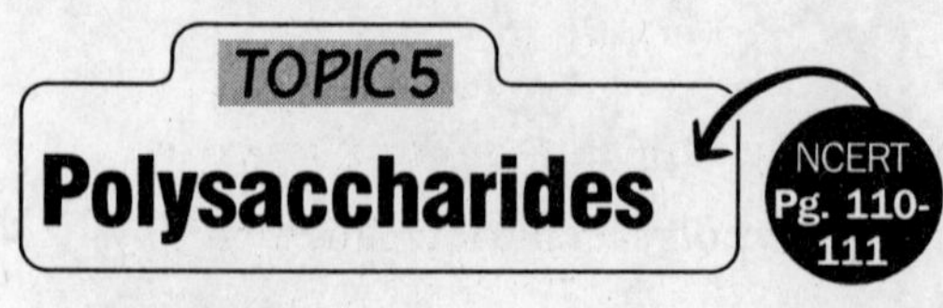

88. Complete the following analogy.

Carbohydrate : ________________ : : Protein : Amino acid

89. Polypeptides are threads containing different monosaccharides as building blocks.
(*Rewrite the statement after correcting the underlined word.*)

____

90. Complete the following analogy with respect to polymer of molecules.

Glycogen : Glucose : : ____________ : Fructose

91. Identify the odd one out from the following compounds.

Glucose, Fructose, Galactose, Sucrose

____

92. Which of the following statements about polysaccharide is incorrect?

(a) Glycogen is the storage product in animals ☐

(b) Cellulose in plant cell wall is a homopolymer ☐

(c) Inulin is a polymer of repeating glucose units ☐

(d) Right end of a polysaccharide is reducing ☐

93. Answer the following questions by considering the diagrammatic representation of a polysaccharide.

(i) It is the branched structure of ________________.

(ii) The given structure is a stored form of glucose

True ☐ False ☐

***94.** Starch forms helical secondary structure and can hold ________ molecules in the helical portion.

***95.** Cellulose possesses complex helices which can hold I_2.

True ☐ False ☐

96. Write the type of carbohydrate found in the following structures /products.

(i) Muscles and liver of animal ________________

(ii) Plant cell wall, paper, cotton fibre ________________

(iii) Exoskeleton of arthropods ________________

***97.** Consider the following statements.

Statement I Cellulose is a heteropolymer formed by joining repeating units of glucose.

Statement II The outer skeleton of insects have a complex polysaccharide called chitin.

Choose the correct option from the following:

(a) Statement I is true, but statement II is false ☐

(b) Statement I is false, but statement II is true ☐

98. Consider the given characteristics.

I. Long chains of sugar and amino acids.

II. Important class of biological polymers.

III. Found in acid insoluble pellet

IV. Function as important source of energy in animal cells.

How many of the above given features appropriately relate to polysaccharides?

(a) 4 ☐ (b) 2 ☐ (c) 3 ☐ (d) 1 ☐

99. Name any two modified sugars used as building blocks in amino sugar.

____

TOPIC 6
Nucleic Acids

NCERT Pg. 111

100. The nucleotide functions as the buildings block of polysaccharides.
(*Rewrite the statement after correcting the underlined word.*)

____

101. A nucleotide has three chemically distinct components, *viz,* ______________, ______________ and ______________.

102. Purines and pyrimidines are the homocyclic rings in nucleic acids.

True ☐ False ☐

103. Match the following columns.

Column I (Nitrogen bases)		Column II (Types of nitrogen base)
A. Purine	1.	Guanine
B. Pyrimidine	2.	Cytosine
	3.	Thymine
	4.	Adenine
	5.	Uracil

A. ______________ B. ______________

104. A nucleotide having ribose sugar is called ______________ and a nucleotide containing deoxyribose sugar is termed ______________.

105. Polysaccharide, polypeptide and polynucleotide comprise the true macromolecular fraction of any living tissue.

True ☐ False ☐

TOPIC 7

Structure of Proteins

NCERT Pg. 111-112

106. In inorganic chemistry, the structure invariably refers to the ______.

107. Up to which level, the structure of a molecule is described in the following fields?

(i) Organic chemistry

(ii) Physics ______

(iii) Biology ______

108. The sequence of amino acid in a protein structure is <u>sequential</u> information.
(*Rewrite the statement after correcting the underlined word.*)

______

109. Which protein structure is studied to determine the first and last amino acid of a protein?

______

***110.** If a protein is imagined as a line, the left end represented by first amino acid is known as C-terminal amino acid.

True ☐ False ☐

***111.** The right hand of protein is represented by the last amino acid and it is known as ______ (N-terminal/C-terminal) amino acid.

***112.** A portion of protein thread is folded in the form of a ______.

***113.** The most common type of helix found in protein is ______ (right/left) handed.

***114.** The linear polypeptide chain folded into a specific coiled structure is known as <u>quaternary</u> structure.
(*Rewrite the statement after correcting the underlined word.*)

______

115. Consider the following statements.

Statement I The primary structure of a protein gives information about the sequence of amino acids.

Statement II The three dimensional structure of a protein is contributed by the tertiary structure.

Choose the correct option from the following.

(a) Statement I is true, but statement II is false ☐

(b) Statement I is false, but statement II is true ☐

(c) Both statements I and II are true ☐

(d) Both statements I and II are false ☐

***116.** Refer to the given figure of structure of proteins and answer the questions that follow.

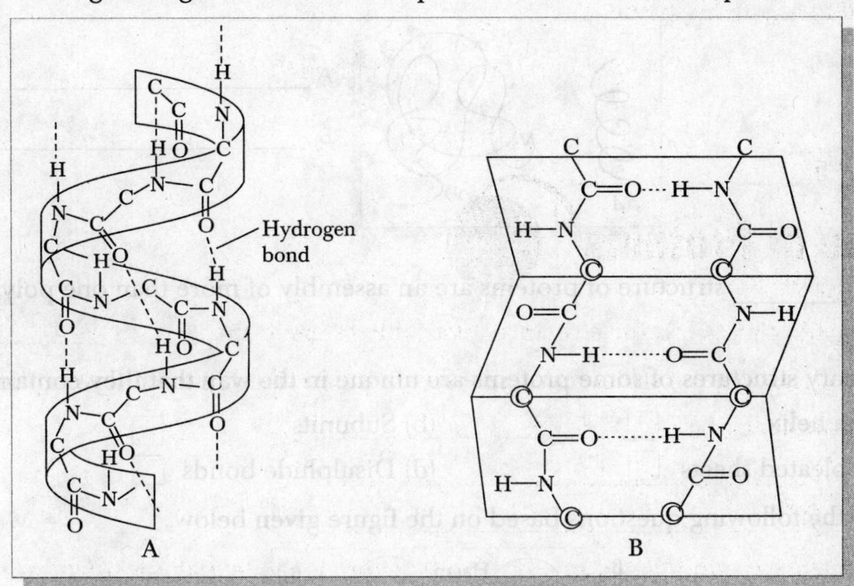

(i) Identify the level of protein structure of figures *A* and *B*.

A. ____________ B. ____________

(ii) Figure *A* is coiled in ____________ (right/left) handed manner.

117. The long protein chain is folded into a hollow woolen ball to form ____________ structure of protein.

118. ____________ (Tertiary/Secondary) structure gives three dimensional structure, and is necessary for many biological activities of proteins.

119. Consider the given structure of protein and answer the questions that follows.

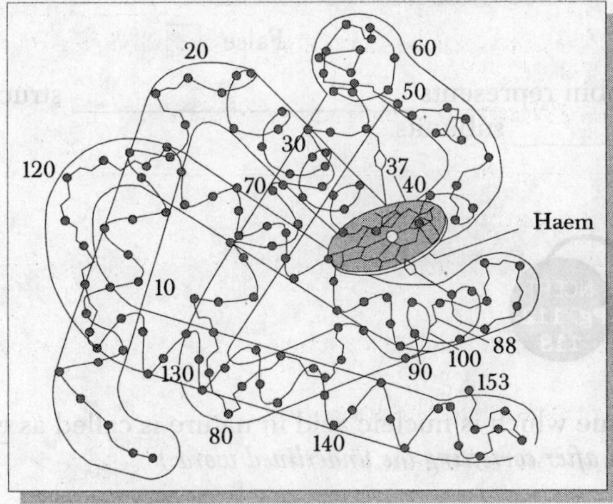

(i) Identify the level of this protein structure. ____________

(ii) Name any two bonds which stabilise this structure. ____________

120. Identify the level of protein structures shown in the diagrams *A* and *B*.

A. ____________________

B. ____________________

121. ____________ structure of proteins are an assembly of more than one polypeptide or subunits.

122. Quaternary structures of some proteins are unique in the way that they contain

(a) Alpha helix ☐ (b) Subunits ☐

(c) Beta pleated sheets ☐ (d) Disulphide bonds ☐

***123.** Answer the following questions based on the figure given below.

(i) Identify the level of structure of the protein. ____________

(ii) The protein subunits are arranged in linear string of spheres.

True ☐ False ☐

***124.** The adult haemoglobin represents ____________ structure of proteins and consists of ____________ subunits.

TOPIC 8 Enzymes

NCERT Pg. 112-118

125. A non-protein enzyme which is nucleic acid in nature is called as <u>exoenzymes</u>. (*Rewrite the statement after correcting the underlined word.*)

____

126. During the tertiary structure formation, the protein chain folds and *criss-crosses* itself to form many ____________ sites.

127. Where does the substrate fit into the enzyme?

____

***128.** Inorganic catalysts and enzymes differ in some context. Identify the effect of the given conditions on both inorganic catalysts and enzymes.

(i) High temperature __________________________

(ii) High pressure __________________________

***129.** Some enzymes isolated from thermophilic organisms are stable and retain their catalytic power at high temperature up to 80-90° C.

True ☐ False ☐

130. How many of the following transformations depicts a chemical reaction?

(i) Change in shape of a molecule.
(ii) Formation of new bonds.
(iii) Ice melts into water.
(iv) Water becomes vapour.
(v) Hydrolysis of starch into glucose.

____

131. The ____________ of a physical or chemical process refers to the amount of product formed per unit time.

132. Answer the following questions, considering the given expression.

$$\text{Rate} = \frac{\delta P}{\delta t}$$

(i) It is not affected by temperature.

True ☐ False ☐

(ii) The rate of reaction __________________ (doubles only /doubles or decreases) by half for every 10°C change in either direction.

133. Consider the following statements.

Statement I The enzymes isolated from thermophilic organisms can withstand high temperatures.

Statement II Enzymes act catalysts by speeding up the rate of reaction but not participating in the reaction.

Choose the correct option from the following.

(a) Statement I is true, but statement II is false ☐

(b) Both statements I and II are true ☐

134. Which of the following statements about an enzyme is correct?

(a) The secondary structure of an enzyme shows the presence of active site. ☐

(b) All enzymes of a living system are denatured at temperatures above 400 C. ☐

(c) The rate of a reaction is the amount of product formed per unit time. ☐

(d) Bonds are only rearranged in the substrate during the transition state. ☐

135. How do the following conditions affect the rate of the reaction?

(i) Catalysed reaction __________________________

(ii) Uncatalysed reaction __________________________

136. Answer the following questions by considering the given equation.

$$CO_2 + H_2O \overset{A}{\rightleftharpoons} H_2CO_3$$

(i) Identify the enzyme A. ________________

(ii) Which of the following graph is correct for the enzyme A? ________________

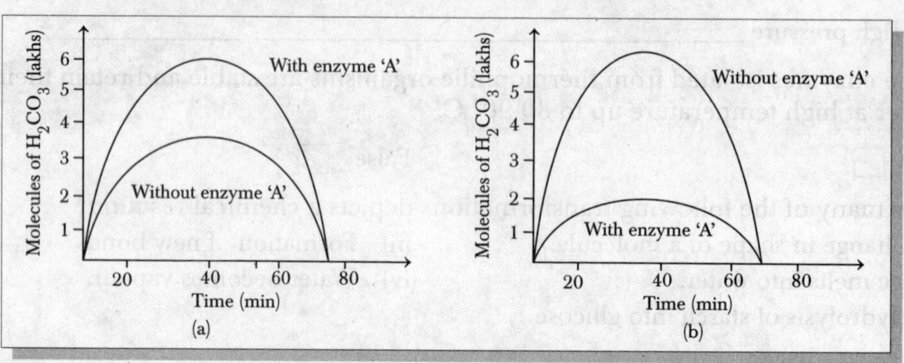

(iii) The enzyme can accelerate the reaction rate by 10 million times as about 600,000 molecules of H_2CO_3 can be formed instead of 200.

True ☐ False ☐

137. Answer the following questions, considering the given metabolic pathway.

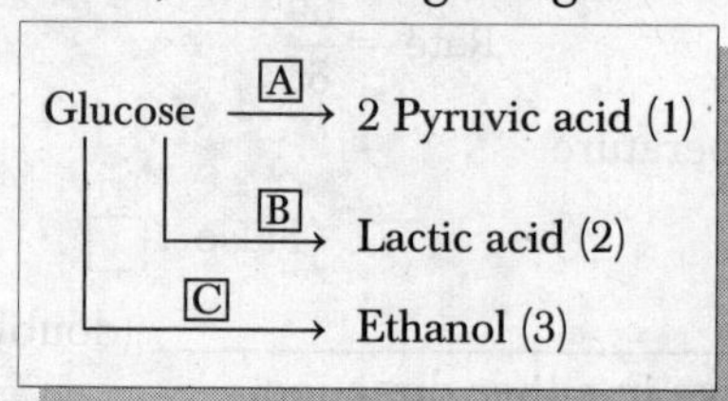

(i) Identify the conditions A and B in which these reactions occur.

A. ________________ B. ________________

(ii) Identify the process C by which ethanol is produced from glucose. C. ________________

(iii) How many enzymes are used in the metabolic pathway 1? ________________.

(iv) The metabolic pathway 3 occurs in ________________.

(v) The metabolic pathway 2 occurs in ________________.

138. The enzyme with three dimensional structures including an active site convert a ________________ into a product.

139. The substrate changes the conformation of active site during the binding process.

True ☐ False ☐

140. Consider the following statements.

Statement I Enzymes can convert a substrate to a product through a transition state.

Statement II Enzymes lower the energy barrier making the transition of 'S' to 'P' easier.

Choose the correct option from the following.

(a) Both statements I and II are true ☐

(b) Both statements I and II are false ☐

141. The substrate binds to the enzyme's active site to form a complex called enzyme substrate complex. This complex remain in non-transition state.
(*Rewrite the statement after correcting the underlined word.*)

____

142. The ____________________ is released from the active site after the expected bond formation or dissociation is completed.

143. In an enzymatic pathway the structure of ____________________ (enzyme/substrate) gets converted into the structure of product.

144. The enzyme produces many altered ____________________ between the stable substrate and the product which are unstable.

145. The peak of energy required for the reaction represents the activation state in which high intermediate is formed during the conversion of reactant to product.
(*Rewrite the statement after correcting the underlined words.*)

____

146. All the molecules of substrate possess energy, which is utilised to collide with other molecules, so as to reach between the reactant and product. This energy is called ____________________.

147. Consider the following image. Which of the following can be concluded from the graph?

(a) A is an enzymatic reaction. ☐
(b) The reaction is endothermic ☐
(c) B is an enzymatic reaction ☐
(d) There is no transition state. ☐

148. Answer the following questions, considering the given graph.

(i) Identify *A*, *B* and *C*.
A.____________________ B.____________________
C.____________________

(ii) Which of the following graph represents lower activation energy? ____________________

(iii) If product is at lower level than substrate, the reaction is an ______________ reaction.

(iv) The rate of reaction in graph 1 is low because of

____

149. The activation energy of any reaction is ______________ (lowered/increased) by enzyme.

150. Given below are four steps of an enzymatic reaction.

(i) E + S (ii) EP

(iii) E+P (iv) ES

Arrange them in proper sequence of enzyme action.

(a) (i), (iv), (iii), (ii) ☐ (b) (iv), (i), (iii), (ii) ☐

(c) (i), (iv), (ii), (iii) ☐ (d) (iv), (i), (ii), (iii) ☐

151. Answer the following questions, considering the given equation.

$$E+S \rightleftharpoons \boxed{A} \longrightarrow EP \longrightarrow E+\boxed{B}$$

(i) Identify *A* and *B*. A.______________ B. ______________

(ii) Complex *A* is less reactive and stable.

True ☐ False ☐

(iii) The released enzyme *E* at the end of reaction is reused.

True ☐ False ☐

(iv) *A* and EP are ______________

(v) Which of the following complex is essential for catalysis? ______________

152. Complete the following flowchart.

Substrate → Binds → Ⓐ of the enzyme → 'Alter' the shape of Ⓑ → Ⓒ of chemical bond of substrate → Ⓓ → Enzyme + Product

A. ______________

B. ______________

C. ______________

D. ______________

153. Enzymes are used in very small concentration because

(i) These are toxic chemical compounds.

(ii) These remain unaltered and thus are reused.

____

154. The activity of an enzyme can be affected by many factors which can alter the ______________ (secondary/tertiary) structure of the protein.

***155.** Each enzyme shows its highest activity at an optimum temperature and pH.

True ☐ False ☐

*156. Answer the following questions by considering the given graph.

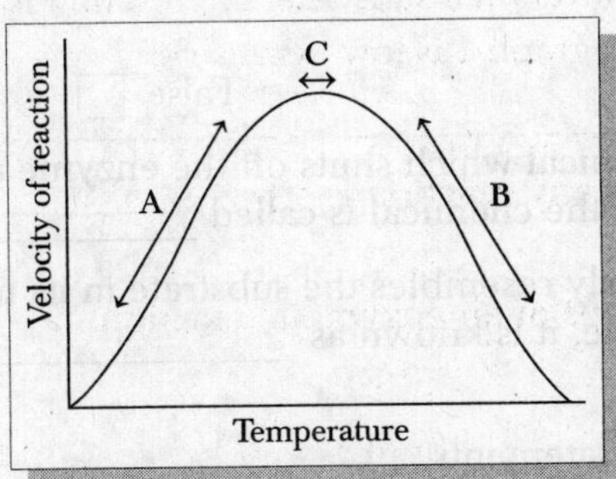

(i) The enzyme remains in inactive state at the slope ____________ .

(ii) Which of the following slope represents optimum temperature? ____________

(iii) During slope ____________ (*A/B*), proteins are denatured.

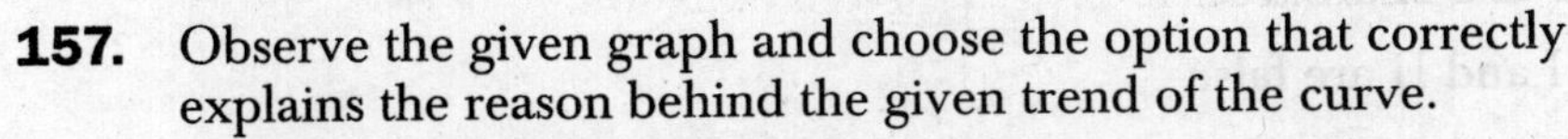

157. Observe the given graph and choose the option that correctly explains the reason behind the given trend of the curve.

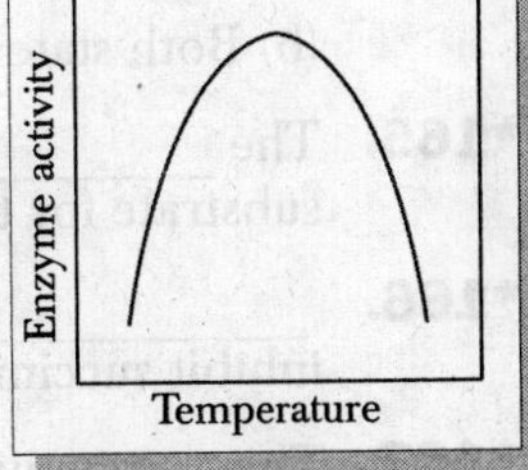

(a) Higher temperature inactivates enzymes ☐

(b) Higher temperature denatures enzymes ☐

(c) Lower temperature denatures enzymes ☐

(d) Lower temperature degrades enzymes ☐

158. The rate of enzymatic activity ____________ with increase in substrate concentration until all the ____________ are saturated with substrate molecules.

159. The maximum velocity of reaction is denoted by ____________, which is not exceeded by any further rise in concentration of the substrate.

160. Answer the following questions by considering the given graph.

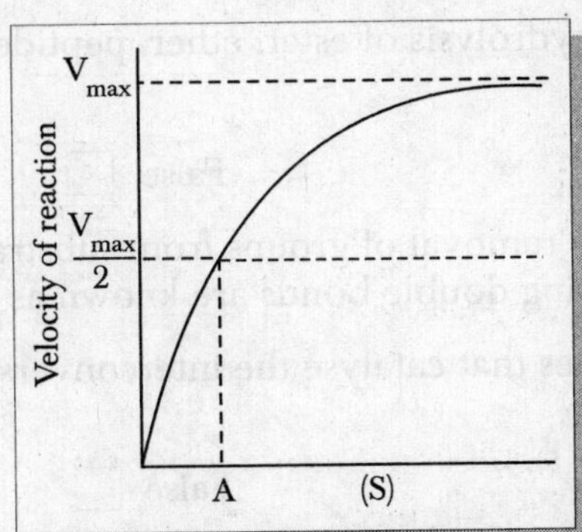

(i) Give relation between velocity of reaction and initial substrate concentration.

____

(ii) At what concentration of substrate, the velocity of reaction becomes independent?

____

(iii) What is '*A*' in this graph? ____________

161. The rate of reaction becomes constant at V_{max} because all the enzyme molecules are used by substrate molecule.

True ☐ False ☐

***162.** The binding of any chemical which shuts off the enzyme activity is called ______ and the chemical is called ______.

***163.** When the inhibitor closely resembles the substrate in its molecular structure and inhibits the activity of the enzyme, it is known as ______ (non-competitive/competitive) inhibition.

***164.** Consider the following statements.

Statement I A competitive inhibitor bears structural similarity with the enzyme.

Statement II In competitive inhibition, the inhibitor binds to the substrate itself.

Choose the correct option from the following:

(a) Both statements I and II are true ☐

(b) Both statements I and II are false ☐

***165.** The ______ (competitive/non-competitive) inhibitor competes with substrate for the substrate binding site of the enzyme due to similar molecular structure.

***166.** ______ closely resembles the substrate succinate in structure due to which it can inhibit succinic dehydrogenase.

***167.** The competitive inhibitors are used in the control of <u>herbicides</u>.
(*Rewrite the statement after correcting the underlined word.*)

______

168. Name the enzyme which catalyse the oxidoreduction of the following reaction.

S(reduced) + S(oxidised) $\rightarrow$ S (oxidised) + S(reduced)

______

169. ______ enzymes catalyse the transfer of a group (other than hydrogen) between a pair of substrate.

170. Hydrolases catalyse the hydrolysis of ester, ether, peptide, glycosidic, C—C, C — halide or P — N bonds.

True ☐ False ☐

171. Enzymes that catalyse the removal of groups from substrates by the mechanisms other than hydrolysis thus, leaving double bonds are known as ______ (ligases/lyases).

172. Ligases include all enzymes that catalyse the interconversion of optical, geometric or positional isomers.

True ☐ False ☐

173. <u>Hydrolases</u> catalyse the joining of bonds like C — O, C — S, C — N, etc.
(*Rewrite the statement after correcting the underlined word.*)

______

174. Match column I with column II.

Column I	Column II
A. Dehydrogenases	1. Transfer of a group other than hydrogen
B. Ligases	2. Catalyse linking of two compounds
C. Lyases	3. Catalyses oxidation and reduction
D. Transferases	4. Removes groups and forms double bonds

	A	B	C	D			A	B	C	D
(a)	3	2	4	1		(b)	3	2	1	4
(c)	3	1	4	2		(d)	3	1	2	4

***175.** Name the non-protein constituent of enzyme which binds to the enzyme to make it catalytically active. __________

***176.** The protein portion of the enzyme is called <u>isozymes</u>.
(*Rewrite the statement after correcting the underlined word.*)

____

***177.** Name all three types of cofactors. __________

***178.** Consider the following statements.

Statement I Apoenzymes are the protein parts of a coenzyme that makes the enzyme catalytically active.

Statement II Co-enzymes are organic compounds which have only transient association with the apoenzyme.

Choose the correct option from the following.

(a) Statement I is true, but statement II is false

(b) Statement I is false, but statement II is true

***179.** __________ (Prosthetic group/Zymogen) are organic compounds which are tightly bound to the __________ (cofactor/apoenzyme).

***180.** Name the prosthetic group of peroxidase and catalase enzyme, which catalyse the breakdown of H_2O_2 to H_2O and O_2. __________

***181.** The association of __________ with the apoenzyme is only transient and it usually occur during the course of catalysis.

***182.** The essential chemical components of many coenzymes are __________

***183.** Many enzymes require <u>vitamin</u> for their activity, which form covalent bonds with active site as well as with the substrate.
(*Rewrite the statement after correcting the underlined word.*)

____

***184.** __________ is a cofactor for the proteolytic enzyme carboxypeptidase.

185. All of the following are cofactors except

(a) Haem (b) Hydrogen (c) NAD (d) Zinc

***186.** Catalytic activity is lost when the cofactor is removed from the enzyme.

True ☐ False ☐

***187.** Match the following columns.

Column I (Cofactors)	Column II (Examples)
A. Prosthetic group	1. Zinc
B. Coenzyme	2. Haem
C. Metal ions	3. NAD and NADP (Nicotinamide Adenine Dinucleotide)

A. ____________ B. ____________ C. ____________

Assertion-Reason Questions

The following questions consist of two statements- Assertion (A) and Reason (R). Answer these questions by selecting the appropriate option given below.

(a) Both A and R are true and R is the correct explanation of A

(b) Both A and R are true, but R is not the correct explanation of A

(c) A is true, but R is false

(d) A is false, but R is true

1. **Assertion** (A) The ash formed by burning a tissue contains only inorganic elements and compounds.

Reason (R) Burning oxidises the carbon compounds into carbon dioxide and water vapour, which is removed.

(a) ☐ (b) ☐ (c) ☐ (d) ☐

2. **Assertion** (A) A zwitter ion is one that carries both positive and negative charges.

Reason (R) Amino acids exist in zwitter ionic forms in solutions of different pH.

(a) ☐ (b) ☐ (c) ☐ (d) ☐

***3.** **Assertion** (A) Secondary metabolites like alkaloids, flavonoids, antibiotics, etc. are useful to human beings.

Reason (R) Secondary metabolites like antibiotics play important roles in physiological processes of human host.

(a) ☐ (b) ☐ (c) ☐ (d) ☐

4. **Assertion** (A) Lipids, despite having a molecular weight of 800 Da, come under the acid insoluble pool.

Reason (R) Cell membranes are majorly composed of lipids and when broken, form vesicular fragments.

(a) ☐ (b) ☐ (c) ☐ (d) ☐

***5. Assertion** (A) Cellulose is a complex polysaccharide that turns blue in colour when reacted with iodine.

Reason (R) Helical secondary structures present in complex polysaccharides can hold I_2 molecules.

(a) ☐ (b) ☐ (c) ☐ (d) ☐

6. Assertion (A) The heterocyclic compounds in DNA could be Adenine, Guanine, Uracil and Cytosine.

Reason (R) DNA contains a deoxyribose sugar, a phosphate group and a nitrogenous base.

(a) ☐ (b) ☐ (c) ☐ (d) ☐

***7. Assertion** (A) Different proteins undergo different levels of folding owing to the function they execute.

Reason (R) Hydrogen bonding and disulphide bonds stabilise the folded structure of most proteins.

(a) ☐ (b) ☐ (c) ☐ (d) ☐

***8. Assertion** (A) The rate of an enzyme catalysed reaction decreases with an increase in temperature.

Reason (R) Most enzymes are proteins in their nature and get degraded at higher temperatures.

(a) ☐ (b) ☐ (c) ☐ (d) ☐

***9. Assertion** (A) The formation of enzyme substrate complex is followed by energy changes involved with transition state progression.

Reason (R) Enzymes catalyse a reaction, by raising the activation energy barrier between the substrate and product.

(a) ☐ (b) ☐ (c) ☐ (d) ☐

10. Assertion (A) After formation of E-P complex, the product is released from the active site of the enzyme.

Reason (R) An enzyme, after releasing the product is used again for another cycle of catalysis.

(a) ☐ (b) ☐ (c) ☐ (d) ☐

Case Based Questions

1. A tissue sample was grinded into a paste using a mortar pestle. The slurry was filtered to obtain the retentate and the filtrate. The acid insoluble retentate was sent for biochemical analysis and four different constituents (A, B, C and D) were identified.

A. Positive iodine test, showing a blue coloration

B. 800 Da component assembled into distinct structure

C. 10 K Da component stabilised by disulfide bridges

D. Polymeric compound with nitrogenous bases

Based on the provided information , answer the following.

(i) Name the possible structure that accounts for blue coloration in A.

(a) Helical primary structure ☐ (b) Helical secondary structure ☐

(c) Beta sheets of primary structure ☐ (d) Beta sheets of secondary structure ☐

(ii) Where in a cell, can we find abundance of the 800 Da component?

(a) Cytoplasm ☐ (b) Mitochondrial matrix ☐

(c) Cell membrane ☐ (d) Cell wall ☐

(iii) Which of the following is true about the primary structure of C?

(a) It forms right handed alpha helices and beta pleated sheets ☐

(b) It provides a linear sequence of arrangement of amino acids ☐

(c) The left end of a chain represents the C-terminal amino acid ☐

(d) It forms left handed alpha helices and beta pleated sheets ☐

(iv) If D has nitrogenous bases A, G, T and C what type of sugar will it contain?

(a) Ribose ☐ (b) Dehydroxyribose ☐

(c) Deoxyribose ☐ (d) Deoxyketose ☐

2. Consider the following graph. In a certain reaction, the addition of a substance 'A' increased the rate of the reaction. Now to the same reaction, addition of substance B had a negative effect on the rate. Substance A normally formed complex with the substrate of the reaction, but presence of substance B inhibited this process. If a graph is plotted, it shows the following result.

Based on this information, answer the following questions.

(i) In the absence of B which of the following situations can decrease the reaction rate?

(a) Increase in substrate concentration ☐ (b) Lowering of the activation energy ☐

(c) Optimum temperature and pH ☐ (d) Saturation of A with substrate ☐

(ii) If A is succinate dehydrogenase, what would be B?

(a) Succinate ☐ (b) Hydrogen ☐

(c) Malonate ☐ (d) Hydroxide ☐

(iii) To which of the following, does B bear structural similarity?

(a) Enzyme ☐ (b) Active site ☐

(c) Substrate ☐ (d) Product ☐

COMPETITION EDGE UP

1. Inhibition of succinic dehydrogenase enzyme by malonate is a classical example of **[NCERT Pg. 117 , NEET 2024]**

(a) Cofactor inhibition ☐
(b) Feedback inhibition ☐
(c) Competitive inhibition ☐
(d) Enzyme activation ☐

2. The cofactor of the enzyme carboxypeptidase is **[NCERT Pg. 118 , NEET 2024]**

(a) Zinc ☐ (b) Niacin ☐
(c) Flavin ☐ (d) Haem ☐

3. Cellulose does not form blue colour with iodine because **[NCERT Pg. 109, NEET 2023]**

(a) It is a helical molecule ☐
(b) It does not contain complex helices and hence cannot hold iodine molecules ☐
(c) It breaks down when iodine reacts with it ☐
(d) It is a disaccharide ☐

4. Given below are two statements.

Statement I A protein is imagined as a line, the left end represented by first amino acid (C-terminal) and the right end represented by last amino acid (N-terminal).

Statement II Adult human haemoglobin, consists of 4 subunits (two subunits of α type and two subunits of β type).

In the light of the above statements, choose the correct answer from the options given below. **[NEET 2023]**

(a) Both statement I and statement II are false ☐
(b) Statement I is true, but statement II is false ☐
(c) Statement I is false, but statement II is true ☐
(d) Both statement I and statement II are true ☐

5. Read the following statements on lipids and find out correct set of statements. **[NCERT Pg. 106, NEET 2022]**

I. Lecithin found in the plasma membrane is a glycolipid.
II. Saturated fatty acids possess one or more C = C bonds.
III. Gingelly oil has lower melting point, hence remains as oil in winter.
IV. Lipids are generally insoluble in water, but soluble in some organic solvents.
V. When fatty acid is esterified with glycerol, monoglycerides are formed.

Choose the correct answer from the options given below.

(a) I, IV and V ☐ (b) III, IV and V ☐
(c) I, II and IV ☐ (d) I, II and III ☐

6. Match List I with List II.

List I (Biological molecules)		List II (Biological functions)
A. Glycogen	(i)	Hormone
B. Globulin	(ii)	Biocatalyst
C. Steroids	(iii)	Antibody
D. Thrombin	(iv)	Storage product

Choose the correct answer from the options given below. **[NEET 2022]**

(a) (A)-(iv), (B)-(ii), (C)-(i), (D)-(iii) ☐
(b) (A)-(ii), (B)-(iv), (C)-(iii), (D)-(i) ☐
(c) (A)-(iv), (B)-(iii), (C)-(i), (D)-(ii) ☐
(d) (A)-(iii), (B)-(ii), (C)-(iv), (D)-(i) ☐

7. Which of the following are not secondary metabolites in plants? **[NCERT Pg. 108, NEET 2021]**

(a) Morphine, codeine ☐
(b) Amino acids, glucose ☐
(c) Vinblastin, curcumin ☐
(d) Rubber, gums ☐

8. Identify the incorrect pair. **[NCERT Pg. 108, NEET 2021]**

(a) Drugs-Ricin ☐
(b) Alkaloids-Codeine ☐
(c) Toxin-Abrin ☐
(d) Lectins-Concanavalin-A ☐

Chapter 10

Cell Cycle and Cell Division

1. In all living organisms, growth and reproduction are the main characteristics of the cell.

True ☐ False ☐

2. Cycles of growth and division allow a ____________ to form a structure consisting of millions of cells.

3. Name the two processes which take place during cell division.

(i) ____________ (ii) ____________

4. Write the scientific word for the process given in the statement.

The sequence of events by which a cell duplicates its genome, synthesises the other constituents of the cell and eventually divides itself in two cells. ____________

5. Cell growth is a continuous process in terms of ____________

***6.** During cell cycle how many times does the DNA synthesis occur? ____________

7. The replicated chromosomes get distributed into the ____________ of daughter cells.

8. The events of cell cycle are under the control of ____________ (cell/genes).

9. Typical eukaryotic cells (human cell) divide once every ____________ hours (12/24).

10. The duration of cell cycle in the cells of all organisms is same.

True ☐ False ☐

11. *Saccharomyces cerevisiae* divides in every ____________ (45 minutes/ 90 minutes).

***12.** Name two basic stages of cell cycle.

(i) ____________ (ii) ____________

***13.** Which phase of cell cycle is the actual phase of cell division? ____________

14. The phase between two successive M-phase is called ____________

*Concepts of all questions bearing * are important for NEET & CUET*

15. What is the approximate percentage duration of cell cycle that comes under interphase in humans? ____________

***16.** Identify the following events of cell cycle on the basis of given statements.

(i) Separation of daughter chromosomes. ____________

(ii) Division of cytoplasm. ____________

17. M-phase is also called as resting phase.
(*Rewrite the statement after correcting the underlined word.*)

____

***18.** Choose the odd one out from the following phases.

G_1-phase, S-phase, G_2-phase, M-phase

____

***19.** The G_1-phase corresponds to the ______ between mitosis and initiation of DNA replication.

20. During G_1-phase, the cell is metabolically active and continuously grows, but does not replicate its DNA.

True ☐ False ☐

21. The amount of DNA per cell reduces during synthesis phase of interphase.

True ☐ False ☐

22. The number of chromosome increases during S-phase of cell cycle.

True ☐ False ☐

***23.** If the initial amount of DNA in a cell is 2C, what is the content of DNA after the synthesis phase gets over in the cell cycle? ____________

24. If the amount of DNA in a plant cell before interphase was 4 q and the number of chromosomes was 32, what would be the amount of DNA and the number of chromosomes respectively after G_2?

(a) 4 q and 32 ☐ (b) 8q and 32 ☐

(c) 4 q and 64 ☐ (d) 8 q and 64 ☐

25. In which phase of cell cycle, the centriole duplicates in the cytoplasm? ____________

26. Name the cell phase which synthesise protein to cause condensation of chromosomes to initiate mitosis. ____________

27. The heart cells enter the G_0-stage and divide occassionally.

True ☐ False ☐

28. Give one word for the given statement.
The cell exiting G_1-phase enter an inactive stage called ____________

29. The cells in G_0-phase can divide depending upon the requirement of the organism.

True ☐ False ☐

30. Consider the following statements.

Statement I The G_1-phase is the longest phase of the cell cycle while M-phase is the shortest.

Statement II Once a cell passes G_1, it becomes irreversibly committed for division.

Choose the correct option from the following.

(a) Both statements I and II are true ☐

(b) Both statements I and II are false ☐

***31.** Match the following columns.

Column I (Phases of interphase)	Column II (Events occur)
A. G_0-phase	1. Synthesis of proteins and enzymes
B. G_1-phase	2. Duplication of DNA
C. G_2-phase	3. Inactive stage of the cell cycle
D. S-phase	4. Cell metabolically active and continuously grow

A. ________ B. ________ C. ________ D. ________

32. Identify *A*, *B*, *C* and *D* in the figure of cell cycle.

A. ________

B. ________

C. ________

D. ________

33. In animals, mitotic cell division is only seen in the ________ somatic cells.

34. The plant cells can show mitotic division in both ________ cells.

35. Name the plant species and stage at which mitosis is seen in haploid cells.

____

36. Consider the following statements and choose the correct ones.

I. A damaged cell exits G_2-stage and enters G_0-stage or quiescent stage.

II. Cells in the G_0-stage do not divide, but are metabolically active.

III. In male honeybees, haploid cells divide by mitosis.

IV. The plants can show mitotic division in the diploid cells only.

Choose the correct answer from the options given below.

(a) I and IV ☐ (b) II and III ☐ (c) I and III ☐ (d) II and IV ☐

TOPIC 2

M Phase

NCERT Pg. 122-125

37. Mitosis is also referred as ________ division.

38. Write the names of stages of karyokinesis in a sequential manner.

____

39. Disappearance of nucleolus, chromosome movement and spindle fibres formation are the characteristic features of mitosis in somatic cells.

True ☐ False ☐

40. In which stage of cell cycle, initiation of condensation of chromosome takes place?

____

41. Identify the given stage and choose the structure that completely disappears at the end of this stage.

A B C D

(a) D ☐ (b) C ☐ (c) A ☐ (d) B ☐

42. The centriole moves to opposite poles of the cell in <u>metaphase</u>.
(*Rewrite the statement after correcting the underlined word.*)

____

43. Consider the following figure of late prophase and answer the given questions.

(i) Name the structures which are formed at this stage by the condensation of chromosomal material.

____

(ii) Name the structure which attach two chromatids of chromosomes.

____

(iii) The centrosomes at the opposite poles radiate out microtubules called

____

44. How many of the cell organelles are not seen at the end of the prophase stage of mitotic cell division?

ER, Golgi body, Nucleolus, Lysosomes, Chloroplast

____

45. The complete disintegration of the ________________ marks the initiation of second phase of mitosis.

46. The morphology of chromosomes can be studied at ________ stage of cell division.

47. Consider the following statements.

Statement I Metaphase is the best stage for study as chromosomes line up at the equator.

Statement II The spindles from opposite poles attach to the kinetochore of the arranged chromosomes.

Choose the correct option from the following.

(a) Both statements I and II are true ☐

(b) Both statements I and II are false ☐

48. Metaphase chromosome is made up of two sister chromatids.

True ☐ False ☐

49. Write the technical term for the sentence given below.

Small disc-shaped structures at the surface of centromeres. ________________

50. The plane of alignment of the chromosomes at metaphase is referred to as

____

51. Observe the diagram given alongside and answer the questions that follow.

(i) Which phase of mitosis is depicted in the given diagram?

____

(ii) Spindle fibres attach to the ________________ of chromosome.

(iii) Chromosomes are moved to spindle equator and get aligned along metaphase plate through spindle fibre to both poles.

True ☐ False ☐

52. Which of the following features about the given stage of cell division is incorrect?

(a) The spindles attach to the kinetochore of the sister chromatids ☐

(b) This is the most widely used stage for karyotyping ☐

(c) Complete disintegration of nuclear envelope. ☐

(d) At the end of this stage, the sister chromatids reach opposite poles. ☐

53. At which stage of mitosis, the two daughter chromatids separate from each other, migrate towards the opposite poles and are now referred to as chromosomes of the future daughter nuclei? ________________

54. During anaphase chromosomes move away from the ____________, the centromere of each chromosome is directed towards ____________.

55. Observe the given diagram of mitotic stage, answer the following questions.

(i) Identify the stage. ____________

(ii) At this stage ____________ split and ____________ separate.

56. Consider the following statements.

Statement I The contraction of the spindle and splitting of the centromeres pull the chromatids.

Statement II Cell organelles like Golgi bodies begin to disappear at the end of anaphase of mitosis.

Choose the correct option from the following.

(a) Statement I is true, but statement II is false ☐

(b) Statement I is false, but statement II is true ☐

57. At the end of anaphase, each chromosome arranged at metaphase plate is split simultaneously.

True ☐ False ☐

58. Metaphase is the shortest phase of mitotic cell division.

True ☐ False ☐

59. The mitotic anaphase differs from metaphase in possessing same number of chromosomes and half number of chromatids.

True ☐ False ☐

60. ____________ is the final stage of karyokinesis in which nuclear envelop develops around the chromosome clusters at each ____________ forming ____________ daughter nuclei.

61. Look at the figure given alongside and answer the following questions.

(i) Identify the stage of mitotic cell division.

____

(ii) Name the cell organelles which reform at this stage.

____

(iii) Chromosomes cluster at opposite spindle poles.

True ☐ False ☐

62. Match the following columns.

Column I (Characteristics)		Column II (Phases of mitosis)	
A.	Chromosomes become arranged in a horizontal plane at the equator	1.	Anaphase
B.	Daughter chromosomes move to opposite poles of the spindle	2.	Prophase
C.	Chromosomes become visible as fine long threads	3.	Telophase
D.	Chromosomes lose their distinctiveness and gradually transform into chromatin network	4.	Metaphase

A.______ B.______ C.______ D.______

63. Give the technical term for the following sentence.

Segregation of duplicated chromosomes into two daughter nuclei. ______

64. Cytokinesis involves the segregation of nuclear content.

True ☐ False ☐

65. Cell furrow appears in the plasma membrane of animal cell during ______

66. Cytoplasmic division occurs *via* cell plate formation in ______

67. What is the significance of the structure labelled as X?

(a) It divides the nucleus into two daughter nuclei. ☐

(b) It forms middle lamella that connects adjacent cells. ☐

(c) It pulls the sister chromatids to the opposite poles. ☐

(d) It divides the cytoplasm centripetally by furrow. ☐

68. When karyokinesis is not followed by cytokinesis, it results in the formation of

______

69. Syncytium is the condition of multinucleate cells.

True ☐ False ☐

70. If the given stage is not succeeded by cytokinesis, where can we find the condition that would arise?

(a) Epidermis of coconut ☐

(b) Endodermis of coconut ☐

(c) Endosperm of coconut ☐

(d) Epiblemma of coconut ☐

71. Formation of liquid endosperm in coconut is the result of no formation of ______ around daughter nuclei.

72. Consider the following statements.

Statement I Cell furrow during cytokinesis proceeds outward and divides the cytoplasm into two.

Statement II Failure of karyokinesis causes multinucleate condition as seen in liquid endosperm of coconut.

Choose the correct option from the following.

(a) Statement I is true, but statement II is false ☐

(b) Both statements I and II are false ☐

73. In some social insects, mitosis can be seen in ____________ cells.

74. Mitosis usually results in the production of ____________ daughter cells with ____________ genetic complement.

75. Mitosis is usually restricted to the ____________ cells.

76. Consider the following statements.

Statement I Mitosis is a characteristic of diploid cells and under no circumstance is observed in haploid cells.

Statement II The regular wear and tear of body cells and tissues is taken care of by the equational division.

Choose the correct option from the following.

(a) Statement I is true, but statement II is false ☐

(b) Statement I is false, but statement II is true ☐

77. Mitosis results into daughter cells with some different genetic constitution.

True ☐ False ☐

78. Give the technical term for the following statement.

The ratio between nuclear content and cytoplasm. ____________

79. ____________ is maintained by a process called cell division.

80. The meristematic cells of plants continuously exhibit the process of ____________

TOPIC 3 Meiosis

NCERT Pg. 125-128

81. The kind of cell division in which chromosome number is reduced to half is called ____________

82. The type of division that ensures the production of haploid phase in the life cycle of sexually reproducing organisms is ____________

83. The precursor cells of meiosis are ____________

84. Some list of cells are given below, mark them as mitosis or meiosis on the basis of division exhibited by them.

(i) Upper layer of epidermal cells. ______________

(ii) Germ cell. ______________

(iii) Cells of lining of gut. ______________

(iv) Blood cells. ______________

85. Meiosis involves two sequential cycles of ______________

86. During meiosis, DNA replication occurs thrice during interphase, M-phase and cytokinesis. (*Rewrite the statement after correcting the underlined phrase.*)

____

87. During meiosis-I, one of the daughter cells receive mixture of maternal and paternal chromosomes.

True ☐ False ☐

88. The important events in meiosis are pairing of ______________ and ______________ between non-sister chromatids of homologous chromosomes.

89. Four haploid cells are formed at the end of meiosis-I only.

True ☐ False ☐

90. Prophase-II of meiotic division is the longest and complex process as compared to similar stage in mitosis. (*Rewrite the statement after correcting the underlined word.*)

____

91. Choose the odd one out among the following.

Leptotene, Crossing over, Zygotene, Pachytene, Diplotene, Diakinesis

____

92. The chromosomes become gradually visible under the light microscope during ______________ stage of meiosis.

93. The compaction of chromosomes occurs during ______________

94. Pairing of homologous chromosomes occurs during leptotene.

True ☐ False ☐

95. Use the technical term for the following sentence.

The process of pairing of chromosomes. ______________

96. Consider the following statements.

Statement I Random chromosomes start pairing up during the zygotene stage of prophase-I.

Statement II Bivalents show distinct structure of four chromatids during the pachytene stage.

Choose the correct option from the following.

(a) Statement I is true, but statement II is false ☐

(b) Statement I is false, but statement II is true ☐

97. The ____________ complex is formed during zygotene stage of meiosis-I.

98. The tetrad or bivalent is formed during zygotene.

True ☐ False ☐

99. How many of the following events do not occur during zygotene?

Formation of synaptonemal complex, Pairing of chromosomes, Appearance of bivalents, Involvement of recombinase

____

100. The complex P is observed during which stage of cell division?

(a) Pachytene ☐

(b) Diplotene ☐

(c) Leptotene ☐

(d) Zygotene ☐

101. Pachytene is relatively longer than zygotene and leptotene.

True ☐ False ☐

102. The paired chromosomes are known as ____________

103. The begining of diplotene is recognised by the dissolution of the

____

104. Name the site where crossing over occurs between non-sister chromatids of the homologous chromosomes.

____

105. Give the biological word for the following sentence.

Exchange of genetic material between the two homologous chromosomes.

____

106. Consider the following statements.

Statement I Recombination nodules mark the sites of genetic exchange during the pachytene stage of prophase-I.

Statement II Crossing over ensures that genetic variability is sustained in species which further contributes to evolution.

Choose the correct option from the following.

(a) Statement I is true, but statement II is false ☐

(b) Both statements I and II are true ☐

107. The crossing over is a non-enzymatic complex process.

True ☐ False ☐

108. Complete the following analogy.

Zygotene : Bivalent : : Pachytene : ____________

109. A mutation in a particular gene formed a defective version of cell division enzyme, that reduced genetic variation in the following generation. The gene encoded for

(a) nuclease ☐ (b) synthetase ☐

(c) polymerase ☐ (d) recombinase ☐

110. The crossed over homologous chromosomes get completely separated at the end of pachytene.

True ☐ False ☐

111. Consider the following figure showing one of the stages of cell cycle and name the structure marked as *A*.

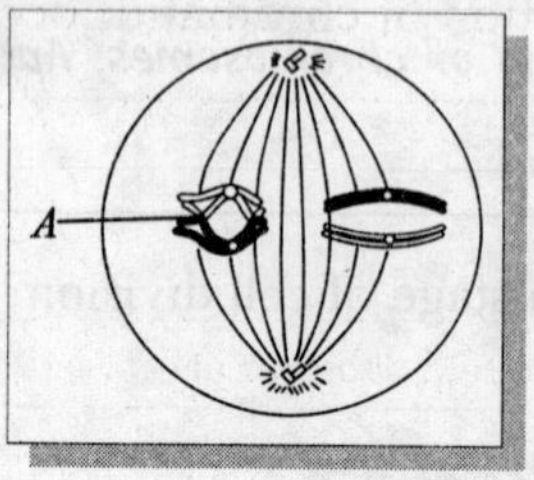

A. ____________

112. The X-shaped structure formed between the non-sister homologous chromosomes is called ____________

113. The meiotic spindle condensation brings out separation of ____________ chromosomes.

114. Consider the following figure and answer the questions given below.

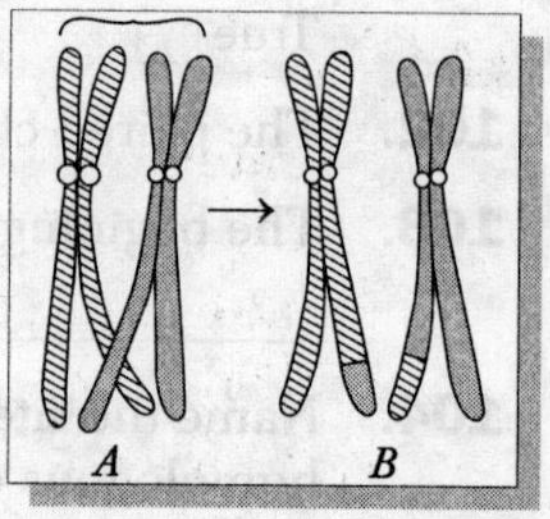

(i) Identify the event *A*. ____________

(ii) At which stage event *A* occurs? ____________

(iii) Event *B* occurs in the substage ____________ of prophase-I of meiosis-I.

115. The diakinesis has intact nuclear envelope and nucleolus.

True ☐ False ☐

116. How many of the following events occur during diakinesis?

Terminalisation of chiasmata, Dissolution of synaptonemal complex, Degeneration of nucleolus, Fully condensed chromosomes

____

117. Name the stages of cell cycle represented by the diagram given below (*A* and *B*).

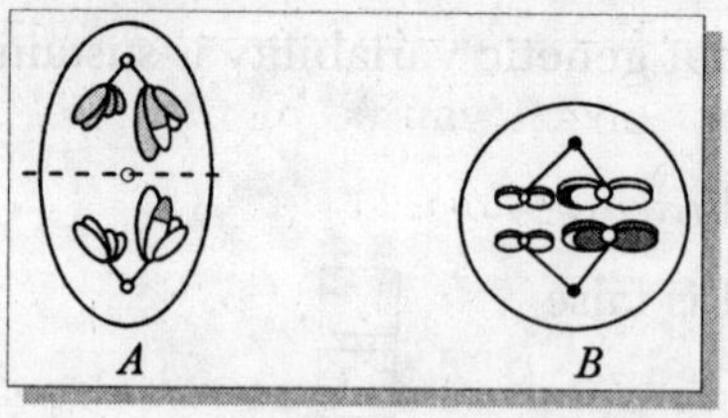

A. ____________

B. ____________

118. Identify the *A* and *B* of the given table considering the given figure.

Number of homologous chromosomes	Number of chromatids	Phase of cell division
Ⓐ	Ⓑ	Telophase-I

A. ____________ B. ____________

119. In which phase of meiosis-II the chromosome become compact?

____

120. Meiosis-II resembles normal mitosis.

True ☐ False ☐

121. Complete the following analogy.

Prophase-I : Centromeric division : ____________

122. Splitting of centromere and hence separation of chromatids occurs during ____________

123. Match the following columns.

Column I	Column II
A. Interkinesis	1. Four haploid daughter cells
B. Metaphase-I	2. Nuclear membrane reappears
C. Telophase-I	3. Stage between two meiotic divisions
D. Telophase-II	4. Chromosome align at equatorial plate

A. ______ B. ______ C. ______ D. ______

124. Consider the following statements.

Statement I Metaphase-II resembles metaphase of mitosis with chromosomes lined up at the equator.

Statement II Cytokinesis at the end of telophase-II produces a tetrad of cells with a ploidy of *n*.

Choose the correct option from the following.

(a) Both statements I and II are true ☐

(b) Both statements I and II are false ☐

125. Tetrad of cells are formed at the end of the ____________ of meiosis.

126. How many of the following are not the significance of meiosis?

Assortment of chromosomes, DNA replication, Crossing over, Mutation, Protein synthesis

____

127. Variations which are important for mutation are caused by meiosis.

(*Rewrite the statement after correcting the underlined word.*) ____________

128. Consider the following statements.

Statement I Both mitotic and meiotic divisions contribute towards evolution of species.

Statement II Crossing over leads to changes and changes accumulating over a long time leads to evolution.

Choose the correct option from the following.

(a) Statement I is true, but statement II is false ☐

(b) Statement I is false, but statement II is true ☐

129. Meiosis results in reduction of chromosome number, maintaining consistency of chromosome number during sexual reproduction and production of genetic variability.

True ☐ False ☐

Assertion-Reason Questions

The following questions consist of two statements- Assertion (A) and Reason (R). Answer these questions by selecting the appropriate option given below.
(a) Both A and R are true and R is the correct explanation of A
(b) Both A and R are true, but R is not the correct explanation of A
(c) A is true, but R is false
(d) A is false, but R is true

***1. Assertion** (A) The interphase is the stage between two mitotic divisions where the cell is metabolically arrested.

Reason (R) In a 24 hour duration, a cell invests minimum time for karyokinesis followed by cytokinesis.

(a) ☐ (b) ☐ (c) ☐ (d) ☐

2. Assertion (A) A cell having 46 chromosomes at the beginning of cell cycle will retain the same number after S-phase.

Reason (R) S-phase is the synthesis phase where synthesis of chromosomes take place in the nucleus of the cell.

(a) ☐ (b) ☐ (c) ☐ (d) ☐

3. Assertion (A) Microscopic observation of the prophase shows distinct chromatids joined at the centromere .

Reason (R) Centrioles that duplicated in the S-phase start moving to the opposite poles in prophase.

(a) ☐ (b) ☐ (c) ☐ (d) ☐

4. Assertion (A) Centromeres of the chromosomes split during the anaphase stage of mitosis.

Reason (R) The contraction of the spindle causes daughter chromosomes to move to opposite poles.

(a) ☐ (b) ☐ (c) ☐ (d) ☐

5. Assertion (A) Microscopic observation reveals telophase to be the reverse of prophase.

Reason (R) Telophase shows rapid condensation of chromosomes and reappearance of nucleolus.

(a) ☐ (b) ☐ (c) ☐ (d) ☐

6. Assertion (A) The progression of cytokinesis in plant cells is centripetal while that in animal cells in centrifugal.

Reason (R) Cell plate acts as the precursor of cell wall, forming the middle lamella that connects adjacent cells.

(a) ☐ (b) ☐ (c) ☐ (d) ☐

7. Assertion (A) Zygotene of prophase-I is the best stage to observe the tetrads under a microscope.

Reason (R) Tetrads are formed between homologous chromosomes by the synaptonemal complex.

(a) ☐ (b) ☐ (c) ☐ (d) ☐

8. Assertion (A) The pachytene stage of prophase-I is important for creating variations in population.

Reason (R) The recombination of the genes between homologous chromosomes is the basis for variations which takes place during pachytene stage.

(a) ☐ (b) ☐ (c) ☐ (d) ☐

9. Assertion (A) Anaphase-II resembles anaphase of mitosis rather than anaphase-I of meiosis.

Reason (R) The contraction of the microtubules pull the daughter chromosomes to opposite poles.

(a) ☐ (b) ☐ (c) ☐ (d) ☐

10. Assertion (A) Meiosis takes place in both germ and somatic cells.

Reason (R) It is a mechanism by which conservation of specific chromosome number is achieved across generations.

(a) ☐ (b) ☐ (c) ☐ (d) ☐

Case Based Questions

1. The given image represents an animal cell at certain stage of division. Observe the image carefully and answer the following questions.

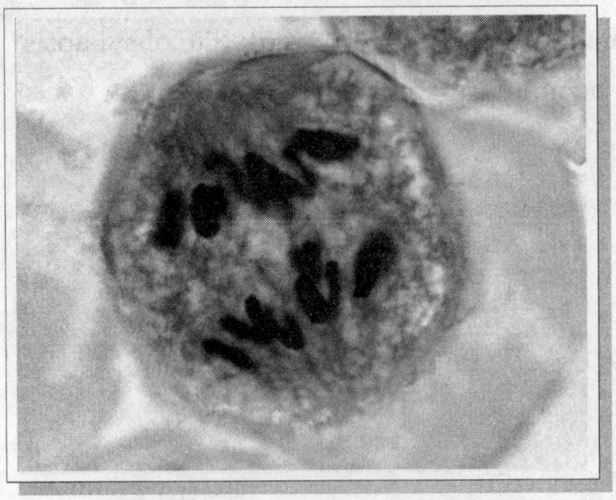

(i) Which particular stage is being represented?

(a) Prophase ☐ (b) Metaphase ☐

(c) Anaphase-I ☐ (d) Anaphase ☐

(ii) Which is the best stage to study the chromosome shape and number?

(a) Metaphase ☐ (b) Anaphase-I ☐

(c) Anaphase-II ☐ (d) Prophase ☐

(iii) Which of the following structures is absent in the given stage?

(a) Spindle fibres ☐ (b) Centrioles ☐

(c) Plasma membrane ☐ (d Nuclear membrane ☐

2. The given image illustrates an electron micrograph of a certain stage of cell division. Study the image carefully and answer the following questions.

(i) Which of the following represents *A* as labelled in the image?

(a) Synaptonemal complex ☐ (b) Recombinant nodule ☐

(c) Centromere ☐ (d) Nucleolar organising region ☐

(ii) What does region *P* represent?

(a) Site of DNA replication ☐ (b) Site of genetic exchange ☐

(c) Site of terminalisation ☐ (d) Site of synapsis ☐

(iii) Which stage is being represented?

(a) Leptotene ☐ (b) Zygotene ☐

(c) Diplotene ☐ (d) Pachytene ☐

COMPETITION EDGE UP

1. Following are the stages of cell division. **[NCERT Pg. 121, NEET 2024]**

A. Gap 2 phase
B. Cytokinesis
C. Synthesis phase
D. Karyokinesis
E. Gap 1 phase

Choose the correct sequence of stages from the options given below:

(a) C-E-D-A-B ☐
(b) E-B-D-A-C ☐
(c) B-D-E-A-C ☐
(d) E-C-A-D-B ☐

2. Given below are two statements:

Statement I Chromosomes become gradually visible under light microscope during leptotene stage.

Statement II The beginning of diplotene stage is recognised by dissolution of synaptonemal complex.

In the light of the above statements, choose the correct answer from the options given below. **[NCERT Pg. 126, NEET 2024]**

(a) Both statement I and statement II are true ☐
(b) Both statement I and statement II are false ☐
(c) Statement I is true, but statement II is false ☐
(d) Statement I is false, but statement II is true ☐

3. Match List I with List II.

	List I (Sub Phases of Prophase-I)		List II (Specific Characters)
A.	Diakinesis	I.	Synaptonemal complex formation
B.	Pachytene	II.	Completion of terminalisation of chiasmata
C.	Zygotene	III.	Chromosomes look like thin threads
D.	Leptotene	IV.	Appearance of recombination nodules

[NCERT Pg. 126, NEET 2024]

(a) A-IV, B-II, C-III, D-I ☐
(b) A-I, B-II, C-IV, D-III ☐
(c) A-II, B-IV, C-I, D-III ☐
(d) A-IV, B-III, C-II, D-I ☐

4. Which of the following stages of meiosis involves division of centromere? **[NCERT Pg. 127, NEET 2023]**

(a) Metaphase-II ☐
(b) Anaphase-II ☐
(c) Telophase ☐
(d) Metaphase-I ☐

5. Among eukaryotes, replication of DNA takes place in **[NCERT Pg 121, NEET 2023]**

(a) S-phase ☐
(b) G_1-phase ☐
(c) G_2-phase ☐
(d) M-phase ☐

6. Which one of the following never occurs during mitotic cell division? **[NCERT Pg. 122 to 125, NEET 2022]**

(a) Movement of centrioles towards opposite poles ☐
(b) Pairing of homologous chromosomes ☐
(c) Coiling and condensation of the chromatids ☐
(d) Spindle fibres attach to kinetochores of chromosomes ☐

7. Select the incorrect statement with reference to mitosis. **[NCERT Pg. 122 to 125, NEET 2022]**

(a) Spindle fibres attach to centromere of chromosomes ☐
(b) Chromosomes decondense at telophase ☐
(c) Splitting of centromere occurs at anaphase ☐
(d) All the chromosomes lie at the equator at metaphase ☐

8. The appearance of recombination nodules on homologous chromosomes during meiosis characterises **[NCERT Pg. 126, NEET 2022]**

(a) bivalent ☐
(b) sites at which crossing over occurs ☐
(c) terminalisation ☐
(d) synaptonemal complex ☐

9. Regarding meiosis, which of the statements is incorrect?

[NCERT Pg. 125, NEET 2022]

(a) DNA replication occurs in S-phase of meiosis-II ☐

(b) Pairing of homologous chromosomes and recombination occurs in meiosis-I ☐

(c) Four haploid cells are formed at the end of meiosis-II ☐

(d) There are two stages in meiosis, meiosis-I and II ☐

10. The fruit fly has 8 chromosomes (2n) in each cell. During interphase of mitosis, if the number of chromosomes at G_1-phase is 8, what would be the number of chromosomes after S-phase ?

[NCERT Pg 121, NEET 2021]

(a) 8 ☐ (b) 16 ☐

(c) 4 ☐ (d) 32 ☐

11. Which stage of meiotic prophase shows terminalisation of chiasmata as its distinctive feature?

[NCERT Pg. 126, NEET 2021]

(a) Leptotene ☐ (b) Zygotene ☐

(c) Diakinesis ☐ (d) Pachytene ☐

12. Which of the following stages of meiosis involves division of centromere?

[NCERT Pg. 127, NEET 2021]

(a) Metaphase-I ☐

(b) Metaphase-II ☐

(c) Anaphase-II ☐

(d) Telophase-II ☐

13. Identify the correct statement with regard to G_1-phase (Gap 1) of interphase. **[NCERT Pg. 121, NEET (Sep.) 2020]**

(a) Reorganisation of all cell components, takes place. ☐

(b) Cell is metabolically active, grows, but does not replicate its DNA ☐

(c) Nuclear division takes place ☐

(d) DNA synthesis or replication takes place ☐

14. Dissolution of the synaptonemal complex occurs during

[NCERT Pg. 126, NEET (Sep.) 2020]

(a) zygotene ☐

(b) diplotene ☐

(c) leptotene ☐

(d) pachytene ☐

Chapter 11

Photosynthesis in Higher Plants

Scan and take Chapter Test

TOPIC 1

What do We Know ? ; Early Experiments

1. Name the physio-chemical process by which plants use light energy to drive the synthesis of organic compound.

____

2. All living forms on earth depends on __________ energy.

3. Photosynthesis is responsible for the release of __________ into the atmosphere by green plants.

4. Photosynthesis transforms __________ energy into __________ energy.

5. Consider the given experiment and identify in which part of the leaf photosynthesis takes place?

Leaf partially covered with black paper → Exposed to sunlight → Tested for starch formation

____

6. Consider the given experiment and answer the following questions.

A leaf enclosed in test tube → Test tube contains (*A*) soaked cotton →

Other half leaf exposed to (*B*) → Placed in sunlight → Tested for the presence of starch

(i) Identify *A* and *B*. __________

(ii) What is the role of *A*? __________

(iii) Which part of the leaf shows positive result for starch? __________

7. Give one conclusion of the above given experiment in Q. 6.

____

8. Name the scientist who proved the essential role of air in the growth of green plants.

____

9. The scientist, who discovered oxygen is

*Concepts of all questions bearing * are important for NEET & CUET*

10. According to Priestley, plants restore the air whatever breathing animals and burning candles remove.

True ☐ False ☐

11. Consider the following statements.

Statement I Priestley performed a set of experiments to reveal the role of air in plant growth from air.

Statement II Jan Ingenhousz provided experimental verification of Priestley's hypothesis.

Choose the correct option from the following.

(a) Both statements I and II are true ☐

(b) Both statements I and II are false ☐

12. "Sunlight is essential for plant" was concluded by __________

13. Jan Ingenhousz did an experiment with an aquatic plant and concluded that all parts of plant release CO_2. (***Rewrite the statement after correcting the underlined words.***)

____

14. Who provided evidence that in green parts of plant glucose is produced and stored as starch ? __________

***15.** The first action spectrum of photosynthesis was observed by__________.

***16.** Write the scientific name of the alga used by Engelman.__________

***17.** Name the scientist who used the following components for setting up an experiment related to photosynthesis.

Prism, Cladophora, Aerobic bacteria

____

18. Consider the following statements.

Statement I The green alga *Spirogyra* was used for Englemann's spectral experiment.

Statement II The action spectrum in Englemann's experiment is a measure of O_2 evolution.

Choose the correct option from the following.

(a) Statement I is true, but statement II is false ☐

(b) Statement I is false, but statement II is true ☐

19. Write the empirical equation representing the process of photosynthesis.

____

***20.** What would happen if in the famous Engelmann's experiment, the aerobic bacteria is replaced with yeast?

(a) Yeast would concentrate at 500 nm ☐

(b) No change in the result ☐

(c) Yeast accumulation will not occur ☐

(d) Yeast would fail to grow in the presence of O_2 ☐

***21.** Name the scientist who proved photosynthesis is a light dependent reaction.

____

22. In photosynthesis, oxygen from an oxidisable compound reduces CO_2 to carbohydrates.

True ☐ False ☐

23. _______________ is the hydrogen donor for purple and green sulphur bacteria.

24. Who demonstrated that O_2 comes from water instead of CO_2 during photosynthesis by using purple and green bacteria in their experiment?

____

25. Write the overall equation for photosynthesis.

____

TOPIC 2

Where Does Photosynthesis Take Place?

NCERT Pg. 136

26. Chloroplasts align along the walls of _______________ cells to get optimum quantity of the incident light.

27. Find the odd one out with respect to chloroplast.

Fluid stroma, Stroma lamellae, Grana, Cisternae

____

28. The membrane system of chloroplast is responsible for _______________ and _______________ synthesis.

29. Stroma of chloroplast is responsible for the synthesis of sugar, which inturn forms starch.

True ☐ False ☐

30. Choose the correct combination of location and synthesised product from the following.

(a) 4 – sugar, 5 – ATP + NADPH ☐

(b) 6 – sugar, 5 – ATP + NADPH ☐

(c) 4 – ATP + NADPH, 5 – sugar ☐

(d) 6 – ATP + NADPH, 5 – sugar ☐

31. Name the reactions which are not directly light driven, but take place in chloroplast.

____

32. Consider the following statements.

Statement I The process of photosynthesis occurs in green, non woody stems apart from leaves.

Statement II Dark reactions indirectly operate upon the products of light reactions.

Choose the correct option from the following.

(a) Both statements I and II are true ☐

(b) Both statements I and II are false ☐

33. Dark reactions are not dependent on ATP and NADPH.

True ☐ False ☐

34. Complete the following analogy.

Light reaction : ______ : : Grana : Stroma : : ______ : Starch

35. Consider the following figure and identify *A*, *B*, *C* and *D*.

A. ______

B. ______

C. ______

D. ______

TOPIC 3

How Many Types of Pigments are Involved in Photosynthesis ?

36. Write the technique that is employed to separate leaf pigments of any green plant.

______

37. Match the following columns.

Column I (Pigments)		Column II (Colour produced on chromatograph)
A. Chlorophyll-*b*	1.	Yellow to yellow orange
B. Carotenoids	2.	Yellow
C. Chlorophyll-*a*	3.	Yellow-green
D. Xanthophylls	4.	Blue-green

A. ______ B. ______ C. ______ D. ______

38.

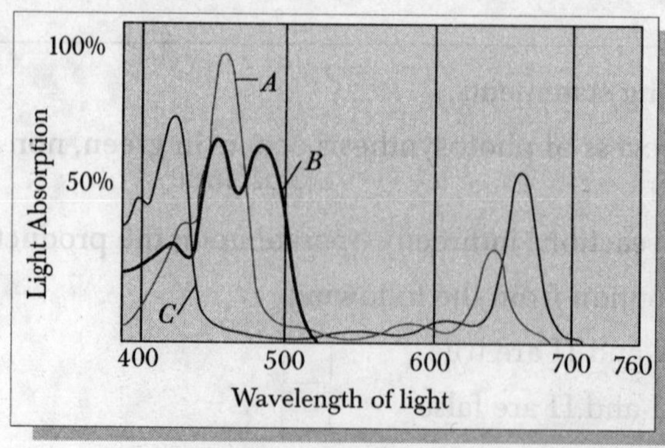

In the image provided, absorption spectra of three photosynthetic pigments along with the wavelength of light are plotted. Which of the following is the chief photosynthetic pigment?

(a) C ☐ (b) A and C ☐ (c) A and B ☐ (d) B ☐

39. The blue and red regions of the spectrum shows __________ (highest/lowest) rate of photosynthesis.

40. Consider the figure given in Q. no. 38 and identify the pigments *A*, *B* and *C*.

A. ______________ B. ______________ C. ______________

41. The absorption spectrum of chlorophyll-*a* is maximum of 660 nm.

True ☐ False ☐

42. ______________ is the chief plant pigment associated with photosynthesis.

43. A graph that plots the effect of different wavelenghts of light on the rate of photosynthesis is called ______________

44. Write the colour spectrum of the first action spectrum of photosynthesis.

____

***45.** Most of the photosynthesis takes place in the blue and red regions of VIBGYOR.

True ☐ False ☐

46. Consider the following statements.

Statement I Both chlorophyll-*a* and *b* molecules appear blue-green on the chromatogram.

Statement II Absorption spectra of chlorophyll-*a* coincides with the action spectra of photosynthesis.

Choose the correct option from the following.

(a) Statement I is true, but statement II is false ☐

(b) Statement I is false, but statement II is true ☐

47. Absorption spectrum of chlorophyll-*a* and the action spectrum of photosynthesis are identical.

True ☐ False ☐

***48.** Write the correct order of light given below on the basis of rate of photosynthesis in decreasing order.

Green, Red, Blue

____

49. What is the wavelength of radiations in visible spectrum? ______________

***50.** Write the range of wavelength in which the rate of photosynthesis is maximum.

____

51. Give a collective term for the following pigments.

Chlorophyll-b, Xanthophylls, Carotenoids

____

52. ________________ pigments transfer the energy to chlorophyll-*a*.

53. Accessory pigments protect chlorophyll-*a* from ________________.

54. Arrange the following in the sequence of energy transfer in photosynthesis.

Phycocyanin, Chlorophyll-a, Carotenoid, Phycoerythrin

____

TOPIC 4

What is Light Reaction ?

NCERT Pg. 138

55. Write the other name for light reaction.________________

56. Arrange the following in the order of its occurrence.

Water splitting, Light absorption, Oxygen release, Formation of ATP and NADPH

____

57. Write the full form of LHC.________________

58. LHCs are present within ________________ and ________________ these are made up of hundreds of pigment molecules bound to ________________.

59. Which of the following statements is not correct?

(a) The antennae pigments protect the chief pigment against photooxidative damage. ☐

(b) The LHC allows wider usage of the spectrum for improving photosynthetic efficiency. ☐

(c) The accessory pigments absorb and transfer photons to the reaction centres. ☐

(d) The reaction centres differ from each other in their absorption maxima. ☐

60. Consider the following statements.

Statement I The LHC pigments absorb incident light of different wavelengths in order to make photosynthesis efficient.

Statement II Several accessory pigments make up the LHC complex of the photosystems.

Choose the correct option from the following.

(a) Both statements I and II are true ☐

(b) Both statements I and II are false ☐

61. How many of the following constitute photosystems (PS)?

Reaction centre, Antennae, ATP synthase, H_2O

____

***62.** Consider the following statements.

Statement I Chlorophyll-*a*, chlorophyll-*b*, xanthophyll and carotenoids form the antennae complex.

Statement II The single chlorophyll-*a* moleule forms the reaction centre.

Choose the correct option from the following.

(a) Statement I is true, but statement II is false ☐

(b) Statement I is false, but statement II is true ☐

***63.** PS-I has absorption peak at ______ and PS-II has absorption peak at ______ .

64. Given figure depicts the Light Harvesting Complex (LHC). Observe the figure and answer the following questions.

(i) Identify *A*, *B* and *C*.

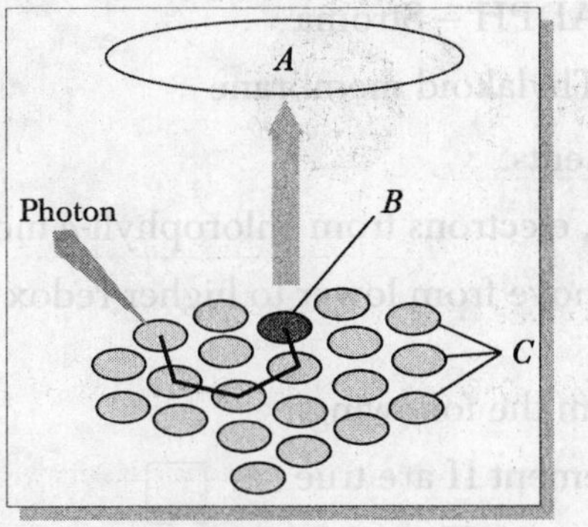

A. ______

B. ______

C. ______

(ii) Name the molecule which forms part *B*. ______

TOPIC 5

The Electron Transport

NCERT Pg. 138-142

65. Electron transport system consists of ______ proteins.

66. Movement of electron in the ETS is downhill in terms of an oxidation-reduction or redox potential scale.

True ☐ False ☐

67. When the chloroplast pigments absorb light, electrons become excited and move ______ in the ETS.

***68.** The electrons in the reaction centre of ______ are excited simultaneously with absorption of light of wavelength ______ .

***69.** Which of the following events, if stopped can stop the electron transport all together?

(a) Photophosphorylation of ATP ☐ (b) Photolysis of water ☐

(c) Reduction of $NADP^+$ ☐ (d) Low CO_2 concentration ☐

***70.** The primary acceptor of electron is located on the ______ (inner/outer) side of the membrane.

71. Arrange the following events of Z-scheme according to the transfer of electrons.

PS-II, Down the electron transport chain to PS-I, Uphill to the acceptor, Down hill to $NADP^+$, Transfer to another acceptor, Excitation of electrons

______

***72.** In Z-scheme of light reaction, the participating pigment systems are ____________ and ____________

***73.** The electron transfer from PS-II to PS-I reduce____________

***74.** Which of the following represents the site of formation of oxygen and NADPH in photochemical reaction?

(a) O_2 – Thylakoid membrane, NADPH – Thylakoid lumen ☐

(b) O_2 –Thylakoid lumen, NADPH – Thylakoid membrane ☐

(c) O_2 – Thylakoid lumen, NADPH – Stroma ☐

(d) O_2 – Stroma, NADPH – Thylakoid membrane ☐

75. Consider the following statements.

Statement I Upon excitation, electrons from chlorophyll-*a* move to a higher energy state.

Statement II The electrons move from lower to higher redox potential through the transport system.

Choose the correct option from the following.

(a) Both statements I and statement II are true ☐

(b) Both statements I and statement II are false ☐

***76.** Given below is the diagrammatic representation of the Z-scheme of light reaction of photosynthesis. Identify *A, B, C* and *D.*

A
B
Light
e^- acceptor
e^- acceptor
D
C
ADP+Pi ATP
Electron transport system
LHC
LHC
$H_2O \rightarrow 2e^- + 2H^+ + [O]$

A. ____________

B. ____________

C. ____________

D. ____________

***77.** Which one directly transfers electrons to $NADP^+$ during light reaction?

(a) PS I ☐ (b) PS II ☐

(c) Cytochromes ☐ (d) Both PS I and PS II ☐

***78.** Write the chemical compound/molecule which supply electrons continuously to PS-II.

____

***79.** The cyclic phosphorylation pathway is operational in which of the following sites?

(a) Thylakoid lumen ☐ (b) Stromal lamellae ☐

(c) Thylakoid membrane ☐ (d) Grana lamellae ☐

***80.** During the light reaction, one molecule of water splits into H^+, O_2 and electrons. (*Rewrite the statement after correcting the underlined phrase.*)

____

***81.** If green plants are incubated with O^{18} labelled water, which molecule (photosynthesis product) will become radioactive? ________________

***82.** The process of cyclic photophosphorylation involves synthesis of ATP coupled with electron transport activated by PS-I. The given process occurs because

(a) NADP reductase and PS-II are absent ☐

(b) there is loss of energy ☐

(c) electrons were not excited ☐

(d) reaction centres were oxidised ☐

***83.** How many H^+ ions are formed from 12 water molecules during non-cyclic photophosphorylation? | 12, 24, 36, 48 |

____

***84.** Consider the following statements.

Statement I The Z-scheme represents cyclical flow of electrons from PS-I to PS-II.

Statement II The final electron acceptor in Z-scheme of photosynthesis is NADPH.

Choose the correct option from the following.

(a) Both statements I and II are true ☐

(b) Both statements I and II are false ☐

85. Select the appropriate words from the box given below to complete the statement.

Water, Oxygen, Carbon dioxide, Photosystem-I, Photosystem-II, Light harvesting centre

The electrons removed from ____________ are provided by __________ by splitting of __________, which creates __________.

***86.** The water splitting complex is associated with PS-II.

True ☐ False ☐

***87.** Consider the following statements.

Statement I Splitting of water ensures continuous flow of electrons to PS-II.

Statement II Splitting of water increases proton concentration in the thylakoid lumen.

Choose the correct option from the following.

(a) Both statements I and II are true ☐

(b) Both statements I and II are false ☐

***88.** Water splitting complex is located on the __________ (inner/outer) side of the membrane of __________ (thylakoid/stroma).

89. The ETC of photosynthesis is bound to ________________ membrane.

90. __________ membranes possess PS-I only, whereas __________ membranes possess both PS-I and PS-II. In cyclic photophosphorylation only ______ works.

***91.** Name the process of synthesis of ATP in cell. __________

***92.** Name any two ATP synthesising organelles. __________

***93.** Write the process where two photosystems work in series from PS-II to PS-I. __________

***94.** When only PS-I is functional, electrons are circulated within the photosystem and the photooxidation occurs due to the cyclic flow of electrons.
(*Rewrite the statement after correcting the underlined word.*)
____

95. Stroma lamellae lacks NADP reductase enzyme.

True ☐ False ☐

96. Complete the following analogy.
Non-cyclic photophosphorylation : Cyclic photophosphorylation : : __________ : ATP

97. __________ photophosphorylation can also occurs when wavelength beyond 680 nm is available for excitation.

98. Consider the following figure of cyclic phosphorylation, answer the given questions.
(i) Identify *A*, *B* and *C*.

C
Light
ATP
e⁻ acceptor
B
A
Chlorophyll P700

A. __________
B. __________
C. __________

(ii) The excited electrons pass onto $NADP^+$.

True ☐ False ☐

***99.** Name the hypothesis of ATP synthesis. __________

100. ATP synthesis is linked to development of a proton gradient across the membrane.

True ☐ False ☐

101. During ATP synthesis, __________ accumulate towards the inside of the thylakoid membrane.

***102.** Protons accumulate in the intermembrane space of the <u>chloroplast</u> when electrons move through ETS during respiration.
(*Rewrite the statement after correcting the underlined word.*)

____

***103.** According to the chemiosmotic theory given by Mitchell, ATPs are synthesised on the membranes of chloroplast due to

(a) K^+ gradient ☐ (b) H^+ gradient ☐
(c) e^- gradient ☐ (d) Na^+ gradient ☐

***104.** Select the appropriate words from the box given below to complete the following paragraph

Outer, Lumen, Inner, Hydrogen, Thylakoid, ER, Potassium, Matrix

Splitting of water takes place on the __________ side of the __________ membrane by which proton or __________ ions are produced that accumulate within the __________ of the thylakoids.

***105.** Consider the given below reaction that shows splitting of water molecule.

$$H_2O \rightarrow 2H^+ + 2e^- + 1/2O_2$$

Choose the fate of H^+ ions thus produced from the above reaction.

(a) Reduction of $NADP^+$ ☐
(b) Formation of proton gradient ☐
(c) Phosphorylation of ATP ☐
(d) Phosphorylation of PS-I ☐

***106.** The NADP reductase enzyme is located on the __________ side of the membrane.

***107.** Complete the following analogy.
Proton increase : __________ : : Proton decrease : Stroma

***108.** After passing on to the electron carrier on the inner side of the membrane, the proton is released into the __________ (inner/outer) side or the __________ (lumen/stroma) side of the membrane.

***109.** The pH of the lumen decreases, while proton gradient is formed across thylakoid membrane.

True ☐ False ☐

110. Proton gradient is broken down due to __________ across the membrane to the stroma.

111. Name the transmembrane channel of the ATPase.__________

112. Name the two parts of ATP synthase enzyme. __________

113. Write the location of CF_0 and CF_1 particles with respect to the thylakoid membrane. (Inside/Outside)

____

114. What is the role of CF_0?

____

115. The breakdown of the proton gradient provides ______________ to cause conformational change in the CF_1 particles of the ATPase.

116. Complete the following sequence.

Splitting of water → Proton pump → (A) → Breakdown of proton gradient → Conformational change of (B) of ATPase → Energy packed ATP release by (C) enzyme

A. ______________ B. ______________ C. ______________

117. Which of the following statement is correct about the chemiosmotic theory?

(a) Chemiosmosis refers to movement of ions against their electrochemical gradient ☐

(b) The primary electron acceptor transfers electron to an electron carrier in stroma ☐

(c) The NADP reductase enzyme picks up hydrogen ions from the thylakoid lumen ☐

(d) Breaking of the proton gradient drives the synthesis of ATP by ATP synthase ☐

118. ATPase has channel that allows electron diffusion back across the membrane.
(*Rewrite the statement after correcting the underlined words.*)

____

119. ATP will be used immediately in the biosynthetic reaction for fixing ______________ and synthesis of ______________.

TOPIC 6

Where are the ATP and NADPH Used?

NCERT Pg. 142-145

120. Write the major products of light reaction.

____

121. Name the phase where ATP and NADPH are used to drive the processes leading to the synthesis of sugar.

____

122. For one CO_2 molecule fixation, ______________ (one/two/three) ATP and ______________ (one/two/three) $NADPH_2$ are used in Calvin cycle.

123. Name the scientist who discovered 3 carbon organic acid as first CO_2 fixation product.

____

124. Answer the following questions with respect to mechanism of photosynthesis.

(i) Write the radioactive atom used by Calvin in his algal photosynthesis studies.

____

(ii) Write the full form of PGA. ______________________________

(iii) Write the chemical name of the first product identified by Calvin as first CO_2 fixation product. ______________________________

(iv) Write the two main pathways of CO_2 assimilation during photosynthesis.

______________________________.

125. Consider the reaction given below

$$\text{Ribulose 1, 5-bisphosphate} \xrightarrow[Q]{CO_2} P$$

Choose the correct combination from the following.

(a) P-3 PGA Q-RuBisCO ☐ (b) P-PEP Q-RuBisCO ☐

(c) P-PEP Q-PEP carboxylase ☐ (d) P-OAA Q-PEP carboxylase ☐

***126.** In C_4 plants the first stable product of CO_2 fixation is ______________________________

***127.** Consider the following statements.

Statement I The biosynthetic phase indirectly depends on light.

Statement II The products of light reactions are used up in sugar synthesis.

Choose the correct option from the following.

(a) Both statements I and II are true ☐

(b) Both statements I and II are false ☐

***128.** The pathway of CO_2 assimilation in which first product is a four carbon atom acid is called ______________________________.

***129.** How many turns of Calvin cycle are needed to make one molecule of glucose?

____

***130.** Calvin cycle does not occur in all photosynthetic plants.

True ☐ False ☐

***131.** Write the primary acceptor of CO_2 in Calvin cycle.

____

***132.** Write the three main stages of Calvin cycle.

____

***133.** ______________________________ is the most crucial step of Calvin cycle.

***134.** In carboxylation, ______________________________ is utilised for carboxylation of RuBP.

***135.** Carboxylation results in the formation of three molecules of 3-PGA.

True ☐ False ☐

***136.** Consider the following statements.

Statement I RuBisCO is the most abundant enzyme in the world.

Statement II The active site of RuBisCO can bind both CO_2 and O_2.

Choose the correct option from the following.

(a) Both statements I and II are true ☐

(b) Both statements I and II are false ☐

***137.** Name the enzyme involved in carboxylation of RuBP. ________

***138.** RuBisCO creates organic carbon from inorganic carbon dioxide in the air.

True ☐ False ☐

***139.** RuBisCO has oxygenation activity only.

True ☐ False ☐

***140.** Name the step of Calvin cycle at which 3-PGA molecule converted into glyceraldehyde-3-phosphate.

____

***141.** Reduction step in the Calvin cycle leads to the formation of ________.

***142.** Reduction involves utilisation of 2 molecules of ATP for ________ and two of NADPH for ________ per CO_2 molecule fixed.

***143.** Fixation of six molecules of CO_2 are required for the formation of <u>six molecules of</u> glucose. (*Rewrite the statement after correcting the underlined words.*)

____

***144.** Study the following figure and identify *A*, *B*, *C* and *D*.

Atmosphere
$CO_2 + H_2O$
A
ADP
(1) Carboxylation
(3) Regeneration
B
ATP
ATP + NADPH
(2) *C*
D
Sucrose and starch
ADP + P_i + $NADP^+$

A. ________

B. ________

C. ________

D. ________

***145.** Complete the table with respect to Calvin cycle.

In	Out
6 CO_2	1 glucose
(A) ATP	(B) ADP
12NADPH	(C) NADP

A. ________

B. ________

C. ________

146. Dark reaction is a misnomer name for biosynthetic phase.

True ☐ False ☐

***147.** Which of the following steps consume ATP?

(a) Carboxylation ☐ (b) Reduction ☐

(c) Regeneration ☐ (d) Both (b) and (c) ☐

148. How many molecules of ATP would be consumed in 5 turns of the Calvin cycle?

(a) 5 ☐ (b) 10 ☐ (c) 15 ☐ (d) 20 ☐

TOPIC 7

The C_4 Pathway

NCERT Pg. 145-147

149. C_4-plants also use C_3-pathway on the main biosynthetic pathway.

True ☐ False ☐

***150.** Leaves of C_4-plant cannot tolerate high temperature.

True ☐ False ☐

151. Name the important process that lacks in C_4-plants. ________

***152.** C_4-leaves have greater productivity of energy.
(*Rewrite the statement after correcting the underlined word.*)

____

***153.** Write the name of cells around vascular bundles of C_4-plants.

____

***154.** Write the technical name of the leaf anatomy of C_4-plants.

____

***155.** Complete the following analogy.

$C_3 : C_4 ::$ ________ : 4- carbon primary CO_2 acceptor.

***156.** The bundle sheath cells of C_4-plants have large number of ________ thick walls ________ to gas exchange and ________ intercellular space.

***157.** Write the other name for C_4-pathway. ________

***158.** How many of the following are C_4 plants?

Sugarcane, Potato, Oat, Sorghum, Maize, Wheat, Rice

____

***159.** How many of the following plants show Kranz anatomy?

Sorghum, Maize, Sugarcane, Potato, Rice, Oat, Pearl millet

***160.** Name the CO_2 acceptor in C_4 pathway. ________

***161.** PEP is present in ________ cells.

162. Consider the following statements.

I. First fixation product in C_4 cycle is a 2-carbon organic acid.

II. NADP reductase enzyme is located on the stroma side of the membrane.

III. OAA was the first stable product of CO_2 fixation which is an organic acid containing 5 carbon atom.

IV. During light reaction the primary acceptor of electron which is located towards the outer side of the membrane transfers its electron not to an electron carrier but to a H^+ carrier.

Choose the incorrect set of statements from the options given below.

(a) II and III ☐ (b) I and IV ☐

(c) I and III ☐ (d) III and IV ☐

***163.** Name the enzyme responsible for primary CO_2 fixation in C_4 pathway.

____

***164.** Mesophyll cells have no __________ enzyme.

***165.** The oxaloacetic acid is present in the __________ cells.

***166.** Consider the following statements.

Statement I PEP carboxylase is found in the mesophyll cells of the leaves.

Statement II Oxaloacetic acid is the first stable product of C_4-pathway.

Choose the correct option from the following.

(a) Both statements I and II are true ☐

(b) Both statements I and II are false ☐

***167.** OAA form malic acid and aspartic acid in the mesophyll cells.

True ☐ False ☐

***168.** Name the location where the C_4 acids are broken down to release CO_2.

____

***169.** Which of the following can be found in the bundle sheath cell ?

(a) PEP carboxylase ☐ (b) Oxaloacetic acid ☐

(c) RuBisCO ☐ (d) Malic acid ☐

***170.** The 3-carbon molecules are transported back to the mesophyll where it converts to aspartic acid.

(*Rewrite the statement after correcting the underlined words.*)

____

***171.** The CO_2 released in the bundle sheath cells enter the Calvin cycle.

True ☐ False ☐

***172.** Name the enzyme present in bundle sheath cells. __________

173. Calvin cycle takes place in __________ of C_4 plants.

***174.** Consider the following figure of Hatch and Slack pathway and identify *A, B, C* and *D.*

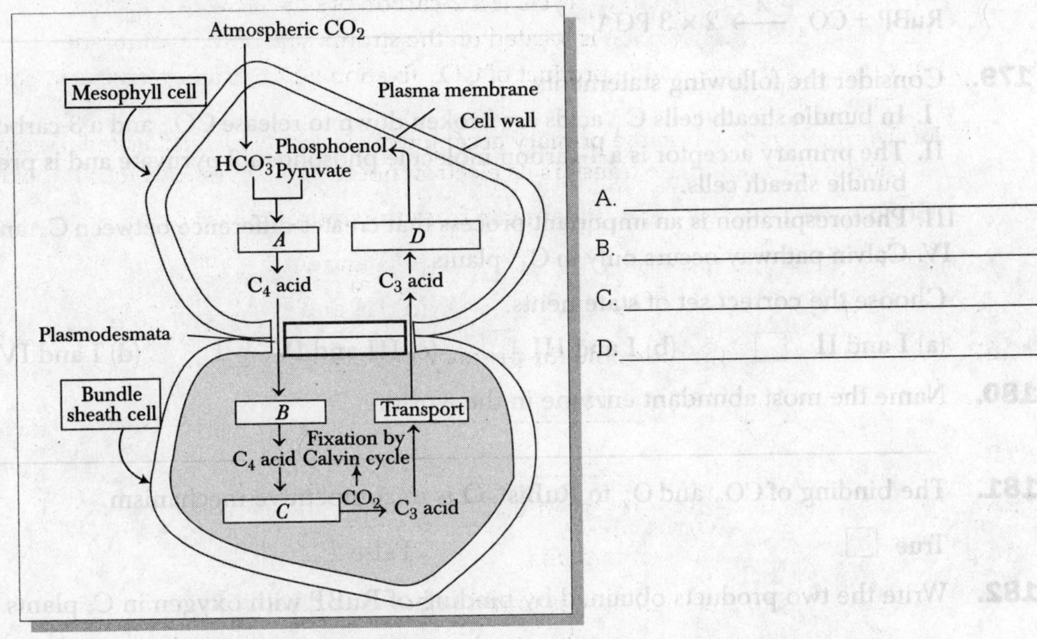

A. __________

B. __________

C. __________

D. __________

175. Which of the following statement about C_4-plants is not correct?

(a) C_4-plants are adapted to withstand dry tropical conditions ☐

(b) Bundle sheath cells compactly arranged in C_4-plants ☐

(c) The C_3 pathway operates in the mesophyll cells of C_4-plants ☐

(d) Oxaloacetic acid is the first stable product of C_4 pathway. ☐

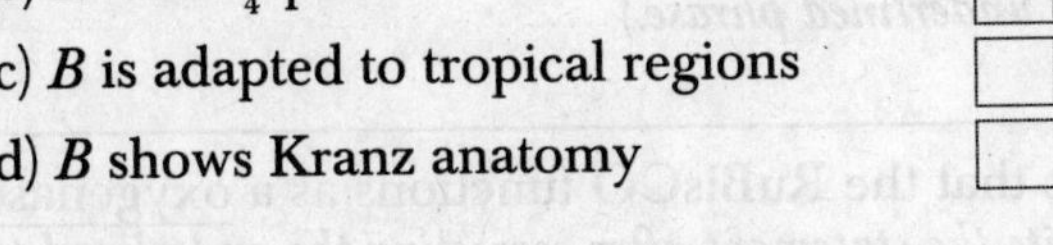

176. In C_4-plants photorespiration does not occur. (*Give reason*)

____

177. In the graph alongside, plant *A* and *B* shows different rates of photosynthesis with temperature. Which of the following options is correct with respect to the graph?

(a) *A* shows greater photorespiration ☐

(b) *A* is a C_4-plant ☐

(c) *B* is adapted to tropical regions ☐

(d) *B* shows Kranz anatomy ☐

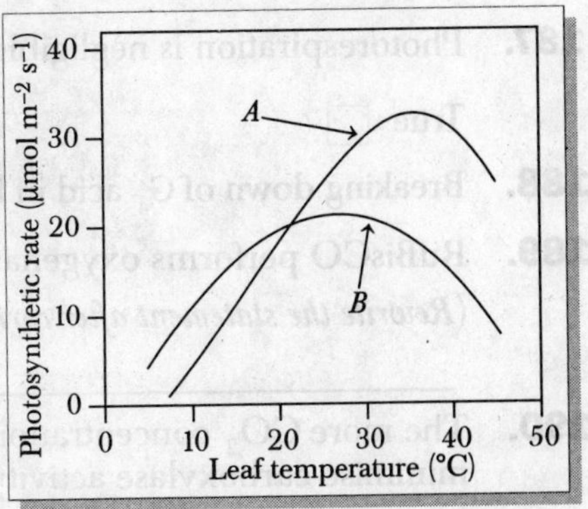

178. Complete the following equation by identifying *A*.

$RuBP + CO_2 \xrightarrow{A} 2 \times 3\ PGA$ ____________

179. Consider the following statements.

I. In bundle sheath cells C_4 acids are broken down to release CO_2 and a 3-carbon molecule.
II. The primary acceptor is a 4-carbon molecule phosphoenol pyruvate and is present in bundle sheath cells.
III. Photorespiration is an important process that creates difference between C_3 and C_4 plants.
IV. Calvin pathway occurs only in C_3 plants.

Choose the correct set of statements.

(a) I and II ☐ (b) I and III ☐ (c) III and IV ☐ (d) I and IV ☐

180. Name the most abundant enzyme in the world.

____

181. The binding of CO_2 and O_2 to RuBisCO is uncompetitive mechanism.

True ☐ False ☐

182. Write the two products obtained by binding of RuBP with oxygen in C_3 plants.

____

183. Photorespiration in ________ plants results in the release of ________ with utilisation of ________.

184. Photorespiration is a wasteful process in C_3-plants.

True ☐ False ☐

185. Consider the following figure and identify *A, B* and *C*.

CO_2 [RuBisCO] O_2

Low temperature
High $CO_2 : O_2$ ratio → [*A*]

High temperature
(*B*): O_2 ratio → [*C*]

A. ____________
B. ____________
C. ____________

186. ____________ (High/Low) photorespiration would occur at low CO_2 concentration in C_3 plants.

187. Photorespiration is negligible in C_3 plants at low light intensities.

True ☐ False ☐

188. Breaking down of C_4 acid in bundle sheath cell ________ intracellular CO_2 concentration.

189. RuBisCO performs oxygenase activity at high CO_2 concentration.
(*Rewrite the statement after correcting the underlined phrase.*)

____

190. The more CO_2 concentration ensures that the RuBisCO functions as a oxygenase, minimise carboxylase activity. (*Rewrite the statement after correcting the underlined phrase.*)

____

TOPIC 9

Factors Affecting Photosynthesis

191. Find the odd one out with respect to internal factors affecting photosynthesis.

Sunlight availability, Mesophyll cells orientation, Number of chloroplasts, Orientation of leaves

____

192. The _______________ factors depend on the genetic predisposition and the growth of the plant.

193. Give a collective term for the following.

CO_2 *concentration, Sunlight, Temperature, Water*

____

194. When the water availability of soil reduces, the rate of photosynthesis decreases due to reduction in

(a) Ambient temperature ☐ (b) Number of abaxial stomata ☐
(c) Enzymatic reactions ☐ (d) Carbon dioxide unavailability ☐

195. Name the factor that comes into effect when several factors affect any biochemical process.

____

196. As a plant performs photosynthesis, (no/two/several) factors affect its rate simultaneously.

____

197. The rate of the biochemical process will be determined by the factor that is nearest to its _______ value.

198. The relationship between incident light and CO_2 fixation rate is _______________ (hyperbolic/parabolic/linear).

199. Light saturation occurs at 20% of full sunlight.

True ☐ False ☐

200. Given below are few statements.

I. C_4 plants have a mechanism that increases the concentration of CO_2 at the enzyme site.
II. Intracellular concentration of CO_2 ensures that the RuBisCO functions as a carboxylase minimising the oxygenase activity.
III. Saturation of light occurs at 20 per cent of the full sunlight.
IV. Decrease in incident light beyond a point causes the breakdown of chlorophyll and a increase in photosynthesis.

Choose the option with incorrect set of statements.

(a) I and II ☐ (b) II and IV ☐
(c) II and III ☐ (d) III and IV ☐

201. At higher light intensity, CO_2 fixation rate does not increase as the factors becomes altered. (*Rewrite the statement after correcting the underlined word.*)

____

202. Increase in incident light beyond ______ point causes breakdown of chlorophyll and decrease in ______.

203. Increase in CO_2 concentration upto ______ (0.05/0.04) per cent can cause an ______ (increase/decrease) in CO_2 fixation rates.

204. Availability of CO_2 level is limiting to the C_4 plants.

True ☐ False ☐

205. C_3-plants respond to ______ (higher/lower) CO_2 concentration by showing ______ (increased/decreased) rates of photosynthesis leading to ______ (higher/lower) productivity.

206. Name any two greenhouse crops.

____

207. The light reactions are more sensitive to temperature than dark reactions. (*Rewrite the statement after correcting the underlined words.*)

____

208. Write the limiting factor among the following.

Green leaves, Optimal light, Optimum CO_2 *concentration, Low temperature*

____

209. The C_4 plants respond to ______ (higher/lower) temperature and show ______ (higher/lower) rate of photosynthesis and C_3 have a much ______ (lower/higher) temperature optimum.

210. Complete the following analogy.

Tropical plants : Temperate plants : : ______ : Lower temperature optimum

211. Water stress causes stomatal closure by reducing CO_2 availability.

True ☐ False ☐

212. Given below are few statements.

I. C_3 plants respond to lower temperatures and show higher rate of photosynthesis.

II. Tropical plants have a higher temperature optimum than the plants adapted to temperate climates.

III. Water stress causes the stomata to close hence increasing the O_2 availability.

IV. Water stress increases the surface area of the leaves.

Choose the option with incorrect set of statements.

(a) I and IV ☐ (b) II and IV ☐

(c) II and III ☐ (d) III and IV ☐

Assertion-Reason Questions

The following questions consist of two statements- Assertion (A) and Reason (R). Answer these questions by selecting the appropriate option given below.
(a) Both A and R are true and R is the correct explanation of A
(b) Both A and R are true, but R is not the correct explanation of A
(c) A is true, but R is false
(d) A is false, but R is true

*1. **Assertion** (A) Engelmann in his experiment with an alga, developed the first absorption spectrum.

Reason (R) In Englemann's experiment, the bacteria concentrated at the site of oxygen evolution.

(a) ☐ (b) ☐ (c) ☐ (d) ☐

*2. **Assertion** (A) ATP and NADPH are produced in the grana of the membrane system.

Reason (R) The enzymatic synthesis of sugar in the stroma is completely light independent.

(a) ☐ (b) ☐ (c) ☐ (d) ☐

*3. **Assertion** (A) In Z-scheme, the PS-II reaction centre receives a continuous supply of electrons.

Reason (R) PS-II gets a steady supply of electrons from splitting of water molecules.

(a) ☐ (b) ☐ (c) ☐ (d) ☐

*4. **Assertion** (A) The proton gradient established across the thylakoid membrane is essential for ATP synthesis.

Reason (R) The concentration of proton on the stromal side decreases as more H^+ is used by NADP reductase.

(a) ☐ (b) ☐ (c) ☐ (d) ☐

*5. **Assertion** (A) The products of photochemical phase are used up in the biosynthetic phase.

Reason (R) In biosynthetic phase, the primary acceptor of CO_2 is a three carbon molecule PGA.

(a) ☐ (b) ☐ (c) ☐ (d) ☐

*6. **Assertion** (A) 6 molecules of CO_2 should be fixed in 6 turns of the cycle to form 1 molecule of glucose.

Reason (R) To fix 3 molecules of CO_2, 3 ATP molecules are consumed in the reduction step.

(a) ☐ (b) ☐ (c) ☐ (d) ☐

*7. **Assertion** (A) The regeneration of RubBP forms the last step in the C_3 pathway of photosynthesis.

Reason (R) RuBP regeneration during the C_3 cycle requires one ATP molecule for phosphorylation.

(a) ☐ (b) ☐ (c) ☐ (d) ☐

***8.** **Assertion** (A) In C_4-plants, Hatch Slack pathway serves as the main biosynthetic pathway.

Reason (R) The mesophyll cells of C_4-plants uses PEP carboxylase for carbon fixation step.

(a) ☐ (b) ☐ (c) ☐ (d) ☐

***9.** **Assertion** (A) The yield and productivity in C_3-plants is much higher than C_4-plants.

Reason (R) C_4-plants increases CO_2 concentration in the bundle sheath cells allowing RuBisCO to function as carboxylase.

(a) ☐ (b) ☐ (c) ☐ (d) ☐

***10.** **Assertion** (A) Atmospheric carbon dioxide is the major limiting factor for photosynthesis.

Reason (R) The carbon dioxide concentration is very low (0.04%) in the atmosphere.

(a) ☐ (b) ☐ (c) ☐ (d) ☐

Case Based Questions

1. Observe the given image and answer the following questions.

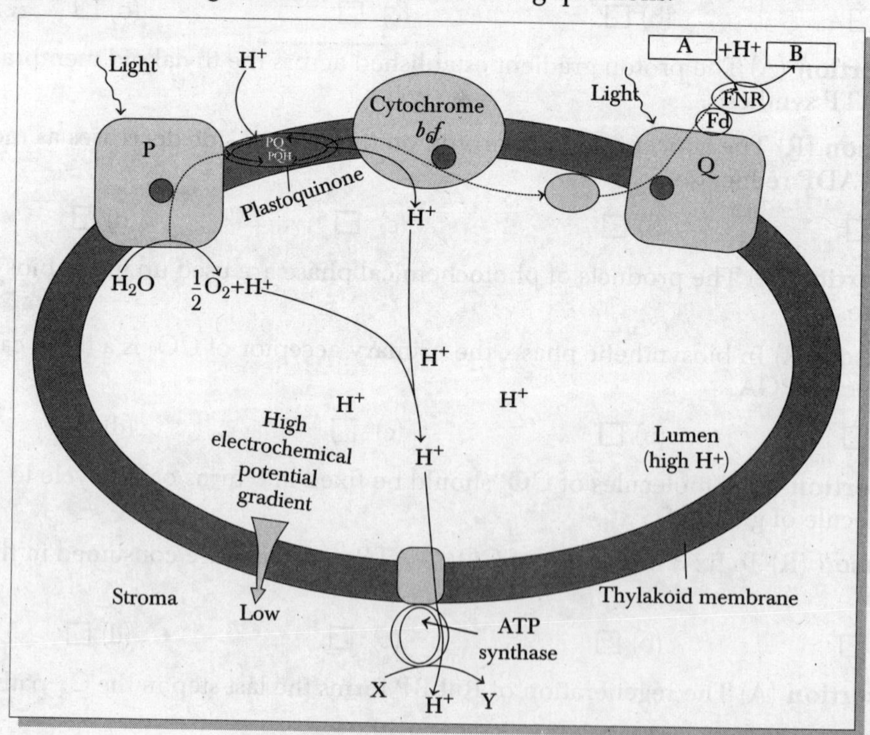

(i) Choose the correct combination of Q and the enzyme that catalyses A to B?

(a) Q-P680, Enzyme - NAP reductase

(b) Q-P700, Enzyme - NAP reductase

(c) Q-P680, Enzyme - ATP synthase

(d) Q-P700, Enzyme - ATP synthase

(ii) In the conversion of X to Y, which of the following is consumed?

(a) Phosphoric acid

(b) Inorganic phosphate

(c) NADP

(d) Reduced NADP

(iii) Which of the following establishes the electrochemical gradient?

(a) H^+ in lumen $>$ H^+ in stroma

(b) H^+ in lumen $<$ H^+ in stroma

(c) H^+ in lumen $=$ H^+ in stroma

(d) H^+ in lumen $=$ H^+ in stroma

***2.** With reference to the graph provided answer the following questions.

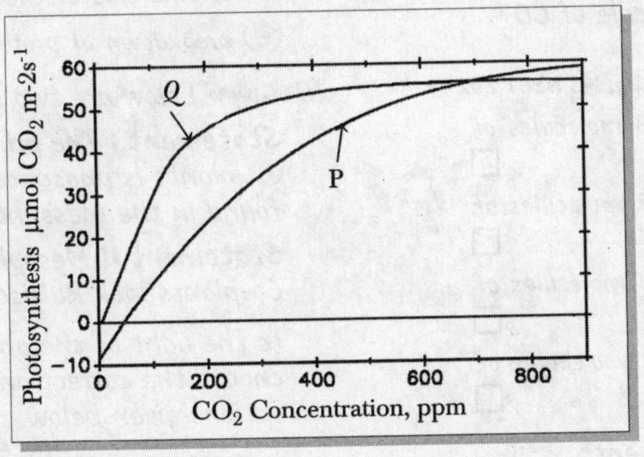

(i) Which of the following plants can be represented by *Q*?

(a) Tobacco

(b) Wheat

(c) *Sorghum*

(d) Bajra

(ii) Which of the following is not produced by Q?

(a) Phosphoglycolate

(b) Phosphoglycerate

(c) Oxaloacetic acid

(d) Malic acid

(iii) A transverse section of which of the following would show elongated palisade mesophyll?

(a) Only P

(b) Both P and Q

(c) Only Q

(d) Absent in both

COMPETITION EDGE UP

1. Which of the following are required for the dark reaction of photosynthesis?

A. Light B. Chlorophyll

C. CO_2 D. ATP

E. NADPH

Choose the correct answer from the options given below

[NCERT Pg. 142, NEET 2024]

(a) A, B and C only ☐

(b) B, C and D only ☐

(c) C, D and E only ☐

(d) D and E only ☐

2. How many molecules of ATP and NADPH are required for every molecule of CO_2 fixed in the Calvin cycle?

[NCERT Pg. 145 NEET 2024]

(a) 2 molecules of ATP and 3 molecules of NADPH ☐

(b) 2 molecules of ATP and 2 molecules of NADPH ☐

(c) 3 molecules of ATP and 3 molecules of NADPH ☐

(d) 3 molecules of ATP and 2 molecules of NADPH ☐

3. Given below are two statements.

Statement I In C_3 plants, some O_2 binds to RuBisCO, hence CO_2 fixation is decreased.

Statement II In C_4 plants, mesophyll cells show very little photorespiration, while bundle sheath cells do not show photorespiration.

In the light of the above statements, choose the correct answer from the options given below.

[NCERT Pg. 147, NEET 2024]

(a) Both statement I and Statement II are true ☐

(b) Both statement I and statement II are false ☐

(c) Statement I is true, but statement II is false ☐

(d) Statement I is false, but statement II is true ☐

4. The reaction centre in PS-II has an absorption maxima at

[NCERT Pg. 138, NEET 2023]

(a) 700 nm ☐ (b) 660 nm ☐

(c) 780 nm ☐ (d) 680 nm ☐

5. Which one of the following is not true regarding the release of energy during ATP synthesis through chemiosmosis? It involves **[NCERT Pg. 140, 141, NEET 2022]**

(a) breakdown of electron gradient ☐

(b) movement of protons across the membrane to the stroma ☐

(c) reduction of $NADP^+$ to $NADPH_2$ on the stroma side of the membrane ☐

(d) breakdown of proton gradient ☐

6. Given below are two statements.

Statement I The primary CO_2 acceptor in C_4-plants is phosphoenolpyruvate and is found in the mesophyll cells.

Statement II Mesophyll cells of C_4-plants lack RuBisCO enzyme.

In the light of the above statements, choose the correct answer from the options given below.

[NCERT Pg. 146, NEET 2022]

(a) Both statement I and statement II are incorrect ☐

(b) Statement I is correct, but statement II is incorrect ☐

(c) Statement I is incorrect, but statement II is correct ☐

(d) Both statement I and statement II are correct ☐

7. What is the role of large bundle sheath cells found around the vascular bundles in C_4-plants? **[NCERT Pg. 145, NEET 2022]**

(a) To increase the number of chloroplast for the operation of Calvin cycle ☐

(b) To enable the plant to tolerate high temperature ☐

(c) To protect the vascular tissue from high light intensity ☐

(d) To provide the site for photorespiratory pathway ☐

8. Which of the following statement is incorrect? [NCERT Pg. 139, 140, NEET 2021]

(a) Both ATP and NADPH + H^+ are synthesised during non-cyclic photophosphorylation ☐

(b) Stroma lamellae have PS-I only and lack NADP reductase ☐

(c) Grana lamellae have both PS-I and PS-II ☐

(d) Cyclic photophosphorylation involves both PS-I and PS-II ☐

9. In light reaction, plastoquinone facilitates the transfer of electrons from [NCERT Pg. 141, NEET (Sep.) 2020]

(a) Cyt-b_6f complex to PS-I ☐

(b) PS-I to $NADP^+$ ☐

(c) PS-I to ATP synthase ☐

(d) PS-II to Cyt-b_6f complex ☐

10. During non-cyclic photophosphorylation, when electrons are lost from the reaction centre at PS-II, what is the source which replaces these electrons? [NCERT Pg. 139, NEET (Oct.) 2020]

(a) Oxygen ☐

(b) Water ☐

(c) Carbon dioxide ☐

(d) Light ☐

11. Which of the following statements is incorrect? [NCERT Pg. 146, NEET (Oct.) 2020]

(a) RuBisCO is a bifunctional enzyme ☐

(b) In C_4-plants, the site of RuBisCO activity is mesophyll cell ☐

(c) The substrate molecule for RuBisCO activity is a 5-carbon compound ☐

(d) RuBisCO action requires ATP and NADPH ☐

Chapter 12

Respiration in Plants

Scan and take Chapter Test

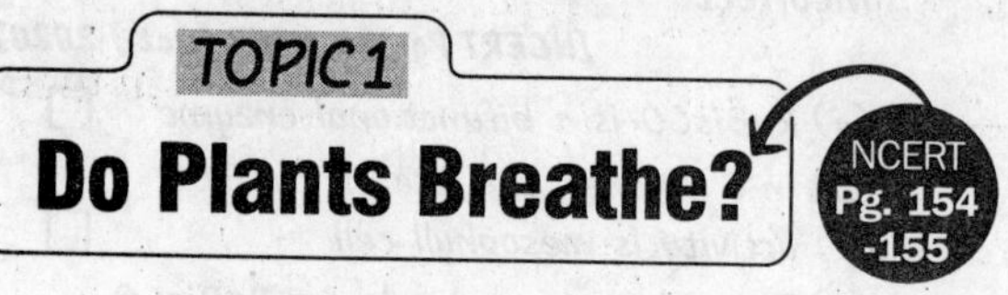

1. How many of the given daily life activities need energy in all living organisms?

   Absorption, Movement, Transport, Reproduction, Breakdown of food, Breathing

   ____

2. All the energy required for life processes is obtained by __________ of some macromolecules that we call 'food'.

3. Green plants and cyanobacteria can prepare their own food by __________.

4. Give the scientific term for the process of trapping light energy and converting it into chemical energy that is stored in the bonds of carbohydrates like glucose, sucrose and starch in plants. __________

5. Animals are __________, they obtain food from plants directly, i.e. __________ or indirectly, i.e. __________.

6. __________ are dependent on dead and decaying matter for food like fungi.

7. Give the scientific term for the mechanism of breakdown of food materials within the cell to release energy and trapping of this energy for synthesis of ATP.

   ____

8. Respiration is a __________ (catabolic/anabolic) and __________ (endergonic/exergonic) process.

9. Complete the following analogy with respect to eukaryotes.

   Photosynthesis : Respiration : : Chloroplasts : __________

10. The breaking of C—C bonds of complex compounds through oxidation within the cells, leading to release of considerable amount of energy is called __________.

11. The compounds that are oxidised during the process of respiration are known as __________.

*Concepts of all questions bearing * are important for NEET & CUET*

12. How many of the following macromolecules can act as respiratory substrates to release energy in plants?

Carbohydrates, Fats, Proteins, Organic acids, Vitamins, Humus, Amino acids

____

13. Respiratory substrates release energy into the cell in a single step.

True ☐ False ☐

14. Name the energy currency of the cell. ______________

15. Plant requires ______________ for respiration to occur and give out ______________ during this process (oxygen/carbon dioxide).

16. For gaseous exchange, plants have ______________ and ______________ in their leaves and stems, respectively.

17. Plants exhibit respiration without respiratory organs. (*Give reasons*)

____

18. All of the following are reasons why plants do not need an elaborate respiratory organ, except

(a) Only little transport of gases is required within a plant body ☐
(b) Different organs of plants respire at rates far lower than animals do ☐
(c) Respiration in plants releases lesser energy in the form of ATP ☐
(d) Cells in a plant body are located close to the surface. ☐

19. State whether following statements are true or false.

(i) There is very little transport of gases from one plant part to another.

True ☐ False ☐

(ii) Roots, stems and leaves respire at rates far higher than animals.

True ☐ False ☐

20. Consider the following statements.

Statement I The tight packing of parenchyma cells allows easy contact with air in plants.

Statement II The lenticels are special pores in stems that are always open for gas exchange.

Choose the correct option from the following.

(a) Statement I is true, but statement II is false ☐
(b) Statement I is false, but statement II is true ☐

21. Complete the biochemical reaction of respiration.

$C_6H_{12}O_6 + 6O_2 \longrightarrow$ ______________ + ______________ + ______________.

22. The gas required during combustion reaction is ______________.

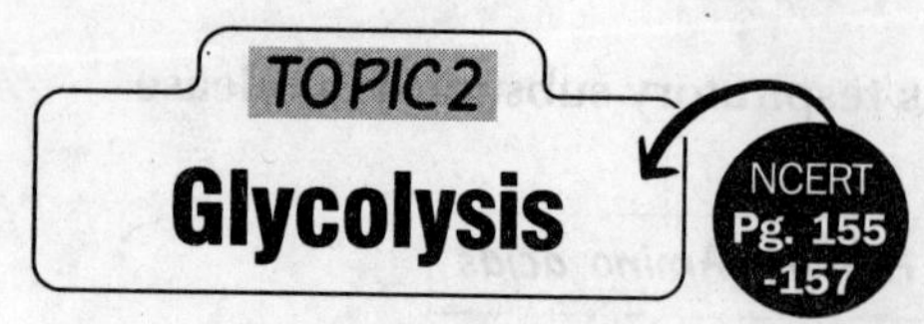

23. In any case (aerobic or anaerobic), all living organisms retain the enzymatic machinery to partially oxidise glucose without the help of oxygen. This breakdown of glucose to pyruvic acid is called ____________________

24. The term glycolysis has originated from two Greek words namely *glycos*, i.e. ____________ *lysis*, i.e. ____________.

25. Glycolysis is also known as EMP pathway. Here, EMP referred to as ____________________

26. Choose the odd one out from the given scientist names.

J. Parnas, Calvin, Otto Meyerhof, Gustav Embden

____

27. In ____________ (aerobic/anaerobic) organisms, glycolysis is the only process in respiration.

***28.** Glycolysis occurs in____________of cell and is present in all living organisms.

29. During glycolysis, one molecule of glucose (6C) is broken down into two molecules of ____________________.

30. Study the flowchart and identify *A* and *B*.

Photosynthesis → End product of photosynthesis (A) → (B) → Glucose, Fructose

A. ____________

B. ____________

31. From the given reaction, identify the correct pair w.r.t *A* and *B*.

$$\text{Sucrose} \xrightarrow{A} \text{Glucose} + \text{Fructose} \xrightarrow{B} \text{Glucose-6-phosphate}$$

(a) *A* – sucrase; *B* – invertase ☐

(b) *A* – invertase; *B* –sucrase ☐

(c) *A* – invertase; *B* – hexokinase ☐

(d) *A* – hexokinase; *B* –invertase ☐

32. The flowchart given below gives the steps involved in glycolysis. Fill in the missing molecules in place of *A*, *B* and *C*.

Glucose
↓
Glucose-6-phosphate
↓
A
↓
B
↓
C ⇌ Triose phosphate (Dihydroxy acetone phosphate)

A. ____________

B. ____________

C. ____________

33. How many reactions are there in glycolysis? ____________

34. Each step of glycolysis uses different enzymes. (*Give reason*)

____

35. Consider the following statements.

Statement I Breakdown of one molecule of glucose yields one molecule of pyruvate in the cytoplasm.

Statement II Fructose1,6-bisphosphate is split into three 2 carbon compounds in the presence of oxygen.

Choose the correct option from the following.

(a) Both statements I and II are true ☐

(b) Both statements I and II are false ☐

36. Which of the following steps of glycolysis reduces NAD^+ to $NADH + H^+$?

(a) Conversion of PGAL to BPGA ☐

(b) Conversion of phosphoenolpyruvate to pyruvic acid ☐

(c) Conversion of fructose1,6-bisphosphate to PGAL ☐

(d) Conversion of PGAL to dihydroxy acetone phosphate ☐

37. Write the reaction of glycolysis where a water molecule is removed.

____

38. The flowchart given below shows some steps in glycolysis. Identify the molecules *A* to *D*.

Glucose ⟶ 1, 3-bisphosphoglyceric acid ⟶ Ⓐ ⟶ Ⓑ ⟶ Ⓒ ⟶ Ⓓ

A. ____________ B. ____________ C. ____________ D. ____________

39. Complete the analogy with respect to ATP in glycolysis.

ATP used : 2 steps :: ATP formed : ____________.

40. How many ATPs are formed during glycolysis? ____________

***41.** Consider the following statements.

Statement I The total ATP formed from oxidation of one glucose molecule to pyruvate is two.

Statement II Two ATP molecules are consumed in phosphorylation of glucose to fructose 6-phosphate.

Choose the correct option from the following.

(a) Statement I is true, but statement II is false ☐

(b) Statement I is false, but statement II is true ☐

42. NADH is ____________ (formed/consumed) during glycolysis.

43. What will happen to glycolytic pathway if cell runs completely out of ATP?

____

44. How many of the following pairs are isomers?

PEP and pyruvate, 3PGA and 2PGA, PGAL and DHAP, Glucose and Fructose Glucose-6-phosphate and Fructose-6-phosphate

____

45. Give the full form of the following.

(i) ATP ____________

(ii) NADH ____________

(iii) PGAL ____________

(iv) DHAP ____________

(v) BPGA ____________

(vi) PEP ____________

46. At the end of glycolysis, ____________ is the net energy gain from one molecule of glucose *via* ____________, but there is also energy stored in the form of ____________.

47. Given below are few steps of glycolysis. Fill in the boxes *A* to *D* by using ATP used and ATP formed.

(i) Glucose → Glucose-6-phosphate – [*A*] ____________

(ii) BPGA → 3PGA – [*B*] ____________

(iii) PEP → Pyruvic acid – [*C*] ____________

(iv) Fructose-6-phosphate → Fructose-1, 6-bisphosphate – [*D*] ____________

***48.** The overall reaction of glycolysis is given below.

Glucose ⟶ 2 Pyruvic acid + 2ATP + $2NADH_2$

True ☐ False ☐

49. Match the following columns.

Column I (Name of compounds)	Column II (Number of carbon atoms)
A. DHAP	1. 6 carbon
B. Glucose	2. 3 carbon
C. Fructose-1, 6-bisphosphate	
D. PEP	

A. ________ B. ________ C.________ D. ________

50. In glycolysis, total ________ ATP molecules are produced and total gain of ATP molecules is ________.

51. How many molecules of NADH are produced when four molecules of phosphoglyceraldehyde are converted into four molecules of pyruvate?

____

52. The reaction forming 3-phosphoglyceric acid in glycolysis is ________ ________ (oxidative phosphorylation/substrate level phosphorylation).

53. There are three major ways in which different cells handle pyruvic acid produced by glycolysis. These are ________, ________ and________

54. Name any three cells where glycolysis occurs.

____

55. In many prokaryotes and unicellular eukaryotes, ________ process takes place in anaerobic condition.

56. Complete the following flowchart showing fermentation.

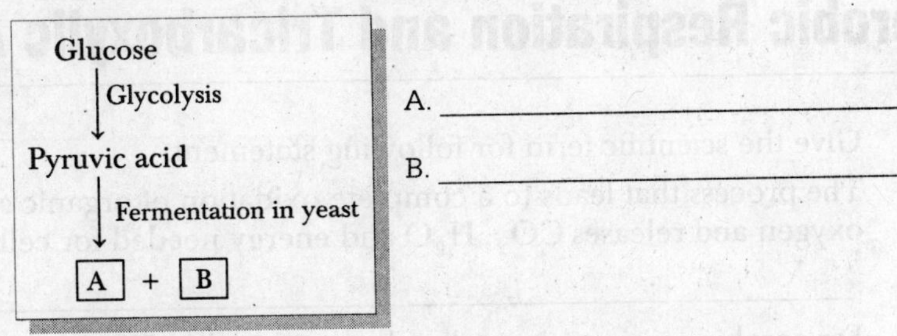

57. In alcoholic fermentation (by yeast), the reduction of pyruvic acid needs two enzymes, i.e. ________ and ________.

58. Study the reaction and answer the following questions.

Glucose
Glycolysis
↓
Pyruvic acid
A
NAD+
↓
Lactic acid

(i) What is the energy rich compound denoted as '*A*'? ______

(ii) Which animal cell also shows this reaction? ______

(iii) Write the enzyme responsible for this process. ______

59. Consider the following statements.

Statement I Pyruvate dehydrogenase catalyses the conversion of pyruvic acid to ethanol.

Statement II NADH + H^+ is the reducing agent which is reoxidised to NAD^+.

Choose the correct option from the following.

(a) Statement I is true, but statement II is false ☐

(b) Statement I is false, but statement II is true ☐

60. Write numerical value to fill in the blanks.

(i) In both lactic acid and alcoholic fermentation not much energy is released, less than ______ per cent of the energy in glucose is released out and not all of it is trapped as ATP.

(ii) Yeasts poison themselves to death when the concentration of alcohol reaches about ______ per cent.

61. How many NAD^+ molecules are formed by alcoholic fermentation of one glucose molecule?

(a) 2 ☐ (b) 1 ☐ (c) 4 ☐ (d) 0 ☐

TOPIC 4

Aerobic Respiration and Tricarboxylic Acid Cycle

NCERT Pg. 158-159

62. Give the scientific term for following statement.

The process that leads to a complete oxidation of organic substances in the presence of oxygen and releases CO_2, H_2O and energy needed for cellular metabolism.

______

63. For aerobic respiration to take place within the '*X*', the product of glycolysis, i.e. pyruvic acid is transported from the cytoplasm into the '*X*'. (Name the cell organelle '*X*')

______

64. Name the two crucial events in aerobic respiration.

______

65. Pyruvate is formed by the glycolytic ____________ (anabolism/catabolism) of carbohydrates in the cytosol. After it enters mitochondrial ____________ (stroma/matrix) it undergoes oxidative ____________ (carboxylation/ decarboxylation) by a complex set of reaction.

***66.** Consider the following equation:

$$Pyruvic\ acid + Co\text{-}A + NAD^+ \xrightarrow[\text{Pyruvate dehydrogenase}]{Mg^{2+}} Acetyl\ Co\text{-}A + CO_2 + NADH + H^+$$

Which of the following correctly identifies the site of the given reaction?

(a) Outer mitochondrial membrane ☐ (b) Inner mitochondrial membrane ☐
(c) Intermembrane space ☐ (d) Mitochondrial matrix ☐

67. Complete the following reaction.

$$\text{Pyruvate} + \boxed{A} + \boxed{B} \xrightarrow[\boxed{C}]{Mg^{2+}} \text{Acetyl Co-A} + \boxed{D} + \boxed{E}$$

A. ____________ B. ____________ C. ____________ D. ____________
E. ____________

68. Consider the following statements.

I. In both lactic acid and alcohol fermentation less than ten per cent of the energy in glucose is released.
II. Conversion of BPGA to PGA is an energy yielding process.
III. Pyruvate is formed by the glycolytic anabolism of carbohydrates in the cytosol.
IV. Pyruvate is transported from the mitochondria into the cytoplasm.

Choose the option with incorrect set of statements.

(a) I, II and III ☐ (b) II, III and IV ☐ (c) I, III and IV ☐ (d) I and III ☐

69. Name the scientist who elucidated TCA cycle. ____________

70. Write another name of TCA cycle. ____________

71. The TCA cycle starts with the condensation of acetyl group with oxaloacetic acid (OAA) to water to yield ____________.

72. Match the following columns.

	Column I		Column II
A.	4 carbon compound	1.	Oxaloacetic acid
B.	3 carbon compound	2.	Pyruvate
C.	5 carbon compound	3.	α-ketoglutaric acid
D.	6 carbon compound	4.	Glucose-6-phosphate

A. ____________ B. ____________ C. ____________ D. ____________

73. Complete the sequence of events in Krebs' cycle in the following flowchart.

Acetyl-Co-A ⟶ Citric acid ⟶ [A] ⟶ [B] ⟶ Fumaric acid ⟶ [C] ⟶ [D]

A. ____________ B. ____________ C. ____________ D. ____________

74. **Write the link reaction between aerobic and anaerobic respiration.**

____

75. **The first 5-C dicarboxylic acid in Krebs cycle which is used in nitrogen metabolism is citric acid.** (***Rewrite the statement after correcting the underlined words.***)

____

76. **Write the missing molecule *X* in the chemical reaction given below.**

Citric acid ⇌ [X] ⟶ α-ketoglutarate

X. ____

77. **Consider the following reaction and identify *X* and *Y*.**

Succinyl Co-A —(Enzyme X; GDP → [Y])→ Succinic acid

X. ______________________ Y. ______________________

78. **The first member of TCA cycle is** ______________________.

79. **Complete the reaction given below.**

Pyruvic acid + [A] + [B] + [C] + ADP + Pi —(Mitochondrial matrix)→ [D] + [E] + 4H⁺ + $FADH_2$ + ATP

A. ______________ B. ______________ C. ______________

D. ______________ E. ______________

80. **Name the molecules from which the given molecules are formed in Krebs cycle.**

(i) OAA ____

(ii) Malic acid ____

(iii) Fumaric acid ____

***81.** **Given below is flowchart of Krebs cycle. Name *X*, *Y* and *Z*.**

Acetyl Co-A
Oxaloacetic acid
Citric acid
Isocitric acid
CO_2
a-ketoglutaric acid (5C)
CO_2
Succinyl-Co-A
Succinic acid
Fumaric acid
Malic acid
X, Y, Z

X. ______________________

Y. ______________________

Z. ______________________

***82.** Which of the following steps involve substrate level phosphorylation?

(a) Conversion of citric acid to isocitrate ☐

(b) Conversion of succinyl Co-A to succinic acid ☐

(c) Conversion of isocitrate to α-ketoglutaric acid ☐

(d) Conversion of malate to oxaloacetate ☐

83. Write the types of reaction occuring in the following.

(i) Succinyl Co-A → OAA ____________

(ii) Citrate → Isocitrate ____________

(iii) Oxalosuccinate → α-ketoglutaric acid ____________

84. Write the name of the process mentioned.

The complete oxidation of pyruvate by the stepwise removal of all the hydrogen atoms, leaving three molecules of CO_2. ____________

85. In two turns of Krebs' cycle, number of molecules of CO_2, NADH, $FADH_2$ and ATP produced are ____________, ____________, ____________ and ____________, respectively.

86. Write the full form of the following.

(i) TCA ____________

(ii) OAA ____________

TOPIC 5

Electron Transport System (ETS) and Oxidative Phosphorylation

NCERT Pg. 159-161

87. Cytochromes are found in ____________ (cristae/matrix) of mitochondria.

88. Electrons from NADH produced in the mitochondrial matrix during TCA cycle are oxidised by complex-I, and electrons are then transferred to <u>cytochrome-*c*</u>.

(*Rewrite the statement after correcting the underlined word.*)

____

89. During ETS, the number of ATP molecules synthesised depends on the nature of ____________.

90. ____________ acts as a mobile carrier for transfer of electrons between complex-III and IV.

91. Give the location of ubiquinone. ____________

92. Cytochrome-*c* oxidase complex contains cytochromes ______, ______ and ______ copper centres.

93. When the electrons pass from one carrier to another *via* complex-I to IV in ETS, they are coupled to complex-V to produce ______.

94. Match the following columns.

Column I (Complexes)	Column II (Respective names)
A. Complex-I	1. ATP synthase
B. Complex-II	2. Cytochrome-*c* oxidase
C. Complex-III	3. Cytochrome-bc_1
D. Complex-IV	4. Succinate dehydrogenase
E. Complex-V	5. NADH dehydrogenase

A. ______ B. ______ C. ______ D. ______
E. ______

95. Given below are few statements.

I. Pyruvic dehydrogenase requires Mg^{2+} for converting pyruvic acid to acetyl Co-A.
II. Oxidative decarboxylation of pyruvic acid takes place in the mitochondrial matrix.
III. Molecule of GTP is synthesised during the conversion of succinyl Co-A to succinic acid.
IV. Electrons from NADH produced in the cytoplasm are oxidised by NADH dehydrogensae.

Choose the option with correct set of statements.

(a) I, III and IV ☐ (b) II, III and IV ☐
(c) I, II and III ☐ (d) I and IV ☐

96. Match Column I with Column II.

Column I	Column II
A. Complex I	1. Oxidation of succinate
B. Complex II	2. Copper centres
C. Complex IV	3. ATP synthesis
D. Complex V	4. Oxidation of NADH + H^+

	A	B	C	D			A	B	C	D	
(a)	4	1	2	3	☐	(b)	4	1	3	2	☐
(c)	4	3	2	1	☐	(d)	4	3	1	2	☐

***97.** Identify *A, B, C, D, E* and *F* in the given figure of electron transport chain.

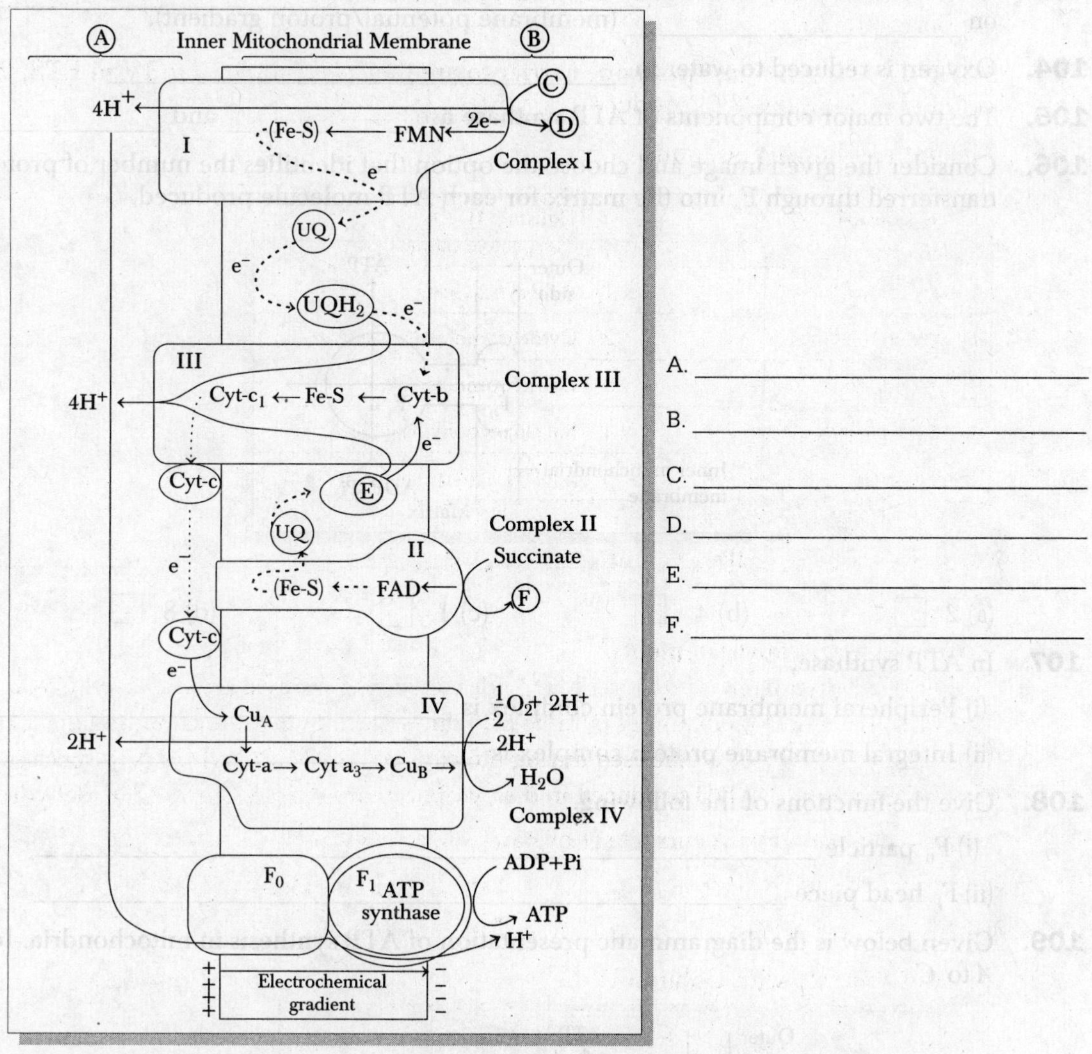

A. ____________________

B. ____________________

C. ____________________

D. ____________________

E. ____________________

F. ____________________

98. Complete the following analogy with respect to ATP molecules produced.

NADH : ____________ ATP :: $FADH_2$: ____________ ATP

99. What is the role of oxygen in ETS? (*Give answer in one line*)

____

100. For production of proton gradient, photosynthesis requires ____________ while, respiration requires ____________.

101. Give the scientific term for the process of formation of ATP by transfer of phosphate group from a substrate to ADP. ____________

102. Give one difference between photophosphorylation and oxidative phosphorylation with respect to oxygen.

____

103. Chemiosmotic theory of ATP synthesis in chloroplasts and mitochondria is based on ____________ (membrane potential/proton gradient).

104. Oxygen is reduced to water in ____________.

105. The two major components of ATP synthase are ____________ and ____________.

106. Consider the given image and choose the option that identifies the number of protons transferred through F_0 into the matrix for each ATP molecule produced.

Outer side
ATP
F_0
F_1
Inner mitochondrial membrane
ADP Pi
Matrix

(a) 2 ☐ (b) 4 ☐ (c) 1 ☐ (d) 8 ☐

107. In ATP synthase,

(i) Peripheral membrane protein complex is ____________

(ii) Integral membrane protein complex is ____________

108. Give the functions of the following.

(i) F_0 particle ____________

(ii) F_1 head piece ____________

109. Given below is the diagrammatic presentation of ATP synthesis in mitochondria. Identify *A* to *C*.

Outer side
ATP
Stalk
A
$2H^+$
B
C
Inner mitochondrial membrane
ADP Pi
Matrix

A. ____________

B. ____________

C. ____________

110. The passage of protons through the channel formed by F_1 is coupled to the catalytic site of the F_0 component.

True ☐ False ☐

111. During passage of electron over ETC, pH of matrix increases.

True ☐ False ☐

TOPIC 6

The Respiratory Balance Sheet and Amphibolic Pathway

112. Fill in the blanks about the assumptions made to calculate net gain of ATP.

(i) There is a sequential, orderly pathway functioning, with one substrate forming the next and with ____________, ____________ and ____________ pathway following one after another.

(ii) The NADH synthesised in glycolysis is transferred into the mitochondria and undergoes ____________.

(iii) ____________ of the intermediate compounds in the respiratory pathway are utilised to synthesise any other compound.

(iv) Only ____________ is being respired, no other alternative substrates are entering in the pathway at any of the intermediary stages.

***113.** The net gain of ATP molecules during aerobic respiration from one molecule of glucose is ____________.

114. NADH is oxidised to NAD^+ rather slowly in fermentation, however the reaction is very vigorous in case of aerobic respiration.

True ☐ False ☐

115. What is the total number of ATP produced by oxidation of NADH during aerobic respiration of one glucose molecule?

(a) 32 ☐ (b) 36 ☐
(c) 38 ☐ (d) 30 ☐

116. How many ATP molecules will be generated in a plant system during complete oxidation of 40 molecules of glucose?

____

117. Out of the three respiratory substrates (carbohydrates, fats and proteins), which one is the most favoured substrate?

____

118. Respiratory pathway is catabolic.
(*Rewrite the statement after correcting the underlined word.*)

____

119. The figure given below describes inter-relationship among metabolic pathways showing respiration mediated breakdown of different organic molecules to CO_2 and H_2O. Identify *A-D*.

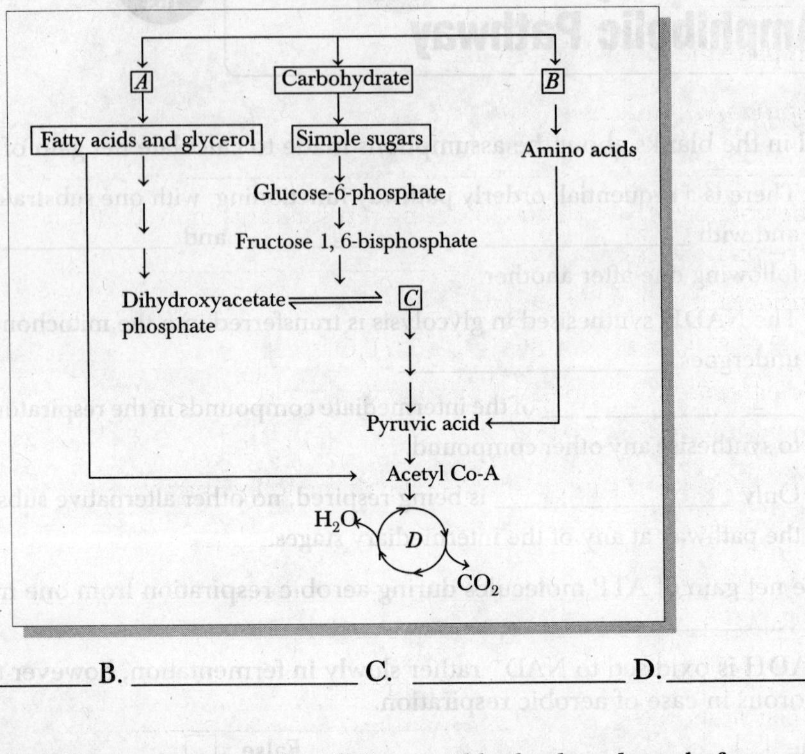

A. ______ B. ______ C. ______ D. ______

120. In which of the following compounds will fatty acid be broken down before entering the respiratory pathway?

(a) Carbon dioxide ☐ (b) Pyruvate ☐

(c) Acetyl Co-A ☐ (d) Glycerol ☐

121. What is the next molecule formed in the respiratory pathway for the given substrates?

(i) Proteins ______

(ii) Fatty acids ______

(iii) Fats ______

122. Consider the following statements.

I. Oxidation of one molecule of NADH gives rise to 2 molecules of ATP while of one molecule of $FADH_2$ produces 3 molecules of ATP.

II. F_1 is a peripheral membrane protein complex and contain the site for synthesis of ATP from ADP and inorganic phosphate.

III. Fats is the favoured substrate for respiration.

IV. Fatty acids would be broken down to acetyl Co-A before entering the respiratory pathway when it is used as a substrate.

Choose the correct set of statement.

(a) I and IV ☐ (b) I and II ☐

(c) II and IV ☐ (d) III and IV ☐

TOPIC 7

Respiratory Quotient

NCERT Pg 163-164

123. Complete the following formula.

Respiratory Quotient = $\frac{X}{Y}$

X. ____________ Y. ____________

124. If the volume of CO_2 liberated during respiration is more than the volume of O_2 used then the respiratory substrate will be ____________.

***125.** Consider the following equation.

$2C_{18}H_{34}O_2 + 51O_2 \longrightarrow 36CO_2 + 34H_2O$

Calculate the RQ from the above reaction.

(a) 0.71 ☐ (b) 0.9 ☐ (c) 1 ☐ (d) 0.07 ☐

126. Write the value of respiratory quotient of the following substrates.

(i) Tripalmitin ____________

(ii) Organic acids ____________

(iii) Fats ____________

(iv) Proteins ____________

(v) Carbohydrates ____________

(vi) Oxalic acid ____________

Assertion-Reason Questions

The following questions consist of two statements- Assertion (A) and Reason (R). Answer these questions by selecting the appropriate option given below.

(a) Both A and R are true and R is the correct explanation of A

(b) Both A and R are true, but R is not the correct explanation of A

(c) A is true, but R is false

(d) A is false, but R is true

1. **Assertion** (A) Energy released by oxidation in respiration is not used directly, but is used to synthesise ATP.

Reason (R) During oxidation within a cell, all the energy contained in respiratory substrates is released in a single step.

(a) ☐ (b) ☐ (c) ☐ (d) ☐

2. **Assertion** (A) Stems have openings called lenticels that allow oxygen from the atmosphere to diffuse in.

Reason (R) The loose packing of parenchyma cells allows the cells in a stem to be in contact with air.

(a) ☐ (b) ☐ (c) ☐ (d) ☐

***3.** **Assertion** (A) Glucose undergoes complete oxidation during glycolysis to form two molecules of pyruvate.

Reason (R) The conversion of phosphoenolpyruvate to pyruvic acid during glycolysis is an energy yielding step.

(a) ☐ (b) ☐ (c) ☐ (d) ☐

***4.** **Assertion** (A) Two ATP molecules are synthesised during fermentation by yeast to produce alcohol.

Reason (R) Fermentation is preceded by glycolysis where two ATP molecules are synthesised per glucose molecule.

(a) ☐ (b) ☐ (c) ☐ (d) ☐

***5.** **Assertion** (A) Pyruvic acid undergoes oxidative decarboxylation in mitochondrial matrix to form acetyl Co-A.

Reason (R) Pyruvate dehydrogenase requires the participation of several factors, including NAD^+ and cofactor A.

(a) ☐ (b) ☐ (c) ☐ (d) ☐

6. **Assertion** (A) The regeneration of NAD^+ and FAD^+ is crucial for continuation of the TCA cycle.

Reason (R) NAD^+ is reduced to $NADH + H^+$ whereas FAD^+ is reduced to $FADH_2$ during the Krebs' cycle

(a) ☐ (b) ☐ (c) ☐ (d) ☐

7. **Assertion** (A) The oxidation of $NADH + H^+$ and $FADH_2$ is coupled to the synthesis of ATP.

Reason (R) Oxidative phosphorylation is driven by the energy of oxidation and reduction.

(a) ☐ (b) ☐ (c) ☐ (d) ☐

***8.** **Assertion** (A) There is a net gain of 38 molecules of ATP during complete oxidation of one molecule of glucose.

Reason (R) Anaerobic respiration only oxidises glucose partially, with a net gain of four ATP molecules per glucose.

(a) ☐ (b) ☐ (c) ☐ (d) ☐

***9.** **Assertion** (A) The respiratory pathway is amphibolic in nature for different respiratory substrates.

Reason (R) Fats and proteins can also act as respiratory substrates and enter the pathway at different points.

(a) ☐ (b) ☐ (c) ☐ (d) ☐

10. **Assertion** (A) Respiratory quotient is the ratio between the volume of O_2 consumed to the volume of CO_2 produced.

Reason (R) The respiratory quotient of fats is always less than 1 while that in proteins is about 0.9.

(a) ☐ (b) ☐ (c) ☐ (d) ☐

Case Based Questions

1. Study the given image carefully and answer the questions that follow.

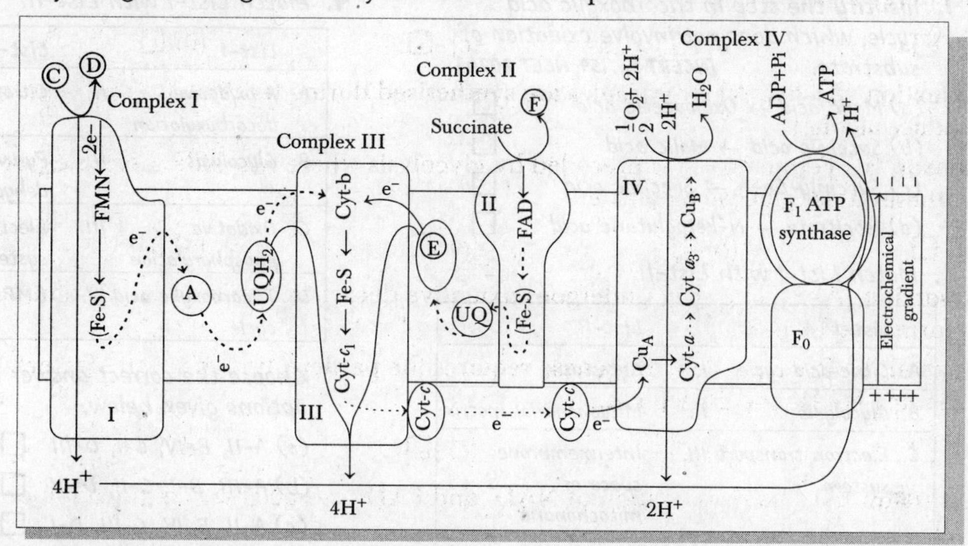

(i) What is the reduced form of A called?

(a) Ubiquinone ☐ (b) Ubiquinol ☐

(c) Ubiquin ☐ (d) Ubiquinal ☐

(ii) Which of the following acts as the mobile carrier of electrons?

(a) Cytochrome-*c* ☐ (b) Cytochrome-bc_1 ☐

(c) Cytochrome-*a* ☐ (d) Cytochrome-a_3 ☐

(iii) Which of the following metals are associated with complex IV?

(a) Mg ☐ (b) Ca ☐ (c) Cu ☐ (d) Na ☐

(iv) Which of the following is the correct combination of the parts of complex V?

(a) F_0 – integral membrane protein F_1 – peripheral membrane protein ☐

(b) F_0 – peripheral membrane protein F_1 – integral membrane protein ☐

(c) F_0 – integral membrane protein F_1 – integral membrane protein ☐

(d) F_0 – peripheral membrane protein F_1 – peripheral membrane protein ☐

2. You are working in a biofuel company that utilises organic waste to produce ethanol through fermentation. Recently, there has been a decrease in ethanol yield. You are asked to investigate the process of identifying the potential causes.

Based on the above case, answer the questions that follow.

(i) During the above process, which of the following cannot be expected as a product?

(a) Ethanol ☐ (b) Carbon dioxide ☐ (c) Oxygen ☐ (d) Lactic acid ☐

(ii) The biofuel company is using organic waste as a substrate. What type of fermentation is most likely used in this process?

(a) Alcoholic fermentation ☐ (b) Lactic acid fermentation ☐

(c) Aerobic respiration ☐ (d) Photosynthesis ☐

(iii) Anaerobic fermentation is a type of cellular respiration. Compared to aerobic respiration, how much ATP is produced during anaerobic fermentation?

(a) Less than seven per cent ☐ (b) More than seven per cent ☐

(c) More than thirteen per cent ☐ (d) Less than thirteen per cent ☐

COMPETITION EDGE UP

1. Identify the step in tricarboxylic acid cycle, which does not involve oxidation of substrate. **[NCERT Pg. 159, NEET 2024]**

(a) Malic acid $\rightarrow$ Oxaloacetic acid ☐
(b) Succinic acid $\rightarrow$ Malic acid ☐
(c) Succinly-Co-A $\rightarrow$ Succinic acid ☐
(d) Isocitrate $\rightarrow$ N-ketoglutaric acid ☐

2. Match List-I with List-II.

List-I	List-II
A. Citric acid cycle	I. Cytoplasm
B. Glycolysis	II. Mitochondrial matrix
C. Electron transport system	III. Intermembrane space of mitochondria
D. Proton gradient	IV. Inner mitochondrial membrane

Choose the correct answer from the options given below. **[NCERT Pg. 155, 159, 160, NEET 2024]**

(a) A-I, B-II, C-III, D-IV ☐
(b) A-II, B-I, C-IV, D-III ☐
(c) A-III, B-IV, C-I, D-II ☐
(d) A-IV, B-III, C-II, D-I ☐

3. Given below are two statements: One is labelled as Assertion (A) and the other is labelled as Reason (R).

Assertion (A) ATP is used at two steps in glycolysis.

Reason (R) First ATP is used in converting glucose into glucose-6-phosphate and second ATP is used in conversion of fructose-6-phosphate into fructose-1-6-diphosphate.

In the light of the above statements, choose the correct answer from the options given below. **[NCERT Pg. 156, NEET 2023]**

(a) Both A and R are true, R is not the correct explanation of A ☐
(b) A is true, but R is false ☐
(c) A is false, but R is true ☐
(d) Both A and R are true and R is the correct explanation of A ☐

4. Match List-I with List-II. **[NEET 2023]**

List-I	List-II
A. A oxidative decarboxylation	I. Citrate synthase
B. Glycolysis	II. Pyruvate dehydrogenase
C. Oxidative phosphorylation	III. Electron transport system
D. Tricarboxylic acid cycle	IV. EMP pahtway

Choose the correct answer from the options given below.

(a) A-II, B-IV, C-I, D-III ☐
(b) A-III, B-I, C-II, D-IV ☐
(c) A-II, B-IV, C-III, D-I ☐
(d) A-III, B-IV, C-II, D-I ☐

5. What is the net gain of ATP when each molecule of glucose is converted to two molecules of pyruvic acid? **[NCERT Pg. 156, NEET 2022]**

(a) 6 ☐ (b) 2 ☐ (c) 8 ☐ (d) 4 ☐

6. What amount of energy is released from glucose during lactic acid fermentation? **[NCERT Pg. 157, NEET 2022]**

(a) More than 18% ☐
(b) About 10% ☐
(c) Less than 7% ☐
(d) Approximately 15% ☐

7. Which of the following statements is incorrect? **[NCERT Pg. 160, NEET 2021]**

(a) During aerobic respiration, role of oxygen is limited to the terminal stage ☐
(b) In ETC (Electron Transport Chain), one molecule of NADH + H^+ gives rise to 2 ATP molecules and one $FADH_2$ gives rise to 3 ATP molecules ☐
(c) ATP is synthesised through complex V ☐
(d) Oxidation-reduction reactions produce proton gradient in respiration ☐

8. The number of substrate level phosphorylation in one turn of citric acid cycle is **[NCERT Pg. 158, NEET (Sep.) 2020]**

(a) one ☐ (b) two ☐
(c) three ☐ (d) zero ☐

Chapter 13

Plant Growth and Development

Scan and take Chapter Test

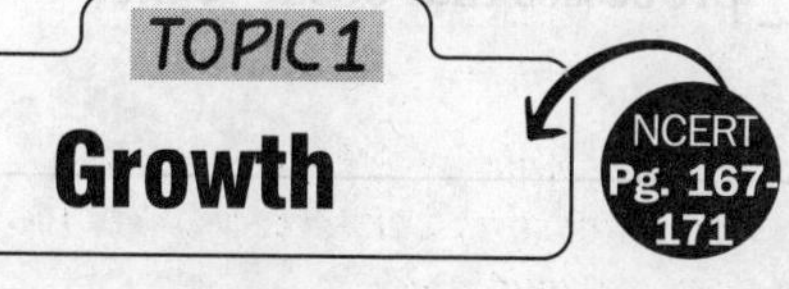

1. During plant growth, ________________ phase precedes flowering.

2. Development is the sum total of two processes, named ________________

3. Refer to the given below diagrams and answer the following questions.

(i) In the given diagrams, name the structures labelled as *A-D*.

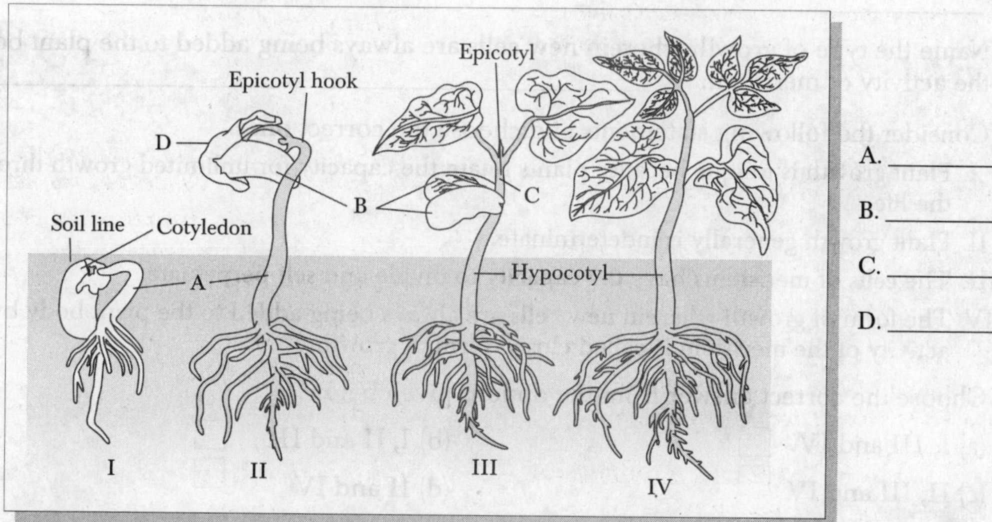

(ii) The given diagrams represent germination and seedling development in <u>maize</u>.
(*Rewrite the statement after correcting the underlined word.*)

____

*Concept's of all questions bearing * are important for NEET & CUET*

4. Consider the following statements.

Statement I The hypocotyl is the part of the embryonal axis that bears the seed leaves.

Statement II Epicotyl extends above the cotyledons and bear the leaf primordia.

Choose the correct option from the following.

(a) Statement I is true, but statement II is false ☐

(b) Both statements I and II are true ☐

***5.** The factors which govern and control developmental processes in plants are either intrinsic or extrinsic.

True ☐ False ☐

6. Read the following characteristics and identify the biological term.

I. Irreversible permanent increase in size of an organ or its parts or even of an individual cell.

II. Most fundamental and conspicuous characteristic of a living being.

____

7. Growth is accompanied by ________________ processes that occur at the expense of ________________.

***8.** An example of growth is ________________ (leaf expansion /swelling of wood piece in water).

9. Name the tissue which enables plants to retain the capacity of unlimited growth throughout their life. ________________

10. How many of the listed characters are displayed by the cells of meristems?

Capacity to divide continuously, Self-perpetuation, Present throughout plant body

____

11. Name the type of growth wherein new cells are always being added to the plant body by the activity of meristem. ________________

12. Consider the following statements and choose the correct ones.

I. Plant growth is unique because plants retain the capacity for unlimited growth throughout the life.

II. Plant growth generally is indeterminate.

III. The cells of meristems have the capacity to divide and self-perpetuate.

IV. The form of growth wherein new cells are always being added to the plant body by the activity of the meristem is called closed form of growth.

Choose the correct answer from the options given below.

(a) I, III and IV ☐ (b) I, II and III ☐

(c) II, III and IV ☐ (d) II and IV ☐

***13.** Refer to the given diagram and answer the following questions.

(i) Name the parts labelled as *A*, *B* and *C*.

A. ____________

B. ____________

C. ____________

(ii) Among the parts *A*, *B* and *C*, choose the odd one out with respect to the type of growth contributed by them. ____________

(iii) Along with part *C*, name other two structures which appear later in life of dicotyledonous plants and gymnosperms. ____________

14. Choose the incorrect combination from the following.

(a) Root length – Primary growth ☐

(b) Cork cambium – Secondary growth ☐

(c) Wood– Primary growth ☐

(d) Vascular cambium – Secondary growth ☐

15. Complete the analogy given below with respect to different meristems and their function.
Apical meristem : Elongation of plant : : ____________ : Increase in girth of associated organs.

16. At cellular level, the growth is principally a consequence of increase in the amount of ____________.

17. How many of the listed parameters are used to measure the growth in plants?

Increase in fresh weight, Increase in length, Dry weight, Increase in cell number, Increase in protoplasm directly

____

18. Match the following columns.

Column I (Various structures of plants)	Column II (Parameters of growth)
A. Maize root apical meristem	1. Increase in size of the cell upto 3,50,000 times
B. Cell in a watermelon	2. Increase in length
C. Dorsiventral leaf	3. Increase in cell number from one to 17500 per hour
D. Pollen tube	4. Increase in surface area

A.________ B.________ C.________ D.________

19. Name the three phases of the period of growth.

____

20. Consider the following statements.

Statement I Plasmodesmata between adjacent plant cells allow exchange of materials between cells.

Statement II The maturation zone lying adjacent to the meristematic zone contains cell with increased vacuolation.

Choose the correct option from the following.

(a) Statement I is true, but statement II is false ☐

(b) Statement I is false, but statement II is true ☐

***21.** Consider the following diagram of root tip and answer the questions that follow

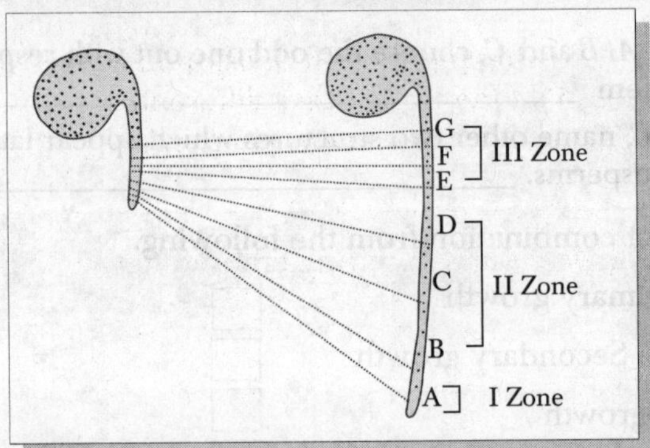

(i) The given diagram shows the parallel line technique for the detection of zones of _______________ .

(ii) Match the following columns considering the above figure.

Column I	Column II
A. I	1. Phase of elongation
B. II	2. Phase of maturation
C. III	3. Meristematic phase of growth

A._______________ B._______________ C._______________

(iii) Choose the odd one out with respect to the cell characteristics of zone I of the above figure.

Constantly dividing, Rich in protoplasm, Large nuclei, Thickened cell walls, Abundant plamodesmata

____

(iv) How many of the listed characteristics are likely to be found in the cells of zone II?

Increased vacuolation, Cell enlargement, Cell attain maxmimum size, New cell wall deposition

____

(v) Mention any two characteristics of cells found in zone III.

(a) ______________ (b) ______________

***22.** Study the diagram given below and identify the *A* and *B* pattern of growth.

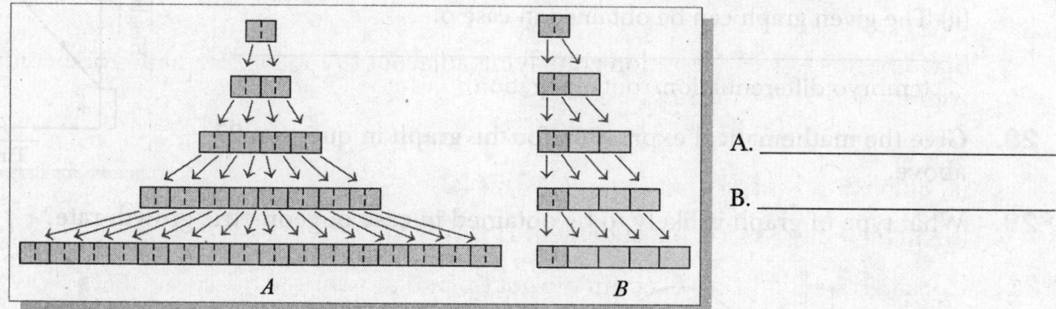

***23.** In geometric growth, following mitotic cell division in actively dividing cells, only one daughter cell continues to divide while other differentiates and matures.

(*Rewrite the statement after correcting the underlined words.*)

____

***24.** The given diagram shows the stages during embryo development. What does *A* and *B* represent in it?

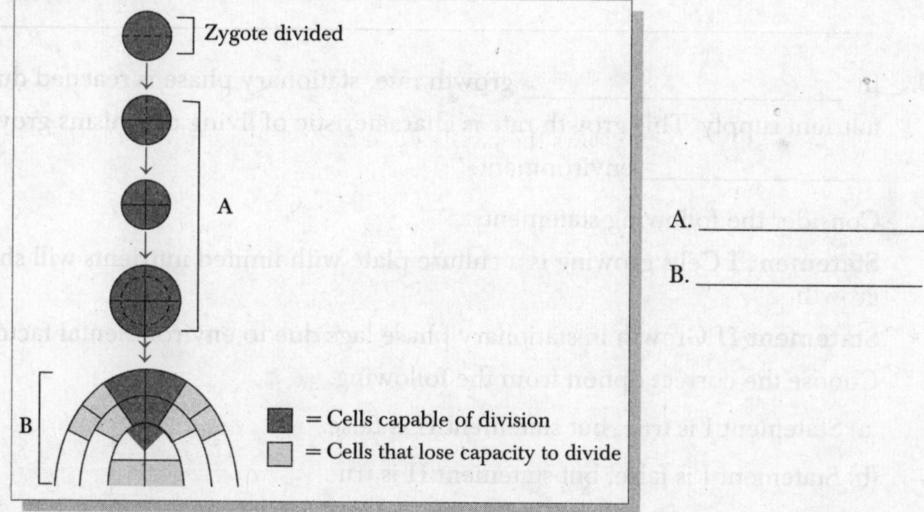

25. In case of geometric growth rate, ______________ (no cell/both the daughter cells) divide following the mitotic cell division.

26. Consider the following statements.

Statement I The mitotic division of zygote resulting in increased cell number is representative of arithmetic growth.

Statement II Simplest example of arithmetic growth is the elongation of root at a constant rate.

Choose the correct option from the following.

(a) Statement I is true, but statement II is false ☐

(b) Statement I is false, but statement II is true ☐

27. Refer to the graph and answer the questions that follow.

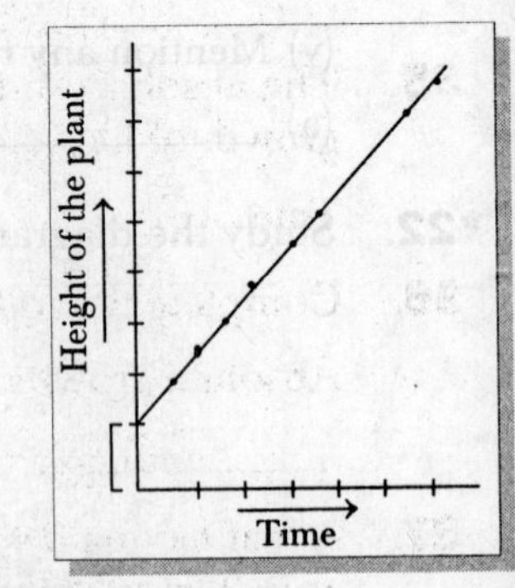

(i) Name the type of growth rate shown in the graph.

____

(ii) The given graph can be obtained in case of ______________________________ (embryo differentiation/root elongation)

28. Give the mathematical expression for the graph in question 27 above.

***29.** What type of graph is likely to be obtained in case of geometric growth rate?

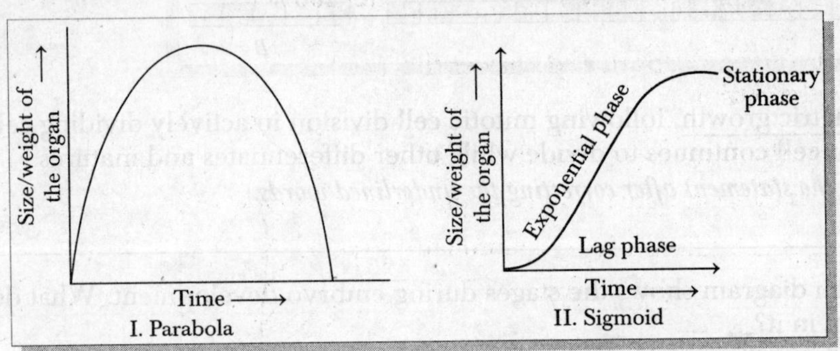

____

30. In ______________________ growth rate, stationary phase is reached due to the limited nutrient supply. This growth rate is characteristic of living organisms growing in ______________________ environment.

31. Consider the following statements.

Statement I Cells growing is a culture plate with limited nutrients will show geometric growth.

Statement II Growth in stationary phase lags due to environmental factors.

Choose the correct option from the following.

(a) Statement I is true, but statement II is false

(b) Statement I is false, but statement II is true

(c) Both statements I and II are true

(d) Both statements I and II are false

32. A tree showing seasonal activities and cells in culture exhibit (sigmoid/linear) growth curve.

33. Give the mathematical expression for exponential/geometric growth rate.

____

34. Give technical term for the following sentence.

The measure of the ability of the plant to produce new plant material.

____

35. The absolute and relative growth rates give the quantitative comparison between the growth of living system.

True ☐ False ☐

36. Complete the following analogy given below with respect to growth patterns.

Absolute growth rate : Total growth per unit time : : Relative growth rate :

____

37. A leaf having a surface area of 25 cm^2 grows to 30 cm^2 in one hour. Calculate its relative growth rate.

(a) 25% ☐ (b) 20% ☐ (c) 100% ☐ (d) 0% ☐

38. Refer to the given diagram and answer the questions that follow.

A′
B′
10 cm^2
55 cm^2
5 cm^2
50 cm^2
A
B

(i) The growth of two leaves *A* and *B* is *A′* and *B′* in the given time is an example of ______________(absolute growth/relative growth) in area.

(ii) Which leaf show much higher relative growth rate? (*A* or *B*)

____

39. Name the device that is used to measure growth rate.

____

40. Name any three essential elements for growth.

____

41. Match the following columns.

Column I (Elements)	Column II (Functions)
A. Water	1. Synthesise protoplasm and acts as a source of energy
B. Oxygen	2. Cell enlargement and provides medium for enzymatic activities
C. Nutrients	3. Release metabolic energy through cellular respiration

A. __________ B. __________ C. __________

42. Any deviation from the optimum temperature range could be detrimental for plant survival.

True ☐ False ☐

43. Consider the following statements.

Statement I A cell placed in hypotonic solution shows a decrease in cell size.

Statement II Gravity can act as a signal to induce phases of growth in plants.

Choose the correct option from the following.

(a) Statement I is true, but statement II is false ☐

(b) Statement I is false, but statement II is true ☐

TOPIC 2

Differentiation, Dedifferentiation and Redifferentiation

***44.** Give biological term for the following sentence.

Process of maturation of cells derived from root apical and shoot-apical meristems and cambium to perform specific functions.

____

45. Maturation of cells derived from apical meristems and cambium is associated with structural changes in cell walls and ______________.

46. The tracheary elements carry water to long distances in plants. To perform this function, their cells would possess following anatomical features during differentiation except one which is

Abundant protoplasm, Strong and elastic cell walls, Lignocellulosic secondary cell walls

____

***47.** Complete the analogy given below related to differentiated cells.

Differentiated cells regain the capacity of division : Dedifferentiation : : ______________________ : Redifferentiation

***48.** Formation of interfascicular cambium and cork cambium from fully differentiated parenchyma cells is an example of <u>redifferentiation</u>.

(*Rewrite the statement after correcting the underlined word.*)

____

***49.** Complete the following analogy with respect to formation of vascular tissue.

Differentiation : Formation of tracheary elements : : ______________ : Specialisation of vascular cambium into secondary xylem and phloem.

***50.** A tumour is an example of ______________.

***51.** The parenchyma cells that are made to divide under controlled laboratory conditions during plant tissue culture represents ______________ (dedifferentiation/redifferentiation).

***52.** Give biological term for the sentence given below.

Process in which the cells once again lose the capacity to divide, but mature to perform specific functions.

____

53. The two types of open growth in plants are

____

54. The differentiation in plants is open because cells/tissues arising out of the ____________ have ____________ at maturity.

55. The final structure at maturity of a cell is determined by the location of cell within.

True ☐ False ☐

56. Complete the following analogy with respect to cell position after differentiation.

Cells away from root apical meristem : Root cap cells : : Cells at the periphery : ____________.

57. Consider the following statements.

Statement I Plant tissue can undergo dedifferentiation to form undifferentiated mass by hormonal stimulation.

Statement II In case of tumours, differentiated cells mass dedifferentiate to acquire cell division property.

Choose the correct option from the following.

(a) Statement I is true, but statement II is false ☐
(b) Statement I is false, but statement II is true ☐
(c) Both statements I and II are true ☐
(d) Both statements I and II are false ☐

TOPIC 3 Development

NCERT Pg. 172-174

58. Give biological term for the sentence given below.

All changes that an organism goes through during its life cycle.

____

59. In plants, development phase is the period between seed germination and ____________ (flowering/senescence)

60. The given diagram shows sequence of developmental processes in a plant cell, identify *A-D*.

Ⓒ
Death
Ⓑ
Meristematic cell
Ⓐ
Differentiation
Expansion (elongation)
Ⓓ
Mature cell

A. ____________
B. ____________
C. ____________
D. ____________

61. The ability of plants to follow different pathways in response to environment or phases of life to form different structures is called <u>heterozygosity</u>.

(*Rewrite the statement after correcting the underlined word.*)

____

62. Choose the odd one out with respect to heterophylly.

Cotton, Buttercup, Coriander, Larkspur

____

63. Consider the following statements.

Statement I Environment serves to be the only stimulant that drives heterophylly in plants.

Statement II Heterophylly of larkspur is an example of plasticity driven by phases of plant growth.

Choose the correct option from the following.

(a) Statement I is true, but statement II is false ☐

(b) Statement I is false, but statement II is true ☐

***64.** Match the following columns.

Column I	Column II
A.	1. Adult larkspur
B.	2. Buttercup in water habitat
C.	3. Juvenile larkspur
D.	4. Terrestrial buttercup

A. ______ B. ______ C. ______ D. ______

65. Complete the flowchart given below.

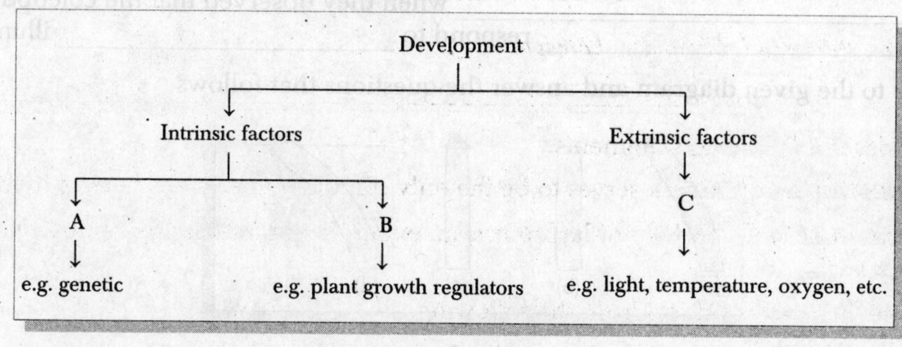

A. ______________ B. ______________ C. ______________

Plant Growth Regulators

66. PGRs are small, simple molecules of diverse ______________. These are also called ______________

67. Match the following columns.

Column I	Column II
A. Indole compounds	1. Kinetin
B. Adenine derivatives	2. ABA
C. Carotenoids derivatives	3. C_2H_4
D. Terpenes	4. GA
E. Gases	5. IAA

A. ______________ B. ______________ C. ______________

D. ______________ E. ______________

68. Choose the odd one out with respect to phytohormones.

Kinetin , Purine, N^6-furfurylamino purine, Ethylene

____

69. The phytohormones which promote cell division, enlargement, tropic growth, flowering, fruiting and seed formation are called ______________. The PGRs which promote dormancy and abscission in response to wounds and stresses are called

____

70. How many of the listed phytohormones are plant growth promoters?

Auxins, Gibberellins, Abscisic acid, Cytokinins

____

71. Discovery of phytohormones began with the observation of ________________ when they observed that the coleoptiles of ________________ respond to ________________ illumination.

72. Refer to the given diagram and answer the questions that follows

(i) What does the experiment demonstrate?

____

(ii) What does the arrow indicate in the diagram?

____

73. In F Skoog experiment, the tobacco stem of callus would proliferate, if nutrient medium is supplemented with yeast extract along with auxins.

True ☐ False ☐

74. F Skoog observed that the internodal segments of tobacco stem proliferate in the presence of auxin and ________________ (coconut milk /ethylene).

75. Match the following columns.

Column I	Column II
A. FW Went	1. Reported symptoms of bakanae disease in rice seedling.
B. E Kurosawa	2. Confirmed release of volatile substances from ripened oranges.
C. Skoog and Miller	3. Crystallised cytokinesis promoting active substance, kinetin.
D. Cousins	4. Isolated auxin from tips of coleoptiles of oat seedlings.

A.________ B. ________ C. ________ D. ________

76. Consider the following statements.

Statement I From Skoog's study it was evident that proliferation of callus needed both auxin and kinetin.

Statement II Cousin's proved that volatile PGR was promoting ripening process in fruits like banana.

Choose the correct option from the following.

(a) Statement I is true, but statement II is false ☐

(b) Statement I is false, but statement II is true ☐

(c) Both statements I and II are true ☐

(d) Both statements I and II are false ☐

77. Auxin was first isolated from the oat seedling.

True ☐ False ☐

78. Auxins are _______________ and _______________ compounds having certain growth regulating properties. These are generally produced by _______________ of the stems and roots.

79. Complete the following analogy given below.

Natural auxins : IAA and IBA : : Synthetic auxins : _______________.

80. Rose plants which are propagated through stem cuttings are often sprayed with synthetic auxin solutions because

(a) auxin promotes shoot elongation ☐ (b) auxin promotes rooting in shoots ☐
(c) auxin promotes cell expansion ☐ (d) auxin promotes cell division ☐

81. Name the hormone which initiates rooting in stem cutting, flowering in pineapples and promotes abscission of older leaves and fruits.

____

82. Name the phenomenon in which the growing apical bud inhibits the growth of lateral or axillary buds.

____

83. In tea plantation and hedge making, apical dominance is inhibited by the removal of _______________.

84. What does the diagram given below depict?

(a) Plant with apical bud (b) Plant with apical bud removed

85. Auxin induces _______________ in tomatoes, 2, 4-D is widely used as _______________ as it kills _______________ and does not affect mature monocotyledonous plants.

86. Consider the following statements.

Statement I Naphthalene acetic acid has been isolated from plants along with IAA and IBA.

Statement II Synthetic auxins are also used in agriculture for killing weeds and unwanted herbs.

Choose the correct option from the following.

(a) Statement I is true, but statement II is false ☐
(b) Statement I is false, but statement II is true ☐

87. Auxins control xylem differentiation and help in cell division.

True ☐ False ☐

88. GA$_1$ is the first gibberellin to be discovered and intensively studied form.

(*Rewrite the statement after correcting the underlined word.*)

____

89. A horticulture farmer who wants to increase his profit margin on apples by increasing their shelf life and on grapes by increasing stalk length should spray the plants a diluted solution of

(a) auxins ☐ (b) cytokinins ☐

(c) gibberellins ☐ (d) ethylene ☐

90. Complete the following analogy given below with respect to function of plant hormone.

Grapes : GA increases length of axis and length of stalk : : Apples :

____

91. Fruits can be left on trees longer so as to extend the shelf life because GA delays ______________ (senescence/parthenocarpy).

92. What is the function of GAs in brewing industry?

____

***93.** Gibberellin helps to increase the yield of sugarcane by 20 tonnes per acre by increasing the ______________

94. Spraying juvenile conifers with GAs hastens the ______________ (seed production/maturity period).

95. Give biological term for the following sentence.

Process of internode elongation just prior to flowering.______________

96. Choose the odd one out with respect to functions of gibberellin.

Beet, Cabbage, Sugarcane, Lettuce

____

97. Cytokinins have specific effect on ______________ and were discovered as chemical called ______________ from the autoclaved herring ______________.

98. Complete the following analogy given below with respect to chemical nature of cytokinin.

Synthetic cytokinin : Kinetin : : Natural cytokinin : ______________.

99. Consider the following statements.

Statement I Auxin stimulates plant growth while cytokinin inhibits plants growth as PGRs.

Statement II Cytokinin causes cell elongation while auxin promotes cell division in plants.

Choose the correct option from the following.

(a) Statement I is true, but statement II is false ☐

(b) Statement I is false, but statement II is true ☐

100. Name any two sources of zeatin.

____

101. Choose the odd one out with respect to the site of cytokinin production.

Root apices, Mature leaves, Young fruits, Developing shoot buds

____

102. Cytokinins help to produce new leaves, ______________ in leaves, lateral shoot growth and __________ shoot formation. It helps to overcome the __________ and promote ______________ .

103. The gaseous PGR, ethylene is synthesised by tissues undergoing senescence and ripening fruits.

True ☐ False ☐

104. Name the hormone which promotes horizontal growth of seedling, fruit ripening and senescence and abscission of leaves and flowers.

____

105. Ethylene inhibits respiratory climactic.

True ☐ False ☐

106. Hormone __________ is found in high concentrations in mature and slightly overripened fruits.

107. Identify whether the ethylene promotes (P) or inhibits (I) the listed processes.

(i) Seed and bud dormancy (P/I). ______________

(ii) Germination in peanut seeds (P/I). ______________

(iii) Internode/petiole elongation in deep water rice plant (P/I). ______________

(iv) Root growth and root hair formation (P/I). ______________

108. Apples are generally wrapped in wax paper. (*Give reason*)

____

109. Match Column I with Column II.

Column I	Column II
A. Auxin	1. Promotes abscission
B. Cytokinin	2. Parthenocarpy
C. Gibberellin	3. Internodal elongation
D. Ethylene	4. Chloroplast formation

	A	B	C	D			A	B	C	D	
(a)	2	1	3	4	☐	(b)	2	4	3	1	☐
(c)	2	4	1	3	☐	(d)	2	1	4	3	☐

110. Mention the function of ethylene in pineapples.

____

111. Name the most widely used compound as source of ethylene in agriculture.

____

112. Choose the odd one out with respect to the ethephon functioning.

Hastens ripening in tomato and apple, Inhibits abscisssion in flowers and fruits, Promotes female flowers in cucumber

____

113. Match the following columns.

	Column I (Phytohormones)		Column II (Plant parts where they are synthesised)
A.	IAA	1.	Tissue undergoing senescence
B.	Cytokinins	2.	Shoot apices
C.	Ethylene	3.	Root apices

A ______ B. ______ C. ______

114. Read the following statements and identify the PGR.

(i) General plant growth and metabolism inhibitor.

(ii) Acts as an antagonist to GAs.

(iii) Known as stress hormone.

____

115. ABA inhibits seed germination and closure of stomata.

True ☐ False ☐

116 ABA helps the seed to withstand desiccation by inducing ______.

117. Consider the following statements.

Statement I In case of water stress in plants, abscisic acid promotes closure of the stomata to conserve water.

Statement II Abscisic acid promotes seed dormancy which allows them to withstand unfavourable conditions.

Choose the correct option from the following.

(a) Statement I is true, but statement II is false ☐

(b) Both statements I and II are true. ☐

118. Name the hormone which acts as antagonistically to ABA. ______

119. Consider the following statements.

Statement I Gibberellins and abscisic acid are antagonist in their mode of actions as PGR.

Statement II Gibberellins promote seed dormancy while abscisic acid breaks seed dormancy.

Choose the correct option from the following.

(a) Statement I is true, but statement II is false ☐

(b) Statement I is false, but statement II is true ☐

120. Expand the following.

(i) IBA ______

(ii) NAA ______

(iii) 2,4-D ______________________

(iv) IAA ______________________

(v) GA ______________________

(vi) ABA ______________________

121. A particular plant species which is adapted to grow in marshy areas would have increased levels of which hormone?

(a) Ethylene ☐ (b) Abscisic acid ☐

(c) Gibberellic acid ☐ (d) Zeatin ☐

122. How many of the following listed events are promoted by more than one PGRs?

Dormancy in seed or buds, Abscission, Senescence, Apical dominance

____

Assertion-Reason Questions

The following questions consist of two statements- Assertion (A) and Reason (R). Answer these questions by selecting the appropriate option given below.
(a) Both A and R are true and R is the correct explanation of A
(b) Both A and R are true, but R is not the correct explanation of A
(c) A is true, but R is false
(d) A is false, but R is true

1. **Assertion** (A) Development of a mature plant from a zygote follows a precise order.

Reason (R) The secondary growth in gymnosperms is due to the apical meristems in root and shoot.

(a) ☐ (b) ☐ (c) ☐ (d) ☐

2. **Assertion** (A) The meristematic zone contains constantly dividing cells found in the root and shoot tips.

Reason (R) The cells of the meristematic zone contain large conspicuous nucleus and with no protoplasm.

(a) ☐ (b) ☐ (c) ☐ (d) ☐

3. **Assertion** (A) In arithmetic growth both the cells follow mitotic division and undergo exponential growth.

Reason (R) The increase in size of a leaf expressed per unit time refers to the absolute growth of the leaf.

(a) ☐ (b) ☐ (c) ☐ (d) ☐

***4.** **Assertion** (A) The realistic growth followed by most living systems is the geometric growth pattern.

Reason (R) Plants growing in a small area, would show a stationary phase of growth right after the log phase.

(a) ☐ (b) ☐ (c) ☐ (d) ☐

***5.** **Assertion** (A) Parenchyma cells of a leaf can be induced hormonally to divide under laboratory conditions.

Reason (R) A tumour formed in a particular organ is a product of redifferentiation of the cells.

(a) ☐ (b) ☐ (c) ☐ (d) ☐

***6.** **Assertion** (A) Buttercups growing in terrestrial habitats have broader leaves than those growing in aquatic habitat.

Reason (R) The pathway for leaf development is triggered by environmental changes due to plasticity of plants.

(a) ☐ (b) ☐ (c) ☐ (d) ☐

***7.** **Assertion** (A) Decapitation is an important practice in tea plantations.

Reason (R) 2,4 D is a synthetic version of auxin that is used for initiating rooting in stems.

(a) ☐ (b) ☐ (c) ☐ (d) ☐

***8.** **Assertion** (A) Gibberellins have been widely used for increasing the shelf-life of apples.

Reason (R) Gibberellins promote senescence in plants thereby increasing the market period.

(a) ☐ (b) ☐ (c) ☐ (d) ☐

***9.** **Assertion** (A) Cytokinins in a way act antagonistically with auxins.

Reason (R) Auxins promote apical dominance while cytokinins help in overcoming the same.

(a) ☐ (b) ☐ (c) ☐ (d) ☐

10. **Assertion** (A) The rise in respiration rate in fruits that hastens the ripening process is caused by gibberellins.

Reason (R) Ethylene is a gaseous hormone that can promote senescence and abscission in plants.

(a) ☐ (b) ☐ (c) ☐ (d) ☐

Case Based Questions

1. Read the following passage and answer the following questions.

Heterophyllous plants produce abrupt changes in leaf morphology in response to environmental factors. Certain plants possess narrow or deeply serrated/lobed leaves. Such leaves are adaptations to underwater conditions and also lack stomata. Thus, depth of water becomes a key factor involved in heterophylly. The phenomenon of heterophylly typically correlates with changes in water depth.

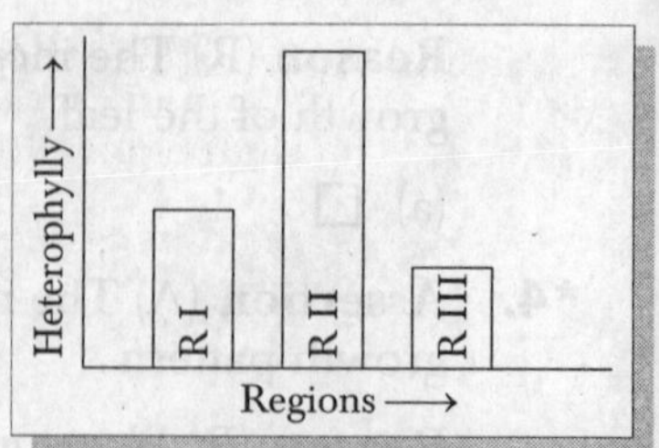

Moreover, light quality can also be effective in inducing the phenomenon of heterophylly. Photoperiod, however, only has a mild impact on leaf morphology orientation. Graph given below is an analysis based on the data collected for over a year in three different areas. Consider the graph and choose the correct answer for the given questions.

(i) Which of the given options is supposed to accurately represent R II?

(a) desert ☐ (b) land ☐

(c) aquatic habitat ☐ (d) arid habitat ☐

(ii) Which among the following is an exception to the phenomenon of heterophylly?

(a) Buttercup ☐ (b) Coriander ☐

(c) Larkspur ☐ (d) Gulmohar ☐

(iii) How would the shape of leaves change with increasing water depth?

(a) Leaves would show resemblance like aerial leaves ☐

(b) They will not show any modification ☐

(c) They will be narrower and lobed ☐

(d) They will be thick ☐

2. The graphs given below show the effect of two hormones A and B on a plant cutting. Observe the graphs carefully and answer the following questions by choosing the correct answer from the options given below.

(i) Identify A and B.

(a) A - Gibberellin, B - ABA ☐ (b) A - Auxin, B - ABA ☐

(c) A - ABA, B - Auxin ☐ (d) A - Cytokinin, B - Auxin ☐

(ii) Hormone B is synthesised

(a) in flowers ☐ (b) in roots ☐

(c) in leaves ☐ (d) in axillary buds ☐

(iii) Apart from the function of rooting, phytohormone A functions in

(a) stem elongation ☐ (b) seed germination ☐

(c) promoting seed dormancy ☐ (d) fruit ripening ☐

COMPETITION EDGE UP

1. Auxin is used by gardeners to prepare weed-free lawns. But no damage is caused to grass as auxin [NEET 2024]
   (a) promote apical dominance
   (b) promotes abscission of mature leaves only
   (c) does not affect mature monocotyledonous plants
   (d) can help in cell division in grasses, to produce growth

2. In tissue culture experiments, leaf mesophyll cells are put in a culture medium to form callus. This phenomenon may be called as [NCERT Pg. 172, NEET 2023]
   (a) dedifferentiation
   (b) development
   (c) senescence
   (d) differentiation

3. Spraying of which of the following phytohormone on juvenile conifers helps in hastening the maturity period, that leads to early seeds production? [NCERT Pg. 176, NEET 2023]
   (a) Gibberellic acid
   (b) Zeatin
   (c) Abscisic acid
   (d) Indole-3-butyric acid

4. Which hormone promotes internode/petiole elongation in deep water rice? [NCERT Pg. 177, NEET 2023]
   (a) Kinetin (b) Ethylene
   (c) 2, 4-D (d) GA_3

5. The gaseous plant growth regulator is used in plants to [NCERT Pg. 177, NEET 2022]
   (a) promote root growth and root hair formation to increase the absorption surface
   (b) help overcome apical dominance
   (c) kill dicotyledonous weeds in the fields
   (d) speed up the malting process

6. Production of cucumber has increased manifold in recent years. Application of which of the following phytohormones has resulted in this increased yield as the hormone is known to produce female flowers in the plants? [NCERT Pg. 177, NEET 2022]
   (a) Gibberellin
   (b) Ethylene
   (c) Cytokinin
   (d) ABA

7. Which one of the following plants does not show plasticity? [NCERT Pg. 173, NEET 2022]
   (a) Coriander
   (b) Buttercup
   (c) Maize
   (d) Cotton

8. Plants follow different pathways in response to environment or phases of life to form different kinds of structures. This ability is called [NCERT Pg. 173, NEET 2021]
   (a) elasticity (b) flexibility
   (c) plasticity (d) maturity

9. The plant hormone used to destroy weeds in a field is [NCERT Pg. 176, NEET 2021]
   (a) IAA (b) NAA
   (c) 2, 4-D (d) IBA

10. The process of growth is maximum during [NCERT Pg. 170, NEET (Sep.) 2020]
    (a) lag phase I
    (b) senescence
    (c) dormancy
    (d) log phase

Chapter 14

Breathing and Exchange of Gases

Scan and take Chapter Test

TOPIC 1

Respiratory Organs

NCERT Pg. 183-185

1. The process of exchange of O_2 from the atmosphere with CO_2 produced by the cells is called ______

2. Consider the following statements.

Statement I Insects use tracheal tubes to circulate oxygen throughout their body.

Statement II Frogs take in oxygen only by cutaneous respiration through their skin.

Choose the correct option from the following.

(a) Statement I is true, but statement II is false ☐

(b) Statement I is false, but statement II is true ☐

3. Name the animal group showing following types of respiration.

(i) Tracheal respiration ______

(ii) Branchial respiration ______

(iii) Pulmonary respiration ______

(iv) Cutaneous respiration ______

4. Match Column I with Column II.

Column I	Column II
A. Coelenterates	1. Branchial respiration
B. Earthworm	2. Cutaneous respiration
C. Grasshopper	3. Simple diffusion
D. Snails	4. Tracheal respiration

	A	B	C	D			A	B	C	D	
(a)	3	2	4	1	☐	(b)	3	2	1	4	☐
(c)	3	1	4	2	☐	(d)	3	1	2	4	☐

*Concepts of all questions bearing * are important for NEET & CUET*

5. Write the correct sequence of air passage in man through the structures given below.

Pharynx, Larynx, Trachea, Bronchi, Alveoli, Nasal passage, Nasal chamber, External nostril, Bronchioles

____

6. Nasopharynx opens through the larynx region into the ______________

7. Which portion of the human respiratory system is called sound box? ______________

8. Larynx is present in between ______________

9. Identify the structures *A*, *B*, *C* and *D* in the human respiratory system.

A
Larynx
B
C
Pleural membrane
Heart
D
Lung
Diaphragm

A. ______________

B. ______________

C. ______________

D. ______________

10. The cartilaginous flap which prevents the entry of food into the larynx during swallowing is ______________

11. Trachea divides into right and left primary bronchi at ________ (5th/6th) thoracic vertebrae.

12. Incomplete cartilaginous rings support all of the following except

Trachea, Bronchi, Initial bronchioles, Alveoli

____

13. Lungs are comprised of network of bronchi, bronchioles and alveoli.

True ☐ False ☐

14. Each lung is enclosed by two membranes called the ______________

15. Consider the following statements.

Statement I The trachea is the only part of conducting zone supported by incomplete cartilaginous rings.

Statement II The lungs are covered by a pericardium whose two layers are tightly packed with one another.

Choose the correct option from the following.

(a) Both statements I and II are true ☐

(b) Both statements I and II are false ☐

16. What is the function of pleural fluid? ______________

17. The outer pleural membrane is in close contact with the ________________ lining whereas the inner pleural membrane is in contact with the ________________ surface.

18. Study the different parts given in the box and identify how many of them are related to conducting part (C) and respiratory/exchange part (R) of respiratory system?

Alveolar duct, Trachea, Bronchi, Larynx, Nasopharynx, External nostrils, Nasal chamber, Terminal bronchioles, Alveoli

____

19. Which of the following represents the conducting zone of the respiratory tract?

(a) P, Q and S
(b) P, Q, R and S
(c) Q, R, S and T
(d) R, S and T

20. Choose the words from the given box to fill in the blanks.

Diaphragm, Ribs, Vertebral column, Sternum

Thoracic chamber is formed dorsally by the ________________, ventrally by the ________________, laterally by the ________________ and on the lower side by the dome-shaped ________________.

21. Write the names of the structure mentioned as *A*, *B* and *C* in the diagram given below.

A. ________________

B. ________________

C. ________________

22. The lungs in the thoracic cavity is protected

(a) dorsally by the ribs and laterally by the vertebral column
(b) dorsally by the vertebral column and laterally by the ribs
(c) ventrally by the vertebral column and laterally by ribs
(d) ventrally by ribs and laterally by vertebral column

***23.** Read the following functions and identify the part of respiratory system to which these functions belong.

(i) Transport the atmospheric air to alveoli.

(ii) Clear air from foreign particles.

(iii) Humidifies and bring air to body temperature.

____

24. Complete the missing words in the flowchart of process of respiration in humans.

Breathing or (A) _______________ by which atmospheric air is drawn in and CO_2 rich alveolar air is released out.

↓

Diffusion of O_2 and CO_2 across (B) _______________

↓

Transport of gases by the (C) _______________

↓

(D) _______________ of O_2 and CO_2 between blood and tissues

↓

Utilisation of O_2 by the cells for (E) _______________ and resultant release of CO_2, i.e. (F) _______________

TOPIC 2

Mechanism of Breathing

NCERT Pg. 185-186

25. Breathing involves two phases, i.e. _______________ during which atmospheric air drawn in and _______________ by which the alveolar air is released out.

26. Inspiration and expiration are active processes.

True ☐ False ☐

27. The movement of air into and out of the lungs is carried by creating a <u>chemical reaction</u> between the lungs and the atmosphere.

(*Rewrite the statement after correcting the underlined words.*)

____

***28.** Which of the following combination is correct for inspiration?

(a) Negative pressure in lungs; positive pressure in atmosphere ☐

(b) Positive pressure in lungs; positive pressure in atmosphere ☐

(c) Negative pressure in lungs; negative pressure in atmosphere ☐

(d) Positive pressure in lungs; negative pressure in atmosphere ☐

***29.** Negative pressure in lungs is achieved when intrapulmonary pressure is _______________ than the atmospheric pressure.

***30.** Expiration takes place when the __________ pressure is greater than the atmospheric pressure.

***31.** Consider the following statements.

Statement I Positive pressure in lungs allows air to move out of the body during expiration.

Statement II Increase in the pulmonary pressure forces air out of the lungs during expiration.

Choose the correct option from the following.

(a) Both statements I and II are true ☐

(b) Both statements I and II are false ☐

***32.** Arrange the following steps of inspiration in correct order of their occurrence.

I. The contraction of external intercostal muscles raises the ribs and sternum.

II. Volume of thorax increases in the dorso-ventral axis.

III. Intrapulmonary pressure decreases.

IV. Diaphragm contraction.

V. Air rushes into the lungs.

VI. Volume of the thorax increases in the anterior-posterior axis.

____

33. Which of the following happens during the given process?

(a) Decrease in dorso-ventral axis ☐

(b) Decrease in antero-posterior axis ☐

(c) Increase in intra pulmonary pressure ☐

(d) Increase in volume of thoracic cavity ☐

***34.** Arrange the following steps of expiration in correct order of their occurrence.

I. Relaxation of external intercostal muscles and return of diaphragm and sternum to their normal position.

II. Air expelled from lungs.

III. Volume of thorax decreases.

IV. Intra-pulmonary pressure increases.

____

***35.** During expiration, the diaphragm becomes __________ (concave/dome/oblique) shaped.

***36.** Consider the following statements.

Statement I During inspiration the ribs and sternum are raised to reduce the dorso-ventral axis.

Statement II The diaphragm contracts and pulls down to increase the antero-posterior axis in inspiration.

Choose the correct option from the following.

(a) Statement I is true, but statement II is false ☐

(b) Statement I is false, but statement II is true ☐

37. Additional muscles required for forceful breathing are ______________________________

38. Write the names of the following muscles.

(i) Inspiratory muscles - contraction of these brings inspiration, e.g.

____

(ii) Expiratory muscles - contraction of these bring expiration, e.g.

____

39. The rate of breathing in a normal healthy human is 70-72 times/minute.
(*Rewrite the statement after correcting the underlined words.*)

____

40. An instrument for measuring the air capacity of lungs is ______________ (Spirometer/Stethoscope).

41. Consider the following statements and choose the correct ones.

I. The movement of air into and out of the lungs is carried out by creating a pressure gradient between the lungs and the atmosphere.

II. The diaphragm and a specialised set of muscles external and internal intercostals between the ribs, help in generation of such gradients.

III. Expiration is initiated by the contraction of diaphragm.

IV. The contraction of internal-intercostal muscles lifts up the ribs and the sternum.

Choose the correct answer from the options given below.

(a) I and II ☐ (b) II and III ☐
(c) I and III ☐ (d) II and IV ☐

***42.** In the diagrams given below complete the labels for mechanism of breathing.

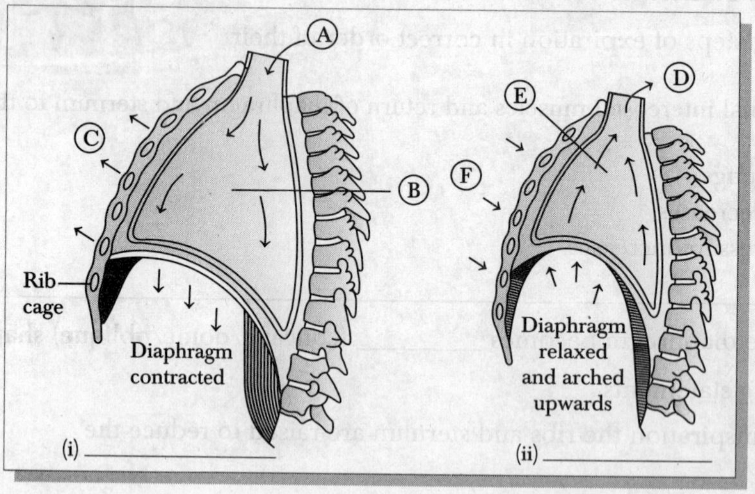

Rib cage
Diaphragm contracted
Diaphragm relaxed and arched upwards

(i) ______________ (ii) ______________

A. ______________
B. ______________
C. ______________
D. ______________
E. ______________
F. ______________

TOPIC 3

Respiratory Volumes and Capacities

***43.** Write the names of the respiratory volume against each statement.

(i) Additional volume of air, a person can inspire by a forcible inspiration.

____

(ii) Additional volume of air, a person can expire by a forcible expiration.

____

(iii) Volume of air remaining in the lungs even after a forcible expiration.

____

(iv) Volume of air inspired or expired during a normal respiration.

____

(v) Total volume of air accommodated in the lungs at the end of a forced inspiration.

____

(vi) Volume of air that will remain in the lungs after a normal expiration.

____

***44.** Consider the following statements.

Statement I A healthy man can inspire or expire approximately 6000 to 8000 mL of air per minute.

Statement II Even after forcible expiration about 500 mL of air still remains in the lungs.

Choose the correct option from the following.

(a) Statement I is true, but statement II is false ☐

(b) Statement I is false, but statement II is true ☐

***45.** Match the following columns.

Column I	Column II
A. Tidal volume	1. 2500-3000 mL of air
B. Inspiratory reserve volume	2. 1000-1100 mL of air
C. Expiratory reserve volume	3. 500 mL of air
D. Residual volume	4. 1200 mL of air

A .________ B. ________ C. ________ D. ________

***46.** Arrange the following in the order of increasing volume.

Tidal volume, Residual volume, ERV, Vital capacity

____

***47.** Different respiratory volumes are given below.

Tidal volume = 500 mL Residual volume = 1000 mL
IRV = 2500 mL ERV = 1000 mL

The Functional Residual Capacity (FRC) is ____________ mL

***48.** The volume of air that a person can inspire after normal expiration is 3500 mL and the tidal volume is 500 mL. Find the volume of air a person can inspire by forceful inspiration.

(a) 4000 mL ☐ (b) 3000 mL ☐ (c) 3500 mL ☐ (d) 4500 mL ☐

***49.** Match the following columns.

Column I	Column II
A. Total Lung Capacity (TLC)	1. IRV + TV
B. Expiratory Capacity (EC)	2. FRC + TV + IRV
C. Inspiratory Capacity (IC)	3. ERV + TV
D. Vital Capacity (VC)	4. ERV + TV + IRV

A. ____________ B. ____________ C. ____________ D. ____________

50. In the given graph mark the following.

Inspiratory reserve volume, Vital capacity, Functional residual capacity, Residual volume, Total lung capacity

A. ____________
B. ____________
C. ____________
D. ____________
E. ____________

TOPIC 4

Exchange of Gases

NCERT Pg. 187-188

51. The exchange of gases in the alveoli of the lungs takes place by ____________ (passive transport/active transport/simple diffusion).

52. What are the two important factors that can affect the rate of diffusion of gases in respiration?

____

53. Give the scientific term for the pressure exerted by an individual gas in a mixture of gases.

____

***54.** Identify *A, B, C* and *D* with respect to partial pressure of oxygen and CO_2 in different mediums.

Respiratory gas	Atmospheric air	Alveoli	Blood (Deoxygenated)	Blood (Oxygenated)	Tissues
O_2	159 mm Hg	(A)	40 mm Hg	(B)	40 mm Hg
CO_2	(C)	40 mm Hg	45 mm Hg	40 mm Hg	(D)

A. ______ B. ______ C. ______ D. ______

55. Consider the following statements.

Statement I In a mixture of CO_2 and O_2 in water, it is found that O_2 dissolves at a higher rate than CO_2.

Statement II Lesser the thickness of the diffusion membrane, faster would be the rate of diffusion.

Choose the correct option from the following.

(a) Statement I is true, but statement II is false

(b) Statement I is false, but statement II is true

***56.** Complete the following sentences.

(i) The partial pressure of CO_2 is ______ (higher/lesser) in systemic veins than in systemic arteries.

(ii) The partial pressure of CO_2 is ______ (higher/lesser) in tissue spaces than in systemic arteries.

***57.** Identify *A* to *D* in the given diagram.

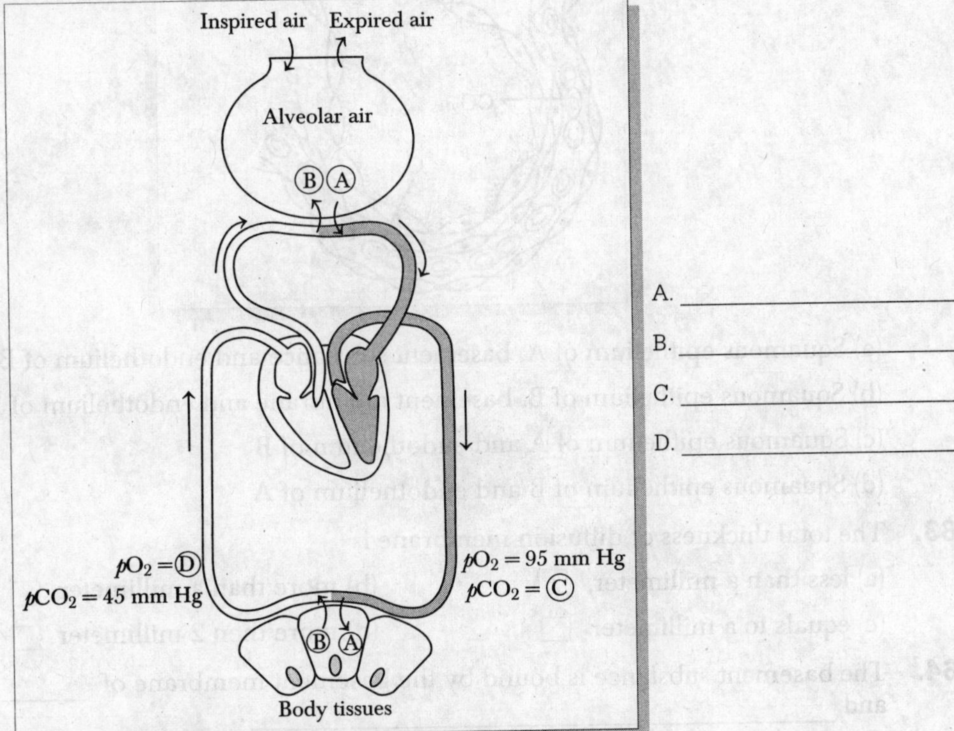

A. ______

B. ______

C. ______

D. ______

58. Which of the following combinations allow exchange of gases at the alveoli?

(a) pO_2 in alveoli > pO_2 in capillary ☐

(b) pO_2 in alveoli = pO_2 in capillary ☐

(c) pCO_2 in alveoli = pCO_2 in capillary ☐

(d) pCO_2 in alveoli > pCO_2 in capillary ☐

59. The solubility of CO_2 in blood is 20-25 times lesser than the solubility of O_2.

True ☐ False ☐

60. Consider the following statements.

Statement I pCO_2 in alveolar capillaries is 5 mm Hg more than pCO_2 in alveolar air

Statement II CO_2 diffuses out of the tissues due to its high partial pressure in the tissues than blood.

Choose the correct option from the following.

(a) Both statements I and II are true ☐

(b) Both statements I and II are false ☐

61. In lungs, the air is separated from the venous blood through ______ and ______.

62. The diffusion membrane is formed of

(a) Squamous epithelium of A, basement substance and endothelium of B ☐

(b) Squamous epithelium of B, basement membrane and endothelium of A ☐

(c) Squamous epithelium of A and endothelium of B ☐

(d) Squamous epithelium of B and endothelium of A ☐

63. The total thickness of diffusion membrane is

(a) less than a millimeter ☐ (b) more than a millimeter ☐

(c) equals to a millimeter ☐ (d) more then 2 millimeter ☐

64. The basement substance is bound by the basement membrane of ______ and ______.

TOPIC 5

Transport of Gases

NCERT Pg. 189-190

65. What percentage of O_2 is transported by RBCs and plasma, respectively in human body?

____

***66.** Blood carries CO_2 in three form. The correct percentages of CO_2 in these forms are

(i) as carbaminohaemoglobin ____________________

(ii) as bicarbonates ____________________

(iii) dissolved form in plasma ____________________

***67.** Consider the following statements.

Statement I Maximum percentage of CO_2 is transported as carbamino-haemoglobin in blood.

Statement II Binding of carbon dioxide with haemoglobin is favoured at the tissue level.

Choose the correct option from the following.

(a) Statement I is true, but statement II is false ☐

(b) Statement I is false, but statement II is true ☐

***68.** Haemoglobin is a ________ coloured ________ containing pigment present in the ________. Oxygen can bind with haemoglobin in a reversible manner to form. Each haemoglobin molecule can carry a maximum of ________ molecules of O_2.

***69.** What are the four factors affecting the binding of haemoglobin with oxygen?

____

***70.** Consider the following statements.

Statement I Binding of oxygen with haemoglobin is an example of oxidation reaction.

Statement II Low pH conditions in the alveoli favours the dissociation of oxygen from haemoglobin.

Choose the correct option from the following.

(a) Statement I is true, but statement II is false ☐

(b) Both statements I and II are false ☐

***71.** Complete the equation by stating the location for '*X*' and '*Y*'.

$$HbO_2 \underset{\text{Association (At 'Y')}}{\overset{\text{Dissociation (At 'X')}}{\rightleftharpoons}} Hb + O_2$$

X. ____________________ *Y*. ____________________

***72.** In an oxygen dissociation curve, what is plotted on the

(i) x-axis ____________________

(ii) y-axis ____________________

***73.** The oxygen dissociation curve is ____________ in shape.

74. After taking a long deep breath we do not respire for few seconds due to more CO_2 in the blood.

True ☐ False ☐

***75.** Every 100 mL of oxygenated blood can deliver around <u>15 mL</u> of oxygen to the tissues under normal physiological conditions.
(*Rewrite the statement after correcting the underlined words.*)

____

***76.** The given graph shows an oxygen dissociation curve for haemoglobin.

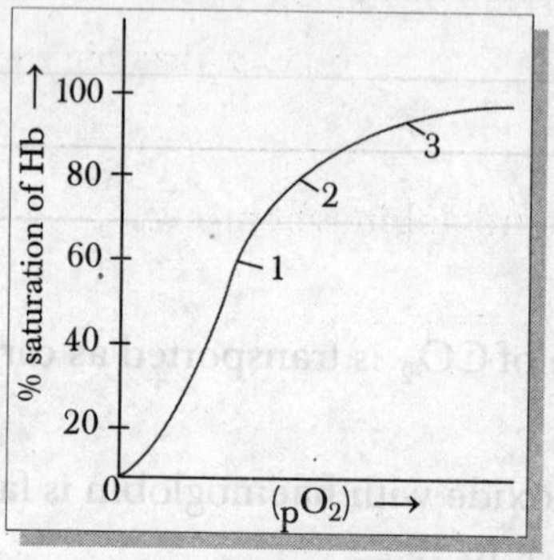

Locate left ventricle, pulmonary vein and vena cava in the given graph with respect to positions 1, 2 and 3. _______________________

***77.** If 1g of Hb carries 1.34 mL of O_2 and 100 mL of blood has 15 g Hb then, how much O_2 will be carried approximately by 100 mL of arterial blood?

____

***78.** Oxygen dissociation curve can be shifted from normal position depending on its various factor. Mention the conditions with respect to pO_2, pCO_2, H^+ ions pH and temperature when

(i) the curve is shifted to right _______________________

(ii) the curve is shifted to left _______________________

***79.** At partial pressure of 40 mm Hg, curve B shows lesser oxygen saturation of haemoglobin than curve A, probably because of

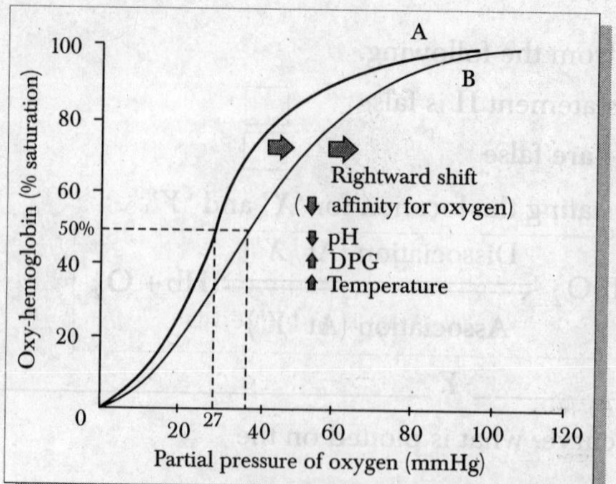

(a) High pO_2 in blood ☐ (b) Low pCO_2 in blood ☐

(c) Increased acidity ☐ (d) Low temperature ☐

***80.** Choose the odd one out for the factors favouring dissociation of oxyhaemoglobin to deliver O_2 to tissue.

$\uparrow pO_2$, $\uparrow pCO_2$, $\uparrow H^+$, $\uparrow$ *Temperature*

____

***81.** The factor which favours the formation of HCO_3^- and H^+ in the blood is _______________ (high pCO_2/low pCO_2).

***82.** A high percentage of CO_2 is transported in dissolved state in comparison to O_2 because

(i) CO_2 has less solubility in plasma. (ii) CO_2 has high solubility in plasma.

____

***83.** CO_2 dissociates from carbaminohaemoglobin when

pO_2 : _______________ :: pCO_2 : _______________

***84.** Identify X in the given equation.

$$CO_2 + H_2O \underset{}{\overset{X}{\rightleftharpoons}} H_2CO_3 \underset{}{\overset{X}{\rightleftharpoons}} H^+ + HCO_3^-$$

X. _______________

***85.** Which of the following conditions favour this reaction?

$HCO_3^- + H^+ \rightarrow H_2CO_3 \rightarrow H_2O + CO_2$

(a) Low pCO_2 ☐ (b) High pCO_2 ☐ (c) Low pO_2 ☐ (d) High pO_2 ☐

86. Every 100 mL of deoxygenated blood delivers approximately _______________ mL of CO_2 to the alveoli.

***87.** Write the correct sequence of CO_2 diffusion by choosing the terms from the box given below.

Capillary basement membrane, Alveolar epithelium, Alveolar epithelial basement membrane, Capillary endothelial membrane, Thin interstitial space

____

TOPIC 6

Regulation of Respiration

NCERT Pg. 190

88. Human beings have a significant ability to maintain and moderate the respiratory rhythm to suit the demands of the body tissues. This is achieved by _______________ system.

89. Respiratory process is regulated by certain specialised centres in the brain. Name them according to the description.

(i) Responsible for regulation of respiration or causes inspiration.

____

(ii) Reduce the inspiratory duration upon stimulation or limit inspiration.

____

***90.** Consider the following statements.

Statement I The primary regulation of respiration is mediated by centres located in the medulla.

Statement II The reduction of inspiration occurs due to signals from the pneumotaxic centres in pons.

Choose the correct option from the following.

(a) Both statements I and II are true ☐

(b) Both statements I and II are false ☐

***91.** Write the location of pneumotaxic centre and respiratory rhythm centre within human brain.

______

92. Chemical regulation of respiration is done *via* ______ area situated adjacent to the rhythm centre in the brain.

93. A person in a congested room shows an increase in the rate of breathing due to

(a) Increase in the CO_2 levels detected by the pons ☐

(b) Decrease in O_2 levels detected by the medulla ☐

(c) Increase in CO_2 level detected by the medulla ☐

(d) Decrease in the O_2 level detected by the pons ☐

94. Receptors associated with aortic arch and carotid artery can recognises changes in ______ and ______ concentration and send necessary signals to ______ for remedial actionb.

95. Respiratory centre of brain is stimulated by ______ (O_2 / CO_2) content in ______ (arterial/venous) blood.

96. Consider the following statements.

Statement I Oxygen levels in the body does not create any significant changes to the respiratory rhythm.

Statement II Suffocation reduces the pH levels in blood activating the chemosensitive area in medulla.

Choose the correct option from the following.

(a) Both statements I and II are true ☐

(b) Both statements I and II are false ☐

97. The role of oxygen in the regulation of respiratory rhythm is ______

TOPIC 7

Disorders of Respiratory System

98. Name the pulmonary disease in which alveolar surface area involved in gas exchange is drastically reduced due to damage in the alveolar walls. ________________

***99.** *Parthenium* pollens can trigger breathing difficulties along with wheezing in certain patients due to
(a) Inflammation of the alveoli ☐
(b) Inflammation of bronchi and bronchioles ☐
(c) Inflammation of pericardium ☐
(d) Inflammation of nasal lining ☐

100. ________________ is a chronic respiratory disorder caused mainly by cigarette smoking.

101. Consider the following statements.
Statement I Cigarette smoking can damage the respiratory surface of the alveolar walls.
Statement II Prolonged exposure to dust can alter the lung surface due to proliferation of fibrous tissue.
Choose the correct option from the following.
(a) Both statements I and II are true ☐ (b) Both statements I and II are false ☐

***102.** A respiratory disorder causing difficulty in breathing, wheezing due to inflammation of bronchi and bronchioles is ________________

Assertion-Reason Questions

The following questions consist of two statements- Assertion (A) and Reason (R). Answer these questions by selecting the appropriate option given below.
(a) Both A and R are true and R is the correct explanation of A
(b) Both A and R are true, but R is not the correct explanation of A
(c) A is true, but R is false
(d) A is false, but R is true

1. Assertion (A) During swallowing the glottis remains covered by a thick muscular flap called epiglottis.
Reason (R) The covering of the glottis during swallowing prevents food from entering the wind pipe.
(a) ☐ (b) ☐ (c) ☐ (d) ☐

2. Assertion (A) The conducting part of the respiratory system prepares the air so that exchange can occur in the alveoli.
Reason (R) The conducting part starts with the external nostrils and end up at the terminal bronchioles.
(a) ☐ (b) ☐ (c) ☐ (d) ☐

3. **Assertion** (A) The process of breathing requires pressure gradient between the lungs and the atmosphere.

Reason (R) For inspiration, there should be a positive pressure in the lungs which would force air from outside to enter the lungs.

(a) ☐ (b) ☐ (c) ☐ (d) ☐

4. **Assertion** (A) During expiration there is decrease in the volume of thoracic cavity which increases intrapulmonary pressure.

Reason (R) During expiration the ribs and sternum lowers down and the diaphragm relaxes and return to original position.

(a) ☐ (b) ☐ (c) ☐ (d) ☐

5. **Assertion** (A) The residual volume of the lungs can be obtained from the total lung capacity and vital capacity.

Reason (R) Residual volume is the sum total of total lung capacity and vital capacity of the lungs.

(a) ☐ (b) ☐ (c) ☐ (d) ☐

6. **Assertion** (A) Carbon dioxide can diffuse much faster than oxygen across the diffusion membrane.

Reason (R) Gases move from region of higher partial pressure to a region of lower partial pressure.

(a) ☐ (b) ☐ (c) ☐ (d) ☐

7. **Assertion** (A) Partial pressure of carbon dioxide in blood capillaries is more than that of respiring cells.

Reason (R) The partial pressure of gases is an important factor that contributes towards the direction of diffusion.

(a) ☐ (b) ☐ (c) ☐ (d) ☐

8. **Assertion** (A) Oxygen binds to haemoglobin at the alveolar surface and gets dissociated at the tissues.

Reason (R) Low pO_2 and High pCO_2 at the lung surface causes the formation of oxyhaemoglobin.

(a) ☐ (b) ☐ (c) ☐ (d) ☐

9. **Assertion** (A) Presence of carbonic anhydrase is crucial in transporting carbon dioxide in blood.

Reason (R) Carbonic anhydrase catalyses the reversible formation of bicarbonates at the tissues.

(a) ☐ (b) ☐ (c) ☐ (d) ☐

10. **Assertion** (A) An increase in pH and CO_2 concentration can alter the breathing rate by neural control.

Reason (R) The chemosensitive area in pons activate in response to changes in pH and CO_2 levels.

(a) ☐ (b) ☐ (c) ☐ (d) ☐

Case Based Questions

1. The graph represents the expiratory reserve volume of two individuals X and Y. Compare the plots and answer the following questions:

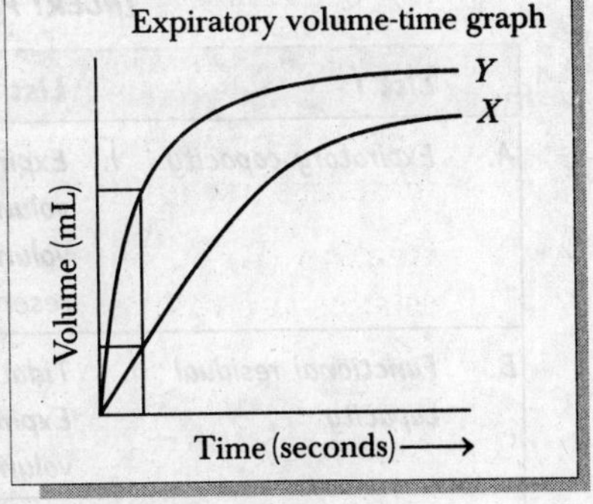

(i) Which of the following conclusions can be derived from the plot?

(a) Both the persons have a normal lung function ☐

(b) X is suffering from a respiratory disease. ☐

(c) Y is suffering from a respiratory disease ☐

(d) Both X and Y have respiratory disorders ☐

(ii) What could be a probable cause of lowering the expiratory volumes?

(a) Loss of elasticity of lung membrane ☐ (b) Infection of the pericardium ☐

(c) Inflammation of the respiratory tract ☐ (d) All of the above ☐

(iii) How is ERV related to FRC?

(a) ERV = FRC + RV ☐ (b) ERV = FRC + TV ☐

(c) ERV = FRC- RV ☐ (d) ERV = FRC – TV ☐

2. The image represents oxygen dissociation curve. The curve shifts to position A and B under certain conditions. With reference to this answer the following questions.

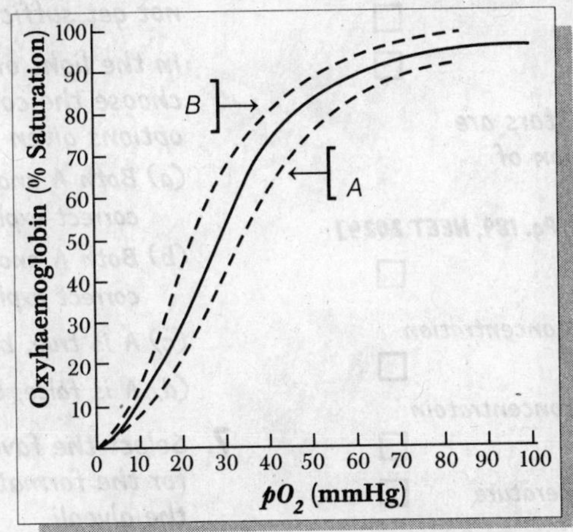

(i) Where would the curve show a shift to position A?

(a) Tissues ☐ (b) Blood capillaries ☐ (c) Alveoli ☐ (d) Conducting system ☐

(ii) Which of the following factors can cause a shift to position B?

(a) Low pO_2 ☐ (b) Low pCO_2 ☐

(c) Low pH ☐ (d) High temperature ☐

(iii) Which of the following pairs support the shift of the curve to A?

(a) Low pO_2, High pCO_2 ☐ (b) Low pO_2, Low pCO_2 ☐

(c) High pO_2, Low pCO_2 ☐ (d) High pO_2, High pCO_2 ☐

COMPETITION EDGE UP

1. Match List I with List II. **[NCERT Pg. 187, NEET 2024]**

	List I		List II
A.	Expiratory capacity	I.	Expiratory reserve volume + Tidal volume + Inspiratory reserve volume
B.	Functional residual capacity	II.	Tidal volume + Expiratory reserve volume
C.	Vital capacity	III.	Tidal volume + Inspiratory reserve volume
D.	Inspiratory capacity	IV.	Expiratory reserve volume + Residual volume

Choose the correct answer from the options given below.

(a) A-II, B-IV, C-I, D-III ☐
(b) A-III, B-II, C-IV, D-I ☐
(c) A-II, B-I, C-IV, D-III ☐
(d) A-I, B-III, C-II, D-IV ☐

2. Which of the following factors are favourable for the formation of oxyhaemoglobin in alveoli? **[NCERT Pg. 189, NEET 2024]**

(a) High pO_2 and high pCO_2 ☐
(b) High pO_2 and lesser H^+ concentration ☐
(c) Low pCO_2 and high H^+ concentratoin ☐
(d) Low pCO_2 and high temperature ☐

3. Vital capacity of lung is **[NCERT Pg. 187, NEET 2023]**

(a) IRV + ERV + TV + RV ☐
(b) IRV + ERV + TV – RV ☐
(c) IRV + ERV + TV ☐
(d) IRV + ERV ☐

4. Which of the following is not the function of conducting part of respiratory system? **[NCERT Pg. 185, NEET 2022]**

(a) Inhaled air is humidified ☐
(b) Temperature of inhaled air is brought to body temperature ☐
(c) Provides surface for diffusion of O_2 and CO_2 ☐
(d) It clears inhaled air from foreign particles ☐

5. Under normal physiological condition in human being every 100 mL of oxygenated blood can deliver .... mL of O_2 to the tissues. **[NCERT Pg. 189, 2022]**

(a) 5 mL ☐ (b) 4 mL ☐
(c) 10 mL ☐ (d) 2 mL ☐

6. Assertion (A) A person goes to high altitude and experiences 'altitude sickness' with symptoms like breathing difficulty and heart palpitations.

Reason (R) Due to low atmospheric pressure at high altitude, the body does not get sufficient oxygen.

In the light of the above statements, choose the correct answer from the options given below. **[NEET 2021]**

(a) Both A and R are true and R is the correct explanation of A ☐
(b) Both A and R are true, but R is not the correct explanation of A ☐
(c) A is true, but R is false ☐
(d) A is false, but R is true ☐

7. Select the favourable conditions required for the formation of oxyhaemoglobin at the alveoli. **[NCERT Pg. 189, NEET 2021]**

(a) High pO_2, low pCO_2, less H^+, lower temperature ☐
(b) Low pO_2, high pCO_2, more H^+, higher temperature ☐
(c) High pO_2, high pCO_2, less H^+, higher temperature ☐
(d) Low pO_2, low pCO_2, more H^+, higher temperature ☐

8. *The partial pressures (in mm Hg) of oxygen (O_2) and carbon dioxide (CO_2) at alveoli (the site of diffusion) are* **[NCERT Pg. 187, NEET 2021]**

(a) $pO_2 = 104$ and $pCO_2 = 40$ ☐

(b) $pO_2 = 40$ and $pCO_2 = 45$ ☐

(c) $pO_2 = 95$ and $pCO_2 = 40$ ☐

(d) $pO_2 = 159$ and $pCO_2 = 0.3$ ☐

9. *Select the correct events that occur during inspiration.* **[NCERT Pg. 185, NEET (Sep.) 2020]**

I. Contraction of diaphragm.

II. Contraction of external inter-costal muscles.

III. Pulmonary volume decreases.

IV. Intra pulmonary pressure increases.

(a) III and IV ☐

(b) I, II and IV ☐

(c) Only IV ☐

(d) I and II ☐

10. *The Total Lung Capacity (TLC) is the total volume of air accommodated in the lungs at the end of a forced inspiration. This includes* **[NCERT Pg. 187, NEET (Oct.) 2020]**

(a) RV, IC (Inspiratory Capacity), EC (Expiratory Capacity) and ERV ☐

(b) RV, ERV, IC and EC ☐

(c) RV, ERV, VC (Vital Capacity) and FRC (Functional Residual Capacity) ☐

(d) RV (Residual Volume), ERV (Expiratory Reserve Volume), TV (Tidal Volume) and IRV (Inspiratory Reserve Volume) ☐

11. *Identify the wrong statement with reference to transport of oxygen.* **[NCERT Pg. 189, NEET 2020]**

(a) Partial pressure of CO_2 can interfere with O_2 binding with haemoglobin ☐

(b) Higher H^+ concentration in alveoli favours the formation of oxyhaemoglobin ☐

(c) Low pCO_2 in alveoli favours the formation of oxyhaemoglobin ☐

(d) Binding of oxygen with haemoglobin is mainly related to partial pressure of O_2 ☐

Chapter 15

Body Fluids and Circulation

1. Fill in the blanks.

(i) In simple organisms like sponges and coelenterates, ___________ circulates in body cavity from the surroundings to facilitate the exchange of O_2, CO_2, nutrients and waste products in cells.

(ii) More complex organisms use special fluids within their bodies to transport such materials. The _________ is the most commonly found body fluid in most of the higher organisms including humans for this purpose.

2. What is the composition of blood?

____

3. Write the percentage of the following.

(i) Plasma in blood _______________________________

(ii) Water in plasma _______________________________

(iii) Protein in plasma _____________________________

4. Blood is slightly _______________ in nature with pH range _______________ .

5. Plasma is a pink coloured, viscous fluid in blood.

True ☐ False ☐

6. Choose the odd one out.

Albumin, Fibrinogen, Globulin, Cellulose

____

*Concepts of all questions bearing * are important for NEET & CUET*

7. Match the following columns.

Column I (Blood proteins)	Column II (Functions)
A. Fibrinogen	1. Defense mechanisms of the body
B. Globulins	2. Osmotic balance
C. Albumins	3. Clotting or coagulation of blood

A. ______ B. ______ C. ______

8. Name the minerals present in plasma. ______

9. What is '*X*' in the formula, Plasma – '*X*' = Serum

X. ______

10. Consider the following statements.

Statement I Fibrinogens are required for coagulation of blood.

Statement II Plasma without clotting factors is called serum.

Choose the correct option from the following.

(a) Both statements I and II are true ☐

(b) Both statements I and II are false ☐

11. Choose the odd one out. *Erythrocytes, Leucocytes, Thrombocytes, Plasma*

______

12. The common names for erythrocytes, leucocytes and thrombocytes are ______, ______ and ______, respectively.

13. How many features are correct for erythrocytes?

(i) Least abundant of all the cells in blood.

(ii) Formed in the red bone marrow in adults.

(iii) Devoid of nucleus in most of the mammals.

______

14. Mammalian RBCs are ______ (sickle/biconcave) in shape.

15. What is the amount of haemoglobin present in 100 mL blood of human?

______

16. Give the scientific term for the following.

(i) Formation of erythrocytes. ______

(ii) The process of formation of blood clot. ______

(iii) The red coloured, iron containing complex protein in red blood cells. ______

17. Give one significant role of RBCs in our body. ______

18. The graveyard of RBCs is <u>kidney</u>.
(*Rewrite the statement after correcting the underlined word.*)

______

19. How many features are true for White Blood Cells (WBCs)?

(i) Lack haemoglobin

(ii) Lifespan ranges from a few hours to few days.

(iii) Enucleate cells.

(iv) Ranges from 6000 – 8000 mm^{-3} of blood approximately in healthy human.

____

***20.** Complete the flowchart depicting the types of leucocytes in human body.

Leucocytes → *A*, *B*

A → *C*, Basophils, *D*

B → *E*, Lymphocytes

Lymphocytes → *F*, *G*

A. ________ B. ________ C. ________ D. ________

E. ________ F. ________ G. ________

21. A person with peanut allergy, having eaten them by mistake would show an increase in which of the following cell type in his blood report?

(a) Lymphocytes ☐ (b) Eosinophils ☐ (c) Neutrophils ☐ (d) Macrophages ☐

22. Choose the odd one out. *Neutrophils, Basophils, Eosinophils, Monocytes*

____

23. Complete the analogy with respect to WBCs.

Neutrophils : Most abundant in the body : : ________ : Least abundant in the body.

24. Consider the following statements.

Statement I B and T cells are a type of WBCs that are actively involved in defence of the body.

Statement II Liver can be called as the cemetery of the red blood cells .

Choose the correct option from the following.

(a) Statement I is true, but statement II is false ☐

(b) Statement I is false, but statement II is true ☐

***25.** Match the following columns.

	Column I (Types of leucocytes/WBCs)		Column II (% of total WBCs)
A.	Neutrophils	1.	20-25%
B.	Basophils	2.	2-3%
C.	Monocytes	3.	6-8%
D.	Eosinophils	4.	0.5 -1%
E.	Lymphocytes	5.	60-65%

A. ________ B. ________ C. ________

D. ________ E. ________

***26.** Choose the odd one out with respect to secretions of basophils.

Histamine, Serotonin, Heparin, Antibodies

____

***27.** Match the following columns.

Column I (WBCs)	Column II (Functions)
A. Eosinophils	1. Involved in inflammatory reactions
B. Basophils	2. Allergic reactions
C. Neutrophils	3. Responsible for immune response
D. Lymphocytes	4. Phagocytic cells
E. Monocytes	

A. ________ B. ________ C. ________ D. ________ E. ________

***28.** How many of the given leucocytes can destroy foreign organisms entering the body?

Eosinophils, Basophils, Neutrophils, Monocytes, Lymphocytes

____

***29.** Identify the cells labelled as *A* to *E*.

A B C D E

A. ______________
B. ______________
C. ______________
D. ______________
E. ______________

30. The largest leucocyte is <u>neutrophil</u>. (*Rewrite the statement after correcting the underlined word.*)

____

31. Match the following columns.

Column I (Formed elements)	Column II (Number in/mm^3 of blood)
A. Erythrocytes	1. 5–5·5 millions
B. Leucocytes	2. 6000–8000
C. Platelets	3. 1,50,000 – 3,50,000

A. ________ B. ________ C. ________

32. A person with dengue hemorrhagic fever have fall in platelet count that could be fatal because

(a) There could be severe dehydration ☐

(b) There could be internal bleeding and plasma leakage ☐

(c) There could be a high persistent fever ☐

(d) There could be a reduction in the WBC count ☐

33. Name the two blood grouping systems used all over the world.

____

34. Write the scientific terms for the following.

(i) Chemicals that can induce immune response. ________________

(ii) Proteins produced in response to antigens. ________________

***35.** ABO blood grouping is based on the presence or absence of __________ (2/4) surface antigens.

***36.** Identify *W* to *Z* in the table given below.

Blood groups	Antigens on RBCs	Antibodies in plasma	Donor's group
A	*(W)*	anti-B	A, O
B	B	anti-A	*(Y)*
AB	A, B	*(X)*	AB, A, B, O
O	Nil	anti-A, B	*(Z)*

W. __________ X. __________ Y. __________ Z. __________

***37.** Consider the following statements.

Statement I People with O negative blood group are called the universal donor due to absence of antibodies in the plasma.

Statement II People with AB blood type can receive blood from anyone due to the absence of antigens.

Choose the correct option from the following.

(a) Both statements I and II are true ☐

(b) Both statements I and II are false ☐

***38.** A person in a serious car accident is given blood from a donor without blood group matching because the donor is

(a) O negative ☐ (b) O positive ☐

(c) AB positive ☐ (d) AB negative ☐

***39.** A sample of blood shows clumping with antiserum-A, but not with antiserum-B. The blood group would be ________ (A/AB/B).

40. Blood groups were discovered by Landsteiner.

True ☐ False ☐

***41.** Rh-factor is concerned with blood grouping. It derives its name from __________ (monkey/chimpanzee).

***42.** It is estimated that about ________ (80%/20%) individuals in the world are Rh positive.

***43.** How many characteristics are true for erythroblastosis foetalis?

(i) Cause severe anaemia

(ii) Cause jaundice

(iii) Could be fatal to the foetus

____

***44.** Consider the following statements and choose the incorrect ones.

I. Rh negative woman can safely deliver her first baby with Rh positive blood without any risk.

II. Rh positive woman carrying Rh negative child in her second pregnancy is administered anti Rh antibodies.

III. Rh antigens of the (Rh^+) foetus do not get exposed to the Rh-ve blood of the mother in the first pregnancy.

IV. An Rh+ve person, if exposed to Rh-ve blood will form specific antibodies against the Rh antigens.

Choose the correct answer from the option given below.

(a) II and IV ☐ (b) III and IV ☐ (c) II and III ☐ (d) I and IV ☐

***45.** In an Rh negative mother, erythroblastosis foetalis can be prevented by administering ________ to the ________ immediately after the delivery of the first Rh positive child.

***46.** What will happen if Rh(– ve) person donates blood to Rh(+ ve) person for the second time?

(i) Destruction of RBC in Rh(+ve) person. ☐

(ii) Nothing will happen to Rh(+ve) person. ☐

Tick ✓ the most accurate box

47. The blood group of the mother was found to be A negative when tested for her first successful pregnancy. However, her subsequent pregnancies suffered the loss of a healthy growing foetus. This condition would occur if

(a) Developing foetus is Rh^- ☐ (b) Developing foetus is Rh^+ ☐

(c) There is lack of proper diet ☐ (d) The mother suffers from a disease ☐

***48.** If a Rh^+ man marries a Rh^- woman then which of the following would happen?

(i) No problem with 1st pregnancy.

(ii) No problem during any pregnancy.

(iii) Problem would be expected in second pregnancy.

____

***49.** If a woman with Rh positive blood becomes pregnant with a Rh-negative child, what would happen in her second pregnancy?

(a) The foetus would suffer from jaundice ☐

(b) Antibodies would form in maternal blood ☐

(c) Antigens would form in foetal blood ☐

(d) No effect on the foetus ☐

***50.** Blood exhibits ________ mechanism in response to an injury or trauma. This is a mechanism to prevent excessive loss of blood from the body.

***51.** Name the dark reddish-brown scum formed at the site of a cut or an injury over a period of time.

____

***52.** $\underline{K^+}$ ions play a very important role in blood clotting.
(*Rewrite the statement after correcting the underlined word.*)

____

***53.** Identify A and B for the given reactions with respect to blood clotting.

$$\text{Prothrombin} \xrightarrow{A} \text{Thrombin}$$

$$\text{Fibrinogen} \xrightarrow{B} \text{Fibrin}$$

A. ______________ B. ______________

54. Consider the following statements.

Statement I Fibrins are formed by the conversion of active fibrinogens by the enzyme thrombokinase.

Statement II Thrombokinase facilitates the conversion of prothrombin to thrombin.

Choose the correct option from the following.

(a) Statement I is true, but statement II is false ☐

(b) Statement I is false, but statement II is true ☐

***55.** Arrange the given steps of mechanism of blood coagulation in the correct sequence of occurrence.

(i) Conversion of prothrombin into thrombin (ii) Coagulum formation

(iii) Thrombokinase formation (iv) Site of injury release tissue thromboplastins

(v) Conversion of fibrinogen into fibrin

***56.** A series of linked ______________ (cascade process) involving a number of ______________ present in the ______________ in an inactivate state is required for coagulation of blood.

***57.** Prothrombin, which helps in clotting of blood is released by the blood platelets and produced in liver.

True ☐ False ☐

58. Name the vitamin which takes part in blood clotting mechanism. ______________

TOPIC 2

Lymph

NCERT Pg. 197

59. Complete the equation for lymph.

Lymph = Blood – (______________ + ______________)

60. Consider the following statements.

Statement I Lymph is actually the tissue fluid flowing through elaborate network of lymphatic vessels.

Statement II Lymph helps in absorption of fats through the lacteals present in the intestinal villi.

Choose the correct option from the following.

(a) Both statements I and II are true ☐

(b) Both statements I and II are false ☐

61. Interstitial fluid or tissue fluid is collected and drained back to the major veins by an elaborate network of vessels called the ____________ system. The fluid present in the system is called ____________.

62. Choose the correct option for lymph.

(i) Colourless/Yellow-coloured fluid. ____________

(ii) Lymphocytes present/Lymphocytes absent ____________

(iii) Absorbs fats/Manufacture proteins____________

63. Choose the odd one out with respect to lymph.

Hormones, Antibodies, Nutrients, RBCs

____

64. Lymph contain specialised lymphocytes which are responsible for ____________ responses of the body.

TOPIC 3

Circulatory Pathways and The Human Circulatory System

NCERT Pg. 197-199

65. Name the animal group in which the following system is present.

(i) Open circulatory system ____________

(ii) Closed circulatory system ____________

66. In open circulatory system, blood pumped by the heart passes through large vessels into open spaces or body cavities called ____________.

67. Advantage of closed circulatory system over open circulatory system includes which of the following?

(i) Closed system can direct blood to specific tissues.

(ii) Exchange of material occurs slowly.

(iii) Closed circulatory system can support higher levels of metabolic activity.

____

68. Choose the incorrect matching pair.

(a) *Pila* - Sinuses ☐

(b) Spider - Sinuses ☐

(c) *Octopus* - Closed circulatory system ☐

(d) Earthworm - Network of blood vessels ☐

69. In closed circulatory system, all the components given in bracket are present except, (heart, blood vessels, sinuses, blood).

____

70. Match the following columns.

Column I (Heart)		Column II (Animals)		Column III (Circulation types)	
A.	3-Chambered	1.	Reptiles	K.	Incomplete double circulation
B.	2-Chambeted	2.	Fishes	L.	Single circulation
C.	4-Chamboted	3.	Birds and mammals	M.	Double circulation
D.	3 Chambered	4.	Amphibians		

A. ________ B. ________ C. ________ D. ________

71. Consider the following statements.

Statement I Reptiles and birds can have a three chambered heart because they are cold blooded animals.

Statement II In fishes the deoxygenated blood from the heart is pumped to the body and returned to gills for oxygenation.

Choose the correct option from the following.

(a) Both statements I and II are true ☐

(b) Both statements I and II are false ☐

72. In amphibians and reptiles, left atrium receives oxygenated blood from gills/lungs/skin.

True ☐ False ☐

73. In reptiles and amphibians, there is no clear cut separation of oxygenated and deoxygenated blood because they have ________.

74. Three major components of human circulatory system include

____

75. Choose the correct option for human heart.

(i) Origin : ectodermal/mesodermal ________

(ii) Situated in : thoracic/abdominal cavity ________

(iii) Position with respect to lungs : between/above________

(iv) Slightly tilted : left/right ________

76. The double-walled membranous bag that protects the heart and enclose pericardial fluid is ________.

77. The nodal musculature of the heart bears the ability of generating action potential without any external stimuli.

True ☐ False ☐

78. Write the location of the following parts in human heart.

(i) Biscuspid valves ________

(ii) Tricuspid valves ________

(iii) Semilunar valves ________

(iv) Chordae tendineae ________

(v) Sino-Atrial (SA) node ________

(vi) Atrio-Ventricular (AV) node ________

79. Match Column I with Column II.

Column I	Column II
A. Pulmonary valves	1. Right atrium and Right ventricle
B. Bicuspid valves	2. Left ventricle and aorta
C. Tricuspid valves	3. Right ventricle and Pulmonary artery
D. Aortic valves	4. Left atrium and left ventricle

	A	B	C	D			A	B	C	D	
(a)	3	4	1	2	☐	(b)	3	4	2	1	☐
(c)	3	2	1	4	☐	(d)	3	2	4	1	☐

80. Give two functions of heart valves.

(i) ____________ (ii) ____________

81. Ventricle is thick-walled as compared to atrium because

(i) It pumps blood to distant structures. ☐

(ii) It does not contain SA and AV nodes. ☐

Tick ☑ *the most accurate box.*

82. The given figure represents a section of a human heart. Indentify the parts labelled as *A* to *E* and write in the space provided.

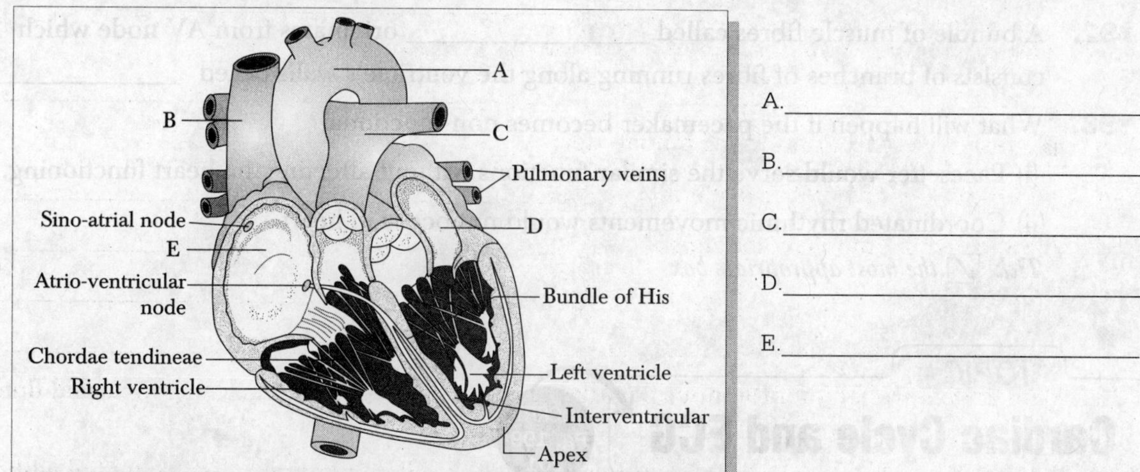

A. ____________

B. ____________

C. ____________

D. ____________

E. ____________

***83.** Consider the following statements.

Statement I Nodal tissue distributed in the upper right corner of right atrium constitutes the SA node.

Statement II SAN initiates the action potential without a stimulus to generate a heart beat confirms its autoexcitable nature.

Choose the correct option from the following.

(a) Both statements I and II are true ☐

(b) Both statements I and II are false ☐

***84.** Arrange the following in correct conduction sequence in heart.

AV node, Bundle of His, Purkinje fibres, SA node, Heart muscles

____

85. What prevents bicuspid and tricuspid valves from collapsing back into atria during powerful ventricular contractions?

____

86. In humans, name the septum which separates the following

(i) Right and left atria ______________

(ii) Left and right ventricle ______________

(iii) Atrium and ventricle of same side ______________

***87.** Give scientific term for following.

Sino-atrial node and atrio-ventricular node. ______________

***88.** Complete the following analogy.
Pacemaker of heart : SA node : Pacesetter of heart : ______________

***89.** The SA node can generate the maximum number of action potential, i.e. ______________.

***90.** SA node is called the pacemaker of heart because

____

***91.** Artificial pacemaker is grafted at the place of ______________.

***92.** A bundle of muscle fibres called ______________ originates from AV node which consists of branches of fibres running along the ventricle's walls called ______________.

***93.** What will happen if the pacemaker becomes non-functional?

(i) Pacesetter would serve the similar functions without affecting the heart functioning. ☐

(ii) Coordinated rhythmic movements would not occur in heart. ☐

Tick ✓ the most appropriate box.

TOPIC 4

Cardiac Cycle and ECG

NCERT Pg. 199-201

***94.** Complete the flowchart of steps of cardiac cycle.

SA node generates action potential
↓
A
↓
B
↓
Atrial diastole
↓
C

A. ______________

B. ______________

C. ______________

***95.** During systole of heart, auricles and ventricles contract ______________ (simultaneously/separately).

***96.** Oxygenated blood is pumped into the aorta and deoxygenated blood is pumped into the pulmonary artery during ______________.

***97.** Consider the given events.

I. Auricular diastole coincides

II. Tricuspid and bicuspid valves close

III. Semilunar valves open

When do the above events occur in a cardiac cycle?

____

***98.** Consider the following statements.

Statement I Ventricular systole increases the ventricular pressure thereby causing the closure of bicuspid and tricuspid valves to prevent backflow of blood into the atria

Statement II The generation of the action potential causes atrial systole and increases blood flow to ventricles.

Choose the correct option from the following.

(a) Both statements I and II are true ☐

(b) Both statements I and II are false ☐

***99.** Contraction of right ventricle pumps blood into ______________ artery.

***100.** During cardiac cycle, about ______________ (90%/50%) of ventricular filling occur prior to atrial contraction. ______________ (10%/50%) ventricular filling occur due to atrial contraction.

***101.** How many of the listed events occur during joint diastole?

(i) All 4 heart chambers are in relaxed state.

(ii) Tricuspid and bicuspid valves open.

(iii) Semilunar valves are closed.

(iv) Action potential is conducting.

(v) Blood flows into left and right ventricles from left and right atria.

____

***102.** Which of the following is an incorrect combination?

(a) Joint Diastole – Closure of semilunar valves ☐

(b) Ventricular systole – Opening of semilunar valves ☐

(c) Joint Diastole – Opening of AV valves ☐

(d) Ventricular systole – Opening of the AV valves ☐

***103.** The sequential event in the heart which is cyclically repeated is called ______________.

***104.** Cardiac cycle consists of systole and diastole of both the atria and ventricles.

True ☐ False ☐

***105.** Write the numerical value of each of the following.

(i) Heart beats per minutes. ____________

(ii) Duration of the cardiac cycle. ____________

(iii) Number of cardiac cycles per minute. ____________

(iv) Stroke volume. ____________

(v) Cardiac output ____________

***106.** Give the scientific term for the following sentences.

(i) The volume of blood pumped out by each ventricle per minute. ____________

(ii) The volume of blood pumped by each ventricle during a cardiac cycle. ____________

107. Name the device that is

(i) Used for hearing prominent heart sound. ____________.

(ii) Used for measuring blood pressure. ____________.

108. Complete the following analogy with respect to a normal person.

The systolic pressure :: 120 mmHg : The diastolic pressure : ____________

109. Complete the equations.

Stroke volume $\otimes$ 'X' = Cardiac output

____

110. A child with a heart rate of 100 beats per minutes shows an increase of 25 % during active sports like kabaddi. With a stroke volume of 70 mL, calculate the cardiac output.

(a) 8000 mL ☐ (b) 5000 mL ☐ (c) 8750 mL ☐ (d) 5750 mL ☐

111. In a cardiac output of 5250 mL per minute, with 75 heartbeats per minute, the stroke volume is ____________.

112. Consider the following statements.

Statement I During exercise the increase in the heart rate causes an increase in the cardiac output.

Statement II The two heart sounds lub and dub are associated with the closure of bi and tricuspid valves respectively, but do not hold clinical significance.

Choose the correct option from the following.

(a) Statement I is true, but statement II is false ☐

(b) Statement I is false, but statement II is true ☐

113. The two prominent heart sounds can be easily heard through a ____________ (Stethoscope/sphygmomanometer).

114. Complete the following analogy given below.

____________ : First heart sound : : ____________: Second heart sound

115. Name the heart sounds.

(i) Produced during closure of the semilunar valve. ____________

(ii) Produced during closure of tricuspid and bicuspid valves. ____________

***116.** Give the full form of ECG. ____________

***117.** Name the machine used to obtain an ECG. ____________

***118.** What does ECG represent? (*Give answer in one line*)

____

119. Which of the following options correctly represents ECG of a normally functioning heart?

(a) ☐

(b) ☐

(c) ☐

(d) ☐

120. Match the following columns.

Column I	Column II
A. P-wave	1. Ventricular depolarisation followed by ventricular contraction
B. QRS complex	2. Atrial depolarisation followed by systole of both atria
C. T-wave	3. Ventricular repolarisation followed by ventricular relaxation

A. __________ B. __________ C. __________

121. Consider the following statements.

Statement I The P-wave in an ECG indicates contraction of the atria due to electrical excitation.

Statement II The repolarisation of the ventricles at the end of systole is indicated by the T-wave.

Choose the correct option from the following.

(a) Both statements I and II are true ☐

(b) Both statements I and II are false ☐

***122.** The electrocardiogram makes the sound '__________pip__________pip__________peeeeeeeeeee' as the patient goes into cardiac arrest.

True ☐ False ☐

***123.** By counting the number of <u>PQ</u> complexes that occur in a given time period, the heartbeat rate of a person can be determined.

(*Rewrite the statement after correcting the underlined word.*)

____

***124.** To obtain a standard ECG, a patient is connected to the machine with three electrical leads at three locations, *viz.* ______________________________

TOPIC 5

Double Circulation and Regulation of Cardiac Activity

125. Give the scientific term for the following sentence.
'The tubes that conduct the blood in our body'.

____

126. Identify *A*, *B* and *C* in the given diagram.

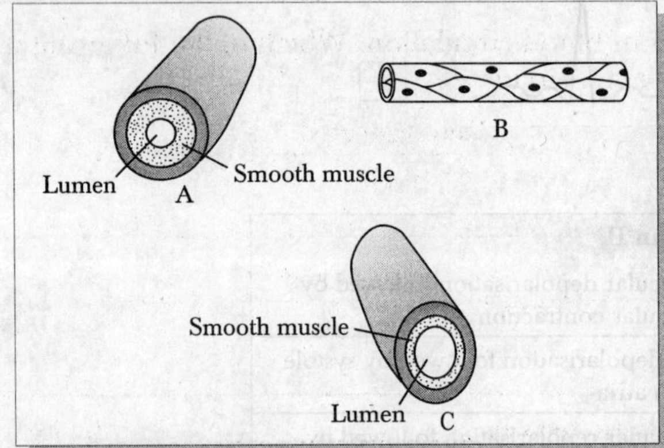

A. ______________________

B. ______________________

C. ______________________

127. Match the following columns.

	Column I (Layers of blood vessels)		Column I (Compositions)
A.	Tunica intima	1.	Fibrous connective tissue with collagen fibres
B.	Tunica media	2.	Smooth muscle fibres
C.	Tunica externa	3.	Squamous epithelium

A. __________ B. __________ C. __________

128. Veins differ from artery in possessing ______________________
(thin tunica media/thin tunica intima)

____

***129.** Given below are differences between '*X*' and '*Y*'. Identify '*X*' and '*Y*'.

X	*Y*
Blood flow is fast.	Blood flow is slow.
Valves absent.	Valves present.
Walls are thick.	Walls are thin.

X. __________ Y. __________

130. What does double circulation mean?
(i) Blood passes through heart twice.
(ii) Heart pumps oxygenated blood, *via.* two major vessels.

____

131. Consider the following statements.

Statement I Pulmonary circulation is responsible for transport of nutrients, O_2, CO_2 and other substances to and from the tissues.

Statement II The blood pumped by left ventricle enters the pulmonary artery while aorta receives blood from right ventricle.

Choose the correct option from the following.

(a) Both statements I and II are true ☐

(b) Both statements I and II are false ☐

132. Complete the equation.

Double circulation = ________________ + ________________.

133. Given below are two pathways of blood circulation. Which of the following represent pulmonary circulation and systemic circulation?

(i) Left ventricle $\xrightarrow[\text{blood}]{\text{Oxygenated}}$ Tissue $\xrightarrow[\text{blood}]{\text{Deoxygenated}}$ Right auricle

____

(ii) Right ventricle $\xrightarrow[\text{blood}]{\text{Deoxygenated}}$ Lungs $\xrightarrow[\text{blood}]{\text{Oxygenated}}$ Left auricle

____

134. Neural signals through sympathetic nerves ________________ the heartbeat while, that through parasympathetic nerves ________________ the rate of heartbeat.

***135.** Name two blood vessels possessing semilunar valves.

____

136. Name the type of circulation that exhibit the following features.

(i) Provides nutrients, oxygen and other essential substances to the tissues.

(ii) Take CO_2 and other harmful substances away for elimination.

(iii) Deoxygenated blood is collected by venules, veins and vena cava and emptied into right atrium.

(iv) Oxygenated blood entering aorta is carried by a network of arteries, arterioles and capillaries to the tissue.

____

137. The blood circulation which starts and ends into capillaries is renal circulation.
(*Rewrite the statement after correcting the underlined words.*)

____

138. Vascular connection between the digestive tracts and liver is called

________________.

139. A vein called pulmonary vein carries the blood from intestine to the liver (hepatic gland).
(*Rewrite the statement after correcting the underlined words.*)

____

140. The hepatic portal vein carries blood from __________ to the __________ before it is delivered to the systemic circulation.

141. Consider the following statements.

Statement I The coronary blood vessels are involved in supplying blood to the heart muscles.

Statement II Blood from the intestine is delivered to the liver before release into circulation by hepatic artery.

Choose the correct option from the following.

(a) Statement I is true, but statement II is false ☐

(b) Statement I is false, but statement II is true ☐

142. Identify the parts labelled as *A*, *B*, *C*, *D* and *E* in the given schematic plan of blood circulation in human.

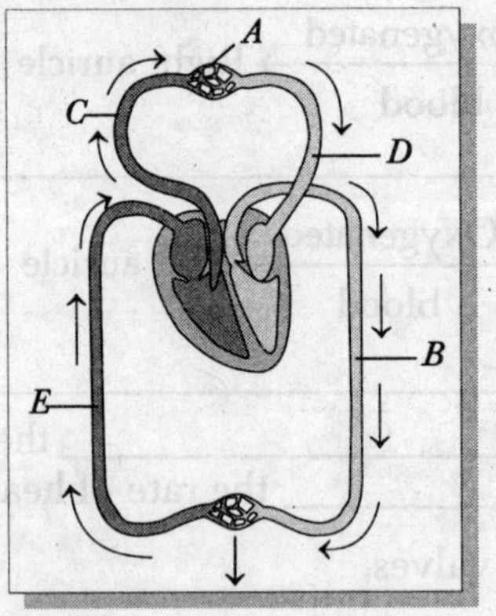

A. __________

B. __________

C. __________

D. __________

E. __________

143. Name the largest vein of the body. __________

144. The given features correspond to which blood vessel in the body?

(i) Narrowest of all blood vessels.

(ii) Permits rapid exchange of materials between blood and tissue.

(iii) Single layer of simple squamous epithelium.

____

145. What is the nature of blood passing through the blood vessels *A*, *B*, *C* and *D*?

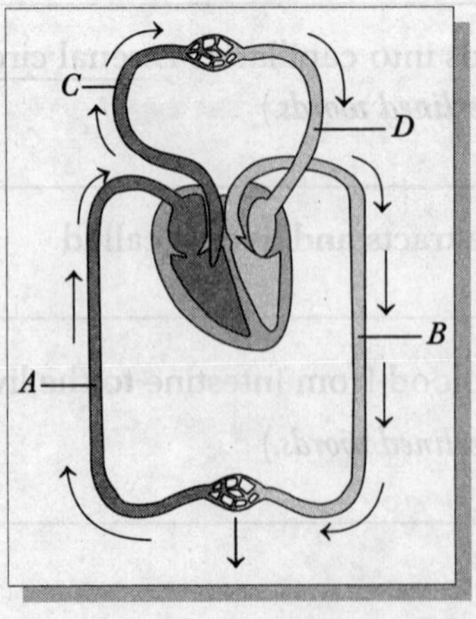

A. __________

B. __________

C. __________

D. __________

146. Match the following columns.

	Column I		Column II
A.	Superior vena cava	1.	Carries deoxygenated blood to lungs
B.	Inferior vena cava	2.	Carries oxygenated blood from lungs
C.	Pulmonary artery	3.	Brings deoxygenated blood from lower part of the body to right atrium
D.	Pulmonary vein	4.	Brings deoxygenated blood from upper part of the body to right atrium

A. ________ B. ________ C. ________ D. ________

147. Normal activities of the heart are regulated intrinsically by specialised muscles called ________, hence the heart is called ________.

148. Cardiac centre lies in which part of brain? ________

149. Cardiac centre can moderate the cardiac functions through <u>somatic</u> neural system.
(*Rewrite the statement after correcting the underlined word.*)

____

150. Consider the following statements.

Statement I Neural signals from medulla control the cardiac output of a person through the somatic branch.

Statement II The adrenal cortex can also influence the heart and thus the cardiac output in a person.

Choose the correct option from the following.

(a) Both statements I and II are true ☐

(b) Both statements I and II are false ☐

151. How can neural signal through the sympathetic nerves (part of ANS) increases cardiac output?

(i) By increasing ventricular systole and rate of heartbeat.

(ii) By decreasing ventricular systole and rate of heartbeat.

____

152. Parasympathetic neural signals decrease cardiac output by (increasing/decreasing) speed of conducting action potential.

____

153. Name the adrenal medullary hormones that can increase the cardiac output.

____

154. A person who is suddenly startled by a rope on a dark road, will show an increase in all of the following, except

(a) Adrenaline hormone increased gasping ☐

(b) Cardiac output ☐

(c) Heart rate ☐

(d) Haemoglobin level ☐

TOPIC 6

Disorders of Circulatory System

155. Write the name of the scientific term given for the following conditions.

(i) High blood pressure ________________

(ii) Low blood pressure ________________

(iii) Chest pain ________________

156. Systolic or Pumping pressure in a normal human is ________________

157. Which value indicates hypertension or high Blood pressure (BP) in humans?

120/80, 110/70, 130/80, 140/ 90

____

158. Consider the following statements.

Statement I A person with unchecked obesity can develop conditions of congestive heart failure.

Statement II Narrowing of blood vessels due to cholesterol deposit might increase blood pressure.

Choose the correct option from the following.

(a) Both statements I and II are true ☐

(b) Both statements I and II are false ☐

159. Given below are the conditions in a person which could lead to different circulatory system disorders. Write the correct disease/disorder name for each condition.

(i) Heart muscle is suddenly damaged by an inadequate blood supply.

____

(ii) Heart does not pump blood effectively due to lung congestion.

____

(iii) When enough oxygen is not reaching to the heart muscle. ________________

(iv) When the heart stops beating. ________________

(v) Deposition of calcium, fibrous tissue and lipids on the wall lining the lumen of large and medium-sized arteries. ________________

160. Deposition of cholesterol in the arteries can cause all of the following except:

(a) Chest pain ☐ (b) High blood pressure ☐

(c) Heart failure ☐ (d) Widening of lumen ☐

Assertion-Reason Questions

The following questions consist of two statements- Assertion (A) and Reason (R). Answer these questions by selecting the appropriate option given below.
(a) Both A and R are true and R is the correct explanation of A
(b) Both A and R are true, but R is not the correct explanation of A
(c) A is true, but R is false
(d) A is false, but R is true

***1.** **Assertion** (A) Rh+ person cannot donate blood to Rh - individual.

Reason (R) Rh antigens are present on the surface of the RBCs of majority people.

(a) ☐ (b) ☐ (c) ☐ (d) ☐

***2.** **Assertion** (A) Low calcium ions in blood can lead to huge blood loss from injured site.

Reason (R) Calcium plays a major role in blood clotting process.

(a) ☐ (b) ☐ (c) ☐ (d) ☐

3. **Assertion** (A) Tissue fluid if accumulates in the interstitial spaces can cause inflammation and damage.

Reason (R) Lymph has the same composition as that of the blood plasma, except that it lacks red blood cells only.

(a) ☐ (b) ☐ (c) ☐ (d) ☐

4. **Assertion** (A) Birds and mammals have a more efficient blood circulatory system compared to reptiles and amphibians.

Reason (R) Double circulation prevents mixing of the blood and increases efficiency of delivering oxygen to the cells.

(a) ☐ (b) ☐ (c) ☐ (d) ☐

***5.** **Assertion** (A) The ventricular systole is initiated by an impulse originating in the sino atrial node.

Reason (R) Ventricular systole causes the AV valves to close while opening the semilunar valves.

(a) ☐ (b) ☐ (c) ☐ (d) ☐

***6.** **Assertion** (A) During ventricular relaxation, the ventricular pressure falls thus closing the semilunar valves.

Reason (R) The closing of the semilunar valves during ventricular diastole prevents blood from flowing back into the ventricles.

(a) ☐ (b) ☐ (c) ☐ (d) ☐

***7.** **Assertion** (A) The QRS complex of an ECG indicates the contraction phase of the ventricles.

Reason (R) The T wave of an ECG denotes that blood is being pumped out of the heart chambers.

(a) ☐ (b) ☐ (c) ☐ (d) ☐

***8.** **Assertion** (A) The pulmonary circulation is necessary for oxygenation of the blood brought by major veins.

Reason (R) The systemic circulation allows distribution of the oxygenated blood to the entire body cells .

(a) ☐ (b) ☐ (c) ☐ (d) ☐

9. **Assertion** (A) Any possible damage to the medulla can alter the cardiac output of a person.

Reason (R) Medulla regulates the sympathetic and parasympathetic branch of the CNS.

(a) ☐ (b) ☐ (c) ☐ (d) ☐

10. **Assertion** (A) A person with untreated hypertension for a prolonged time can cause damage of vital organs.

Reason (R) A high blood pressure above 140/90 mm Hg can damage the arteries supplying blood to vital organs like brain and kidney.

(a) ☐ (b) ☐ (c) ☐ (d) ☐

Case Based Questions

***1.** In order to determine general health status or to monitor and to diagnose any one or a variety of diseases that affect blood cells, usually a person undergoes a CBC or Complete Blood Count.

CBC involves a group of tests that evaluate the cells circulating in our blood. One such report is shown below. Analyse the report carefully and answer the following questions by choosing the correct options.

Component	Your Value	Standard Range	Units Flag
White Blood Cell Count	14	4.0-11.0	K/uL
Red Blood Cell Count	5.20	4.40-6.00	M/uL
Haemoglobin	16.0	13.5-18.0	g/dL
Platelet Count	149	150-400	K/uL L
Differential Type	Automated		
Neutrophil %	92	49.0-74.0	%
Lymphocyte %	75	26.0-46.0	% L
Monocyte %	13	2.0-12.0	% H
Eosinophis %	7	0.0-5.0	% H
Basophil%	1	0.0-2.0	%
Abs. Neutrophil	10	2.0-8.0	K/uL
Abs. Lymphocyte	7	2.0-5.1	K/uL
Abs. Monocyte	2	0.0-0.0	K/uL
Abs. Eosinophil	0.4	0.0-0.5	K/uL
Abs. Basophil	0.0	0.0-0.2	K/uL

(i) What possible conclusion can be made from the following report about the person?

(a) The person is suffering from hypertension ☐

(b) The person is suffering from an infectious disease ☐

(c) The person is suffering from a deficiency disease ☐

(d) The person has a very weak immune system ☐

(ii) What is the mode of action of neutrophils?

(a) Antibody secretion ☐ (b) Antiallergic stimulation ☐

(c) Anti-inflammatory reaction ☐ (d) Phagocytosis ☐

(iii) The person's blood would show an increase in all of the following, except

(a) Histamine ☐ (b) Serotonin ☐

(c) Fibrin ☐ (d) Heparin ☐

(iv) Which type of cells would be involved in long time memory of possible infection?

(a) B lymphocytes ☐ (b) Monocytes ☐

(c) Macrophages ☐ (d) T lymphocytes ☐

2. The image shows the ECG report of a healthy person and another person (*X*) with a cardiovascular disease. The person with the given disease complained about chest pain while doing exercise or any other physical activity. The persons medical history details about cholesterol deposition. Based on the provided information, answer the following.

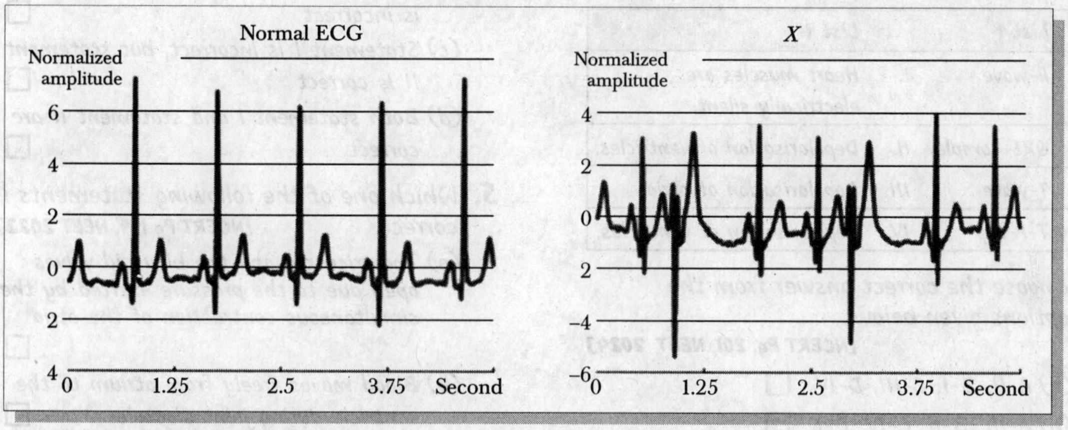

Normal ECG — Normalized amplitude; 0, 1.25, 2.5, 3.75 Second

X — Normalized amplitude; 0, 1.25, 2.5, 3.75 Second

(i) What does the QRS complex of X suggest?

(a) Problems with ventricular systole ☐ (b) Problems with atrial systole ☐

(c) Problems with ventricular diastole ☐ (d) Problems with atrial diastole ☐

(ii) Which of the following disease is X most likely suffering from?

(a) Congestive heart failure ☐ (b) Hypertension ☐

(c) Coronary artery disease ☐ (d) Cardiac arrest ☐

(iii) Which of the following could be the reason for X's condition?

(a) Narrowing of the arteries ☐ (b) Losing elasticity of veins ☐

(c) Narrowing of the veins ☐ (d) Losing elasticity of arteries ☐

COMPETITION EDGE UP

1. *Following are the stages of pathway for conduction of an action potential through the heart.*

A. AV bundle

B. Purkinje fibres

C. AV node

D. Bundle branches

E. SA node

Choose the correct sequence of pathway from the options given below.

[NCERT Pg. 199, NEET 2024]

(a) E-C-A-D-B ☐

(b) A-E-C-B-D ☐

(c) B-D-E-C-A ☐

(d) E-A-D-B-C ☐

2. *Match List I with List II.*

	List I		List II
A.	P-wave	I.	Heart muscles are electrically silent.
B.	QRS-complex	II.	Depolarisation of ventricles.
C.	T-wave	III.	Depolarisation of atria.
D.	T-P gap	IV.	Repolarisation of ventricles.

Choose the correct answer from the options given below.

[NCERT Pg. 201, NEET 2024]

(a) A-II, B-I, C-III, D-IV ☐

(b) A-III, B-II, C-IV, D-I ☐

(c) A-III, B-IV, C-I, D-II ☐

(d) A-II, B-I, C-IV, D-III ☐

3. *Which of the following statements are correct?*

A. Basophils are most abundant cells of the total WBCs.

B. Basophils secrete histamine, serotonin and heparin.

C. Basophils are involved in inflammatory response.

D. Basophils have kidney shaped nucleus.

E. Basophils are agranulocytes.

Choose the correct answer from the options given below.

[NCERT Pg. 194, NEET 2023]

(a) C and E only ☐

(b) B and C only ☐

(c) A and B only ☐

(d) D and E only ☐

4. *Given below are two statements.*

Statement I The coagulum is formed of network of threads called thrombins.

Statement II Spleen is the graveyard of erythrocytes.

In the light of the above statements, choose the most appropriate answer from the options given below.

[NCERT Pg. 194, NEET 2022]

(a) Both statement I and statement II are incorrect ☐

(b) Statement I is correct, but statement II is incorrect ☐

(c) Statement I is incorrect, but statement II is correct ☐

(d) Both statement I and statement II are correct ☐

5. *Which one of the following statements is correct?* **[NCERT Pg 199, NEET 2022]**

(a) The tricuspid and the bicuspid valves open due to the pressure exerted by the simultaneous contraction of the atria ☐

(b) Blood moves freely from atrium to the ventricle during joint diastole ☐

(c) Increased ventricular pressure causes closing of the semilunar valves ☐

(d) The Atrio-Ventricular Node (AVN) generates an action potential to stimulate atrial contraction ☐

6. *Persons with 'AB' blood group are called as "universal recipients". This is due to* **[NEET 2021]**

(a) Absence of antigens-A and B on the surface of RBCs ☐

(b) Absence of antigens-A and B in plasma ☐

(c) Presence of antibodies, anti-A and anti-B on RBCs ☐

(d) Absence of antibodies, anti-A and anti-B in plasma ☐

7. Match the following columns and select the correct option.

[NCERT Pg. 194, NEET (Sep.) 2020]

	Column I		Column II
A.	Eosinophils	1.	Immune response
B.	Basophils	2.	Phagocytosis
C.	Neutrophils	3.	Release histaminase destructive enzymes
D.	Lymphocytes	4.	Release granules containing histamine

A B C D

(a) 4 1 2 3 ☐

(b) 1 2 4 3 ☐

(c) 2 1 3 4 ☐

(d) 3 4 2 1 ☐

8. Which of the following conditions causes erythroblastosis foetalis?

[NCERT Pg. 196, NEET (Oct.) 2020]

(a) Mother Rh+ve and foetus Rh –ve ☐

(b) Mother Rh–ve and foetus Rh +ve ☐

(c) Both mother and foetus Rh –ve ☐

(d) Both mother and foetus Rh +ve ☐

9. The QRS complex in a standard ECG represents

[NCERT Pg. 202, NEET (Sep.) 2020]

(a) Depolarisation of auricles ☐

(b) Depolarisation of ventricles ☐

(c) Repolarisation of ventricles ☐

(d) Repolarisation of auricles ☐

Chapter 16

Excretory Products and their Elimination

Scan and take Chapter Test

TOPIC 1

Human Excretory System

NCERT Pg. 205-208

1. The process of excretion involves the removal of ______________________.

*2. How many of the given molecules are excreted from the animal body?

Ammonia, Urea, Uric acid, Carbon dioxide, Oxygen, Water, Na^+, K^+, Cl^-, Phosphate, Sulphate

____

3. Give common term for the following.

Ammonia, Urea, Uric acid

____

4. Complete the following analogy given below.

______________ : Most toxic nitrogenous waste : : ______________ : Least toxic nitrogenous waste.

5. Nitrogenous wastes which require large amount of water and least amount of water for their excretion are ____________ and ____________, respectively.

6. Ammonia is insoluble and is generally excreted by active transport through gill surfaces as ammonium ions.

True ☐ False ☐

7. Kidneys do not play any significant role in the removal of ammonia.

True ☐ False ☐

8. Terrestrial animals do not excrete ammonia to ______________ (conserve water/conserve energy).

*Concepts of all questions bearing * are important for NEET & CUET*

9. Which of the following represents the correct combination of molecule X and the gland Y where the reaction takes place?

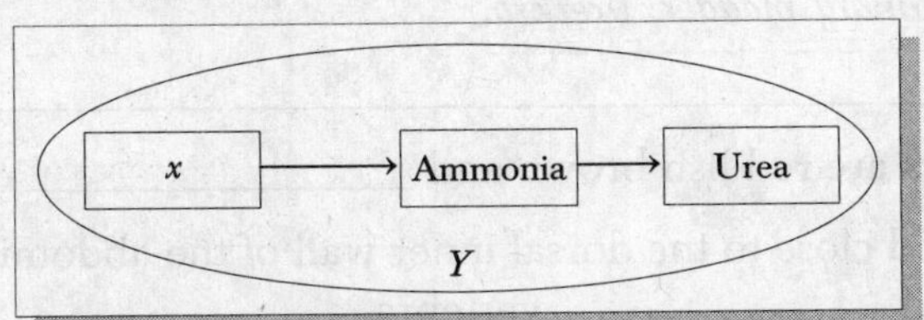

(a) X – Lipid, Y – Liver ☐
(b) X – Protein, Y – Liver ☐
(c) X – Lipid, Y – Gall bladder ☐
(d) X – Protein, Y – Gall bladder ☐

10. Identify *A, B* and *C* in the given table.

Type of animals	Excretory wastes	Representative animal groups
Ammonotelic	Ammonia	*B*
Ureotelic	Urea	*C*
Uricotelic	*A*	Reptiles and birds

A. ________ B. ________ C. ________

***11.** Given below are animal species. Mention the type of excretory process shown by them.

(i) Frog, Human, Alligators ________
(ii) Pigeon, Lizard, Cockroach ________
(iii) Rohu, *Clarias*, *Pila*, Prawn ________

12. Excretion of nitrogenous waste in the form of pellet or paste is known as <u>ammonotelism</u>.
(*Rewrite the statement after correcting the underlined word.*)

____

13. Give the common excretory structure for the following.

Platyhelminthes , Rotifers, Some annelids, Cephalochordates

____

***14.** Match Column I with Column II.

Column I	Column II
A. Flame cells	1. Prawns
B. Malpighian tubules	2. Earthworms
C. Green glands	3. *Planaria*
D. Nephridia	4. Cockroaches

	A	B	C	D			A	B	C	D	
(a)	3	4	1	2	☐	(b)	3	4	2	1	☐
(c)	3	2	4	1	☐	(d)	3	2	1	4	☐

15. How many of the listed parts of excretory system are found in humans?

Kidneys, Ureters, Urinary bladder, Urethra

____

16. In humans, kidneys are reddish-brown and ______________ shaped structure.

17. Kidneys are situated close to the dorsal inner wall of the abdominal cavity between the ______________ and ______________ vertebra.

18. Each kidney of an adult human measures

(i) In length ______________ (ii) In width ______________

(iii) In thickness ______________ (iv) In weight ______________

19. Towards the centre of the inner concave surface of the kidney, a notch is present which is called ______________.

20. Name the described part in each statement.

(i) Part of kidney which is the gateway for ureter, nerves and blood vessels. ______________

(ii) Inner to the hilum of kidney is a broad funnel-shaped space. ______________

(iii) Projections in renal pelvis. ______________

21. Identify and label the structures mentioned as *A* to *E* in the given figure.

B
E
Medulla
Cortex
Renal artery
Renal vein
C (with pure blood)
A
D
X

A. ______________

B. ______________

C. ______________

D. ______________

E. ______________

X. ______________

22. The outer layer of human kidney is composed of a tough ______________. Inside the kidney, the two zones, an outer ______________ and an inner ______________ is present.

23. Consider the following statements.

Statement I Portion of the cortex between the medullary pyramids form the columns of Bertini.

Statement II The ureter and the blood vessels enter the kidney through the hilum.

Choose the correct option from the following.

(a) Statement I is true, but statement II is false

(b) Statement I is false, but statement II is true

(c) Both statements I and II are true

(d) Both statements I and II are false

24. Columns of Bertini in the kidneys of mammals are formed as extensions of ____________________ (cortex in pelvis/ medulla in pelvis/cortex in medulla).

25. With respect to the direction of flow of substances into and out of the kidney, which of the following is wrongly labelled?

(a) *B* and *C* ☐ (b) *A* and *B* ☐ (c) *A* and *C* ☐ (d) *A*, *B* and *C* ☐

26. Recognise the figure *X* and label the parts *A* to *F*.

A. ____________________

B. ____________________

C. ____________________

D. ____________________

E. ____________________

F. ____________________

X. ____________________

27. Arrange the given structures of mammalian kidney from outside capsule till the ureter.

Renal capsule, Renal pelvis, Ureter, Renal calyx, Medullary pyramid, Cortex

____

28. Each kidney has nearly ____________________ million complex tubular structures called nephrons.

29. The structural and functional unit of human kidney is

30. Name the two major parts of a nephron. ____________________

***31.** Complete the following analogy with respect to glomerulus.

Blood enters : Afferent arteriole : : Blood leaves : ____________________

32. The diameter of the efferent arterioles is less than the afferent arterioles because

(a) to allow maximum reabsorption of water

(b) to ensure secretion of ions

(c) to allow filtration under pressure

(d) to ensure reabsorption of ions

33. Renal corpuscle is also known as ____________________.

34. Complete the flowchart depicting the components of nephron.

Nephron
- Renal capsule
  - Glomerulus
  - B
- A
  - C
  - Loop of Henle
  - D

A. __________ B. __________ C. __________ D. __________

***35.** A diagrammatic representation of a nephron showing blood vessels, ducts and tubule is given below. How many of its parts are correctly labelled? Also write the correct labels for the incorrect ones.

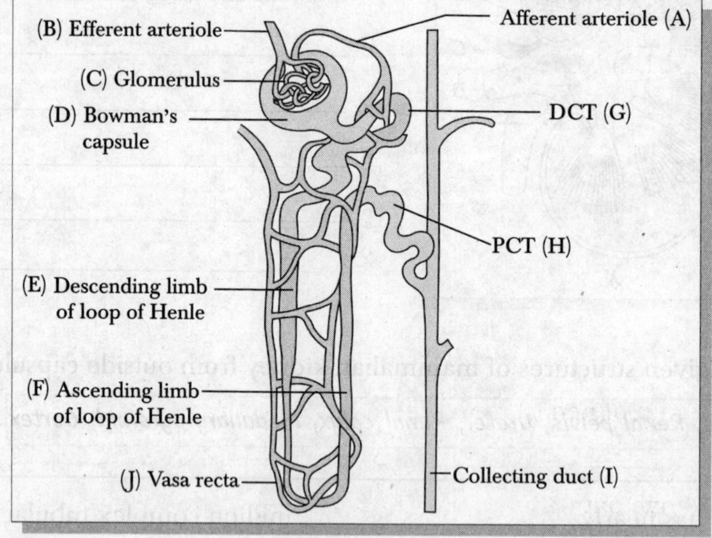

***36.** Give the full form of the following.

(i) PCT ____________________

(ii) DCT ____________________

***37.** Identify the structure based on the given description in a nephron.

(i) A tuft of capillaries formed by the afferent arteriole. ____________________

(ii) A fine branch of renal artery. ____________________

(iii) Double-walled cup-like structure enclosing glomerulus. ______

(iv) A hairpin-shaped part of renal tubule having ascending and descending limb. ______

***38.** Complete the flowchart depicting the flow of tubular fluid in the nephron.

Bowman's capsule
↓
A
↓
B
↓
C
↓
D
↓
Collecting duct

A. ______

B. ______

C. ______

D. ______

39. Which of the following statement about the nephrons is not correct?

(a) The bowman's capsule and the glomerulus together form the malpighian body ☐

(b) The proximal convoluted tubule lies closer to the malpighian body ☐

(c) The collecting duct carries the glomerular filtrate to the ureters ☐

(d) The distal convoluted tubule of many nephrons open into the collecting duct ☐

40. Many collecting ducts converge and through medullary pyramids in the calyces open into the renal pelvis.

True ☐ False ☐

***41.** Complete the flowchart depicting the passage of urine in humans.

Collecting tubule
↓
A
↓
B
↓
C
↓
Outside the body

A. ______

B. ______

C. ______

42. Name the two types of nephron present in human kidneys.

______

***43.** Choose the odd one out with respect to structure in cortical region of kidney.

PCT, DCT, Malpighian corpuscle, Loop of Henle

______

***44.** Name the type of nephron in which

(i) Loop of Henle is too short and extends very little into the medulla. ______

(ii) Loop of Henle is very long and runs deep into the medulla. ______

45. The efferent arteriole emerging from the glomerulus forms a fine capillary network around the renal tubule called ______ capillaries.

46. *Vasa recta* run parallel to the ________________.

***47.** Consider the following statements.

Statement I Majority of the nephrons present is a kidney are cortical nephrons.

Statement II Vasa recta is highly reduced in juxtamedullary nephrons.

Choose the correct option from the following.

(a) Statement I is true, but statement II is false ☐

(b) Statement I is false, but statement II is true ☐

48. Match the following columns.

Column I		Column II
A. Ureters	1.	Canal-like structure extending from the neck of the bladder to exterior
B. Urinary bladder	2.	Paired, narrow, tubular structures to carry urine from kidneys
C. Urethra	3.	Pear-shaped muscular sac-like structure in the pelvic cavity.

A. ________________ B. ________________ C. ________________

49. Sphincter muscles are present in which of the following structures?

Ureters, Urinary bladder, Urethra

____

TOPIC 2
Urine Formation and Function of the Tubules

NCERT Pg. 208-210

50. Urine formation involves three processes. Name them.

(i) ____

(ii) ____

(iii) ____

51. The part of nephron which performs the first step in urine formation is ________________.

52. On an average ________________ mL of blood is filtered by the kidneys per minute which constitute roughly ________________ (1/3rd/1/5th) of the blood pumped out by each ventricle of heart in a minute.

53. The glomerular capillary blood pressure causes filtration of blood through 3 layers, i.e.

(i) ____

(ii) ____

(iii) ____

54. Give the scientific term given to the epithelial cells of Bowman's capsule.

____

55. Filtration slits or slit pores present between podocytes allow filtration of blood, that filter almost all the constituents of the plasma except proteins.

True ☐ False ☐

56. In the nephron, the blood from the afferent arteriole filters into the lumen of the ______________. This process is called as ultrafiltration.

57. The following diagram represents the Malpighian body. Answer the questions based on it.

(i) Label parts *A* to *D*.

A. ______________

B. ______________

C. ______________

D. ______________

(ii) Name the special cells forming the visceral layer in the above diagram. ______________

(iii) What process takes place in the glomerulus? ______________

58. What would happen if the diameter of *X* and *Y* were exchanged?

(a) Reversal of pressure gradient ☐ (b) Reversal of osmolarity ☐

(c) Increased rate of ultrafiltration ☐ (d) No effect on urine formation ☐

59. $'X' = \dfrac{\text{Amount of filtrate formed by the kidney}}{\text{Minute}}$

What is '*X*' in the above formula?

X. ______________________________

***60.** GFR in a healthy individual is approximately

(i) ______________ ml/minute (ii) ______________ L /day

***61.** The kidneys have built in mechanisms for the regulation of GFR. One such efficient mechanism is carried out by ____________

***62.** JGA is a special sensitive region formed by cellular modification in the PCT and efferent arteriole at the location of their contact.

(*Rewrite the statement after correcting the underlined words.*)

____

***63.** A fall in GFR can activate the ____________ to release ____________ hormone which can stimulate the glomerular blood flow and thereby the GFR back to normal.

64. Of the total filtrate, nearly how much (in per cent) of it is reabsorbed by the renal tubule?

____

65. Name the cells present in different segments of nephrons which perform reabsorption.

____

***66.** Choose the odd one out for the substances which are actively reabsorbed in the nephron.

Glucose, Amino acids, Na^+ ions, Nitrogenous wastes

____

***67.** Which of the following does not depend on ATP for transport across the renal tubules?

(a) Glucose ☐ (b) Na^+ ☐ (c) Urea ☐ (d) Amino acids ☐

***68.** During urine formation, the tubular cells secretes substances into the filtrate. How many of the given substances are secreted into the filtrate?

K^+, H^+, Ammonia, Water

____

69. Consider the following statements.

Statement I 1.5 litres of urine output per day in contrast to 180 litres of GF, suggests that 99% of filtrate is reabsorbed.

Statement II Reabsorption of filtrate takes place at the highest rate in the proximal convoluted tubules.

Choose the correct option from the following.

(a) Both statements I and II are true ☐

(b) Both statements I and II are false ☐

***70.** Tubular secretion is an important step in urine formation because

(i) it maintains ionic and acid-base balance of body fluids.

(ii) it increases the amount of urine to be excreted out of the body.

____

***71.** Choose the odd one out with respect to tubules of the nephron.

PCT, Henle's loop, Collecting duct, Bowman's capsule

____

72. Name the epithelial tissue lining PCT. ____________

***73.** What percentage of electrolyte and water is reabsorbed by PCT?

____

***74.** Given below are some substances in the PCT which are either reabsorbed or being filtered. Identify them.

HCO_3^-, $NaCl$, H_2O, Nutrients, K^+, H^+, NH_3^+

(i) Reabsorbed in the PCT. ______________________________

(ii) Selective secretion into the filtrate. ______________________________

***75.** Which of the following is not a function of PCT?

(a) Reabsorption of nutrients like glucose ☐

(b) Maintains the pH and ion balance ☐

(c) Secretion of H^+ and K^+ ions in the filtrate ☐

(d) Reabsorption of water and electrolytes ☐

***76.** Choose the correct option for the given statements about loop of Henle.

(i) Reabsorption is ______________ (minimum/maximum) in this segment.

(ii) The descending limb of loop of Henle is__________(impermeable/permeable) to electrolytes.

77. What does 2 and 3 marked in the image indicate?

(a) 2 – Secretion, 3 – Reabsorption ☐

(b) 2 – Reabsorption, 3 – Secretion ☐

(c) 2 – Reabsorption, 3 – Ultrafiltration ☐

(d) 2 – Secretion, 3 – Utrafiltration ☐

***78.** Write the correct name of limb of Henle's loop.

	Water	Electrolytes
Impermeable	*A*	*B*
Permeable	*C*	*D*

A. ______________ B. ______________ C.______________ D.______________

***79.** In the Henle's loop, as the concentrated filtrate pass upward, it gets diluted due to the passage of electrolytes to the ______________.

***80.** If loops of Henle were absent from mammalian nephrons, the urine would be more ______________ (dilute/concentrated).

***81.** Conditional reabsorption of Na^+ and water takes place in the ______________ (DCT/PCT).

82. Consider the following statements.

Statement I The ascending limb is impermeable to water, but allows transport electrolytes of actively or passively.

Statement II Only the PCT of the renal tubules are actively involved in maintaining the pH balance.

Choose the correct option from the following.

(a) Statement I is true, but statement II is false ☐

(b) Statement I is false, but statement II is true ☐

***83.** The long duct of collecting tubule extends from the cortex of the kidney to the inner parts of the medulla.

True ☐ False ☐

***84.** Identify the regions *A*, *B*, *C* and *D* in the given figure and choose the correct statement related to them.

(i) Large amount of water is reabsorbed from this region to produce concentrated urine.

(ii) It is capable of reabsorption of HCO_3^- and selective secretion of H^+ and K^+ ions to maintain pH and $Na^+ - K^+$ balance in the blood.

(iii) Vitamins, hormones, chloride ions, etc., are reabsorbed from the filtrate here.

(iv) In this tubule, the filtrate first becomes hypertonic to blood plasma and then becomes hypotonic to blood plasma.

A
B
C
D

A. ______________

B. ______________

C. ______________

D. ______________

85. Collecting duct allows passage of small amounts of urea into the medullary interstitium to keep up the osmolarity.

True ☐ False ☐

***86.** Match the following columns.

Column I	Column II
A. Proximal convoluted tubule	1. Formations of concentrated urine
B. Distal convoluted tubule	2. Reabsorption of large amount of water
C. Henle's loop	3. Reabsorption of 70-80% of electrolyte
D. Collecting duct	4. Ionic balance

A. ________ B. ________ C. ________ D. ________

***87.** Match Column I with Column II.

Column I	Column II
A. PCT	1. Minimum reabsorption
B. Loop of Henle	2. Reabsorption of HCO_3^-
C. DCT	3. H^+ and K^+ secretion
D. Collecting duct	4. Conditional reabsorption

	A	B	C	D			A	B	C	D	
(a)	2	1	4	3	☐	(b)	2	1	3	4	☐
(c)	2	3	1	4	☐	(d)	2	3	4	1	☐

***88.** **Study the figure and write the correct names for *A* to *E* substances from the following.**

H^+, H_2O, Urea, NaCl, HCO_3^-

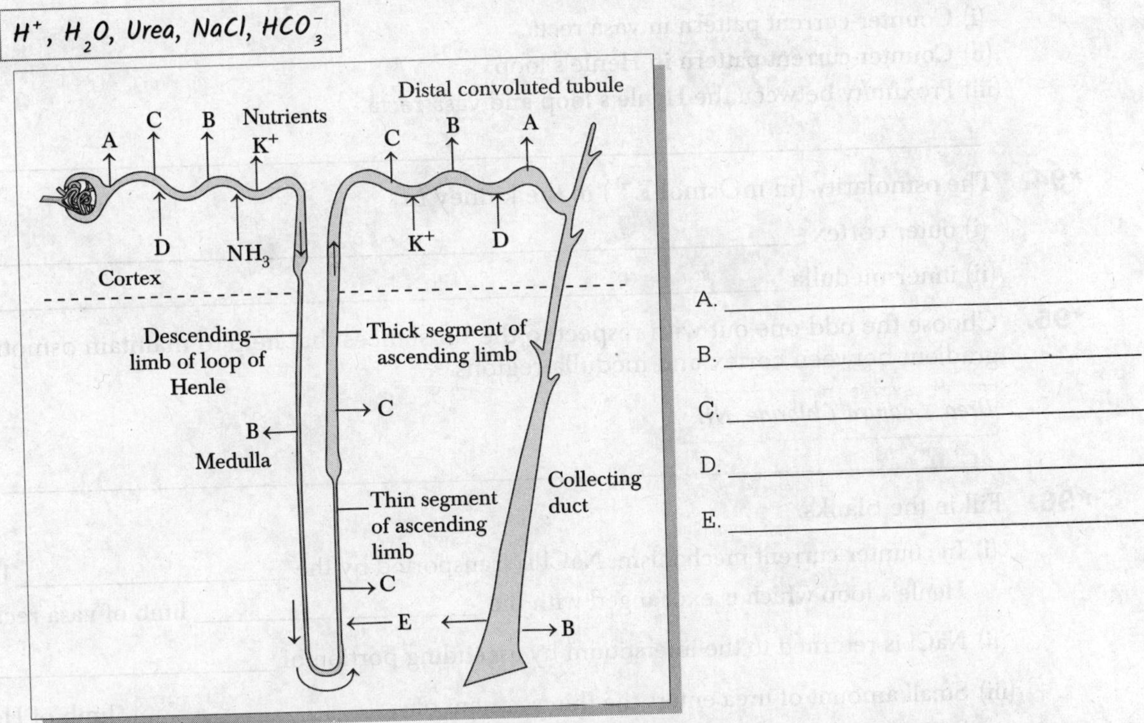

A. ________

B. ________

C. ________

D. ________

E. ________

***89.** **Under normal condition, which one is completely reabsorbed in the renal tubule?**

Urea, Salts, Uric acid, Glucose, H_2O, Na^+ ions, K^+ ions

____

90. Give the scientific term for the process mentioned below as '*X*' and '*Y*'.

'*X*'	'*Y*'
It is absorption of selected material from the nephric filtrate into the blood of peritubular blood capillaries.	It is removal of selected material from the blood of the peritubular blood capillaries into the nephric filtrate.
It takes place by diffusion and active process.	It takes place by active transport.

X. ________ Y. ________

TOPIC 3

Mechanism of Concentration of the Filtrate

NCERT Pg. 210-212

91. Mammals have the ability to produce ________ (hypotonic/hypertonic) urine.

92. Out of the following segments, which of the following segments play an important role in counter current mechanism?

PCT, Vasa recta, DCT, Henle's loop, Collecting duct

____

***93.** How many factors help in maintaining an increased osmolarity towards the inner medullary interstitium?

(i) Counter-current pattern in vasa recta.

(ii) Counter-current pattern in Henle's loop.

(iii) Proximity between the Henle's loop and vasa recta.

____

***94.** The osmolarity (in mOsmol L^{-1}) in the kidney in

(i) outer cortex ________

(ii) inner medulla ________

***95.** Choose the odd one out with respect to the substances that help to maintain osmotic gradient between cortex and medulla regions.

Urea, Sodium Chloride, NH_3

____

***96.** Fill in the blanks.

(i) In counter-current mechanism, NaCl is transported by the ________ limb of Henle's loop which is exchanged with the ________ limb of vasa recta.

(ii) NaCl is returned to the interstitium by ascending portion of ________.

(iii) Small amount of urea enters the thin segment of ________ limb of Henle's loop which is transported back to the interstitium by the ________.

***97.** In the given diagrammatic representation of counter-current mechanism, what is the osmolarity (mOsmol L^{-1}) at *P, Q, R* and *S* regions?

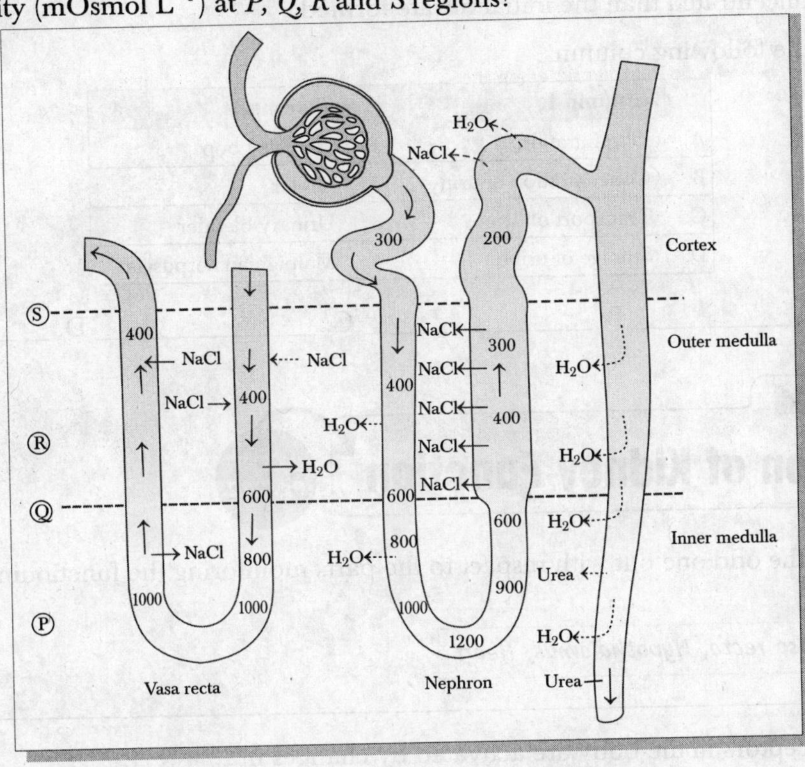

P. ______ Q. ______ R. ______ S. ______

98. The counter-current mechanism helps to ______

***99.** Consider the following statements.

Statement I Only NaCl gradient is sufficient to concentrate the urine in the collecting duct.

Statement II Only concentration of urine in collecting duct is due to the osmolarity of medullary interstitium.

Choose the correct option from the following.

(a) Statement I is true, but statement II is false ☐

(b) Statement I is false, but statement II is true ☐

100. The increase in osmolarity from 300 to 1200 mOsmol/L is due to

(a) Hypertonicity of medullary interstitium ☐

(b) Hypotonicity of loop of Henle ☐

(c) Hypertonicity of loop of Henle ☐

(d) Hypotonicity of medullary interstitium ☐

***101.** What possible effect would be produced in the absence of counter current mechanism?

(a) Body would produce highly concentrated urine ☐

(b) Body would produce very dilute urine ☐

(c) There would be no effect on urine concentration ☐

(d) Body would reduce urine output volume ☐

102. Human kidneys can produce urine nearly ________________ (twenty/four) times concentrated than the initial filtrate formed.

103. Match the following columns.

	Column I		Column II
A.	Ultrafiltration	1.	Henle's Loop
B.	Concentration of urine	2.	Ureter
C.	Transport of urine	3.	Urinary bladder
D.	Storage of urine	4.	Malpighian corpuscle

A. ____________ B. ____________ C. ____________ D. ____________

TOPIC 4

Regulation of Kidney Function

NCERT Pg. 212

104. Choose the odd one out with respect to the parts monitoring the functioning of the kidneys.

JGA, Vasa recta, Hypothalamus, Heart

____

105. Osmoreceptors in the body are activated by changes in ____________ volume, ____________ volume and ____________ concentration.

106. Complete the sequence for the regulation of kidney function.

An excess loss of water from body → Stimulates (A) → Releases (B) hormone → From osmoreceptors of (C) → Increases water permeability of (D) and (E) tubule → Prevention of diuresis

A. ____________ B. ____________ C. ____________

D. ____________ E. ____________

***107.** Osmoregulation is the function of ________________ (oxytocin/vasopressin).

***108.** An increase in body fluid volume can switch on the osmoreceptors and suppress ADH release.

True ☐ False ☐

***109.** What would be the appropriate response of the body to counter a sudden drop in blood pressure?

(a) Increase ADH and Angiotensin II ☐
(b) Increase ADH and decrease Angiotensin II ☐
(c) Increase Angiotensin II and Decrease ADH ☐
(d) Decrease ADH and Angiotensin II ☐

***110.** Complete the flowchart.

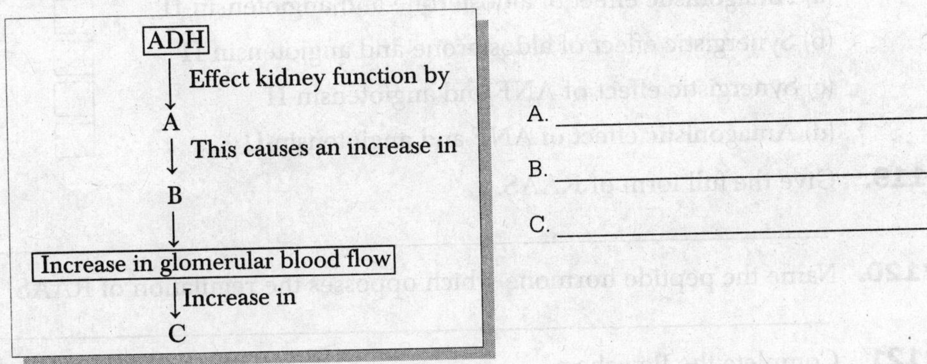

A. ____________

B. ____________

C. ____________

111. What cause the JG cells to release renin?

(i) Fall in GFR and blood pressure. (ii) Increased GFR and blood pressure.

____

***112.** Complete the flowchart.

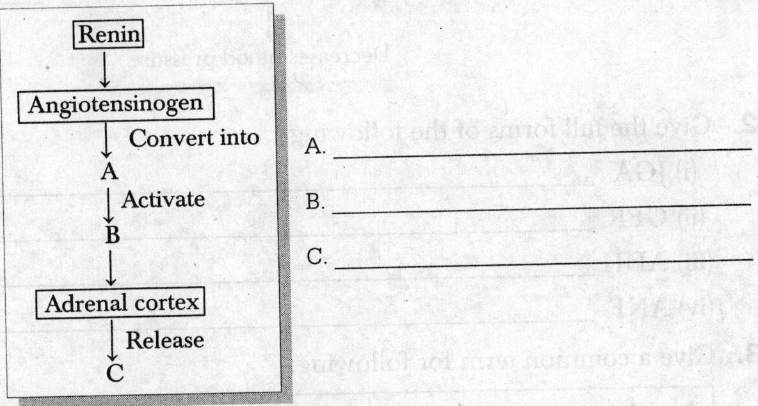

A. ____________

B. ____________

C. ____________

***113.** Give the two functions of angiotensin-II.

____

***114.** Choose the correct option, if vasoconstrictions occur in the body.

(i) Glomerular blood pressure ____________ (increase/decrease)

(ii) GFR ____________ (increase/decrease)

(iii) Aldosterone secretion ____________ (starts/stops)

(iv) ____________ (Reabsorption/Secretion) of Na^+ and water in the DCT occurs.

115. Renin-angiotensin mechanism controls ____________ (ultrafiltration/blood pressure).

***116.** Choose the odd one out from the following.

Glomerular filtration, Antidiuretic hormone, Hypertonic urine, Aldosterone.

____

***117.** Renin causes reabsorption of Na^+ and water from the distal parts of the tubule.

(Rewrite the statement after correcting the underlined word.)

____

***118.** A fall in GFR is countered by

(a) Antagonistic effect of aldosterone and angiotensin-II

(b) Synergistic effect of aldosterone and angiotensin-II

(c) Synergistic effect of ANF and angiotensin-II

(d) Antagonistic effect of ANF and angiotensin-II

119. Give the full form of RAAS.

____

***120.** Name the peptide hormone which opposes the regulation of RAAS.

____

***121.** Complete the flowchart.

Increased blood pressure
↓
ANF releases from the (A)
↓
Causes (B)
↓
Decreases blood pressure

A. ______________________________

B. ______________________________

***122.** Give the full forms of the following.

(i) JGA ______________________________

(ii) GFR ______________________________

(iii) ADH ______________________________

(iv) ANF ______________________________

***123.** Give a common term for following.

Angiotensinogen-II, ANF, ADH, Aldosterone

____

TOPIC 5 Micturition

NCERT Pg. 212-213

124. Give the scientific term used for the expulsion of urine from the urinary bladder.

____

125. Given below is the outline of principal event of urination. Arrange them in ascending order.

(i) Stretch receptors on the wall of urinary bladder send signal to the CNS.

(ii) The bladder fills with urine and becomes distended.

(iii) Micturition.

(iv) CNS passes on motor messages to initiate the contraction of bladder.

____

126. PNS receives signals from the stretch receptors present on the wall of the bladder.

True ☐ False ☐

127. During urination, contraction of smooth muscles of the bladder and relaxation of urethral sphincter causing the release of urine.

True ☐ False ☐

128. Micturition occurs when ______ (urethra relaxes/urethra contracts).

129. The neural mechanism that causes urination is called ______.

130. Urine is a light ______ coloured watery fluid which is slightly ______ in pH.

131. Answer the following questions in numbers only.

(i) The pH of a normal human urine. ______

(ii) The amount of urine excreted by an adult per day in litres. ______

(iii) The amount of urea excreted with urine per day (in gm) in an adult. ______

132. Urine contains 95% of ______ and only 5% of ______ in it.

133. There is no ______ (vitamin/glucose) normally found in the urine.

TOPIC 6

Role of Other Organs in Excretion

NCERT Pg. 213

134. Give the common function of lungs, kidneys, liver and skin.

______

135. How much CO_2 is removed per minute by human lungs?

______

136. ______ is the largest gland of the body, which functions as both secretory and excretory organs.

137. How many of the given substances are excreted from the liver.

Bile, Degraded steroid hormones, Vitamins, Drugs, Cholesterol, NaCl, Urea, Lactic acid

______

138. Bile comprises of two pigments, namely ______ and ______

139. Sweat glands and sebaceous glands are common in their nature as they both have

______

140. Complete the following analogy given below.

______ : Secretes watery fluid with NaCl : : ______.

Secretes sebum.

141. What is the composition of sweat?

______

142. Choose the odd one out with respect to substances eliminated by sebum from body.

Sterols, Lactic acid, Hydrocarbons, Waxes

143. Give the function of the following.

(i) Sweat ____________

(ii) Sebum ____________

TOPIC 7

Disorders of the Excretory System

NCERT Pg. 213-214

144. Given below are some abnormalities in the urine. Give the scientific term against each.

(i) Presence of excess urea in blood. ____________

(ii) Presence of abnormally high ketone bodies in urine. ____________

(iii) Presence of glucose in urine. ____________

***145.** Uremia is highly harmful and may lead to ____________.

***146.** Name the process of removal of urea from the blood of a person with kidney failure.

____

***147.** Dialysing unit (artificial kidney) contains a fluid which is almost same as plasma except that it has ____________

***148.** Consider the following statements.

Statement I Filtered blood coming out of the dialysis unit must be treated with anti heparin.

Statement II Once filtered by dialysis, the blood is transferred back to the body through an artery.

Choose the correct option from the following.

(a) Statement I is true, but statement II is false ☐

(b) Statement I is false, but statement II is true ☐

***149.** Arrange the following in stepwise manner w.r.t dialysis.

(i) Blood is passed into a vein.

(ii) Blood is mixed with heparin.

(iii) Blood is mixed with anti-heparin.

(iv) Blood is drained from a convenient artery.

(v) Blood is passed through coiled and porous cellophane tube bathing in dialysis fluid.

(vi) Removal of nitrogenous wastes from blood.

***150.** What is the ultimate method in the correction of acute renal failure?

____

***151.** How many assumptions are correct with respect to kidney transplant?
(i) It is the ultimate method where drug or dialysis do not help.
(ii) Close relatives are often used as kidney donors to minimise risk of rejection.
(iii) Blood is treated with heparin before feeding to the dialysis unit.

____

***152.** Give common name for the kidney disorder mentioned below.
Renal calculi ______________________

***153.** Choose the correct option for the following.
(i) Chemical composition of renal calculi, besides uric acid is ______________ (barium chloride/calcium oxalate).
(ii) Diabetes insipidus is characterised by ______________ (concentrated/dilute) urine.
(iii) Diabetes insipidus is caused due to the deficiency of (ADH/ANF). ______________

***154.** During diuresis in a person,
(i) volume of excreted urine increases.
(ii) volume of excreted urine decreases.

____

155. Which of the following statements about glomerulonephritis is correct?
A. It is a liver disorder.
B. It is related to functioning of kidney.
C. Crystallised calcium salts are found in patient.
D. Inflammation in glomerulus of nephron is found.
(a) Only A ☐ (b) B and C ☐ (c) C and D ☐ (d) B and D ☐

Assertion-Reason Questions

The following questions consist of two statements- Assertion (A) and Reason (R). Answer these questions by selecting the appropriate option given below.
(a) Both A and R are true and R is the correct explanation of A
(b) Both A and R are true, but R is not the correct explanation of A
(c) A is true, but R is false
(d) A is false, but R is true

1. **Assertion** (A) Ammonia is the least toxic nitrogenous waste and requires minimal water for elimination.
Reason (R) The high solubility of ammonia in water allows its excretion by simple diffusion across body surfaces.
(a) ☐ (b) ☐ (c) ☐ (d) ☐

2. **Assertion** (A) Vasa recta originating from the peritubular capillaries is highly reduced in cortical nephrons.

Reason (R) The peritubular capillaries are fine branches that originate from the afferent arterioles.

(a) ☐ (b) ☐ (c) ☐ (d) ☐

***3.** **Assertion** (A) 180 litres of glomerular filtrate is formed per day while the urine out put is 1.5 litres only.

Reason (R) The glomerular filtrate is produced at a high pressure.

(a) ☐ (b) ☐ (c) ☐ (d) ☐

4. **Assertion** (A) The entire plasma portion of the blood is passed into the lumen of Bowman's capsule.

Reason (R) The arrangement of the podocytes creates intricate filtration slits that allow this filtration.

(a) ☐ (b) ☐ (c) ☐ (d) ☐

***5.** **Assertion** (A) Urine gets concentrated as it flows through the descending limb of the loop of Henle.

Reason (R) The urine becomes diluted again as it travels through the ascending branch of Henle's loop.

(a) ☐ (b) ☐ (c) ☐ (d) ☐

***6.** **Assertion** (A) NaCl is added to the medullary interstitium from the ascending limb of Henle's loop.

Reason (R) NaCl from Henle's loop is exchanged with the descending limb of the vasa recta.

(a) ☐ (b) ☐ (c) ☐ (d) ☐

***7.** **Assertion** (A) Flow of filtrate in the two limbs of the Henle's loop sets a counter current.

Reason (R) Counter current mechanism help in maintaining a decreasing osmolarity towards the inner medullary interstitium.

(a) ☐ (b) ☐ (c) ☐ (d) ☐

***8.** **Assertion** (A) A person with severe dehydration will lower the secretion of vasopressin from the posterior pituitary.

Reason (R) Vasopressin secretion depends on the signals received by the hypothalamus from the osmoreceptors.

(a) ☐ (b) ☐ (c) ☐ (d) ☐

***9.** **Assertion** (A) A fall in the GFR will give signal to the body to increase angiotensin-II.

Reason (R) Angiotensin-II formed from angiotensin I is a powerful vasoconstrictor.

(a) ☐ (b) ☐ (c) ☐ (d) ☐

***10.** **Assertion** (A) In haemodialysis, anti-heparin is added to the blood before passing it to the dialysing unit.

Reason (R) The composition of the dialysing fluid is the same as that of plasma except nitrogenous waste.

(a) ☐ (b) ☐ (c) ☐ (d) ☐

Case Based Questions

1. Humans can excrete hyper-osmotic or hypo-osmotic urine depending on the availability of water in the body. Regulation of kidney functioning is controlled by both neural system and hormones.

The given image illustrates along with basic structural and functional unit of kidney called nephron. Answer the following questions based on the provided image.

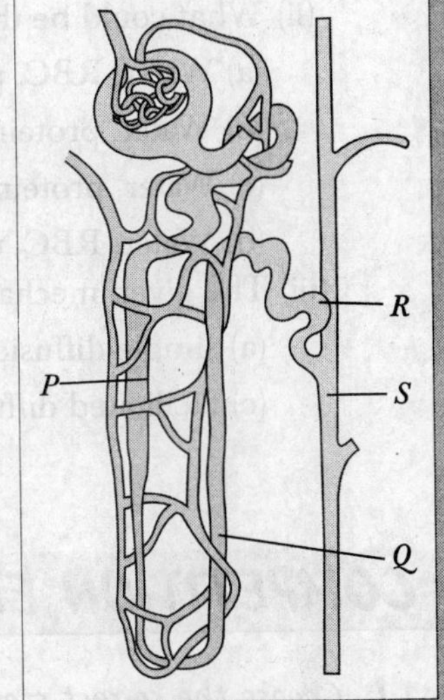

(i) Which of the following pair represents hypertonic condition of the filtrate?

(a) P and Q ☐ (b) P and R ☐

(c) Q and R ☐ (d) P and S ☐

(ii) Which of the following about Q is correct?

(a) It is permeable to water ☐

(b) It is permeable to electrolyte ☐

(c) It is impermeable to electrolyte ☐

(d) It is freely permeable ☐

(iii) What will happen if Henle's loop is absent in the functional nephron?

(a) There will be no urine formation ☐

(b) The urine will be more concentrated ☐

(c) The urine will be more dilute ☐

(d) There will be no change in the quality and quantity of urine formed ☐

2. In the given image a process is being performed on a person which involves drawing blood from the artery and passing it into an artificial unit X. Answer the following questions based on the given information.

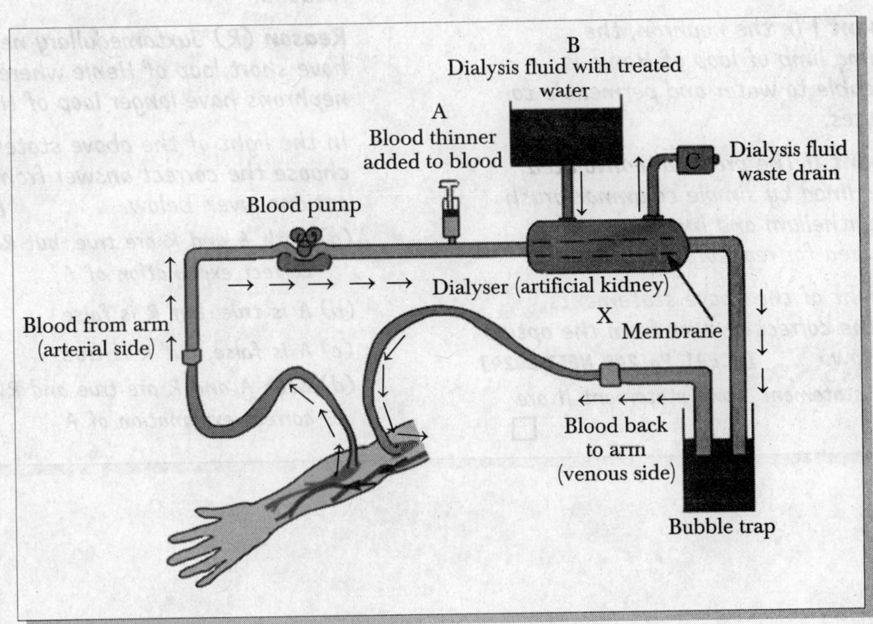

(i) Before passing the blood into X, it is treated with A which is

(a) albumin ☐ (b) platelets ☐
(c) heparin ☐ (d) fibrin ☐

(ii) What could be the possible composition of fluid B that is added to the unit X?

(a) Water, RBC, proteins, hormones ☐
(b) Water, proteins, hormones, urea ☐
(c) Water, proteins, hormones, ions ☐
(d) Water, RBC, urea, proteins ☐

(iii) The given mechanism works on the principle of

(a) simple diffusion ☐ (b) active transport ☐
(c) facilitated diffusion ☐ (d) osmosis ☐

COMPETITION EDGE UP

1. Choose the correct statement given below regarding juxta medullary nephron. **[NCERT Pg. 208, NEET 2024]**

(a) Juxta medullary nephrons are located in the columns of Bertini. ☐
(b) Renal corpuscle of juxta medullary nephron lies in the outer portion of the renal medulla. ☐
(c) Loop of Henle of juxta medullary nephron runs deep into medulla. ☐
(d) Juxta medullary nephrons outnumber the cortical nephrons. ☐

2. Given below are two statements.

Statement I In the nephron, the descending limb of loop of Henle is impermeable to water and permeable to electrolytes.

Statement II The proximal convoluted tubule is lined by simple columnar brush border epithelium and increases the surface area for reabsorption.

In the light of the above statements, choose the correct answer from the option given below. **[NCERT, Pg. 209, NEET 2024]**

(a) Both statement I and statement II are true ☐
(b) Both statement I and statement II are false ☐
(c) Statement I is true, but statement II is false ☐
(d) Statement I is false, but statement II is true ☐

3. Given below are two statements, one is labelled as **Assertion** (A) and the other is labelled as **Reason** (R).

Assertion (A) Nephrons are of two types: Cortical and juxtamedullary, based on their relative position in cortex and medulla.

Reason (R) Juxtamedullary nephrons have short loop of Henle whereas, cortical nephrons have longer loop of Henle.

In the light of the above statements, choose the correct answer from the options given below. **[NEET 2023]**

(a) Both A and R are true, but R is not the correct explanation of A ☐
(b) A is true, but R is false ☐
(c) A is false, but R is true ☐
(d) Both A and R are true and R is the correct explanation of A ☐

4. Which of the following statements are correct?

A. An excessive loss of body fluid from the body switches off osmoreceptors.

B. ADH facilitates water reabsorption to prevent diuresis.

C. ANF causes vasodilation.

D. ADH causes increase in blood pressure.

E. ADH is responsible for decrease in GFR.

Choose the correct answer from the options given below. [NEET 2023]

(a) B, C and D only ☐

(b) A, B and E only ☐

(c) C, D and E only ☐

(d) A and B only ☐

5. The increase in osmolarity from outer to inner medullary interstitium is maintained due to [NCERT Pg. 211, NEET (Oct.) 2020]

I. close proximity between Henle's loop and vasa recta

II. counter-current mechanism

III. selective secretion of HCO_3^- and hydrogen ions in PCT.

IV. higher blood pressure in glomerular capillaries

(a) Only II ☐

(b) III and IV ☐

(c) I, II and III ☐

(d) I and II ☐

6. Select the correct statement. [NCERT Pg. 212, NEET (Oct.) 2020]

(a) Atrial Natriuretic Factor increases the blood pressure ☐

(b) Angiotensin-II is a powerful vasodilator ☐

(c) Counter-current pattern of blood flow is not observed in vasa recta ☐

(d) Reduction in Glomerular Filtration Rate (GFR) activates JG cells to release renin ☐

7. Which of the following would help in prevention of diuresis? [NEET (Sep) 2020]

(a) Reabsorption of Na^+ and water from renal tubules due to aldosterone ☐

(b) Atrial natriuretic factor causes vasoconstriction ☐

(c) Decrease in the secretion of renin by JG cells ☐

(d) More water reabsorption due to undersecretion of ADH ☐

8. Presence of which of the following conditions in urine are indicative of diabetes mellitus? [NCERT Pg. 313 NEET (Sep.) 2020]

(a) Uremia and Renal calculi ☐

(b) Ketonuria and Glycosuria ☐

(c) Renal calculi and Hyperglycaemia ☐

(d) Uremia and Ketonuria ☐

Chapter 17

Locomotion and Movement

Scan and take Chapter Test

TOPIC 1

Types of Movement, Muscle and Mechanism of Muscle Contraction

1. Movement is one of the significant features of both plants and animals.

True ☐ False ☐

2. Name a unicellular organism which shows movement by streaming of protoplasm.

____

3. How many of the listed structures in human body show movement?

Tongue, Ear pinna, Eyelids, Limbs, Jaws

____

4. Some movements result in change of place or location. Such voluntary movements are called ______________.

5. Complete the following analogy with respect to locomotory structures in different animals.

Cilia : ______________ Tentacles : ______________ :

6. All movements are locomotion, but all locomotions are not movements.

True ☐ False ☐

7. Locomotion performed by animals vary with their ______________.

8. The purpose of locomotion in living beings is to

(i) search of food, shelter, mate and climatic conditions.

(ii) derive metabolic energy for survival.

____

9. Name the three types of movements exhibited by cells in human body.

____

*Concepts of all questions bearing * are important for NEET & CUET*

10. Match Column I with Column II.

Column I	Column II
A. *Paramoecium*	1. Flagella
B. *Amoeba*	2. Pseudopodia
C. *Hydra*	3. Cilia
D. *Euglena*	4. Tentacles

	A	B	C	D			A	B	C	D
(a)	3	2	4	1		(b)	3	2	1	4
(c)	1	2	3	4		(d)	1	2	4	3

11. Consider the following statements.

Statement I Amoeboid movement which uses pseudopodia is limited only to *Amoeba.*

Statement II Cytoskeletal elements like microfilaments are also involved in amoeboid movement.

Choose the correct option from the following.

(a) Statement I is true, but statement II is false

(b) Statement I is false, but statement II is true

(c) Both statements I and II are true

(d) Both statements I and II are false

12. Passage of ova through the female reproductive tract is facilitated by ______________

13. Choose the odd one out with respect to the type of movement.

(i) Macrophages, Leucocytes, Microfilaments, Jaws______________

(ii) Tongue, Hands, Feet, Basophils______________

14. Ciliary movement in humans occurs in ______________ organs which are lined by ______________ epithelium.

15. Given below are locations where ciliary movement occurs in human body. Write the functions of this movement.

(i) Trachea ______________

(ii) Fallopian tube ______________

16. Name the property of muscles effectively used for locomotion.

____

17. Locomotion requires a perfect coordinated activity of ______________, ______________ and ______________ systems.

18. Origin of muscle is ______________ (ectodermal/endodermal/mesodermal).

19. How much of the body weight is contributed by muscles in humans?

____

20. Name the four properties exhibited by the muscle.

____

21. The criteria used for classification of muscles is
(i) location, appearance, nature of activity regulation.
(ii) number of myofibrils and their appearance.
____

22. What is the other mame given to skeletal muscles?
____

23. During vigorous exercise, lactic acid can accumulate in ____________ muscles.

24. Smooth muscles is a name given to ____________ muscle.

25. Complete the following table by filling blanks *A-H*.

Skeletal muscles	Visceral muscles	Cardiac muscles
Associated with skeletal components of body	(A)	(B)
(C)	(D)	Striated
Voluntary	(E)	(F)
(G)	Performs various functions like transport of food through digestive tract	(H)

A. ________ B. ________ C. ________ D. ________
E. ________ F. ________ G. ________ H. ________

26. Visceral muscles have a striped appearance and are smooth in appearance.
True ☐ False ☐

27. Name the muscle present in the following structures.

Alimentary canal, Stomach, Reproductive tract

____

28. Write two functions performed by visceral muscles.
(i) ______________________________
(ii) ______________________________

***29.** Skeletal muscle is made up of a number of muscle bundles known as ____________.

***30.** A layer surrounding each muscle bundle is called ____________, which is made up of ____________ tissue.

***31.** Muscle fibres are basically muscle cells present inside each muscle bundle.
True ☐ False ☐

***32.** Give the scientific terms for the following components of muscle fibre.
(i) Plasma membrane ____________
(ii) Cytoplasm ____________
(iii) Endoplasmic reticulum ____________

33. In the diagrammatic cross-sectional view of a muscle, label the parts *A* to *D*.

A. ____________________

B. ____________________

C. ____________________

D. ____________________

***34.** Anatomical unit of the skeletal muscle is muscle bundle.
(*Rewrite the statement after correcting the underlined words.*)

____

35. Muscle fibre is a syncitium due to the presence of ____________________ .

***36.** The storehouse of Ca^{2+} ions in muscle fibre is ____________________ (sarcolemma/sarcoplasmic reticulum).

***37.** The characteristic feature of muscle fibre is the presence of large number of myofibril in the sarcoplasm.

True ☐ False ☐

***38.** Consider the image given in Q. 33. Which of the following is not correct about structure *A*?

(a) It is line by a double layered membrane called sarcolemma ☐

(b) It is syncitium as the sarcoplasm contains many nuclei. ☐

(c) The sarcoplasm is the store house of calcium ions. ☐

(d) It contains myofibrils with light and dark bands. ☐

***39.** Consider the following statements.

Statement I Sarcoplasm of muscle fibres contain parallelly arranged myofilaments.

Statement II Striated appearance of myofibrils is due to actin and myosin proteins.

Choose the correct option from the following.

(a) Statement I is true, but statement II is false ☐

(b) Statement I is false, but statement II is true ☐

(c) Both statements I and II are true ☐

(d) Both statements I and II are false ☐

***40.** Each myofibril has alternate dark and light bands. The light bands contain ____________ protein whereas dark bands contain ____________ protein.

41. The functional unit of contraction of muscle fibre is ____________________ .

***42.** How many features are true for a sarcomere?

(i) These are the sections of myofibrils joined end to end all along the muscle fibre.

(ii) It is the area between two M-lines.

(iii) It comprises of one full A-band and half I-band.

____

***43.** Match the following columns.

Column I	Column II
A. I-band	1. Light band of actin filament
B. A-band	2. Dark band of myosin filament
C. M-line	3. Thin fibrous membrane present in the middle of A-band
D. Z-line	4. It is central part of thick filament not overlapped by thin filament
E. H-zone	5. Elastic fibre bisecting I-band

A. ______________ B. ______________ C. ______________

D. ______________ E. ______________

44. The given image shows a muscle fibre. Which of the following is the correctly identifies structure *X* and *Y*?

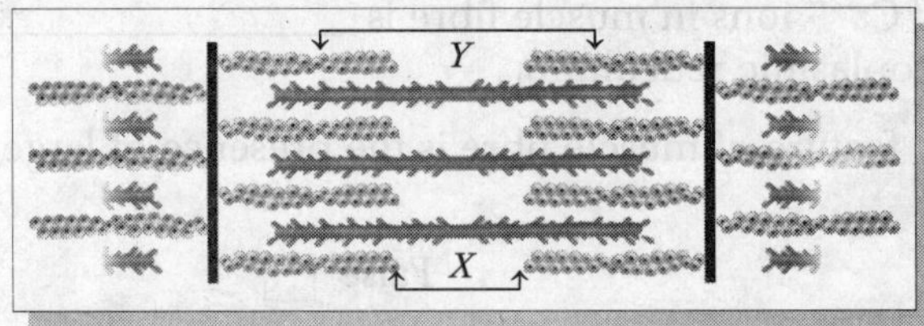

(a) X–H-zone, Y–I-band ☐ (b) X–H-zone, Y–A-band ☐

(c) X–Z-line, Y–I-band ☐ (d) X–Z-line, Y–A-band ☐

***45.** Action filaments are called ______________ filaments, whereas myosin filaments are called ______________ filaments.

***46.** Give the full form of the following.

(i) I-band ______________

(ii) A-band ______________

***47.** In a resting stage, the edges of thin filaments on either side of the thick filaments partially overlap the free ends of the thick filaments thus, leaving the central part of the thick filament.

True ☐ False ☐

***48.** Label the parts *A* to *G* in the diagrammatic representation of anatomy of a muscle fibre showing a sarcomere.

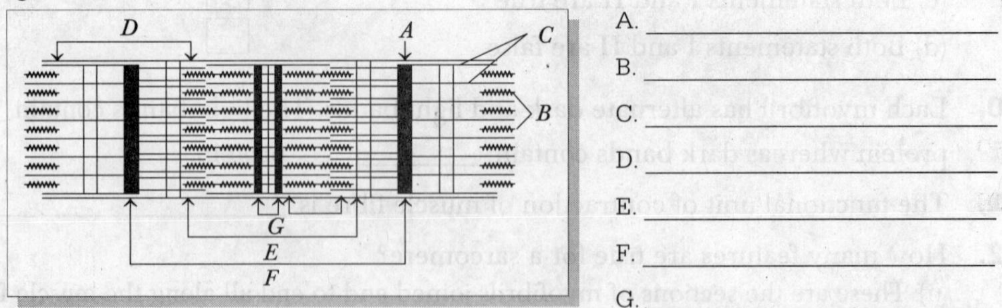

A. ______________

B. ______________

C. ______________

D. ______________

E. ______________

F. ______________

G. ______________

***49.** Consider the following statements.

Statement I The thick filaments in the 'A' band are held together by a thin fibrous membrane called 'Z' line.

Statement II The centre of each 'I' band of the thin filaments is an elastic fibre called 'M' line which bisects it.

Choose the correct option from the following.

(a) Statement I is true, but statement II is false ☐
(b) Statement I is false, but statement II is true ☐
(c) Both statements I and II are true ☐
(d) Both statements I and II are false ☐

50. Central part of thick filament which is not overlapped by thin filaments is known as ____________

51. Name the following based on the description given below.

(i) Two contractile proteins which help to shorten muscle fibre.

____

(ii) Two regulatory proteins which determine when the muscle should contract.

____

***52.** Each actin (thin) filament is made up of two ____________ actins that are helically wound to each other.

53. ____________ actin is a polymer of monomeric ____________ actin.

54. Consider the following statements.

I. Skeletal muscles are primarily involved in locomotory actions and changes of body postures.
II. The portion of the myofibril between two successive '*m*' lines is considered as the functional unit of contraction.
III. Each thick filament is parallelly wound to each other.
IV. Myofilaments are the structure which is parallelly arranged in the sarcoplasm.

Choose the option with correct sets of statements.

(a) I and III ☐ (b) II and IV ☐ (c) I and IV ☐ (d) II and III ☐

55. Tropomyosin masks the binding sites for myosin on actin filaments during resting state.

True ☐ False ☐

56. Identify *A*, *B* and *C* in the given diagram of actin (thin) filament.

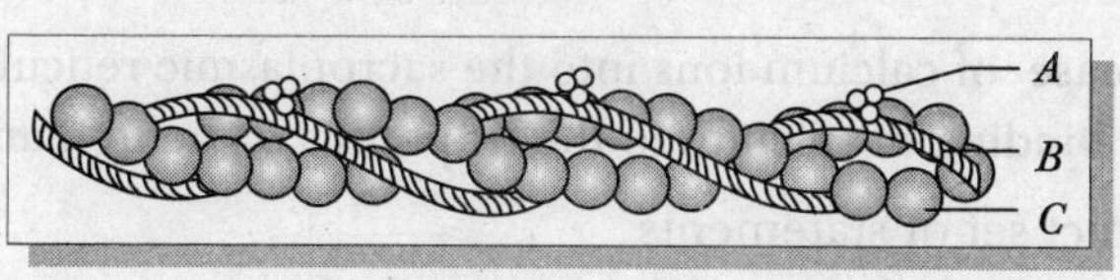

A. ____________
B. ____________
C. ____________

57. Myosin filament is a polymer of monomeric protein called ____________.

58. Identify *A*, *B*, *C* and *D* in the given diagram of myosin monomer.

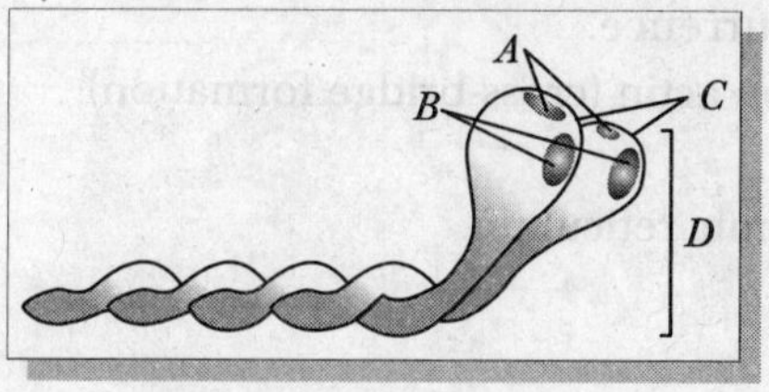

A. ____________
B. ____________
C. ____________
D. ____________

***59.** Give the full form of the following.

(i) HMM ____________________

(ii) LMM ____________________

***60.** A defective actin filament, lacks troponin on the tropomyosin filaments. Which of the following events would not occur?

(a) Winding of the two F actin filaments ☐ (b) Binding of myosin to the actin ☐

(c) ATP hydrolysis by the HMM ☐ (d) Masking the binding site for myosin ☐

***61.** The HMM component project outward at regular distance and angle from the surface of polymerised myosin filament and form a ____________________.

***62.** The globular head of HMM is an active ATPase enzyme and it contains

ATP binding sites, Actin binding sites, Myosin binding sites, Troponin binding sites, Calcium binding sites

____

***63.** Name the theory that best explain the mechanism of muscle contraction.

____

***64.** Contraction of muscle fibres takes place by the sliding of the thin filaments over the thick filaments.

True ☐ False ☐

65. Muscle contraction is initiated by a signal sent by CNS, *via* __________ neurons.

66. Complete the following equation.
Motor unit = Motor neuron + ____________________

67. Give the scientific term for the following sentence.
The junction between a motor neurons and the sarcolemma of the muscle fibre.

____________________.

68. When a neural signal reaches neuromuscular junction and releases neurotransmitters ____________________ is generated.

69. Consider the following statements.

I. Tropomyosin also run close to the 'F' actins throughout its length.

II. Contraction of a muscle fibres takes place by the sliding of the thick filaments over the thin filaments.

III. Acetylcholine causes the release of calcium ions into the sacroplasmic reticulum.

IV. Increased Ca^{2+} levels cause binding of calcium to the troponins on actin filaments.

Choose the option with incorrect set of statements

(a) I and II ☐ (b) I and III ☐

(c) II and III ☐ (d) II and IV ☐

***70.** Given below is the sequence of events which causes muscle contraction. Arrange them correctly in the order of their occurrence.

I. Myosin binds with active sites on actin (cross-bridge formation).

II. Nerve impulse.

III. Release of Ca^{2+} from sarcoplasmic reticulum.

IV. Acetylcholine is released.

V. Sarcomere shortens.

VI. Action potential generated in sarcolemma.
VII. Spread of impulses over sarcolemma on T-tubules.

71. During contraction, __________ bands get shorten whereas __________ bands retain the length.

72. Choose the correct order for contraction of muscles from the following options.

(a) Ca^{2+} binds to troponin → Cross bridge formation → ATP hydrolysis → Sliding of filaments ☐

(b) Ca^{2+} binds to troponin → ATP hydrolysis → Cross-bridge formation → Sliding of filaments ☐

(c) ATP hydrolysis → Ca^{2+} binds to troponin → Cross-bridge formation sliding of filaments ☐

(d) ATP hydrolysis → Ca^{2+} binds to troponin → Sliding of filaments → Cross-bridge formation. ☐

73. Identify *A*, *B*, *C* and *D* in the given diagram of muscle contraction.

A. __________

B. __________

C. __________

D. __________

74. Fill in the blanks by choosing the correct pair from the box.

Sarcoplasmic reticulum and sarcoplasm, Myosin head and actin filament Calcium ions and troponin.

(i) Muscle contraction is initiated by the binding of __________ to __________.

(ii) Cross-bridge is formed between __________ and __________ during muscle contraction.

(iii) Action potential causes calcium ions to diffuse from the __________ into __________.

75. Given below are few statements.

I. Motor-end plate is the junction between motor neuron and sacroplasm of muscle fibre.
II. The formation of cross- bridge requires energy from hydrolysis of ATP.
III. Relaxation occurs when calcium is pumped back to the sacroplasmic cisternae.
IV. Myosin releases the ADP and P_1 which results in state of relaxation.

Choose the option with correct set of statements.

(a) I, II and IV ☐ (b) I, II and III ☐
(c) II, III and IV ☐ (d) I, III and IV ☐

76. Give the scientific term used for the reduction in the force of contraction of muscle after prolonged stimulation. ____________________

77. Repeated activation of the muscles lead to lactic acid accumulation thus, causing fatigue due to aerobic breakdown of glucose .
(*Rewrite the statement after correcting the underlined phrase.*)

____

78. A red coloured oxygen storing pigment in muscle is ____________________ (myoglobin/ haemoglobin).

79. Complete the following analogy given below.
Aerobic muscle : Anaerobic muscle : : Red muscle fibres : ____________________.

80. Complete the table by writing more or less in the blanks.

Characteristics	Red muscle fibres	White muscle fibres
A. Myoglobin content	________	________
B. Number of mitochondria	________	________
C. Number of sarcoplasmic reticulum	________	________
D. Amount of oxygen stored	________	________

81. An organ used vigorously, requires huge amount of ATP for its activities. Which of the following is not correct about the muscle fibres abundant here?

(a) The muscle fibres can utilize huge amounts of oxygen for ATP production. ☐

(b) The muscle fibres appear red in colour due to the presence of myoglobin. ☐

(c) The muscle fibres have huge number of sarcoplasmic reticulum in the sarcoplasm. ☐

(d) The muscle fibres have huge number of mitochondria and respire aerobically. ☐

82. Identify the state of the sarcomere in the diagram *A*, *B* and *C* given below.

I-band
H-zone
A-band
Ⓐ
Z-line
Z-line
Z-line
Ⓑ
Ⓒ
Two Sarcomeres

A. ____________________

B. ____________________

C. ____________________

TOPIC 2

Skeletal System

NCERT Pg. 224-226

83. Complete the analogy given below.

Bones : Cartilage : : Calcium salts : ________.

84. ________ has slightly pliable matrix whereas ________ has a very hard matrix.

85. Write the number of bones present in axial and appendicular skeleton.

Human Skeletal System

Axial system/skeleton A. ________

Appendicular system/skeleton B. ________

86. Write the common term for the following.

(i) Skull, Vertebral column, Sternum, Ribs. ________

(ii) Cranial bones, Facial bones, Hyoid, Ear ossicles. ________

87. (i) In the given diagram of human skull, identify the bones labelled as *A-H*.

A. ________
B. ________
C. ________
D. ________
E. ________
F. ________
G. ________
H. ________

(ii) How many of the bones shown in diagram form cranial bones?

____

88. Choose the odd one out from the following.

(i) Frontal, Temporal, Maxilla, Sphenoid ________

(ii) Vomer, Nasals, Mandible, Ethmoid ________

(iii) Cervical, Thoracic, Zygomatic, Coccyx ________

89. Write the number of bones in the following.

(i) Cranial ________ (ii) Facial ________

(iii) Hyoid ________ (iv) Middle ear ________

90. Name the hard protective covering of the brain ________

91. How many of the listed bones are paired in humans and how many are unpaired?

Frontal, Parietal, Temporal, Occipital, Sphenoid, Ethmoid

Paired ________

Unpaired ________

92. Write the location of hyoid bone ________________

93. Ear ossicles are present in the ________________ part of ear.

94. Choose the odd one out with respect to ear ossicle.

Malleus, Hyoid, Incus, Stapes

____

***95.** The skull in human articulates with the superior region of the vertebral column with the help of two occipital condyles, thus it is known as ________________ skull.

96. Name the bone which is present at the base of buccal cavity and also included in the skull.

____

97. First vertebra called ________________ articulates with the occipital condyles.

98. Name a facial bone that is not found in pair ________________

99. The main framework of the trunk is constituted by ________________. It provides places for the attachment of the ribs and bones of pelvis.

100. Our vertebral column is formed by ________________ serially arranged units called vertebrae and is dorsally placed.

101. Each vertebrae has a central hollow portion through which spinal cord passes. This hollow portion of vertebrae is called ________________.

102. Human vertebral formula is $C_7T_5L_{12}S_4C_4$.

True ☐ False ☐

103. Examine the figure of vertebral column (right lateral view) and identify *A, B, C, D, E* and *F*.

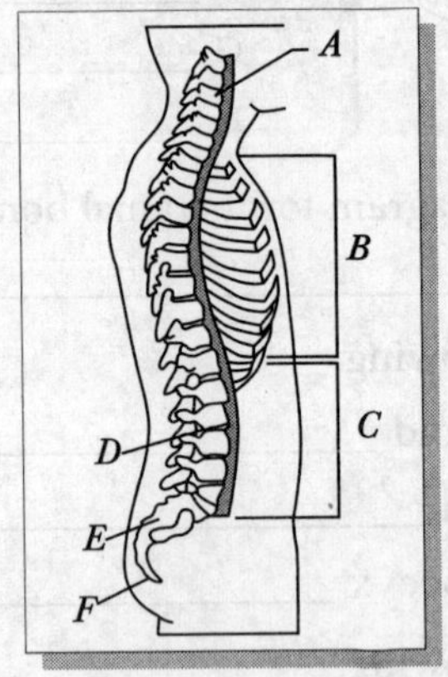

A. ________________
B. ________________
C. ________________
D. ________________
E. ________________
F. ________________

104. ________________ and ________________ are fused bones of vertebral column.

105. Complete the following analogy given below.

First vertebrae : Second vertebrae. : : Atlas : ________________

106. What are the functions of vertebral column in humans?

(i) ________________
(ii) ________________
(iii) ________________

***107.** Identify the bone based on the description
(i) Flat in shape
(ii) Present in the ventral midline of thorax
(iii) True ribs are attached to it

____

***108.** Give the scientific name for the following.
(i) Breast bone ______________________________
(ii) False ribs ______________________________

***109.** Each typical rib in human is a thin flat bone connected ______________ to the vertebral column and ______________ to the sternum.

***110.** Typical ribs are ______________ (monocephalic/bicephalic/tricephalic).

***111.** Match the following columns.

	Column I (Ribs)		Column II (Numbers)		Column III (Locations)
A.	True ribs	1.	First 7 pairs	P.	Attached to vertebral column dorsally and to seventh rib ventrally
B.	False ribs	2.	8th, 9th and 10th pairs	Q.	Do not connect ventrally
C.	Floating ribs	3.	11th and 12th pairs	R.	Attached to vertebral column dorsally and to sternum ventrally

A. ______________ B. ______________ C. ______________

***112.** Which of the following options represents vertebrochondral ribs?
(a) Ribs 1 to 7 ☐ (b) Ribs 8,9 and 10 ☐
(c) Ribs 11 and 12 ☐ (d) Rib 12 ☐

113. Name the cartilage which helps to join sternum with ribs.

114. Complete the equation.

______________ + Ribs + ______________ = Ribcage

115. Identify *A*, *B* and *C* in the given figure of ribcage.

A. ______________
B. ______________
C. ______________

116. Write the number of bones in the given flowchart.

Appendicular skeleton (126 bones)
Limbs (A)
Girdle (B)
Pectoral girdle (C)
Pelvic girdle (D)

A. ________ B. ________ C. ________ D. ________

117. Each limb (upper to lower) consists of how many bones? ________

118. Give common names for the following.

(i) Femur, Tibia, Fibula, Tarsals. ________

(ii) Humerus, Ulna, Radius, Carpals. ________

119. Complete the following based on the number of bones present in human body.

(i) Phalanges = ______ × 2 = ______

(ii) Carpals = ______ × 2 = ______

(iii) Metacarpals = ______ × 2 = ______

(iv) Tarsals = ______ × 2 = ______

(v) Metatarsals = ______ × 2 = ______

120. Give the scientific names of the following bones.

(i) Digits ________

(iii) Thigh bone ________

121. Match Column I with Column II.

Column I	Column II
A. Carpals	1. Palm bones
B. Tarsals	2. Knee cap
C. Patella	3. Ankle bone
D. Metacarpals	4. Wrist bone

	A	B	C	D			A	B	C	D
(a)	4	3	2	1		(b)	4	3	1	2
(c)	4	1	2	3		(d)	4	1	3	2

122. Write the phalangeal/digital formula for human hand/foot. ________

123. Complete the following analogy

Longest bone : Smallest bone : : ________ : ________

124. ________ is a cup-shaped bone that covers the knee ventrally.

125. Give one common function of pectoral girdle and pelvic girdle.

____

126. Consider the following flowchart and identify *A-E*.

Girdle
- Pectoral
  - *A*
  - *B*
- Pelvic
  - *C*
  - *D*
  - *E*

A. ____________ B. ____________ C. ____________ D. ____________ E.

127. A person with a localised fracture in the pelvic girdle, will not have any effect on

(a) Ilium ☐ (b) Coxal ☐ (c) Ischium ☐ (d) Clavicle ☐

128. In the given figure of right pectoral girdle and upper arm, how many labels are correctly named? Also rewrite the incorrect ones correctly.

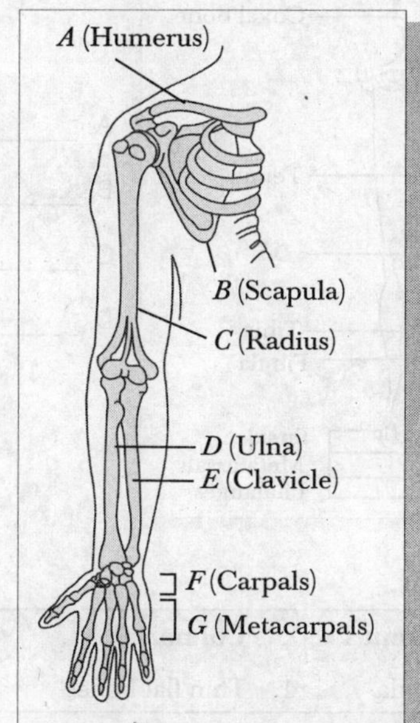

____

***129.** ____________ (Clavicle/Scapula) bone is situated in the dorsal part of the thorax between the second and seventh ribs.

***130.** Give the scientific names given to each of the following.

(i) Collar bone ____________________________

(ii) Shoulder blade ____________________________

***131.** Scapula has a slightly elevated ridge called ____________ which projects as a flat expanded process called the ____________. The latter articulates with the clavicle.

***132.** For articulation of head of humerus, a depression is found in scapula called as <u>occipital cavity</u>. (*Rewrite the statement after correcting the underlined words.*)

____

133. How many curvatures are present in clavicle? ____________

***134.** Pelvic girdle consists of __________ (three/two) coxal bones. Each coxal bone is formed by the fusion of __________ (three/two) bones.

135. Each coxal bone is formed by the fusion of three bones namely,

____

***136.** Complete the following analogy given below.

Glenoid cavity : __________ : : Pectoral girdle : Pelvic girdle

***137.** Two halves of pelvic girdle articulate ventrally at a fibrocartilaginous joint called __________ (Sutures/Pubic symphysis).

***138.** Name the cavity through which the femur bone articulates. ____________

139. Identify *A, B, C* and *D* in the figure given below.

A
B
C
Coxal bone
Femur
D
Tibia
Fibula
Tarsals
Metatarsals
Phalanges

A. ____________
B. ____________
C. ____________
D. ____________

***140.** Match the following columns.

Column I	Column II
A. Scapula	1. Thin flat bones
B. Sternum	2. Long slender bone
C. Clavicle	3. Dagger-shaped bone
D. Ribs	4. Large triangular flat bone

A. __________ B. __________ C. __________ D. __________

TOPIC 3 Joints

NCERT Pg. 226-227

141. How many statements are correct for joints?

(i) These are essential for all types of movements involving bony parts.

(ii) They connect bones and cartilages only.

(iii) These are structural arrangement of tissues.

____

142. Force generated by the muscle is used to carry out movement through joints. In this case, joint acts as point of ____________________ (effort/fulcrum/resistance).

143. Name different types of joints found in human body.

____

***144.** Match the following columns.

Column I	Column II
A. Cartilaginous joints	1. Immovable joints
B. Fibrous joints	2. Imperfectly movable or slightly movable joints
C. Synovial joints	3. Perfectly movable or freely movable joints

A. __________ B. __________ C. __________

***145.** Sutures are fixed, immovable or fibrous joints in which articulating bones are held together by dense fibrous tissue.

True ☐ False ☐

***146.** Complete the flowchart.

Flat *A* bones —fuses to form→ *B* —form→ *C* of brain

A.__________ B.__________ C.__________

147. Give an example of cartilaginous joint. ____________________

148. Synovial joints in humans are characterised by the presence of fluid-filled called ________________ between the articulating surfaces of the two bones.

149. Articular cartilage of synovial joint is ______________ (fibro/elastic/hyaline) cartilage.

150. Cartilaginous joints help in locomotory movements.

True ☐ False ☐

***151.** How many types of synovial joints are present in human body? ______________

***152.** Name the common term given to these joints.

Knee joint, Elbow joint, Interphalangeal joint

____

153. Which of the following joints will show only limited movement?

(a) Saddle joint ☐ (b) Vertebrae ☐

(c) Gliding joint ☐ (d) Sutures ☐

***154.** Give one example of each type of joint.

(i) Ball and socket joint____________________

(ii) Pivot joint ____________________

(iii) Gliding joint ____________________

***155.** Match the following columns.

Column I		Column II	
A.	Between humerus and pectoral girdle	1.	Ball and socket joint
B.	Between the carpals	2.	Pivot joint
C.	Between carpals and metacarpals of thumb	3.	Saddle joint
D.	Between atlas and axis	4.	Gliding joint

A. ________ B. ________ C. ________ D. ________

TOPIC 4

Disorders of Muscular and Sketetal System

***156.** Choose the odd one out with respect to the symptoms of myasthenia gravis.

Fatigue, Tremors, Paralysis of skeletal muscle, Weakening of muscles

____

***157.** Arthritis is a disease caused by degradation of bone.
(*Rewrite the statement after correcting the underlined words.*)

158. Choose the odd one out with respect to arthritis.

Rheumatoid arthritis, Gout, Osteoarthritis, Osteoporosis

____

***159.** Match the following columns.

Column I (Disorders)	Column II (Features)
A. Myasthenia gravis	1. Degeneration of skeletal muscles
B. Muscular dystrophy	2. Neuromuscular junction affected
C. Tetany	3. Low Ca^{2+} in body fluid
D. Arthritis	4. Inflammation of joints

A. ________ B. ________ C. ________ D. ________

***160.** A person suffering from arthritis may experience how many of the listed symptoms?

Swelling in joint, Pain in joint, Sweating, Softness in bones, Fusion of joint, Tissue degeneration

____

161. Name the type of arthritis based on the description given below.

Sodium urate or uric acid crystal accumulate in joints. ________________

162. Name an age related disorder characterised by decreased bone mass and increased chances of fracture.________________

163. Choose the correct option for osteoporosis in each statement.

(i) Osteoporosis occurs more in ______________________ (men/women).

(ii) Decreased level of ______________________adrenaline/oestrogen) is a common cause.

(iii) It occurs due to ______________________ (high level/deficiency) of calcium in the body.

164. ______________________ is a symptom characterised by rapid spasms in muscles due to hypocalcemia.

Assertion-Reason Questions

The following questions consist of two statements- Assertion (A) and Reason (R). Answer these questions by selecting the appropriate option given below.

(a) Both A and R are true and R is the correct explanation of A

(b) Both A and R are true, but R is not the correct explanation of A

(c) A is true, but R is false

(d) A is false, but R is true

1. **Assertion** (A) Macrophages and leucocytes in blood exhibit movement which is quite similar to that of *Amoeba*.

Reason (R) In amoeboid movement, pseudopodia is extended by the stream of protoplasmic content.

(a) ☐ (b) ☐ (c) ☐ (d) ☐

***2.** **Assertion** (A) The fascicles of a muscle is held together by a fibrous tissue layer called fascia.

Reason (R) Each fascia contains huge number of muscle fibres that contain myofilaments.

(a) ☐ (b) ☐ (c) ☐ (d) ☐

***3.** **Assertion** (A) The I bands are light while the A bands are dark comprising thin and thick filaments respectively.

Reason (R) The centre of the I band has elastic Z line while the centre of A band has fibrous M line.

(a) ☐ (b) ☐ (c) ☐ (d) ☐

***4.** **Assertion** (A) At rest, the thin filaments partially overlap the thick filaments at the free ends.

Reason (R) Edges of thick filament, overlapped by thin filaments is called the 'H' zone.

(a) ☐ (b) ☐ (c) ☐ (d) ☐

5. **Assertion** (A) Troponin is present at regular intervals on tropomyosin unit of the F-actin filaments.

Reason (R) Troponin masks the active binding site of myosin protein on the actin filaments at rest.

(a) ☐ (b) ☐ (c) ☐ (d) ☐

6. **Assertion** (A) The globular head of Heavy Meromyosin (HMM) has binding sites for ATP.

Reason (R) The head and short arm components of HMM projects outward to form crossarm.

(a) ☐ (b) ☐ (c) ☐ (d) ☐

***7.** **Assertion** (A) Acetylcholine is released in response to a signal, into the neuromuscular junction.

Reason (R) Stimulus causes release of Ca^{2+} ions from the Sarcoplasmic reticulum to sarcolemmma.

(a) ☐ (b) ☐ (c) ☐ (d) ☐

***8.** **Assertion** (A) Formation of the cross bridge pulls the actin filaments towards the centre of 'I' band.

Reason (R) During contraction, the 'I' bands get reduced, whereas the 'A' bands retain the length.

(a) ☐ (b) ☐ (c) ☐ (d) ☐

9. **Assertion** (A) Each rib is a thin flat bone connected dorsally to the vertebral column and ventrally to the sternum.

Reason (R) Each rib has two articulation surfaces on its ventral end and is hence called bicephalic.

(a) ☐ (b) ☐ (c) ☐ (d) ☐

***10.** **Assertion** (A) Synovial joints allow for a wide range of movement.

Reason (R) Synovial joints have a smooth cartilage lining and synovial fluid lubricating the space between bones.

(a) ☐ (b) ☐ (c) ☐ (d) ☐

Case Based Questions

***1.** Consider the following image and answer the questions that follow.

(i) Which of the following best defines the condition of the muscle fibres?

(a) A-relaxed B-relaxed ☐ (b) A-relaxed B-contracted ☐

(c) A-contracted B-relaxed ☐ (d) A-contracted B-contracted ☐

(ii) Which of the following does not lead to situation A ?
   (a) Release of acetylcholine at the neuromuscular junction ☐
   (b) Release of calcium ions into the sarcoplasm ☐
   (c) Binding of calcium with a subunit of troponin ☐
   (d) Synthesis of ATP by the HMM of myosin ☐

(iii) Which of the following remains unaltered in B?
   (a) I band ☐ (b) Z line ☐
   (c) A band ☐ (d) Actin ☐

2. John, a 65 year old man complains of pain and stiffness in his lower back, which worsens when he bends forward or stands for prolonged periods. He also notices pain radiating down his left leg. Upon examination, his physician suspects a herniated or slipped disc in the lumbar region. Based on the following situation answer the questions that follow.

(i) Which structure is most likely affected, causing the mentioned symptoms?
   (a) Ligments ☐ (b) Intervertebral discs ☐
   (c) Synovial fluid ☐ (d) Articular cartilage ☐

(ii) Which of the following activities or position is likely to alleviate John's symptoms?
   (a) Standing ☐ (b) Sitting ☐
   (c) Bending forward ☐ (d) Lifting heavy objects ☐

(iii) Which structure connects one vertebra to another and provides stability to the spine?
   (a) Intervertebral discs ☐ (b) Ligaments ☐
   (c) Muscles ☐ (d) Spinal nerves ☐

COMPETITION EDGE UP

1. Match List I with List II.

List-I		List-II
A. Fibrous joints	I.	Adjacent vertebrae, limited movement
B. Cartilaginous joints	II.	Humerus and pectoral girdle, rotational movement
C. Hinge joints	III.	Skull, do not allow any movement
D. Ball and socket joints	IV.	Knee, help in locomotion

Choose the correct answer from the options given below.

[NCERT Pg. 227, NEET 2024]

(a) A-IV, B-II, C-III, D-I ☐
(b) A-I, B-III, C-II, D-IV ☐
(c) A-II, B-III, C-I, D-IV ☐
(d) A-III, B-I, C-IV, D-II ☐

2. Match List-I with List-II.

List-I	List-II
A. Cartilaginous joint	I. Between flat skull bones
B. Ball and socket joint	II. Between adjacent vertebrae in vertebral column
C. Fibrous joint	III. Between carpal and metacarpal of thumb
D. Saddle joint	IV. Between humerus and pectoral girdle

Choose the correct answer from the options given below.

[NCERT Pg. 227, NEET 2023]

(a) A-II, B-IV, C-I, D-III ☐
(b) A-I, B-IV, C-III, D-II ☐
(c) A-II, B-IV, C-III, D-I ☐
(d) A-III, B-I, C-II, D-IV ☐

3. Which of the following statements are correct regarding skeletal muscle?

A. Muscle bundles are held together by collagenous connective tissue layer called fascicle.

B. Sarcoplasmic reticulum of muscle fibre is a store house of calcium ions.

C. Striated appearance of skeletal muscle fibre is due to distribution pattern of actin and myosin proteins.

D. M line is considered as functional unit of contraction called sarcomere.

Choose the most appropriate answer from the options given below. **[NCERT Pg. 219, NEET 2023]**

(a) B and C only ☐
(b) A, C and D only ☐
(c) C and D only ☐
(d) A, B and C only ☐

4. Given below are two statements, one is labelled as Assertion (A) and the other is labelled as Reason (R).

Assertion (A) Osteoporosis is characterised by decreased bone mass and increased chances of fractures.

Reason (R) Common cause of osteoporosis is increased levels of oestrogen. **[NEET 2022]**

In the light of the above statements, choose the most appropriate answer from the options given below.

(a) Both (A) and (R) are correct, but (R) is not the correct explanation of (A) ☐
(b) (A) is correct, but (R) is not correct ☐
(c) (A) is not correct, but (R) is correct ☐
(d) Both (A) and (R) are correct and (R) is the correct explanation of (A) ☐

5. Which of the following is a correct match for disease and its symptoms? **[NCERT Pg. 222, NEET 2022]**

(a) Tetany-High Ca^{2+} level causing rapid spasms ☐
(b) Myasthenia gravis–Genetic disorder resulting in weakening and paralysis of skeletal muscle ☐
(c) Muscular dystrophy–An autoimmune disorder causing progressive degeneration of skeletal muscle ☐
(d) Arthritis–Inflammed joints ☐

6. During muscular contraction, which of the following events occur? **[NCERT Pg. 222, NEET 2021]**

I. 'H'-zone disappears.
II. 'A'-band widens.
III. 'I'-band reduces in width.
IV. Myosine hydrolyses ATP, releasing the ADP and Pi.
V. Z-lines attached to actins are pulled inwards.

Choose the correct answer from the options given below.

(a) I, III, IV and V ☐
(b) I, II, III and IV ☐
(c) II, III, IV and V ☐
(d) II, IV, V and I ☐

7. Match the List I with List II. **[NCERT Pg. 225, NEET 2021]**

List I	List II
A. Scapula	1. Cartilaginous joints
B. Cranium	2. Flat bone
C. Sternum	3. Fibrous joints
D. Vertebral column	4. Triangular flat bone

Choose the correct answer from the options given below.

	A	B	C	D			A	B	C	D	
(a)	1	3	2	4	☐	(b)	2	3	4	1	☐
(c)	4	2	3	1	☐	(d)	4	3	2	1	☐

8. Chronic autoimmune disorder affecting neuro-muscular junction leading to fatigue, weakening and paralysis of skeletal muscle is called as **[NCERT Pg. 227, NEET 2021]**

(a) arthritis ☐
(b) muscular dystrophy ☐
(c) myasthenia gravis ☐
(d) gout ☐

9. Match the following columns and select the correct option. **[NCERT Pg. 225, NEET (Sep.) 2020]**

Column I	Column II
A. Floating ribs	1. Located between second and seventh ribs
B. Acromion	2. Head of the humerus
C. Scapula	3. Clavicle
D. Glenoid cavity	4. Do not connect with the sternum

	A	B	C	D			A	B	C	D	
(a)	1	3	2	4	☐	(b)	3	2	4	1	☐
(c)	4	3	1	2	☐	(d)	2	4	1	3	☐

Chapter 18

Neural Control and Coordination

Scan and take Chapter Test

TOPIC 1

Introduction and Human Neural System

1. The function of organ and organ system in our body must be coordinated to maintain ______.

2. Name the process of interaction and complementation of functions of two or more organs. ______

3. The increased supply of oxygen necessitates an increase in the rate of ______ increased blood flow and increased heartbeat.

4. ______ system and ______ system coordinate and integrate all the activities of the organs.

5. The endocrine system provides chemical integration through <u>enzymes</u>.

(Rewrite the statement after correcting the underlined word.)

______

6. The endocrine system provides an organised network of point-to-point connections for a quick coordination.

True ☐ False ☐

7. Complete the following analogy given below.

Endocrine system : Nervous system : : Hormone : ______

8. Name the specialised cells which detect, receive and transmit different kinds of stimuli and which makes neural system. ______

9. Presence of brain with ganglia and better organised neural system is found in ______ (*Hydra* /insects)

______

10. Consider the following statements.

Statement I Lower invertebrates like *Hydra* has a rudimentary nervous system.

Statement II Vertebrates have a complex system of nerves, ganglia and a centrally located brain.

*Concepts of all questions bearing * are important for NEET & CUET*

Choose the correct option from the following.

(a) Statement I is true, but statement II is false

(b) Statement I is false, but statement II is true

(c) Both statements I and II are true

(d) Both statements I and II are false

11. Write the two parts of the human neural system.

____

***12.** The CNS includes the PNS and ANS and is the site of information processing and control. (*Rewrite the statement after correcting the underlined words.*)

____

***13.** The PNS comprises of all the nerves of the body associated with brain and __________.

14. Write the two nerve fibres of PNS.__________

15. Afferent nerve fibres transmit impulses from __________ to __________.

16. Consider the following statements.

Statement I Neural system and endocrine system function in a synchronised fashion.

Statement II The afferent and efferent fibres are parts of the central nervous system.

Choose the correct option from the following.

(a) Statement I is true, but statement II is false

(b) Statement I is false, but statement II is true

(c) Both statements I and II are true

(d) Both statements I and II are false

17. Efferent fibres transmit regulatory signals from the CNS to the brain. (*Rewrite the statement after correcting the underlined word.*)

____

***18.** Choose the correct combinations from the following.

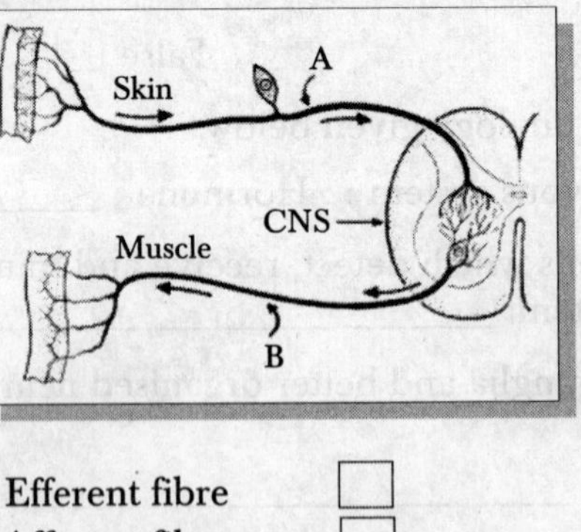

(a) A – Afferent fibre, B – Efferent fibre

(b) A – Efferent fibre, B – Afferent fibre

(c) A – Motor fibre, B – Sensory fibre

(d) A – Sensory fibre, B – Afferent fibre

19. The PNS includes somatic neural system and __________.

20. The system that transmits impulse from the CNS to skeletal muscles is__________.

21. Which of the following are involved in the image given below?

(a) Somatic neural system, skeletal muscles ☐
(b) Autonomic neural system, skeletal muscles ☐
(c) Somatic neural system, smooth muscles ☐
(d) Parasympathetic neural system, skeletal muscles ☐

22. Somatic neural system relays impulses from CNS to voluntary organs.

True ☐ False ☐

23. The system that transmits impulse from the CNS to the involuntary organs and smooth muscles of the body ______________.

24. Write the two parts of autonomic neural system.

____

25. Consider the following statements.

Statement I The autonomic nervous system is associated with involuntary functions of the body.

Statement II Fear is triggered by the parasympathetic part of autonomic nervous system.

Choose the correct option from the following.

(a) Statement I is true, but statement II is false ☐
(b) Statement I is false, but statement II is true ☐
(c) Both statements I and II are true ☐
(d) Both statements I and II are false ☐

***26.** The flowchart given below is the functional organisation of the human nervous system. Identify *A*, *B*, *C*, *D* and *E* in the following flowchart.

A. ______________
B. ______________
C. ______________
D. ______________
E. ______________

***27.** A person on encountering a snake, becomes tensed up with a racing heart, rapid breathing, dilated pupil and dried mouth, due to the stimulation of which branch of the nervous system?

(a) Parasympathetic branch of somatic nervous system ☐
(b) Sympathetic branch of autonomic nervous system ☐
(c) Parasympathetic branch of autonomic nervous system ☐
(d) Sympathetic branch of somatic nervous system ☐

***28.** Visceral nervous system is a part of ____________ and comprises of______, ______, ______ and plexuses. It constitutes the connection between ____________ and the viscera.

29. Given below are few statements.

I. Increased supply of oxygen necessitates an increase in the rate of respiration.

II. Hormones are chemicals secreted by endocrine system.

III. *Hydra* is composed of ganglions and neural tissues.

IV. Insects are composed of network of neurons.

V. PNS is the site of processing information and control.

Choose the option with incorrect set of statements

(a) I, III and V ☐ (b) II, III and V ☐
(c) II, III and IV ☐ (d) III, IV and V ☐

TOPIC 2

Neuron as Structural and Functional Unit of Neural System

NCERT Pg. 231-232

***30.** Write the three major parts of a neuron. ____________

31. ____________ are the short fibres which branch and project out of the cell body.

32. The cluster of rough endoplasmic reticulum in cell body and dendrites are called ____________.

***33.** Dendrites and ____________ of neuron transmit impulses towards and away from the cell body.

34. Which of the following structures in the given alongside image of the neuron, found in somatic and autonomic nervous system, is wrongly labelled?

(a) Node of Ranvier ☐
(b) Axon ☐
(c) Myelin sheath ☐
(d) Nissl's granules ☐

35. Name the bulb-like structure present on the distal end of axon branches.

____

***36.** Which of the following represents the correct pathway of impulse generation ?

(a) Dendrite → Cyton → Axon → Synapse ☐
(b) Dendrite → Axon → Cyton → Synapse ☐
(c) Dendrite → Cyton → Synapse → Axon ☐
(d) Dendrite → Axon → Synapse → Cyton ☐

37. Write a technical name for the following.

(i) Neuron with one axon and two or more dendrites. ______________

(ii) Neuron with one axon and a cell body. ______________

38. Name the chemical present in the synaptic vesicles of synaptic knob.

____

39. Identify the correct pair.

(i) Bipolar neuron–Cornea
(ii) Multipolar neuron–Cerebral cortex
(iii) Unipolar neuron–Embryonic stage

____

40. Choose the correct combination from the following.

X Y

(a) X–Found in cerebral cortex, Y–Found in embryonic stage ☐
(b) X–Bipolar neuron, Y–Multipolar neuron ☐
(c) X–Unipolar neuron, Y–Bipolar neuron ☐
(d) X–Found in embryonic stage, Y–Found in cerebral cortex ☐

41. Name the neuron with one axon and one dendrite.

____

***42.** Myelinated nerve fibres are enveloped by the ______________ cells.

43. Name the cell wraps around the axons of motor and sensory neurons and are involved in neurogeneration.

____

44. Periodic gap in insulating sheath on axon that facilitate rapid nerve conduction are called ______________.

***45.** Match the following columns.

Column I		Column II
A. Spinal nerves	1.	Myelinated nerve fibre
B. Autonomic neural system	2.	Non-myelinated nerve fibre
C. Cranial nerves		
D. Somatic neural system		

A. ______________ B. ______________ C. ______________ D. ______________

46. Consider the following figure and identify *A-G*.

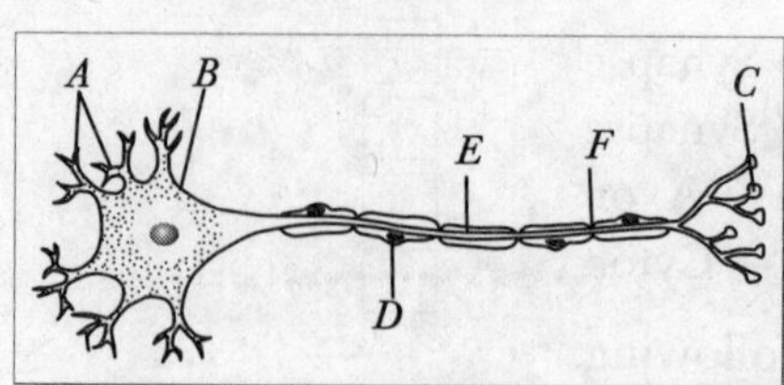

A. ____________
B. ____________
C. ____________
D. ____________
E. ____________
F. ____________

TOPIC 3

Generation, Conduction and Transmission of Nerve Impulse

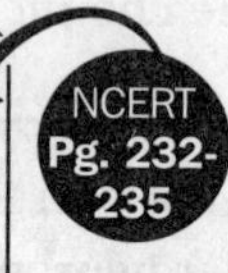

47. "Neurons are excitable cells." Give reason.

____

48. The ion channels present on the neuronal membrane are ____________ (permeable/semipermeable/selectively permeable).

***49.** In the resting phase, axonal membrane is comparatively more permeable to ____________ and impermeable to ____________.

50. During resting phase, the membrane is impermeable to negatively charged proteins. Consequently inside the axoplasm, there is high concentration of ____________ and low concentration of ____________

51. Which of the following represents correct combination?

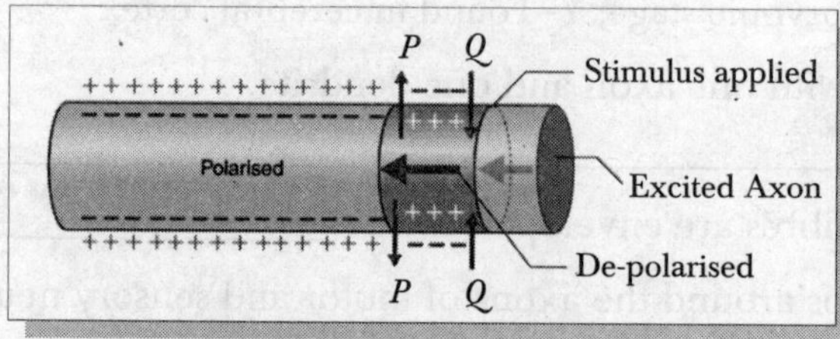

(a) P – Na^+, Q – negatively charged proteins
(b) P – Na^+, Q – K^+
(c) P – K^+, Q – Na^+
(d) P – positively charged proteins, Q – Na^+

***52.** Maintenance of the ionic gradients across the resting membrane is done by

____.

53. For the maintenance of ionic gradients across the resting membrane, the sodium-potassium pump transports ____________ outwards for ____________ into the cell.

54. Which of the following statements is not correct?

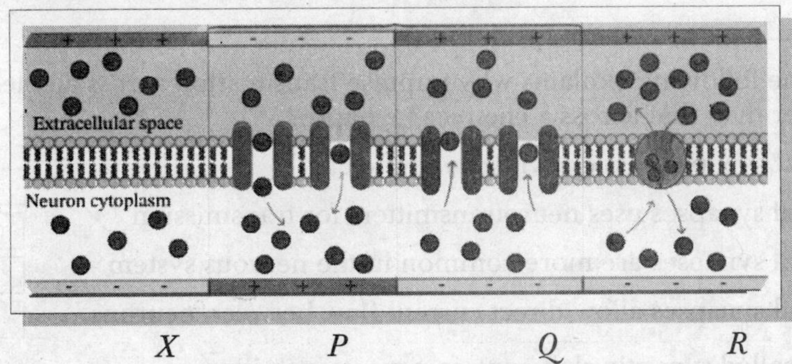

(a) *P* represent reversal of polarity thus initiating action potential
(b) *X* shows the resting polarised state of neuronal membrane
(c) Rapid efflux of potassium ions at *Q* conducts the impulses forward
(d) Resting membrane potential across the neuron is restored at *R*

***55.** The electrical potential difference across the polarised plasma membrane when concentration of K^+ is high inside the axon and low outside, it is known as action potential. (*Rewrite the statement after correcting the underlined words.*)

____

56. When a stimulus is applied at a site on the polarised membrane, the membrane at that site becomes freely permeable to _______________.

***57.** During the propagation of a nerve impulse, the action potential results in the movement of K^+ ions from extacellular fluid to intracellular fluid.

True ☐ False ☐

58. The electrical potential difference across the plasma membrane is called ....

***59.** During the transmission of nerve impulse through a nerve fibre, the potential on the inner side of the plasma membrane has which type of electric charge?

____

60. A wave of action potential is termed as _______________.

***61.** What is the function of *'Q'* represented in the image?

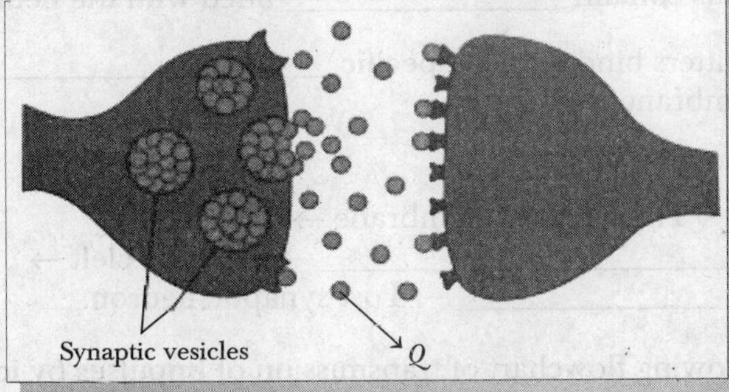

(a) It conducts impulses in the post-synaptic neuron
(b) It generates action potential in the pre-synaptic neuron
(c) It conducts impulses in the pre-synaptic neuron
(d) It restores membrane potential in post-synaptic neuron

***62.** A nerve impulse is transmitted from one neuron to another through the junctions called ____________________.

63. Which of the following explains why impulse transmission across an electrical synapse is always faster than that across a chemical synapse?

(a) Electrical synapses have a wider synaptic cleft ☐

(b) Electrical synapses uses neurotransmitters for transmission ☐

(c) Chemical synapses are more common in the nervous system ☐

(d) Electrical synapses allow direct current flow between neurons. ☐

64. Small sacs called synaptic cleft contain neurotransmitters.
(*Rewrite the statement after correcting the underlined words.*)

____

***65.** Name the junction between pre-synaptic and post-synaptic neurons.

____

66. What is the composition of an electrical synapse?

(a) Pre-synaptic neuron, synaptic cleft, post-synaptic neuron ☐

(b) Pre-synaptic neuron, neurotransmitter, post-synaptic neuron ☐

(c) Pre-synaptic neuron, neurotransmitter, synaptic cleft, post-synaptic neuron ☐

(d) Pre-synaptic neuron and post-synaptic neuron ☐

67. Write the technical term for the gap between a pre and post-synaptic neurons.

____

68. The occurrence of synaptic cleft is usually found in electrical synapses.

True ☐ False ☐

69. "Electrical synapses are rare in our system" Give reason.

____

70. Write a general term for the chemicals that are involved in the transmission of impulses at the synapses. ____________________

71. The axon-terminals contain ________________ filled with the neurotransmitters.

72. The neurotransmitters bind to their specific ____________________ present on the post-synaptic membrane.

***73.** Complete the following sequence.

Synaptic vesicles → Pre-synaptic membrane →
________________________ → Synaptic cleft →
________________________ → Post-synaptic neuron.

74. Complete the following flowchart of transmission of impulses by identifying *A*, *B*, and *C*.

Ⓐ of pre-synaptic membrane → Rupturing of synaptic vesicle → Propagation of post-synaptic Ⓑ → Ⓒ of transmitter.

A. ____________________ B. ____________________ C. ____________________

75. Consider the following figure. Identify *A, B, C, D, E* and *F.*

B
C
A
F
E
D

A. ______
B. ______
C. ______
D. ______
E. ______
F. ______

***76.** Write any two examples of neurotransmitter. ______

TOPIC 4

Central Nervous System

NCERT Pg. 235-236

77. Spinal cord acts as 'command and control system' of the body.

True ☐ False ☐

78. The brain is covered by a layers of protective coverings called ______.

79. The site for processing of vision is ______.

80. Find the odd one out from the following .

Duramater, Arachnoid, Piamater, Sphenoid

______

81. Duramater maintains contact with the brain tissue.

True ☐ False ☐

82. Piamater is the toughest among all the meninges.
(*Rewrite the statement after correcting the underlined word.*)

______

***83.** Find the odd one out from the following parts of brain.

Cerebrum, Cerebellum, Thalamus, Hypothalamus

______

84. Consider the following statements.

I. Axon is a long fibre which consist of branched proximal end.
II. Unmyelinated nerve fibre is commonly found in autonomous and somatic neural system.
III. Rise in the stimulus induce permeability to Na^+.
IV. Cerebrum is the part of hindbrain.

Choose the option with incorrect set of statements

(a) I and III ☐ (b) III and IV ☐
(c) II and IV ☐ (d) I and IV ☐

85. Name the nerve fibres that connects cerebral hemispheres.

____

***86.** The layer of cells which cover cerebral hemisphere is called <u>corpus cortex.</u>
(Rewrite the statement after correcting the underlined word.)

____

87. Identify the structure labelled as '*X*' in the given image.

(a) Corpus luteum ☐ (b) Corpora quadrigemina ☐
(c) Cerebral aqueduct ☐ (d) Corpus callosum ☐

88. Cerebral cortex is referred to as ______________ which consists of motor, sensory and associated areas.

89. Association areas are responsible for intersensory associations, memory and communications.

True ☐ False ☐

90. Fibres of the tracts are covered by ______________ which constitute the inner part of cerebral hemisphere.

91. Choose the correct option from the following.

(a) Grey matter : white matter : : cerebral cortex : myelin sheath ☐
(b) Grey matter : white matter : : myelin sheath : cerebral cortex ☐
(c) Grey matter : white matter : : dura mater : pia mater ☐
(d) Grey matter : white matter : : cerebrum : cerebellum ☐

92. Write the part of the forebrain that is the coordinating centre for sensory and motor signaling. ______________________________

***93.** The inner parts of cerebral hemispheres and a group of associated deep structures form a complex structure called the ______________ system.

***94.** Find the odd one out from the following words. .

Pons, Amygdala, Hippocampus

____

***95.** Hypothalamus contains several groups of ______________ which secrete hormones called ______________ hormones.

***96.** Midbrain is located between thalamus/hypothalamus of the forebrain and ______________ of the hindbrain.

97. Name the canal that passes through the midbrain. ______________

98. Write the technical name for the lobes on the dorsal portion of midbrain.

____

99. The __________, __________ and __________ form the brain stem.

100. Which part of the brain is most likely damaged, in a person who is showing abnormal growth coupled with altered emotions and fluctuations in body temperature?

(a) Amygdala ☐ (b) Hippocampus ☐ (c) Hypothalamus ☐ (b) Thalamus ☐

101. Find the odd one out from the following words.

Pons, Thalamus, Medulla, Cerebellum

____

***102.** Match the following columns.

Column I (Parts of brain)		Column II (Features)
A. Hypothalamus	1.	Neurosecretory cells
B. Midbrain	2.	Centre to control cardio-vascular reflexes
C. Pons	3.	Corpora- quadrigemina
D. Medulla	4.	Fibres interconnecting different region of brain

A. __________ B. __________ C. __________ D. __________

***103.** Consider the following statements.

I. Functions like intersensory associations, memory and communication are controlled by association areas.

II. Concentration of neural cell bodies give colour to the cerebral cortex.

III. Pons, hippocampus and amygdala are the parts of forebrain.

IV. Ventral portion of the midbrain consists of round swellings.

V. Sexual behaviour is controlled by hypothalamus.

Choose the option with correct set of statements

(a) I, III and V ☐ (b) I, II and V ☐ (c) II and IV ☐ (d) I, IV and V ☐

104. Name the part of the hindbrain that is connected to the spinal cord.

____

105. __________ has very convoluted surface to provide additional space for the neurons.

***106.** Consider the following figure, identify *A, B, C, D* and *E*.

A. __________

B. __________

C. __________

D. __________

E. __________

107. Which of the following is not controlled by the medulla oblongata?

(a) Heart rate ☐ (b) Vision ☐
(c) Cough reflex ☐ (d) Secretion of HCl ☐

108. 'Cerebellum has very convoluted surface'. State reason.

____

109. Different regions of brain are interconnected by ______________.

***110.** Match the following columns.

Column I (Parts of brain)		Column II (Functions)	
A.	Cerebrum	1.	Controls the pituitary
B.	Cerebellum	2.	Controls vision and hearing
C.	Hypothalamus	3.	Maintains body posture
D.	Midbrain	4.	Site of intelligence

A.________ B.________ C.________ D.________

111. A person who experienced a sudden blow on the neck at the basal part of the brain, started hyperventilating indicative of serious damage to the

(a) Cerebrum ☐ (b) Hypothalamus ☐
(c) Medulla ☐ (d) Amygdala ☐

Assertion-Reason Questions

The following questions consist of two statements- Assertion (A) and Reason (R). Answer these questions by selecting the appropriate option given below.

(a) Both A and R are true and R is the correct explanation of A
(b) Both A and R are true, but R is not the correct explanation of A
(c) A is true, but R is false
(d) A is false, but R is true

1. **Assertion** (A) Organs like lungs, heart, intestine remain connected with the CNS through the PNS.

Reason (R) The visceral branch of the PNS relays information between the CNS and the viscera.

(a) ☐ (b) ☐ (c) ☐ (d) ☐

2. **Assertion** (A) The dendrites conduct nerve impulses outward from the cell body.

Reason (R) Conduction of impulses relies on the rapid depolarisation of neuronal membrane.

(a) ☐ (b) ☐ (c) ☐ (d) ☐

3. **Assertion** (A) Nerves arising from the brain and spinal cord are always myelinated.

Reason (R) Myelin sheath insulates a neuron for faster conduction of nerve impulses.

(a) ☐ (b) ☐ (c) ☐ (d) ☐

4. **Assertion** (A) The resting membrane potential across a neuron is maintained by the sodium-potassium pump.

Reason (R) The active transport of two sodium ions inside and three potassium ions outside causes polarisation of the axon.

(a) ☐ (b) ☐ (c) ☐ (d) ☐

5. **Assertion** (A) Stimulus induced Na^+ permeability is an irreversible phenomenon.

Reason (R) Rise in K^+ permeability, causes efflux of K^+ thus returning the resting potential.

(a) ☐ (b) ☐ (c) ☐ (d) ☐

***6.** **Assertion** (A) A chemical synapse contains neurotransmitters that are always excitatory in function.

Reason (R) A chemical synapse includes a cleft between the pre and post synaptic membranes.

(a) ☐ (b) ☐ (c) ☐ (d) ☐

***7.** **Assertion** (A) Receptors on the post synaptic membranes play a critical role in transmission of impulses.

Reason (R) Neurotransmitters bind to the receptors which facilitates the opening of ion channels for generating a new potential.

(a) ☐ (b) ☐ (c) ☐ (d) ☐

***8.** **Assertion** (A) Emotional behaviour of a person under different circumstances is under neural control.

Reason (R) The thalamus located at the base of the fore brain, drives the emotional behaviour of a person.

(a) ☐ (b) ☐ (c) ☐ (d) ☐

***9.** **Assertion** (A) Damage to the medulla of the hindbrain can cause instant death of a person.

Reason (R) The medulla has a respiration control centre which regulates breathing of a person.

(a) ☐ (b) ☐ (c) ☐ (d) ☐

10. **Assertion** (A) Injury to the cerebellum can alter the way a person sits and walks.

Reason (R) Cerebellum of the hindbrain controls the balance and coordination of the body.

(a) ☐ (b) ☐ (c) ☐ (d) ☐

Case Based Questions

1. The graph represents the variation of a neuronal membrane potential with time. Study the graph and answer the questions given below.

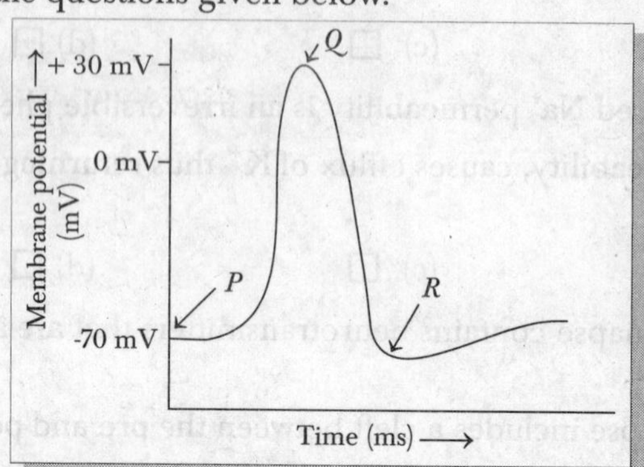

(i) Which of the following maintains *P*?

(a) Impermeability of resting membrane towards potassium ions ☐

(b) Pumping of two sodium ions outwards and three potassium ion inwards ☐

(c) Low K^+ concentration and high Na^+ concentration in the axoplasm ☐

(d) Pumping of three sodium ions outward and two potassium ion inwards ☐

(ii) What causes the rise in membrane potential from *P* to *Q*?

(a) Influx of sodium ions ☐ (b) Efflux of sodium ions ☐

(c) Influx of potassium ions ☐ (d) Efflux of potassium ions ☐

(iii) How does *Q* reduce to the level of *R*?

(a) Due to diffusion of K^+ inside the membrane ☐

(b) Due to diffusion of Na^+ outside the membrane ☐

(c) Due to diffusion of K^+ outside the membrane ☐

(d) Due to diffusion of Na^+ inside the membrane ☐

2. A person met with a devastating car accident, which rushed him to the emergency of a hospital. He had multiple fractures in his hands, but the doctors were more worried about the damage to his brain. After operation, the doctor tested him by pricking a needle to his leg. There was no sensation. Slowly, more serious symptoms started appearing, like the inability to swallow his food, problems with digestion, and difficulty in breathing. When he tried to make his movement, there was lack of coordination and he could not walk straight. With reference to the given passage, answer the following questions:

(i) Which possible part of the brain was most severely affected?

(a) Medulla ☐ (b) Cerebrum ☐ (c) Thalamus ☐ (d) Hypothalamus ☐

(ii) The inability to walk was suggestive of the fact that there was also damage to the

(a) Cerebrum ☐ (b) Pons ☐ (c) Cerebellum ☐ (d) Hypothalamus ☐

(iii) Why was he unable to feel the pricking of the needle?

(a) Neurons were unable to generate action potential in response to the stimulus ☐

(b) Transmission of nerve impulses between brain and spinal cord was affected ☐

(c) The neurotransmitters were unable to generate a new action potential ☐

(d) There was loss of insulation of the axon due to damage to the myelin sheath ☐

COMPETITION EDGE UP

1. Given below are two statements.

Statement I The cerebral hemispheres are connected by nerve tract known as corpus callosum.

Statement II The brain stem consists of the medulla oblongata, pons and cerebrum.

In the light of the above statements choose the mot appropriate answer from the options given below.

[NCERT Pg. 236, NEET 2024]

(a) Both statement I and statement II are true ☐

(b) Both statement I and statement II are false ☐

(c) Statement I is true, but statement II is false ☐

(d) Statement I is false, but statement II is true ☐

2. The parts of human brain that helps in regulation of sexual behaviour, expression of excitement, pleasure, rage, fear, etc. are

[NCERT Pg. 236, NEET 2023]

(a) Corpora quadrigemina and hippocampus ☐

(b) Brain stem and epithalamus ☐

(c) Corpus callosum and thalamus ☐

(d) Limbic system and hypothalamus ☐

3. Select the incorrect statement regarding synapses. **[NCERT Pg. 234, NEET 2022]**

(a) Electrical current can flow directly from one neuron into the other across the electrical synapse ☐

(b) Chemical synapses use neurotransmitters ☐

(c) Impulse transmission across a chemical synapse is always faster than that across an electrical synapse ☐

(d) The membranes of pre-synaptic and post-synaptic neurons are in close proximity in an electrical synapse ☐

4. Which of the following is associated with decrease in cardiac output?

[NCERT Pg. 231, NEET (Oct.) 2020]

(a) Sympathetic nerves ☐

(b) Parasympathetic neural signals ☐

(c) Pneumotaxic centre ☐

(d) Adrenal medullary hormones ☐

5. Which part of the brain is responsible for thermoregulation?

[NCERT Pg. 236, NEET (National) 2019]

(a) Hypothalamus ☐

(b) Corpus callosum ☐

(c) Medulla oblongata ☐

(d) Cerebrum ☐

6. Which of the following structures or regions is incorrectly paired with its functions?

[NCERT Pg. 236, Cancelled [AIPMT 2018]

(a)	Medulla oblongata	Controls respiration and cardiovascular reflexes
(b)	Limbic system	Consists of fibre tracts that interconnect different regions of brain controls movement
(c)	Hypothalamus	Production of releasing hormones and regulation of temperature, hunger and thirst
(d)	Corpus callosum	Band of fibers connecting left and right cerebral hemispheres

(a) ☐ (b) ☐

(c) ☐ (d) ☐

Chapter 19

Chemical Coordination and Integration

Scan and take Chapter Test

TOPIC 1

Endocrine Glands, Hormones and Human Endocrine System

1. Name the substance, that integrates and coordinates all the metabolic activities within the organism. ____________

2. Consider the following statements.

Statement I Hormones are protein sources that act as intracellular messengers and control different bodily processes.

Statement II Hormones can be produced only by specialised exocrine glands.

Choose the correct option from the following.

(a) Statement I is true, but statement II is false

(b) Both statements I and II are false

3. The ____________ and the ____________ system jointly coordinate and regulate the physiological functions in the body.

4. Endocrine glands are also known as ____________ glands.

5. Enzyme is a chemical produced by endocrine glands and released into the blood.

(*Rewrite the statement after correcting the underlined word.*)

____

6. Name the chemical which is non-nutrient, acts as intercellular messenger and is produced in trace amount.

____

7. The ____________ and ____________ producing diffused tissues/cells located in different parts of our body constitute the endocrine system.

*Concepts of all questions bearing * are important for NEET & CUET*

8. (i) Consider the following sequence of endocrine gland and rearrange the correct sequence from top to bottom.

Thymus → Pituitary → Adrenal → Ovary → Pancreas

(ii) Consider the given diagram and answer the following questions.

(a) Identify glands *A* to *F*.

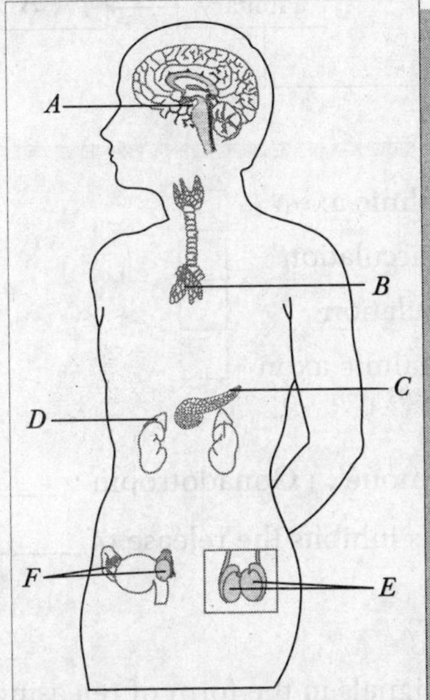

A. ______

B. ______

C. ______

D. ______

E. ______

F. ______

(b) Which of the above given glands functions as both exocrine and endocrine?

______

(c) Which of the above given glands controls female secondary sexual character?

______

9. Name any four organs other than endocrine system that produce hormones.

______

TOPIC 2

The Hypothalamus

NCERT Pg. 240

10. Hypothalamus contains several groups of neurosecretory cells called ______ (chroma/nuclei) which produce hormones.

11. The hormones released by hypothalamus regulate the synthesis and secretion of pineal gland.

True ☐ False ☐

***12.** (i) Name the two types of hormones released by hypothalamus.

______

(ii) ______ hormones are hypothalamic hormones that stimulate the secretion of pituitary hormone.

(iii) ________________ are hypothalamic hormones that inhibit the secretion of pituitary hormone.

(iv) The hypothalamic releasing and inhibitory hormones reach the pituitary gland through portal circulation and regulate the functions of ________________ pituitary.

***13.** In the given representation, choose the correct combination that represents *A* (hormone secreted by pituitary) and *B* (pathway of GnRH to pituitary)

Hypothalams → B (GnRH) → Pituitary → A

(a) A – Somatostatin , B – Hypothalmic axon ☐

(b) A – Gonadotrophin, B – Portal circulation ☐

(c) A– Somatostatin, B – Portal circulation ☐

(d) A – Gonadotrophin, B – Hypothalmic axon ☐

***14.** Complete the following analogy.

Releasing hormone : Inhibiting hormone : : Gonadotropin : ____________

***15.** Somatostatin from the hypothalamus inhibits the release of _______ hormone from the pituitary.

***16.** Consider the following statements.

Statement I Hypothalamus sends signals in the form of releasing hormones in order to regulate anterior pituitary.

Statement II The anterior pituitary or the front lobe of pituitary is under the direct regulation of hypothalamus.

Choose the correct option from the following.

(a) Statement I is true, but statement II is false ☐

(b) Statement I is false, but statement II is true ☐

TOPIC 3

The Pituitary Gland

NCERT Pg 241-242

17. Pituitary gland is lodged in the cavity of the sphenoid bone, called neural lobe. (*Rewrite the statement after correcting the underlined words.*)

____

***18.** Pituitary gland is anatomically divided into ________________ and ________________.

***19.** Write the names of the two portions of adenohypophysis.

____

20. A tumor in which part of the following might result in an abnormal increase in body size and facial features?

(a) Pars distalis ☐
(b) Pars nervosa ☐
(c) Pars intermedia ☐
(d) Neurohypophysis ☐

***21.** Identify the odd one out from the following hormones.

Prolactin, Thyroid stimulating hormone, Melanocyte stimulating hormone, Luteinizing hormone

____

22. Consider the following statements.

Statement I Pituitary secretes trophic hormones that regulate secretions of other endocrine glands.

Statement II ACTH from anterior pituitary stimulates adrenal cortex to secrete steroid hormones.

Choose the correct option from the following.

(a) Statement I is true, but statement II is false ☐

(b) Both statements I and II are true ☐

23. How many of the given hormones are released from the portion *A* in the figure of pituitary gland?

Hypothalamus
Hypothalamic neurons
A

(a) Growth hormone ☐
(b) Prolactin hormone ☐
(c) Melanocyte stimulating hormone ☐
(d) Oxytocin ☐

24. Consider the following statements.

Statement I The adenohypophysis secretes the hormone that causes uterine contraction.

Statement II During child birth oxytocin causes uterine contraction for expulsion of the foetus.

Choose the correct option from the following.

(a) Statement I is true, but statement II is false ☐

(b) Statement I is false, but statement II is true ☐

25. A 25 year old lady with a height of 221 cm (~69 cm more than that of normal average female of same age) showed certain statural abnormalities but a normal blood pressure. However, she often complained of pain in knees and joints.

Identify the cause behind the case discussed.

(a) Non-functional pars intermedia ☐

(b) Improper functioning of pars distalis ☐

(c) Genetic disorders. ☐

(d) Hypersecretion of LH ☐

***26.** Give full form of the following abbreviation of hormones.

(i) GnRH ____________________

(ii) GH ____________________

(iii) PRL ____________________

(iv) TSH ____________________

(v) ACTH ____________________

(vi) LH ____________________

(vii) FSH ____________________

(viii) MSH ____________________

27. Posterior pituitary is also known as ____________________.

***28.** Which portion of pituitary gland releases oxytocin and vasopressin hormones.

29. The synthesis site of vasopressin and oxytocin hormones is ____________________ (neurohypophysis/hypothalamus).

30. A person with hyposecretion of vasopressin would show :

(a) High electrolyte concentration in blood ☐

(b) High electrolyte concentration in urine ☐

(c) A highly concentrated urine with low output ☐

(d) High glucose concentration in urine ☐

***31.** Complete the following flowchart.

Pituitary Gland

Adenohypophysis → Pars distalis, [A]

Neurohypophysis → [B], Infundibulum

A. ____________________

B. ____________________

***32.** (i) The WWE fighter 'The Great Khali' suffered from gigantism during his adult hood. This condition is known as____________

____________________.

(ii) Deficiency of adenohypophysis secretion leads to a condition called

(iii) ____________________ (Hyperpituitarism/Hypopituitarism) causes disorders in the acidophil cells developing gigantism and acromegaly.

33. Name the hormones named as gonadotropins.

____

34. Luteinizing hormone stimulates the synthesis and secretion of ____________________ (androgens/glucocorticoids) from testis.

35. In males spermatogenesis is regulated by ____________________ and ____________________.

36. Complete the following actions of gonadotropins in females.

(i) LH induces ovulation of ________________ follicles.

(ii) FSH induces development of the ________________ follicles.

37. Melanin containing cells are known as ________________.

38. The darkening of the skin in humans is due to ________________ (TSH/MSH).

39. Oxytocin acts on the smooth muscles of our body and stimulates their contraction.

True ☐ False ☐

40. Which hormone is given to induce labor pain during pregnancy? ________________

41. Vasopressin stimulates milk ejection from the mammary gland.

(*Rewrite the statement after correcting the underlined word.*)

____

42. Vasopressin stimulates resorption of water and electrolytes by the ________________ of kidney and reduces loss of water through ________________.

43. Which hormone is also known as anti-diuretic hormone? ________________

44. In which of the following condition blood becomes diluted?

(i) ADH is released.

(ii) ADH is not released.

____

45. Give one word for the following conditions.

(i) A condition in which ADH is deficient. ________________

(ii) A condition in which ADH is hyperactive. ________________

46. Consider the following statements.

Statement I Pars intermedia secretes only one hormone that controls skin pigmentation.

Statement II ACTH stimulates the secretion of mineralocorticoids from adrenal cortex.

Choose the correct option from the following.

(a) Statement I is true, but statement II is false ☐

(b) Statement I is false, but statement II is true ☐

47. Identify the incorrect statement with respect to pituitary gland.

(a) In humans, the pars intermedia is almost merged with pars distalis. ☐

(b) FSH and androgens regulate spermatogenesis in males. ☐

(c) Acromegaly though a serious condition, can be detected at early stages. ☐

(d) Oxytocin and vasopressin are synthesised by hypothalamus and stored by posterior pituitary. ☐

TOPIC 4

Pineal and Thyroid Glands

NCERT Pg. 242-243

48. Name the gland which is present on the dorsal side of forebrain. ________

49. Melatonin regulates ________ rhythm of body, maintain ________ cycle, regulates body ________ and influence menstrual cycle.

50. Name the hormone released by pineal gland. ________

51. A person who travelled from India to USA often feels sleepy, tired and difficult to concentrate because of the change in the time zone which is producing altered secretion of

(a) Pituitary hormone melanin
(b) Pineal hormone melatonin
(c) Pineal hormone melanin
(d) Pituitary hormone melatonin

52. Consider the following statements.

Statement I Melatonin is referred to as sleep hormone.

Statement II It controls sleep - wake cycle, pigmentation and menstrual cycle.

Choose the correct option from the following.

(a) Statement I is true, but statement II is false
(b) Both statements I and II are true

53. The thyroid gland is composed of two lobes which are located on either side of the larynx. (*Rewrite the statement after correcting the underlined word.*)

____

54. The thyroid gland is composed of ________ and ________.

55. The thyroid gland secretes thyroxine or ________, triiodothyronine and ________.

56. Consider the following statements.

Statement I Cancer in the thyroid gland can reduce the secretion of the thyroid hormone.

Statement II Hypersecretion of thyroid hormones can affect the metabolism of the body.

Choose the correct option from the following.

(a) Statement I is true, but statement II is false
(b) Statement I is false, but statement II is true

57. Write the full form of the following abbreviation.

(i) T_3 ________
(ii) T_4 ________
(iii) TCT ________

***58.** Identify the labelled parts *A*, *B* and *C* in the diagram given below.

C
A
B

A. ________
B. ________
C. ________

***59.** Which of the following statements about thyroid gland is correct?

(a) Thyroid gland consists of four lobes located on either side of trachea ☐

(b) Thyroxine also called triiodothyronine requires iodine for its synthesis ☐

(c) Thyroid hormone regulates the electrolyte-water balance of the body ☐

(d) Cretinism in children occurs due to hyperthyroidism during pregnancy ☐

***60.** Dietary iodine is converted into iodide and absorbed in the blood from where it is actively transported into the thyroid gland.

True ☐ False ☐

***61.** Consider the following reaction and answer the given question.

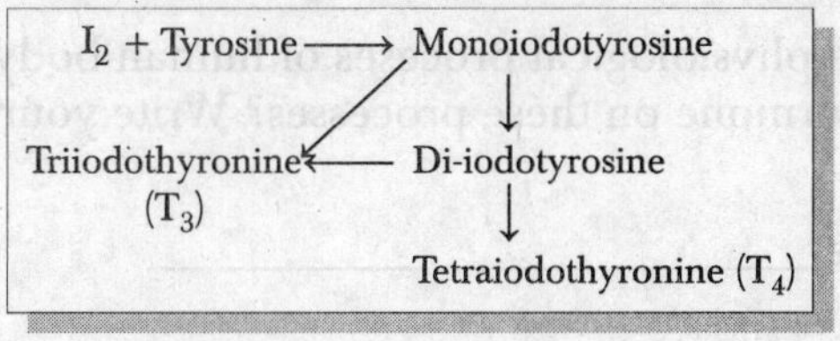

I_2 + Tyrosine ⟶ Monoiodotyrosine ↓ Di-iodotyrosine ↓ Tetraiodothyronine (T_4)

Triiodothyronine (T_3) ⟵ Di-iodotyrosine (+ Monoiodotyrosine)

(i) This reaction takes place in which gland? ____________

62. ____________ disorder is caused by insufficient thyroxine secretion or reduced iodine in our diet.

63. The enlargement of thyroid gland is commonly known as ________ (cretin/goitre).

***64.** Name the condition in which a pregnant lady gives birth to a baby with stunted growth, mental retardation, low IQ and abnormal skin.

____

***65.** Which of the following could be the possible cause of the given condition represented in the image?

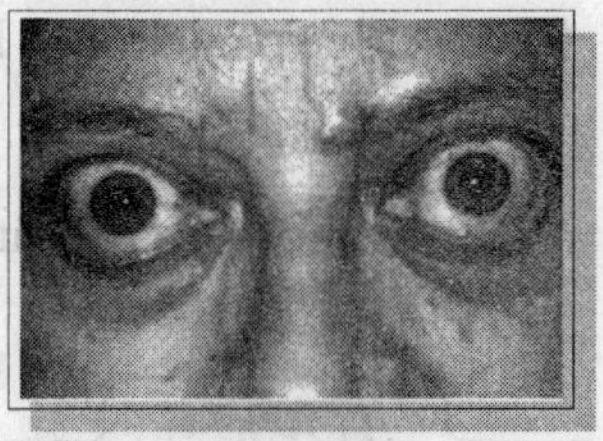

(a) Hypersecretion of thyroid hormone ☐

(b) Hyposecretion of thyroid hormone ☐

(c) Hypersecretion of posterior pituitary ☐

(d) Hyposecretion of posterior pituitary ☐

66. ____________ is a condition in which, the rate of synthesis and secretion of the thyroid hormones is increased to abnormal high levels.

67. Due to hyperthyroidism, enlargement of thyroid gland takes place, this disease is known as ____________ (exophthalamic goitre/Hashimoto's disease).

***68.** Consider the following flowchart of regulation of thyroid hormone, identify *A* ?

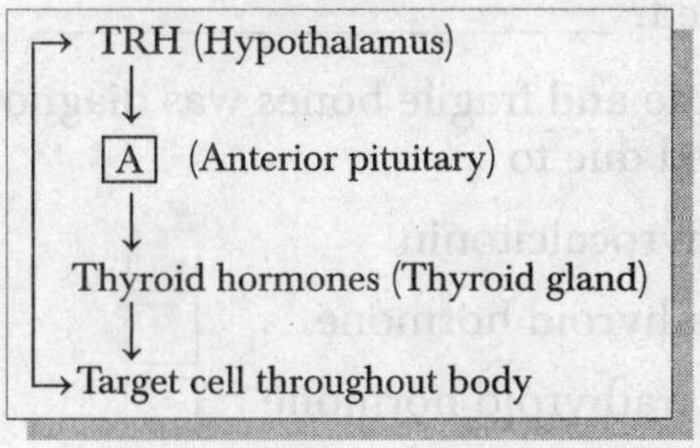

TRH (Hypothalamus)
↓
A (Anterior pituitary)
↓
Thyroid hormones (Thyroid gland)
↓
Target cell throughout body

A. ____________

***69** Which condition occurs, when the part *A* from the above flowchart is inhibited?

____

***70.** Consider the following statements.

Statement I Only T_4 levels are sufficient to determine the functioning of the thyroid gland.

Statement II Thyroid hormones also play a role in the RBC formation and maintaining the salt-water balance.

Choose the correct option from the following.

(a) Statement I is true, but statement II is false

(b) Statement I is false, but statement II is true

***71.** Thyroxine is essential for normal growth, skeletal maturation and mental development.

True False

***72.** Given below are some physiological proceses of human body. What is the effect of increased thyroxine hormone on these processes? Write your answer by only mentioning increase or decrease.

(i) Basal metabolic rate ____________

(ii) Protein synthesis ____________

(iii) Glucose absorption ____________

***73.** Name a protein hormone secreted from thyroid gland. ____________

***74.** Calcitonin is secreted by the C-cells in the ____________ (thyroid/pineal) gland.

***75.** Calcitonin reduces the reabsorption of calcium from bones and inhibits absorption of calcium by the renal tubules.

(*Rewrite the statement after correcting the underlined word.*)

____

***76.** Thyrocalcitonin lowers the blood calcium levels in blood plasma.

True False

77. Exopthalmic goitre is a form of hyperthyroidism and is also known as ____________.

TOPIC 5

Parathyroid Gland

NCERT Pg. 243

***78.** By considering the given figure answer the following questions.

(i) Identify gland *A*. ____________

(ii) Which hormone is secreted from gland *A* ?

(iii) Where is gland *A* situated? ____________

A

***79.** An aged woman with brittle and fragile bones was diagnosed with age related osteoporosis caused due to

(a) Demineralisation by thyrocalcitonin

(b) Mineralisation by parathyroid hormone

(c) Demineralisation by parathyroid hormone

(d) Mineralisation by thyrocalcitonin

*** 80.** Complete the following analogy.

Parathyroid hormone : Hypercalcemic : : ____________ : Hypocalcemic

***81.** The secretion of parathyroid hormone is regulated by the circulating levels of <u>chlorine</u> ions. (*Rewrite the statement after correcting the underlined word.*)

____

***82.** Parathyroid hormone increases the Ca^{2+} levels in the ____________.

***83.** PTH acts on bones and stimulates the process of bone deposition.

True ☐ False ☐

***84.** Parathyroid hormone stimulates ____________ of Ca^{+2} by the renal tubules and ____________ Ca^{2+} absorption from the digested food.

***85.** Consider the following statements.

Statement I The parathyroid hormone secreted by the parathyroid gland is chemically a peptide.

Statement II PTH stimulates reabsorption of Ca^{2+} ions from the digested food.

Choose the correct option from the following.

(a) Statement I is true, but statement II is false ☐

(b) Statement I is false, but statement II is true ☐

***86.** Consider the following flowchart of regulation of parathyroid hormone and identify *A*.

Plasma Ca^{+2} ↓ ⟶ Parathyroid gland ⟶ PTH↑ ⟶ Ⓐ

____

87. The parathyroid gland secretes excessive amounts of parathormone, this condition is known as ____________.

***88.** Differentiate between thyrocalcitonin and parathyroid hormone on the basis of action on calcium in human body.

____

TOPIC 6

Thymus and Adrenal Glands

NCERT Pg. 243-245

***89.** The <u>parathyroid</u> gland is a lobular structure located between lungs behind sternum on the ventral side of aorta. (*Rewrite the statement after correcting the underlined word.*)

____

90. Thymosin is a ____________ hormone secreted by ____________.

91. Consider the following statements.

Statement I People aged between 70-80 years usually show less immunity due to degenerating thymus.

Statement II Thymosins aid in differentiation of T-lymphocytes which provide cell mediated immunity.

Choose the correct option from the following.

(a) Statement I is true, but statement II is false ☐

(b) Both statements I and II are true ☐

92. Thymus is an endocrine gland as well as lymphatic gland.

True ☐ False ☐

93. Thymus gland plays an important role in both ageing and immunity.

True ☐ False ☐

94. Complete the following analogy.

T-lymphocytes : Cell-mediated immunity : : B-lymphocytes :

____

95. Choose the correct combination of P and Q:

Considering the below given representation.

Thymus → P → Differentiaton of T-cells → X

Thymus → P → Q → Production of antibodies

(a) P - Thymosin Q - Humoral ☐

(b) P - Thymosin Q - Cell mediated ☐

(c) P - Thyroxine Q - Humoral ☐

(d) P - Thyroxine Q - Cell mediated ☐

96. The older people have low immunity. (*Give reason*)

____

97. How many pairs of adrenal gland are found in human body?

____

98. Adrenal glands are present at the ________ part of each ________.

99. The centrally located tissue is called the adrenal cortex and outside this lies the adrenal medulla.

True ☐ False ☐

100. Consider the following statements.

Statement I The fear response of the body on sudden encounter with a barking dog is due to effect of catecholamines.

Statement II Catecholamines stimulate glycogenolysis to increase the blood glucose level during stress.

Choose the correct option from the following.

(a) Statement I is true, but statement II is false ☐

(b) Both statements I and II are true ☐

101. Complete the following flowchart.

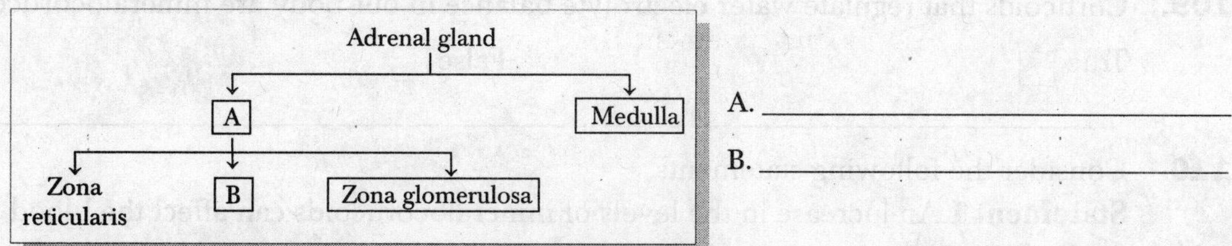

A. ____________________

B. ____________________

***102.** Which hormones are secreted by part *A* in the given diagram of adrenal gland ?

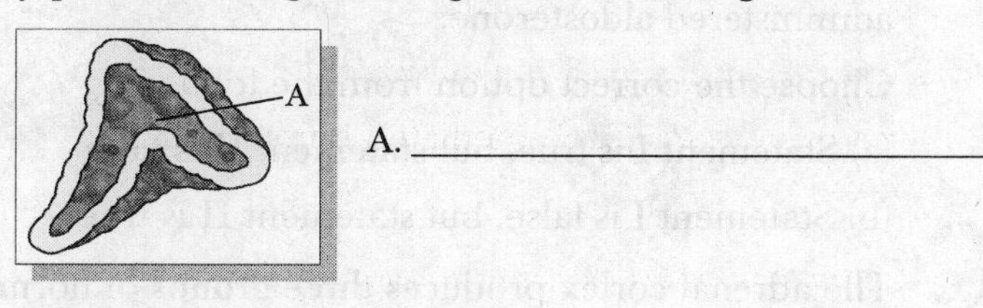

A. ____________________

103. A person with serious allergic infection is administered with

(a) Aldosterone ☐ (b) Cortisol ☐ (c) Paracetamol ☐ (d) Norepinephrine ☐

104. Match Column I with Column II.

Column I	Column II
A. Cortisol	1. Emergency/Stress
B. Aldosterone	2. Secondary sexual features
C. Sex steroids	3. Anti-inflammatory reactions
D. Epinephrine	4. Reabsorption of Na+

	A	B	C	D			A	B	C	D	
(a)	3	4	2	1	☐	(b)	3	4	1	2	☐
(c)	3	1	2	4	☐	(d)	3	1	4	2	☐

105. ______________ and ______________ are commonly called as catecholamines.

106. Medulla hormones are known as emergency hormones or corticoids.
(*Rewrite the statement after correcting the underlined word.*)

____

107. Emergency hormones ____________ alertness, pupilary ____________ and stimulate the breakdown of ____________ resulting in an increase concentration of glucose in blood.

108. Complete the following table with suitable words.

	Human systems	Effect of adrenaline	Effect of nor-adrenaline
(i)	Blood pressure	(A)	Increase
(ii)	Systolic	Increase	(B)
(iii)	Diastolic	(C)	Increase
(iv)	Respiration	(D)	Stimulated
(v)	Kidney	Renal vessel constrictor	(E)
(vi)	CNS	(F)	Increase alertness, arousal and attention

A. ______________ B. ______________ C. ______________

D. ______________ E. ______________ F. ______________

109. Corticoids that regulate water electrolyte balance in our body are mineralocorticoids

True ☐ False ☐

____

110. Consider the following statements.

Statement I An increase in the levels of mineralocorticoids can affect the blood pressure of a person.

Statement II A person with a heightened immune response to a foreign body is often administered aldosterone.

Choose the correct option from the following.

(a) Statement I is true, but statement II is false ☐

(b) Statement I is false, but statement II is true ☐

111. The adrenal cortex produces three groups of hormones from cholesterol.

True ☐ False ☐

112. Which pair of hormones can produce similar effect in the body?

(a) Androgen- Aldosterone ☐ (b) Vasopressin- Aldosterone ☐

(c) Androgen- Cortisol ☐ (d) Vasopressin- Cortisol ☐

113. Give a collective term for the following chemicals.

Glucocorticoids, Mineralocorticoids, Androgens

____

114. Complete the following analogy.

Adrenal medulla : Adrenal cortex : : ____________ : Corticoids

115. Match the following columns.

	Column I (Hormones)		Column II (Functions)
A.	Glucocorticoids	1.	Regulate the balance of water and electrolyte
B.	Androgens	2.	Carbohydrate metabolism
C.	Mineralocorticoids	3.	Development of secondary sex characters

A. ____________ B. ____________ C. ____________

116. Glucocorticoids stimulate ____________, ____________ and ____________

117. Glucocorticoids inhibit cellular uptake and utilisation of ketones.

(*Rewrite the statement after correcting the underlined word.*)

____

118. Give a collective term for the following chemicals.

Cortisol, Cortisone, Hydrocortisone

____

119. Cortisol is involved in maintaining the cardio-vascular system only.

True ☐ False ☐

120. ________________ (Cortisol/Aldosterone) produces anti-inflammatory reactions and suppresses the immune response.

121. Name the corticoid hormone, which acts in the given reaction.

Pyruvate → Glycerol → Glucose

____

122. The secretion of glucocorticoids is stimulated by ________________ from the anterior pituitary.

123. Some steps are incorrect in the following diagrammatic representation of regulation of glucocorticoids secretion. Redraw the flowchart with correct step.

Hypothalamus
↓
Corticotrophin Releasing Factor (CRF)
↓
Anterior lobe of pituitary gland
↓
ACTH
↓
Adrenal cortex
↓
Lower blood glucocorticoid level

____

124. ________________ is the chief mineralocorticoid hormone in our body.

125. Write the effect of aldosterone by mentioning Yes/No on following processes.

(i) Excretion of K^+ and phosphate ions. ________________

(ii) Reabsorption of Na^+. ________________

(iii) Maintenance of electrolyte. ________________

(iv) Reduce the number of lymphocytes. ________________

(v) Maintenance of osmotic pressure. ________________

(vi) Maintenance of blood pressure. ________________

126. What will happen to aldosterone when the sodium level falls in blood?

____

127. Androgenic steroids are secreted by the adrenal ________________ (medulla/cortex) which play a role in the growth of axial hair, pubic hair and facial hair during puberty.

128. Androgens are associated with deposition of protein in muscles, especially in females.

True ☐ False ☐

***129.** Complete the following analogy with respect to adrenal cortex secretion.

Hyposecretion : Hypersecretion : : ________________ : Cushing's syndrome

***130.** How many symptoms are related to Addison's disease.

Acute weakness, Vomiting, Mental clouding, Hyperglycaemia, High BP, Acidosis, Renal failure, Fatigue

____

TOPIC 7

Pancreas

NCERT Pg. 245-246

131. Pancreas is a composite gland which acts as both ________ and ________ gland.

132. The endocrine part of pancreas consists of villi.
(*Rewrite the statement after correcting the underlined word.*)

____

***133.** Normal blood glucose level of body is maintained by a peptide hormone, i.e. ________.

***134.** Glucagon acts on the liver cells and stimulates glycolysis and gluconeogenesis.
(*Rewrite the statement after correcting the underlined word.*)

____

***135.** Insulin acts mainly on ________ and ________.

***136.** Complete the following analogy with respect to blood glucose level.

Insulin : ________ : : Hypoglycemic : Hyperglycemic

***137.** Match the following columns.

Column I	Column II
A. Glucagon	1. Increased blood sugar
B. Insulin	2. Decreased blood sugar
C. Somatostatin	3. Reduces cellular uptake of glucose
	4. Inhibit the secretion of glucagon and insulin
	5. Enhanced cellular uptake of glucose

A. ________ B. ________ C. ________

138. Name the hormone which acts antagonistic to insulin.

____

***139.** Insulin deficiency results in a disorder called diabetes insipidus.
(*Rewrite the statement after correcting the underlined word.*)

____

***140.** ________ is associated with loss of glucose through urine and formation of harmful compounds known as ________

***141.** Consider the following statements.

Statement I The α-cells of the islets stimulates the process of glycogenolysis.

Statement II Pancreas is a heterocrine gland.

Choose the correct option from the following.

(a) Statement I is true, but statement II is false ☐

(b) Both statements I and II are true ☐

142. Diabetic patients are successfully treated with glucagon therapy.

True ☐ False ☐

143. A person with traces of glucose and ketone bodies in the urine, show under secretion of

(a) Hypoglycemic hormone ☐ (b) Hyperglycemic hormone ☐

(c) Hypercalcemic hormone ☐ (d) Hypocalcemic hormone ☐

TOPIC 8

Testis and Ovary

NCERT Pg. 246-247

144. The testes are situated inside the abdominal cavity within a pouch called scrotum.

True ☐ False ☐

145. Name the organ which acts as primary sex organ as well as an endocrine gland in male.

____

146. Testis is composed of ______________ and ______________

147. Androgens mainly testosterone are produced by Leydig cells or interstitial cells.

True ☐ False ☐

148. Given below are few statements. Choose the correct ones

I. Testis performs dual functions as primary sex organ as well as an endocrine gland.

II. Interstitial cells present in the intertubular spaces produce a group of hormones called androgens.

III. Androgens play an inhibitory role in the process of spermatogenesis.

IV. Androgens act on peripheral neural system and influence the male sexual behaviour (libido).

Choose the correct answer from the options given below.

(a) I and II ☐ (b) II and III ☐

(c) III and IV ☐ (d) I and IV ☐

149. Androgens play a major stimulatory role in the process of erythropoietin.
(*Rewrite the statement after correcting the underlined word.*)

____

150. How many actions are stimulated by androgens from the given box?

Act on CNS, Catabolic effect on protein metabolism, Influence libido, Aggressiveness, Growth of facial hairs

____

151. Match Column I with Column II

Column I (Type of cells)	Column II (Hormone secreted)
A. Interstitial cells	1. FSH
B. Corpus luteum	2. Progesterone
C. Ovary	3. Testosterone
D. Pituitary	4. Oestrogen

	A	B	C	D			A	B	C	D
(a)	3	2	4	1		(b)	3	2	1	4
(c)	3	1	4	2		(d)	3	1	2	4

152. Name primary female sex organ which produces one ovum during each menstrual cycle.

153. The ovarian steroids in females are ____________ and ____________.

154. Consider the following statements.

Statement I Progesterone secreted by the corpus luteum maintains the pregnancy of a female.

Statement II In non-pregnant women the progesterone levels fall after the release of the ovum.

Choose the correct option from the following.

(a) Statement I is true, but statement II is false

(b) Both statements I and II are true

155. Consider the following flowchart, identify hormones *A* and *B*.

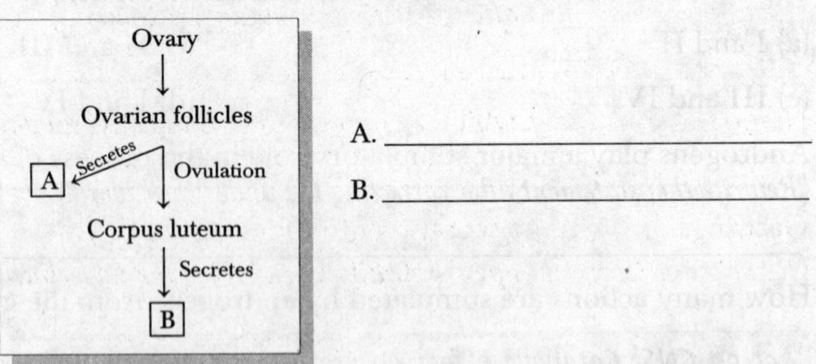

156. Name the hormone which stimulates female secondary sex organs and helps in development of growing ovarian follicles and mammary gland.

157. Complete the following analogy considering 14th day of menstrual cycle.

FSH : LH : : Decrease : ____________.

158. ____________ (Progesterone/Oestrogen) is a luteal hormone which is synthesised by corpus luteum.

159. Progesterone is a ____________ hormone.

160. In the presence of progesterone, the thickening of the endometrium decreases.

True ☐ False ☐

161. ____________ (Progesterone/Relaxin) also acts on the mammary glands and stimulates the formation of alveoli and milk secretion.

162. Oestrogens and progesterone are ____________ (decreased/increased) at the commencement of menstrual cycle.

TOPIC 9

Hormones of Heart, Kidney and Gastrointestinal Tract

NCERT Pg. 247

163. The atrial wall of our heart secretes a peptide hormone called ____________.

164. Complete the following flowchart.

Blood pressure increased
↓
ANF is secreted
↓
A
↓
Reduce blood pressure

A. ____________

***165.** Erythropoiesis is stimulated by a peptide hormone called ____________.

***166.** The Henle's loop cells of kidney produce erythropoietin.
(*Rewrite the statement after correcting the underlined words.*)

____

167. Name the hormones which are secreted from gastro-intestinal tract.

168. Gastrin stimulates the secretion of renin and amylase.
(*Rewrite the statement after correcting by changing the underlined words.*)

____

169. Secretin is a peptide hormone secreted by the small intestine.

True ☐ False ☐

170. Secretin stimulates secretion of ____________ and ____________.

171. GIP acts on both pancreas and gall bladder.

True ☐ False ☐

172. ____________ (CCK/GIP) inhibits gastric secretion and motility.

173. Match the following columns.

	Column I (Hormones)		Column II (Characteristics)
A.	Gastrin	1.	Stimulates secretion of pancreatic enzymes
B.	Secretin	2.	Acts on gastric gland
C.	CCK	3.	Acts on exocrine pancreas

A. __________ B. __________ C. __________

174. Consider the following statements.

Statement I Erythropoiesis is regulated by the endocrine action of the juxtaglomerular cells.

Statement II CCK acts on the pancreas and gall bladder to stimulate secretion of bile juice and pancreatic enzymes.

Choose the correct option from the following.

(a) Statement I is true, but statement II is false ☐

(b) Both statements I and II are true ☐

TOPIC 10

Mechanism of Hormone Action

***175.** Hormones bind to the specific proteins, i.e. __________ to produce their effects on target tissues.

***176.** Where are the hormone receptors present?

____

***177.** Membrane bound receptors are present on the cell membrane of the target cells.

True ☐ False ☐

***178.** __________ receptors are present inside the target cell.

***179.** Hormone binds to its receptor leading to the formation of <u>peptide</u> receptor complex. (*Rewrite the statement after correcting the underlined word.*)

____

***180.** Target tissues change their biochemical nature to form hormone-receptor complex.

True ☐ False ☐

***181.** Give a common biological terms for the following groups on the basis of chemical nature of hormones.

(i) Melatonin, Catecholamines, Adrenaline, Nor-adrenaline __________

(ii) ADH, Oxytocin, ACTH, Calcitonin __________

(iii) Insulin, Glucagon, Parathyroid, Relaxin __________

***182.** Hormones which interact with membrane bound receptors, generate enzymes. (*Rewrite the statement after correcting the underlined word.*)

____

***183.** Give a scientific collective term for the following.

Cyclic AMP, IP_3, Ca^{++}

____

***184.** Name the group of hormones which interact with intracellular receptors.

____

***185.** Consider the given diagram of mechanism of protein hormone action. Identify *A*, *B* and *C*.

A. ______________

B. ______________

C. ______________

***186.** Why do steroid hormones act on intracellular receptors while peptide hormones mediate their function through cell surface receptors?

(a) Steroids cannot bind to cell surface proteins ☐

(b) Steroids are not electrostatically stable on membranes ☐

(c) Steroids are hydrophobic, hence can pass the membrane ☐

(d) Steroids are hydrophilic, hence cannot bind proteins. ☐

***187.** ______________ and ______________ do not bind to the cell surface receptors.

***188.** Steroid and thyroid hormones are water soluble.

True ☐ False ☐

189. Consider the following statements.

Statement I Steroid hormones act by altering the gene expression of the target cells.

Statement II Iodothyronine acts on the target cells by binding to the intracellular receptors.

Choose the correct option from the following.

(a) Statement I is true, but statement II is false ☐

(b) Both statements I and II are true ☐

190. Consider the following figure of mechanism of steroid hormone action. Identify *A* and *B*.

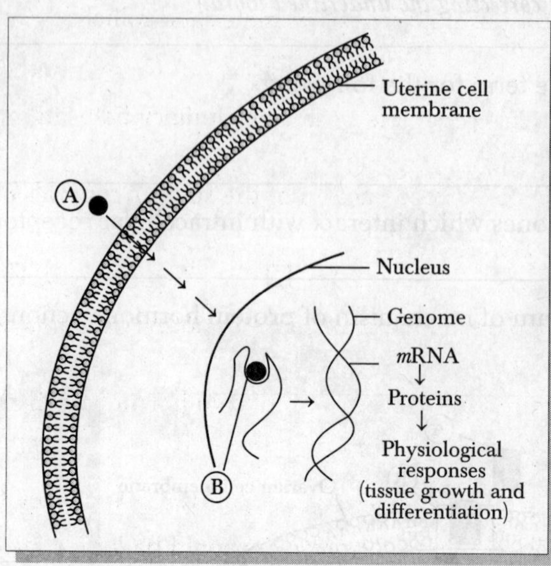

____

***191.** Steroid hormones have their receptor localised inside the <u>mitochondria</u>.
(*Rewrite the statement after correcting the underlined word.*)

____

***192.** ____________, ____________ and ____________ hormones are water soluble, which cannot pass through the lipid membrane.

Assertion-Reason Questions

The following questions consist of two statements- Assertion (A) and Reason (R). Answer these questions by selecting the appropriate option given below.
(a) Both A and R are true and R is the correct explanation of A
(b) Both A and R are true, but R is not the correct explanation of A
(c) A is true, but R is false
(d) A is false, but R is true

1. **Assertion** (A) Hormones are proteins that are secreted by ductless glands of the human body.

Reason (R) Apart from dedicated endocrine glands, hormones are also secreted by major organs.

(a) ☐ (b) ☐ (c) ☐ (d) ☐

***2.** **Assertion** (A) Height of a person can be said to be under the control of hypothalamus.

Reason (R) Somatostatin secreted by the hypothalamus inhibits secretion of growth hormone.

(a) ☐ (b) ☐ (c) ☐ (d) ☐

***3. Assertion** (A) Pars nervosa is under direct neuronal regulation of the hypothalamus.

Reason (R) FSH regulates spermatogenesis in males and follicle development in females.

(a) ☐ (b) ☐ (c) ☐ (d) ☐

4. Assertion (A) Oxytocin secreted by the posterior pituitary helps in milk production in the mammary gland.

Reason (R) Oxytocin also causes contraction of the smooth muscles of the uterus during child birth.

(a) ☐ (b) ☐ (c) ☐ (d) ☐

***5. Assertion** (A) Iodine deficiency in diet can cause hypothyroidism, a condition often faced with people living in hilly areas.

Reason (R) Iodine is required for synthesis of thyroid hormone called thyroxine.

(a) ☐ (b) ☐ (c) ☐ (d) ☐

***6. Assertion** (A) Thyroid hormone deficiency can alter the blood calcium levels.

Reason (R) Hyper secretion of thyroid hormones could be indicative of cancer.

(a) ☐ (b) ☐ (c) ☐ (d) ☐

***7. Assertion** (A) Parathyroid hormone is a peptide hormone which is hypercalcemic in nature.

Reason (R) Along with thyrocalcitonin, parathyroid hormone regulates calcium balance.

(a) ☐ (b) ☐ (c) ☐ (d) ☐

8. Assertion (A) While watching a horror movie one may often see erection of body hairs (piloerection).

Reason (R) Under stressful situation the adrenal cortex is stimulated to secrete emergency hormones.

(a) ☐ (b) ☐ (c) ☐ (d) ☐

***9. Assertion** (A) Reduced activity of the adrenal cortex can affect the blood pressure of a person.

Reason (R) Cortisol is the primary glucocorticoid that regulates carbohydrate metabolism.

(a) ☐ (b) ☐ (c) ☐ (d) ☐

10. Assertion (A) Glucose balance in the blood is regulated by the coordinated processes of glycogenesis and glycogenolysis.

Reason (R) Hyposecretion of insulin by the α-cells of Islets of Langerhans can raise the blood glucose level causing diabetes.

(a) ☐ (b) ☐ (c) ☐ (d) ☐

Case Based Questions

***1.** A person was admitted to a hospital with an extreme case of dehydration. The situation prompted the doctors to administer fluids immediately. After few hours the patient was feeling better, however his urine frequency and output was increased abnormally. On testing the urine sample, doctors found that the electrolyte level in urine was higher than normal. Other parameters were normal. He was diagnosed with the condition *X* and was administered appropriate dosage of *Y*. With reference to the given passage answer the following questions:

(i) Identify the possible condition *X*, he was suffering from.

(a) Diabetes mellitus ☐ (b) Diabetes Insipidus ☐
(c) Hypoglycemia ☐ (d) Adenohypophysis ☐

(ii) Which hormone is responsible in preventing diuresis?

(a) Insulin ☐ (b) Glucagon ☐
(c) Vasopressin ☐ (d) Oxytocin ☐

(iii) Which part of the pituitary is involved in regulating the urine output?

(a) Neurohypophysis ☐ (b) Pars distalis ☐
(c) Pars intermedia ☐ (d) Adenohypophysis ☐

***2.** The given image illustrates, a hormone acting on its target cell. Hormone binding causes changes downstream, one of which is the action of enzyme Adenylyl cyclase that catalyzes the conversion of ATP into a second messenger A. Answer the following questions based on this information:

(i) What could possibly be the hormone?

(a) Testosterone ☐ (b) Progesterone ☐
(c) Cortisol ☐ (d) FSH ☐

(ii) Identify the molecule labelled A.

(a) GTP ☐ (b) Na+ ☐
(c) Cyclic AMP ☐ (d) Phosphate ☐

(iii) Which type of hormones can easily cross the plasma membrane barrier?

(a) Peptide hormones ☐ (b) Protein hormones ☐
(c) Steroid hormones ☐ (d) Polypeptide hormones ☐

COMPETITION EDGE UP

1. Given below are two statements; one is labelled as Assertion A and the other is labelled as Reason (R).

Assertion (A) FSH acts upon ovarian follicles in female and Leydig cells in male.

Reason (R) Growing ovarian follicles secrete oestrogen in female while interstitial cells secrete androgen in male human being.

In the light of the above statements, choose the correct answer from the options given below.

[NCERT Pg. 241, NEET 2024]

(a) Both A and R are true and R is the correct explanation of A ☐

(b) Both A and R are true, but R is not the correct explanation of A ☐

(c) A is true, but R is false ☐

(d) A is false, but R is true ☐

2. Match List I with List II.

List I	List II
A. Exophthalmic goitre	I. Excess secretion of cortisol, moon face and hypergylcemia.
B. Acromegaly	II. Hyposecretion of thyroid hormone and stunted growth.
C. Cushing's syndrome	III. Hypersecretion of thyroid hormone and protruding eye balls.
D. Cretinism	IV. Excessive secretion of growth hormone.

Choose the correct answer from the options given below.

[NCERT Pg. 241, 242, 243, NEET 2024]

(a) A-I, B-III, C-II, D-IV ☐

(b) A-IV, B-II, C-I, D-III ☐

(c) A-III, B-IV, C-II, D-I ☐

(d) A-III, B-IV, C-I, D-II ☐

3. Which of the following is not a steroid hormone? **[NCERT Pg. 248, NEET 2024]**

(a) Cortisol ☐

(b) Testosterone ☐

(c) Progesterone ☐

(d) Glucagon ☐

4. Which one of the following are not under the control of thyroid hormone?

A. Maintenance of water and electrolyte balance.

B. Regulation of basal metabolic rate.

C. Normal rhythm of sleep-wake cycle.

D. Development of immune system.

E. Support the process of RBCs formation.

Choose the correct answer from the options given below. **[NEET 2023]**

(a) B and C only ☐ (b) C and D only ☐

(c) D and E only ☐ (d) A and D only ☐

5. Which of the following are not the effects of parathyroid hormone? **[NCERT Pg. 244, NEET 2022]**

I. Stimulates the process of bone reabsorption.

II. Decreases Ca^{2+} level in blood.

III. Reabsorption of Ca^{2+} by renal tubules.

IV. Decreases the absorption of Ca^{2+} from digested food.

V. Increases metabolism of carbohydrates.

Choose the most appropriate answer from the options given below.

(a) II, IV and V ☐ (b) I and V ☐

(c) II and III ☐ (d) I and III ☐

6. Erythropoietin hormone which stimulates RBCs formation is produced by **[NCERT Pg. 247, NEET 2021]**

(a) Juxtaglomerular cells of the kidney ☐

(b) Alpha cells of pancreas ☐

(c) The cells of rostral adenohypophysis ☐

(d) The cells of bone marrow ☐

7. Presence of which of the following conditions in urine are indicative of Diabetes Mellitus? **[NEET 2020]**

(a) Uremia and renal calculi ☐

(b) Ketonuria and glycosuria ☐

(c) Renal calculi and hyperglycaemia ☐

(d) Uremia and ketonuria ☐

8. Match the following columns and select the correct option from the codes given below. **[NEET (Oct.) 2020]**

Column I	Column II
A. Pituitary hormone	1. Steroid
B. Epinephrine	2. Neuropeptides
C. Endorphins	3. Peptides, proteins
D. Cortisol	4. Biogenic amines

	A	B	C	D			A	B	C	D	
(a)	4	1	2	3	☐	(b)	3	4	2	1	☐
(c)	4	3	1	2	☐	(d)	3	4	1	2	☐

Answers

Chapter-1

The Living World

1. Species
2. Biodiversity
3. Nomenclature
4. (b) Both statements I and II are true.
5. Identified
6. (i) **ICBN**–International Code for Botanical Nomenclature
(ii) **ICZN**–International Code of Zoological Nomenclature
7. Generic name and specific epithet
8. Carolus Linnaeus
9. Genus
10. Italics, Latin
11. Capital, small
12. (a) Statements I and III are correct.
13. (d) *Mangifera indica* Linn.
14. Name of the author who first described the species.
15. *Columba LIVEA* is odd one out, as it is incorrectly written scientific name.
16. Classification
17. Taxa
18. Systematics
19. Systematics is odd one out. Rest all are basic processes in taxonomy while systematics is the branch of biology that deals with comparative and evolutionary relationship between organisms.
20. (b) Both statements I and II are true.
21. (c) *S*
22. Hierarchy
23. Taxon
24. Entities, morphological
25. Smallest
26. Species
27. Genus and species
28. (a) Leopard and tiger are related organisms in the evolution tree.
They have several common features and they both belong to the same genus–*Panthera.*
29. 2 (Potato, brinjal)
30. Lion – *Panthera leo*, Leopard – *Panthera pardus*, Tiger– *Panthera tigris*
31. False. Genus comprises of related species which has more characters in common in comparison to species of other genera.
32. (d) Wheat
33. They belong to same family – Felidae and different genus – *Felis* (cat) and *Panthera* (tiger).
34. Aceae, idae
35. (b) A-Polymoniales
B-Solanaceae
36. Polymoniales
37. (i) Felidae
(ii) Polymoniales
38. Ales
39. (b) These can be corrected as Gorillas, gibbons, monkeys and humans belong to same order Primata.
Animals of the same order show more similarities than those of the same class.
40. Division
41. Class
42. Family, Class
43. It will decreases.
44. (b) X and Y
45. (c) Muscidae
46. (a) A-3, B-4, C-1, D-2
47. (b)
48. (c) Statements I, III and IV are incorrect.
49. (i) Chordata (Phylum),
(ii) Monocotyledonae (Class)
50. I. Carnivora, II. Primata, III. Canidae, IV. Felidae, V. Hominidae
51. Chordata is odd one out. Housefly belongs to phylum–Arthropoda.
52. IV → I → II → III → V
53. (b) *Petunia* and *Datura* have more similarities than Convolvulaceae and Solanaceae.
Wheat and mango relates at the level of division.
54. A-4, B-3, C-2, D-1.
55. *Cicer* and *Petunia* (Genus), Asteraceae and Solanaceae (Family), Primata and Rodentia (Order).
56. (i) Genus, (ii) Taxonomic categories, (iii) Order, (iv) Family

Competition Connect

1. Increase in number of individuals and increase in mass.
2. Cell division
3. (b) In plants, the growth by cell division occurs continuously throughout their life span, whereas in animals, the growth is seen only upto a certain age.
4. True
5. (b) Both statements I and II are true.
6. Accumulation of material on the surface
7. A-1, B-2, C-4, D-3
8. Fragmentation
9. Reproduction, growth
10. 3 (Mules, sterile worker bees as well as an infertile human couple do not reproduce).
11. Metabolism
12. True
13. (a) Metabolism is a defining feature of all living organisms without exception.
14. True
15. Photoperiod
16. Self consciousness
17. 3 (Metabolism, cellular organisation and consciousness).
18. (b) Atomic level → Molecular level → Cellular level → Tissue → Organ → Organ system → Individual
19. (b) Statements I, III and V are correct.

Assertion-Reason Questions

1. (c) A is true, but R is false. R can be corrected as
The number of species that are known and described range between 1.7-1.8 million.
2. (a) Both A and R are true and R is the correct explanation of A.
3. (b) Both A and R are true, but R is not the correct explanation of A.
4. (b) Both A and R are true, but R is not the correct explanation of A.
5. (a) Both A and R are true and R is the correct explanation of A.
6. (c) A is true, but R is false. R can be corrected as
External and internal structure, along with the structure of cell, development process and ecological information of organisms are essential to assign a taxa.
7. (b) Both A and R are true, but R is not the correct explanation of A.
8. (b) Both A and R are true, but R is not the correct explanation of the A.
9. (d) A is false, but R is true. A can be corrected as
Members of a species can interbreed freely.
10. (d) A is false, but R is true. R can be corrected as
Panthera and *Felis* are placed under the same family Felidae.

Case Based Questions

1. (i) (c) (ii) (a) (iii) (b) (iv) (b)
2. (i) (d) (ii) (d) (iii) (a)

Competition Edge Up

1. (d) 2. (a) 3. (d)
4. (a) 5. (d) 6. (c)

Chapter-2

Biological Classification

1. Aristotle
2. Red Blood cells (RBCs)
3. Carolus Linnaeus
4. True
5. All of them except nuclear membrane composition.
6. (b) Five kingdom classification by RH Whittaker took the phylogeny of organisms into consideration.
7. Monera
8. Presence of cell wall in their cells.
9. *A*–Prokaryotic, *B*–Present (non-cellulosic made up of polysaccharide and amino acid), *C*–Present, *D*–Multicellular/loosetissue
10. *A*–Autotrophs–Plantae, *B*–Heterotrophs–Animals and fungi, *C*–Both autotrophs and heterotrophs–Monera and Protista
11. Bacteria
12. (i) True
(ii) False. Bacteria can surive in extreme habitats like hotsprings, deserts, snow and deep oceans.
(iii) True
13. *A*–Cocci, *B*–Bacilli, *C*–Spirilla, *D*-Vibrio
14. Simple, complex
15. (i) Heterotrophic,
(ii) Chemosynthetic
16. Chemoautotrophic, photoautotrophic
17. A-2, B-1, C-3
18. Thermoacidophiles
19. Methanogens
20. (b) Biogas production requires anaerobic digestion by methane forming methanogens.
21. Eubacteria
22. Blue-green algae
23. (a)
24. True
25. Heterocyst
26. Heterocyst
27. *X* - *Nostoc*, *A*–Heterocyst, *B*–Mucilagenous sheath.
28. *Methanococcus* is odd one out as it is a methanogen bacterium.
29. (i) Chemosynthetic autotrophic bacteria
(ii) Photosynthetic autotrophic bacteria
(iii) Chemosynthetic autotrophic bacteria
30. (b) They play a great role in recycling nutrients.
31. All of the given options are economic importances of heterotrophic bacteria, except biogas production and coagulation of blood.
32. Influenza is odd one out as it is a viral disease.
33. *X* – Binary fission, *A*–Cell wall, *B*–Cell membrane, *C*–DNA
34. Spores by sporulation
35. (c) Orgainsm *A* is bacteria and organism *B* is mycoplasma.
36. *Mycoplasma*
37. (b) Mycoplasma are smallest living cells that do not possess cell wall.
38. (b) Statement II and III are incorrect.
39. Protista
40. 4 (Single-celled, eukaryotic, membrane bound organelles, connecting links between plants, animals and fungi)
41. Cell fusion, zygote formation
42. Chrysophytes
43. Diatoms
44. Diatomaceous earth
45. Biogas production is not done by diatomite.
46. Diatoms
47. Photosynthetic
48. True
49. Dinoflagellates
50. *Gonyaulax*
51. Pellicle; two unequal
52. (d) Protein
53. 2 (One long and one short)
54. Chloroplast, heterotrophic
55. A–Dinoflagellates, *B*–Euglenoid (*Euglena*)
56. (a) The gritty texture of diatomaceous earth is used in filtration of oils and syrups.
57. Saprophytic protists

58. True

59. *Plasmodium*

60. Sporangia, cellulose, air currents

61. (b) Both statemants I and II are true

62. Protozoans

63. *Entamoeba histolytica*

64. *Trypanosoma*

65. *X*–*Paramecium*, *A*-Cilia, *B*-Oral groove, *C*-Mouth pore, *D*-Anal pore

66. (b) *Paramecium*

67. (i) Amoeboid protozoan,
(ii) Ciliated protozoan

68. Parasites, *Plasmodium*

69. A-3, B-4, C-1, D-2

70. (a) Heterotrophic

71. (i) Common mushroom
(ii) Toad stools

72. Yeast

73. *Puccinia*

74. Warm and humid

75. Yeast

76. Hyphae, mycelium

77. False. Coenocytic hyphae have no septal walls in its filaments.

78. (b) A–Septate, B–Coenocytic

79. Chitin and polysaccharides

80. Fungi, algae

81. (a) Mycorrhizal association between plants and fungi provides benefit to both the species.

82. (i) Saprophytes
(ii) Parasites
(iii) Mycorrhiza

83. Vegetative means-Fragmentation, Budding, Fission.
Asexual spores-Conidia, Zoospores, Sporangiospores.
Sexual spores-Oospore, Basidiospore, Ascospore.

84. Plasmogamy → Karyogamy → Meiosis in zygote for haploid spore formation.

85. Plasmogamy

86. (c) Statements II, III and IV are correct.

87. Nuclei

88. (d) Conidia-$2n$

89. Ascomycetes, Basidiomycetes

90. True

91. Phycomycetes

92. Phycomycetes

93. Isogamous, anisogamous or oogamous

94. (b) Zoospores are endogenously produced in the sporangium of Phycomycetes.
The gametes produced by *Rhizopus* and *Mucor* are either similar in morphology (isogamous) or dissimilar (anisogamous or oogamous).

95. *A*–*Mucor*, *B*–*Saccharomyces*, *C*–*Penicillium*

96. (b) Both statements I and II are true

97. Conidiospores

98. *Penicillium notatum*

99. (i) Conidia, basidiospores
(ii) Zoospores, aplanospores, ascospores

100. *Ascus*

101. *Neurospora*

102. (i) Ascomycetes
(ii) Basidiomycetes

103. Basidiomycetes

104. Basidiomycetes

105. Exogenously, basidium

106. 4

107. Ascomycetes, Basidiomycetes

108. (i) Basidiocarp
(ii) Multinucleate and aseptate
(iii) *Albugo*

109. (i) *Rhizopus* (ii) *Agaricus*
(iii) *Ustilago* (iv) *Puccinia*

110. (b) Imperfect fungi are so named because only the asexual or vegetative phases of these fungi are known.

111. Deuteromycetes is odd one as it is known as imperfect fungi because only the asexual phases of reproduction are known. All other given classes show both sexual and asexual reproduction.

112. Deuteromycetes

113. (c) *Agaricus*-basidiospores

114. (i) Aplanospores,
(ii) Ascospores
(iii) Basidiomycetes

115. A-2, B-1, C-4, D-3.

116. *A*–Ascomycetes, *B*–Mycelium aseptate and coenocytic, *C*–*Trichoderma* *D*–Basidiomycetes, *E*–*Agaricus*

117. Insectivorous plant – bladderwort and venus flytrap and parasitic plant-*Cuscuta*

118. Plantae

119. Sporophytic, gametophytic

120. (i) True
(ii) False. Higher animals have elaborated sensory and neuromotor mechanisms.
(iii) True

121. Kingdom–Plantae-Chlorophyll, cellulose present and alternation of generation
Kingdom–Animalia - Glycogen present, holozoic nutrition and mobility.

122. Viruses, viroids and prions

123. Non-cellular

124. True

125. Venom or poisonous fluid

126. *X*-Tobacco masaic virus, *A*-*ss*RNA, *B*-Capsid

127. DJ Ivanowsky

128. A–3, B–1, C–2

129. DNA or RNA (Both *ds* and *ss*)

130. True

131. (b) Both statements I and II are true.

132. (i) Nucleoprotein particle
(ii) *ds*DNA virus
(iii) Bacteriophage

133. (i) Plants-*ss*RNA
(ii) Animals-*ss*RNA, *ds*RNA and *ds*DNA

134. *X*-Bacteriophage, *A*–Head, *B*–Collar, *C*–Sheath, *D*–Base plate, *E*-Tail fibre

135. (b) P

136. (i) Capsid
(ii) Capsomeres

137. All are caused by virus/viral infections

138. AIDS

139. 5 (All of the given symptoms are shown by plants infected with virus except leaf spots.) Majority of leaf spots are caused by fungi.

140. Viroid

141. RNA, protein

142. Potato spindle tuber disease, potato spindle tuber viroid

143. Prions

144. (a) Misfolded protein

145. Mad cow disease of cattle

146. Creutzfeldt-Jakob Disease

147. Phycobiont, mycobiont

148. (i) Prepare food for fungi,
(ii) Provide shelter, absorb nutrients and water for algae.

149. Less

150. (b) The mycobiont absorbs mineral nutient for its algal partner in the mutualistic relationship lichens accumulate in the areas with low Air Quality Index (AQI) and are indications of pollution.

151. (i) Prions
(ii) Viroid

Assertion-Reason Questions

1. (a) Both A and R are true and R is the correct explanation of A.

2. (c) A is true, but R is false. It can be corrected as
Chemosynthetic bacteria oxidise various inorganic substances like nitrates, nitrites etc. and use the released energy for their ATP production.

3. (a) Both A and R are true and R is the correct explanation of A.

4. (b) Both A and R are true, but R is not the correct explanation of A. It can be corrected as
Oceans which show red tides can be of scenic beauty, but could probably be dead because red dinoflagellates (e.g. *Gonyaulax*) undergo rapid multiplication to make the sea appear red while releasing toxins that kill other organisms.

5. (c) A is true, but R is false. R can be corrected as
The fungal fruiting bodies undergo reductional division to form haploid spores in them.

6. (d) A is false, but R is true. A can be corrected as
Claviceps are sac fungi with a mycelium which is septate and branched.

7. (a) Both A and R are true and R is the correct explanation of A.

8. (c) A is true, but R is false. R can be corrected as
The genetic material which is DNA or RNA is responsible for the virulence of the virus.

Case Based Questions

1. (i) (b) (ii) (c) (iii) (b)
2. (i) (d) (ii) (c) (iii) (d)

Competition Edge Up

1. (b) **2.** (a) **3.** (d) **4.** (c) **5.** (b)
6. (a) **7.** (d) **8.** (d)

Chapter-3

Plant Kingdom

1. False. Blue-green algae are the members of kingdom–Monera.

2. Kingdom–Plantae includes algae, bryophytes, pteridophytes, angiosperm and gymnosperm.

3. Embryology is the odd one out. Rest of the options were the superficial morphological characters used in earlier system of classification.

4. Linnaeus

5. Vegetative, sexual

6. External, internal

7. George Bentham and Joseph Dalton Hooker

8. Evolutionary

9. True

10. A-4, B-3, C-1, D-2

11. (a) Cytotaxonomy is based on cytological information like chromosome number, structure and behaviour.

12. Algae

13. Lichen

14. Algae reproduce by vegetative, asexual and sexual methods.

15. (i) *Chlamydomonas*, (ii) *Volvox*, (iii) *Ulothrix*.

16. Vegetative

17. True

18. Zoospores

19. *Ulothrix; Spirogyra*

20. Isogamy

21. (d) Isogamous : *Fucus*

22. (c) Fusion between large non-motile female and smaller motile male gamete.

23. *Spirogyra*

24. Oogamous

25. Algae

26. Marine algae

27. *Laminaria, Sargassum*

28. Hydro-colloids e.g. Brown algae–algin, red algae–carrageen

29. Agar

30. *Gelidium* and *Gracilaria*

31. *Chlorella*,

32. Chlorophyceae, Phaeophyceae, Rhodophyceae

33. (a) A-2, B-3, C-1, D-4

34. *A*–Chlorophyceae, *B*–Phaeophyceae, *C*–Red algae

35. Chlorophyll-*a* and *b*.

36. Hexagonal is odd one out. Rest of the options represent the shapes of chloroplasts in different species of algae However, hexagonal shape is not identified.

37. Pyrenoids

38. True

39. Cellulose, pectose

40. False. Vegetative reproduction in Chlorophyceae takes place by fragmentation.

41. False. Flagellated zoospores are produced in zoosporangia.

42. (b) Both statements I and II are true.

43. *Volvox* and *Ulothrix*

44. Phaeophyceae

45. *Ectocarpus*

46. Xanthophylls, carotenoids

47. Fucoxanthin

48. (b) *Fucus* is a member of phaeophyceae/(brown algae). The shades of brown observed in these members is due to the variable amount of fucoxanthin present in them.

49. False. Food is stored as complex carbohydrates in Phaeophyceae.

50. Laminarin, mannitol

51. Algin
52. Holdfast
53. Stipe
54. (a) A-stipe, B-Holdfast
55. Frond
56. False. Asexual reproduction in most brown algae occurs by biflagellated zoospores.
57. Pyriform
58. *Fucus, Dictyota*
59. (i) *Laminaria*, (ii) *A*–Holdfast, *B*–Stipe, *C*–Frond.
60. (i) *Fucus*, (ii) *A*–Air bladder, *B*–Frond, *C*–Midrib.
61. (i) *Dictyota*, (ii) Fucoxanthin
62. *r*-phycoerythrin
63. False. Red algae occur at both surfaces of water and also at deep ocean depths.
64. False. The thalli of most red algae are multicellular.
65. Floridean starch, amylopectin, glycogen
66. True
67. False. Red algae reproduce sexually by non-motile gametes.
68. Oogamous
69. *Porphyra* and *Gelidium*
70. *Porphyra*
71. A-2, B-4, C-1, D-3
72. (b) Statements II, III and V are correct.
73. *A*–Chlorophyll-*a* and *b*, *B*–Floridean starch, *C*–Cellulose and algin, *D*–Absent
74. Amphibian
75. True
76. False. Bryophytes are more differentiated than algae.
77. Rhizoids
78. True
79. True
80. Gametophyte, Haploid
81. Archegonium
82. Antherozoids
83. Sporophyte
84. Sporophyte, gametophyte
85. (a) The gametophyte is haploid while the sporophyte is diploid.
86. Meiosis, gametophyte
87. *Sphagnum*
88. (b) Species of *Sphagnum*, a moss have long been used as packaging material for trans-shipment of living material due to their water holding capacity.
The flask-shaped structure present in bryophytes is archegonium. It produces a single egg.
89. Lichens
90. Liverworts and Mosses
91. Thalloid
92. Gemmae
93. (d) *Marchautia*
94. Gemma cups
95. True
96. False. During sexual reproduction in liverwort, male and female sex organs are produced either on different or same thalli.
97. Holdfast is odd one out. Rest of the options are differentiation of sporophyte whereas holdfast attaches the brown algae to the substratum.
98. Capsule
99. (i) *A*–Archegoniophore, *B*–Gemma cup, *C*-Rhizoids
(ii) Haploid
100. Protonema stage
101. Leafy
102. Rhizoids
103. False. Leafy stage bears sex organs.
104. Fragmentation, budding, secondary protonema.
105. (b) Both statements I and II are true.
106. Sporophyte
107. False. *Funaria* and *Sphagnum* are called mosses.
108. Peat moss
109. (i) *A*–Capsule, *B*–Seta, *C*–Rhizoids, *D*–Sporophyte, *E*–Gametophyte.
(ii) *Funaria*
110. (i) *A*–Antheridial branch, *B*–Archegonial branch.
(ii) *Sphagnum*
111. Pteridophytes
112. Terrestrial
113. (b) Xylem and phloem
114. Sporophytic plant body.
115. Sporophyte
116. Macrophylls
117. Sporophylls
118. Strobili or Cones
119. Reductional
120. Prothallus
121. (b) The spore mother cells of the sporangia divide mitotically to produce spores.
122. (i) Need of water for fertilisation.
(ii) The pteridophytic gametophytes require cool, damp, shady places to grow.
123. Antheridia, archegonia, antherozoids, archegonium.
124. Sporophyll → Strobili → Sporangia → Spore mother cell → Spores
125. Homosporous
126. Large and small spores
127. (b) Both statements I and II are true.
128. *A*–Strobilus, *B*–Node, *C*–Branch
129. *A*–*Selaginella*, *B*–Fern, *C*–*Salvinia*
130. True
131. Sporophyte
132. Female gametophyte
133. Seed habit
134. (b) In the evolutionary history, pteridophytes have succeeded bryophytes and are among the first terrestrial plants to have seed habit.
Selaginella possess smaller leaves or microphylls whereas ferns have large leaves or macrophylls.
135. Heterospory
136. Psilopsida, Lycopsida, Sphenopsida, Pteropsida.
137. Water
138. Require the presence of water for fertilisation.
139. A-4, B-3, C-2, D-1
140. Ovary wall
141. *Sequoia*
142. Tap
143. Mycorrhiza
144. Coralloid
145. (b) Both statements I and II are true.
146. False. Needle-like leaves reduce surface area in conifers, which help to reduce water loss.
147. (i) Thick cuticle, (ii) Sunken stomata
148. False. Gymnosperms are heterosporous.
149. Haploid, sporophylls, cone

150. Lax or compact strobili
151. Male strobili or microsporangiate
152. Pollen grain
153. True
154. False. Male cones and megasporophylls are borne on different trees in *Cycas.*
155. (c) Microsporophyll and microsporangia
156. Megaspore mother cell, nucellus, ovule
157. Meiotically, four
158. Archegonia
159. (b) In gymnosperms the development of pollen grain occurs within the microsporangia of the megasporophyll in gymnosperm.
160. True
161. False. In gymnosperms, the male and female gametophytes do not have an independent free-living existence.
162. *A*–Microsporangium, *B*–Pollen tube, *C*–Archegonia, *D*–Embryo, *E*-Seeds.
163. (i) *Ginkgo*, (ii) *A*–Dwarf shoot, *B*–Long shoot, *C*–Seeds.
164. Flowers
165. False. Seeds are enclosed by fruits in angiosperms.
166. (b) Both statements I and II are true.
167. *Wolfia*
168. Dicotyledons
169. (i) Dicotyledons, (ii) Monocotyledons
170. (c) *Eucalyptus*

Assertion-Reason Questions

1. (b) Both A and R are true, but R is not the correct explanation of A.
2. (b) Both A and R are true, but R is not the correct explanation of A.
3. (c) A is true, but R is false. R can be corrected as
The sporophyte of liverworts contains two copies of the genome and are diploid.
4. (a) Both A and R are true and R is correct explanation of A.
5. (d) A is false, but R is true. A can be corrected as
The spread of living pteridophytes is limited and restricted to narrow geographical regions.
6. (b) Both A and R are true but R is not the correct explanation of A.
7. (a) Both A and R are true and R is correct explanation of A.
8. (b) Both A and R are true, but R is not the correct explanation of A.

Case Based Questions

1. (i) (a) (ii) (b) (iii) (c)
2. (i) (c) (ii) (d) (iii) (a) (iv) (b)

Competition Edge UP

1. (c) **2.** (d) **3.** (a) **4.** (b) **5.** (b)
6. (a) **7.** (c) **8.** (a) **9.** (c) **10.** (a)
11.(c) **12.**(a)

Chapter-4

Animal Kingdom

1. False. All members of Animalia are multicellular, they do not exhibit the same pattern of organisation of cells.
2. *A*–Aschelminthes, annelids, arthropods, molluscs, echinoderms, hemichordates, chordates.
B–Ctenophores, coelenterates
C–Platyhelminthes
D–Poriferans
3. Porifera
4. The type of symmetry found in animals are asymmetrical, radial and bilateral.
5. *A*-Platyhelminthes
B-Coelenterata
C-Echinodermata
6. (d)
7. *A*–Bilateral symmetry, *B*–Radial symmetry
8. *A*-Mesoglea, *B*-Ectoderm, *C*-Endoderm, *D*-Mesoderm
9. (a)
10. (i) Diploblastic, (ii) Mesoderm
11. Coelom
12. *A*-Annelids (coelomate), *B*-Aschelminthes (pseudocoelomate), *C*-Platyhelminthes (acoelomate).
13. True coelom
14. (i) Pseudocoelom
(ii) Acoelomates
15. Segmentation
16. Earthworm
17. False. Notochord is a mesodermally derived rod-like structure formed on the dorsal side during embryonic development in chordates.
18. *A*–Cellular level *B*–Acoelomata, *C*–Bilateral, *D*–Aschelminthes, *E*–Coelomates
19. Porifera
20. Asymmetrical
21. Porifera
22. Ostia, spongocoel, osculum
23. 6(All of them except digestion because it is intracellular)
24. (b) Both statements I and II are true.
25. Choanocytes
26. (c) Skeleton is made up of spongin fiores.
27. Spicules or spongin fibres
28. Hermaphrodite
29. Fragmentation
30. True
31. *A*-*Sycon* (Scypha), *B*-*Euspongia* (Bath sponge), *C*-*Spongilla* (Fresh water sponge)
32. Indirect development
33. Phylum–Coelenterata
34. (i) The diagram given below represents cnidoblast which is used for anchorage, defence and for the capture of prey.
(ii) Nematocyst
35. Hypostome
36. (i) Coral
(ii) Both intracellular and extracellular
37. (a) The polyps can form medusae asexually while the reverse occurs sexually.
38. Medusa
39. Asexually, sexually
40. Metagenesis
41. *A*-Medusa , *B*-Polyp

42. (b) They are free swimming like *Aurelia*.

43. (i) *Physalia*, (ii) *Adamsia*, (iii) *Pennatula*, (iv) *Gorgonia* (v) *Meandrina*

44. Sea walnuts or comb jellies.

45. (i) True
(ii) True
(iii) False. Ctenophores exhibit both extracellular and intracellular digestion.

46. Bioluminescence

47. (b) In *Pleurobrachia* and *Ctenoplana* reproduction takes place only by sexual method.
Bioluminescence is the property whereby living organisms can emit light.

48. (i) *Pleurobrachia*
(ii) Present
(iii) Sexual
(iv) External
(v) Indirect

49. Only coelomate is odd one out. Platyhelminthes are acoelomates. Other mentioned options are characteristics of phylum–Platyhelminthes.

50. Hooks, suckers

51. Flame cells

52. (i) True
(ii) False. Common name of *Fasciola* is liver fluke. Tapeworm is the common name of *Taenia*.

53. (b)

54. Phylum-Aschelminthes

55. Dioecious, pseudocoelomates, complete alimentary canal

56. (a) Development in Aschelminthes may be direct (the young ones resemble the adult) or indirect.

57. (b)

58. Phylum–Aschelminthes

59. Annelida

60. Metameres

61. (c) *Ascaris*

62. Parapodia

63. (d) Statements I, II and IV are incorrect.

64. Nephridia

65. True

66. *Nereis* is odd one out as, it is dioecious, rest are monoecious.

67. Arthropoda

68. Phylum–Arthropoda

69. (c) Chitin

70. Head, thorax and abdomen

71. (b)

72. 7(All of them except radial symmetry). Arthropods exhibit bilateral symmetry.

73. (a)

74. Malpighian tubules is odd one out as they are not sensory structures in arthropods. These are excretory structure.

75. Statocysts

76. Malpighian tubules

77. (i) *Bombyx*
(ii) *Culex/Aedes/Anopheles*

78. A-4, B-1, C-2, D-3

79. Calcareous shell

80. Mantle

81. True

82. Calcareous, head, muscular foot

83. Mantle cavity

84. Radula

85. (d)

86. (b) Feather-like gills present in the mantle cavity are involved with respiration and excretion.

87. *A*-Annelida, *B* - Malpighian tubules, *C* - Open, *D* - Mollusca, *E* - Feather-like gills

88. A–2, B–5, C–4, D–3, E–1

89. *A* - *Pila*, Mollusca
B - *Locusta*, Arthropoda
C - *Hirudinaria*, Annelida,

90. Bilateral

91. Tissue level organisation is odd one out. Echinoderms have organ system level of body organisation.

92. Presence of water vascular system (ambulacral system).

93. True

94. (c) Excretion

95. (i) *Antedon*
(ii) *Echinus*
(iii) *Cucumaria*

96. (i) Absent
(ii) Triploblastic
(iii) Sexual
(iv) Dioecious
(v) *Asterias*

97. (a) An excretory system is absent in the members of the phylum-Echinodermata.

98. True

99. Stomochord

100. (d) Stomochord

101. Hemichordata

102. Closed circulation is odd one out as in it, circulatory system is of open type.

103. *X*-*Balanoglossus*
A-Proboscis,
B-Collar, *C*-Trunk

104. (a) A-4, B-3, C-2, D-1

105. (b) Both statements I and II are true

106. Phyla–Echinodermata, Hemichordata

107. A notochord, a dorsal hollow nerve cord and paired pharyngeal gill slits are the three characteristics of phylum-Chordata

108. *A* - Nerve cord, *B* - Notochord, *C* - Post-anal tail, *D* - Gill slits

109. Cephalochordates, urochordates

110. (b) Lencelet

111. (i) Ventral heart
(ii) Coelomate
(iii) Invertebrates
(iv) Urochordates
(v) *Ascidia*

112. Cartilaginous or bony vertebral column.

113. (i) False. All vertebrates are chordates, but all chordates are not vertebrates.
(ii) True

114. Proboscis

115. Well-developed skull

116. *A* - Urochordata
B - Cephalochordata
C - Cyclostomata
D - Pisces
E - Tetrapoda

117. Cyclostomes

118. (a) Lamprey and hagfish show indirect development in the ocean habitats.

119. *Carcharodon*

120. (i) *Torpedo*,
(ii) *Trygon*

121. (i) *Exocoetus*
(ii) *Pterophyllum*
(iii) *Scoliodon*
(iv) *Pristis*
(v) *Betta*
(vi) *Myxine*
(vii) *Asterias*

122. 2, 1 and 1
123. Air bladder
124. Air bladder
125. (i) False. It belongs to class-Osteichthyes
(ii) True
126. Chondrichthyes
127. (b) There are four pairs of gills in Rohu and *Catla* for respiration.
128. (a) *A*–Placoid scales
B–Cycloid scales
129. A-2, 4, B-1, 3.
130. *A*-Sucking mouth, *B*-Terminal mouth, *C*-Scales absent, *D*-Placoid scales, *E*-Marine, *F*-Marine, *G*-6-15 pairs of gill slits, *H*-4 pairs of gills with operculum.
131. (i) *D*
(ii) *B* and *C* are cartilaginous fishes, *D* is bony fish
(iii) *A*
(iv) *B, C, D*
(v) *D*
(vi) *A-Petromyzon, B- Scoliodon, C-Pristis, D-Catla*
132. (i) Head, trunk
(ii) Tympanum
(iii) Cloaca
(iv) three, two auricles, one ventricle
133. Nephridia is odd one out as it helps in excretion in annelids.
134. (d) Operculum
135. (i) *Rana tigrina*
(ii) External
(iii) Gills
(iv) Indirect
136. Creeping or crawling
137. Class–Reptilia
138. (a) Both reptiles and amphibians are poikilothermous.
139. Internal fertilisation and direct development are features specific to reptiles.
140. (i) Crocodile, alligators
(ii) Snakes, lizards
(iii) Viper, cobra
141. (i) Tortoise, (ii) Toad, (iii) Tree frog, (iv) Garden lizard, (v) Wall lizard, (vi) Krait
142. Pneumatic bones
143. False. In birds, the forelimbs are modified into wings. The hindlimbs are modified for walking, swimming or clasping.
144. Oil
145. Crop and gizzard
146. (i) Lungs
(ii) Beak
147. A-2, B-1, C-4, D-3
148. *A*-Neophron, *B-Struthio, C-Psittacula, D-Pavo*
Out of these, *B* is a flightless bird.
149. Hairs on their body, warm-blooded, presence of mammary glands.
150. 4(All of them, exept viviparous and teeth). Teeth are present in mammals only and birds are oviparous.
151. (d) Statements III and IV are correct.
152. A-Platypus (it is oviparous), *B*- Bat (has wings for flying), *C*-Whale (has flippers and no hindlimbs)
153. Diaphragm is present in bats, but not present in birds.
154. (c) *Ornithorhynchus*
155. 4 (Molluscs, fishes, aquatic arthropods, tadpoles)
156. *A*-Arthropoda, *B*- Chordata, *C*-Butterfly, *D*-elephant
Note Students can opt for other relevant phylum and examples related to given classes.
157. Lungs
158. (i) *Pteropus,*
(ii) *Balaenoptera,*
(iii) *Macaca,*
(iv) *Rattus*

Assertion-Reason Questions

1. (b) Both A and R are true, but R is not the correct explanation of A.
2. (b) Both A and R are true, but R is not the correct explanation of A.
3. (a) Both A and R are true and R is the correct explanation of A.
4. (b) Both A and R are true, but R is not the correct explanation of A.
5. (b) Both A and R are true, but R is not the correct explanation of A.
6. (c) A is true, but R is false. R can be corrected as
Asterias has a complete digestive system with ventrally located anus.
7. (d) A is false, but R is true. A can be corrected as
Chordates differ from non-chordates in having a mesodermally derived notochord.
8. (a) Both A and R are true and R is the correct explanation of A.
9. (c) A is true, but R is false. R can be corrected as
Amphibians like frogs are cold blooded animals that show external fertilisation
10. (a) Both A and R are true and R is the correct explanation of A.

Case Based Questions

1. (i) b (ii) (b) (iii) (a)
2. (i) b (ii) (a) (iii) (c) (iv) (b)

Competition Edge Up

1. (a) **2.** (b) **3.** (b) **4.** (a) **5.** (a)
6. (d) **7.** (a) **8.** (a) **9.** (b) **10.** (a)

Chapter-5

Morphology of Flowering Plants

1. Morphology, roots, stems, leaves, flowers, fruits.
2. Root, shoot
3. False. The direct elongation of the radicle leads to the formation of primary root in majority of the dicotyledonous plants.
4. Secondary, tertiary
5. (i) *A*–Primary root, *B*–Secondary root, *C*–Internode, (ii) Tap root system, (iii) Monocot
6. (b) Presence of tap roots.
7. i-c-2, ii-a-1, iii-b-3
8. The main functions of the root system include
1. Absorption of water,
2. Food storage,
3. Plant growth regulator production.
9. Root cap
10. (i)-c-2, (ii)-a-3, (iii)-b-1
11. (d) Statements III and IV are incorrect.

12. Ascending
13. Stem develops from the plumule of the embryo of a germinating seed.
14. Nodes, internodes
15. True
16. The two main functions of stem are- (i) It conducts water, minerals and photosynthates. (ii) It stores food.
17. Leaf
18. Axillary bud
19. Shoot apical meristems, acropetal
20. (i) *A*–Stipule, *B*–Petiole, *C*–Axillary bud, *D*–Leaf base, *E*–Lamina
(ii) Leaf base
(iii) Monocotyledons
21. Leguminous plants
22. Stipules
23. Petiole
24. Lamina, leaf blade, midrib
25. (a) D (petiole)
26. Veins
27. Venation
28. Reticulate, parallel
29. (c) Wheat
30. Simple
31. Compound
32. False. A bud is present in the axil of petiole in both simple and compound leaves, but not in the axil of leaflets of compound leaf.
33. Pinnately
34. Palmately
35. *A*–It is pinnately compound leaf found in neem. *B*–It is palmately compound leaf found in silk cotton.
36. Phyllotaxy
37. Alternate
38. (c) more than two
39. Node, opposite
40. False. In whorled phyllotaxy, more than two leaves arise at a node and form a whorl.
41. (i)-b-2, (ii)-a-3, (iii)-c-1
42. Flower
43. Internodes
44. Laterally
45. True
46. Inflorescence
47. Acropetal
48. Basipetal
49. (d) They show acropetal succession
50. *A*–Racemose inflorescence *B*–Cymose inflorescence
51. False. A typical flower has four different kinds of whorls arranged successively on the swollen end of the pedicel called thalamus.
52. Calyx and corolla are accessory organs, while androecium and gynoecium are the reproductive organs of a flower.
53. Bisexual, unisexual
54. Radial symmetry
55. 3 (Mustard, *Datura*, Chilli), all of them are actinomorphic flowers.
56. False. Zygomorphic flower can be divided into two similar halves only in one particular vertical plane.
57. Zygomorphic
58. *Canna*, asymmetric
59. 3, 4, 5
60. Bracteate, Ebracteate.
61. (a) A-2, B-4, C-3, D-1
62. Perigynous
63. False. In epigynous flowers, the margin of thalamus grows upward enclosing the ovary completely and getting fused with it.
64. (i)-c-2, (ii)-b-3, (iii)-a-1
65. Hypogynous flower – Mustard, China rose and brinjal.
Perigynous flower – Plum and peach.
Epigynous flower – Guava, cucumber and ray florets of sunflower.
66. Calyx, sepals
67. False. When sepals are united calyx is known as gamosepalous when sepals are free it is termed as polysepalous.
68. *A*–Androecium, *B*–Gynoecium, *C*–Corolla, *D*–Calyx, *E*–Pedicel
69. A-3, B-4, C-2, D-1
70. Insects, pollination
71. Aestivation is the mode of arrangement of sepals or petals in a floral bud.
72. Valvate
73. Twisted aestivation
74. 2 (*Cassia*, Gulmohur), shows imbricate aestivation.
75. (d)
76. *A* – Valvate, *B* – Twisted, *C* – Imbricate, *D* – Vexillary
77. False. In angiosperms, each anther is usually bilobed and each lobe has two chambers.
78. Pollen sacs
79. Staminode
80. (a) If stamens are attached to perianth, they are called epiphyllous.
81. Lily
82. Polyandrous situation,
83. Monoadelphous, diadelphous, polyadelphous
84. (c) Polyadelphous
85. China rose, pea
86. Stigma, style, ovary
87. Ovary, style, stigma
88. False. The stigma is usually at the tip of the style and is the receptive surface for pollen grain.
89. Placenta
90. Apocarpous
91. Syncarpous
92. Placentation
93. False. In marginal placentation, the placenta forms a ridge along the ventral suture of the ovary and the ovules are borne on this ridge forming two rows.
94. Axile
95. Parietal placentation
96. False septum, parietal
97. Free central
98. Basal placentation
99. (c) Ovary becomes two chambered due to false septum.
100. A-3 B-5 C-2 D-1 E-4
101. Fruit
102. Parthenocarpic
103. (i) *A*–Epicarp, *B*–Mesocarp, *C*–Seed, *D*–Endocarp, (ii) Mango, (iii) Drupe.
104. (b) Coconut develops from monocarpellary superior ovary and bear single seed.
105. Coconut
106. Fertilised, seed coat, embryo
107. Radicle, embryonal axis, cotyledons
108. Seed coat, testa
109. Hilum

110. (c) Only B
111. Micropyle
112. (i) *A*–Cotyledons, *B*–Plumule, *C*–Radicle, *D*–Seed coat, *E*–Micropyle, *F*–Hilum
(ii) A–Cotyledons
113. Bean/Gram/Pea
114. They are all examples of non-endospermic seeds. Their endosperm is completely consumed in embryo nourishment.
115. Monocotyledonous
116. Aleurone layer
117. (b) I and II
118. False. Monocotyledonous seeds consist of one large and shield-shaped cotyledon known as scutellum.
119. Coleoptile, coleorhiza
120.

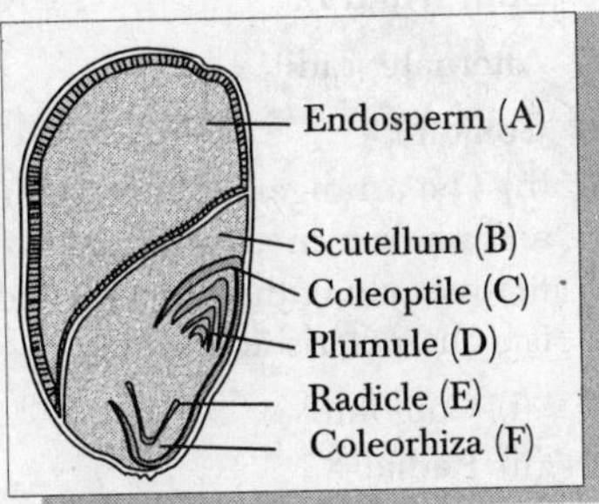

121. (a) The aleurone layer that separates the embryo is rich in protein.
122. The labelled part *A* is endosperm. It is present in *Castor* and maize seeds.
123. (b) Q (coleorhiza)
124. (i) Br, (ii) K, (iii) C, (iv) P, (v) A, (vi) G, (vii) $\underline{G}$, (viii) G, (ix) ⊕, (x) %
125. Floral diagram, number, arrangement
126. False. The position of the mother axis with respect to the flower is represented by a dot on the top of the floral diagram.
127. Cohesion, adhesion
128. $\oplus$ ⚥ $K_{(5)}\ \overset{\frown}{C_{(5)}\ A_5}\ \underline{G}_{(2)}$
129. (c) $\oplus K_5$
130. Potato family
131. All of them are the features of Solanaceae family, except non-endospermic character.
132. Alternate, simple, rarely pinnately compound, exstipulate and reticulate venation.
133. Cymose
134. False. The calyx and corolla of *Solanum nigrum* are five in number, united and with valvate aestivation.
135. (b) Leaves of the members of Solanaceae family are rarely pinnately compound. Potato plants are gamosepalous, gamopetalous, epipetalous with valvate aestivation.
136. (i) *Solanum nigrum*
(ii) Bicarpellary, syncarpous
(iii) Five, epipetalous
(iv) $\oplus$ ⚥ $K_{(5)}\ \overset{\frown}{C_{(5)}\ A_5}\ \underline{G}_{(2)}$
137. 6 (Belladonna, ashwagandha, tomato, brinjal, chilli, tobacco)
138. (i) Belladonna/Ashwagandha
(ii) *Petunia*

Competition Connect

1. Tap, adventitious
2. Prop root
3. Prop root
4. Stilt
5. (a) Respiration
6. False. Pneumatophores come out of the ground and grow vertically upwards.
7. (i) *Rhizophora*, (ii) True
8. (c) is mismatched pair. Pneumatophores help to get oxygen for respiration.
9. Adventitious, sweet potato
10. All of them are underground stem and are modified to store food.
11. (a) Cucumber-tendrils, *Citrus* thorns
12. Tendrils
13. All of them possess stem tendril.
14. (b) Both statements I and II are true.
15. Thorns
16. True
17. Thorns are found in *Citrus* and *Bougainvillea*.
18. Flattened, fleshy cylindrical
19. Runner
20. This is the species of *Oxalis* which shows runner type of modification.
21. Stolons
22. Offsets
23. False. Suckers are the lateral branches originating from the basal and underground portion of the stem, grow horizontally and give rise to leafy shoots.
24. A-4, B-3, C-1, D-2
25. Petiole, leaves
26. Venus flytrap, pitcher plant
27. *A*-Support (tendril), *B*–Protection (spine), *C*–Storage (fleshy leaves)
28. (b) In peas, leaves are modified into tendrils that support in climbing.
29. (i) Leaves are alternate, pinnately compound, pulvinate leaf base, stipulate, reticulate venation.
(ii) racemose, (iii) False. Flowers are bisexual and zygomorphic.
(iv) The plant twig (a) is of *Pisum sativum.*
30. 2 (Gamopetalous, twisted aestivation).
31. False. The calyx of pea flower is five in number with gamosepalous and valvate/imbricate condition.
32. (i) Androecium – Anther is ten in number, diadelphous, anther dithecous.
(ii) Gynoecium – Ovary superior, monocarpellary, unilocular, style single.
(iii) % ⚥ $K_{(5)}C_{1+2+(2)}A_{(9)+1}\underline{G}_1$
33. (i) Dye - *Indigofera*, (ii) Fibres - Sunhemp, (iii) Fodder - *Sesbania, Trifolium*,
(iv)Medicine - Muliathi,
(v) Ornamentals - Lupin, sweet pea
34. Members of Fabaceae family.
35. False. Flowers of Malvaceae family are bisexual.
36. Actinomorphic
37. 2 (epipetalous, syncarpous)
38. Crucifers
39. Brassicaceae
40. True

41. The seed of cabbage plant gets nourishment through endosperm.

42. Basal

43. (a) Sunflower has inferior ovary and is referred to as hypogynous.

44. Zygomorphic, actinomorphic

45. All except ebracteate

46. Poaceae

47. Wheat, jowar, sugarcane, oats.

48. parallel, one

49. superior, hypogynous

50. (i) Used as food for domesticated animals.
(ii) Sugarcane is used in production of sugar and gur.

51. (c) Flowers contain a stalk or pedicel

52. (b) Malvaceae–actinomorphic; Graminae–zygomorphic

Assertion-Reason Questions

1. (d) A is false, but R is true. A can be corrected as
The fine thread like structures present in the region of maturation are the root hairs.

2. (a) Both A and R are true and R is correct explanation of A.

3. (a) Both A and R are true and R is the correct explanation of A.

4. (c) A is true, but R is false. R can be corrected as
In guava plants, a pair of leaves arise from a single node and lie opposite to each other.

5. (a) Both A and R are true and R is correct explanation of A.

6. (b) Both A and R are true, but R is not the correct explanation of A.

7. (d) A is false, but reason is true. A can be corrected as
Castor seeds undergo double fertilisation and contain endosperm which provides food to the developing embryo.

8. (d) A is false, but R is true. A can be corrected as
Monocot seeds like maize contain endosperm that nourishes the embryo.

9. (a) Both A and R are true and R is correct explanation of A.

10. (c) A is true, but R is false. R can be corrected as
Flowers of Malvaceae family have many carpels and all the carpels remain fused.

Case Based Questions

1. (i)-(d), (ii)-(b), (iii)-(c), (iv) (c)
2. (i)-(a), (ii)-(a), (iii)-(d)

Competition Edge Up

1. (d) **2.** (a) **3.** (a) **4.** (c) **5.** (c) **6.** (d)
7. (d) **8.** (b) **9.** (a) **10.** (a) **11.** (a)

Chapter-6

Anatomy of Flowering Plants

1. Epidermal tissue system, ground or fundamental tissue system and vascular tissue system.

2. Epidermal cells, stomata, epidermal appendages.

3. Epidermis

4. False. Epidermis is made up of elongated, compactly arranged cells and forms a continuous layer.

5. Parenchymatous, vacuole

6. Cuticle

7. Roots have to absorb water and nutrients freely from the soil and the presence of cuticle would prevent it.

8. Transpiration, gaseous exchange

9. (c) Leaf epidermis

10. False. Bean-shaped guard cells are found in dicot and dumb-bell-shaped guard cells are found in monocot.

11. True

12. Thin, thickened

13. Guard cells

14. Subsidiary cells.

15. Epidermal cells

16. B–Dumb-bell-shaped stomata

17. Root hairs

18. Trichomes

19. False. Trichomes in the shoot system are usually multicellular.

20. True

21. Transpiration

22. (c) Unicellular elongations

23. False. Ground tissue constitutes all tissues except epidermis and vascular bundles.

24. Parenchyma, collenchyma, sclerenchyma

25. Mesophyll

26 Mesophyll is odd one out. All of them are part of the epidermal tissue system except mesophyll.

27. Phloem, xylem

28. False. Cambium is absent in monocot plants.

29. Open

30. Cambium is absent in monocotyledons, hence they do not show secondary growth.

31. (b) Dicot stem

32. (i) *B*, (ii) *A*, (iii) *A*, (iv) *B*, (v) *A*, (vi) Both *A* and *B*.

33. Alternate, radii

34. Conjoint

35. (b) The arrangement of xylem and phloem in an alternate manner along the different radii is a characteristic of roots.

36. (i) Conjoint
(ii) Radial
(iii) Conjoint

37. (c) Conjoint type of vascular bundles are more common in stems and roots.

38. Epiblema

39. Epiblema

40. Cortex

41. Endodermis

42. Endodermal layer

43. Casparian strips

44. Pericycle, parenchymatous

45. False. In dicot root, pith is usually absent.

46. *B*–Cortex, *C*–Endodermis, *D*–Xylem

47. (b) Pericycle is the thick walled parenchymatous layer present inner to the endodermis.
The parenchymatous cells between xylem and phloem in dicot roots forms the conjunctive tissue.

48. Root hair → Epidermis → Cortex → Endodermis → Pericycle → Phloem → Pith

49. (d) Stele

50. Cortex is odd one out. All of them constitute stele except cortex.

51. Dicot root

52. Radial, polyarch

53. (d) Vascular bundles are conjoint open type.

54. Casparian strip is present in endodermal cell C.

55. (b) Monocot roots have epidermal appendages that help in absorption of water and minerals.

56. (i) Monocot root
(ii) Monocot root
(iii) Dicot root

57. True

58. Hypodermis, cortical layer endodermis

59. Collenchymatous

60. (a) Hypodermis – collenchyma, cortical layer – parenchyma

61. Starch grain, starch sheath

62. Hypodermis, endodermis

63. Pericycle

64. A-2, B-1, C-4, D-3

65. *A*–Pith, *B*–Vascular bundle, *C*–Pericycle, *D*–Medullary ray

66. (a) Parenchyma

67. Medullary rays

68. False. The vascular bundles in dicot stem are arranged in a ring.

69. (b) Both statements I and II are true.

70. Pith

71. *A*–Phloem, *B*–Cambium *C*–Metaxylem, *D*–Pericycle, *E*–Protoxylem, *F*–Pith.

72. (d) I, III and IV

73. Sclerenchymatous

74. Closed

75. Monocot

76. (a) *A* can show secondary growth.

77. False. Dicotyledonous leaf is also known as dorsiventral leaf.

78. Adaxial

79. *A*–Bundle sheath cells, *B*–Spongy mesophyll, *C*–Palisade mesophyll

80. False. The abaxial surface of leaf bears more stomata than adaxial in dicot.

81. Mesophyll

82. (c) Bundle sheath

83. (i) Palisade parenchyma,
(ii) Spongy parenchyma

84. Veins, midrib

85. (a) The vascular bundles are surrounded by a layer of thick walled bundle sheath cells in a dicot leaf.

86. Bundle sheath

87. Isobilateral leaf

88. Stomata, palisade, spongy

89. (c) Presence of epidermis, mesophyll and vascular bundles.

90. Bulliform cell

91. Bulliform cell, exposed

92. Bulliform cell

93. Parallel venation

94. *A*–Adaxial epidermis, *B*–Mesophyll cell, *C*–Xylem

95. (d) 2

Competition Connect

1. Anatomy

2. Plant anatomy

3. True

4. Yes

5. Meristematic and permanent tissues

6. Meristems

7. (i) Present
(ii) Absent
(iii) Absent

8. Apical meristem

9. *A*–Leaf primordium, *B*–Shoot apical, *C*–Meristematic zone, *D*–Axillary bud

10. Distant region

11. *A*–Initials of central cylinder and cortex, *B*–Root apical meristem, *C*–Cortex, *D*–Protoderm, *E*–Root cap.

12. Axillary bud, branch or a flower

13. Intercalary meristem.

14. Leaves, internodes

15. Bamboo can grow about 60 cm/day because of the presence of intercalary meristem.

16. Intercalary meristem

17. Intercalary meristem, apical meristem

18. Lateral meristem

19. Lateral meristem

20. Fascicular vascular cambium, interfascicular cambium and cork cambium.

21. (b) Both statements I and II are true.

22. True

23. *A*–Secondary meristem, *B*–Apical meristem, *C*–Intercalary meristem, *E*–Ground meristem.

24. Permanent or mature cells.

25. Dermal tissues, ground tissues, vascular

26. False. The cells of permanent tissue have definite shape, size and function and they loose the power of division.

27. (i) Simple tissues
(ii) Complex tissues

28. 3 (Sclerechyma, parenchyma, collenchyma).

29. Parenchyma

30. Thin, cellulose

31. Photosynthesis, secretion

32. (b) Parenchyma cells are specialised cells responsible for functions like photosynthesis, storage, secretion.

33. living

34. *X*–Intercellular space

35. Collenchyma

36. (c) Suberin

37. Collenchyma

38. 3 (Having protoplasts, oval cells, contain chloroplast)

39. Fibres

40. Fibres

41. Sclereids

42. The gritty texture of guava is due to presence of sclereids.

43. (i) *A*–Pits, *B*–Lumen
(ii) Tea, legumes

44. (i) Parcenchyma tissues,
(ii) Sclerenchyma tissues,

45. Sclerenchymatous cells provide mechanical support because these are lignified, dead and without protoplast.

46. (b) Collenchyma tissue provides support, structure, mechanical strength to leaf veins, petiole and stem of young plants.
Sclereids are spherical, highly thickened dead cells, having narrow lumen.

47. Complex tissue

48. Xylem

49. Mechanical strength

50. Seive tube is odd one out, as it is a part of phloem. Other four are the parts of xylem.

51. Tracheids

52. False. Vessels are the most advance type of conductive element in xylem.

53. (b) Lignin

54. Vessel

55. *A*–Tracheid, *B*–Vessel

56. Lignified, devoid

57. Perforated

58. (b) Both statements I and II are true.

59. Xylem fibres

60. Xylem parenchyma

61. Parenchyma cells

62. Ray parenchymatous cell

63. (i) Protoxylem
(ii) Metaxylem

64. Periphery, centre

65. Stem

66. False. In exarch condition, protoxylem lies towards the periphery whereas metaxylem lies towards the centre.

67. Sieve tube elements, companion cells, phloem parenchyma and phloem fibres.

68. Albuminous

69. *A*–Sieve tube element, *B*–Phloem parenchyma, *C*–Companion cell

70. Companion cells and sieve tubes

71. Peripheral, nucleus

72. Living

73. Sieve tubes

74. Companion cells

75. (b) They are present in all vascular plants.

76. (c) Statements I, II and III are in correct.

77. 2 (Companion cells, phloem parenchyma)

78. A-2, B-3, C-1

79. Phloem fibres

80. Thick, protoplasm, dead

81. Lignified, cellulose

82. Sieve tubes

83. Metaphloem

84. Secondary

85. Patches, complete ring

86. (a) Apical meristem

87. Intrafascicular cambium

88. False. Interfascicular cambium is formed by the medullary rays.

89. (b) The cambial ring becomes active and begins to cut off new cells, both towards the inner and the outer sides.
The cells cut off towards pith, mature into secondary xylem.

90. *A*–Phellem, *B*–Phellogen, *C*–Medullary rays, *D*–Secondary xylem

91. False. Due to less activity of cambium in winter, it produces fewer xylary elements having narrow vessels.

92. Spring wood, early wood

93. Heartwood

94. Sapwood

95. (b) Spring wood-light colour, wide vessels
Autumn wood-dark colour, narrow vessels

96. A-4, B-6, C-5, D-1, E-2, F-3

97. (c) It arises in the outer octex of woody plants and forms cork for protection.

98. Phellogen, rectangular

99. False. Phellogen cuts of cells on both sides, i.e. outer cell is known as phellem and inner cell is known as phelloderm.

100. Periderm

101. Bark

102. Hard

103. Lenticels

104. *A*–Complimentary cells, *B*–Secondary cortex

105. Lenticels

106. *A*–Cortex, *B*–Vascular cambium, *C*–Secondary xylem, *D*–Primary xylem

Assertion-Reason Questions

1. (a) Both A and R are true and R is correct explanation of A.

2. (c) A is true, but R is false. R can be corrected as
The thin cells of parenchyma are closely packed or have small intercellular spaces between them.

3. (c) A is true, but R is false. R can be corrected as
Sclerenchyma is a simple permanent tissue that provides mechanical strength.

4. (d) A is false, but R is true. A can be corrected as
In stems, protoxylem lies towards the centre while metaxylem lies towards the periphery of the organ.

5. (d) A is false, but R is true. A can be corrected as
The stomatal pore is lined by guard cells with outer thin walls and inner thick walls.

6. (b) Both A and R are true, but R is not the correct explanation of A.

7. (c) A is true, but R is false. R can be corrected as
The endodermal cells have a deposition of water impermeable waxy material called suberin in the form of casparian strips.

8. (a) Both A and R are true and R is correct explanation of A.

9. (a) Both A and R are true and R is correct explanation of A.

10. (a) Both A and R are true and R is the correct explanation of A.

Case Based Questions

1. (i) d (ii) d (iii) c
2. (i) a (ii) b (iii) b

Competition Edge Up

1. (d) **2.** (a) **3.** (a) **4.** (c) **5.** (a)
6. (d) **7.** (d) **8.** (a) **9.** (d) **10.** (b)

Chapter-7

Structural Organisation in Animals

1. Epithelial, connective, muscular, neural

2. (a) Basic tissues forming an organisation. prove essential for more efficient and better coordinated activities of millions of cells constituting an organism.

3. Mimicry

4. (c) To protect against extreme heat

5. Endothermy is odd one out because frogs do not have constant body temperature.

6. False. The skin of frog is slippery and smooth due to the presence of mucus.

7. Head, trunk

8. (i) Nictitating membrane
(ii) 4
(iii) 5
(iv) Swimming, leaping burrowing

9. (a) A-3, B-1, C-4, D-2

10. (ii) Male frog can be distinguished from female frog by the presence of vocal sacs and copulatory pad on the first digit of the forelimb.

11. Carnivores

12. (i) False. In frog, excess of the bile juice secreted by the liver is stored in gall bladder.
(ii) False. In frog, for the digestion of food, walls of the stomach secrete HCl and gastric juice.
(iii) True

13. (b) Liver-bile, Stomach-HCl

14. *A*–Gall bladder, *B*–Lung, *C*–Fat bodies, *D*–Kidney, *E*–Rectum, *F*–Urinary bladder

15. (b) The pancreas is a digestive gland that produces pancreatic juice containing digestive enzymes that aid in digestion of food.

16. (i) False. Frogs respire on land and in the water by two different methods. In water, skin act as aquatic respiratory organ (cutaneous respiration.)
(ii) True
(iii) True

17. Skin

18. Closed type

19. Two atria and one ventricle

20. (c) I and III

21. Right atrium

22. (c) A-Sinus venosus
B-Conus arteriosus

23. Vena cava

24. Ventral

25. Veins

26. Intestine

27. Renal portal system

28. (i) Pulmonary respiration
(ii) Pericardium

29. (a) The composition of lymph is different from blood as it lack few proteins and RBCs.

30. 4(All of them except blood without RBC and WBC).

31. Paired kidney, ureters, urinary bladder and cloaca

32. (i) Urinogenital ducts
(ii) Nephrons
(iii) Excretory and reproductive ducts
(iv) Ureotelic animal

33. Highly evolved neural system and endocrine glands

34. 10

35. (i) Olfactory lobes, unpaired diencephalon and paired cerebral hemispheres
(ii) Optic lobes
(iii) Cerebellum and medulla oblongata

36. (b) Both statements I and II are true.

37. Cellular aggregations around nerve endings

38. (a) Hearing-Tympanum with external ears.

39. (b) A-4, B-2, C-1, D-3

40. A–3, B–1, C–2, D–4

41. 10-12

42. 3(Urine, sperm, faecal matter).

43. Testes → Vasa efferentia (*A*) → Kidney → Bidder's canal (*B*) → Urinogenital duct → Cloaca (*C*)

44. (b) Vasa efferentia are 10-12 in number that arises from the testis in frogs and opens into the Bidder's canal.

45. *A*–Vasa efferentia, *B*–Testis, *C*–Adrenal gland, *D*–Fat body, *E*–Kidney

46. *A*–Oviduct, *B*–Ovary, *C*–Ova, *D*–Cloaca, *E*–Urinary bladder

47. True

48. 22500-3000 ova.

49. (d) Fertilisation takes place inside the female body in the water.

50. (i) External
(ii) Tadpole
(iii) Metamorphosis
(iv) Muscular legs

51. (b) III and IV.

Competition Connect

1. Tissues

2. 4, 2

3. Structure and function

4. Epithelial tissue

5. (i) Compound epithelium
(ii) Simple epithelium

6. Squamous, cuboidal and columnar epithelium.

7. *A* - Squamous epithelium, *B* - Simple cuboidal epithelium, *C* - Simple columnar epithelium, *D* - Columnar cells bearing cilia

8. A-2-M, B-3-N, C-4-K, D-1-L

9. (i) Cuboidal epithelium
(ii) Ciliated columnar epithelium
(iii) Squamous epithelium
(iv) Columnar epithelium

10. (i) Simple squamous epithelium
(ii) Simple cuboidal epithelium and columnar epithelium
(iii) Ciliated epithelium

11. Ciliated epithelium

12. Glandular, unicellular and multicellular

13. *A*– (i) Multicellular, (ii) Cluster of cells, (iii) Cells of salivary gland.
B– (i) Unicellular, (ii) Isolated cells, (iii) Goblet cells of alimentary canal.

14. (a) A-1, B-2, C-4, D-3

15. Exocrine and Endocrine glands.

16. Sweat glands and mammary glands.

17. Hormones

18. Endocrine glands

19. 3 Statements (i, iii and iv) are related to compound epithelium. Statement II is incorrect and can be corrected as. It has limited role in secretion and absorption.

20. (i) True (ii) True

21. Cell junctions

22. A-2, B-3, C-1

23. Blood

24. *X*-Areolar tissue, *A*-Macrophages, *B*-Fibroblast, *C*-Collagen fibres, *D*-Mast cells

25. (i) Fibres
(ii) Bone, adipose and cartilage

26. Loose connective tissue

27. Areolar tissue

28. Adipose tissue

29. *X*-Adipose tissue, *A*-Fat storage area, *B*-Nucleus, *C*-Plasma membrane

30. (i) Dense connective tissue
(ii) Dense regular tissue
(iii) Dense irregular tissue

31. (a) Skin is a dense irregular connective tissue that has fibroblasts and collagen oriented differently.

32. (b) B

33. *A*-Dense irregular connective tissue, *B*-Dense regular connective tissue

34. A-2, B-4, C-1, D-3

35. Cartilage

36. Tip of nose, outer ear, joints between adjacent bones of vertebral column.

37. Bone

38. Osteocytes, lacunae

39. Bone marrow

40. Blood

41. *A*–Collagen fibres, *B*–Cartilage cell (chondrocytes)

42. A–3, B–1, C–2, D–4

43. Myofibrils

44. A-1-M, B-3- L, C-2-K

45. *A* – Multinucleate
B – Uninucleate
C – Non-striated and spindle-shaped, *D* – Striated, Cylindrical with intercalated discs, *E* – Voluntary, *F* – Involuntary, *G* – Very rapid contraction and soon get fatigued, *H* – Rapid contraction and never get fatigued, *I* – Present attached to skeletal bones, *J* – Wall of internal organs such as the blood vessel, stomach and intestine

46. True

47. Neural tissue

48. Neuron

49. *A*-Axon, *B*-Cell body with nucleus, *C*-Dendrite, *D*-Neuroglea

50. Neuroglial cell

51. Brain and spinal cord

52. True

53. Insecta, Arthropoda

54. Head, thorax and abdomen

55. Chitin

56. Sclerites

57. Sternites

58. True

59. *A* – Prothoracic leg,
B – Mesothorax,
C – Metathorax,
D – Tegmina, *E* – Anal cerci

60. 6

61. Flexible neck

62. Chewing and biting

63. Tongue

64. *A* – Mandible, *B* – Maxilla, *C* – Labium, *D* – Labrum

65. (c) Hypopharynx-tongue

66. *A*–Labrum, *B*–Mandible, *C*–Hypopharynx, *D*–Maxilla, *E*–Labium

67. 3 (Prothorax, mesothorax and metathorax).

68. (b) The head of cockroach has 6 fused segments and show mobility in all directions. Cockroach head is connected with thorax by a short extension of the prothorax known as the neck.

69. (i) All the three thoracic segments, i.e. prothorax mesothorax and metathorax
(ii) Mesothorax, metathorax

70. 3 statements, i.e. (i), (ii) and (iii) are correct. Forewings are not used in flight.

71. 10

72. Boat-shaped

73. Brood or Genital pouch

74. Gonopore

75. Anal cerci

76. *A*–Salivary gland, *B*–Crop *C*–Gizzard, *D*–Malpighian tubules, *E*–Ileum

77. Crop

78. Foregut and midgut

79. 100-150

80. Midgut and hindgut

81. Malpighian tubules

82. Pharynx → Oesophagus → Crop → Gizzard → Ileum → Colon → Rectum

83. *A*–Anterior aorta, *B*–Alary muscles, *C*–Chambers of heart

84. False. Blood of a cockroach contains colourless plasma and haemocytes.

85. Abdomen

86. *A*–Heart, *B*–To sinuses

87. network of trachea

88. Oxygen, sphincters

89. Diffusion

90. Fat bodies, nephrocytes and urecose glands

91. True

92. Supra-oesophageal ganglion

93. Mandible

94. Dorsal, 2000 hexagonal

95. ommatidia

96. (d) III and IV

97. (ii) More sensitive with less resolution

98. *A*–Phallic gland
B–Testis
C–Seminal vesicle
D–Ejaculatory duct

99. *A*–Collaterial glands, *B*–Genital chamber, *C*–Vestibulum, *D*–Spermatheca, *E*–Gonapophyses

100. Mushroom gland

101. (i) Male Gonapophysis or phallomere
(ii) phallomere

102. (i) Seminal vesicles
(ii) Spermatophores

103. True

104. (b) The mushroom shaped gland in a male cockroach is located in 6th, 7th abdominal segment.

105. A–3, B–1, C–2, D–4

106. (i) Oothecae

107. (b) Development of *P. americana* is paurometabolous, i.e. there is development through nymphal stage.

108. Wing pads

109. Both forewings and hindwings develop

110. (i) Omnivorous, (ii) Dioecious, (iii) Coelomate, (iv) Serious pest and vector of several diseases.

Assertion-Reason Questions

1. (d) A is false, but R is true. A can be corrected as
Tubular parts of nephrons are made up of cuboidal epithelium.

2. (b) Both A and R are true, but R is not the correct explanation of A.
Most of the epithelial cells are packed together with little intercellular spaces as they form a continuous barrier between the interior and exterior of the body.

3. (d) A is false, but R is true. A can be corrected as
In cockroaches two antenna arise from sockets located in front of the eyes.

4. (c) A is true, but R is false. R can be corrected as
Malpighian tubules help in removal of excretory products like uric acid from the haemolymph.

5. (a) Both A and R are true and R is the correct explanation of A.

6. (a) Both A and R are true and R is the correct explanation of A.

7. (c) A is true, but R is false. R can be corrected as
Male frogs bear a copulatory pad on the first digit of the forelimbs which are absent in female frogs.

8. (a) Both A and R are true and R is the correct explanation of A.

9. (a) Both A and R are true and R is the correct explanation of A.

10. (a) Both A and R are true and R is the correct explanation of A.

Case Based Questions

1. (i) (b) (ii) (d) (iii) (d)
2. (i) (b) (ii) (a) (iii) (c)

Competition Edge Up

1. (c) **2.** (b) **3.** (a) **4.** (b) **5.** (a)
6. (a) **7.** (c) **8.** (a) **9.** (c) **10.** (a)

Chapter-8

Cell : The Unit of Life

1. Unicellular, multicellular
2. Cell
3. Antonie von Leeuwenhoek
4. Robert Hooke
5. Electron microscope
6. Matthias Schleiden
7. Animal
8. Presence of cell wall
9. Cells, its product
10. A-2, B-3, C-4, D-1
11. Cell theory, new cells were formed.
12. New cells are derived from pre-existing cells.
13. False. Rudolf Virchow modified the hypothesis of Schleiden and Schwann to give the cell theory a final shape, according to which all living organisms are composed of cells and all cells arise from pre-existing cells.
14. These are considered to be exceptions to cell theory.
15. Nucleus
16. Eukaryotic cell
17. Cytoplasm
18. Cytoplasm
19. All of them are absent in prokaryotes, except ribosomes.
20. Lysosomes is the odd one out as all of them contain ribosomes, except lysosomes.
21. Centrosome
22. An ostrich
23. A-3, B.-4, C-1, D- 2
24. (a) A-3, B-1, C-4, D-2
25. Nerve cell
26. Red blood cell
27. 7.0 µm
28. *A*–Round and biconcave, *B*–Amoeboid, *C*–Long and narrow, *D*–Round and oval, *E*–Branched and long *F*–Elongated
29. (b) Both statements I and II are true.
30. 3 (i, ii, iii). Prokaryotic cell does not contain defined nucleus and peroxisomes.
31. Comma-shaped
32. All of them possess cell wall, except *Mycoplasma.*
33. Naked, nuclear
34. Plasmid
35. 3(i, ii, iii). Plasmids are of different types thus, (iv) is not correct.
36. (i) Prokaryotic
(ii) False. The size of this cell range between 1-2 µm.
37. Three
38. two
39. Hans Christian Gram
40. Gram positive, Gram negative
41. False. The composition and thickness of glycocalyx is different among different bacteria.
42. Slime layer
43. Capsule
44. (iii). As cell wall prevent bursting of cell.
45. Plasma membrane
46. Glycocalyx → Cell wall → Plasma membrane
47. Mesosome
48. 3 (Form of vesicles, Tubules, Lamellae)
49. 6(i, ii, iii, iv, v, vi)
50. Cyanobacteria
51. Flagella
52. True

53. (a) The capsule in a bacterial cell lies outside the bacterial cell. It increases the adherence of the bacteria to surfaces.
54. Filament, hook, basal body
55. Filament
56. A-3, B-2, C-1
57. Fimbriae
58. (b) Q
59. Plasma membrane
60. 15nm to 20nm
61. (a) Prokaryotic ribosomes are made up to two sub-units 50S and 30S, which when present together, form 70S prokaryotic ribosomes.
62. False. The prokaryotic ribosome is made up of 60% *r*RNA and 40% ribosomal protein.
63. Polyribosomes or Polysome
64. Inclusion bodies
65. Inclusion bodies
66. Blue-green, purple and green photosynthetic bacteria.
67. Eukaryotic cell
68. Eukaryotic cell
69. True
70. Plant cell
71. Centrioles
72. *A*–Nucleolus, *B*–Rough endoplasmic reticulum, *C*–Smooth endoplasmic reticulum, *D*–Vacuole
73. *A*–Microvilli, B–Plasma membrane, C–Cytoplasm *D*–Ribosome, *E*–Centriole
74. Electron microscope
75. Phospholipids
76. False. In bilayer membrane, the lipids polar head lies towards the outer side and tails towards the inner side.
77. Polar head of lipid bilayer
78. Saturated
79. A-2, B-3, C-1
80. Integral, peripheral
81. Peripheral protein
82. Integral
83. (a) Position on the membrane
84. False. Integral membrane proteins are difficult to extract.
85. False. Singer and Nicolson proposed a cell membrane structure model known as fluid mosaic model.
86. Lateral
87. Fluidity
88. (i) *A*–Peripheral protein, *B*–Phospholipid bilayer, *C*–Integral protein, *D*–Cholesterol,
(ii) Fluid mosaic model
89. False. Glycolipids and cholesterol are usually present in the membrane of the animal cells.
90. 5(ii, iii, v, vi, vii)
91. Selectively permeable
92. Only certain molecules to pass through, impermeable.
93. (b) The cell membrane possesses a hydrophobic core that prevents the polar molecules to cross the membrane freely.
94. Passive
95. Neutral solutes
96. Diffusion
97. Osmosis
98. Protein
99. Facilitated diffusion
100. The entry of glucose in erythrocytes takes place *via* facilitated diffusion.
101. Active
102. False. A process of transport which require energy in the form of ATP is known as active transport.
103. The transport of Na^+/K^+ takes place by active transport.
104. A-4, B-3, C-2, D-1
105. Non-living
106. Fungi, plants
107. False. The cell wall gives shape to the cell and protects the cell from mechanical damage and infection.
108. False. The cell wall helps in cell to cell interaction and provides barrier to undesirable macromolecules.
109. 4(cellulose, galactans, mannans, calcium carbonate).
110. A-3, B-2, C-1
111. (b) The middle lambella that glues the adjacent plant cells, is made up of calcium pectate.
112. (d) Transport of nutrients
113. Secondary wall → Primary wall → Middle lamella
114. Primary wall
115. Holds or glues
116. False. The plasmodesmata pass through the cell wall and middle lamella.
117. Plasmodesmata
118. All of these are the part of endomembrane system, except peroxisomes.
119. Coordinated
120. Endoplasmic reticulum
121. Luminal (inside ER), Extraluminal (Cytoplasm)
122. Ribosomes
123. Ribosome absent
124. Protein
125. RER
126. Lipid molecule and steroid hormones.
127. *A*-Rough Endoplasmic Reticulum (RER), *B*-Smooth Endoplasmic Reticulum (SER)
128. (a) The RER is involved in protein synthesis while SER synthesises lipids. Both of these combine together to form plasma membrane *via* membrane biogenesis.
129. Camillo Golgi (1898)
130. Golgi apparatus
131. False. The Golgi apparatus consist of many flat, disc-shaped sacs or cisternae.
132. 0.5μm, 1.0 μm
133. Parallel
134. This is Golgi apparatus. *A*–Cisternae
135. (b) Both statements I and II are true.
136. Cell membrane, nucleus
137. Forming
138. (i) Different, but interconnected
139. (d) All of the above would be altered.
140. Packaging
141. (ii) Materials to be packaged in the form of vesicles from the ER fuses with the *cis* face of the Golgi apparatus and move towards the maturing face.
142. Vesicles
143. True
144. *Trans*
145. True
146. Glycoproteins, glycolipids
147. Vesicular

148. False. Lysosomes are formed by the process of packaging in the Golgi apparatus.
149. Hydrolytic enzyme
150. All of these are hydrolytic enzymes, present in lysosomes.
151. (d) Lysosomes
152. Acidic
153. True
154. (ii), Lysosomes contain hydrolytic enzyme, these enzymes are capable of digesting the substances of their own cell.
155. Vacuole
156. 5 (Water, sap, carbon dioxide, anthocyanin and excretory product)
157. Tonoplast
158. 90%
159. False. The tonoplast facilitates the transport of a number of ions and other materials against concentration gradient.
160. (a) Movement of ions across the tonoplast occurs actively from cytoplasm to the vacuoles.
161. Ions concentration of cytoplasm < Ions concentration of vacuole
162. Contractile vacuole
163. Food vacuole
164. A-2, B-1, C-4, D-3
165. False. Mitochondria, unless specifically stained are not easily visible under the microscope.
166. Meristematic cell
167. Shape, size
168. Shape–sausage or cylindrical shaped and size–diameter (0.2-1.0 μm) and length (1.0-4.1 μm)
169. Double
170. Two
171. *A*–Matrix, *B*–Crista, *C*–Inner membrane.
172. Matrix
173. (b) B
174. Outer membrane
175. Inner membrane
176. Cristae
177. Mitochondria
178. ATP, powerhouse
179. Matrix
180. (a) Sperm cells have increased number of mitochondria in order to facilitate the movement of sperm.
181. 70S
182. Fission
183. Plastids
184. Pigments
185. Chloroplasts, chromoplasts, leucoplasts
186. A-2, B-1, C-3
187. Aleuroplasts
188. Rhodoplast is odd one out as all other options are types of leucoplast.
189. (a) A-2, B-3, C-1, D-4
190. Carotene, xanthophyll
191. (b) Statements II, IV and V are correct.
192. Mesophyll
193. 1, 20-40
194. True
195. Inner membrane
196. Stroma
197. Stroma
198. (i) *B*–Granum or integral thylakoid, (ii) *A*–Thylakoid, (iii) Stroma lamellae
199. Stroma lamellae
200. True
201. Stroma
202. Ribosomes
203. Cytoplasmic ribosome
204. Ribosomes
205. George Palade (1953)
206. Ribosomes
207. (i) Eukaryotic cell, (ii) Prokaryotic cell
208. (i) 80S (ii) 70S
209. Density, size
210. False. The ribosomes are organised by nucleosome and are made out of RNA and protein.
211. False. The sedimentation coefficient is a measure of density and size.
212. Cytoskeleton
213. 3 (Mechanical support, motility, shape of the cell).
214. Cytoskeleton elements
215. Cilia and flagella
216. False. Cilia are small structures which work like oars, causing the movement of either the cell or the surrounding fluid.
217. Longer, movement
218. Different
219. Plasma membrane
220. Axoneme, microtubules
221. 9 + 2 arrangement
222. (i) *A*–Central microtubule *B*–Central sheath, *C*–Peripheral microtubules (doublets), *D*–Interdoublet bridge, *E*–Radial spoke
(ii) Nine pairs at periphery and 1 pair at centre.
223. (b) Radial spoke
224. Bridges
225. Radial spoke
226. Nine
227. Centriole, basal
228. (a) Cilia and flagella emerge from centriole like structure called basal bodies.
229. (b) Peripheral triplets of centrioles
230. False. The two cylindrical structures of a centrosome is called centrioles.
231. Amorphous pericentriolar material.
232. Perpendicular
233. Tubulin, triplet
234. (i) Hub, (ii) Radial spoke
235. Cilia, flagella
236. Spindle apparatus
237. (b) Both statements I and II are true.
238. Chromatin
239. Nucleoprotein, nucleoli
240. Perinuclear
241. True
242. Ribosomes
243. (i) *A*–Nuclear pore, *B*–Nucleolus, *C*–Nucleoplasm, *D*–Nuclear membrane
(ii) *A*–Nuclear pore
(iii) *C*–Nucleoplasm.
244. 2
245. (c) Ribosomes would not be synthesised
246. Zero. Both of these lack nucleus.
247. Nucleoli
248. False. The content of nucleolus is continuous with rest of the nucleoplasm because it is not a membrane bound structure.
249. Nucleoli
250. A-3, B-4, C-1, D-2.
251. *Paramecium*
252. Chromatin, chromosomes

253. DNA, histones, non-histones, RNA
254. 2, 46
255. Centromere
256. (c) kinetochore
257. (i) *A*–Kinetochore
(ii) *B*–Chromatids
258. Centromere
259. A-3, B-2, C-4, D-1
260. (i) Metacentric, (ii) Telocentric
261. Sub-metacentric
262. Acrocentric
263. False. A few chromosomes have non-staining secondary constrictions at a constant location, it gives the appearance of a small fragment called satellite.
264. (a) Statements I and II are incorrect.
265. Microbodies

Assertion-Reason Questions

1. (a) Both A and R are true and R is correct explanation of A.
2. (c) A is true, but R is false. R can be corrected as
The cell wall provides resistance against the water pressure within.
3. (d) A is false, but R is true. A can be corrected as
Prokaryotic cells lack important organelles like mitochondria, but contain mesosomes that perform cellular respiration.
4. (d) A is false, but R is true. A can be corrected as
The presence of polysomes in a cell cannot confirm its prokaryotic or eukaryotic nature as polysomes can be present in both prokaryotes and eukaryotes.
5. (c) A is true, but R is false. R can be corrected as
Peripheral membrane proteins are easier to extract out of the membrane compared to the integral ones.
6. (d) A is false, but R is true. A can be corrected as
The hydrolases present in the lysosomal compartments are activated at acidic pH.
7. (b) Both A and R are true and R is not the correct explanation of A.

Case Based Questions

1. (i) b (ii) a (iii) c (iv) d
2. (i) a (ii) d (iii) c

Competition Edge Up

1. (a) **2.** (b) **3.** (d) **4.** (c) **5.** (a)
6. (b) **7.** (b) **8.** (b) **9.** (a) **10.** (a)
11.(b)

Chapter-9

Biomolecules

1. Carbon, hydrogen, oxygen, nitrogen.
2. True
3. *A*–0.5, *B*–18.5, *C*–46.6, *D*–3.3, *E*–2.8
4. Trichloroacetic acid
5. (i) Cheesecloth or cotton
(ii) *A*–Acid soluble pool, *B*–Acid insoluble pool,
(iii) Acid soluble pool (*A*)
6. Separation
7. Analytical technique gives an idea of molecular formula and structure of the organic compound.
8. Biomolecules
9. Wet weight
10. Ash
11. (i) *A*–Burn, (ii) Calcium, magnesium
12. Sulphate, phosphate
13. Hydrogen, oxygen, chlorine, carbon
14. Organic, inorganic
15. (i) Chemistry student can identify functional groups like aldehydes, ketones, aromatic compounds, etc.
(ii) Biology student can identify amino acid, nucleotide bases, fatty acids, etc.
16. Amino acids
17. α-amino acids
18. (ii) The chemical formula of methane is CH_4 in which four valence position of carbon is occupied by hydrogen. Similarly in amino acids, the four valence position occupied by four substituent groups.
19. Hydrogen, carboxyl group, amino group, variable group
20. False. On the basis of the nature of *R*-group there are many amino acids.
21. Twenty
22. Glycine
23. A-3, B-1, C-4, D-2
24. Alanine
25. False. The physical and chemical properties of amino acids are dependent on amino, carboxyl and *R*-functional groups.
26. Amino
27. Basic
28. Neutral
29. Arginine is odd one out, because all of them are neutral amino acids, except arginine.
30. (a) Valine is a neutral amino acid while lysine is basic.
31. Acidic
32. All of them are aromatic amino acid.
33.
34. (c) Molecule with overall charge as O.
35. (i) *B*, (ii) *A*, (iii) *C*
36. Insoluble, Fatty acids
37. Carboxyl
38. 16
39. (d) Carbohydrate group; $-CH_3$; C_2H_5; 1 to 19.
40. (i) Without double bond,
(ii) With one or more double bonds.
41. Trihydroxy propane
42. True
43. Monoglycerides, diglycerides, triglycerides
44. (b) Both statements I and II are true.
45. Lower
46. Phosphorylated, cell membrane
47. Palmitic acid

48. (i) *A*– $(CH_2)_{14}$, (ii) *A*–OH, *B*–OH

49. (b) Lecithin, Cell membrane

50. 3, as shown below

$$\begin{array}{l} \qquad\qquad\qquad\quad CH_2-O-\overset{\displaystyle O}{\overset{\|}{C}}-R_1 \\ R_2-\overset{\displaystyle O}{\overset{\|}{C}}-O-\underset{\displaystyle A}{CH} \\ \qquad\qquad\qquad\quad CH_2-O-\overset{\displaystyle O}{\overset{\|}{C}}-R_3 \end{array}$$

51. (i) Cholesterol (ii) steroid

52. Nitrogen base

53.

O, HN, O, N, H

54. Nucleosides

55. Nucleoside

56. Nucleotide

57. Nucleotide

58. (b) Adenylic acid, uridylic acid, thymidylic acid, etc. are nucleotide while adenosine thymine, cytidine, etc. are nucleoside.
Nitrogenous bases when found attached to sugar and phosphate are nucleotides.

59.

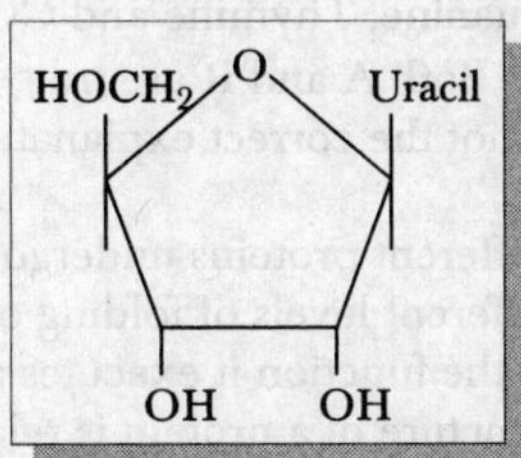

60. The new structure formed in Adenosine

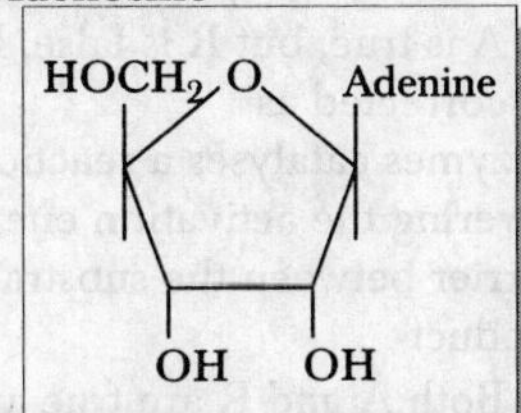

61. (c) Phosphate

62. Nucleotides

63. Metabolites

64. False. The metabolites which are required for the growth and maintenance of cellular functions are called primary metabolites.

65. 3 (Alanine, thiamine, uridine)

66. True

67. Secondary metabolites

68. A-4, B-1, C-2, D-6, E-3 F-7, G-5

69. Rubber, drugs, spices, scents, pigments.

70. (a) A-4, B-5, C-1, D-2

71. 18 to 800

72. True

73. Biomolecules

74. Acid soluble

75. (i) 800, (ii) Insoluble, (iii) (b)

76. Polymerisation

77. Cytoplasmic

78. A-4, B-1, C-3, D-2

79. Water > Protein > Carbohydrate > Lipid

80. Amino acids, peptide

81. Homopolymer

82. Dietary proteins

83. Essential

84. Serine

85. A-3, B-1, C-5, D-6, E-2, F-4

86. RuBisCO (Ribulose Bisphosphate Carboxylase Oxygenase)

87. (b) The amino acids that are taken into the body through diet are the essential amino acids. Since, they are not naturally synthesised in our bodies.

88. Monosaccharides

89. Polysaccharides

90. Inulin

91. All of them are monosaccharides except sucrose.

92. (c) Inulin is a polymer of repeating glucose units.

93. (i) Glycogen (ii) True

94. Iodine

95. False. Cellulose does not contain complex helices and hence cannot hold I_2.

96. (i) Glycogen, (ii) Cellulose, (iii) Chitin

97. (b) Cellulose, an important component of plant cell wall is a homopolymer and not a heteropolymer.

98. 3

99. Glucosamine, N-acetyl galactosamine

100. Nucleic acids

101. Monosaccharide, heterocyclic compound, phosphoric acid

102. False. Purine and pyrimidines posses heterocyclic ring in nucleic acids.

103. A-1, 4; B-2, 3, 5

104. Ribonucleotide, deoxyribonucleotide

105. True

106. Molecular formulae

107. (i) Two dimensions, (ii) Three dimensions, (iii) Four levels

108. Positional

109. Primary structure

110. False. If a protein is imagined as a line, the left end represented by first amino acid is known as N-terminal amino acid.

111. C-terminal

112. Helix

113. Right

114. Secondary

115. (c) Both statements I and II are true.

116. (i) *A*–α-helix, *B*–β-pleated sheet, (ii) Right

117. Tertiary

118. Tertiary

119. (i) Tertiary structure,
(ii) van der Waals' forces, electrostatic bond and hydrogen bond.

120. *A* – Secondary structure,
B – Tertiary structure

121. Quaternary

122. (b) Subunits

123. (i) Quaternary structure,
(ii) False. The protein subunits are arranged one upon each other in the form of a cube.

124. Quaternary structure, 4

125. Ribozymes.

126. Active

127. The active site of an enzyme is a crevice or pocket into which substrate fits.

128. (i) Inorganic catalyst works efficiently at high temperature while enzyme gets denatured.

(ii) High pressure is favourable for inorganic catalyst while it affects the efficiency of enzyme.

129. True

130. 2 (ii, v)

131. Rate

132. (i) False. It is affected by temperature.
(ii) Doubles or decreases

133. (b) Both statements I and II are true.

134. (c) The rate of a reaction is the amount of product formed per unit time.

135. (i) The rate of the reaction will increase due to the catalysis process of enzymes.
(ii) The rate of the reaction would not be affected due to the absence of enzymes.

136. (i) Carbonic anhydrase, (ii) (a), (iii) True

137. (i) *A*–Aerobic condition, *B*–Anaerobic condition,
(ii) *C*–Fermentation,
(iii) 10 different enzymes (during glycolysis)
(iv) Yeast, (v) Skeletal muscles of human.

138. Substrate (S)

139. False. The substrate does not change the conformation of active site during binding process.

140. (a) Both statements I and II are true.

141. Transition

142. Product

143. Substrate

144. Structural state

145. Transition state

146. Activation energy

147. (c) B is an enzymatic reaction

148. (i) *A*–Activation energy without enzyme, *B*–Activation energy with enzyme, *C*–Transition state,
(ii) Graph (2),
(iii) Exothermic, (iv) The rate of graph 1 is low because of large activation energy.

149. Lowered

150. (c) i, iv, ii, iii

151. (i) *A*–ES, *B*–P, (ii) False. Complex *A* is short lived and reactive
(iii) True
(iv) Intermediate complex
(v) E + S

152. *A*–Active site, *B*–Enzyme, *C*–Breakdown, *D*–Enzyme-Product complex

153. (ii) Enzymes are used in very small concentrations because the chemical reactants do not cause any alteration in the composition or physiology of the enzyme. The same enzyme molecule can be used again and again.

154. Tertiary

155. True

156. (i) Slope *A*, (ii) *C*, (iii) *B*

157. (b) Higher temperature denatures enzymes

158. Increases, active sites

159. V_{max}

160. (i) Velocity of reaction α initial substrate, (ii) High concentration, (iii) K_m (Michaelis - Menten's constant)

161. True

162. Inhibition, inhibitor

163. Competitive

164. (b) Competitive inhibitor bears structural similarities with the substrate.
Due to its close structural similarity with the substrate the inhibitor competes with the substrate for substrate binding site of the enzyme. As a result, the substrate fails to bind.

165. Competitive

166. Malonate

167. Bacterial pathogens.

168. Oxidoreductases/ dehydrogenases

169. Transferases

170. True

171. Lyases

172. False. Isomerases include all enzymes that catalyse the interconversion of optical, geometric or positional isomers.

173. Ligases

174. (a) A-3, B-2, C-4, D-1

175. Cofactor

176. Apoenzymes.

177. Prosthetic group, coenzyme, metal ions.

178. (b) Apoenzyme is the protein part of the enzyme which remains inactive without the cofactor.

179. Prosthetic group, apoenzyme

180. Haem

181. Coenzyme

182. Vitamin

183. Metal ions

184. Zinc

185. Hydrogen

186. True

187. A-2, B-3, C-1

Assertion-Reason Questions

1. (a) Both A and R are true and R is the correct explanation of A.

2. (b) Both A and R are true, but R is not the correct explanation of A.
A zwitter ion is one that carries both positive and negative charges because of its ionizable nature in solutions of different pH.

3. (a) Both A and R are true and R is the correct explanation of A.

4. (a) Both A and R are true and R is the correct explanation of A.

5. (d) A is false, but R is true. A can be corrected as
Cellulose does not contain complex helices and thus do not turn blue in colour when reacted with iodine.

6. (d) A is false, but R is true. A can be corrected as
The heterocyclic compounds in DNA could be Adenine, Guanine, Thymine and Cytosine.

7. (b) Both A and R are true, but R is not the correct explanation of A.
Different proteins undergo different levels of folding owing to the function it executes as structure of a protein is related to the function it performs.

8. (a) Both A and R are true and R is the correct explanation of A.

9. (c) A is true, but R is false. R can be corrected as
Enzymes catalyses a reaction, by lowering the activation energy barrier between the substrate and product

10. (a) Both A and R are true and R is the correct explanation of A.

Case Based Questions

1. (i) (b) (ii) (c) (iii) (b) (iv) (c)

2. (i) (d) (ii) (c) (iii) (c)

Competition Edge Up

1. (c) **2.** (a) **3.** (b) **4.** (c) **5.** (b) **6.** (c) **7.** (b) **8.** (a)

Chapter-10

Cell Cycle and Cell Division

1. True
2. Single cell
3. (i) DNA replication, (ii)–Cell growth
4. Cell cycle
5. Cytoplasmic increase
6. One
7. Nucleus
8. Genes
9. 24
10. False. Duration of cell cycle is different in different organisms.
11. 90 minutes
12. (i) Interphase (ii) M-phase/mitosis phase
13. M-phase or mitosis phase
14. Interphase
15. 95%
16. (i) – Karyokinesis, (ii) – Cytokinesis
17. Interphase
18. M-phase is odd one out. Other three are stages of interphase.
19. Interval
20. True
21. False. Amount of DNA per cell becomes double during synthesis phase of interphase.
22. False. The number of chromosome does not increase during S-phase of cell cycle.
23. 4C
24. (b) 89 and 32
25. S-phase
26. G_2-phase
27. False. The heart cells enter the G_0-stage and do not exhibit division.
28. Quiescent stage (G_0-phase)
29. True
30. (a) Both statements I and II are true.
31. A-3, B-4, C-1, D-2
32. *A*–Interphase, *B*–S-phase, *C*–G_2-phase, *D*–M-phase
33. Diploid
34. Diploid and haploid
35. Gametophyte of bryophyte, e.g. *Riccia.*
36. (b) Statements II and III are correct.
37. Equational
38. Prophase, Metaphase, Anaphase, Telophase.
39. True
40. Prophase
41. (b) C
42. Prophase
43. (i) Mitotic chromosomes (ii) Centromere (iii) Asters
44. 3 (ER, Golgi body, nucleolus)
45. Nuclear envelope
46. Metaphase
47. (a) Both statements I and II are true.
48. True
49. Kinetochore
50. Metaphase plate
51. (i) Metaphase (ii) Kinetochores (iii) True
52. (d) At the end of this stage the sister shromatids reach opposite poles
53. Anaphase
54. Equatorial plate, pole
55. (i) Anaphase, (ii) Centromeres, chromatids
56. (a) Cell organelles like Golgi bodies disappear at the end of prophase of mitosis.
57. False. At the onset of anaphase, each chromosome arranged at metaphase plate is split.
58. False, Anaphase is the shortest phase of mitotic cell division.
59. True
60. Telophase, pole, two
61. (i) Telophase, (ii) Nucleolus, Golgi complex and endoplasmic reticulum (iii) True.
62. A–4, B–1, C–2, D–3
63. Karyokinesis
64. False, Cytokinesis involves the segregation of cytoplasmic content.
65. Cytokinesis
66. Plant cell
67. (b) It forms middle lamella that connects afdjacent cells.
68. Multinucleate condition
69. True
70. (c) Endosperm of coconut
71. Cell wall
72. (b) Cell furrow during cytokinesis proceeds inward and divides the cytoplasm into two. Failure of cytokinesis causes multinucleate condition as seen in liquid endosperm of coconut.
73. Haploid
74. Diploid, identical
75. Diploid
76. (b) Mitosis is usually restricted to the diploid cells only, but in some lower plants and in some social insects haploid cells also divide by mitosis.
77. False. Mitosis results into daughter cells with identical genetic complement.
78. Nucleocytoplasmic ratio
79. Nucleocytoplasmic ratio
80. Mitotic cell division
81. Meiotic cell division
82. Meiosis
83. Germ cell and diploid cells
84. (i) Mitosis, (ii) Meiosis, (iii) Mitosis, (iv) Mitosis
85. Cell division and nuclear division
86. Once during S-phase
87. True
88. Homologous chromosome, recombination
89. False. Meiosis-I ends with the formation of two daughter cells.
90. Prophase-I
91. Crossing over is odd one out. Rest others are substages of prophase-I.
92. Leptotene
93. Leptotene
94. False. Pairing of homologous chromosomes occurs during zygotene.
95. Synapsis
96. (b) Homologous chromosomes start pairing up during the zygotene type of prophase-I.
97. Synaptonemal
98. True
99. 1 (Involvement of recombinase).
100. (a) Pachytene
101. True

102. Homologous chromosomes
103. Synaptonemal complex
104. Recombination nodules
105. Crossing over
106. (b) Both statements I and II are true.
107. False. Crossing over is an enzyme mediated process.
108. Recombination nodule
109. (d) Recombinase
110. False. Recombination between homologous chromosomes is completed at the end of pachytene, leaving the chromosomes linked at the sites of crossing over.
111. *A*–Chiasmata
112. Chiasmata
113. Homologous
114. (i) Crossing over,
(ii) Pachytene,
(iii) Diakinesis
115. False. At the end of diakinesis, nuclear envelope and nucleolus disappear.
116. 3 (Terminalisation of chiasmata, degeneration of nucleolus, fully condensed chromosomes).
117. *A*–Anaphase-I, *B*–Metaphase-I
118. *A*–0, *B*–4
119. Prophase-II
120. True
121. Anaphase-II
122. Anaphase-II
123. A-3, B-4, C-2, D-1
124. (a) Both statements I and II are true
125. Telophase-II
126. 2 (DNA replication and protein synthesis).
127. Evolution
128. (b) Meiotic divisions contribute towards evolution of species.
129. True

Assertion-Reason Questions

1. (d) A is false, but R is true. A can be corrected as
The interphase is the stage between two mitotic divisions where the cell is metabolically active.

2. (c) A is true, but R is false. R can be corrected as
S-phase is the synthesis phase where synthesis of DNA takes place in the nucleus of the cell.

3. (b) Both A and R are true, but R is not the correct explanation of A.
Microscopic observation of the prophase shows distinct chromatids joined at the centromere as during prophase the condensation of the chromosomes begins.

4. (a) Both A and R are true and R is the correct explanation of A.

5. (c) A is true, but R is false. R can be corrected as
Telophase shows rapid decondensation of chromosomes and reappearance of nucleolus.

6. (d) A is false, but R is true. A can be corrected as
The progression of cytokinesis in plant cells is centrifugal while that in animal cells in centripetal.

7. (d) A is false, but R is true. A can be corrected as
Pachytene of prophase-I is the best stage to observe the tetrads under a microscope.

8. (a) Both A and R are true and R is the correct explanation of A.

9. (b) Both A and R are true, but R is not the correct explanation of A.
Anaphase-II resembles anaphase of mitosis rather than anaphase-I of meiosis because anaphase-II is equational division while anaphase-I is reductional division.

10. (d) A is false, but R is true. A can be corrected as
Meiosis takes place in germ cell only as it is a reductional division in which number of chromosomes is reduced to half.

Case Based Questions

1. (i) (d) (ii) (a) (iii) (d)
2. (i) (c) (ii) (b) (iii) (c)

Competition Edge Up

1. (d) **2.** (a) **3.** (c) **4.** (b) **5.** (a)
6. (b) **7.** (a) **8.** (b) **9.** (a) **10.** (a)
11. (c) **12.** (c) **13.** (b) **14.** (b)

Chapter-11

Photosynthesis in Higher Plants

1. Photosynthesis
2. Light
3. Oxygen
4. Light, chemical.
5. Photosynthesis occurr only in the green parts (uncovered part) of the leaves.
6. (i) *A*–KOH, *B*–Air
(ii) KOH absorbs the carbon dioxide present in the test tube.
(iii) The exposed part of leaf tested positive for starch.
7. The experiment showed that CO_2 is required for photosynthesis.
8. Joseph Priestley (1733-1804)
9. Priestley
10. True
11. (a) Both statements I and II are true.
12. Jan Ingenhousz
13. Only green parts of plant release O_2.
14. Julius von Sachs
15. TW Engelmann
16. *Cladophora*
17. Engelmann
18. (b) TW Engelmann in order to demonstrate his spectral experiment used green alga *Cladophora.*
19. $CO_2 + H_2O \xrightarrow{\text{Light}} [CH_2O] + O_2$
20. (c) Yeast accumulation will not occur.
21. Cornelius van Niel
22. False. In photosynthesis, hydrogen from an oxidisable compound reduces CO_2 to carbohydrates.
23. Hydrogen Sulphide (H_2S)
24. Cornelius van Niel
25. $6\,CO_2 + 12H_2O \xrightarrow{\text{Light}} C_6H_{12}O_6 + 6H_2O + 6O_2$
26. Mesophyll
27. Cisternae is odd one out, as it is the part of mitochondria. Rest other options are the parts of chloroplast.

28. ATP and NADPH.
29. True
30. (a) 4-sugar 5-ATP + NADPH
31. Dark reactions
32. (a) Both statements I and II are true.
33. False. Dark reaction are dependent on ATP and NADPH.
34. Dark reaction, ATP/NADPH
35. *A* - Stroma lamella, *B* - Grana, *C* - Stroma, *D* - Ribosomes.
36. Paper chromatography.
37. A - 3, B - 1, C - 4, D - 2.
38. (a) c
39. Highest
40. *A* - Chlorophyll-*b*, *B* - Carotenoids, *C* - Chlorophyll-*a*.
41. True
42. Chlorophyll-*a*
43. An action spectrum
44. Blue and red regions of the spectrum.
45. True
46. (b) Chlorophyll-*a* appears bright or blue-green in the chromatogram, while chlorophyll '*b*' appears yellow-green.
47. False. Absorption spectrum of chlorophyll-*a* and the action spectrum of photosynthesis are not identical.
48. Red > Blue > Green
49. 390-760 nm
50. 400 - 700 nm
51. Accessory pigments
52. Accessory
53. Photooxidations
54. Phycocyanin → Phycoerythrin → Carotenoid → Chlorophyll-*a*
55. Photochemical reaction
56. Light absorption → Water splitting → Oxygen release → Formation of NADPH and ATP.
57. Light Harvesting Complex.
58. PS-I, PS-II, proteins
59. (a) The antennae pigments protect the chief pigment against photo oxidative damage.
60. (a) Both statements I and II are true.
61. 2 (Reaction centre and antennae)
62. (b) Each photosystem has all the pigments (except chlorophyll '*a*') forming a light harvesting complex called antennae.
63. 700 nm; 680 nm
64. (i) *A*–Primary acceptor, *B*–Reaction centre, *C*–Pigment molecules
(ii) Chlorophyll-*a*
65. Cytochrome
66. True
67. Uphill
68. PS-I, 700 nm
69. (b) Photolysis of water
70. Outer
71. PS-II → Uphill to the acceptor → Down the electron transport chain to PS-I → Excitation of electrons → Transfer to another acceptor → Downhill to $NADP^+$
72. PS-I and PS-II
73. $NADP^+$ to NADPH + H^+
74. (c) O_2–Thylakoid lumen, NADPH – Stroma
75. (a) Both statements I and II are true.
76. *A*–Photosystem-II
B–Photosystem-I
C–$NADP^+$
D–NADPH
77. (a) PS I
78. H_2O
79. (b) Stroma lamellae
80. $2H^+$, [O] and 2 electrons.
81. O_2
82. NADP reductase and PS-II are absent.
83. H_2O gives $2H^+$; $12 \times 2 = 24\ [H^+]$
84. (b) The Z-scheme represents the non-cyclic flow of electrons from water to $NADP^+$.
At the end, the electrons are finally accepted by $NADP^+$.
85. Photosystem-I, photosystem-II, water, oxygen.
86. True
87. (a) Both statements I and II are true.
88. Inner, thylakoid
89. Thylakoid
90. Stroma lamellae, grana lamella, PS-I
91. Phosphorylation
92. Mitochondrion and chloroplasts
93. Non-cyclic photophosphorylation.
94. Phosphorylation
95. True
96. ATP + NADPH
97. Cyclic
98. (i) *A*-ETS, *B*-ADP + Pi, *C*-PS-I
(ii) False. The excited electron does not pass onto $NADP^+$, it is cycled back to PS-I.
99. Chemiosmotic hypothesis.
100. True
101. Proton
102. Mitochondria
103. (c) H^+ gradient
104. Inner, thylakoid, hydrogen, lumen
105. (b) Formation of proton gradient
106. Stroma
107. Thylakoid lumen
108. Inner, lumen.
109. True
110. Movement of proton
111. CF_0
112. CF_0 and CF_1
113. CF_0 - Inside, CF_1 - Outside
114. It forms a transmembrane channel that carries out facilitated diffusion of proton across the membrane.
115. Energy
116. *A*–Proton gradient, *B*–F_1 particles, *C*–ATPase
117. (d) Breaking of the proton gradient drives the synthesis of ATP by ATP synthase.
118. H^+ diffusion
119. Carbon dioxide (CO_2), sugars
120. ATP, NADPH and O_2
121. Biosynthetic phase
122. Three, two
123. Melvin Calvin
124. (i) ^{14}C (Carbon-14).
(ii) Phosphoglyceric acid
(iii) 3-phosphoglyceric acid
(iv) C_3 pathway and C_4 pathway
125. (a) P-3PGA Q-RuBisCO
126. Oxaloacetic Acid (OAA)
127. (a) Both statements I and II are true.
128. C_4-pathway
129. 6
130. False. Calvin cycle occurs in all photosynthetic plants.
131. Ribulose Bisphosphate (RuBP)

132. Carboxylation, reduction and regeneration.
133. Carboxylation
134. Carbon dioxide
135. False. Carboxylation results in the formation of two molecules of 3-PGA.
136. (a) Both statements I and II are true.
137. RuBP carboxylase - oxygenase (RuBisCO)
138. True
139. False. RuBisCO has both carboxylation and oxygenation property.
140. Reduction
141. Glucose
142. Phosphorylation, reduction
143. One molecule
144. *A*-Ribulose 1, 5 - bisphosphate, *B*-3-Phosphoglycerate, *C*-Reduction, *D*-Triose phosphate
145. *A*-18, *B*-18, *C*-12
146. True
147. Both (b) and (c)
148. 15
149. True
150. False. Leaves of C_4-plant can tolerate high temperature.
151. Photorespiration
152. Biomass
153. Bundle sheath cells
154. Kranz anatomy
155. 3-carbon primary CO_2 acceptor
156. Chloroplast, impervious, no
157. Hatch and Slack pathway
158. 3(*Sorghum,* Sugarcane, Maize).
159. 4(Sugarcane, maize, *Sorghum,* pearl millet).
160. Phosphoenolpyruvate (PEP)
161. Mesophyll
162. (c) I and III
163. PEP Carboxylase
164. (c) RuBisCO
165. Mesophyll
166. (a) Both statements I and II are true.
167. True
168. Bundle sheath cells
169. RuBisCO
170. Phosphoenol pyruvate.
171. True
172. RuBisCO enzyme
173. Bundle sheath cells
174. *A*-Fixation, *B*-Transport, *C*-Decarboxylation, *D*-Regeneration.
175. (c) The C_3 pathways operates in the mesophyll cells of C_4 plants.
176. C_4 plants have mechanism that increases the concentration of CO_2 at the enzyme site.
177. (b) A is a C_4 plant
178. *A* - RuBisCO
179. (b) I and III
180. RuBisCO
181. False. The binding of CO_2 and O_2 to RuBisCO is competitive mechanism.
182. Phosphoglycerate and phosphoglycolate
183. C_3, CO_2, ATP
184. True
185. *A*–Calvin cycle *B*–Low CO_2 *C*–Photorespiration
186. High
187. True
188. Increase
189. Low CO_2 concentration.
190. Carboxylase, minimise oxygenase activity.
191. Sunlight availability is odd one out. Rest of the options are internal factors affecting photosynthesis.
192. Internal
193. External factors affecting photosynthesis.
194. (d) Carbon dioxide unavailability
195. Law of limiting factor
196. Several
197. Minimal
198. Linear
199. False. Light saturation occurs at 10% of full sunlight.
200. (d) III and IV
201. Limiting
202. Chlorophyll, photosynthesis
203. 0.05, increase
204. False. Availability of CO_2 level is limiting to the C_3 plants.
205. Higher, increased, higher
206. Tomato and bell pepper.
207. Dark, light reaction.
208. Low temperature
209. Higher, higher, lower.
210. Higher temperature optimum
211. True
212. (d) III and IV are incorrect.

Assertion-Reason Questions

1. (d) A is false, but R is true. A can be corrected as
Engelman in his experiment with an alga, developed the first action spectrum.
2. (c) A is true, but R is false. R can be corrected as
The enzymatic synthesis of sugar in the stroma is dependent on the products of light reaction.
3. (a) Both A and R are true and R is the correct explanation of A.
4. (b) Both A and R are true, but R is not the correct explanation of A.
The proton gradient established across the thylakoid membrane is essential for ATP synthesis as the breakdown of this gradient leads to the synthesis of ATP by ATP synthase enzyme.
5. (c) A is true, but R is false. R can be corrected as
In biosynthetic phase, the primary acceptor of CO_2 is a five carbon molecule RuBP.
6. (c) A is true, but R is false. R can be corrected as
To fix 3 molecules of CO_2, 9 ATP molecules are consumed in the reduction step.
7. (b) Both A and R are true, but R is not the correct explanation of A.
The regeneration of RuBP forms the last step in the C_3 pathway of photosynthesis so that RuBP can be reused in the Calvin cycle for continuous fixation of carbon.
8. (d) A is false, but R is true. A can be corrected as
In C_4 plants C_3 pathway serves as the main biosynthetic pathway.
9. (d) A is false, but R is true. A can be corrected as
The yield and productivity in C_4 plants is much higher than C_3 plants.
10. (b) Both A and R are true, but R is not the correct explanation of A.

Atmospheric carbon dioxide is the major limiting factor for photosynthesis as increase in concentration upto 0.05 per cent can cause an increase in CO_2 fixation rates, beyond this the levels can become damaging over longer periods.

Case Based Questions

1. (i) (b) (ii) (b) (iii) (a)
2. (i) (c) (ii) (a) (iii) (b)

Competition Edge Up

1. (c) **2.** (d) **3.** (c) **4.** (a) **5.** (a) **6.** (d)
7. (a) **8.** (d) **9.** (d) **10.** (b) **11.** (b)

Chapter-12

Respiration in Plants

1. 5 (All of them need energy except breakdown of food because it releases energy.)
2. Oxidation
3. Photosynthesis
4. Photosynthesis
5. Heterotrophs, herbivores, carnivores
6. Saprophytes
7. Cellular respiration
8. Catabolic, exergonic
9. Mitochondria
10. Respiration
11. Respiratory substrates
12. 4 (Carbohydrates, fats, proteins, organic acids).
13. False. Respiratory substrates release energy (in the form of ATP) in a series of slow stepwise reactions controlled by enzymes.
14. ATP
15. Oxygen, carbon dioxide
16. Stomata, lenticels
17. Each plant part takes care of its own gaseous needs. Plants do not present great demands for gaseous exchange. Almost all living cells in a plant have their surface exposed to air.
18. (c) Respiration in plants release uses energy in the form of ATP.
19. (i) True
(ii) False. Roots, stems and leaves respire at rates far lower than animals.
20. (b) The loose packing of parenchyma cells allows easy contact with air in plants.
21. $6CO_2 + 6H_2O$ + Energy
22. O_2 (Oxygen)
23. Glycolysis
24. Sugar, splitting
25. EMP–Embden, Meyerhof and Parnas.
26. Calvin is odd one out. All of the given scientists proposed scheme of glycolysis except Calvin, he proposed Calvin cycle of photosynthesis.
27. Anaerobic
28. Cytoplasm
29. Pyruvic acid (3C)
30. *A*–Sucrose, *B*–Invertase
31. (c) *A* – invertase, *B* – hexokinase
32. *A*-Fructose-6-phosphate, *B*-Fructose-1, 6-bisphosphate, *C*-Triose phosphate (Glyceraldehyde-3-phosphate).
33. 10
34. Each step involves a different chemical reactions.
35. (b) Breakdown of one molecule of glucose yields two moelcule of pyruvic acid in the cytoplasm. Fructose 1, 6-bisphosphate is split into dihydroxyacetone phosphate and 3- phosphoglyceraldehyde.
36. (a) Conversion of PGAL to BPGA.
37. 2x 2-phosphoglycerate→ 2 Phosphoenol Pyruvate (PEP) + H_2O
38. *A*–3-phosphoglyceric acid, *B*–2-phosphoglycerate *C*–Phosphoenol pyruvate, *D*–Pyruvic acid
39. 2 steps
40. 4 molecules of ATP
41. (a) One ATP molecule is consumed in phosphorylation of glucose to fructose - 6 - phosphate.
42. Formed
43. Glycolysis will stop as its first and third step need ATP.
44. 4 pairs are isomers (PEP and pyruvate are not isomers).
45. (i) Adenosine Triphosphate
(ii) Nicotinamide Adenine Dinucleotide
(iii) Phosphoglyceraldehyde
(iv) Dihydroxyacetone Phosphate
(v) Bisphosphoglyceric acid
(vi) Phosphoenol Pyruvate
46. 68 KJ, ATP, NADH + H^+
47. *A*–ATP utilised, *B*–ATP formed, *C*–ATP formed, *D*–ATP utilised
48. True
49. A-2, B-1, C-1, D-2
50. 4, 2
51. 4
52. Substrate level phosphorylation
53. Alcoholic fermentation, lactic acid fermentation, aerobic respiration.
54. Muscle cells, nerve cells and RBCs
55. Fermentation
56. *A*–Ethanol, *B*–CO_2
57. Pyruvic acid decarboxylase and alcohol dehydrogenase.
58. (i) *A*– NADH + H^+
(ii) Muscle cells during exercise
(iii) Lactate dehydrogenase
59. (b) Pyruvic acid decarboxylase and alcohol dehydrogenase catalyses the conversion of pyruvic acid to ethanol.
60. (i) 7
(ii) 13
61. 2
62. Aerobic respiration
63. Mitochondria
64. TCA (Tricarboxylic Acid) and ETS (Electron Transport System)
65. Catabolism, matrix, decarboxylation
66. (d) Mitochondrial matrix
67. *A*–Co-A, *B*–NAD^+, *C*–Pyruvate dehydrogenase, *D*–CO_2, *E*–NADH + H^+
68. (c) I, III and IV
69. Hans Krebs
70. Krebs' cycle or Citric acid cycle
71. Citric acid
72. A-1, B-2, C-3, D-4
73. *A*–α–ketoglutaric acid, *B*–Succinic acid, *C*–Malic acid, *D*–OAA
74. Pyruvic acid + NAD^+ + Co-A → Acetyl Co-A + CO_2 + $NADH_2$
75. α-ketoglutaric acid
76. *X*–Isocitrate

77. *X*–Succinyl Co-A Synthetase
Y–GTP

78. Oxaloacetic acid

79. *A*–4NAD$^+$, *B*–FAD$^+$, *C*–2H_2O, *D*–3CO_2, *E*–4NADH

80. (i) Malic acid
(ii) Fumaric acid
(iii) Succinic acid

81. *X*–NADH + H^+, *Y*–$FADH_2$, *Z*–GTP

82. (b) Conversion of succinyl Co-A to succinic acid.

83. (i) Oxidation
(ii) Isomerism
(iii) Decarboxylation

84. Tricarboxylic acid cycle

85. 4CO_2, 6NADH, 2$FADH_2$, 2ATP

86. (i) Tricarboxylic Acid Cycle
(ii) Oxaloacetic Acid

87. Cristae

88. Ubiquinone

89. Electron donor

90. Cytochrome-*c*

91. Within the inner membrane of mitochondria.

92. *a*, a_3 and two

93. ATP

94. A-5, B-4, C-3, D-2, E-1

95. (c) I, II and III

96. (a) A-4, B-1, C-2, D-3

97. *A*-Inter-membrane space, *B*-Matrix, *C*-NADH+ H^+, *D*-NAD$^+$, *E*-UQH_2, *F*-Fumarate

98. 3 molecules, 2 molecules

99. Oxygen derives the whole process by removing hydrogen from the system. It is the final hydrogen acceptor resulting in the formation of H_2O.

100. Light energy, energy of oxidation reduction

101. Oxidative phosphorylation

102. In photophosphorylation, oxygen is evolved, while in oxidative phosphorylation, oxygen is used.

103. Proton gradient

104. Electron transport chain

105. F_1, F_0

106. 2

107. (i) F_1, (ii) F_0

108. (i) It forms the channel through which protons cross the inner membrane.
(ii) It provides site for the synthesis of ATP from ADP and inorganic phosphate.

109. *A*-2H^+, *B*-F_0, *C*-F_1.

110. False. The passage of protons through the channel formed by F_0 is coupled to the catalytic site of the F_1 component.

111. True

112. (i) Glycolysis, TCA cycle and ETS
(ii) Oxidative phosphorylation
(iii) None
(iv) Glucose

113. 38

114. True.

115. 30

116. 1520 (38 ATP by 1 glucose $40 \times 38 = 1520$ ATP).

117. Glucose (carbohydrate)

118. Amphibolic.

119. *A*-Fats, *B*-Proteins, *C*-Glyceraldehyde-3-phosphate, *D*-Krebs cycle

120. Acetyl Co-A

121. (i) Amino acids
(iii) Acetyl Co-A
(iv) Glycerol and fatty acid

122. (c) II and IV

123. $RQ = \dfrac{\text{Volume of } CO_2 \text{ evolved } (X)}{\text{Volume of } O_2 \text{ consumed } (Y)}$

124. Greater

125. 0.71

126. (i) 0.7
(ii) More than one
(iii) Less than one
(iv) Less than one
(v) 1
(vi) 4

Assertion-Reason Questions

1. (c) A is true, but R is false. R can be corrected as
During oxidation within a cell, all the energy contained in respiratory substrates is released in a series of slow step-wise reactions controlled by enzymes.

2. (b) Both A and R are true, but R is not the correct explanation of A.

3. (d) A is false, but R is true, A can be corrected as
Glucose undergoes partial oxidation during glycolysis to form two molecules of pyruvate.

4. (a) Both A and R are true and R is the correct explanation of A.

5. (c) A is true, but R is false. R can be corrected as
Pyruvate dehydrogenase requires the participation of several coenzymes, including NAD+ and Coenzyme-A.

6. (a) Both A and R are true and R is the correct explanation of A.

7. (a) Both A and R are true and R is the correct explanation of A.

8. (c) A is true, but R is false. R can be corrected as
Anaerobic respiration only oxidises glucose partially, with a net gain of two ATP molecules per glucose.

9. (b) Both A and R are true, but R is not the correct explanation of A.

10. (d) A is false, but R is true. A can be corrected as
Respiratory quotient is the ratio between the volume of CO_2 evolved to the volume of O_2 consumed.

Case Based Questions

1. (i) (b) (ii) (a) (iii) (c) (iv) (a)
2. (i) (c) (ii) (a) (iii) (a)

Competition Edge Up

1. (c) **2.** (b) **3.** (d) **4.** (c) **5.** (b)
6. (c) **7.** (b) **8.** (a)

Chapter-13

Plant Growth and Development

1. Vegetative

2. Growth and differentiation

3. (i) *A*–Hypocotyl
B–Cotyledons
C–Epicotyl
D–Seed coat
(ii) Bean (dicot).

4. (b) Both statements I and II are true.

5. False. The factors which govern and control developmental processes in plants are both intrinsic and extrinsic.

6. Growth

7. Metabolic, energy

8. Leaf expansion

9. Meristematic tissue (meristems)

10. 2 (Capacity to divide continuously, self perpetuations). Meristems are not found throughout the plant body, but at certain location only.

11. Open form of growth

12. (b) Statements I, II and III are correct.

13. (i) *A*-Shoot apical meristem
B-Root apical meristem
C-Vascular cambium
(ii) C is the odd one as it contributes to secondary growth whereas both *A* and *B* contribute to primary growth in plants.
(iii) Vascular cambium, lateral meristem and cork cambium.

14. (c) Wood-primary growth is incorrect combination.

15. Lateral meristem

16. Protoplasm.

17. 4 (All of them except increase in protoplasm directly). It is difficult to measure the increase in protoplasm directly. Therefore, some quantity is measured which is more or less proportional to it.

18. A-3, B-1, C-4, D-2

19. Meristematic phase, elongation phase and maturation phase.

20. (a) The cells lying just next to the meristematic zone, represent the phase of elongation. The cells in this phase have increased vacuolation.

21. (i) Elongation
(ii) A-3, B-1, C-2
(iii) Thickened cell wall is odd term because cells in zone I possess primary (thin) cell walls.
(iv) 3 (Increased vacuolation, cell enlargement, new cell wall deposition)
(v) (a) Maximal size of cell and wall thickening,
(b) Protoplasmic modifications

22. *A*–Geometric growth
B–Arithmetic growth

23. Arithmetic growth

24. *A*–Geometric phase,
B–Arithmetic phase

25. Both the daughter cells

26. (b) The mitotic division of zygote resulting in increased cell number is a representative of geometric growth.

27. (i) Arithmetic growth
(ii) Root elongation

28. $L_t = L_o + rt$, where, L_t = Length at time 't', L_0 = Length at time zero, r = growth rate/elongation per unit time.

29. II, sigmoid-shaped

30. Geometric, natural

31. (c) Both statements I and II are true.

32. Sigmoid

33. $W_1 = W_0 e^{rt}$, where, W_1 = Final size (Weight, Height, Number, etc.), W_0 = Initial size, r = Growth rate, t = Time of growth, e = Base of natural logrithms.

34. Efficiency index

35. True

36. Growth per unit initial parameter at a given time.

37. (b) 20%

38. (i) Absolute growth.
(ii) *A*. Both leaves gained 5 cm area, but leaf *A* gained 100% of its original area while leaf *B* gained only 10% of its area.

39. Auxanometer

40. Water, oxygen, macro and micronutrient

41. A-2, B-3, C-1.

42. True

43. (b) A cell placed in hypotonic solution would show an increase in cell size due to inward movement of water into the cell, thereby making it swell.

44. Differentiation

45. Protoplasm

46. Abundant protoplasm would not be found in differentiated tracheary cells, on the contrary, these cells would lose their protoplasm.

47. Dedifferentiated cells lose the capacity of division.

48. Dedifferentiation

49. Redifferentiation

50. Dedifferentiation

51. Dedifferentiation

52. Redifferentiation

53. Determinate and indeterminate.

54. Same meristem, different structure

55. True

56. Epidermis

57. (c) Both statements I and II are true.

58. Development

59. Senescence

60. *A*-Plasmatic growth,
B-Senescence,
C-Cell division,
D-Maturation

61. Plasticity

62. Buttercup is odd one out as it shows heterophylly due to environment whereas other three show heterophylly in different stages of life cycle.

63. (b) Apart from environment, the phases of life of the plant to form different kind of structures drive heterophylly in plants.

64. A-3, B-2, C-4, D-1

65. *A*-Intracellular, *B*-Intercellular, *C*-Environment

66. Chemical composition, Phytohormones.

67. A-5, B-1, C-2, D-4, E-3

68. Ethylene is odd one out as it is a gaseous hormone while other three are adenine derivatives.

69. Plant growth promoters, Plant growth inhibitors

70. 3 (Auxins, gibberellins, cytokinins). Abscisic acid is plant growth inhibitor.

71. Charles Darwin and Francis Darwin, canary grass, unilateral

72. (i) The experiment demonstrates that tip of coleoptile is the source of auxin.
(ii) The arrows indicate the direction of light.

73. True

74. Coconut milk

75. A-4, B-1, C-3, D-2
76. (c) Both statements I and II are true.
77. False. Auxins was first isolated from human urine.
78. Natural, synthetic, growing apices
79. NAA and 2, 4-D
80. (b) Auxin promote rooting in shoot.
81. Auxins
82. Apical dominance
83. Shoot tips
84. Figure. (a)-Apical dominance in plants. Figure (b)-Growth of lateral buds into branches after decapitation
85. Parthenocarpy, herbicide, dicotyledonous weeds
86. (b) NAA is a synthetic auxin, i.e. it has been made artificially. However, it is extensive by use in agriculture.
87. True
88. GA_3.
89. (c) Gibberellins
90. GA elongates and improves the fruit's shape.
91. Senescence
92. Speeding up the malting process.
93. Length of the stems.
94. Maturity period
95. Bolting
96. Sugarcane is odd one out as it is not rosette plant. GAs promote stem elongation in it whereas other three plants are rosette which show bolting by application of GAs.
97. Cytokinesis, kinetin, sperm DNA
98. Zeatin
99. (b) Both auxin and cytokinin are plant growth promoters, i.e they stimulate plant growth.
100. Coconut milk and corn-kernels.
101. Mature leaves is odd one out as cytokinins are produced in the region of rapid cell division.
102. Chloroplast, adventitious, apical dominance, nutrient mobilisation
103. True
104. Ethylene
105. False. Ethylene promotes respiratory climatic or rise in rate of respiration.
106. Ethylene
107. (i) Inhibits (ii) Promotes (iii) Promotes (iv) Promotes
108. It is because wax prevents entry of O_2 to apple, this checks the cellular respiration and overripening of fruit by preventing ethylene formation.
109. (b) A-2, B-4, C-3, D-1
110. Initiate flowering and synchronizing fruit set.
111. Ethephon
112. Inhibit abscission in flowers and fruits is odd one out as ethephon accelerates this process.
113. A-2, B-3, C-1.
114. Abscisic acid
115. False. ABA inhibits seed germination but promotes the closure of stomata.
116. Dormancy
117. (b) Both statements I and II are true.
118. Gibberellic acid
119. (a) Gibberellin have been found to break seed dormancy whereas ABA being stress hormone, promote seed dormancy during unfavourable conditions.
120. (i) Indole Butyric Acid
(ii) Naphthalene Acetic Acid
(iii) 2, 4-Dichlorophenoxyacetic acid
(iv) Indole-3-Acetic Acid
(v) Gibberellic Acid
(vi) Abscisic Acid
121. (a) Ethylene
122. 2(Abscission and senescence are promoted by both ethylene and ABA).

Assertion-Reason Questions

1. (c) A is true, but R is false. R can be corrected as
The secondary growth in gymnosperms is due to the lateral meristems in root and shoot.
2. (c) A is true, but R is false. R can be corrected as
The cells of the meristematic zone contains large conspicuous nucleus and are rich in protoplasm.
3. (d) A is false, but R is true. A can be corrected as
In arithmetic growth only one daughter the cell follow mitotic division while the other matures and differentiates.
4. (b) Both A and R are true, but R is not the correct explanation of A.
5. (c) A is true, but R is false. R can be corrected as
A tumour formed in a particular organ is a product of dedifferentiation of the cells
6. (a) Both A and R are true and R is the correct explanation of A.
7. (b) Both A and R are true, but R is not the correct explanation of A.
8. (c) A is true, but R is false. R can be corrected as
Gibberelins delay senescence in plants thereby increasing the market period
9. (a) Both A and R are true and R is the correct explanation of A.
10. (d) A is false, but R is true. A can be corrected as
The rise in respiration rate in fruits that hastens the ripening process is caused by ethylene.

Case Based Questions

1. (i) (c) (ii) (d) (iii) (c)
2. (i) (d) (ii) (b) (iii) (a)

Competition Edge Up

1. (c) **2.** (a) **3.** (a) **4.** (b)
5. (a) **6.** (b) **7.** (c) **8.** (c)
9. (c) **10.** (d)

Chapter-14

Breathing and Exchange of Gases

1. Breathing
2. (a) Frogs can respire through their moist skin (cutaneous respiration) and through lungs.
3. (i) Insects,
(ii) Aquatic arthropods, molluscs and fishes
(iii) Amphibians, reptiles, birds, mammals
(iv) Earthworms, frogs
4. (a) A-3, B-2, C-4, D-1
5. External nostril → Nasal passage → Nasal chamber →Pharynx → Larynx → Trachea → Bronchi → Bronchioles → Alveoli

6. Trachea
7. Larynx
8. Epiglottis and trachea
9. *A* – Epiglottis, *B* – Trachea, *C* – Bronchus, *D* – Alveoli
10. Epiglottis
11. 5th
12. Alveoli
13. True
14. Pleura
15. (b) The tracheae, primary, secondary and tertiary bronchi and initial bronchioles are supported by incomplete cartilaginous rings.
The lungs are covered by pleura whose two layers consists of pleural fluid between them.
16. It reduces friction on the lung surface.
17. Thoracic, lung
18. C = 7; trachea, bronchi, larynx, nasopharynx, external nostrils, nasal chamber, terminal bronchiole.
R = 2 ; alveoli and alveolar duct.
19. (b) P, Q, R and S
20. Vertebral column, sternum, ribs, diaphragm
21. *A*–Alveolar sac, *B*–Secondary bronchus, *C*–Bronchioles
22. (b) Dorsally by the vertebral column and laterally by the ribs.
23. Conducting part of respiratory system.
24. *A*–Pulmonary ventilation, *B*–Alveolar membrane, *C*–Blood, *D*–Diffusion, *E*–Catabolic reactions, *F*–Cellular respiration
25. Inspiration, expiration
26. False. Inspiration is an active process whereas expiration is passive process.
27. Pressure gradient
28. (a) Negative pressure in lungs; positive pressure in atmosphere
29. Less
30. Intrapulmonary
31. (a) Both statements I and II are true.
32. IV → VI → I → II → III → V
33. (d) Increase in volume of thoracic cavity
34. I → III → IV → II
35. Dome
36. (b) During inspiration the ribs and sternum are raised to increase the volume of thoracic - chamber in the dorso - ventral axis.
37. Internal intercostals and abdominal muscles
38. (i) Diaphragm muscle and external intercostal muscles.
(ii) Abdominal muscle and internal intercostal muscles.
39. 12-16 times/minute.
40. Spirometer
41. (a) Statements I and II are correct.
42. (i) Inspiration ; *A*–Air entering the lungs, *B*–Volume of thorax increased, *C*–Ribs and sternum raised.
(ii) Expiration ; *D*–Air expelled from lungs, *E*–Volume of thorax decreased, *F*–Ribs and sternum returned to original position.
43. (i) Inspiratory Reserve Volume (IRV)
(ii) Expiratory Reserve Volume (ERV)
(iii) Residual Volume (RV)
(iv) Tidal Volume (TV)
(v) Total Lung Capacity (TLC)
(vi) Functional Residual Capacity (FRC).
44. (a) Even after forcible expiration about 1100 mL to 1200 mL of air remains in the lungs.
45. A - 3, B - 1, C - 2, D 4
46. $\underset{(500\text{ mL})}{\text{Tidal volume}} < \underset{(1000\text{ mL})}{\text{ERV}} < \underset{(1200\text{ mL})}{\text{RV}} < \underset{(4500\text{ mL})}{\text{Vital capacity}}$
47. FRC = ERV + RV
= 1000 + 1000 = 2000 mL
48. (b) 3000 mL
49. A - 2, B - 3, C - 1, D - 4
50. *A* – Inspiratory reserve volume, *B* – Total lung capacity, *C* – Functional residual capacity, *D* – Residual volume, *E* – Vital capacity
51. Simple diffusion
52. Solubility of the gases as well as the thickness of the membranes involved.
53. Partial pressure
54. *A* – 104mm Hg, *B* – 95mm Hg, *C* – 0.3mm Hg, *D* – 45mm Hg
55. (b) In a mixture of CO_2 in water it is found that CO_2 dissolves at a higher rate then O_2.
56. (i) Higher
(ii) Higher
57. *A*–O_2, *B*–CO_2, *C*–40 mm Hg, D–40 mm Hg.
58. (a) pO_2 in alveoli > pO_2 in capillary
59. False. In comparison to solubility of O_2 in blood, the solubility of CO_2 is 20-25 times higher.
60. (a) Both statements I and II are true
61. Squamous epithelium, endothelium of alveolar capillaries.
62. (a) Squamous epithelium of A. basement substance and endothelium of B.
63. (a) less than a millimetre.
64. Squamous epithelium, single layer endothelial cells of capillaries.
65. 97% and 3%
66. (i) 20-25%, (ii) 70%, (iii) 7%
67. (b) Maximum percentage of CO_2 is transported as bicarbonate in blood.
68. Red, iron, RBCs, oxyhaemoglobin, four
69. Partial pressure of O_2(pO_2), partial pressure of CO_2(pCO_2), hydrogen ion concentration, temperature.
70. (b) Binding of oxygen with haemoglobin results in the formation of oxyhaemoglobin.

Low pH conditions in the tissues favours the dissociation of oxygen from haemoglobin.

71. *X* is tissue, *Y* is alveoli in lungs.

72. (i) Partial pressure of oxygen (mm Hg)
(ii) Percentage saturation of haemoglobin with oxygen.

73. Sigmoid (or S-shaped).

74. False. After taking a long deep breath we do not respire for few seconds due to less CO_2 in the blood.

75. 5mL

76. 1. Vena cava (60%) because vena cava carry deoxygenated blood, but still some oxygen is there,
2. Left ventricle (80%),
3. Pulmonary vein (95-100%) Because pulmonary vein carry oxygenated blood.

77. If 1 gm Hb carry 1.34 mL of O_2 and 100 mL of blood has 5g of Hb then 100 mL of blood will carry $1.34 \times 15 = 20.1$ mL or 20 mL of O_2 approximately.

78. (i) Shift to right ↓ in pO_2, ↑ in pCO_2, ↑ in H^+ ions, ↓ in pH, ↑ in body temperature.
(ii) Shift to left ↑ in pO_2, ↓ in pCO_2, ↓ in H^+ ions, ↑ in pH, ↓ in body temperature.

79. (c) Increased acidity

80. pO_2 ↑ odd one out. All other factors favour dissociation of oxyhaemoglobin.

81. High pCO_2

82. (ii) Because CO_2 has high solubility in plasma.

83. Increases, decreases

84. *X*-Carbonic anhydrase

85. (a) Low pCO_2

86. 4

87. Capillary endothelial membrane → Capillary basement membrane →Thin interstitial space → Alveolar epithelial basement membrane → Alveolar epithelium

88. Neural

89. (i) Respiratory rhythm centre
(ii) Pneumotaxic centre

90. (a) Both statements I and II are true.

91. Pons and medulla, respectively.

92. Chemosensitive

93. (c) Increase in CO_2 level detected by the medulla

94. CO_2, H^+, rhythm centre

95. CO_2, arterial

96. (a) Both statements I and II are true.

97. Insignificant

98. Emphysema

99. (b) Inflammation of bronchi and bronchioles

100. Emphysema

101. (a) Both statements I and II are true

102. Asthma

Assertion-Reason Questions

1. (d) A is false, but R is true. A can be corrected as
During swallowing food the glottis remains covered by a elastic cartilaginous flap called epiglottis.

2. (b) Both A and R are true, but R is not the correct explanation of A.

3. (c) A is true, but R is false. R can be corrected as
For inspiration, there should be a negative pressure in the lungs which would force air from outside to enter the lungs.

4. (a) Both A and R are true and R is the correct explanation of A.

5. (c) A is true, but R is false. R can be corrected as
Residual volume is the difference of total lung capacity and vital capacity.

6. (b) Both A and R are true, but R is not the correct explanation of A.

7. (d) A is false but R is true. A can be corrected as
Partial pressure of carbon dioxide in blood capillaries is less than that of respiring cells.

8. (c) A is true, but R is false. R can be corrected as
Low pCO_2 and high pO_2 at the lung surface causes the formation of oxyhaemoglobin

9. (a) Both A and R are true and R is the correct explanation of A.

10. (c) A is true, but R is false. R can be corrected as
The chemosensitive area in medulla activate in response to changes in pH and CO_2 levels

Case Based Questions

1. (i) (b) (ii) (d) (iii) (c)
2. (i) (a) (ii) (b) (iii) (a)

Competition Edge Up

1. (a) **2.** (b) **3.** (c) **4.** (c) **5.** (a) **6.** (a)
7. (a) **8.** (a) **9.** (d) **10.** (d) **11.** (b)

Chapter-15

Body Fluids and Circulation

1. (i) Water
(ii) Blood

2. Fluid matrix, plasma and formed elements.

3. (i) Plasma constitutes 55% of blood
(ii) 90-92% of water in plasma.
(iii) 6-8% of protein in plasma.

4. Alkaline, 7.3–7.5

5. False. Plasma is a straw coloured, viscous fluid in blood.

6. Cellulose is odd one out. Rest all are protein found in blood.

7. A-3, B-1, C-2

8. Na^+, Ca^{2+}, Mg^{2+}, HCO_3^-, Cl^-, etc.

9. '*X*'-Clotting factors

10. (a) Both statement I and II are true.

11. Plasma is odd one out. It is not a part of formed elements.

12. Red blood cells, white blood cells, platelets.

13. 2 (ii, iii) are correct for erythrocytes. Statement (i) is not correct. It can be corrected as
Erythrocytes are the most abundant of all the cells in the blood.

14. Biconcave

15. 12-16 gms

16. (i) Erythropoiesis
(ii) Coagulation
(iii) Haemoglobin

17. RBCs help in transport of respiratory gases (O_2 and CO_2).

18. Spleen

19. 3(i, ii, iv). Incorrect feature can be corrected as WBCs are nucleated cells

20. *A*-Granulocytes, *B*-Agranulocytes, *C*-Neutrophils, *D*-Eosinophils, *E*-Monocytes, *F*-T-lymphocytes, *G*-B-lymphocytes.

21. (b) Eosinophils

22. Monocytes is odd one out. Others are granulocytes.

23. Basophils

24. (a) Spleen is known as the cemetery of red blood cells.

25. A-5, B-4, C-3, D-2, E-1.

26. Antibodies is odd one out. These are not released from basophils but are released from lymphocytes.

27. A-2, B-1, C-4, D-3, E-4.

28. 3 (Neutrophils, lymphocytes and monocytes)

29. *A*-Monocyte, *B*-Eosinophil, *C*-Basophils, *D*-Neutrophil, *E*-T-Lymphocyte

30. Monocyte

31. A-1, B-2, C-3

32. (b) There could be internal bleeding and plasma leakage

33. ABO blood grouping and Rh blood grouping

34. (i) Antigen
(ii) Antibodies

35. 2

36. *W*–A, *X*–Nil, *Y*–B,O, *Z*– O

37. (b) People having O negative blood group are universal donors since they lack surface antigens on their RBCs.
People having AB blood group are universal recepients due to the absence of antibodies, anti-A and anti-B in the plasma.

38. (a) O negative

39. A

40. True

41. Monkey

42. [illegible]

43. [illegible] iii), i.e. all of the given characteristics are true.

44. (a) Statements II and IV are incorrect.

45. Anti Rh antibodies, mother

46. (ii) Nothing happens to Rh (+ve) person.

47. (b) Developing foetus is Rh^+

48. (i) and (iii), i.e. no problem in 1st pregnancy and problem would be expected in second pregnancy.

49. (d) No effect on the foetus

50. Coagulation or clotting

51. Clot or coagulam

52. Ca^{2+}

53. *A*-Thrombokinase, *B*-Thrombin

54. (b) Fibrins are formed by the conversion of inactive fibrinogens in plasma by the enzyme thrombin.

55. (iv) → (iii) → (i) → (v) → (ii)

56. Enzymic reactions, factors, plasma.

57. True

58. Vitamin-K

59. RBCs + some proteins

60. (a) Both statements I and II are true

61. Lymphatic, lymph

62. (i) Colourless
(ii) Lymphocytes present
(iii) Absorbs fats

63. RBCs is odd one out as they are not present in lymph.

64. (b) Immune

65. (i) Arthropods and molluscs
(ii) Annelids and chordates

66. Sinuses

67. (i) and (iii). Its disadvantage is that in closed circulatory system, exchange of material occurs slowly.

68. (c) Octopus-closed circulatary system is an incorrect match

69. Sinuses are not present in closed circulatory system.

70. A-1– K, B-2–L, C-3–M, D-4–K

71. (b) Amphibians and reptiles (except crocodile) have 3-chambered heart with 2 atria and a single ventricle.
In fishes the heart pumps out deoxygenated blood which is oxygenated by the gills and supplied to body parts. The deoxygenated blood from there is returned to the heart.

72. True

73. One ventricle

74. Heart, blood vessels, blood

75. (i) Mesodermal
(ii) Thoracic cavity
(iii) Between
(iv) Left

76. Pericardium

77. True

78. (i) Opening between left atrium and left ventricle.
(ii) Opening between right atrium and right ventricle.
(iii) Opening of the right and left ventricles into pulmonary artery and aorta, respectively.
(iv) Ventricles of heart.
(v) Right upper corner of the right atrium.
(vi) Lower left corner of the right atrium.

79. (a) A-3, B-4, C-1, D-2.

80. (i) Valves allow flow of blood in one direction, i.e. from atria to ventricle and from ventricles to pulmonary artery or aorta.
(ii) Valves prevent backflow of blood.

81. (i) Ventricles pump blood out of the heart to distant tissues therefore their walls are thicker than atria.

82. *A*-Aorta, *B*-Vena cava, *C*-Pulmonary artery, *D*-Left atrium, *E*-Right atrium

83. (a) Both statements I and II are true.

84. SA node → AV node → Bundle of His → Purkinje fibres → Heart muscles

85. *Chordae tendineae*

86. (i) Interatrial septum
(ii) Interventricular septum
(iii) Atrio-ventricular septum

87. Nodal tissue

88. AV node

89. 70–75 min^{-1}

90. It initiates and maintains the rhythmic contractile activity of heart.

91. Sino-atrial (SA) node

92. Bundle of His, Purkinje fibres

93. (ii), i.e. Cardiac muscles will not undergo coordinated rhythmic movements.

94. *A*-Atrial systole. *B*-Ventricular systole, *C*-Joint diastole.
95. Separately
96. Ventricular systole
97. Ventricular systole
98. (a) Both statements I and II are true.
99. Pulmonary
100. 90%, 10%
101. 4, i.e. i, ii, iii, v (Action potential is not generated during joint diastole).
102. (d) Ventricular systole-opening of AV valves is incorrect combination.
103. Cardiac cycle
104. True
105. (i) 72 times per minute
(ii) 0.8 Seconds
(iii) 72 cycles per minute
(iv) 70 mL of blood
(v) 5000 mL or 5 L of blood (approximately)
106. (i) Cardiac output
(ii) Stroke volume
107. (i) Stethoscope
(ii) Sphygmomanometer
108. 80 mmHg
109. Heart rate
110. (c) Cardiac output = Stroke volume × heart rate (Beats per minute)
$= 70 \text{ mL} \times 125 (100 + 25\% \text{ of } 100)$
$= 8750 \text{ mL}$
111. 70 mL
$5250 = \text{stroke volume} \times 75$
$\Rightarrow \text{Stroke volume} = \frac{5250}{75} = 70$
112. (a) The first heart sound lub is associated with the closure of tricuspid and bicuspid, whereas the second heart sound dub is associated with the closure of semilunar valves, respectively. Both the sounds hold clinical diagnostic importance.
113. Stethoscope
114. Lub, dub
115. (i) Dub
(ii) Lub
116. Electrocardiogram
117. Electrocardiograph
118. ECG is graphical representation of the electrical activity of the heart during a cardiac cycle.
119. (d)
120. A-2, B-1, C-3
121. (a) Both statements I and II are true.
122. False
The electrocardiograph (monitoring machine) makes the sound pip-pip-peeeee as the patient goes into cardiac arrest.
123. QRS
124. One to each wrist and to the left ankle
125. Blood vessels
126. *A*-Artery, *B*-Capillary, *C*-Vein
127. A-3, B-2, C-1
128. Thin tunica media
129. *X*-Arteries, *Y*- Veins
130. (i) It means that the blood passes through the heart twice for each circuit of the body.
131. (b) Systemic circulation is responsible for transport of nutrients, O_2, CO_2 and other substances to and from the tissue. The blood pumped by the right ventricle enters the pulmonary artery whereas left ventricle pumps blood into the aorta.
132. Double circulation = Pulmonary circulation + Systemic circulation
133. (i) Systemic circulation
(ii) Pulmonary circulation
134. Increases, decreased
135. Aorta and pulmonary artery
136. Systemic circulation
137. Portal circulation
138. Hepatic portal system
139. hepatic portal vein
140. Intestine, liver
141. (a) Hepatic portal vein carries deoxygenated blood from the intestine to the liver before getting released to the systemic circulation.
142. *A*–Lungs, *B*–Dorsal aorta, *C*–Pulmonary artery, *D*–Pulmonary vein, *E*–Vena cava
143. Inferior vena cava
144. Capillaries
145. *A*–Deoxygenated, *B*–Oxygenated, *C*–Deoxygenated, *D*–Oxygenated
146. A-4, B-3, C-1, D-2
147. Nodal tissue, myogenic
148. Medulla oblongata
149. Autonomic nervous system
150. (b) Neural centre in the medulla oblongata can moderate the cardiac function through ANS. Neural signals *via* sympathetic nerves can moderate the cardiac output.
Hormones of the adrenal medulla can also increase the cardiac output.
151. (i) By increasing the rate of heartbeat and strength of ventricular contraction.
152. Decreasing
153. Epinephrine
154. (d) Haemoglobin level
155. (i) Hypertension
(ii) Hypotension
(iii) Angina pectoris
156. 120 mm Hg
157. 140/90
158. (a) Both statements I and II are true.
159. (i) Heart attack
(ii) Heart failure (Congestive heart failure)
(iii) Angina pectoris
(iv) Cardiac arrest
(v) Atherosclerosis (Coronary artery disease)
160. (d) Widening of lumen

Assertion-Reason Questions

1. (b) Both A and R are true, but R is not the correct explanation of A. It can be corrected as
An Rh + person cannot donate blood to Rh - individual because this would result in formation of anti Rh antibodies in the blood of the recipient and would cause clumping and destruction of RBCs.
2. (a) Both A and R are true and R is the correct explanation of A.
3. (c) A is true, but R is false. R can be corrected as
Lymph has the same composition as that of the blood plasma except that it lacks red blood cells and large proteins.
4. (a) Both A and R are true and R is the correct explanation of A.
5. (d) A is false, but R is true. A can be corrected as

The atrial systole is initiated by an impulse originating in the sino atrial node

6. (a) Both A and R are true and R is the correct explanation of A.

7. (c) A is true, but R is false. R can be corrected as

The T wave of an ECG denotes the return of ventricles to relaxation or repolarisation.

8. (b) Both A and R are true, but R is not the correct explanation of A.

The pulmonary circulation is necessary for oxygenation of the blood brought by major veins because it carries the deoxygenated blood through the pulmonary artery, to the lungs.

9. (c) A is true but R is false. R can be corrected as

Medulla regulates the sympathetic and parasympathetic branch of the ANS

10. (a) Both A and R are true and R is the correct explanation of A.

Case Based Questions

1. (i) (b) (ii) (d) (iii) (c) (iv) (a)

2. (i) (a) (ii) (c) (iii) (a)

Competition Edge UP

1. (a) **2.** (b) **3.** (b) **4.** (c) **5.** (b)

6. (d) **7.** (d) **8.** (b) **9.** (b)

Chapter-16

Excretory Products and their Elimination

1. Metabolic wastes from the body.

2. 10 (All of them except oxygen). Oxygen is not excreted out.

3. Nitrogenous wastes in animals.

4. Ammonia, uric acid

5. Ammonia, uric acid

6. False. Ammonia is readily soluble and is generally excreted by diffusion across body surfaces or through gill surfaces (in fish) as ammonium ions.

7. True

8. Conserve water

9. (b)

10. A-Uric acid, *B*-Aquatic amphibians, bony fishes and aquatic insects,
C-Mammals, terrestrial amphibians and marine fishes.

11. (i) Ureotelism, (ii) Uricotelism (iii) Ammonotelism

12. Uricotelism

13. Protonephridia

14. (a) A-3, B-4, C-1, D-2

15. 4, i.e. All of them are the parts of human excetory system.

16. Bean

17. T_{12} (last thoracic) L_3 (third lumbar)

18. (i) 10-12 cm, (ii) 5-7 cm
(iii) 2-3 cm, (iv) 120-170 g

19. Hilum

20. (i) Hilum
(ii) Renal pelvis
(iii) Calyces

21. The figure '*X*' is of human urinary system.
A-Ureter, *B*-Inferior vena cava, *C*-Dorsal aorta, *D*-Urethra, *E*-Pelvis

22. Renal capsule, cortex, medulla

23. (c) Both statements I and II cre true.

24. Cortex in medulla

25. (c)

26. The figure '*X*' is the diagrammatic representation of LS of kidney in humans. *A*-Renal column, *B*-Renal pelvis, *C*-Renal artery, *D*-Renal vein, *E*-Calyx, *F*-Medullary pyramid

27. Renal capsule → Cortex → Medullary pyramid → Renal calyx

28. One

29. Nephron

30. Glomerulus and renal tubule

31. Efferent arteriole

32. (c) To allow filtration under pressure

33. Malpighian body

34. *A*-Renal tubule, *B*-Bowman's capsule, *C*-Proximal Convoluted Tubule (PCT), *D*-Distal Convoluted Tubule (DCT).

35. 6 parts are correctly labelled, *viz. C, D, E, F, I, J* (*A*-Efferent arteriole, *B*-Afferent arteriole, *G*-PCT, *H*-DCT)

36. (i) PCT - Proximal Convoluted Tubule
(ii) DCT - Distal Convoluted Tubule

37. (i) Glomerulus
(ii) Afferent arteriole
(iii) Bowman's capsule
(iv) Henle's loop

38. A-Proximal convoluted tubule, *B*-Descending limb of loop of Henle,
C-Ascending limb of loop of Henle, *D*-Distal convoluted tubule.

39. (c) The collecting duct carries the glomerular filtrate to the ureters.

40. True

41. A-Ureter, *B*-Urinary bladder, *C*-Urethra

42. Cortical nephron and juxta medullary nephron.

43. Loop of Henle is odd one out as it dips into the medulla region of kidney.

44. (i) Cortical nephron
(ii) Juxta medullary nephron

45. Peritubular

46. Henle's loop.

47. (a) Vasa recta is absent or highly reduced in cortical nephrons.

48. A-2, B-3, C-1

49. Urethra

50. (i) Glomerular filtration
(ii) Reabsorption
(iii) Secretion

51. Glomerulus

52. 1100-1200, 1/5th

53. (i) The endothelium of glomerular blood vessels
(ii) A basement membrane
(iii) The epithelium of Bowman's capsule.

54. Podocytes

55. True

56. Bowman's capsule

57. (i) *A*-Afferent arteriole
B-Efferent arteriole
C-Bowman's capsule
D-Proximal convoluted tubule
(ii) Podocytes
(iii) Ultra filtration

58. (a) Reversal of pressure gradient

59. Glomerular Filtration Rate (GFR)

60. (i) 125 (ii) 180

61. Juxta Glomerular Apparatus (JGA)

62. Distal Convoluted Tubule (DCT) and afferent arteriole.

63. JG cells, renin

64. About 99% of the filtrate has to be reabsorbed by the renal tubule.

65. Tubular epithelial cells

66. Nitrogenous wastes is odd one out as these are reabsorbed passively in the nephron.

67. (c) Urea

68. 3 (K^+, H^+, ammonia)

69. (a) Both statements I and II are true.

70. (i) It helps in the maintenance of ionic and acid-base balance of the body fluids.

71. Bowman's capsule is odd one out as it is not a tubule.

72. Simple cuboidal brush-bordered epithelium.

73. 70-80 per cent of electrolytes and water is reabsorbed by PCT

74. (i) HCO_3^-, NaCl, H_2O, nutrients
(ii) H^+, NH_3^+, K^+

75. (c) Secretion of H^+ and K^+ ions in the filtrate

76. (i) Minimum
(ii) impermeable

77. (b) 2-Reabsorption 3-Secretion

78. A-Ascending limb
B-Descending limb
C- Descending limb *D*-Ascending limb

79. Medullary fluid

80. Dilute

81. DCT

82. (a) Only the DCT of the renal tubules are actively involved in maintaining the pH balance.

83. True

84. A-PCT-(iii), *B*-Henle's loop-(iv), *C*-DCT-(ii), *D*-Collecting duct-(i)

85. True

86. A-3, B-4, C-1, D-2

87. (a) A-2, B-1, C-4, D-3

88. *A*–HCO_3^-, *B*–H_2O, *C*–NaCl, *D*–H^+, *E*–Urea

89. Glucose

90. '*X*' is tubular reabsorption, '*Y*' is tubular secretion.

91. Hypertonic

92. Vasa recta, Henle's loop

93. 3, i.e. All of them.

94. (i) 300
(ii) 1200

95. NH_3 is the odd one out.

96. (i) Ascending, descending,
(ii) Vasa recta
(iii) Ascending, collecting duct

97. *P*-1200 mOsmol L^{-1}, *Q*-900 mOsmol L^{-1},
R-600 mOsmol L^{-1},
S-300 mOsmol L^{-1}

98. Counter-current mechanism helps to maintain a concentration gradient in the medullary interstitium.

99. (b) NaCl is transported by the ascending limb of Henle's loop which is exchanged with the descending limb of vasa recta. NaCl is returned to the interstitium by the ascending perstion of vasa recta.

100. (a) Hypertonicity of medullary interstitium

101. (b) Body would produce very dilute urine

102. Four

103. A-4, B-1, C-2, D-3

104. Vasa recta is odd one out.

105. Blood, body fluid, ionic

106. *A*-Hypothalamus, *B*-ADH, *C*-Neurohypophysis, *D*-DCT, *E*-Collecting duct

107. Vasopressin

108. False. An increase in body fluid volume can switch off the osmoreceptors and suppress ADH release.

109. (a) Increase ADH and angiotensin II.

110. A-Constriction of blood vessels, *B*-Blood pressure, *C*-GFR

111. (i) A fall in Glomerular Filtration Rate (GFR) or glomerular blood flow and blood pressure.

112. A-Angiotensin-I, *B*-Angiotensin-II, *C*-Aldosterone

113. Vasoconstriction and release of aldosterone.

114. (i) Increase (ii) Increase
(iii) Starts, (iv) Reabsorption

115. Blood pressure

116. Glomerular filtration is odd one out as rest options are concerned with kidney function and regulation.

117. Aldosterone

118. (b) Synergistic effect of aldosterone and angiotensin-II

119. Renin-Angiotensin-Aldosterone System.

120. Atrial-Natriuretic Factor (ANF)

121. A- Heart (atria), *B*-Vasodilation

122. (i) Juxta Glomerular Apparatus
(ii) Glomerular Filtration Rate
(iii) Antidiuretic hormone
(iv) Atrial Natriuretic Factor

123. Hormones

124. Micturition

125. (ii) → (i) → (iv) → (iii)

126. False, CNS receives signals from the stretch receptors present on the wall of the bladder.

127. True

128. Urethra relaxes

129. Micturition reflex

130. Yellow, acidic

131. (i) 6.0
(ii) 1-1.5
(iii) 25-30 gm

132. Water, other substances

133. Glucose

134. Help in the elimination of excretory wastes.

135. 200 mL/minute

136. Liver

137. 5 NaCl, urea and lactic acid are not excreted from the liver.

138. Bilirubin, biliverdin

139. Secretory glands on skin

140. Sweat gland, sebaceous gland

141. NaCl, small amount of urea, lactic acid, etc.

142. Lactic acid is odd one out as it is not a part of sebum.

143. (i) It provides cooling effect on the body surface and also helps in removal of wastes.
(ii) It provides protective oily covering for the skin.

144. (i) Uremia
(ii) Ketonuria
(iii) Glycosuria

145. Kidney failure

146. Hemodialysis

147. No urea

148. (a) Once filtered by dialysis, the blood is transferred back to the body through a vein.

149. (iv) → (ii) → (v) → (vi) → (iii) → (i)

150. Kidney transplantation

151. 3, i.e. All of the given assumptions are correct.

152. Kidney stones

153. (i) Calcium oxalate
(ii) Dilute
(iii) ADH

154. Volume of excreted urine increases.

155. (d) B and D

Assertion-Reason Questions

1. (d) A is false, but R is true. A can be corrected as
Uric acid is the least toxic nitrogenous waste and requires minimal water for elimination.

2. (c) A is true but, R is false. R can be corrected as
The peritubular capillaries are fine branches that originate from the efferent arterioles.

3. (b) Both A and R are true, but R is not the correct explanation of A.
180 litres of Glomerular filtrate is formed while the urine out put per day is 1.5 litres only because 90% of the filtrate is reabsorbed by the renal tubules.

4. (d) A is false, but R is true. A can be corrected as
The entire plasma portion of the blood except the proteins,are passed into the lumen of Bowman's capsule.

5. (b) Both A and R are true but, R is not the correct explanation of A.
As the urine flows through the descending limb of the loop of Henle, it gets concentrated because the descending loop is permeable to water, but impermeable to electrolytes.

6. (b) Both A and R are true, but R is not the correct explanation of A.
NaCl is added to the medullary interstitium from the ascending limb of Henle's loop to maintain a concentration gradient in the interstitium that would help in concentrating the urine in the collecting ducts.

7. (c) A is true, but R is false. R can be corrected as
Counter current mechanism help in maintaining an increasing osmolarity towards the inner medullary interstitium.

8. (d) A is false, but R is true. A can be corrected as
A person with severe dehydration will increase the secretion of vasopressin from the posterior pituitary.

9. (a) Both A and R are true and R is the correct explanation of A.

10. (b) Both A and R are are true, but R is not the correct explanation of A.
In haemodialysis, heparin is added to the blood before passing it to the dialysing unit because heparin is an anticoagulant and prevents blood clotting.

Case Based Questions

1 (i) (d) (ii) (b) (iii) (c)
2 (i) (c) (ii) (c) (iii) (a)

Competition Edge Up

1. (c) **2.** (b) **3.** (b) **4.** (a) **5.** (d)
6. (d) **7.** (a) **8.** (b)

Chapter-17

Locomotion and Movement

1. True

2. *Amoeba*

3. 4(All of them except ear pinna)
Ear pinna does not show movement.

4. Locomotion

5. *Paramoecium, Hydra*

6. False. All locomotions are movements, but all movements are not locomotion.

7. Habitats

8. (i) Locomotion is performed for search of food, shelter, mate, suitable breeding grounds, favourable climatic conditions or to escape from enemies and predators.

9. Amoeboid, ciliary and muscular

10. (a) A-3, B-2, C-4, D-1

11. (b) Amoeboid movement which uses pseudopodia is not limited only to *Amoeba* as specialised cells in our body like macrophages and leucocytes also exhibit the same movement.

12. Ciliary movement

13. (i) Jaws is odd one out. Rest show amoeboid movement.
(ii) Basophils is odd one out. Rest show muscular movement.

14. Internal tubular, ciliated.

15. (i) Helps in removing dust particles and some of the foreign substance inhaled along with atmospheric air.
(ii) Passage of ova and fertilised zygote.

16. Contractile property

17. Muscular, skeletal and neural

18. Mesodermal

19. 40-50%

20. Excitability, contractility, extensibility and elasticity.

21. (i) Location, appearance and nature of regulation of their activities.

22. Striated muscles

23. Skeletal

24. Visceral

25. *A*-Located in the inner walls of hollow visceral organs, *B*-Muscles of heart, C-Striated, *D*-Non-striated, *E*-Involuntary, *F*-Involuntary, *G*-Primarily involved in locomotory actions, *H*-Pumping of heart

26. False, visceral muscles do not exhibit any striation (non-striated muscle) and are smooth in appearance.

27. Visceral or smooth muscle

28. (i) Transportation of food through the digestive tract
(ii) Transport of gametes through the genital tract.

29. Fascicle

30. Fascia, collagenous connective

31. True

32. (i) Sarcolemma
(ii) Sarcoplasm
(iii) Sarcoplasmic reticulum

33. *A* - Fascicles (muscle bundles)
B - Muscle fibres (muscle cells)
C - Sarcolemma
D - Blood capillaries

34. Muscle fibre

35. Many nuclei

36. Sarcoplasmic reticulum

37. True

38. (b) It is syncitium as the sarcoplasm contains many nuclei.

39. (c) Both statements I and II are true.

40. Actin, myosin

41. Sarcomere

42. 2 statements, i.e. (i) and (iii) are true. Statement (ii) is false because sarcomere is the area between two Z-lines.

43. A-1, B-2, C-3, D-5, E-4

44. (b) X-H zone, Y-A band

45. Thin, thick

46. (i) Isotropic band
(ii) Anisotropic band

47. True

48. *A* - Z-line, *B* - Myosin filament, *C* - Actin filaments, *D* - I-band (light band), *E* - A-band, *F* - Sarcomere, *G* - H-zone

49. (d) The thick filaments in the 'A' band are held together by a thin fibrous membrane called 'M' line. The centre of each 'I' band of the thin filaments is an elastic fibre called 'Z' line which bisects it.

50. H-zone

51. (i) Actin and myosin
(ii) Troponin and tropomyosin

52. 'F' (filamentous)

53. Filamentous, globular

54. (c) I and IV.

55. False. Troponin masks the active binding sites for myosin on actin filaments during resting state.

56. *A*–Troponin, *B*–Tropomyosin, *C*–F-actin

57. Meromyosin

58. *A*–Actin binding site, *B*–ATP binding site, *C*–Myosin head, *D*–Cross arm (HMM)

59. (i) Heavy Meromyosin
(ii) Light Meromyosin

60. (d) Masking the binding site for myosin

61. Cross arm

62. ATP binding sites, actin binding sites

63. Sliding filament theory

64. True

65. Motor

66. Muscle fibre

67. Neuromuscular junction or motor end plate.

68. An action potential.

69. (c) II and III

70. II $\rightarrow$ IV $\rightarrow$ VI $\rightarrow$ VII $\rightarrow$ III $\rightarrow$ I $\rightarrow$ V

71. I, A

72. (b) Ca^{2+} binds to troponin$\rightarrow$ ATP hydrolysis $\rightarrow$ cross-bridge fromation $\rightarrow$ sliding of filaments

73. *A*-Cross-bridge, *B*-Sliding/ rotation, *C*-Breaking of cross-bridge, *D*-ATP

74. (i) Calcium ions and troponin
(ii) Myosin head and actin filament.
(iii) Sarcoplasmic reticulum sarcoplasm

75. (c) II, III and IV

76. Muscle fatigue

77. Anaerobic breakdown of glycogen

78. Myoglobin

79. White muscle fibres

80. A-Red - more, White - less, B-Red - more, White - less, C-Red - less, White - more, D- Red - more, White - less

81. (c) The muscle fibres have huge number of sarcoplasmic reticulum in the sarcoplasm.

82. *A* - Relaxed state of sarcomere, *B* - Contracting state of sarcomere, *C* - Maximally contracted state of sarcomere.

83. Chondroitin salts

84. Cartilage, bone

85. A-80, B-126

86. (i) Axial skeleton
(ii) Skull bones

87. (i) *A*-Parietal, *B*-Frontal, *C*-Maxilla, *D*-Hyoid, *E*-Temporal, *F*-Occipital, *G*-Ethmoid, *H*-Sphenoid
(ii) Only 6 labels represent cranial bones, i.e. frontal bone, parietal bones, temporal bones, occipital bone, sphenoid bone and ethmoid bone.

88. (i) Maxilla is odd one out as it is facial bone (Rest are cranial bones).
(ii) Ethmoid is odd one out as it is cranial bone (Rest are facial bones).
(iii) Zygomatic is odd one out as it is facial bone (Rest are bones of vertebral column).

89. (i) 8 bones
(ii) 14 bones
(iii) 1 bone
(iv) 3 bones × 2 ears = 6 bones

90. Cranium

91. Paired – 2 (Parietal and temporal) Unpaired-4 (Frontal, occipital, sphenoid, ethmoid)

92. At the base of the buccal cavity

93. Middle

94. Hyoid is odd one out. It is not an ear ossicle.

95. Dicondylic

96. Hyoid

97. Atlas

98. Mandible
99. Vertebral column
100. 26
101. Neural canal
102. False. Human vertebral formula is $C_7T_{12}L_5S_{1(5)}Co_{1(4)}$
103. *A*-Cervical vertebra, *B*-Thoracic vertebra, *C*-Lumbar vertebra, *D*-Intervertebral disc, *E*-Sacrum, *F*-Coccyx
104. Sacrum, coccyx
105. Axis
106. (i) Protects the spinal cord
(ii) Supports the head
(iii) Provides surface for attachment for ribs and musculature of back
107. Sternum
108. (i) Sternum
(ii) Vertebrochondral ribs
109. Dorsally, ventrally
110. Bicephalic
111. A-1-R, B-2-P, C-3-Q
112. (b) Ribs 8, 9 and 10
113. Hyaline cartilage
114. Thoracic vertebrae, sternum
115. *A*-Sternum, *B*-Vertebral column , *C*-Ribs.
116. A-120, B-6, C-4, D-2
117. 30 bones
118. (i) Hindlimb bones
(ii) Forelimb bones
119. (i) Phalanges $= 14 \times 2 = 28$
(ii) Carpals $= 8 \times 2 = 16$
(iii) Metacarpals $= 5 \times 2 = 10$
(iv) Tarsals $= 7 \times 2 = 14$
(v) Metatarsals $= 5 \times 2 = 10$
120. (i) Phalanges
(ii) Femur
121. (a) A-4, B-3, C-2, D-1
122. 2, 3, 3, 3, 3
123. Femur, stapes
124. Patella
125. Help in the articulation of limbs.
126. *A*-Clavicle, *B*-Scapula, *C*-Ilium, *D*-Ischium, *E*-Pubis
127. (d) Clavicle
128. 3 are correctly labelled, i.e. *B, F, G*. Rest are incorrect and can be corrected as *A*-Clavicle, *C*- Humerus, *D*-Radius, *E*-Ulna
129. Scapula
130. (i) Clavicle
(ii) Scapula
131. Spine, acromion process
132. Glenoid cavity
133. Two
134. Two, three
135. Ilium, ischium and pubis
136. Acetabulum
137. Pubic symphysis
138. Acetabulum
139. *A*-Ilium, *B*-Pubis, *C*-Ischium, *D*-Patella
140. A-4, B-3, C-2, D-1
141. 2 statements (i) and (iii) are correct.
Statement (ii) is incorrect because joints are contact between bones or between bones and cartilages.
142. Fulcrum
143. Joints are of three types, i.e. fibrous, cartilaginous and synovial.
144. A-2, B-1, C-3
145. True
146. *A*-Skull, *B*-Sutures, *C*-Cranium
147. Joints between the adjacent vertebrae in the vertebral column.
148. Synovial cavity
149. Hyaline
150. False. Synovial joints help in locomotory movements.
151. 5 (Ball and socket, hinge, saddle, pivot, gliding)
152. Hinge joint
153. (b) Vertebrae
154. (i) Between humerus and pectoral girdle
(ii) Between atlas and axis
(iii) Between carpals
155. A-1, B-4,C-3, D-2
156. Tremors is odd one out as they are not a symptom of Myasthenia gravis.
157. Inflammation of joints
158. Osteoporosis is odd one out as it is not a type of arthritis.
159. A-2, B-1, C-3, D-4
160. 4 (Swelling in joint, pain in joint, fusion of joint, tissue degeneration). Softness in bones and sweating are not the symptoms of arthritis.
161. Gout
162. Osteoporosis
163. (i) Women , (ii) Oestrogen
(iii) Deficiency
164. Tetany

Assertion-Reason Questions

1. (b) Both A and R are true but R is not the correct explanation of A. Macrophages and leucocytes in blood exhibit movement which is quite similar to that of amoeba as they exhibit amoeboid movement by protoplasmic extensions.
2. (d) A is false but R is true. A can be corrected as
The fascicles of a muscle is held together by a collagenous connective tissue layer called fascia.
3. (b) Both A and R are true but R is not the correct explanation of A. The I bands are light while the A bands are dark comprising thin and thick filaments respectively as they are made up of actin and myosin protein, which gives them the alternate banding pattern.
4. (c) A is true but R is false. R can be corrected as
The central part of thick filament, not overlapped by thin filaments is called the 'H' zone.
5. (a) Both A and R are true and R is the correct explanation of A.
6. (b) Both A and R are true but R is not the correct explanation of A. The globular head of Heavy Meromyosin (HMM) has binding sites for ATP as the globular he[illegible] is an active ATPase enzyme.
7. (c) A is true but R is false. R [illegible] be corrected as
Stimulus causes release of [illegible] ions from the Sarcoplasn[illegible] reticulum into the sarco[illegible]
8. (d) A is false but R is t[illegible] be corrected as
Formation of the cr[illegible] pulls the actin filar[illegible] the centre of 'A' b[illegible]
9. (c) A is true but [illegible] be corrected a[illegible]
Each rib has [illegible] surfaces on [illegible] hence call[illegible]
10. (a) Bot[illegible] is[illegible]

Case Based Questions

1. (i) (c) (ii) (d) (iii) (c)
2. (i) (b) (ii) (b) (iii) (b)

Competition Edge Up

1. (a) 2. (a) 3. (a) 4. (b) 5. (d)
6. (a) 7. (d) 8. (c) 9. (c)

Chapter-18

Neural Control and Coordination

1. Homeostasis
2. Coordination
3. Respiration
4. Neural, endocrine
5. Hormones
6. False. The neural system provides an organised network of point-to-point connection for a quick coordination.
7. Neurotransmitter
8. Neurons
9. Insects
10. (c) Both statements I and II are true.
11. Central Neural System (CNS) and Peripheral Neural System (PNS).
12. Brain and spinal cord

Spinal cord
fferent and efferent fibres
Tiss es/Organs, CNS
fferent and efferent
rt of the peripheral
em.
sues/organs
nt fibre, B –
ural system
22. system
23. A ral system,
24. Symp
25. parasy al system
(a) Fear is ral system and
26. A-Sympathetic neural system.
B-Peripher d by the
C-Autonomic neu autonomic

D–Sympathetic neural system, *E*–Parasympathetic neural system

27. Sympathetic branch of autonomic nervous system.
28. Peripheral nervous system, nerves, fibres, ganglia, CNS
29. (d) III, IV and V.
30. Cell body, dendrites and axon
31. Dendrites
32. Nissl's granules
33. Axon
34. Axon
35. Synaptic knob
36. (a) Dendrite → Cyton → Axon → Synapse
37. (i) Multipolar neuron
(ii) Unipolar neuron
38. (c) Neurotransmitters
39. (ii) and (iii) are correct pair.
(i) is incorrect and can be corrected as
Bipolar neuron-Retina of an eye.
40. (d) X – found in embryonic stage, Y – found in cerebral cortex.
41. Bipolar
42. Schwann
43. Schwann cells
44. Nodes of Ranvier
45. A-1, B-2, C-1, D-2
46. *A*-Dendrites, *B*-Cell body, *C*-Axon terminal, *D*-Schwann cells, *E*-Axon, *F*-Node of Ranvier, *G*-Synaptic knob
47. Neurons are excitable cells because their membranes are in a polarised state.
48. Selectively permeable
49. Potassium ion (K^+), Sodium ion (Na^+).
50. Potassium, sodium
51. (c) $P - K^+, Q - Na^+$
52. Active transport of ions by the sodium potassium pump.
53. $3Na^+$, $2K^+$
54. (c) Rapid efflux of potassium ions at *Q*, conducts impulse forward.
55. Resting potential
56. Na^+
57. False. During the propagation of a nerve impulse, the action potential results in the movement of Na^+ ions from extracellular fluid to intracellular fluid.
58. Action potential
59. First negative then positive and again back to negative.
60. Nerve impulse
61. (a) It conducts impulses in the post synaptic neuron.
62. Synapse
63. (d) Electrical synapses allow direct current flow between neurons.
64. Synaptic vesicles
65. Synapse
66. (d) Pre-synaptic neuron and post-synaptic neuron.
67. Synaptic cleft
68. False. The occurrence of synaptic cleft is usually found in chemical synapses.
69. Electrical synapses are rare in our system as chemical synapses are more widespread and provide greater flexibility due to the use of neurotransmitters.
70. Neurotransmitters
71. Vesicle
72. Receptors
73. Neurotransmitters, Receptors on post-synaptic membrane.
74. *A*– Depolarisation, *B*–Action potential, *C*–Hydrolysis
75. *A*-Synaptic cleft, *B*-Axon, *C*-Pre-synaptic membrane, *D*-Neurotransmitter, *E*-Receptor, *F*-Post-synaptic membrane
76. Acetylcholine and epinephrine
77. False. Brain acts as 'command and control system' of the body.
78. Cranial meninges
79. Brain
80. Sphenoid is odd one out. Rest others are the layer of cranial meninges.
81. False. Piamater maintains contact with the brain tissue.
82. Duramater
83. Cerebellum is odd one out. Rest of the options are the parts of forebrain.
84. (d) I and IV
85. Corpus callosum
86. Cerebral cortex
87. (d) Corpus callosum
88. Grey matter
89. True
90. Myelin sheath

91. (a) Grey matter : white matter : : cerebral cortex : myelin sheath.
92. Thalamus
93. Limbic
94. Pons is odd one out. Rest of the options are parts of the limbic system.
95. Neurosecretory cells, hypothalamic hormone.
96. Pons
97. Cerebral aqueduct
98. Corpora quadrigemina
99. Midbrain, pons and medulla oblongata.
100. (c) Hypothalamus
101. Thalamus is odd one out. Rest of the options are the parts of hindbrain.
102. A-1, B-3, C-4, D-2
103. (b) I, II and V
104. Medulla
105. Cerebellum
106. *A*-Cerebral hemisphere, *B*-Corpus callosum, *C*-Midbrain, *D*-Thalamus, *E*-Hypothalamus
107. (b) Vision
108. Cerebellum has very convoluted surface to provide additional space to neurons.
109. Fibre tracts
110. A-4, B-3, C-1, D-2
111. (c) Medulla

Assertion-Reason Questions

1. (a) Both A and R are true and R is the correct explanation of A.
2. (d) A is false, but R is true. A can be corrected as
The dendrites conduct nerve impulses inward to the cell body.
3. (a) Both A and R are true and R is the correct explanation of A.
4. (c) A is true, but R is false. R can be corrected as
The active transport of three sodium ions outside and two potassium ions inside causes polarisation of the axon.
5. (d) A is false, but R is true. A can be corrected as
Stimulus induced Na^+ permeability is short lived and is reversed on repolarisation of the membrane.
6. (d) A is false, but R is true. A can be corrected as
A chemical synapse contains transmitters that are either excitatory or inhibitory in function.
7. (a) Both A and R are true and R is the correct explanation of A.
8. (c) A is true, but R is false. R can be corrected as
The limbic system of the forebrain drives the emotional behaviour of a person.
9. (a) Both A and R are true and R is the correct explanation of A.
10. (a) Both A and R are true and R is the correct explanation of A.

Case Based Questions

1. (i) (d) (ii) (a) (iii) (c)
2. (i) (a) (ii) (c) (iii) (b)

Competition Edge UP

1. (c) **2.** (d) **3.** (c) **4.** (b)
5. (a) **6.** (b)

Chapter-19

Chemical Coordination and Integration

1. Hormones
2. (b) Hormones are non-nutrient chemicals that act as intercellular messengers and control different bodily functions.
Hormones are produced by endocrine glands like pituitary, pineal, thyroid, adrenal, etc.
3. Neural system, endocrine
4. Ductless
5. Hormone
6. Hormone
7. Endocrine glands, hormone
8. (i) Pituitary → Thymus → Pancreas → Adrenal → Ovary
(ii) (a) *A*–Pituitary gland, *B*-Thymus, *C*–Pancreas, *D*-Adrenal, *E*-Testis, *F*–Ovary
(b) Pancreas
(c) Ovary
9. Gastrointestinal tract, liver, kidney and heart.
10. Nuclei
11. False. The hormones released by hypothalamus regulate the synthesis and secretion of pituitary hormone.
12. (i) Releasing hormones and inhibiting hormones
(ii) Releasing
(iii) Inhibiting
(iv) Anterior
13. (b) A – Gonadotrophin, B – Portal circulation
14. Somatostatin
15. Growth hormone
16. (a) The posterior pituitary is under the direct neural regulation of hypothalamus.
17. Sella tursica
18. Adenohypophysis, neurohypophysis
19. Pars distalis and pars intermedia.
20. (a) Pars distalis
21. Melanocyte stimulating hormone is odd one out. All hormones are released from pars distalis except melanocyte stimulating hormone which is secreted by pars intermedia.
22. (b) Both statements I and II are true.
23. 2 (i, ii)
24. (b) The hormone that causes uterine contractions is oxytocin. It is actually synthesised by hypothalamus and transported axonally to neurohypophysis where it is stored and released.
25. (b) Improper functioning of pars distalis
26. (i) Gonadotrophin Releasing Hormone,
(ii) Growth Hormone,
(iii) Prolactin,
(iv) Thyroid Stimulating Hormone,
(v) Adrenocorticotrophic Hormone,
(vi) Luteinizing Hormone,
(vii) Follicle Stimulating Hormone,
(viii) Melanocyte Stimulating Hormone
27. Neurohypophysis
28. Posterior pituitary
29. Hypothalamus
30. (a) High electrolyte concentration in blood
31. *A*–Pars intermedia, *B*–Pars nervosa

32. (i) Acromegaly,
(ii) Hypopituitarism,
(iii) Hyperpituitarism
33. LH and FSH
34. Androgens
35. FSH, androgens
36. (i) Graafian, (ii) Ovarian
37. Melanocytes
38. MSH
39. True
40. Oxytocin
41. Oxytocin
42. Distal tubules, urine (diuresis)
43. Vasopressin
44. (i) ADH is released.
45. (i) Diabetes insipidus,
(ii) Antidiuresis
46. (a) Adrenocortico Trophic Hormone (ACTH) stimulates the synthesis and secretion of glucocorticoids from adrenal cortex.
47. (c) Acromegaly though a serious condition, can be detected at early stages.
48. Pineal gland
49. Diurnal, sleep-wake, temperature
50. Melatonin
51. (b) Pineal hormone melatonin
52. (b) Both statements 1 and II are true.
53. Trachea
54. Follicles, stromal tissues
55. Tetraiodothyronine, thyrocalcitonin
56. (b) Due to cancer of the thyroid gland or due to development of nodules of thyroid glands, the rate of synthesis and secretion of thyroid hormone increases abnormally high leading to hyperthyroidism.
57. (i) Triiodothyronine,
(ii) Tetraiodothyronine,
(iii) Thyrocalcitonin
58. *A*–Thyroid gland, *B*–Trachea, *C*–Vocal cord
59. (c) Thyroid hormone regulates the electrolyte-water balance of the body.
60. True
61. (i) Thyroid gland
62. Hypothyroidism
63. Goitre
64. Cretinism because of hypothyroidism
65. (a) Hypersecretion of thyroid hormone
66. Hyperthyroidism
67. Exophthalmic goitre
68. *A* – TSH
69. Hypothyroidism
70. (b) Both T_3 and T_4 levels are sufficient to determine the functioning of thyroid gland. T_3 test checks for the levels of triiodothyronine and is usually prescribed if T_4 tests show elevation.
71. True
72. (i) Increase,
(ii) Increase,
(iii) Increase
73. Thyrocalcitonin (TCT)
74. Thyroid
75. Reabsorption
76. True
77. Graves' disease
78. (i) *A*–Parathyroid gland,
(ii) Parathyroid hormone,
(iii) Parathyroid glands are present on the back side of the thyroid gland.
79. (c) Demine ralisation by parathyroid hormone.
80. Thyrocalcitonin
81. Calcium
82. Blood
83. False. PTH acts on bones and stimulates the process of bone resorption.
84. Reabsorption, increases
85. (a) PTH stimulates absorption of Ca^{2+} from digested food.
86. *A*–Increase plasma Ca^{+2}
87. Hyperparathyroidism
88. Thyrocalcitonin decreases the calcium level in blood whereas parathyroid hormone increases the calcium level in blood.
89. Thymus
90. Peptide, thymus
91. (b) Both statements I and II are true.
92. True
93. True
94. Humoral immunity.
95. (a) P-Thymosin Q-Humoral
96. Thymus is degenerated in old individuals resulting in a decreased production of thymosin. As a result, the immune responses of old persons become weak.
97. One pair
98. Anterior, kidney
99. False. The centrally located tissue is called the adrenal medulla and outside this lies the adrenal cortex.
100. (b) Both statements I and II are true.
101. *A*-Cortex, *B*-Zona fasciculata
102. Adrenaline and nor-adrenaline
103. (b) Cortisol
104. (a) A - 3, B - 4, C - 2, D - 1
105. Adrenaline, nor-adrenaline
106. Hormones of fight or flight
107. Increase, dilation, glycogen
108. *A*-Increase, *B*-Increase, *C*-Incrase, *D*-Stimulated, *E*-Renal vessel constrictor, *F*-Increase mental anxiety.
109. True
110. (a) A person with heightened immune response to a foreign body is often administered glucocorticoids particularly cortisol.
111. True
112. (b) Vasopressin aldosterone
113. Corticoids
114. Catecholamines
115. A-2, B-3, C-1
116. Gluconeogenesis, lipolysis, proteolysis
117. Amino acids
118. All of these are the examples of glucocorticoids.
119. False. Cortisol is involved in maintaining the cardio-vascular system and kidney functions.
120. Cortisol
121. Cortisol
122. Adrenocorticotrophic Hormone (ACTH)
123. Hypothalamus → CRF → Anterior lobe of pituitary gland → ACTH → Adrenal cortex
Raised blood glucocorticoid level
124. Aldosterone
125. (i) Yes, (ii) Yes, (iii) Yes, (iv) No, (v) Yes, (vi) Yes

126. More aldosterone is secreted
127. Cortex
128. False. Androgens are associated with deposition of protein in muscles especially in males.
129. Addison's disease
130. 6 (Acute weakness, vomiting, mental clouding, acidosis, renal failure and fatigue).
131. Exocrine, endocrine
132. Islets of Langerhans
133. Glucagon/Insulin
134. Glycogenolysis
135. Hepatocytes, adipocytes
136. Glucagon
137. A-1, 3, B-2, 5, C-4
138. Glucagon
139. Mellitus
140. Diabetes mellitus, ketone bodies
141. (b) Both statements I and II are true.
142. False. Diabetic patients are successfully treated with insulin therapy.
143. (a) Hypoglycemic hormone
144. False. Testes are situated outside the abdominal cavity within pouch called scrotum.
145. Testis
146. Seminiferous tubules, Interstitial tissues
147. True
148. (a) Statements I and II are correct.
149. Spermatogenesis
150. 4(Act on CNS, influence libido, aggressiveness, growth of facial hairs).
151. (a) A-3, B-2, C-4, D-1
152. Ovary
153. Oestrogen, progesterone
154. (b) Both statements I and II are true.
155. *A*–Oestrogen, *B*–Progesterone
156. Oestrogen
157. Increase
158. Progesterone
159. Pregnancy
160. False. In the presence of progesterone, the thickening of the endometrium increases.
161. Progesterone
162. Decreased
163. Atrial Natriuretic Factor (ANF)
164. *A*–Dilation of blood vessels
165. Erythropoietin
166. Juxtaglomerular
167. Gastrin, secretin, Cholecystokinin (CCK) and Gastric Inhibitory Peptide (GIP).
168. Hydrochloric acid, pepsinogen
169. True
170. Water, bicarbonate ions
171. False. CCK acts on both pancreas and gall bladder.
172. GIP
173. A-2, B-3, C-1
174. (b) Both statements I and II are true.
175. Hormone receptor.
176. Target tissues
177. True
178. Intracellular
179. Hormone
180. False. Hormone-receptor complex formation leads to certain biochemical changes in the target tissue.
181. (i) Amines, (ii) Peptides (iii) Proteins
182. Second messengers
183. Secondary messengers
184. Steroid hormones and iodothyronines
185. *A*–Hormone (e.g. FSH), *B*–Receptor, *C*–Generation of second messenger, e.g. *c*AMP, Ca^{+2}
186. (b) Steroids are hydrophobic, hence can pass the membrane
187. Steroid hormone, thyroid hormone
188. False. Steroid and thyroid hormones are lipid soluble.
189. (b) Both statements I and II are true.
190. *A*–Hormone (e.g. oestrogen), *B*–Hormone-receptor complex.
191. Nucleus
192. Protein, polypeptide, amino acid derivatives.

Assertion-Reason Questions

1. (d) A is false but R is true. A can be corrected as
Hormones are non-nutrient chemicals that are secreted by ductless glands of the human body.
2. (a) Both A and R are true and R is the correct explanation of A.
3. (b) Both A and R are true but R is not the correct explanation of A.
4. (d)A is false but R is true. A can be corrected as
Oxytocin secreted by the posterior pituitary helps in milk ejection from the mammary gland.
5. (a) Both A and R are true and R is the correct explanation of A.
6. (b) Both A and R are true, but R is not the correct explanation of A.
7. (b) Both A and R are true, but R is not the correct explanation of A.
8. (c) A is true but R is false. R can be corrected as
Under stressful situation the adrenal medulla is stimulated to secrete emergency hormones.
9. (b)Both A and R are true, but R is not the correct explanation of A.
10. (c) A is true but R is false. R can be corrected as
Hyposecretion of insulin by the β-cells of Islets of Langerhans can raise the blood glucose level causing diabetes.

Case Based Questions

1. (i) (b) (ii) (c) (iii) (a)
2. (i) (d) (ii) (c) (iii) (c)

Competition Edge Up

1. (d) **2.** (d) **3.** (d) **4.** (b) **5.** (a)
6. (a) **7.** (b) **8.** (b)